An Index to Literature

in

The New Yorker

Volumes I-XV, 1925-1940

by

Robert Owen Johnson

The Scarecrow Press, Inc.

Metuchen, N.J. 1969

The Library of Congress Cataloged the Original Printing of
This Title as:

Johnson, Robert Owen.
An index to literature in the New Yorker. Metuchen, N. J., Scarecrow Press, 1969–71.

3 v. 22 cm.

CONTENTS: [1] Volumes I-XV, 1925–1940.—[2] Volumes XVI-XXX, 1940–1955.—[3] Volumes XXXI-XLV, 1955–1970.

1. The New Yorker—Indexes. I. Title.

AP2.N6764 051 71–7740
SBN 8108–0272–4 (v. 1) varies MARC

Library of Congress rev 2
69 [r71z²3]

Table of Contents

I wish to dedicate this volume to my researchers: Mary Smith Adams, Daniel A. Brewer, William H. Day, Barbara A. Johnson, David W. Johnson, Susan J. Umberger.

R. O. J.

Introduction

It may be easiest to begin by listing departments this index does not include: On and Off the Avenue, Tables for Two, Motors and Motoring, Horse Shows and Hunts, and all sports columns (The Race Track, Football, Polo, Tee and Green, and the like).

In addition, I have had to exclude The Art Galleries and Musical Events, The Sky Line and, most regretfully, the cartoons. Howard Brubaker's Of All Things, which appeared in most early issues, has not been listed.

I have been unable to identify contributors to Talk of the Town, for it is The New Yorker's policy not to make such matters public.

This volume indexes Volumes I through XV of The New Yorker (February 21, 1925, through February 10, 1940), and is organized into three sections, Original Material, Reviews, and Name Index. Into the first section I have attempted to put every imaginative work, prose and verse, ranging from Thurber's "The Secret Life of Walter Mitty" to several score four-line verses, untitled and unsigned, which appeared in early issues.

Further, I have included each Profile, Reporter at Large, Wayward Press, Onward and Upward with the Arts, New York Childhood, Annals of Crime, and the like. A complete listing of these departments, with their identifying abbreviations, is found on p. xiii. With some hesitation I have included all Letters from Paris, Letters from London (and letters from other cities), as well as Our Footloose Correspondents.

The first section also contains subject references to literary figures and their works. The former range as far afield as stage designers and the one motion picture actor whose inclusion seems undebatable, Charlie Chaplin. These references are taken from sources such as Talk of the Town, Profiles, Paris and London Letters, Alexander Woollcott's Shouts and Murmurs, and parodies. I have tried to avoid listing only brief mentions, although at times a good anecdote, though short, proved irresistible.

A word about my method of identifying entries in the first section: each title, when not part of a series such as The Wayward Press, has been designated either Prose or Verse. I have not attempted to distinguish among doggerel, verse and various genres of poetry, nor have I tried to identify prose as humor, satire, personal narrative, and the like. Such identification, in a project which will index some 2300 issues, is impossible.

Titles appearing under a general heading which is used more than eight times are identified by an abbreviation standing for that heading. Thus, each title in the Reporter at Large series is identified as RL, and Newman Levy's Weekend Verses are WV. Profiles are identified as PR followed by the last name of the subject in parenthesis.

My only inconsistency in this matter has been determined, as is usual in such cases, by practicality: W. E. Farbstein's Stories of Today, five or six short poems under each heading, are identified by the series heading only. So many verses were published that a separate listing for each would have greatly increased the size of this index.

In the second section I have listed by title every Theatre, Current Cinema and Book review of some substance, the point of demarcation being 15 lines. Each entry contains the reviewer's last name in parenthesis; the reviewers are listed in the name index as are the authors of the works reviewed. A small letter r after each identifying number indicates that the reference is to a reviewer.

Each title in the first two sections is identified by a number, the numbers ranging from 1 to 17957, with original material in numbers 1 to 11889 and reviews from 11890 to 17957. Users of this index who wish a complete listing of a particular author's work, both original material and reviews, should consult the third section, Name Index, and look up all the numbers listed after his name. To repeat, authors of works reviewed are also listed in this section.

About the asterisks and daggers: they are, unfortunately, most important, and a reader who fails to observe them may possibly grump about inaccuracy of page designation. From October 5, 1929 to April 2, 1960, The New Yorker published both a New York edition and an Out-of-Town edition. In many cases pagination is not the same, a fact that may cause users some trouble, but probably not nearly as much as that caused the compiler. A second but closely related matter is that only libraries in the metropolitan New York area can be expected to have a complete set of one edition.

Libraries as close (or as far away) as those at Yale and Wesleyan have mixed sets; the same may be expected in Dubuque and other distant parts. I have found that the microfilm edition, although basically Out-of-Town, has at least one issue from the New York edition mixed in. The early New Yorker's apparently nonchalant mailing habits seem to be at issue here.

The two editions, when they differ, do so because of advertising; but articles and poems may have been rearranged and may bear different page numbers in the final two-thirds of each issue. Pagination may differ by only a few pages or by 40 or 50; it is impossible to generalize.

Furthermore, for a few months in late 1934 and early 1935, Theatre reviews were run a week later in the Out-of-Town edition. This practice appears to have ended on March 30, 1935, but I have been unable to determine when it began; The New Yorker kept no records of this type for its Out-of-Town edition.

Thus, the asterisks and daggers. An asterisk in the volume, page and date designator signifies that the entry is from the Out-of-Town edition, and warns a reader using a New York edition that he may have to look elsewhere in the same issue. All entries from late 1929 on that do not have an asterisk have been standardized to the New York edition, and a user who has an Out-of-Town edition may have to look elsewhere. Fortunately, Theatre, Current Cinema and Book reviews are in their same relative positions in all issues.

A dagger is used for Theatre reviews which appear on successive weeks in late 1934 and early 1935. All such reviews have been standardized to the New York edition and marked by a dagger. Users of the index who have an Out-of-Town edition will have to look for these reviews a week later.

How can the reader identify an issue from the Out-of-Town edition? By a small five-pointed star appearing just before the date on the cover. One final remark on the matter: pages may not differ, especially in slim issues published during the summer months and after Christmas. And they do not differ, usually, for items found in approximately the first third of each issue. But a little uncertainty and detective work may increase the user's pleasure.

This index has made an attempt to identify articles signed by pseudonyms and initials and, in a few cases, those which are anonymous. To this purpose The New Yorker's library was of great help, although not always able to identify very early authors, for the staff kept few records of this sort at first.

A list of identifications appears on p. 423; this list should not be taken as definitive, and it is for roughly the first ten years of the magazine's publication only. The New Yorker understandably wishes to protect the identity of its authors after the mid-1930's. In all cases where I have been able to identify the person behind the pseudonym, I have included entries under the legal name. Thus, articles signed by Guy Fawkes are listed under Robert Benchley, and all of Patience Eden's poems are listed under Martha Banning Thomas.

My acknowledgments: I especially wish to thank the Research Committee at Washington State University for a grant which has enabled me to employ the researchers listed in the dedication (my wife Barbara, who helped a great deal, worked, as do most faculty wives, without pay); and I wish to thank my superiors in the chain of command for the sabbatical leave which made this volume possible.

I have used the following libraries, and gratefully acknowledge their help: the Washington State University Library, the University of Idaho Library, the Sterling Memorial Library at Yale University, the Olin Memorial Library at Wesleyan University, the New Haven Public Library, and The New Yorker's library.

I wish to thank Mr. Milton Greenstein, vice president of The New Yorker, for his permission to use the library; and my special thanks go to Miss Ebba Jonsson, who organized the library, and to her two gracious assistants, Mrs. Helen Stark and Miss Elizabeth Smith. They helped me with the identifications mentioned above, and served me coffee and cookies each afternoon.

My son and daughter, David and Susan, helped me a great deal by alphabetizing and filing thousands of slips. Finally, my appreciation to Dr. Ralph R. Shaw, editor of Scarecrow Press, for his enthusiastic encouragement from the very beginning.

Pullman, Washington
May 1969

Symbols and Abbreviations

Abbreviations for Series

*	
†	
AC	Annals of Crime
BR	Broadway Rackets
CP	Current Press
DL	Down-town Lyrics
DOL	Doldrums
FP	Foreign Parts
FPI	Famous Poems Illustrated
HHT	Hotels Here and There
LYMA	Let Your Mind Alone!
ME	Manhattan Epitaphs
ML	Magic Letters
MLHT	My Life and Hart Times
MM	The Making of a Magazine
MNL	My Own, My Native Land
NESD	Notes for an East Side Dictionary
NYC	A New York Childhood
OFC	Our Footloose Correspondents
OLD	Open Letters Department
OMEU	Our Own Modern English Usage
ORR	Our Roving Reporters
OSB	Our Own Sob Ballads
OUWA	Onward and Upward With the Arts
OW	Over the Waves
PP	Pavement Profiles
PR	Profile
RC	The Ritz Carltons
RL	A Reporter at Large
SH	Songs of Hotels

SM	Shouts and Murmers
TA	Thoughts in the Aquarium
TT	Talk of the Town
TWNY	That Was New York
WATN	Where Are They Now?
WP	The Wayward Press
WV	Weekend Verses

Original Material

The ABC of the Lausanne pact. Prose. Frank Sullivan. 8:11-12 Jy30'32. 1
À bas Ben Adhem. Verse. Ogden Nash. 6:32 D13'30. 2
A la carte-1928. Prose. Robert Barry. 3:83 F11'28. 3
A la mayonnaise. Prose. Hildegarde Angell. 2:20-1 Jy10'26. 4
A la queue Leu Leu. Prose. Mary Poore. 12:72-3*My16'36. 5
A. M. Verse. William Rose Benét. 9:14 Jy29'33. 6
A. Pickus calling. OFC. Helen Kay. 14:67-8*Ap9'38. 7
ATC. Prose. Robert M. Coates. 3:72-3 S17'27. 8
Abandoned farms. Verse. Winifred Welles. 15:20*Jy1'39. 9
Abandoned orchard. Verse. Bernice Kenyon. 9:42 Ap8'33. 10
Abby, this is your father. Prose. S. J. Perelman. 15:26-8*D16 '39. 11
Abdication of a jester. Verse. Ogden Nash. 12:23*Mr28'36. 12
Abie's Irish Rose. (Play) TT. 3: 14-15 My28'27. 13
Abie's Irish Rose. (Play) TT. 1: 3 O10'25. 14
Aboard the Mayflower. Prose. Homer Joseph Dodge. 2:13-15 Jy17'26. 15
The abolition riots of 1834. TWNY. Herbert Asbury. 8:52-7 N5'32. 16
About dogs. NESD. John J. Holzinger. 10:85 Mr17'34. 17
About duty. Verse. Price Day. 7:71 Ap18'31. 18
About Mr. Hamson's book on food. Prose. William A. Krauss. 13:66-7*My8'37. 19
About my mother. Verse. Clinch Calkins. 3:21 Je4'27. 20
About New Yorkers. Prose. Katharine Brush. 11:22*D21'35. 21
About nothing at all. Verse. Fillmore Hyde. 2:21 Ag21'26. 22
About this time of year. Prose. Patricia Collinge. 5:73-4 N2 '29. 23
About this time of year. Prose. Ed. B. Graham. 2:54-5 O30'26. 24
About with the booksy. Prose. Maddy Vegtel. 10:19-20*Ja19 '35. 25
Absolutely free! Prose. A. B. Bernd. 6:88-90 Je7'30. 26
Absolution. Prose. Morley Callaghan. 7:20-1 D5'31. 27
Absolutism and the independents. Prose. Weare Holbrook. 2:25 Mr20'26. 28
Abstraction-flowers. PR (O'Keeffe) Robert M. Coates. 5:21-4 Jy6 '29. 29
Acacia Island. Verse. Muna Lee. 6:20 Mr15'30. 30
Accepted. ME. Alfred Kreymborg. 3:93 My7'27. 31
Accident. Verse. Jean Batchelor. 5:88 N30'29. 32
An accident in the field. Prose. Robert M. Coates. 14:23-6*D3 '38. 33
Accident near Charlottesburg. Prose. William A. Krauss. 12:58-9*My16'36. 34
The accident room. RL. F. A. Fender. 7:46-54 O24'31. 35
According to formula. Verse. Arthur H. Folwell. 3:51 F26'27. 36
Accoucheur. Prose. S. N. Behrman. 7:20-4 F6'32. 37
Achievement. Prose. Edward L. Gordy. 11:76-7*My11'35. 38
Achievement. Verse. Nancy Byrd Turner. 5:53 S28'29. 39

All for love. Prose. Alan Marshall. 13:79-82*Mr13'37. 204
All is not lost. Verse. Martha Banning Thomas. 5:78 Ja4'30. 205
All most comical. Prose. Anthony Armstrong. 15:48-9* N25'39. 206
All quiet on the eastern front. Prose. Ring Lardner. 7:14-16* Je27'31. 207
All quiet on the western front. (Novel) Alexander Woollcott. 5:32 Jy27'29. 208
All souls. Prose. Alice Frankforter. 10:44-6 N3'34. 209
All the king's horses. PR (Hildreth). Niven Busch, Jr. 5:20-3 Ag24'29. 210
All the news that's fit to sell. Prose. Thomas S. Bosworth. 3:96-7 My21'27. 211
All the news that's fitted to print. Prose. Corey Ford. 1:21 Ja 30'26. 212
All the perfumes of 125th Street. Prose. Wolcott Gibbs. 7:19-20 N7'31. 213
All the years of her life. Prose. Morley Callaghan. 11:17-19* Je8'35. 214
All things considered. SM. Alexander Woollcott. 9:34 Je3'33. 215
All things considered. SM. Alexander Woollcott. 9:30 Ag5'33. 216
All we need is horse sense. Prose. George S. Kaufman. 11:20*My25'35. 217
All you can hold for five bucks. RL. Joseph Mitchell. 15:35-42*Ap15'39. 218
Allergy met a bear. Verse. Ogden Nash. 12:16*Ag8'36. 219
Allerton House for men. SH. Newman Levy. 4:31 N17'28. 220
The alley. Prose. Louise Davidson. 11:55*Ja11'36. 221
Allie bobs oop again. OW. Ring Lardner. 8:24-7 Jy30'32. 222
Alligator's idol. PR (Goodman). Henry Anton Steig. 13:27-34* Ap17'37. 223
"Allo! Allo!" Prose. Florence Helm. 2:56-7 My1'26. 224
Alma martyr. Prose. Cornelia Otis Skinner. 12:52-3*Je13'36. 225
Alma mater's eggs. RL. E. B. White. 8:36-42*Ap16'32. 226
Alma mother. Prose. Jack Cluett. 6:54-6 Je21'30. 227
Almighty dollar. Prose. Hannah Lees. 9:52-4 My27'33. 228
Almost anybody's litany. Prose. Baird Leonard. 3:17 Ja7'28. 229
Almost Grimm. Prose. Oliver Claxton. 2:20 Ja1'27. 230
Almost Grimm again. Prose. Oliver Claxton. 3:38-40 My14 '27. 231
Aloha oe. Prose. Jack Cluett. 5:90-1 F23'29. 232
Alone. Prose. Eugene Joffe. 12:29-30*S26'36. 233
Along this path . . . Verse. Elspeth O'Halloran. 5:28 My11 '29. 234
Alphabet vinaigrette. Verse. Raymond Holden. 11:19*S28'35. 235
Also ran. PR (Thomas). Henry F. Pringle. 5:28-31 N9'29. 236
Alt wein. PR (Bodanzky). Hollister Noble. 6:23-6 Mr15'30. 237
The alumnae bulletin. Prose. John O'Hara. 4:101 My5'28. 238
Always. Prose. E. B. White. 2:31 My8'26. 239
Amalie and the Mister. Prose. Mary Rose Himler. 9:43-4 Jy 22'33. 240
Amateur. Verse. Anon. 1:20 Mr28 '25. 241
Amateur. Verse. Philip G. Wylie. 3:89 Mr5'27. 242
Amateur at work. PR (Turnesa). Noel F. Busch. 15:21-6*S9'39. 243
The amateur gadgeteer. Prose. Reed Johnston. 4:59-60 Ja19'29. 244
The amateur gardener. NESD.

Apostrophe to a sparrow loafing outside my office window. Verse. Margaret Fishback. 7:48 S26'31. 405
Apostrophe to a tom-cat. Verse. Katharine D. Morse. 4:60 Ap14 '28. 406
Apostrophic notes from the new-world physics. Verse. E. B. White. 10:24 O6'34. 407
The apotheosis of the handsaw. OUWA. Lucille Fletcher. 14:55-7*My7'38. 408
Apparitions. Verse. Peggy Bacon. 10:22*N17'34. 409
Appeal. Verse. Margaretta Manning. 3:47 S3'27. 410
An appeal to Emily Post. OLD. Patricia Collinge. 10:26-7*D29 '34. 411
Appeal to Gertrude. Verse. Melville Cane. 10:84 N3'34. 412
Appearance of evil. Prose. Frances Warfield. 11:24-6*Jy13'35. 413
Appendix to politics. Verse. John Strong Newberry. 7:52 Mr28 '31. 414
The appetizer. Verse. Persis Greely Anderson. 6:25 Ap12 '30. 415
Apple cart. Verse. Lucy Hale Sturges. 3:103 D10'27. 416
Apple time. Verse. Richard Peckham. 7:20 O31'31. 417
Apples. Verse. Dorothy Dow. 4:85 S22'28. 418
Apples in New Hampshire. Verse. Marie Gilchrist. 8:20 O1'32. 419
Applicant. Verse. Philip G. Wylie. 2:40 S11'26. 420
Applied cravatology. Prose. Dearing Ward. 3:28-9 Ja14'28. 421
Appreciation. Prose. John O'Hara. 5:97-8 Ap13'29. 422
Apprehensive survey. Verse. Phyllis Mc Ginley. 10:21 N3 '34. 423
Approach to the infinite. RL. Morris Markey. 10:58-64 F17 '34. 424
Après la guerre finie. WP. Robert Benchley. 11:43-5*F23'35. 425
April. Verse. Lenore G. Marshall. 11:29*Ap27'35. 426
April fool! WATN. James Thurber. 13:22-6*Ag14'37. 427
April ice. Verse. Jean Batchelor. 6:107 Ap5'30. 428
April wren. Verse. Frances M. Frost. 7:17 Ap18'31. 429
Apropos the circus. Verse. Anon. 2:34 Ap17'26. 430
Aquarium. Verse. Frances M. Frost. 7:47 Ja2'32. 431
Aquarium reverie. Verse. Mary C. McCall, Jr. 2:80 O2'26. 432
Arbitration. RL. Jack Alexander. 13:52-61*Ap24'37. 433

(No entry) 434
Architecture and building. NESD. John J. Holzinger. 10:56 Mr24 '34. 435
Architecture triumphant. Prose. Creighton Peet. 2:17 Jy10'26. 436
Arctic agrarian. Verse. Louis Untermeyer. 7:19 My2'31. 437
Are there more than one Otto Kahn? Prose. Rube Goldberg. 3:22-3 Ap9'27. 438
Are we leaving tomorrow? Prose. John O'Hara. 14:17-18*Mr19 '38. 439
Are wives women? Verse. Marjorie Allen Seiffert. 7:47 O17 '31. 440
Are women getting anywhere? Prose. James Thurber. 6:17-18 S6'30. 441
Are you a coward? 'Tis only conscience, Hamlet asserts. Prose. Herbert Asbury. 1:12 Je27'25. 442
Are you giving a party? Prose. Maddy Vegtel. 11:85*Ap6'35. 443
Are you going my way? No, never. Verse. Ogden Nash. 13:17*Jy3

Aunt Bina. Prose. Helen Bishop. 12:44-6*Jy11'36. 577
Aunt Katherine. Prose. George Cecil Cowing. 7:75-6 Ap11'31. 578
Aunt Martha's method. Prose. Chester T. Crowell. 13:61* My15'37. 579
Aunt Mary's doctor. SM. Alexander Woollcott. 5:44 My4'29. 580
Aunt Rachel. Prose. Maddy Vegtel. 12:51-3*Ap11'36. 581
Aunts at the opera. Prose. John Chapin Mosher. 2:20-1 D25'26. 582
Authority. Verse. Joseph Anthony. 7:18 S5'31. 583
The author's road to fame. Prose. B. B. 1:25 My16'25. 584
Autobiographical novel. Prose. Fleta Campbell Springer. 3:80-1 O8'27. 585
Autobiography. Verse. Charmé Seeds. 10:28 S1'34. 586
The autobiography of Alice B. Sullivan. Prose. Frank Sullivan. 9:13-14 Jy1'33. 587
The autobiography of Alice B. Toklas. (Parody) Frank Sullivan. 9:13-14 Jy1'33. 588
Autobiography with adjuration. Verse. Samuel Hoffenstein. 8: 20-1 Je11'32. 589
Autocrat of the card table. PR (Work). Helena Huntington Smith. 3:18-19 Ja14'28. 590
Autograph. Prose. Sally Benson. 14:18-19*Ja7'39. 591
Automation. Verse. Paul G. Gumbinner. 4:81 My26'28. 592
Automobile men. Prose. George Cecil Cowing. 9:66 S30'33. 593
Auto-phlebotomy at the Times. Prose. Tracy Hammond Lewis. 2:57-8 My8'26. 594
Autres bêtes, autres moeurs. Verse. Ogden Nash. 6:29 N15 '30. 595
Autumn lament. Verse. Margaret Fishback. 3:91 O1'27. 596
Autumn morning. Verse. Gerald Raftery. 14:64*O28'38. 597
The Autumn of the heart. Verse. Helene Mullins. 12:52*My16'36. 598
Autumn song. Verse. Marjorie Allen Seiffert. 6:105 O4'30. 599
Autumnal heart. Verse. Rachel Field. 15:36*O7'39. 600
Autumnal query: New York City. Verse. Henry Morton Robinson. 7:59 O3'31. 601
Autumnal reverie. Verse. Franklin P. Adams. 13:65*O16'37. 602
Autumnal song. Verse. Frances M. Frost. 12:32*N7'36. 603
Autumnal sowing. Verse. Frances M. Frost. 6:27 O18'30. 604
Avast and belay. Prose. John O'Hara. 15:22-3*O7'39. 605
Ave atque Farley. Verse. Ogden Nash. 11:34*D14'35. 606
Ave atque vale. Verse. Ruth Lambert Jones. 13:45*O9'37. 607
Ave Galento! Verse. Morris Bishop. 15:23*Je24'39. 608
The avenue. RL. Morris Markey. 2:28-30 D25'26. 609
The avenue at St. Patrick's. Verse. James Kevin Mc Guinness. 1:19 Ag22'25. 610
Avenue progress. Verse. Anon. 2: 36 N13'26. 611
The average American. Verse. W. E. Faberstein. 7:18*Je13'31. 612
Average cop. PR (Williams). St. Clair McKelway. 9:23-7 F10 '34. 613
The aviary. NESD. John J. Holzinger. 10:67 S1'34. 614
Aviation for amateurs. Prose. Wolcott Gibbs. 4:64-5 Je16'28. 615
Avocado, or the future of eating. Prose. S. J. Perelman. 13:28-9*My1'37. 616
Awake. Verse. Elizabeth Bohm. 14:46*Jy9'38. 617
Away from it all. Verse. Hortense Flexner. 15:56*Ag26'39. 618
Away from it all. Verse. Ogden

The Berne boy. Prose. Emanuel Eisenberg. 9:56-7 My20'33. 789

Best boy I ever had. Prose. Anthony Amstrong. 14:31*D10 '38. 790

The best dressed man has amnesia. Prose. John Chapin Mosher. 2:21 Jy31'26. 791

The best hotel in the world. HHT. Donald Moffat. 9:44-8 Ap 29 '33. 792

The best people. SM. Alexander Woollcott. 5:30 D28'29. 793

The best things come in small packages. Prose. Sally Benson. 15:15-17*D23'39. 794

Best wishes. Prose. Hugh Troy. 11:67*S14'35. 795

Betrayal. Prose. Arthur Kober. 7:38-40 O17'31. 796

Betrothal. Prose. James Reid Parker. 15:62*F18'39. 797

Better banditry. Prose. Owen P. White. 1:6 Je20'25. 798

Better to have loved and lost. Prose. Oliver Claxton. 3:74 Ja 28'28. 799

A better understanding. Prose. Sally Benson. 10:96-9 My19'34. 800

Betty at bridge. Verse. Martha Banning Thomas. 3:65 F26'27. 801

Between the dark and the daylight. Verse. Morris Bishop. 10:28 Ja19'35. 802

Between the halves. Prose. John O'Hara. 5:85-9 O12'29. 803

Beware of china pigs. Prose. Edith Owen. 8:64-6*Mr5'32. 804

Beware the Brazilian navy. Prose. Ruth McKenney. 13:28-33*Jy10 '37. 805

Bewitched baby. Verse. Jacqueline Embry. 5:28 Ap27'29. 806

Biarritz. Verse. Kenneth Allan Robinson. 8:14 Ag6'32. 807

Bibliophile. Prose. A. B. Bernd. 8:55-6 Je4'32. 808

Bibliophile. Verse. Elspeth O'Halloran. 3:84 My14'27. 809

Bicycles and automobiles. Prose. Gertrude Carver. 8:41-3 Ja28 '33. 810

Big business. RL. Morris Markey. 10:79-84 Ap14'34. 811

A big edition. WP. Robert Benchley. 7:52-8 N21'31. 812

Big evening. Prose. Gordon Sager. 14:55-6*Mr19'38. 813

Big for her age. Prose. Louise Field Cooper. 11:48*Ja25'36. 814

The big game. Prose. Herman J. Mankiewicz. 1:11-12 N14'25. 815

Big hookup. Verse. Martha Banning Thomas. 9:57 Ja13'34. 816

The big inflammables. Prose. Cornelia Otis Skinner. 15:20-2*Ag19'39. 817

Big Jim. PR (Farley). Alva Johnston. 7:23-7 N28'31. 818

The big man. Verse. Anon. 3:81 N12'27. 819

The big man. Verse. Adrienne M. Murphy. 4:17 Jy7'28. 820

Big Nemo. PR (Woollcott). Wolcott Gibbs. 15:24-9*Mr18'39; 15:24-9*Mr25'39; 15:22-7*Ap1 '39. 821

The big parade. (Film) TT. 1:5 D26'25. 822

A big proposition. Prose. Henrietta Fort Holland. 11:19-20*Je 8'35. 823

Big race. RL. Morris Markey. 12:31-4*O24'36. 824

Big red. PR (Man O'War). Arthur Bartlett. 13:24-31*D18'37. 825

The big red team. RL. John R. Tunis. 6:56-66 N8'30. 826

Big ship. RL. Morris Markey. 10:69-74 My19'34. 827

Big shot-at. PR (Diamond). Joel Sayre. 7:24-7*Je13'31. 828

Big wind from Kansas. TWNY. Herbert Asbury. 9:44-51 Je10 '33. 829

Bigger and better bathtubs. Prose. Nancy Hoyt. 3:54-5 Mr5'27. 830

frey T. Hellman. 15:20-5*Ja 27'40. 874
The black eagle. PR (Julian). Morris Markey. 7:22-5*Jy11 '31; 7:20-3*Jy18'31. 875
The black hat. PR (Gest). Gilbert W. Gabriel. 1:7-8 Je27'25. 876
The black list. Prose. John Chapin Mosher. 5:33-4 N23'29. 877
Black Lucifer. Verse. Witter Bynner. 2:36 N13'26. 878
Black madness. Prose. Carroll Carroll. 11:67*Je8'35. 879
Black magic. Verse. Henrietta Fort Holland. 7:83 O31'31. 880
The black magic of Barney Haller. Prose. James Thurber. 8: 13-14 Ag27'32. 881
Black mass. Verse. Nicholas Samstag. 3:38 O29'27. 882
The black sheep. Prose. Frank Sullivan. 10:17-18 Je2'34. 883
Blackout. Prose. A. O. N. 7:44 F 21'31. 884
The Blackstone revels. RL. Morris Markey. 2:36-40 F5'27. 885
Blarney Stone. Prose. Frances Crane. 11:60*Je22'35. 886
Bleak moment. Prose. Wolcott Gibbs. 15:17-18 F10'40. 887
The bleakest job. Prose. Corey Ford. 2:20 My29'26. 888
The bleakest job. Prose. Corey Ford. 2:24 Jy24'26. 889
The bleakest job. Prose. Corey Ford. 2:24 Jy31'26. 890
The blenny. TA. Will Cuppy. 8: 24 O22'32. 891
Bless our home. Prose. Grace L. Daly. 9:51-3 Mr11'33. 892
"Blessed be the artist . . ." Verse. Hans Stengel. 1:14 Ag 1'25. 893
Blessed city. Prose. Russell Maloney. 15:18-19*S9'39. 894
A blessed event. OUWA. E. B. White. 11:29-36*Ja25'36; 11: 31-5*F1'36. 895
Blessed Mother Cabrini. RL. Morris Gilbert and Russell Maloney. 14:34-8*N5'38. 896
Blest! Prose. Thomas Langan. 2: 24 S25'26. 897
Blind bulls-and-bears. RL. Morris Markey. 1:13-14 Ja16'26. 898
Blind . . . deaf . . . dumb. PR (Keller). Robert M. Coates. 5:24-6 Ja25'30. 899
Blind sailor-man. Verse. Martha Banning Thomas. 5:44 S14'29. 900
The blind spot. Prose. Donald Moffat. 7:15-17 Ag22'31. 901
Bliss. Verse. Arthur Guiterman. 1:40 N7'25. 902
Bliss. Prose. John Chapin Mosher. 7:28-9 D12'31. 903
Blitz vs. Prentiss. Prose. Donald Thompson. 5:101-103 Mr23'29. 904
Blonde oblivion. Verse. M. M. 3: 107 N26'27. 905
Bloom. Verse. Peggy Bacon. 3:87 N26'27. 906
Blossoms on Lexington. Prose. Travis Hoke. 10:99-100 Ap7'34. 907
Blotters: an absorbing medium. Prose. Corey Ford. 1:22 My9 '25. 908
The Blotz. Prose. Frank Sullivan. 7:20-1 O24'31. 909
A blue basket. Prose. Murdock Pemberton. 14:65*F11'39. 910
Blue harvest. Verse. Frances M. Frost. 6:33 S27'30. 911
Blue heritage. Prose. Theodore Pratt. 8:23 N12'32. 912
Blue hyacinths. Prose. Dawn Powell. 9:22-4 Jy15'33. 913
Blue night. Verse. Frances M. Frost. 7:17*Jy18'31. 914
Blue notes on the program. Prose. Weare Holbrook. 1:28 F13'26. 915
The blue Pacific. Prose. G. Schwabe. 13:51-2*Ap3'37. 916
Blue wild asters. Verse. David Morton. 12:77*S19'36. 917
Bluebeard. Verse. Persis Greely Anderson. 5:104 O5'29. 918
Bluebeard. Verse. Helene Mullins. 4:29 D8'28. 919

The Bluebeard series. SM. Alexander Woollcott. 9:32 Mr18'33. 920
Blumey. PR (Blumenthal). Alva Johnston. 8:19-23 F4'33; 8:21-4 F11'33. 921
Blushes and tears. RL. James Thurber. 8:34-9 S24'32. 922
Boarding-house pastoral. Verse. Grace Hazard Conkling. 4:86 S15'28. 923
The boat race. Prose. Frances Crane. 6:34-8 Ap12'30. 924
Boat ride. Verse. Elinore Blaisdell. 4:28 Ap14'28. 925
A bob ballad. Verse. James Kevin McGuinness. 1:18 Mr7'25. 926
Bobbing for words. Prose. Robert Benchley. 8:14-16 Jy16'32. 927
Bobs comes to New York. Prose. Richard Lockridge. 10:42-6 S 8'34. 928
Bodenheim, Maxwell. TT. 5:13-14 Je15'29. 929
Bodenheim, Maxwell. TT. 1:1-2 Jy25'25. 930
The body beautiful. Prose. S. J. Perelman. 11:15-16 Jy6'35. 931
Boggains in the Bronx. Prose. Arthur Kober. 10:18-20*Ja12 '35. 932
Bohemia. Verse. Dorothy Parker. 3:25 S17'27. 933
Bojangles. PR (Robinson). St. Clair McKelway. 10:26-8 O6 '34; 10:30-4 O13'34. 934
Boshevik businessman. PR (Bogdanov). William C. White. 9: 16-20 Jy15'33. 935
The bomb, the chickens, and the traffic light. Prose. Russell Maloney. 14:53-4*Mr12'38. 936
Bon voyage. Verse. Rosemary Carr Benét. 2:66-7 O2'26. 937
Bon voyage. Prose. Margaret Fishback. 4:64-6 S8'28. 938
Bon voyage. Prose. Dawn Powell. 9:17-18 Ap22'33. 939
Bon voyage. Prose. Jean Graham Townley. 4:65-6 D22'28. 940
Bon voyage, say we. Prose. John Chapin Mosher. 2:13-14 Jy10 '26. 941
Bon voyage yourself. Prose. Burdette Kinne. 6:69-71 Je21'30. 942
Bone-tired. Verse. Hortense Flexner. 14:60*F4'39. 943
Boo, beau! Prose. Wolcott Gibbs. 6:25 N8'30. 944
Book note. SM. Alexander Woollcott. 10:36-9 Mr10'34. 945
Book of etiquette answered. Prose. Clara Janson. 1:23 Je6'25. 946
A book of one's own. Prose. F. Soctt Fitzgerald. 13:19*Ag21 '37. 947
Book review. Verse. Grace Hazard Conkling. 4:59 S1'28. 948
Book review. Verse. E. B. White. 6:26 O25'30. 949
Book review. Verse. E. B. White. 6:26 D13'30. 950
Book review. Verse. E. B. White. 7:14*My23'31. 951
Book review. Verse. E. B. White. 9:29 D16'33. 952
Books, current--London. Janet Flanner. 16:65-6*Je17'39. 953
The bookworm turns. Verse. John Holmes. 11:32*Mr16'35. 954
A boon to Babbits. Prose. Ernest F. Hubbard. 1:11 F21'25. 955
Boost New York. Prose. Robert Benchley. 5:12 Ag24'29. 956
Boot and saddle. Prose. Alice Frankforter. 5:30-1 D7'29. 957
The bootleg baby carriage. Prose. Angelica Gibbs.]5:52-3*Ja20 '40. 958
Bootleggers. Prose. Vera Caspary. 5:92-3 Mr30'29. 959
A bootlegger's story. Prose. Jean. 2:25-6 S25'26; 2:29-30 O2'26; 2: 30-1 O9'26; 2:36-9 O16'26. 960
Boots and saddles. RL. Morris Markey. 12:33-40*Ap25'36. 961
Boots of empire. Prose. Ruth Suckow. 12:32*Ja30'37. 962

Booze. RL. Morris Markey. 3:30-3 D31'27. 963
Bored. Verse. Margaret Widdemer. 7:21*Je13'31. 964
Boredom squared and cubed. Verse. Morris Bishop. 10:14 Ag11'34. 965
Borough of cemeteries. Prose. Irwin Shaw. 14:13-15*Ag13'38. 966
The boss. ME. Alfred Kreymborg. 3:18 Ag27'27. 967
The boss. PR (Goodman). Helena Huntington Smith. 10:24-8 N3 '34. 968
Boss Hague, the bandwagon, and beer. RL. Alva Johnston. 8:17-20 Jy16'32. 969
Boss of the circus/big top. PR (Gumpertz). Alva Johnston. 9:27-30 My6'33; 9:21-3 My13'33. 970
The boss' present. Prose. John O'Hara. 4:56-62 D1'28. 971
The boss talks. Prose. John O'Hara. 5:43-5 Ag3'29. 972
Boss without cigar. PR (Simpson). Noel F. Busch. 15:21-7*O28 '39. 973
Boston. Verse. Katharine D. Morse. 5:90 Mr23'29. 974
Boston baby. Verse. K. C. Sappington. 9:52 Je17'33. 975
The Boston hat. Verse. Leslie Nelson Jennings. 9:36 Mr11'33. 976
Bostonian through looking-glass. PR (Ames). Niven Busch, Jr. 5:30-3 O19'29. 977
Botany exam. Prose. Robert Benchley. 6:15 Je14'30. 978
"Both insidious and invidious . . ." Verse. Anon. 1:29 Ja2'26. 979
Bottom the weaver. Verse. Jean Batchelor. 7:25 Ja23'32. 980
Bound to succeed. Prose. Hildegarde Dolson. 11:34-5*Jy27'35. 981
Bourdet, Édouard. TT. 2:26 D11 '26. 982
Bourget, Paul. Janet Flanner. 11:51*F15'36. 983
A bout with care. ML. John Strong Newberry. 9:53 Ap22'33. 984
Bow wow. Prose. John O'Hara. 15:21-3*My13'39. 985
Bowery bum. PR (McGoorty). Russel Crouse. 7:23-6 O31'31. 986
Bowling Green. DL. Burke Boyce. 3:99 S10'27. 987
A box to hide in. Prose. James Thurber. 6:25 Ja24'31. 988
The boxer. Prose. Alice Frankforter. 7:70-1 Ap25'31. 989
Boxing taught without punishment. PR (O'Brien). A. J. Liebling. 13:20-6*Ja8'38. 990
Boxwood. Verse. Anne Hamilton. 8:59*Ap23'32. 991
The boy and I. Prose. Barry Blake. 4:25-7 Mr3'28. 992
The boy and I. Prose. Barry Blake. 4:24-5 Mr24'28. 993
Boy dressing. Verse. Mark Van Doren. 12:17*Mr21'36. 994
Boy friend. Prose. Robert M. Coates. 12:69-70*Ap4'36. 995
Boy from Boston. WATN. James Thurber. 12:23-5*Ap18'36. 996
Boy, go out and get me a shingle. RL. Morris Markey. 11:27-30* Ag3'35. 997
A boy in a barn. PR (Cook). Marc Connelly. 4:29-31 Mr31'28. 998
Boy meets bullfinch. PR (Chapman). Geoffrey T. Hellman. 15:22-7*Mr4'39. 999
Boy meets girl meets foot. Prose. S. J. Perelman. 15:18-19*My13 '39. 1000
Boy on earth. Verse. Frances M. Frost. 13:52*F5'38. 1001
Boy orator grows older. PR (Sirovich). Richard O. Boyer. 14:24-30*N5'38. 1002
Boy wanted. PR (Lipton). Anthony Gibbs. 6:30-3 S13'30. 1003
Boy wonder. Prose. Zelda F. Popkin. 9:40-2 Ag12'33. 1004
The boys. PR (John-Frederics, Inc.) Margaret Case Harriman.

11:21-4*D28'35. 1005
Boys are funny. Prose. Margaret Ford. 11:70*Ap13'35. 1006
The boys from Syracuse. PR (Lee and Shubert). A. J. Liebling. 15:26-30*N18'39; 15:23-7*N25 '39; 15:33-7*D2'39. 1007
The boys in blue. RL. Arthur Bartlett. 14:36-42*My14'38. 1008
The boys in blue. RL. Morris Markey. 2:22-3 Mr27'26. 1009
The boys look 'em over. Prose. Arthur Kober. 8:45-7 Je18'32. 1010
The boyswillbe boys. Prose. Spud Johnson. 3:63-5 Mr19'27. 1011
Brackett, Charles. TT. 1:2-3 N 28'25. 1012
The Bradley Martins step out. TWNY. McAlister Coleman. 4: 32-43 F2'29. 1013
Brahmin. Verse. Nicholas Samstag. 3:67 S24'27. 1014
Branch library. RL. Frances Hackett. 8:30-6*F27'32. 1015
Brass tacks. Verse. Margaret Fishback. 3:87 Mr19'27. 1016
Brave new world. RL. Richard O. Boyer. 14:68-76*N12'38. 1017
Brave new world. Prose. Judith Fay. 12:44-50*D19'36. 1018
Brave new world. Prose. Horton Heath. 12:54-6*N7'36. 1019
Bread alone. Prose. John O'Hara. 15:17-18*S23'39. 1020
A bread and butter letter. Prose. Katie Spaeth. 3:76-7 Ap9'27. 1021
Bread-and-butter letters. Verse. Franklin P. Adams. 13:24*Je 26'37. 1022
The bread and butter note. Prose. Ordway Teed. 2:51-2 Ap17'26. 1023
"Bread--what is it?" Prose. John Forbes. 4:38-9 F25'28. 1024
Break of day. Prose. Dan Wickenden. 15:39-40*Mr25'39. 1025
Breakfast of a literary family. Prose. Marion Lay. 8:53-4 Ja 14'33. 1026
Breakfast with Dorothy Thompson. Prose. E. B. White. 15:19-20*My27'39. 1027
Breakfast with peers. Prose. E. B. White. 4:18 S1'28. 1028
Breakfast with the blackbirds of the Rue Blanche. Prose. Nancy Hoyt. 3:42-9 Ap23'27. 1029
Breakfast with the President. Prose. James Thurber. 3:28 N 12'27. 1030
The breaking up of the Winships. Prose. James Thurber. 11:15-16*Ja11'36. 1031
The breaks. SM. Alexander Woollcott. 6:42 My10'30. 1032
Breathing spell. Prose. John Chapin Mosher. 9:22-3 Je10'33. 1033
Breezes about town. Prose. Margaret Fishback. 3:41 Ag27'27. 1034
Br'er rabbit ball. Prose. Ring Lardner. 6:73-7 S13'30. 1035
The Brevoort. SH. Newman Levy. 4:32 N10'28. 1036
Brezonek off Broadway. Prose. Frederick Packard. 15:50-1 My 13'39. 1037
The bride. Prose. Morley Callaghan. 9:22-4 S23'33. 1038
The bride of Berchtesgaden. Prose. Ludwig Bemelmans. 15: 18-21*S23'39. 1039
Bride of the Sound. Prose. Howard Brubaker. 1:12 O10'25. 1040
Bridge. Verse. H. C. N. 2:41 Ap10 '26. 1041
Bridge, bowl, and bookrest. Prose. Ford Madox Ford. 7:22-3 My2 '31. 1042
Bridge for three. Prose. Alice Frankforter. 8:57-8*Mr12'32. 1043
Bridge, poker, pinochle. NESD. John J. Holzinger. 10:99 S22 '34. 1044
Bridge trolley. DL. Burke Boyce. 3:97 My14'27. 1045
The bridle. Prose. Josie Turner. 3:82 My28'27. 1046
Brief blossoming. Verse. Frances M. Frost. 6:26 Ap19'30. 1047

Brief dust of glory. Prose. H. L. Mencken. 15:25-32*Ag5'39. 1048

Brief history. Prose. Wolcott Gibbs. 7:22*Je13'31. 1049

A brief history of the Hippodrome. Prose. T. H. Bliss. 1:29 My9 '25. 1050

Brief lessons in the law. Prose. José Schorr. 13:67-8*Mr13'37.

Brief meeting. RL. Morris Markey. 11:28-32*Jy27'35. 1052

A brief study of dendrophilism. Prose. Robert Benchley. 9:17-18 F18'33. 1053

The bright decade. Verse. Henrietta Fort Holland. 9:53 O28 '33. 1054

The bright emperor. Prose. James Thurber. 8:16-17 Ag20'32. 1055

Bright thought. Verse. Dearing Ward. 3:73 Ja14'28. 1056

A brighter income-tax return. Prose. John C. Emery. 8:47-8*Mr5'32. 1057

Bring needle beer back! Prose. Robert Benchley. 9:12 Ap22 '33. 1058

Bring on the whipped cream. Verse. Margaret Fishback. 5:97 Mr2'29. 1059

Bringing her out. Prose. Norman R. Jaffray. 4:48-50 Ja19'29. 1060

Bringing up a bond. Prose. Katherine Sproehnle. 2:19 Je26'26. 1061

Bringing up the city fathers. PR (McKee). Henry F. Pringle. 3:19-22 S10'27. 1062

Britain's best. PR (Lillie). Henry F. Pringle. 7:22-5 S19'31. 1063

Britannia, Britannia! Verse. Phyllis McGinley. 9:16 Mr4'33. 1064

British Board of Film Censors. Conrad Aiken. 11:45-6*D28'35. 1065

The British language. Prose. Frances Crane. 4:105-107 O13 '28. 1066

British tableware. Verse. Arthur Guiterman. 12:46*My23'36. 1067

Britton, Nan. TT. 3:14-15 O22'27. 1068

The broadcasting industry. RL. Morris Markey. 4:42-6 Mr3'28. 1069

Broadcasting the testimonial dinner. Prose. Tom Sims. 4:115-16 N10'28. 1070

Broadway blues. Verse. Charles Norman. 3:42 Ap9'27. 1071

Broadway bulletin. Prose. James Thurber. 6:25 O4'30. 1072

Broadway chiseller. PR (Franklin). Meyer Berger. 11:22-6*Ap20'35. 1073

Broadway lambs invade fair Vevey. Prose. Frank Ward O'Malley. 3:42-5 Je11'27. 1074

The Broadway lights, fantastic. Verse. Carroll Carroll. 4:88 Ja5'29. 1075

Broadway. (Play) TT. 2:14 S25'26. 1076

Broadway rackets. Prose. Jack Wynn. 3:28-30 Ag6'27. 1077

Broadway rackets. Prose. Jack Wynn. 3:23-4 Ag13'27. 1078

Broadway rackets. Prose. Jack Wynn. 3:25-6 Ag27'27. 1079

Broadway rackets. Prose. Jack Wynn. 3:27-8 S10'27. 1080

Broadway rackets. Prose. Jack Wynn. 3:28-9 S24'27. 1081

Broadway rackets. Prose. Jack Wynn. 3:101-104 O15'27. 1082

Broadway rackets. Prose. Jack Wynn. 3:85-8 O29'27. 1083

Broadway rackets. Prose. Jack Wynn. 3:104-110 N19'27. 1084

Broadway Rapsody. Verse. Wolcott Gibbs. 15:18*F18'39. 1085

Broadway storekeeper. PR (Yereshevsky). A. J. Liebling. 14:24-7*O15'38. 1086

Broadway view. Prose. Elmer Davis. 7:16-17 F28'31. 1087

Broccoli in Manhattan. Prose. Florence Brobeck. 3:59 S10'27. 1088

Broken arcs. Prose. William Rose

Benét. 3:15-16 Ja28'28. 1089
The broken engagement. Prose. Arthur Kober. 6:128-9 D6'30. 1090
Broken heart. Prose. Esther Evarts. 15:40-1* D30'39. 1091
Broker. ME. Alfred Kreymborg. 3:24 Ap23'27. 1092
Broker. Prose. Henry Roth. 15: 45-8*N18'39. 1093
Bronx belle. Prose. Arthur Kober. 11:17-18*Jy27'35. 1094
Bronx blues. Verse. Charles Norman. 3:83 F19'27. 1095
Bronx nocturne. Prose. Arthur Kober. 10:58-60 N10'34. 1096
The Bronx palace. RL. Geoffrey T. Hellman. 9:50-4 Ap8'33. 1097
Bronx Park. Verse. Anon. 1:41 Ja30'26. 1098
Bronx pastoral. Prose. Arthur Kober. 10:19-21 F17'34. 1099
Brooklyn Bridge. DL. Burke Boyce. 2:15 Ja22'27. 1100
The Brooklyn enigma. TWNY. Frances Warfield. 10:67-76 S 8'34. 1101
Brooklyn rooming house. Prose. John Cheever. 11:76-7*My25 '35. 1102
The Brooklyn Theatre disaster. TWNY. Herbert Asbury. 6: 39-43 Ap26'30. 1103
Brooklynese champion 1926. Verse. M. F. 2:53 S11'26. 1104
Brother. Prose. John O'Hara. 12: 23-4*Jy18'36. 1105
Brothers in N. G. S. Prose. Frank Sullivan. 9:13-14 Je24'33. 1106
Broun, Heywood. Anon. 1:14 F21 '25. 1107
Broun, Heywood. Edmund R. Brown. 3:83-4 N5'27. 1108
Broun, Heywood. PR. Heywood Broun. 3:18-22 O1'27. 1109
Broun, Heywood. PR. R. A. 3: 18-22 O1'27. 1110
Broun, Heywood. Siste Viator. 1:1 Mr7'25. 1111
Broun, Heywood. TT. 4:13 My 26'28. 1112
Broun, Heywood. TT. 6:17-18 O 25'30. 1113
Broun, Heywood. TT. 10:15 S22 '34. 1114
The brown derby and the bee. PR (Smith). Arthur Krock. 2:16-18 My29'26. 1115
The brown suit. Prose. John D. Follett. 11:28*Ja11'36. 1116
Brownstone. Prose. Niven Busch, Jr. 4:21-3 Ap14'28. 1117
Brownstone. Verse. Wayland Wiles Williams. 3:105 Ap23'27. 1118
Brownstone with bath. TWNY. Joseph Wyler. 14:40-2*Ja28'39. 1119
The browsing room. SM. Alexander Woollcott. 8:38 N19'32. 1120
Brussels letter. Janet Flanner. 12:26*Jy18'36. 1121
Bryant Park. Verse. Arthur Guiterman. 9:59 Je24'34. 1122
Bryant Park. NYC. Mary Heaton Vorse. 6:19-21 Jy26'30. 1123
Buck Mulligan. TT. 15:16-17 O21 '39. 1124
Bucolic interlude. RL. Morris Markey. 11:42-9*S14'35. 1125
Buddha in East Fifty-third Street. Prose. Florence Marks. 12:41-2*Je6'36. 1126
Budding censors. Prose. Leonard Hatch. 3:87 S17'27. 1127
Buffalo. Prose. John Cheever. 11: 50-3*Je22'35. 1128
A bugler's progress. PR (Lasky). Alva Johnston. 13:18-24*Jy10 '37. 1129
The build-up. Prose. Arthur Kober. 8:58-61 S10'32. 1130
The building. MM. Corey Ford. 1:24 Ja2'26. 1131
The building climber. Verse. Jean Batchelor. 5:23 Ag17'29. 1132
Built upon sand. Prose. John Chapin Mosher. 15:22-3*Je24 '39. 1133
Bull Hill. Verse. Arthur Guiterman. 7:19*Je27'31. 1134
Bulletin. Verse. Parke Cummings. 4:59 Jy21'28. 1135
Bunco. Prose. Emile C. Schnurmacher. 2:32-3 My8'26. 1136

Button, button. Prose. Helen Riesenfeld. 9:65-7 My6'33. 1178
Button vs. Paine. Prose. Wolcott Gibbs. 8:12-14 Jy30'32. 1179
Buy it, put it away, and forget about it. Prose. Groucho Marx. 5:54-8 My4'29. 1180
By a grasshopper to an ant. Verse. Martha Banning Thomas. 7:71*Je13'31. 1181
By an inexpert accountant. Verse. Anon. 4:81 O20'28. 1182
By faculty action. Prose. James Reid Parker. 11:40-2*F1'36. 1183
By the boys themselves. Prose. Oliver LaFarge. 14:26-8*My 14'38. 1184
By the people. RL. Morris Markey. 11:47-50*F16'35. 1185
By their desks. Prose. Stanley Jones. 5:39 My4'29. 1186
By way of introduction. SM. Alexander Woollcott. 7:34 O24'31. 1187
By way of nutshells. RL. Morris Markey. 2:23-4 My1'26. 1188
By way of Yonkers. Prose. John O'Hara. 13:28-30*F27'37. 1189
Bye low baby. Prose. E. B. White. 4:25-6 Mr17'28. 1190
Byrnes, Oscar. TT. 15:14*My27 '39. 1191

C

C. Dewey of Hoboken. TWNY. Leigh Mitchell Hodges. 14:65-7*O22'38. 1192
The cad. Prose. Charles O'Neill. 12:54-6*Je27'36. 1193
Cadenza. Verse. Leslie Nelson Jennings. 11:78*D21'35. 1194
Cads and gentlemen. Prose. W. E. Farbstein. 8:20 Jy2'32. 1195
Café des enfants--2 a.m. Verse. J. C. Norton. 3:43 F19'27. 1196
Café royal. RL. Leo Rosten. 13:37-43*Ap10'37. 1197
Cafeteria. Prose. Arthur Kober. 6:47-8 O11'30. 1198
Cain, James M. (Parody) James Thurber. 10:19-20 Mr10'34. 1199
Cain, James M. (Parody) James Thurber. 11:17-18*F16'35. 1200
Cairo. FP. H. L. Mencken. 10:34 Jy28'34. 1201
Calculations in a country club. Verse. Morris Bishop. 11:14* Ag3'35. 1202
Caldwell, Erskine. (Parody) James Thurber. 12:21-2*Mr28'36. 1203
Calendar. Verse. Frances M. Frost. 8:17 D3'32. 1204
Calendar for New Yorkers. Verse. Phyllis McGinley. 13:49*Ja8'38. 1205
Calendar for the month. Verse. Nate Salisbury. 2:30 O16'26. 1206
A calendar of success. Prose. Sigmund Spaeth. 3:100-101 Ap30 '27. 1207
Calendars. Prose. Anthony Armstrong. 5:22-3 Ja4'30. 1208
California asserts herself. Verse. Anon. 1:19 Mr7'25. 1209
California--dun't esk. Prose. J. F. 2:30-1 N27'26. 1210
California, here we stay! SM. Alexander Woollcott. 9:28 Je10 '33. 1211
Californiana. Verse. Leslie Nelson Jennings. 6:32 D20'30. 1212
Californiana. Verse. Leslie Nelson Jennings. 6:31 Ja10'31. 1213
Californiana. Verse. Leslie Nelson Jennings. 6:42 F7'31. 1214
Californiana. Verse. Leslie Nelson Jennings. 7:35 F21'31. 1215
Californiana. Verse. Leslie Nelson Jennings. 8:85*Mr19'32. 1216
Californiana. Verse. Leslie Nelson Jennings. 8:26 Je11'32. 1217
Californiana. Verse. Leslie Nelson Jennings. 9:46 My6'33. 1218
The caliph complex. Prose. Ben Hecht. 2:30-1 D4'26. 1219
The call. Prose. Alice Frankforter. 14:67-8*D17'38. 1220

Guinness. 1:8 Ag1'25. 1266
Careless Cinderella. Prose. Oliver Claxton. 3:31 F26'27. 1267
Carib fantasy. Verse. Muna Lee. 6:41 D27'30. 1268
Carib garden. Verse. Muna Lee. 9:70 Ja13'34. 1269
Caribbean island. Verse. Frances M. Frost. 10:37 S15'34. 1270
Caribbean marsh. Verse. Muna Lee. 8:25 Ja7'33. 1271
Caribbean noon. Verse. Muna Lee. 10:98 O20'34. 1272
Caricature. Verse. V. Valerie Gates. 4:84 O6'28. 1273
Carillon. Verse. Arthur Guiterman. 7:95 Ap11'31. 1274
Carmel's alley. Prose. Alan Campbell. 14:51*Je18'38. 1275
Carnival in Fourteenth Street. Verse. Henrietta Fort Holland. 4:59 Je9'28. 1276
Carnival in town. RL. Morris Markey. 11:41-8*Mr23'35. 1277
A carol for children. Verse. Ogden Nash. 11:18*D21'35. 1278
The carp. TA. Will Cuppy. 8:23 Jy9'32. 1279
Carrousel. Verse. Anne Herendeen. 6:21 My31'30. 1280
Carrousel. Verse. E. B. White. 11:25*D21'35. 1281
Carrousel horse. Verse. Alice Rayfiel Siegmeister. 7:53*Jy18 '31. 1282
Carrousel tune. Verse. Rollin Kirby. 2:16 Jy17'26. 1283
Carry me back. Prose. Sally Benson. 14:13-15*Ag27'38. 1284
Cartography. Verse. Louise Bogan. 14:12*Jy23'38. 1285
Cartography. Prose. Philip G. Wylie. 2:20 Ap10'26. 1286
The cartoon situation. Prose. Wolcott Gibbs. 5:18 D28'29. 1287
The case against women. Prose. James Thurber. 12:15-16*O 24'36. 1288
The case for the daydreamer. LYMA. James Thurber. 12:20-1*D19'36. 1289
Case number 4278. Prose. Nunnally Johnson. 3:26 Jy16'27. 1290
A case of abandonment. RL. St. Clair McKelway. 10:44-51 Jy14 '34. 1291
A case of bibliocide. Prose. Samual Hopkins Adams. 15:39-42* O21'39. 1292
The case of Captain Huntley-Graham, Pratt. Theodore Pratt, 14:61-2*Mr19'38. 1293
The case of Colonel Bradshaw. Prose. S. J. Perelman. 13:56* Je5'37. 1294
The case of Herman Kemmerborn. Prose. Philip Curtiss. 9:21-3 Je24'33. 1295
The case of Mr. Chow. Prose. Emily Hahn. 13:19-21*N6'37. 1296
The case of Mrs. Nash. Prose. Mollie Panter-Downes. 14:48-53*N12'38. 1297
The case of the laughing butler. Prose. James Thurber. 12:15-16*O31'36. 1298
The case of the pleasing taxi-driver. Prose. Ogden Nash. 12: 25-6*My30'36. 1299
Case of the poisoned bun. RL. Morris Markey. 9:34-7 Ag19 '33. 1300
Case report 7007. RL. Chester T. Crowell. 7:32-4 Ja2'32. 1301
Cash and carry. PR (Pyle). Alva Johnston. 4:31-4 D8'28. 1302
Casino, I love you. Prose. E. B. White. 5:18-19 Je15'29. 1303
Casino-place. Prose. Frances Crane. 7:36-8 S26'31. 1304
Cassandra drops into verse. Verse. Dorothy Parker. 1:5 F28'25. 1305
Castle for sale. RL. Brendan Gill. 14:32-40*N26'38. 1306
Castle in New Hampshire. Prose. Richard Lockridge. 8:15-16 F4 '33. 1307
A castle in Spain. Prose. Sylvia Townsend Warner. 12:22-5*Ja2 '37. 1308
Casuals of the keys. Prose. James Thurber. 8:17-18*My7'32. 1309
A cat. Prose. Philip G. Wylie. 2:

Charmed circle. Verse. Henrietta Fort Holland. 13:32*Mr6 '37. 1395
Charming hostesses. Verse. Morris Bishop. 10:28 S15'34. 1396
Charon. Verse. Persis Greely Anderson. 5:123 N2'29. 1397
Charwoman. Verse. Anon. 2:70 O9'26. 1398
A chat with the Bishop. Prose. Elmer Rice. 6:15-16 Ja10'31. 1399
Chaucer for Gotham. Verse. Anon. 2:61 My1'26. 1400
Chaucer for Gotham. Verse. Philip G. Wylie. 2:50 My15'26. 1401
Cheap dance-halls. Prose. Maxwell Bodenheim. 2:25 Je12'26. 1402
Checking up. WP. Robert Benchley. 4:36-40 Mr3'28. 1403
Cheer up! Verse. Fillmore Hyde. 3:24 Ja28'28. 1404
Cheerful imbecility. Verse. Arthur Guiterman. 8:71*My7'32. 1405
Chemistry. Verse. E. B. White. 11:21*N9'35. 1406
Cher maître (L. G.). Verse. Emanuel Eisenberg. 9:12 Jy15 '33. 1407
The cherry. Verse. Anon. 1:35 F13'26. 1408
The chestnut man. PP. Burke Boyce. 3:34 D17'27. 1409
The chestnut man. Verse. Leslie Nelson Jennings. 2:74 F5'27. 1410
Chestnut market a gamble as usual. Verse. Anon. 2:85 N6'26. 1411
Chevaux 40, hommes 8. Prose. Wolcott Gibbs. 5:19-20 Jy20 '29. 1412
Chez Alice Foote. Verse. Margaretta Manning. 4:105 S15'28. 1413
Chez authoress. Prose. Parke Cummings. 2:16 D25'26. 1414
Chez Niny. SM. Alexander Woollcott. 6:36 My31'30. 1415
Chez nous. Prose. Emily Hahn. 10:39-46 F17'34. 1416
Chicago. Verse. Florence Kiper Frank. 5:77 Ap6'29. 1417
Chief justice. PR (Hughes). Henry F. Pringle. 11:20-4*Je29'35; 11:18-22*Jy6'35; 11:18-23*Jy13'35. 1418
Chief operator. PR (Gifford). Jack Alexander. 13:22-7*Je5'37; 13:22-7*Je12'37; 13:22-8*Je19'37. 1419
Child. Verse. Arthur Guiterman. 7:23*Jy18'31. 1420
Child of evil. Verse. Frances Park. 3:61 Je11'27. 1421
The child who was mother to a woman. PR (Sanger). R. Hale. 1:11-12 Ap11'25. 1422
The child wonder. PR (Loos). Edward E. Paramore, Jr. 2:25-8 N6'26. 1423
Children first. Prose. Frances Woodward Prentice. 7:49-50* Jy4'31. 1424
The children of Lynn. Prose. Forbes Watson. 2:30-1 F5'27. 1425
Children of the kingdom. RL. Carl Carmer. 12:26-36*Mr21'36; 12:43-9*Mr28'36. 1426
Children's books. John Holmes. 11:26-32*D21'35. 1427
The children's half-hour. Verse. D'Annunzio Cohen. 12:24*Je6 '36. 1428
The children's hour. Verse. Phyllis McGinley. 8:25 S10'32. 1429
Children's hour. Prose. Katherine Sproehnle. 5:21-3 My18'29. 1430
The children's hour: Peter Rabbit to Winnie-the-Pooh. OUWA. John Holmes. 11:26-32*D21'35. 1431
Children's poetry. Dorothy Mills and Morris Bishop. 13:32-7*N 13'37. 1432
The children's quarter of an hour. Verse. Margaret Fishback. 5: 111 O5'29. 1433
A child's garden of extroversion. Prose. S. J. Perelman. 15:16-

17*S2'39. 1434

A child's garden of reverses. Verse. David McCord. 8:19 N19'32. 1435

A child's guide to New York. Verse. Wolcott Gibbs. 15:20* My13'39. 1436

Child's play. Prose. E. B. White. 1:17 D26'25. 1437

A child's primer of transit. Verse. Margaret Fishback. 2:43 Ja22 '27. 1438

Chimes chanty. DL. Burke Boyce. 3:53 Mr5'27. 1439

China painting: prince of dull sports. Prose. S. J. Perelman. 9:13-14 Jy8 '33. 1440

Chinatown. Verse. Katharine D. Morse. 4:28 Je23'28. 1441

Chinatown. Verse. John Ogden Whedon. 4:38 S15'28. 1442

Chinatown bus. Verse. Anon. 2: 14Jy 31'26. 1443

Chinese opera. Verse. Edith Franklin Wyatt. 9:16 S9'33. 1444

Chinese prelude. Prose. Alice Frankforter. 9:38-40 Je10'33. 1445

Chinese theatre. Prose. Stephen Graham. 3:17 Ag6'27. 1446

The chiseller. Prose. Morley Callaghan. 6:15-17 Ag16'30. 1447

Chiseller. Prose. Arthur Kober. 7:82-4 O10'31. 1448

The choice. Verse. David McCord. 14:30*D10'38. 1449

Choir practice. RL. Morris Markey. 3:30-4 F18'28. 1450

Cholly. Prose. James Thurber. 7:17-18 S19'31. 1451

Chorus girl. Prose. Arthur Kober. 6:85-7 Ap5'30. 1452

A Christmas book review. Verse. Henrietta Fort Holland. 12:54* D19'36. 1453

Christmas crisis. Prose. Joseph Fulling Fishman. 8:43-4 D24 '32. 1454

Christmas Eve. Prose. Kay Boyle. 7:13-15 D26'31. 1455

Christmas Eve. Verse. Muna Lee. 8:35 D24'32. 1456

Christmas Eve in old New York. Prose. Fairfax Downey. 2:75 D18'26. 1457

The Christmas fund. Prose. John Forbes. 3:38-40 D17'27. 1458

Christmas "greedings." Prose. Jack Cluett. 3:29 D24'27. 1459

Christmas guide. Verse. Margaret Fishback. 9:20 D16'33. 1460

Christmas in many lands. Verse. Franklin P. Adams. 12:25*D26 '36. 1461

Christmas is a state of mind. Prose. Donald Moffat. 6:23-4 D13'30. 1462

Christmas is for children. Prose. G. F. Willison. 6:45-8 D27'30. 1463

Christmas list. Verse. Margaret Fishback. 3:98 D3'27. 1464

The Christmas shopper's dream. Verse. Baird Leonard. 2:33 D 18'26. 1465

A Christmas story. Prose. William Maxwell. 12:13-15*D26'36. 1466

Christmas story. RL. Joseph Mitchell. 14:22-5*D24'38. 1467

Christmas suggestions. Prose. G. L. H. 1:31 D19'25. 1468

A Christmas swallow. Prose. Berry Fleming. 5:53-5 D21'29. 1469

Christmas week. Verse. Parke Cummings. 2:74 D18'26. 1470

Christopher. Verse. Raphael McCord. 3:24 Ja21'28. 1471

Christopher K. A. P. L. A. N. Prose. Leo Rosten. 14:16-19* O8'38. 1472

Chromium linings. Prose. Franklin P. Adams. 13:30*N6'37. 1473

Chronic. Verse. Kenneth Phillips Britton. 4:72 Mr17'28. 1474

Chronicle of a crime. Prose. James Thurber. 3:58-9 Ja21'28. 1475

The church of Africa. Prose. Eleanor Gilchrist. 15:67*Je10 '39. 1476

The church of dumb creatures.

Verse. Laura Benét. 7:24 O10 '31. 1477
Churches courageous. DL. Burke Boyce. 2:26 D25'26. 1478
Churchill, Winston. (Novelist) TT. 6:11-12 Je7'30. 1479
"Chutspo." PR (Cantor). S. N. Behrman. 8:23-7 D10'32. 1480

(No entry) 1481
Chutzbah. Prose. Jerome Weidman. 12:42-4*F29'36. 1482
The cicada. Verse. Caroline Slade. 10:56 Je16'34. 1483
Cider song. Verse. Mildred Weston. 7:27 N7'31. 1484
Cigarette pictures. NYC. Arthur H. Folwell. 5:24-7 My4'29. 1485
Cinderella. Prose. George Cecil Cowing. 5:98-100 My25'29. 1486
The cinema cherub. PR (Jannings). Elsie McCormick. 3:20-3 Ja 28'28. 1487
Circe is with us again. Verse. Martha Banning Thomas. 3:17 N5'27. 1488
Circulating library. SM. Alexander Woollcott. 9:32 Mr25'33. 1489
The circulation problem if any. MM. Corey Ford. 1:26 O31'25. 1490
Circumstances alter cases. Prose. Nancy Hoyt. 2:21 Ja22'27. 1491
"The circus dancer prances . . ." Verse. Selma Robinson. 2:38 Mr27'26. 1492
Cirque d'hiver. Verse. Elizabeth Bishop. 15:23*Ja27'40. 1493
Citation. Verse. Leslie Nelson Jennings. 10:50 D22'34. 1494
Citation for a medal. Verse. Phyllis McGinley. 15:65*O14 '39. 1495
Cities. Verse. Charles Norman. 5:28 S14'29. 1496
The city. Verse. Arthur Davison Ficke. 12:16*O24'36. 1497
City beautification. Prose. Sigi Smun. 2:37 Ag7'26. 1498
City block. Verse. Ruth Lambert Jones. 5:93 O5'29. 1499
City block. RL. A. J. Liebling. 13:35-44*N27'37. 1500
City-bred. Verse. Ruth Fitch Bartlett. 4:73 S15'28. 1501
City bred. Verse. Elizabeth Gunn. 6:56 Ag23'30. 1502
City evening. Verse. E. B. White. 3:15 Ag6'27. 1503
City Hall Park. DL. Burke Boyce. 2:23 Ja15'27. 1504
City moon. Verse. Winfield Townley Scott. 15:34*Ja20'40. 1505
The city of light. Prose. James Thurber. 13:50-1*O23'37. 1506
The city of madness. Prose. Harold Standish Corbin. 1:6 Je 27'25. 1507
City songs. Verse. Mark Van Doren. 5:25 N9'29. 1508
City stars. Verse. Jean Batchelor. 6:27 F22'30. 1509
City's April. Verse. Frances Park. 3:29 Ap9'27. 1510
Civic pride at Thirty-fourth. Verse. Margaret Fishback. 7:112 D5'31. 1511
Civic virtue. Prose. Alice Frankforter. 9:67-8 O28'33. 1512
Civics and lavender water. Prose. Baird Leonard. 1: 9-10 N7'25. 1513
Civil service. Prose. Jack Cluett. 4:91-2 N17'28. 1514
The Civil War phone-number association. Prose. James Thurber. 8:17-18 O15'32. 1515
A civilized metropolis. Prose. Gilbert Seldes. 2:28-9 O16'26. 1516
The civilized one. Verse. Anon. 1:24 F6'26. 1517
Clam churning must go. Prose. Frank Sullivan. 10:17*Ja26'35. 1518
The clam man. DL. Burke Boyce. 2:24 Ja1'27. 1519
Clancy. Prose. Max Miller. 10:26-8 Jy14'34. 1520
Clarissa. Prose. Winifred Willis. 15:49-50*Ja6'40. 1521
The class-concious gambler. Prose. Ruth McKinney. 12:95-6*D12

'36. 1522
Class in pronunciation. Verse. Ellen Mc Loughlin. 7:65*Je13 '31. 1523
The class of '28 gets down to business. Prose. Zelda F. Popkin. 4:92-4 O27'28. 1524
Classmates, stay 'way from my door. Verse. Margaret Fishback. 15:61*Je10'39. 1525
Claustrophobia. Verse. Harold Willard Gleason. 5:58 Mr2'29. 1526
A clean conscience never relaxes. Verse. Ogden Nash. 12:15*S26 '36. 1527
Cleaning out my desk I come upon old tenants of a locket. Verse. Martha Banning Thomas. 4:96 Mr31'28. 1528
Clearing the air. Prose. Clinch Calkins. 5:45-7 N16'29. 1529
Cleric. Verse. Peggy Bacon. 3: 34 Ap16'27. 1530
The cliché expert reveals himself in his true colors. Prose. Frank Sullivan. 12:16-17*Ag1 '36. 1531
The cliché expert takes the stand. Prose. Frank Sullivan. 11:15-16*Ag31'35. 1532
The cliché expert tells all. Prose. Frank Sullivan. 12:16-17*Je20 '36. 1533
The cliché expert testifies on a Roosevelt hater. Prose. Frank Sullivan. 14:18-20*Je18'38. 1534
The cliché expert testifies as a toper. Prose. Frank Sullivan. 12:21-3*O17'36. 1535
The cliché expert testifies on crime. Prose. Frank Sullivan. 12:19-20*My23'36. 1536
The cliché expert testifies on Europe. Prose. Frank Sullivan. 15:18-19*Jy15'39. 1537
The cliché expert testifies on literary criticism. Prose. Frank Sullivan. 13:15-16*Jy24'37. 1538
The cliché expert testifies on love. Prose. Frank Sullivan. 11:19-20*N16'35. 1539
The cliché expert testifies on the movies. Prose. Frank Sullivan. 12:15-16*F13'37. 1540
The cliché expert testifies on vacations. Prose. Frank Sullivan. 13:15-16*Ag21'37. 1541
The cliché expert testifies on war. Prose. Frank Sullivan. 12:13-14*Jy18'36. 1542
Clinic joust. Verse. E. B. White. 3:30 Mr5'27. 1543
Clinging vine. Verse. Peggy Bacon. 10:22 Ag11'34. 1544
The clipping bureau. Prose. Newman Levy. 7:97-8 D5'31. 1545
The clock. Verse. Witter Bynner. 6:129 D6'30. 1546
The clock. RL. Morris Markey. 6:35-9 Jy26'30. 1547
The cloister and the bench. PR (Cardozo). Babette Deutsch. 6: 25-8 Mr22'30. 1548
Closeup. Prose. Emanuel Eisenberg. 8:26-7 O15'32. 1549
Cloth collector. Prose. Archibald Pyne. 7:26-7 Ap18'31. 1550
Cloud. Verse. Mildred Weston. 14: 60*O8'38. 1551
Clouds. Verse. Fillmore Hyde. 8: 20*Ap16'32. 1552
Clown. Prose. Peter Pansy. 1:35 O24'25. 1553
Club car. Prose. Nancy Hale. 7: 42-3 D26'31. 1554
Clubs is trumps. Prose. Parke Cummings. 2:42-3 Mr13'26. 1555
Clytemnestra: Long Island style. RL. Elmer Davis. 3:32-6 My7 '27. 1556
Coal country. Verse. Frances M. Frost. 11:83 D7'35. 1557
The coal fields. Prose. John O'Hara. 4:85-8 O20'28. 1558
The coal situation. Verse. Anon. 1:47 F6'26. 1559
Cobbler. Verse. Peggy Bacon. 3: 32 Jy16'27. 1560
The cockerel. Verse. Mark Van Doren. 12:22*Ag29'36. 1561
Cockleshells for a mantelpiece. Prose. Frances Crane. 10:77-

8 S29'34. 1562
Cocktail. Verse. Grace Hazard Conkling. 4:23 O20'28. 1563
A cocktail is a lovely drink. Prose. C. Knapp. 4:52-3 Mr17 '28. 1564
The cocktail season. Verse. Margaret Fishback. 8:63 Ja7'33. 1565
Cocktailana. Prose. Gilbert Seldes. 2:29 Ja29'27. 1566
A cocky mick. PR (Kenlon). Henry F. Pringle. 2:15-16 Je12 '26. 1567
Cocteau, Jean. Janet Flanner. 5: 56 Ag24'29. 1568
Cocteau, Jean. Janet Flanner. 7: 46 Ja30'32. 1569
The codfish. TA. Will Cuppy. 8: 25 S17'32. 1570
Coenties Slip. DL. Burke Boyce. 2:56 N27'26. 1571
Coffee and liqueurs. Prose. Bessie Breuer. 7:16-19 S26'31. 1572
The coffee cup. Verse. Frances Park. 3:38 Ag6'27. 1573
Coffee pot. Prose. John O'Hara. 7:70-3 D12'31. 1574
The co-founder. WATN. Greer Williams. 14:26-30*N12'38. 1575
Cohan, George M. PR. Gilbert Seldes. 10:27-31 Mr17'34; 10: 23-7 Mr24'34. 1576
Coiffeur pour dames. PR (Antoine). Bessie Breuer. 7:23-6 N21'31. 1577
Coiffeur pour dames. Prose. Alice Frankforter. 5:87-90 My 18'29. 1578
Coincidentally. Prose. W. E. Farbstein. 7:19 N28'31. 1579
The coke situation. Prose. Frank Sullivan. 3:15-16 F4'28. 1580
Colby, Natalie Sedgwick. TT. 4:21 Mr19'27. 1581
The cold house. Prose. John O'Hara. 14:15-16*Ap2'38. 1582
Cold thoughts. Verse. Hortense Flexner. 12:66*N14'36. 1583
Colette, Sidonie Gabrielle. TT. 11:10*Je1'35. 1584
Colette, Sidonie Gabrielle. Janet Flanner. 6:57-9 Ag9'30. 1585
Collaboration on books, husband and wife. TT. 15:9*Jy15'39. 1586
Collection. SM. Alexander Woollcott. 6:40 S27'30. 1587
The collector. Prose. Alice Frankforter. 8:56-7 Je18'32. 1588
The collector. Prose. John W. Thomason, Jr. 8:20-1 Ja7'33. 1589
The collectors. Prose. William A. Krauss. 14:83-6*D3'38. 1590
Collector's luck. Prose. G. M. Hurley. 8:41-2*Mr12'32. 1591
College days. MLHT. James Thurber. 9:15-17 S23'33. 1592
College luncheon. Prose. Alice Frankforter. 5:32-5 Ja4'30. 1593
College of salesmanship. Prose. Harold Bergman. 6:56-8 S20 '30. 1594
Collisions. Verse. Clarence Day. 9:23 Ja27'34. 1595
Colloque sentimental. Prose. Emanuel Eisenberg. 8:37-8 Jy 30'32. 1596
The colloquium. Prose. James Reid Parker. 12:59-60*O10'36. 1597
Colloquy with a matron. Prose. John Chapin Mosher. 2:28-9 O 23'26. 1598
Colonel of the 7th. PR (Tobin). Victor Weybright. 11:20-4*Ja11 '36. 1599
Colonel Peyton and the risks of war. Prose. William A. Krauss. 13:66-7*S25'37. 1600
Colonel Woodcock's caller. Verse. E. B. White. 7:27 S19'31. 1601
The colonel's leg. Prose. Wolcott Gibbs. 5:19-20 Mr9'29. 1602
Color. Prose. T. H. Wenning. 7:19-20 Ap25'31. 1603
Color nut. PR (Twyefort). Richard O. Boyer. 15:23-7*S23'39. 1604
The color of mice. Prose. E. B. White. 4:19-20 S22'28. 1605
Color scheme. Verse. Leslie Nel-

son Jennings. 11:74*D14'35. 1606
Coloratura salesmanship. PR (Elliot). Alva Johnston. 8:21-5 S17'32. 1607
The colossus of children. PR (Dreiser). Waldo Frank. 1:6-7 Ag15'25. 1608
Columbia Encyclopedia. Titus Oates. 12:41-4*Mr21'36. 1609
Come as someone else. PR (Maxwell). Janet Flanner. 9:24-7 N25'33. 1610
Come clean, Mr. Guest! Verse. Ogden Nash. 9:16 S23'33. 1611
Come over to my house. Prose. Robert McLaughlin. 15:29-33* Jy15'39. 1612
Come seven. Prose. T. H. Wenning. 11:72*My25'35. 1613
Come, sweet culture, prithee come! Verse. E. B. White. 9:26 S30'33. 1614
Come, ye disconsolate. PR (Campbell). Charles Mac Arthur. 2:25-8 N20'26. 1615
The comeback. Prose. Dawn Powell. 15:15-17*Ag26'39. 1616
Comet. PR (Schiaparelli). Janet Flanner. 8:19-23*Je18'32. 1617
Comeuppance for an infidel. Prose. Margaret Case Harriman. 15:50-1*S23'39. 1618
Comfort for winebibbing gallants. Verse. Anon. 2:35 My29'26. 1619
The comforter. Prose. Alice Frankforter. 7:29 Mr14'31. 1620
The comforter. Prose. Arthur Kober. 4:46-8 Ap14'28. 1621
Comforting Pullman facts. Verse. S. M. Moffatt. 7:56 O10'31. 1622
Comics face starvation as gag men near wit's end. OW. Ring Lardner. 9:24-7 Jy8'33. 1623
The coming of age of applied myology. OUWA. Carlton Brown. 13:40-54*D4'37. 1624
Coming out. Prose. Louise Bogan. 9:22 O14'33. 1625
The coming struggle for food. Prose. Clifford Orr. 14:52-3* F11'39. 1626
Commager, H. S. (Parody) James Thurber. 14:15*O8'38. 1627
Command performance. Prose. Frances Crane. 9:22-3 N25'33. 1628
Commandeered. Prose. Richard Lockridge. 8:16-17 D3'32. 1629
The commander. PR (Booth). Virgilia Peterson Ross. 6:22-5 Je21'30. 1630
Comme il faut. Prose. Rose C. Feld. 13:47-51*N20'37. 1631
Commencement. Prose. Gertrude Carver. 8:62-4 Je11'32. 1632
Comment made while riding on the Twenty-third Street ferry. Verse. Philip G. Wylie. 2:37 Ap10'26. 1633
Comments from a country garden. Verse. Elizabeth Coatsworth. 6:77 S13'30. 1634
The committee. Prose. Marc Connelly. 4:22-4 Ap7'28. 1635
Committee on Christmas joy. Prose. Paul Hollister. 6:38-45 D6'30. 1636
Common denominator. Prose. Jerome Barry. 10:21 Mr10'34. 1637
Communicated. SM. Alexander Woollcott. 9:34 S16'33. 1638
Communication. Verse. William Rose Benét. 4:34 Mr10'28. 1639
Communication. Verse. William Pynne. 3:65 F18'28. 1640
Community barter. Prose. Robert Benchley. 9:13 Ap15'33. 1641
The community players. Prose. James Reid Parker. 7:84-5 Ap11'31. 1642
Community silver lining. Verse. Wallace Cox. 4:85 My5'28. 1643
Commuters. Verse. Esther Johnston. 3:104 Ap23'27. 1644
Compagnon de voyage. Verse. Carroll Carroll. 5:36 My4'29. 1645
Companioned thus. Verse. Harold Lewis Cook. 13:25*Je12'37. 1646
Comparative values. Verse. Mar-

twenty-six. Prose. Marion E. Arnold. 5:88-90 Ap13'29. 1686
Condensed statement. Prose. George Cecil Cowing. 9:55-6 Ja20'34. 1687
Conditioned reaction. Verse. Anna Mary Wells. 4:86 O13'28. 1688
Conditions at the pool. Prose. John O'Hara. 5:45-7 Jy6'29. 1689
Conducted by the spirits. PR (Toscanini). Samuel Chotzinoff. 5:23-6 F23'29. 1690
Coney Island. Verse. Fillmore Hyde. 2:29 Je5'26. 1691
Coney Island night. Prose. Maxwell Bodenheim. 2:14 Jy31'26. 1692
The conference. Prose. Charlton Andrews. 4:38-40 Ap21'28. 1693
A conference. Verse. Arthur Guiterman. 7:78*My23'31. 1694
The conference. Prose. Arthur Kober. 6:103-105 O4'30. 1695
Confession. Verse. Fillmore Hyde. 2:30 N6'26. 1696
Confession. Verse. Richard Peckham. 6:83 N29'30. 1697
Confession. Prose. Charles G. Shaw. 4:25-7 N17'28. 1698
The confession. Prose. Frank Sullivan. 6:18-20 Ap5'30. 1699
Confessional. Prose. Anon. 1:22 Ap18'25. 1700
Confessions of a book-lover. Prose. Thomas Longan. 3:88-91 Ap9'27. 1701
Confessions of a born spectator. Verse. Ogden Nash. 12:28*Ja 16'37. 1702
Confessions of a bus-booster. Prose. Paul Gould. 4:58-63 D 8'28; 4:55-6 D15'28. 1703
Confessions of a gate-crasher. Prose. Thomas Longan. 2:57-60 Ja22'27. 1704
Confessions of a semi-pro great lover. Prose. Al Graham. 12: 90-1*N14'36. 1705
Confessions of an amateur champion. Prose. Wont Tell. 2:28-9 S11'26. 1706
The confessions of an old coupe. Verse. Martha Banning Thomas. 2:12 Ag7'26. 1707
Confidence voiced in New Yorker as birthday dawns. Prose. Charles MacArthur. 3:30-1 F 19'27. 1708
Confirmation for a rumor. Verse. Phyllis McGinley. 10:27*D8'34. 1709
Confiteor. Prose. Brendan Gill. 15:45-6*S2'39. 1710
Confusion in Gemini. Prose. Sally Benson. 10:19-21 Mr24'34. 1711
Congenial souls wanted. Prose. Robert Benchley. 3:17 Jy2'27. 1712
A congenital lecturer abroad. Verse. Miriam Vedder. 7:55 S5'31. 1713
Congratulations. Verse. Parke Cummings. 5:42 N23'29. 1714
Congress. Prose. Loring M. Black. 1:13 Ja9'26. 1715
Congress in session. Prose. Robert M. Coates. 13:38-9*Je26'37. 1716
Congressional record. Verse. David McCord. 15:40*Ap8'39. 1717
Conjugation. Verse. Marjorie Allen Seiffert. 5:89 O26'29. 1718
Conjure--. Verse. Leslie Nelson Jennings. 5:18 Mr30'29. 1719
Conjury. Verse. Ruth Lambert Jones. 5:99 S28'29. 1720
A Connecticut lad. Verse. E. B. White. 9:29 O14'33. 1721
Connecticut Spring. Verse. Frances M. Frost. 10:33 Ap7'34. 1722
Connelly, Marc. TT. 6:12 Mr15'30. 1723
Connelly, Marc. TT. 1:1 My9'25. 1724
Connoisseur. Verse. Mildred Weston. 7:47 Ja30'32. 1725
Conqueror. Prose. Irma Brandeis. 7:56-7 S5'31. 1726
The conqueror. Prose. Cecelia Winkler. 15:70*N11'39. 1727
Conrad, Joseph. TT. 4:18-19 Mr3

'28. 1728
The conscious vs. the unconscious. LYMA. James Thurber. 13:19-21*F20'37. 1729
Consequently therefore. Verse. Frances M. Frost. 6:28 N29 '30. 1730
Conservative. Verse. Hortense Flexner. 9:74 S9'33. 1731
Conserving our leaders. Prose. Robert Benchley. 8:31-2 Jy9 '32. 1732
Consider Mr. Barsh. Prose. Ellis Parker Butler. 7:50-3 O10 '31. 1733
Consider the dog. Verse. John Strong Newberry. 5:38 N30'29. 1734
Consolation of religion. Verse. Anon. 2:56 My22'26. 1735
Consolatory thought. Verse. Parke Cummings. 3:59 My28 '27. 1736
Console consolation. Prose. John Forbes. 6:56-7 My24'30. 1737
Console conversation. Prose. John Forbes. 4:34 N17'28. 1738
The constant Jay. Verse. Ring Lardner. 1:20 Ap18'25. 1739
Construction. Prose. E. B. White. 2:48 N6'26. 1740
The construction of our sentences. MM. Corey Ford. 1:36 O10 '25. 1741
Constructive criticism. Prose. Albert Carroll. 4:97 Mr24'28. 1742
Consumer's complaint. Verse. Will Scarlet. 11:74*D21'35. 1743
Contented crusader. PR (Sumner). Alva Johnston. 13:22-7*F20'37. 1744
The continental angle. Prose. Zelda Fitzgerald. 8:25 Je4'32. 1745
Contract bridge. Prose. Jack Cluett. 4:80-2 Je23'28. 1746
Contredanse. Verse. Elizabeth Coatsworth. 14:23*F26'38. 1747
Contretemps in the Bronx. Prose. Arthur Kober. 14:23-5*Ap16 '38. 1748
Contribution to science. Prose. James Reid Parker. 13:65-8* Mr6'37. 1749
Convalescence. Verse. David McCord. 12:17*Ag22'36. 1750
Convalescence. Verse. David McCord. 12:18*S12'36. 1751
Convalescence. Verse. David McCord. 12:28*O10'36. 1752
Convalescence. Verse. David McCord. 12:18*O31'36. 1753
Convent. Verse. Jerome Barry. 5:62 O19'29. 1754
The convention. Prose. C. Knapp. 4:66-8 Je9'28. 1755
Convention. Prose. John O'Hara. 5:80-2 Je15'29. 1756
The convention secretary sells Gurlick to the delegates. Prose. Samuel Taylor Moore. 2:20 Ag 28'26. 1757
The convention situation. Prose. Michael Scully. 7:55-7 Mr21'31. 1758
Convention trailer. Prose. Arthur Kober. 9:57-9 S9'33. 1759
Conversation. Prose. E. L. Masters. 4:21 Jy14'28. 1760
Conversation at Loch Ness. Verse. Clarence Day. 10:25 Mr17'34. 1761
Conversation in the black maria. Prose. John Chapin Mosher. 4: 26-7 Ap21'28. 1762
A conversation in the faculty club. Prose. Morris Bishop. 15:24-5* F25'39. 1763
Conversation in the telephone booth of an Eighth Avenue Liggett's drugstore. Prose. Sidney Skolsky. 4:82-3 Ja5'29. 1764
Conversation is an art. Verse. Lee Wilson Dodd. 8:25*My14'32. 1765
Conversation piece. Prose. Louise Bogan. 9:13-14 Ag12'33. 1766
Conversation with a Russian. Prose. John O'Hara. 6:43-5 Mr 29'30 1767
Conversations on bootlegging. RL. Morris Markey. 4:36-42 My5'28;

4:34-40 My12'28; 4:36-44 My 19'28; 4:38-48 My26'28. 1768
Conversion to atheism. Verse. Miriam Vedder. 7:35 Mr28'31. 1769
A convert to equitation. Prose. John O'Hara. 6:51-3 My3'30. 1770
Cook's tour. Verse. John Holmes. 11:22*S14'35. 1771
Cool and comfortable. Prose. Patricia Collinge. 15:66*Jy8 '39. 1772
Cool-throated hound. Verse. Mark Van Doren. 9:23 Je10'33. 1773
"A coonskin coat . . ." Verse. Anon. 1:31 Ja2'26. 1774
Coöperation. Verse. Persis Greely Anderson. 7:78 N7'31. 1775
The cop and the driver. Prose. Langdon Post. 2:111-13 D11'26. 1776
The cop in the silk shirt. PR (Coughlin). Niven Busch, Jr. and A. Barr Gray. 2:22-4 S25 '26. 1777
Cop into college man. RL. James Thurber. 6:47-52 Mr29'30. 1778
Cop is copped copping coppers. Prose. Nate Salisbury. 1:22 Ap11'25. 1779
Cops and robbers. Prose. James Reid Parker. 11:56-9*Ja11'36. 1780
Cop's cop. PR (Mulrooney). Milton MacKaye. 7:22-6 O17'31. 1781
The copy-desk muse. Anon. 3:85 S24'27. 1782
Copyright. Prose. Parke Cummings. 13:65-6*F27'37. 1783
Coq d'or. Verse. Anon. 4:82 Je 23'28. 1784
Coq d'or. Verse. Nicholas Samstag. 3:54 Ag20'27. 1785
Coquette. Prose. George Milburn. 8:22-3 Ja28'33. 1786
Corn-fed. Prose. Henry Anton. 12:18-21*S19'36. 1787
The Cornell-Penn imbroglio. Prose. Frank Sullivan. 5:27 N 16'29. 1788
The corner--reminiscences of Hammerstein's Victoria. Prose. Loney Haskell. 6:38-47 D13'30; 6:50-6 D20'30. 1789
Cornet. Prose. Theodore Pratt. 3:87 Ap30'27. 1790
Corpora delictorum. SM. Alexander Woollcott. 5:42 N2'29. 1791
Corporal Moses Smith and the liberation of South America. TWNY. Morris Bishop. 13:50-5*S25'37. 1792
The corporal of St.-Aignan. SM. Alexander Woollcott. 8:30-2 D31'32. 1793
The corpse on the speakeasy floor. RL. Edmund Pearson. 9:40-5 Ap1'33. 1794
Correct weight 1 cent. Verse. Mildred Weston. 12:56*Mr28'36. 1795
Correspondence. Prose. Winifred Willis. 7:65-6 O10'31. 1796
A correspondence in the "Times." Sylvia Townsend Warner. Prose. 14:22-3*Ap23'38. 1797
Correspondence with a tailor. Prose. Wolcott Gibbs. 13:57-8* Mr13'37. 1798
Cosmetic counter. Verse. Jean Batchelor. 6:22 Mr1'30. 1799
The cosmopolite. Verse. Carroll Carroll. 2:87 D11'26. 1800
"Cosmos." PR (Butler). Alva Johnston. 6:28-32 N8'30; 6:33-41 N15'30. 1801
The Cossack. Prose. Robin Kinkead. 13:50-4*Mr13'37. 1802
The Costellos clean the boiler. RL. Edmund Pearson. 9:31-4 Ag26'33. 1803
The costume balls. Prose. Frank Sullivan. 2:13-14 Mr13'26. 1804
Costume piece. Prose. Alice Frankforter. 9:97-9 D16'33. 1805
Counsel. Verse. Sydney King Russell. 5:19 Je8'29. 1806
Counsel for the defense. PR (Lawes). Helena Huntington

Smith. 2:15-17 Jy10'26. 1807
Counselor. Prose. T. H. Wenning. 6:27-8 O4'30. 1808
The counter man. Prose. Leonard Hall. 1:11 Jy4'25. 1809
Counter-irritant. Prose. Sally Benson. 15:15-17*Jy22'39. 1810
Counter-revolution. Prose. John K. Hutchens. 11:44-5*Ag17'35. 1811
Counterpoint. Prose. Wolcott Gibbs. 13:15-16*Ag28'37. 1812
Counterpoint. Verse. Ruth Lambert Jones. 5:17 Mr9'29. 1813
Counterpoint. Verse. Baird Leonard. 14:52*Jy16'38. 1814
Counterpoint. Verse. Baird Leonard. 14:55*S17'38. 1815
Counterpoint. Verse. Baird Leonard. 14:50*F4'39. 1816
Counterpoint. Verse. Baird Leonard. 15:32*Ap8'39. 1817
Country fire. Prose. Brendan Gill. 14:54-5*O1'38. 1818
Country life in America. Verse. Martha Banning Thomas. 3:19 Jy9'27. 1819
Country mushrooms. Verse. Grace Hazard Conkling. 5:40 O19'29. 1820
Country night. Verse. Frances M. Frost. 13:37*Ag28'37. 1821
Country night. Verse. Selma Robinson. 7:48 S12'31. 1822
Country sentiment. Verse. Grace Hazard Conkling. 4:82 O27'28. 1823
Country weekend. Verse. Martha Banning Thomas. 7:46 N14'31. 1824
Coup. Prose. Carroll Carroll. 11:42*Ag3'35. 1825
Couple. Prose. E. B. White. 3:94-5 My14'27. 1826
A couple of hamburgers. Prose. James Thurber. 11:20-2*N16'35. 1827
Couplets on literary matters. Verse. John Holmes. 12:29* My9'36. 1828
Courage. Verse. Paul M. Saunders. 15:56*S9'39. 1829
The courageous one. Verse. E. B. White. 5:22 Mr23'29. 1830
The course of true love. Prose. Robert M. Coates. 13:16-17* Ag7'37. 1831
Courtesy of Coca-Cola. PR (McNamee). Geoffrey T. Hellman. 6:20-2 Ag9'30. 1832
Courtesy of the Gideons. Prose. A. B. Bernd. 7:42 Ap4'31. 1833
Courtroom pastorale. RL. Richard O. Boyer. 14:38-43*S10'38. 1834
Courtroom warrior. PR (Buckner). Alva Johnston. 8:21-3*Mr12'32; 8:24-7*Mr19'32. 1835
The courtship of Erato. Prose. Carroll Carroll. 2:80-1 N13'26. 1836
The courtship of Milton Barker. Prose. Wolcott Gibbs. 14:17-21* Ap9'38. 1837
Courtship through the ages. Prose. James Thurber. 15:23-4*D9'39. 1838
Cousin Bob. Prose. George Cecil Cowing. 6:27 D13'30. 1839
Cousin Larry. Prose. Dorothy Parker. 10:15-17 Je30'34. 1840
Cousin Marie and the Reich. Prose. Anna Mary Wells. 14:81-3*N19'38. 1841
Cousin Penelope. Verse. Dearing Ward. 3:56 D17'27. 1842
Couturière casualty. Verse. Jean Batchelor. 9:74 O7'33. 1843
The covert wagon. Verse. Margaret Fishback. 8:26 D24'32. 1844
Coward, Noel. TT. 1:3 N14'25. 1845
Coward, Noel. TT. 1:2 S5'25. 1846
Coward, Noel. PR. Alexander Woollcott. 4:21-5 Ja19'29. 1847
Coward, Noel. (Parody) Wolcott Gibbs. 13:14 My8'37. 1848
Cows wit wings. Verse. E. B. White. 4:29 Mr17'28. 1849
Cowslips. Prose. Howard Cushman. 4:44 My19'28. 1850
The crack of doom. Prose. E. B.

White. 9:19-20 O14'33. 1851
Cracked ceilings. Prose. Corey Ford. 1:17 N7'25. 1852
Cracker. Prose. Theodore Pratt. 10:55-7*Ja19'35. 1853
Cracker conquered. Prose. Theodore Pratt. 12:55-6*O3'36. 1854
Crackers and milk. Prose. Stanley Jones. 4:90-1 O13'28. 1855
The cradle of civilization. Prose. Dorothy Parker. 5:23-4 S21'29. 1856
Cradle piece. Verse. Frances M. Frost. 7:18 S19'31. 1857
Cradle song. Verse. Frances M. Frost. 9:18 Ap22'33. 1858
Crane, Nathalia. TT. 11:10-11* Ja18'36. 1859
Crane, Stephen. TT. 12:14*N7'36. 1860
Crank letter. Verse. Gerald Raftery. 15:95*D16'39. 1861
Crap game. Prose. Daniel Fuchs. 13:19-20*D25'37. 1862
A crash in Tin Pan Alley. Prose. John Ogden Whedon. 5:89-92 Ap6'29. 1863
Crashes and screams. Prose. Russell Maloney. 14:60-1*S17 '38. 1864
Crashing a trip to Europe. Prose. Sam Marx. 3:65-70 Jy2'27. 1865
Crashing into banquets. Prose. Epicure. 3:76-7 S24'27. 1866
Crashing "the ladder." Prose. P. M. R. 3:67-8 Je11'27. 1867
Crashing the opera. Prose. Henry Carlton. 4:65-6 Mr17'28. 1868
A craven's craving. Verse. Jean Batchelor. 15:40*S16'39. 1869
Crazy but charming. Prose. Alan Campbell. 15:56-8*F18'39. 1870
The crazy club. Prose. Frank Sullivan. 3:25-6 S24'27. 1871
Crazy over horses. PR (Hertz). Helena Huntington Smith. 6:22-5 Je7'30. 1872
Cream of the jest. Verse. Phyllis McGinley. 6:83 O18'30. 1873
The creative life. Prose. Hannah Lees. 10:34-6 S29'34. 1874
The creatures. Verse. Marjorie Allen Seiffert. 6:75 O4'30. 1875
A credit to the college. Prose. James Reid Parker. 13:53-5* My22'37. 1876
Credulity. Verse. Anon. 3:103 N19 '27. 1877
Crêpe. Verse. Robert Hyde. 5:119 O12'29. 1878
Crescendo. Verse. Margaret Fishback. 12:61*Ap11'36. 1879
Cricket. Prose. Alice Frankforter. 9:28-30 Ag26'33. 1880
Crime and punishment. TWNY. Herbert Asbury. 7:30-3*Ag1'31. 1881
Crime and punishment. Verse. Dorothy Dow. 4:39 F25'28. 1882
Crime and punishment. RL. Morris Markey. 3:28-32 Ja21'28. 1883
The crime at Mrs. Ward's. Prose. Donald Moffatt. 6:18-20 My31 '30. 1884
Crime for all. WP. Robert Benchley. 5:43-8 My18'29. 1885
Crime in the Cumberlands. RL. James Thurber. 12:30-5*F29 '36. 1886
Crime passionel. RL. Morris Markey. 3:36-40 Ap2'27. 1887
Crime passionnel. RL. Morris Markey. 3:28-32 Jy9'27. 1888
The crime wave. NESD. John J. Holzinger. 9:37 Ag26'33. 1889
Crimes of the movies. Verse. W. E. Farbstein. 7:22*Jy25'31. 1890
Criminal city. Prose. Elmer Davis. 2:31 Ja29'27. 1891
Criminal item. RL. Morris Markey. 3:36-40 F26'27. 1892
The crimson menace. RL. Morris Markey. 6:44-50 My17'30. 1893
A crisis. RC. Fillmore Hyde. 3: 16-17 My28'27. 1894
Crisis at Valley Forge. Verse. John Holmes. 11:23*Jy13'35. 1895

Crisis in Japan. OFC. Helen Mears. 14:60-5*S10'38. 1896
Crisp new bills for Mr. Teagle. Prose. Frank Sullivan. 11:17-19*D21'35. 1897
The critic. Prose. Mary F. Watkins. 9:47-51 Ja13'34. 1898
The critic delivers a guarded opinion. Prose. Sigmund Spaeth. 3:23 Ap16'27. 1899
The critic on the pan. Verse. John Holmes. 12:18*S5'36. 1900
Critique. Verse. Gertrude Curtis Ryan. 8:63*Ap30'32. 1901
Critique. Prose. E. B. White. 3:30 N5'27. 1902
Critique of the newer poetry. Prose. Frank J. O'Donnell. 1:24 Jy25'25. 1903
Croak. Verse. Peggy Bacon. 4:22 F9'29. 1904
Crocus. Verse. Anon. 2:36 Mr20 '26. 1905
Croesus in politics. PR (Mellon). Homer Joseph Dodge. 4:18-21 Ag4'28. 1906
The crooners' paradise. OW. Ring Lardner. 8:22-7 Jy16'32. 1907
Croquet. SM. Alexander Woollcott. 6:36 S20'30. 1908
Cross-country gamut. Prose. James Thurber. 3:40-2 F11'28. 1909
Cross-lots. Verse. Marie Gilchrist. 7:25 Ja2'32. 1910
Cross-section. Prose. G. Schwabe. 3:48 S17'27. 1911
The cross-talkers. Prose. Lillian Day. 7:58-60 S19'31. 1912
Crossed heart. Verse. Frances M. Frost. 6:70 My31'30. 1913
Crosstown. Prose. Marquis James. 1:15 O3'25. 1914
The crosstown-bus situation. Prose. James Thurber. 8:20-1*My14'32. 1915
Crossing Manhattan Bridge. Verse. Philip G. Wylie. 2:47 Ap17'26. 1916
Crossing the Alps. Verse. Baird Leonard. 3:68 F26'27. 1917
Crossing the color line. Verse. Alfred Kreymborg. 7:19 D12 '31. 1918
The Croydon exhumations. WP. Robert Benchley. 5:30-6 Ag31 '29. 1919
The crucial game. OW. Ring Lardner. 8:40-2 O22'32. 1920
Cruciform. Verse. Winifred Welles. 14:21*Ag6'38. 1921
Cruise blues. Verse. Mildred Weston. 15:65*F18'39. 1922
Cruise captain's chantey. Verse. Phyllis McGinley. 12:24*F22'36. 1923
Cruise hostess. Verse. Franklin P. Adams. 13:47*Ja8'38. 1924
Cruise life on the ocean's wave. Verse. Franklin P. Adams. 13:43*Ag21'37. 1925
Crumbs. Verse. Elizabeth Coatsworth. 6:93 N15'30. 1926
Crusader. WATN. James Thurber. 12:22-4*Jy4'36. 1927
The cry from Macedonia. Verse. Rollin Kirby. 3:34 Mr5'27. 1928
A cry in the night. Prose. A. B. Bernd. 7:50*My23'31. 1929
The crying abuse and the gentlemanly waiter. Prose. G. Beck. 5:80-1 My4'29. 1930
Crying need. Prose. A. B. Bernd. 2:21 Mr27'26. 1931
The crystal slipper. RL. Morris Markey. 11:29-38*Ja18'36. 1932
Crystals of progress. Prose. Richard Lockridge. 11:65-7*Ap 13'35. 1933
Cubit-adder. PR (Hoopingarner). Russell Lord. 8:21-4*Ap16'32. 1934
Cuisine unexcelled. Prose. Waverly L. Root. 2:36-7 D4'26. 1935
Cul-de-sac. Verse. Ted Robinson, Jr. 6:50 My3'30. 1936
The culinary expert takes the stand. Prose. Frank Sullivan. 11:17-18*F8'36. 1937
Culinary note. Verse. Leslie Nelson Jennings. 9:42 Je24'33. 1938
Cultural note. Verse. Charmé

Seeds. 14:74*N26'38. 1939
The culture business. PR (Pond). Milton MacKaye. 8:18-22 Ag27 '32; 8:22-5 S3'32. 1940
Culture on the hoof. OUWA. Gilbert Seldes. 12:37-43*Je27'36. 1941
The cup of day. Verse. Robert P. Tristram Coffin. 9:14 Je24'33. 1942
Curaçao. Prose. Alice Frankforter. 9:53-8 O21'33. 1943
The curb in the sky. Prose. James Thurber. 7:17-18 N28 '31. 1944
Curb markets. Verse. Arthur Guiterman. 7:60 S26'31. 1945
Curb service. Prose. Theodore Pratt. 13:48-9*Ja8'38. 1946
Curbstone art: grouping. Prose. Corey Ford. 1:13 Je20'25. 1947
Cure. Prose. Wolcott Gibbs. 10:30-1 My26'34. 1948
Cure. Prose. Frances Warfield. 9:24 O21'33. 1949
Curfew must not ring to-night. FPI. James Thurber. 15:26-7*Je17'39. 1950
Curkden and the goosegirl. Verse. Helene Mullins. 4:66 S1'28. 1951
Curl up and diet. Verse. Ogden Nash. 11:20*Je8'35. 1952
Current films (Paris). Janet Flanner. 14:54 Ap9'38. 1953
The current press. Prose. Morris Markey. 1:15-16 S19'25. 1954
The current press. Prose. Morris Markey. 1:15-16 O24'25. 1955
The current press. Prose. Morris Markey. 1:11-12 D5'25. 1956
The current press. Prose. Morris Markey. 1:22-3 F6'26. 1957
The current press. Prose. Morris Markey. 2:22-3 Mr20'26. 1958
The current press. Prose. Morris Markey. 2:23-4 Ap24'26. 1959
The current press. Prose. Morris Markey. 2:26-8 My29'26. 1960
The current press. Prose. Morris Markey. 2:26-30 Je26'26. 1961
The current press. Prose. Prenez Garde. 1:16-17 Ag15'25. 1962
Customers for costumes. Prose. G. M. Hurley. 7:50-2 Mr28'31. 1963
The customers' man. Prose. Robert Winsmore. 3:83-5 N19'27. 1964
The customs. RL. Morris Markey. 3:36-40 S17'27. 1965
Cut out the favoritism. Verse. Etaoin Shrdlu. 1:26 Mr28'25. 1966
Cut that waste! Prose. Ellis Parker Butler. 6:67-8 N8'30. 1967
Cute quaint. Prose. Theodore Pratt. 2:61 D4'26. 1968
Cycle. Verse. Jerome Barry. 12:18*Ja2'37. 1969
Cycle. Verse. J. H. 8:16 S10'32. 1970
Cycle. Verse. Ruth Lambert Jones. 5:53 O19'29. 1971
A cycle of Broadway. TWNY. Walter Prichard Eaton. 9:51-61 F10'34. 1972
Cynara. Prose. Clifford Orr. 10:107-108 N10'34. 1973
Cynthia and Cecily. Prose. Maddy Vegtel. 10:22 N3'34. 1974
Czar and elder. PR (Hays). Alva Johnston. 9:18-21 Je10'33; 9:16-19 Je17'33. 1975
Czar of song. PR (Buck). Alva Johnston. 8:22-5 D17'32; 8:19-22 D24'32. 1976

D

Da Capo. SM. Alexander Woollcott. 5:38 Ap6'29. 1977
The dada city. Prose. Robert M. Coates. 6:16-17 Ag23'30. 1978
The dada city. Prose. Robert M. Coates. 6:32-3 Ag30'30. 1979
The dada city. Prose. Robert M. Coates. 6:40-2 S6'30. 1980
Daddy dear. Prose. Sally Benson.

15:25-7*D9'39. 1981
The daddy of Sunday painters. PR (Peters). Murdock Pemberton. 1:11-12 Jy11'25. 1982
The daemon. Verse. Louise Bogan. 14:25*Ap2'38. 1983
Daguerrotype. Prose. Wolcott Gibbs. 5:18 Jy27'29. 1984
Daily papers. Verse. Margaret Widdemer. 3:19 My28'27. 1985
The daily round. Prose. Frederick Packard. 5:66-8 S7'29. 1986
Daily strength for daily need. Verse. Margaret Fishback. 4:44 My19'28. 1987
The daisy chain. Prose. Dawn Powell. 9:19-20 S30'33. 1988
Dallas, Texas. OFC. Michael Scully. 8:48*My7'32. 1989
Damn Mr. Archer! Prose. James Reid Parker. 10:58-9 Mr10'34. 1990
The damned hotel. Prose. Robert M. Coates. 13:16-17*My8'37. 1991
Dance-motif for a masque. Verse. Grace Hazard Conkling. 4:25 Ja19'29. 1992
Dance team. PR (De Marcos). Margaret Case Harriman. 15:22-7*Ja6'40. 1993
The dance will end at midnight. Verse. Robert Hillyer. 14:20* S16'38. 1994
Dancing Hamlet. PR (Draper). Russell Maloney. 14:20-5*Ja 7'39. 1995
Dancing in the Bronx. Prose. Arthur Kober. 11:47-50*Jy13 '35. 1996
Danger: keep out. Prose. Miriam Vedder. 7:46 Ag22'31. 1997
Dangerous tendencies of the Gotham Jehu. Prose. Stanley Walker. 1:35 O10'25. 1998
Daniel Webster, the hay fever, and me. Prose. E. B. White. 14:14-15*Jy30'38. 1999
D'Annunzio, Gabriele. Clifton Fadiman. 14:57-8*Je11'38. 2000
Danse macabre. Verse. Robert Strunsky. 11:45*Ag3'35. 2001
Dante and --. PR (Fairfax). Ring Lardner. 4:16-17 Jy7'28. 2002
Daphne's daughter. Prose. Emanuel Eisenberg. 9:68-72 My13'33. 2003
The dark Christmas on Wildwood Road. Verse. Morris Bishop. 10:22*D22'34. 2004
Dark leader. PR (Johnson). Robert Wohlforth. 9:22-6 S30'33. 2005
Dark November. Verse. Robert Hillyer. 14:17*N26'38. 2006
Dark party. Prose. D. B. Wyndham Lewis. 7:23-5 Mr7'31. 2007
Darkest Africa. Prose. Alice Frankforter. 6:23-4 Ag9'30. 2008
D'Artagnan of the courts. PR (Borotra). John R. Tunis. 6:24-7 S6'30. 2009
A dash of canary. Prose. Sigmund Spaeth. 2:24 Mr6'26. 2010
Dat ole diablerie in advertising copy. Prose. Robert Wohlforth. 6:90-2 Ap5'30. 2011
Date with romance. Prose. Mollie Panter-Downes. 15:23-4*O 14'39. 2012
Dated. Verse. Martha Banning Thomas. 5:58 N16'29. 2013
Daughter of her father. PR (Frick). John McCarten. 15:21-5*Jy15 '39; 15:23-6*Jy22'39. 2014
David. Prose. Ellen Vorse. 8:57-8 F4'33. 2015
Davis, Owen. TT. 10:22 O13'34. 2016
Dawn in Central Park. Verse. Carroll Carroll. 2:48 Ja22'27. 2017
The dawn of speech. Prose. Arthur H. Folwell. 1:31 Mr14'25. 2018
The dawn of the moving picture. SM. Alexander Woollcott. 8:30 S24'32. 2019
Dawns about town. Prose. Margaret Fishback. 3:45 O22'27. 2020
The day. Verse. Theodore Spencer. 15:58*D2'39. 2021
Day at the races. RL. Morris Markey. 2:36-8 S18'26. 2022

Day-before-yesterday man. PR (Jones). Geoffrey T. Hellman. 15:24-30*Ap29'39. 2023
Day by day. Prose. Morley Callaghan. 8:13-15 Ag20'32. 2024
Day, Clarence. TT. 8:7*Ap2'32. 2025
Day, Clarence. TT. 1:10-11*Ja11 '36; 11:9*Ja25'36. 2026
A day in Albany. RL. Jack Alexander. 13:42-51*My8'37. 2027
Day in court. RL. Morris Markey. 2:32-4 S25'26. 2028
"A day in thy courts." Prose. Franklin P. Adams. 2:29 O9 '26. 2029
A day in town. Prose. Anon. 1: 7-8 S19'25. 2030
A day like today. Prose. John O'Hara. 14:14-15*Ag6'38. 2031
Day off. Verse. Marion Canby. 9:27 S30'33. 2032
Day on the beach. Prose. John Chapin Mosher. 8:19-21 S3'32. 2033
The day the bonus came. Prose. John Chapin Mosher. 12:44*Je 27'36. 2034
The day the dam broke. MLHT. James Thurber. 9:11-13 Jy29 '33. 2035
A day with La Guardia. RL. Jack Alexander. 13:35-49*O16'37. 2036
A day with Senator Wagner. RL. Brendan Gill. 15:44-50*Ap22'39. 2037
Daylight saving. Verse. Dorothy Parker. 3:26 Jy2'27. 2038
Days. Prose. John O'Hara. 14:21* Ap30'38. 2039
Days like that. Prose. Robert M. Coates. 13:60-1*S11'37. 2040
Dayton, Tennessee. Prose. Marquis James. 1:6-9 Jy11'25. 2041
De minimis. Verse. Sara Henderson Hay. 5:63 O26'29. 2042
De mortuis. Verse. Henrietta Fort Holland. 14:32*Jy30'38. 2043
De profundis. Verse. Ruth Lambert Jones. 5:107 S14'29. 2044
De rigueur. Verse. Margaretta Manning. 4:57 My19'28. 2045
De senectute. PR (Root). Henry F. Pringle. 11:21-6*F1'36; 11: 21-5*F8'36; 11:22-7*F15'36. 2046
De senectute. SM. Alexander Woollcott. 5:30 F15'30. 2047
Deacon gets tilt for tat. OW. Ring Lardner. 8:26-32 Ag20'32. 2048
The dead city. Verse. Clinch Calkins. 3:17 S10'27. 2049
Dead Letter Office. Verse. William Rose Benét. 9:25 Je3'33. 2050
Dead letters. Prose. Margaret Fishback. 2:65-6 O30'26. 2051
Dead man's bathroom. Prose. Russell Maloney. 12:19-20*Ja 23'37. 2052
Deadlock. Verse. Margaret Fishback. 4:107 Mr17'28. 2053
The deadly parallels. Prose. Frank Sullivan. 7:17 Ap18'31. 2054
Dean of the theatre. PR (Frohman). Alva Johnston. 9:21-3 O28'33; 9:21-4 N4'33. 2055
Dear, dead dumbshow. Verse. Morris Bishop. 12:25*F29'36. 2056
The dear Dimmers. Prose. Clifford Orr. 8:26-7 O1'32. 2057
Dear editor. Verse. Hortense Flexner. 14:64*My14'38. 2058
Dear Jack. Verse. Helene Mullins. 12:110*D5'36. 2059
Dear little Margaret. Prose. Angelica Gibbs. 15:59-61*Mr4'39. 2060
Dear Margery. Prose. Frances Warfield. 10:32-3 My5'34. 2061
Dear Mr. Smith--. Verse. Hortense Flexner. 14:28*Mr26'38. 2062
Dear old boob. Prose. Frank Sullivan. 8:17-19 My21'32. 2063
A dear old couple. Prose. Marc Connelly. 4:19-20 Mr24'28. 2064
Dear old golden rule days. Prose. John Chapin Mosher. 10:29-30 S15'34. 2065

Dear old Paris. Prose. Frank Sullivan. 8:15-16 S17'32. 2066
Dearest Edith. PR (Wharton). Janet Flanner. 5:26-8 Mr2'29. 2067
Death. Verse. William Butler Yeats. 5:21 Ap27'29. 2068
Death at dinner. Prose. Helene Fredric. 10:97-8 Mr24'34. 2069
Death in Fortieth Street. Verse. Phyllis McGinley. 10:76 Ap14 '34. 2070
Death in the family. Prose. Jerome Weidman. 15:65-6*Ap1 '39. 2071
Death in the rumble seat. Prose. Wolcott Gibbs. 8:15 O8'32. 2072
Death of a dog. WATN. James Thurber. 14:24-7*Ag20'38. 2073
Death of a traitor. Prose. Emily Hahn. 14:49-51*D17'38. 2074
The death of Colonel Peyton. Prose. William A. Krauss. 13: 72-3*O30'37. 2075
The death of Santa Claus. Prose. Clifford Orr. 9:14-16 O23'33. 2076
Death on the front porch. Prose. James Reid Parker. 10:83-6 S8'34. 2077
Death, without sting. RL. Jack Alexander. 12:40-6*Ja16'37. 2078
De Brancovan, Anna. Janet Flanner. 9:30 My27'33. 2079
Debtor. Verse. Sara Henderson Hay 6:26 My17'30. 2080
Debunkers. Verse. Alfred Kreymborg. 7:18 N28'31. 2081
Débutantes at a concert. Verse. Edith Franklin Wyatt. 14:57* Mr12'38. 2082
The debutante's good-night. Verse. Baird Leonard. 2:44 Mr20'26. 2083
Decalcomania. Prose. R. C. Washburn. 3:92-3 My7'27. 2084
December evening. Verse. Frances M. Frost. 7:17 D26'31. 2085
December fugitive. Verse. Henry Morton Robinson. 13:31*D18'37. 2086
December night. Verse. Anon. 2: 61 D18'26. 2087
The deceptrices. Verse. William Carlos Williams. 15:20*Ag12 '39. 2088
Deck the hall. Verse. Mildred Weston. 6:87 D20'30. 2089
Declaration. Verse. Leslie Nelson Jennings. 3:83 Ja7'28. 2090
Declaration. SM. Alexander Woollcott. 6:30 Jy5'30. 2091
Decline and fall of the ape. Prose. Will Cuppy. 7:16-17*Ag15'31. 2092
The decline of the art of conversation. Prose. Oliver Claxton. 3:16-17 Ag6'27. 2093
The decline of the gesture. Prose. Oliver Claxton. 3:21 My7'27. 2094
The decline of the sport of kings. Prose. Paxton Hibben. 3:30-4 My28'27. 2095
Decline of winking. Prose. Richard Lockridge. 11:35-6*Ap27'35. 2096
Declining an invitation to a picnic. Verse. George Abell. 5:105 Je 15'29. 2097
The declining function. Prose. Ellin Mackay. 1:15-16 D12'25. 2098
Decorative art. Verse. Persis Greely Anderson. 6:100 N22'30. 2099
Deep in the forest. Prose. Sylvia Townsend Warner. 13:18-20*Je 19'37. 2100
The deep-sea squid farm. MM. Corey Ford. 1:1 S19'25. 2101
Deep South. Prose. Nathan Asch. 13:73-5*Ap10'37. 2102
The deep talkers. Prose. Arthur Kober. 6:101-103 Ap12'30. 2103
The deep, tangled Kaufman. PR (Kaufman). Alexander Woollcott. 5:26-9 My18'29. 2104
Defeat. Prose. Mary C. McCall, Jr. 5:102-103 Mr16'29. 2105

Dispirited. Verse. Carroll Carroll. 5:42 Ap13'29. 2233

Dispossessed. Verse. Hortense Flexner. 12:30*Mr14'36. 2234

Dispraising tact. Verse. Marjorie Allen Seiffert. 6:85 S27'30. 2235

Dissent. SM. Alexander Woollcott. 8:34*Mr19'32. 2236

Dissertation on furniture. Verse. Phyllis McGinley. 11:16*Jy6 '35. 2237

The distance fiend. Verse. Arthur H. Folwell. 1:11 F21'25. 2238

Distant drums. Prose. Frank B. Elser. 11:30-2*Mr9'35. 2239

Distinction. Verse. Ruth Lambert Jones. 5:39 Ag3'29. 2240

A distinguished American abroad. Prose. Anon. 4:85-6 N3'28. 2241

Distinguished citizens of 1931. Prose. W. E. Farbstein and Joseph P. Pollard. 7:21-2 D19 '31. 2242

The distracted gardener. Verse. Martha Banning Thomas. 6:101 My24'30. 2243

District leader. PR (Hines). Jack Alexander. 12:21-6*Jy25'36; 12:18-23*Ag1'36; 12:18-24*Ag8 '36. 2244

Dithers and jitters. Prose. Cornelia Otis Skinner. 13:21*Ap 24'37. 2245

A ditty of dreadful days. Verse. A. K. Laing. 3:42 D17'27. 2246

Divide by twelve. Prose. Frances Warfield. 9:28-9 N25'33. 2247

Divine discontent. Verse. Florence S. Edsall. 9:78 O14'33. 2248

Divine plan. Verse. Hortense Flexner. 11:22*Jy6'35. 2249

Divine worship. Prose. Donald Gordy. 7:52-3*Ag8'31. 2250

Division. Verse. Jean Batchelor. 5:33 O19'29. 2251

Divorce. Prose. John O'Hara. 7:77-9 Ap11'31. 2252

Divorce: its cause and cure. Prose. Winifred Willis. 15:53*Ja13'40; 15:40-2 F3'40. 2253

Dixie and Al. RL. Morris Markey. 3:28-33 Ja28'28. 2254

The dizzy rise (and ensuing bust) of simplified spelling. OUWA. H. L. Mencken. 12:37-44*Mr7 '36. 2255

Do ducks speak? Prose. Oliver Claxton. 3:85 My21'27. 2256

Do or dial. Prose. Bella Cohen. 3:39-40 N5'27. 2257

Do or diaphragm. PR (Robinson-Duff). S. N. Behrman. 11:22-7*My25'35. 2258

Do re mi. Prose. Wolcott Gibbs. 11:23-4*O12'35. 2259

Do we execute innocent people? RL. Edmund Pearson. 11:32-9*Je22'35. 2260

Do-X. RL. Morris Markey. 7:59-63 S12'31. 2261

Do you believe in signs? Prose. Oliver Claxton. 4:87 Ap28'28. 2262

Do you care about the armadillo? the cassowary? WP. Scudder Middleton. 11:35-42*N2'35. 2263

Do you know—? Prose. John O'Hara. 4:41 Jy14'28. 2264

Do you know my garden? Prose. Maddy Vegtel. 11:43-4*Ag10'35. 2265

"Do you know the spumonito . . ." Verse. M. M. 3:63 N5'27. 2266

Do you like it here? Prose. John O'Hara. 15:17-18*F18'39. 2267

Doc Marlowe. Prose. James Thurber. 11:19-21*N2'35. 2268

The doctor. Verse. E. B. White. 2:83 F5'27. 2269

A doctor a day. Prose. Heywood Broun. 3:19-21 O29'27. 2270

A doctor a day. Prose. Heywood Broun. 3:15-17 N5'27. 2271

A doctor a day. Prose. Heywood Broun. 3:30-1 N12'27. 2272

A doctor a day. Prose. Heywood Broun. 3:31-2 N26'27. 2273

A doctor a day. Prose. Heywood Broun. 3:38-42 D10'27. 2274

Dr. Andrews passes by. Prose. Oriana Atkinson. 12:71-2*S19 '36. 2275

Dr. Baldin. Prose. Emily Hahn. 13:23-5*Ja1'38. 2276
Dr. Bonte's chickens. SM. Alexander Woollcott. 8:30*Ap2'32. 2277
Dr. C-dm-n's diary. Prose. Nunnally Johnson. 2:39 F27'26. 2278
Dr. Frankenstein and Mr. Sweeney. Prose. Wolcott Gibbs. 8:16-17* F27'32. 2279
Doctor Freeme's own petard. Prose. Frank Sullivan. 8:19-21*Mr5'32. 2280
The doctor looks at art. Verse. Hortense Flexner. 12:54*F6'37. 2281
"The doctor looks" at his garden. Verse. Morris Flexner. 11:27* Je8'35. 2282
Doctor Maclure. SM. Alexander Woollcott. 5:62 N23'29. 2283
Doctor of movies. PR (Hays). Arthur Krock. 2:21-2 My8'26. 2284
Doctor Samuel Johnson. Verse. Robert Hillyer. 14:25*F11'39. 2285
Dr. Spencer's clock. Prose. Franklin P. Adams. 11:20*F1 '36. 2286
Dr. Stoke's statue. Prose. Robert Nathan. 8:16-17 F11'33. 2287
Doctor Straton. Verse. Fillmore Hyde. 1:37 Ja30'26. 2288
The doctor will see you now. Verse. Kenneth Fearing. 15:26* Ap1'39. 2289
Dr. Wyeth's son. Prose. John O'Hara. 10:25-6 Jy28'34. 2290
The doctors' ball. Prose. George Cecil Cowing. 6:74-5 Mr29'30. 2291
The documents in the case. Prose. Russell Maloney. 15: 33*Ap29'39. 2292
Dodsworth. (Novel) TT. 5:12 Mr 9'29. 2293
Does mankind progress? Verse. Anon. 2:51 My15'26. 2294
Does Whelen own the Whelan Drug Stores? Prose. Geoffrey T. Hellman. 15:57-8*Je24 '39. 2295
Dog. Verse. Virginia Woods Bellamy. 13:70*D4'37. 2296
The dog. Verse. Laura Benét. 6: 88 My24'30. 2297
Dog and sea gulls. Verse. Robert P. Tristram Coffin. 13:29*N13 '37. 2298
Dog around the block. Verse. E. B. White. 6:27 D6'30. 2299
Dog gone. Prose. Oliver Claxton. 3:85 Je4'27. 2300
Dog lover. Prose. Sally Benson. 7:45-7*Jy25'31. 2301
The dog parade. Verse. Arthur Guiterman. 15:33*S16'39. 2302
Dog race. RL. Morris Markey. 10:73-8 S15'34. 2303
The dog show. Prose. Alice Frankforter. 5:32-5 F15'30. 2304
Dog story. Prose. Ludwig Bemelmans. 15:18-20*Ag12'39. 2305
Dog to walk. Prose. Alice Frankforter. 9:51-3 Ap22'33. 2306
Dog's best friend. PR (Blair). Geoffrey T. Hellman. 14:27-33* D3'38. 2307
The doily menace. Prose. E. B. White. 5:15 Jy20'29. 2308
Dole. Verse. Ruth Lambert Jones. 5:107 S21'29. 2309
Dole. RL. Morris Markey. 11:36-44*My4'35. 2310
The dollar. Prose. Frank Sullivan. 9:20-1 N11'33. 2311
A doll's house for Nora. SM. Alexander Woollcott. 9:28-30 Jy29'33. 2312
Dolly and Polly, Billy and Cholly. PR (Paul). Margaret Case Harriman. 13:23-7*O16'37; 13:22-7*O23'37. 2313
Domestic employment agency. Prose. Ruth Leigh. 3:42-4 O22 '27. 2314
Domestic setback. Prose. Richard Lockridge. 7:18-20 S19'31. 2315
Done into movies. Prose. Stephen Leacock. 3:59-61 F4'28. 2316
Don't bank on it. Prose. Margaret Ford. 11:56-7*My25'35. 2317
Don't bother to dress. Prose. John

Je22'35. 2360
Doyle, Arthur Conan. John Cowmos. 4:50 O6'28. 2361
Draft board nights. MLHT. James Thurber. 9:17-19 S30'33. 2362
"A draft of XXX Cantos." Verse. Lee Wilson Dodd. 9:69 My20 '33. 2363
The dragon hunters. RL. Russell Owen. 3:32-8 My21'27. 2364
Dragonfly. Verse. Edith Franklin Wyatt. 12:45*Jy18'36. 2365
Drama critics, New York. TT. 14:11-12*Ap9'38. 2366
The drama-lovers. Prose. George Cecil Cowing. 5:35 D14'29. 2367
A dramatic critic reports a wedding. Prose. Nat N. Dorfman. 1:34 Ja23'26. 2368
A dramatic criticism. Prose. Philip G. Wylie. 2:30 O2'26. 2369
Dramatic note. Verse. Arthur Guiterman. 2:50 Ap24'26. 2370
Dramatis personae. Prose. James Reid Parker. 13:26-7*Mr13'37. 2371
Dream cases. Prose. Robert Benchley. 12:17*Mr21'36. 2372
Dream children: a reverie. Prose. E. B. White. 5:20-1 Ap20'29. 2373
Dream come true. Prose. Maddy Vegtel. 11:57-8*N16'35. 2374
Dream of a lowbrow. Verse. Parke Cummings. 2:93 N13'26. 2375
Dream poetry. Prose. Edmund Wilson. 13:50-2*Jy31'37. 2376
A dream walking. PR (Dali). Margaret Case Harriman. 15:22-7* Jy1'39. 2377
Dreiser, Theodore. PR. Waldo Frank. 1:6-7 Ag15'25. 2378
Dreiser, Theodore. TT. 1:10 Ja 23'26. 2379
Dreiser, Theodore. TT. 6:13 Mr 1'30. 2380
The dress rehearsal. Prose. Alice Frankforter. 5:35 O12'29. 2381
The dress rehearsal. Prose. Arthur Kober. 3:14-15 Ja28 '28. 2382
Dressed up like a fire engine. TWNY. Herbert Asbury. 6:39-46 Mr1'30. 2383
Dressing-room number four. Prose. Patricia Collinge. 5:53 O26'29. 2384
Dressing table. Verse. Margaretta Manning. 4:21 S8'28. 2385
Drift. RL. Morris Markey. 7:49-53 O17'31. 2386
Drinking customs. Prose. Anthony Armstrong. 12:38-41*Ag15'36. 2387
Drinking days. NESD. John J. Holzinger. 9:32 F10'34. 2388
Drinking song. Verse. Anon. 2:41 Mr13'26. 2389
Drive slow, man chortling. Verse. Ogden Nash. 15:20*O21'39. 2390
The driving of the rivet. Verse. E. B. White. 5:21 F15'30. 2391
Drop that other shoe Frank Gallop! Prose. Frank Sullivan. 14: 17-18*F19'38. 2392
Drypoint. Verse. Rollin Kirby. 2: 14 Ag28'26. 2393
Du côté de chez hillis. Prose. Eleanor Gilchrist. 14:29-30*S3 '38. 2394
Dubious compensation. Verse. Margaret Fishback. 4:47 Je23'28. 2395
Dudelsackpfeifer. Prose. Frank Sullivan. 7:19-20 Ja9'32. 2396
The duel. Prose. Morley Callaghan. 10:21-2 S22'34. 2397
Duet. Verse. James Thurber. 4:31 N17'28. 2398
Dug in the Bronx. Prose. Arthur Kober. 10:18-20*Ja26'35. 2399
Dusk in fierce pajamas. Prose. E. B. White. 9:16-17 Ja27'34. 2400
Dust. Verse. Dorothy Leonard. 5:64 Ja4'30. 2401
Dusty answer. SM. Alexander Woollcott. 10:34 Je9'34. 2402
Dutch cleaning. Prose. Maddy Vegtel. 10:55-6 S15'34. 2403
Duties of the clergy. Verse. Clarence Day. 11:46*D28'35. 2404

The dutiful child. Prose. John C. Emery. 10:85-6 Je16'34. 2405
Duty copy. WP. Robert Benchley. 6:30-3 N1'30. 2406
Dynamite is like a mill pond. Prose. John O'Hara. 9:44-7 O 14'33. 2407

E

'E. Prose. Thomas Wolfe. 13: 22-6 Jy17'37. 2408
E. M. D. --please write. SM. Alexander Woollcott. 10:28 Je23'34. 2409
An ear for an ear. Verse. Olive Ward. 9:26 O7'33. 2410
Ear, nose, and throat. Prose. Cornelia Otis Skinner. 14:25-6*O22'38. 2411
Ear pictures. Prose. E. B. White. 10:24-5 S22'34. 2412
Early aviation. Prose. Donald Ogden Stewart. 4:22-3 Mr24 '28. 2413
Early morning. Verse. Rachel Field. 10:74 My12'34. 2414
Ears errant. ML. John Strong Newberry. 9:54 Ap29'33. 2415
An earthbound boy. Verse. E. B. White. 14:29*My21'38. 2416
Earth's pensive passenger. Verse. Morris Bishop. 8:24 N5'32. 2417
East fifty-seven. Verse. Parke Cummings. 2:83 Ja29'27. 2418
East Hampton. Verse. Eleanor Hoysradt. 7:23*Jy25'31. 2419
East is West. Prose. Elizabeth Oñativia. 8:42 Ag27'32. 2420
East of the Avenue. Prose. Thomas Edgelow. 1:15 N14'25. 2421
East River. RL. Morris Markey. 4:36-40 Ap7'28. 2422
East Seventies. Prose. Mary F. Watkins. 9:61-2 My13'33. 2423
East side. RL. Morris Markey. 2:26-30 Ja1'27. 2424
East side night life. Prose. Zelda F. Popkin. 2:68-9 Je5'26. 2425
East side song-hit parade. Verse. John J. Holzinger. 13:40*Jy3'37. 2426
East side song-hit parade. Verse. John J. Holzinger. 13:40*Jy10 '37. 2427
East side song-hit parade. Verse. John J. Holzinger. 13:48*Jy31 '37. 2428
East side song-hit parade. Verse. John J. Holzinger. 13:62*S18 '37. 2429
East side song-hit parade. Verse. John J. Holzinger. 13:73*O30 '37. 2430
East side song-hit parade. Verse. John J. Holzinger. 13:75*N13 '37. 2431
East side song-hit parade. Verse. John J. Holzinger. 13:59*N27 '37. 2432
East side song-hit parade. Verse. John J. Holzinger. 13:79*D11 '37. 2433
East side, west side. Prose. Baird Hall. 2:50 Ag28'26. 2434
East side-west side. Prose. Baird Hall. 2:58 S11'26. 2435
East side-west side. Prose. Baird Hall. 2:45 O2'26. 2436
Easter query. Verse. Martha Banning Thomas. 4:86 Ap7'28. 2437
Easterly gale. Verse. Martha Banning Thomas. 13:85*D18'37. 2438
Eastern standard. Verse. E. B. White. 2:26 S25'26. 2439
Eastside—westside. Verse. Howard Cushman. 1:46 D12'25. 2440
Ebenezer's war on crime. OFC. Alberta Williams. 12:62-3*Ja9 '37. 2441
The eccentric Cornburys. TWNY. Herbert Asbury. 8:40-5 O1'32. 2442
Echo. Prose. Sidney Skolsky. 1:19 F28'25. 2443
Echo. Verse. Mildred Weston. 7:39 Jy18'31. 2444
Eclectic. Verse. Elizabeth Coatsworth. 6:24 D27'30. 2445
An economist at work. Prose. Raymond Holden. 12:64-5*F22'36. 2446
Economy's home, sweet home.

Prose. John C. Emery. 1:28 My30'25. 2447
Eden with serpent. Prose. Wolcott Gibbs. 11:17-19*Ap20'35. 2448
Edgar Street. Verse. Burke Boyce. 2:35 S4'26. 2449
Edith Carr and I. Prose. Frances Warfield. 10:29-30 S22'34. 2450
Edith Emmet that was. Prose. Lillian Day. 6:52-6 O4'30. 2451
Editor & Publisher. Robert Benchley. 10:60-6 Je9'34. 2452
Editorials. Prose. Joseph Fulling Fishman. 3:32-3 N5'27. 2453
The editor's easy chair. SM. Alexander Woollcott. 5:58 O12 '29. 2454
Educating the public. WP. Robert Benchley. 5:34-42 Mr2'29. 2455
Education. Prose. Kay Boyle. 12: 23-4*O17'36. 2456
Education. Verse. Baird Leonard. 6:87 O18'30. 2457
The education of a prince. PR (Romanoff). Alva Johnston. 8:19-23 O29'32; 8:28-32 N5'32; 8:24-8 N12'32; 8:24-8 N19'32; 8:24-9 N26'32. 2458
The education of an anarchist. Prose. Wolcott Gibbs. 10:20-1 Mr3'34. 2459
The education of Mr. Galbraith. Prose. Douglass Welch. 13:28-9*Ap10'37. 2460
Educational efforts. Verse. Clarence Day. 11:21*Jy13'35. 2461
Educational note. Verse. Leslie Nelson Jennings. 9:61 N4'33. 2462
Educator. PR (Robinson). Geoffrey T. Hellman. 9:28-31 N18'33. 2463
Edward Damper. Prose. Wolcott Gibbs. 8:16 N26'32. 2464
Edward's grandson. PR (Edward, Prince of Wales). Anthony Gibbs. 7:27-30 O3'31; 7:26-9 O10'31. 2465
Eeny meeny miny mo. Prose. E. B. White. 6:21-2 D20'30. 2466
"Eeeny, meeny, mynamo . . ." Verse. Arthur Guiterman. 5:19 Mr9'29. 2467
Effable, scrutable English. Prose. Robert M. Coates. 13:22-3*S18 '37. 2468
Efficency experts. Verse. Persis Greely Anderson. 7:90 N14'31. 2469
Ego. Verse. Peggy Bacon. 8:41 Ja21'33. 2470
Ego. Verse. Alice Corbin. 10:20 Mr3'34. 2471
The egotist. PR (Poiret). Janet Flanner. 3:23-5 O29'27. 2472
Egyptologist. PR (Winlock). Geoffrey T. Hellman. 9:16-19 Jy29 '33. 2473
Eheu, fugaces. NYC. Donald Moffat. 5:22-4 Jy20'29. 2474
The eight-day crossing. Prose. Alice Frankforter. 4:44-5 Ag 25'28. 2475
Eight men in a boat. WATN. James Thurber. 12:20-5*S5'36. 2476
Eight o'clock sharp. Prose. Robert Benchley. 5:23-5 Ap6'29. 2477
Eighth Avenue. Verse. Jean Batchelor. 6:91 S13'30. 2478
Eighth Avenue. Prose. John Forbes. 4:40 D15'28. 2479
Eighth Street. Verse. Rollin Kirby. 2:28 O30'26. 2480
El cartero. Prose. Theodore Pratt. 9:50-1 Mr25'33. 2481
El comandante. Prose. Theodore Pratt. 9:48-9 Mr18'33. 2482
El tio. Prose. Theodore Pratt. 9: 75-6 S16'33. 2483
Elastic plots. Verse. Mary Carolyn Davies. 8:14 Jy23'32. 2484
Elder. Verse. Peggy Bacon. 10:62 Ag25'34. 2485
The elderly bachelor. Prose. S. F. 5:68-9 N9'29. 2486
Election day is a holiday. Verse. Ogden Nash. 8:23 N5'32. 2487
Elegiac. Verse. Robert A. Simon. 2:35 Je19'26. 2488
Elegiac poetry. Annemarie Ewing

and Morris Bishop. 15:35-40* Mr18'39. 2489
Elegies for a passing world. Verse. Edmund Wilson. 10:19* Ja26'35. 2490
Elegy. Verse. W. E. Farbstein. 7:44 S12'31. 2491
Elegy. Verse. Arthur Guiterman. 1:25 S19'25. 2492
Elegy for Janes. Verse. Rosemary Carr Benét. 5:21 My25 '29. 2493
Elegy for Twelfth Night. Verse. Phyllis McGinley. 15:38*Ja6 '40. 2494
Elegy with a pewter lining. Verse. Phyllis McGinley. 15:19*Ag19 '39. 2495
Elephant. Verse. Virginia Woods Bellamy. 15:43*Ap22'39. 2496
The elephant comes in. Prose. Richard Lockridge. 9:26-7 D2 '33. 2497
Elevated. Prose. E. B. White. 2:107 D4'26. 2498
The elevator starter. Prose. John O'Hara. 6:80 Mr15'30. 2499
Elevator weather. Prose. Robert Benchley. 6:15 Jy12'30. 2500
Eleven a. m. Prose. Ruth Overton. 2:69 S18'26. 2501
Eleven-forty. Prose. Theodore Pratt. 2:77-8 O9'26. 2502
Elfin. Verse. Leslie Nelson Jennings. 5:45 Ag3'29. 2503
Eliot, T. S. H. W. Eliot, Jr. 9:51 Mr25'33. 2504
Eliot, T. S. TT. 8:11 Ja7'33. 2505
Eliot, T. S. TT. 8:12 Ja21'33. 2506
Eliot, T. S. TT. 9:12 Mr11'33. 2507
Eliot, T. S. (Parody) Betty Morrow. 13:27*O16'37. 2508
Elizabeth. Prose. Alice Frankforter. 7:60 D5'31. 2509
Ella and the Chinee. Prose. John O'Hara. 7:57-9 Ja23'32. 2510
Ellen. Prose. Morley Callaghan. 9:15-16 Mr4'33. 2511
Ellis, Havelock. (Parody) Robert Benchley. 12:17*Mr21'36. 2512
Elmer Gantry. (Novel) TT. 2:20-1 N6'26. 2513
Elsa Maxwell. Prose. Frank Sullivan. 6:15-16 Ja31'31. 2514
Elsie Dinsmore at a night club. Prose. Josie Turner. 3:26-7 O 29'27. 2515
Elsie Dinsmore at Palm Beach. Prose. Josie Turner. 4:15-17 Ja26'29. 2516
Elsie Dinsmore at the costume ball. Prose. Josie Turner. 5:15-17 Ag24'29. 2517
Elsie Dinsmore books. G. B. Stern. 12:52-5*Mr14'36. 2518
Elsie Dinsmore entertains at tea. Prose. Josie Turner. 5:19-20 Ap27'29. 2519
Elsie Dinsmore goes shopping. Prose. Josie Turner. 3:23-4 D 17'27. 2520
Elsie Dinsmore plays cards. Prose. Josie Turner. 4:15-16 Je9'28. 2521
Elsie Dinsmore plays nurse. Prose. Josie Turner. 3:17-19 Ja28'28. 2522
Elsie Dinsmore's ride. Prose. Josie Turner. 3:16-17 Ja7'28. 2523
Elsie Dinsmore's weekend. Prose. Josie Turner. 3:23-4 Jy30'27. 2524
Elsie reread. OUWA. G. B. Stern. 12:52-5*Mr14'36. 2525
Emancipated cats. Prose. John Tucker Battle. 1:31 N14'25. 2526
Embarrassment in the presence of the ladies of the chorus. Prose. Heywood Broun. 3:22-4 O15'27. 2527
Embassy. Prose. Jay Franklin Carter. 11:20-4*Ag17'35. 2528
Embittered Spring song. Verse. Jean Batchelor. 8:49*My14'32. 2529
The emerald. Verse. Raymond Holden. 5:36 O26'29. 2530
The emerald boss. PR (McCooey). Niven Busch, Jr. 3:25-8 Mr12 '27. 2531
Emergency lunches. RL. Frances

Warfield 8:32-8*Ap30'32. 2532
Emigrants at the zoo. Prose. Barbara Heggie. 15:71*Je10 '39. 2533
Emigrant's song. Verse. Wolcott Gibbs. 4:85 Je9'28. 2534
Emil. Prose. Sylvia Townsend Warner. 14:19-21*O29'38. 2535
Emil and Oscar. Prose. Arthur H. Folwell. 3:59 F26'27. 2536
Emily Post (1272 B.C.). Verse. Persis Greely Anderson. 5:94 S28'29. 2537
Emmet handles the cosmos. Prose. Brendan Gill. 13:22-4* Ag28'37. 2538
Emotional crisis. Prose. Elspeth O'Halloran. 4:28 Mr3'28. 2539
The Emperor Jones. PR (Jones). Gilbert Seldes. 7:25-8 My9'31. 2540
The Emperor Jones. (Film) TT. 9:10 Jy22'33. 2541
Employees who on June 15th completed eight (8) months continuous service will receive a vacation of one (1) week. Verse. Margaret Fishback. 3: 34 Ag6'27. 2542
Employment agency. Verse. Elias Lieberman. 14:26*Jy16'38. 2543
The employment situation. Verse. Margaret Fishback. 3:61 N26 '27. 2544
En famille. Prose. Alice Frankforter. 5:63-6 Je15'29. 2545
En passant. Verse. Baird Leonard. 1:13 Ja9'26. 2546
En rapport. Verse. Hortense Flexner. 7:20 My9'31. 2547
En route. Prose. Thyra Samter Winslow. 3:15-16 Ag6'27. 2548
Enchanted iles. SM. Alexander Woollcott. 9:38 F25'33. 2549
Enchantment. Verse. George Russell. 6:26 Ap5'30. 2550
Encore une fois. Verse. Lee Wilson Dodd. 7:17 Ja2'32. 2551
Encounter. Prose. Robert M. Coates. 9:21-2 Ap8'33. 2552
Encounter. Verse. Catharine Connell. 5:38 My25'29. 2553
Encounter. RL. Morris Markey. 9:44-53 Ja27'34. 2554
Encounter with the past. Prose. Richard Lockridge. 11:73*My 18'35. 2555
Encyclopedia Britannica. Verse. Ogden Nash. 7:67 Mr21'31. 2556
The end. Prose. Louise Field Cooper. 14:40*Ag6'38. 2557
The end. Verse. Dorothy Homans. 1:11 Ag8'25. 2558
The end in sight. Prose. John Chapin Mosher. 10:16-18 Jy28 '34. 2559
End of a world's fair. Prose. Mildred Gilman. 9:42-50 O21 '33. 2560
The end of Summer. Verse. Martha Banning Thomas. 5:66 S21 '29. 2561
End of Summer. Prose. Winifred Willis. 14:63-4*O8'38. 2562
End of the line. Prose. Richard Lockridge. 12:71*My16'36. 2563
The end of the season. Prose. Robert Benchley. 1:15 Ja2'26. 2564
End of the tether. RL. Morris Markey. 9:42-7 F18'33. 2565
Endorsement of an attitude. Verse. Martha Banning Thomas. 3:40 F4'28. 2566
Enemy of society. RL. Hickman Powell. 12:88-96*D5'36. 2567
Enfant terrible. PR (Rivera). Geoffrey T. Hellman. 9:25-8 My20 '33. 2568
Enfant terrible. PR (Feldman). Newman Levy. 4:22-5 Ag25'28. 2569
Enfants cordiales. Prose. Rosemary Carr Benét. 3:39-40 Mr5 '27. 2570
Engagement-book. Verse. Grace Hazard Conkling. 4:50 N17'28. 2571
Engagements for tomorrow. Verse. Kenneth Fearing. 14:24*F4'39. 2572
Engaging frankness. Verse. W. E. Farbstein. 14:24*My28'38. 2573

The engine. Verse. Louise Bogan. 6:21 Ja3'31. 2574
England, my England. Prose. Robert Nathan. 10:36 Ap28'34. 2575
England's most photographed female. PR (Nuthall). John R. Tunis. 6:20-2 Ag23'30. 2576
The English author who consented to be interviewed. Prose. Fillmore Hyde. 2:15-16 My1'26. 2577
English B-1 convenes. Prose. Paul Horgan. 6:77-9 S27'30. 2578
English hearts are honest oak. Prose. James Reid Parker. 9:24-6 Ag26'33. 2579
English in fifteen minutes. Prose. Frederick Packard. 8:48-9*My 14'32. 2580
English spoken. Prose. Theodore Pratt. 8:51-2 O1'32. 2581
English usage. TT. 12:9-10*Ja 30'37. 2582
Englishmen never speak to strangers in trains. Prose. Donald Moffat. 6:15-17 Ag30'30. 2583
Enigma. Prose. Mary Heaton Vorse. 6:26 N8'30. 2584
Enigma. Prose. Frances Warfield. 7:20 Ja23'32. 2585
Enigma in Altman's. Verse. Phyllis McGinley. 11:16*Ja18'36. 2586
Ennobling our criminals. Prose. Waldo Frank. 1:21 My30'25. 2587
Ennui. Verse. Parke Cummings. 3:49 F4'28. 2588
Ennui. Verse. Oliver Jenkins. 5:92 Ap6'29. 2589
Ennui. Verse. M. M. 3:85 N19'27. 2590
The enquiring reporter. See The inquiring reporter. (No entry) 2591
Entente cordiale. Verse. Mildred. Weston. 10:28 Je9'34. 2592
The entertainers. Verse. Persis Greely Anderson. 7:75 My16'31. 2593
The enthusiast. Prose. Winifred Willis. 7:54-5 F13'32. 2594
Entirely unnecessary verses. Verse. Martha Banning Thomas. 4:30 N10'28. 2595
The epic of Augustus Jones. Verse. E. O. Laughlin. 10:37*D 29'34. 2596
Epic of the soul. Verse. Gertrude Curtis Ryan. 7:55 Ap25'31. 2597
Epicure. Prose. Jack Cluett. 7:48 Ja23'32. 2598
Epicure. Verse. Ruth Lambert Jones. 6:108 D13'30. 2599
Epigrams in a cellar. Verse. Christopher Morley. 3:15 D31 '27. 2600
Epilogue for a marionette show. Verse. Arthur Guiterman. 9:56 Ja20'34. 2601
Episode. Prose. Philip Berman. 1:22 D12'25. 2602
Episode of the cherry tree. Verse. Mildred Weston. 8:20*F20'32. 2603
An epistle of Paul. OW. Ring Lardner. 8:30-4 S3'32. 2604
Epistle to a hasty goer. Verse. Emanuel Eisenberg. 8:14 F4'33. 2605
Epistle to the trade. Verse. A. K. Laing. 4:71 Ja26'29. 2606
Epitaph. Verse. Anon. 1:7 Jy18 '25. 2607
Epitaph. Verse. Ruth Lambert Jones. 8:19 S10'32. 2608
Epitaph. Prose. Robert Nathan. 7:20-4 S26'31. 2609
Epitaph. Verse. Susan Weaver. 8:55*Ap23'32. 2610
Epitaph for a certain hostess. Verse. Ruth Lambert Jones. 4:112 D15'28. 2611
Epitaph for a dead lady. Verse. Charles Norman. 4:15 Jy28'28. 2612
Epitaph for a good girl. Verse. Leslie S. Pearl. 4:36 Je30'28. 2613
Epitaph for a grim woman. Verse. Martha Banning Thomas. 8:18 S24'32. 2614
Epitaph for a Persian kitten. Verse. Miriam Vedder. 7:81

Mr14'31. 2615
Epitaph for one who shall be nameless. Verse. Edward J. Fitzgerald. 11:62*S28'35. 2616
Epitaphs for authors. Verse. Kenneth Phillips Britton. 1:37 F13'26. 2617
Epitaphs for authors. Verse. Kenneth Phillips Britton. 2:34 Mr20'26. 2618
Epithalamiom. Verse. Elspeth O'Halloran. 3:16 Je25'27. 2619
Epithalamion. Verse. Phyllis McGinley. 12:23*My30'36. 2620
Equine. Verse. William Rose Benét. 8:28 My21'32. 2621
Equinox. Verse. Robert Hillyer. 14:20*Mr19'38. 2622
Ere the cold come. Verse. Harold Lewis Cook. 12:24*O31'36. 2623
The erg man. WATN. James Thurber. 12:20-1*O31'36. 2624
Erin goes bragh. Verse. T. H. Bliss. 1:22 My23'25. 2625
The erloff. Prose. John O'Hara. 15:22-3 F3'40. 2626
Ernest, the Indian. Prose. Wolcott Gibbs. 12:19-20*My2'36. 2627
Erskine, John. PR. Helena Huntington Smith. 3:27-9 D10'27. 2628
Erskine, John. TT. 2:11-12 Ja15 '27. 2629
Escalator. Verse. Mildred Weston. 11:70*O12'35. 2630
An escapade. Prose. Morley Callaghan. 4:22-5 N24'28. 2631
Escape. Verse. Grace Hazard Conkling. 5:26 D28'29. 2632
Escape. Verse. Frances M. Frost. 5:46 O12'29. 2633
Escape. Verse. Frances M. Frost. 6:18 Mr1'30. 2634
The escape. Verse. Mark Van Doren. 5:19 Ja25'30. 2635
Escape from the Bronx. Prose. Arthur Kober. 11:15-18*Ag10 '35. 2636
The escape of William J. Sharkey. TWNY. Herbert Asbury. 7:39-44 Mr7'31. 2637
Escapists, fie! Verse. Morris Bishop. 15:17*Jy29'39. 2638
Eschatology. Verse. Morris Bishop. 6:25 Ja3'31. 2639
The essay menace. Prose. Frank Sullivan. 5:18-19 Mr2'29. 2640
Essay on dignity. Prose. James Thurber. 11:19-20*Ja4'36. 2641
Essay on man. Verse. Arthur Guiterman. 14:42*O8'38. 2642
Essayage. Prose. Christopher Morley. 4:14 Jy21'28. 2643
Essence of chic Paris. PR (Guitrys). Ferdinand Tuohy. 2:29-32 D18'26. 2644
Essence of the campaign. Prose. Marquis James. 1:36-7 S12'25. 2645
Essences. Verse. E. B. White. 5:18 Jy6'29. 2646
The estate. Verse. Martha Banning Thomas. 4:135 D15'28. 2647
The Eternal Road. TT. 11:10-11* Ja25'36. 2648
Eternal things. Verse. Marjorie Allen Seiffert. 6:28 D20'30. 2649
Ethel bites the dog. Prose. James Reid Parker. 7:75-7 N28'31. 2650
Etiquette. Verse. Mary Ballard Duryee. 14:51*Je11'38. 2651
Etiquette. Verse. Sylvia Fuller. 2:68 S11'26. 2652
Etiquette. Verse. Benjamin Musser. 2:48 Jy17'26. 2653
Eton--Harrow. Prose. Frances Crane. 9:34-5 Jy15'33. 2654
Étude pharmacopoeia. Prose. Bessie Breuer. 7:16-18 N7'31. 2655
Etymology of "Joe Maffon." Prose. Carlton Brown. 11:66-7*F8'36. 2656
Euphemism. H. L. Mencken. 11: 39-42 Ag31'35. 2657
Europe in the U. S. A. Verse. Max Lief. 1:22 Mr21'25. 2658
(No entry) 2659
Euterpe. NESD. John J. Holzinger. 9:73 S23'33. 2660
The évacués. WATN. Frances

Russell. 13:42-8*Ja22'38. 2661
Evadne. Prose. John Chapin Mosher. 5:100-101 Ap27'29. 2662
Eva's deathbed revisited. Prose. Prose. Wolcott Gibbs. 15:15-16*D30'39. 2663
Even at the aquarium. Verse. S. F. 2:43 O16'26. 2664
Even beauty--. Verse. Marjorie Allen Seiffert. 6:20 My3'30. 2665
Evening, a public park. Verse. Rolfe Humphries. 13:22*My8 '37. 2666
Evening hymns. Verse. Clarence Day. 10:24 Ap14'34. 2667
Evening in Patchin Place. Verse. Charles Norman. 4:82 S15'28. 2668
Evening of a lady. Prose. Phyllis Ryan. 3:102-103 D3'27. 2669
An evening on ice. Prose. E. B. White. 3:30 Mr19'27. 2670
Evening prayer. Verse. Elspeth O'Halloran. 4:26 Mr17'28. 2671
The evening primrose. Verse. Dorothy Parker. 5:14 Ag24'29. 2672
The evening's at seven. Prose. James Thurber. 8:15 O22'32. 2673
Ever after. Prose. Oliver Claxton. 3:65 Ap16'27. 2674
Ever staunch and true, alma mater, to you. OUWA. Morris Bishop. 13:86-96*D11'37. 2675
Every darn time. Prose. Gerold Frank. 14:28-9*Ag6'38. 2676
Every man for himself. Verse. Wood Kahler. 5:104 Mr23'29. 2677
Every twenty-four hours. Prose. Beatrice Kaufman. 4:59-62 Jy 14'28. 2678
Everyreporter, or the big spitfire. Prose. Frank Sullivan. 4:23 N 10'28. 2679
Everything flows. RL. St. Clair McKelway. 11:66-70*N23'35. 2680
Everything is wild. Prose. James Thurber. 8:13-14*Ap2'32. 2681
Everything will be o. k. RL. Brendan Gill. 15:35-9*Je3'39. 2682
Evolution of a diplomat. Prose. Rose C. Feld. 11:71-2*Ap13'35. 2683
The evolution of a movie scenario. Prose. Sidney Skolsky. 3:84 O 15'27. 2684
Evolution of a movie title. Prose. W. B. C. 1:20 My23'25. 2685
Evolution of a problem child. PR (Hague). John McCarten. 13:20-5*F12'38; 14:21-6*F19'38. 2686
Evolution of a valentine. Verse. Margaret Fishback. 5:49 F15 '30. 2687
Ex tempore. Verse. Margaretta Manning. 4:62 Jy14'28. 2688
Exam time. Prose. Robert Benchley. 2:13 Je12'26. 2689
Exasperating. Verse. Le Baron Cooke. 1:15 S12'25. 2690
Excavation. RL. Morris Markey. 3:28-32 Je18'27. 2691
Excavations about town. Prose. Margaret Fishback. 4:95-6 Ap 14'28. 2692
Excavations in Ur. Verse. Joseph Auslander. 7:21 My2'31. 2693
Exceedingly rich talk. Prose. Freudy. 1:23 Jy25'25. 2694
Excelsior. Prose. W. E. Farbstein. 9:28 D30'33. 2695
Excelsior. FPI. James Thurber. 15:28-9*Mr11'39. 2696
Exceptional eighth of October. Verse. Miriam Vedder. 6:101 O11'30. 2697
[Excerpts from a letter written by Mr. Louis Brock . . .] OUWA. Louis Brock. 9:67-8 Ja27'34. 2698
Exchange Alley. DL. Burke Boyce. 3:15 Jy2'27. 2699
Exclamation points and colons. OMEU. James Thurber. 5:20-1 Jy20'29. 2700
Exclusive. SM. Alexander Woollcott. 5:45 Ap20'29. 2701
Excursion. RL. Morris Markey. 3: 36-40 Mr12'27. 2702

F

Father and pugdogs and rubber trees. Prose. Clarence Day. 11:16-19*S28'35. 2829

Father and the crusader's third wife. Prose. Clarence Day. 8:15 F11'33. 2830

Father and the French court. Prose. Clarence Day. 8:14 Ja 21'33. 2831

Father Bill. PR (Cashin). Henry F. Pringle. 3:19-21 Ja7'28. 2832

Father brightens the sick room. Prose. Clarence Day. 9:14-16 Je24'33. 2833

Father buys us a boat. Prose. Clarence Day. 11:14-16*Jy20 '35. 2834

Father declines to be killed. Prose. Clarence Day. 11:18-20*Je15'35. 2835

Father, Delmonico's, and Buffalo Bill. Prose. Clarence Day. 11:25-7*Ap13'35. 2836

A father does his best. Verse. E. B. White. 7:18*Je20'31. 2837

Father Duffy. SM. Alexander Woollcott. 8:30-2 Jy16'32. 2838

Father feels starved. Prose. Clarence Day. 9:14-15 Ap22 '33. 2839

Father finds guests in the house. Prose. Clarence Day. 9:23-5 Ja6'34. 2840

Father gets a surprise. Prose. Clarence Day. 12:16-17*Ap11 '36. 2841

Father gives mother an allowance. Prose. Clarence Day. 13:22-4*Je26'37. 2842

Father has a bad night. Prose. Clarence Day. 9:22-3 D23'33. 2843

Father has trouble with the land of Egypt. Prose. Clarence Day. 10:18-21 F24'34. 2844

Father hires a cook. Prose. Clarence Day. 9:22-3 Mr25'33. 2845

Father interferes with the 23rd Psalm. Prose. Clarence Day. 11:22*Mr16'35. 2846

Father invests in a livery. Prose. Clarence Day. 12:21-4*My9 '36. 2847

Father is firm with his ailments. Prose. Clarence Day. 9:19-21 My20'33. 2848

Father isn't much help. Prose. Clarence Day. 9:17-18 D2'33. 2849

Father keeps cows. Prose. Clarence Day. 13:14-16*Jy31'37. 2850

Father lets in the telephone. Prose. Clarence Day. 9:18-20 My13'33. 2851

Father objects to exploring. Prose. Clarence Day. 11:31-3*Ag3'35. 2852

Father opens my mail. Prose. Clarence Day. 10:28-31 My5'34. 2853

Father plans to get out. Prose. Clarence Day. 11:17-18*Je29'35. 2854

Father puts Mother on horseback. Prose. Clarence Day. 13:17-19* Je12'37. 2855

Father sends me to the World's Fair. Prose. Clarence Day. 9:30-4 Jy1'33. 2856

Father sews on a button. Prose. Clarence Day. 10:24-5 Mr10'34. 2857

Father tackles the Bible. Prose. Clarence Day. 11:20-2*My18'35. 2858

Father teaches me to be prompt. Prose. Clarence Day. 10:21-2 Mr31'34. 2859

Father thumps on the floor. Prose. Clarence Day. 9:17-18 Ap29'33. 2860

Father tries to make Mother like figures. Prose. Clarence Day. 9:13-15 Ja20'34. 2861

Father visits the war. Prose. Clarence Day. 11:18-20*F15'36. 2862

Father wakes up in the village. Prose. Clarence Day. 10:19-21 My19'34. 2863

Father's home disappears. Prose. Clarence Day. 11:16-19*Ag17 '35. 2864

Father's method of courtship.

Hugh O'Connor. 11:78-82*D14 '35. 2908
Field day in the city. Verse. Margaret Fishback. 8:28 Je 25'32. 2909
Field mouse. Verse. Frances M. Frost. 7:24 O3'31. 2910
Fiery recollection. Verse. Elizabeth Coatsworth. 12:17*Je27 '36. 2911
Fifteen and five. Prose. Newman Levy. 4:17-18 Ja26 '29. 2912
The fifteen biggest men in America. Prose. Alva Johnston. 5: 17-19 Ja25'30. 2913
Fifteen dollars a week. Prose. Horton Heath. 7:32 N28'31. 2914
Fifteen-minutes-for-efficiency. Prose. John O'Hara. 5:47-50 Mr30'29. 2915
Fifteen years ago. SM. Alexander Woollcott. 8:28 D3'32. 2916
Fifth Avenue. Verse. Grace Hazard Conkling. 4:136 D8'28. 2917
Fifth Avenue at 3 p. m. Prose. Anon. 1:19 F21'25. 2918
Fifth Avenue fantasia. Verse. Arthur Guiterman. 6:86 My10'30. 2919
A Fifth Avenue maverick. PR (Vanderbilt). William Boardman Knox. 1:11-12 D26'25. 2920
Fifth Avenue's nize baby. PR (Winter). Niven Busch, Jr. 2:15-17 Jy3'26. 2921
Fifth in hand. Prose. G. Schwabe. 4:97-8 My5'28. 2922
Fifty. Verse. Elspeth O'Halloran. 5:27 Ap13'29. 2923
Fifty-cent meal. Prose. John O'Hara. 4:63-4 Ja12'29. 2924
59th & B'way & 8th. Verse. Paul G. Gumbinner. 3:107 Ap9'27. 2925
57th Street day. Prose. Elise Jerard. 1:19-20 F6'26. 2926
Fifty years ago. NYC. Babette Deutsch. 5:21-4 F1'30. 2927
Fifty years of Wall Street. PR (Content). Matthew Josephson. 8:22-6 O1'32. 2928
Fifty years young. Prose. Sally Benson. 9:51-3 Ag19'33. 2929
The fight. RL. Morris Markey. 2:25-6 Jy31'26. 2930
Figs. Prose. Theodore Pratt. 7:51-2*My23'31. 2931
Figs à la Palermitain. Prose. Geoffrey Kerr. 3:52-3 D24'27. 2932
Figures of speech. Prose. Ernest F. Hubbard. 1:19 Mr14'25. 2933
Filling that hiatus. Prose. Robert Benchley. 8:17-18 S24'32. 2934
Fin de saison--Palm Beach. Prose. E. B. White. 10:24-5 Ap 7'34. 2935
Final addition. Verse. David McCord. 9:16 Je10'33. 2936
Final exams. WP. Robert Benchley. 4:36-8 Je2'28. 2937
Final orders given by a very ill country gentleman to his grief-stricken secretary. Verse. James Thurber. 14:19*Ap23'38. 2938
Final retort. Verse. Louis Untermeyer. 12:16*Jy18'36. 2939
Finals at Lost Lake. Prose. Richard Lockridge. 11:57*S28'35. 2940
Financial advice. Prose. Dorothy Mills Emery. 7:20-1 D12'31. 2941
Financial letters. Prose. Katherine Sproehnle. 3:30 Ap23'27. 2942
Financial statement. Verse. Ogden Nash. 14:23*Ja28'39. 2943
Financially speaking. Prose. Samuel James. 3:42-3 Jy9'27. 2944
The fine-and-dandy spirit. RL. Carlton Brown. 13:65-9*My22 '37. 2945
A fine feminine frenzy. Verse. Margaret Fishback. 3:79 Mr5 '27. 2946
A fine game. Prose. Gilbert Seldes. 2:14-15 Ja1'27. 2947
A fine turkey dinner. Prose. Brendan Gill. 15:49-51*D23'39. 2948
The finest. RL. Morris Markey.

3:36-42 Ap9'27. 2949
Finette. Prose. Donald Moffat. 11: 15-16*Je15'35. 2950
Finger in the pie. Prose. James Reid Parker. 12:54-6*D5'36. 2951
The finger man. Prose. John Chapin Mosher. 7:14-16 F13 '32. 2952
Finger wave. Verse. Persis Greely Anderson. 6:54 Je14'30. 2953
The finical financier. Verse. Fillmore Hyde. 2:32 O2'26. 2954
Finished. Verse. Peggy Bacon. 8:49 Ja14'33. 2955
Finished basement. Prose. Norman Matson. 10:18-20*N24'34. 2956
Finnigan. WATN. James Thurber. 12:19-20*O31'36. 2957
Fire. Prose. Bronz. 1:39 N7'25. 2958
Fire. Prose. Theodore Pratt. 2: 21 Ja15'27. 2959
The fire alarm. Verse. Margaret Fishback. 2:34 Ag7'26. 2960
Fire-boat. DL. Burke Boyce. 4: 31 Mr31'28. 2961
Fire buckets and the battle watch. TWNY. Herbert Asbury. 5:48-54 Ja18'30. 2962
Fire-killer. Prose. Selma Robinson. 12:28-32*S19'36. 2963
Fire next door. Prose. Philip G. Wylie. 6:38-40 Mr29'30. 2964
Fire sign. PR (Brice). Niven Busch, Jr. 5:25-7 Ap20'29. 2965
Firebug-catcher. PR (Brophy). St. Clair McKelway. 11:18-23*Ja 18'36; 11:20-4*Ja25'36. 2966
Fires under the melting pot. NYC. Joseph Gollomb. 5:29-32 S14 '29. 2967
Firmament. Verse. Jean Batchelor. 6:22 Ap12'30. 2968
First aid. NESD. John J. Holzinger. 9:56 O7'33. 2969
The first and last appearance of a character in fiction named Bailey. Prose. Donald Ogden Stewart. 4:17-19 Ag11'28. 2970
First Avenue. RL. Morris Markey. 3:68-73 D10'27. 2971
The first car through. Prose. Robert M. Coates. 12:16-18*F 22'36. 2972
The first churchman. PR (Manning). Alva Johnston. 7:24-36 F 28'31. 2973
The first day. Prose. Alice Frankforter. 9:44-6 S23'33. 2974
First day. Prose. Oliver La Farge. 14:25-7*Mr5'38. 2975
The first day. Prose. James Reid Parker. 11:64*O5'35. 2976
First families, move over! Verse. Ogden Nash. 11:21*N16'35. 2977
The first fire engines. TWNY. Herbert Asbury. 5:40-6 Ja25'30. 2978
The first fortnight. RL. Morris Markey. 9:38-43 D23'33. 2979
First frost. Verse. Elspeth O'Halloran. 7:89 N7'31. 2980
The first lady. PR (Coolidge). Paul A. Burns. 2:17-18 My15'26. 2981
The first lawyer. TWNY. Russel Crouse. 6:47-8 F22'30. 2982
First lesson. Verse. Phyllis McGinley. 10:17*Ja12'35. 2983
First lines of telephone dialogues. Prose. Arthur H. Folwell. 4:24 S29'28. 2984
The first newspaper. TWNY. Foster Rhea Dulles. 5:26-30 Jy13 '29. 2985
A first night. Prose. Arthur Kober. 3:17-19 F4'28. 2986
First night. Verse. E. B. White. 8:23 F4'33. 2987
The first-nighter. Prose. Arthur Kober. 2:101-103 D11'26. 2988
The first of the Barrymores. Prose. Virginia Tracy. 6:29-32 O11'30. 2989
First offence. Prose. Kay Boyle. 10:19-20*Ja5'35. 2990
The first one. Prose. Nancy Hale. 12:23-5*D5'36. 2991
First person plural. Prose. Jerome Barry. 10:65-7 O13

Florida. Verse. Fred G. Steelman. 1:29 N14'25. 3036

Florida--off season. Prose. Mildred Gilman. 11:79-80*My11 '35. 3037

Florida Special. Verse. David McCord. 15:27*F18'39. 3038

The flour riot of 1837. TWNY. Herbert Asbury. 7:56-60 N14 '31. 3039

Flower lover no. 1. PR (Scheepers). Richard O. Boyer. 14: 18-24*Je25'38. 3040

Flower show. Verse. Sara Van Alstyne Allen. 14:39*Mr19'38. 3041

The flower show. Prose. Alice Frankforter. 6:23-4 Mr22'30. 3042

Flower wagon. Verse. Burke Boyce. 6:48 My31'30. 3043

The flowering down east. Prose. Agnes Burke Hale. 14:53-4*Ap 23'38. 3044

Flowers appear on the earth. Prose. Dorothy Thomas. 12:53-5*My16'36. 3045

Flowers for the occasion. Prose. John Chapin Mosher. 11:20*O 12'35. 3046

A flowery description. Verse. Martha Banning Thomas. 2:82 O16'26. 3047

The flurry in Dickens. SM. Alexander Woollcott. 10:32-6 My19 '34. 3048

Flush: a biography. SM. Alexander Woollcott. 9:24 S2'33. 3049

Flying Dutchman. PR (Fokker). Doree Smedley and Hollister Noble. 6:20-4 F7'31. 3050

The flying Dutchman of Central Park West. Verse. Newman Levy. 5:36 Ja4'30. 3051

Flying horses. Prose. Benedict Thielen. 15:15-17*Ag12'39. 3052

Flying moment. Verse. Frances M. Frost. 9:15 Jy8'33. 3053

Flying over Ethiopian mountain ranges. Verse. E. B. White. 13: 26*D11'37. 3054

Flying slow. RL. E. B. White. 7: 43-8*My23'31. 3055

Flying trapeze. Verse. Harold Willard Gleason. 5:40 Jy6'29. 3056

Fodder. Verse. Peggy Bacon. 2:42 D4'26. 3057

The foddle-doddle-banker-o. Verse. Fillmore Hyde. 6:29 Ja17'31. 3058

Fog. Verse. Grace Hazard Conkling. 5:78 S28'29. 3059

Fog on the Hudson. Verse. Lindley Williams Hubbell. 6:22 S6 '30. 3060

Folk cookery. Prose. Sylvia Townsend Warner. 12:65*Je13'36. 3061

Folk-lore. SM. Alexander Woollcott. 7:36 D12'31. 3062

The follies of Florenz Ziegfeld. Prose. The professor. 1:9-10 Mr14'25. 3063

The follow-up. Prose. John O'Hara. 4:37 Jy7'28. 3064

Follow-up. Prose. Katherine Sproehnle. 5:36-8 Mr16'29. 3065

The follow-up man. Prose. George S. Chappell. 4:46-7 Ag11'28. 3066

Food. Verse. Parke Cummings. 2: 47 N13'26. 3067

Food. Verse. Nancy Hoyt. 2:65 F5 '27. 3068

Food for the ironists. RL. Morris Markey. 5:26-35 Je29'29. 3069

Food for thought. Verse. Will Scarlet. 15:33*My6'39. 3070

Food fun for the menfolks. Prose. James Thurber. 12:15-17*O3 '36. 3071

Foodstuffs. NESD. John J. Holzinger. 9:34 O14'33. 3072

Fooled again. Verse. Anon. 1:35 Ja23'26. 3073

Fool's song. Verse. Lee Wilson Dodd. 6:111 My10'30. 3074

Foot it featly. Verse. Jean Batchelor. 11:52 Jy13'35. 3075

Football girls--and why. Prose. Katharine Brush. 3:88-9 N5'27. 3076

The football season. Prose. Frank

Sullivan. 4:23-5 O13'28. 3077
Foot-note on a flapper. Verse. Martha Banning Thomas. 2:58 Je5'26. 3078
Foot-notes. SM. Alexander Woollcott. 7:30 Ja16'32. 3079
Footnote. Verse. Richard Armour. 15:73*My20'39. 3080
Footnote. Verse. Hortense Flexner. 13:51*F20'37. 3081
Footnote on a business. RL. Morris Markey. 7:58-63 F28'31. 3082
Footnote on civilization. Verse. A. B. Bernd. 7:79 Ap11'31. 3083
A footnote on match covers. Prose. Gilbert Seldes. 2:22 Ja22'27. 3084
Footnote on the yellow peril. Prose. S. J. Perelman. 12:14* Ja30'37. 3085
A footnote to a footnote. Prose. Russell Maloney. 15:26*Jy15 '39. 3086
A footnote to eulogy. Prose. Wolcott Gibbs. 13:30*F5'38. 3087
Footnote to government. RL. Morris Markey. 10:63-70 Mr 24'34. 3088
A footnote to history. SM. Alexander Woollcott. 6:32 Ap5'30. 3089
Footnotes on a course of study. Prose. James Thurber. 12:17-18*N7'36. 3090
Footnotes on the popular song. OUWA. Sigmund Spaeth. 10: 89-94 N3'34. 3091
The footprint in the sidewalk. Verse. Myron H. Broomell. 15:62*N4'39. 3092
For a child born at dawn. Verse. Frances M. Frost. 7:17*Ag8 '31. 3093
For a female cat named Walt Disney. Verse. Mary Ballard Duryee. 15:32*Mr4'39. 3094
For a good boy/girl. Verse. Elinor Wylie. 3:25 My28'27. 3095
For a Manhattan nursery. Verse. Philip G. Wylie. 2:26 Ja8'27. 3096
For a very little theatre. Prose. Wolcott Gibbs. 4:31 Je2'28. 3097
For Alpha Delta Phi. SM. Alexander Woollcott. 8:32 S17'32. 3098
For an amorous lady. Verse. Theodore Roethke. 14:25*Ja7 '39. 3099
For an architect. Verse. Philip G. Wylie. 2:39 O30'26. 3100
For an easy enthusiast. Verse. Ruth Lambert Jones. 8:26 O8 '32. 3101
For an old dance. Verse. Louise Bogan. 5:17 F1'30. 3102
For any improbable she. Verse. Ogden Nash. 6:93 O4'30. 3103
For any occasion. PR (Schling). Margaret Case Harriman. 12: 18-23*Jy18'36. 3104
For art's sake. Prose. Alice Frankforter. 5:51-2 Ja25'30. 3105
For art's sake. Prose. Nancy Hale. 10:17-19 Mr31'34. 3106
For Christmas. Prose. Patricia Collinge. 5:158-61 D7'29. 3107
For city Spring. Verse. Stephen Vincent Benét. 11:27*Ap13'35. 3108
For herself. Verse. Marie Gilchrist. 8:16*Ap23'32. 3109
For I have learned. Verse. Mark Van Doren. 9:28 S16'33. 3110
For infants only. Prose. Geoffrey T. Hellman. 14:21*D17'38. 3111
For lonely hearts. RL. Morris Markey. 5:40-5 D28'29. 3112
For mayor, Mr. Hylan. Prose. Pier Glass. 1:9 S12'25. 3113
For 100% censorship. Prose. Maxwell Bodenheim. 1:16 Ja2'26. 3114
For our discomfort. SM. Alexander Woollcott. 7:30 Ja2'32. 3115
For our own good. WP. Robert Benchley. 5:50-8 D7'29. 3116
For Pete's sake. Prose. G. Schwabe. 3:82-3 N5'27. 3117
For posterity. Verse. Martha

lass Welch. 11:40-3*S7'35. 3201
French conversation. Prose. Elizabeth Wilder. 10:30*Ja19 '35. 3202
French II-A. Prose. Morris Bishop. 6:33 O11'30. 3203
French hold off at naval parley. Prose. Reed Johnston. 6:38-40 Ap5'30. 3204
French in fifteen minutes--vive le tariff wall. Prose. Fredrick Packard. 7:50-1 Ap25'31. 3205
The French Lily. PR (Pons). Janet Flanner. 7:20-3 Ja16'32. 3206
French one. Prose. Morris Bishop. 6:47-9 D6'30. 3207
French propaganda. Prose. Robert Benchley. 9:18-19 Ap29'33. 3208
A friend in need will be around in five minutes. Verse. Ogden Nash. 15:27*Jy8'39. 3209
Friend of a friend. Prose. T. H. Wenning. 7:14-15 Ja30'32. 3210
Friend of the family. Prose. Sally Benson. 14:17-19*My7'38. 3211
The friends of my father. Prose. Maddy Vegtel. 14:69-70*S24'38. 3212
Friends of the dumb. RL. Robert Littell. 8:26-30 Ag27'32. 3213
Friends of the professor. Prose. Francis Steegmuller. 11:76-7* Mr16'35. 3214
Friendship is like that. Prose. G. Schwabe. 5:101-102 My11 '29. 3215
Frigidity in men. Prose. E. B. White. 5:23-5 S28'29. 3216
Frogs. Verse. Frances M. Frost. 12:76*Ap4'36. 3217
From A to Z. Verse. Ruth Fitch Bartlett. 4:78 Ap14'28. 3218
From a Manhattan tomb. Verse. Ogden Nash. 6:20 Ja31'31. 3219
From a Mexican window. Prose. Charles Kaufman. 10:16-18 Je 16'34. 3220
From a sandlot grandstand. RL. Alvin F. Harlow. 12:32-9*S26 '36. 3221
From a zealous non-worker. Prose. Ring Lardner. 6:26-7 N29'30. 3222
From an office. Verse. E. B. White. 2:29 N20'26. 3223
From an office window. Verse. Phyllis Reid. 3:32 S24'27. 3224
From another world. Verse. Louis Untermeyer. 14:27*Ap30'38. 3225
From butterfly to grub. Verse. Dorothy Dow. 4:34 Ag18'28. 3226
"From considerable lucre I would part ..." Verse. Anon. 1:26 F13'26. 3227
From lust to love in daily installments. OUWA. Ruth McKenney. 13:48-52*Je26'37. 3228
From Madrid to the mirror. PR (Moore). John K. Winkler. 4:23-6 My26'28. 3229
From Paris. Prose. Argus. 1:24 Jy11'25. 3230
From rags to rags. Prose. Ruth McKenney. 14:17-19*Jy16'38. 3231
From St. Luke's. Verse. Peggy Bacon. 2:56 F12'27. 3232
From the book of etiquette. Prose. Clara Janson. 1:21 My23'25. 3233
From "The book of etiquette." Prose. Clara Janson. 1:13 Je 27'25. 3234
From the book of etiquette. Prose. Clara Janson. 1:23Ag8'25. 3235
From the Bronx. Verse. Sylvia Fuller. 2:49 Ag28'26. 3236
From the diary of a transatlantic aviatrix. Prose. Arthur Moss. 3:94 N12'27. 3237
From the diary of a would-be pedestrian. Prose. Charles G. Shaw. 1:20 My16'25. 3238
From the last row on a first night. Prose. Charles G. Shaw. 1:16 Mr14'25. 3239
From the New England primer.

Verse. Franklin P. Adams. 14:20*My28'38. 3240
From the opinions of a New Yorker. Verse. Anon. 1:14 F21'25. 3241
From the record. PR (West Forty-seventh Street Police Station). Meyer Berger. 14:22-7*N19'38; 14:22-8*N26'38. 3242
Front boy. PR (Boomer). Niven Busch, Jr. 3:22-4 S24'27. 3243
Front-page news. Prose. Donald Marshall. 15:42-4*N4'39. 3244
Frontispiece. Prose. James Reid Parker. 12:73-5*Ap11'36. 3245
Frost, Robert. PR. Raymond Holden. 7:24-7*Je6'31. 3246
Frost, Robert. (Parody) E. E. 1: 16*Mr28'25. 3247
Frou-frou, or the future of vertigo. Prose. S. J. Perelman. 14: 15*Ap16'38. 3248
Frozen moment. Verse. Kenneth W. Porter. 11:20*S21'35. 3249
Frozen music or solidified static. Prose. Lewis Mumford. 7:28-36*Je20'31. 3250
Fruits of a dull Monday. WP. Robert Benchley. 3:23-4 D24 '27. 3251

(No entry) 3252
The fruits of culture. Verse. Lee Wilson Dodd. 8:75*Mr19'32. 3253
The fruits of journalism. Prose. Nunnally Johnson. 2:27 Ja8'27. 3254
Frustrated. Verse. Anon. 2:48 My 15'26. 3255
Frustration. Verse. Dorothy Parker. 3:25 Jy23'27. 3256
Führer. PR (Hitler). Janet Flanner. 12:20-4*F29'36; 12:27-31* Mr7'36; 12:22-6*Mr14'36. 3257
Full fathom five. SM. Alexander Woollcott. 5:40 Je22'29. 3258
Fuller Brush romance. Prose. G. Schwabe. 3:50-2 D17'27. 3259
Fun. Prose. Carroll Carroll. 3:40-2 My28'27. 3260
Fun for the kiddies. Prose. John O'Hara. 5:76-8 Je1'29. 3261
Fun in the terminal. Prose. Howard Cushman. 5:47-8 O12'29. 3262
Fun with chemistry. Prose. Raymond Holden. 13:36-40*S18'37. 3263
Funeral of a lady marionette. Verse. Ruth Brown. 5:106 Mr 23'29. 3264
Funerals and taxis. Prose. Eleanor Pálffy. 8:63-5*Ap9'32. 3265
Funiculi, funicula. Prose. Gertrude Curtis Ryan. 8:33-5 Jy23 '32. 3266
Funk at Wagnalls. Verse. Phyllis McGinley. 11:29*S21'35. 3267
The funniest man you ever saw. Prose. James Thurber. 7:13-14*Ag15'31. 3268
Funny-legs. PR (Chaplin). Waldo Frank. 1:9-10 My23'25. 3269
The funny man. Prose. John Chapin Mosher. 5:21-2 My4'29. 3270
Furnished apartment for rent. Prose. Gilbert Seldes. 2:13 Ap 10'26. 3271
Furnished bachelor. Prose. Charles G. Shaw. 2:29 N27'26. 3272
Furry fury. Verse. Jean Batchelor. 13:35*Ag21'37. 3273
Furs and scales. Verse. Arthur Guiterman. 5:26 Mr23'29. 3274
The further nationalist movement. Prose. Theodore Pratt. 8:46-7 Je11'32. 3275
The further off from England. Verse. Phyllis McGinley. 14: 43*Ja21'39. 3276
The fury. Prose. Robert M. Coates. 12:15-18*Ag15'36. 3277
Futchin in the Bronx. Prose. Arthur Kober. 13:33-5*D4'37. 3278
Future conditional. Prose. Wolcott Gibbs. 13:14*My8'37. 3279
The future of element 87. Prose. James Thurber. 7:17 O31'31. 3280
The future of hotels. Prose. Joseph Fulling Fishman. 1:45-6 D12'25. 3281

'27. 3921
Genealogical trees. Verse. Arthur Guiterman. 11:30*Je8'35. 3922
Genealogy. Verse. Witter Bynner. 6:74 S20'30. 3923
The general. Verse. Persis Greely Anderson. 5:75 Ja11'30. 3924
The general. Prose. Arthur H. Folwell. 3:45 Jy23'27. 3925
The General. PR (Johnson). Matthew Josephson. 10:21-5 Ag18 '34; 10:23-8 Ag25'34; 10:22-8 S1'34. 3926
General director. PR (Johnson). Robert A. Simon. 11:30-3*D14 '35. 3927
General good news. WP. Robert Benchley. 3:26-8 Ja14'28. 3928
A general survey of early Summer in town and country. Verse. E. B. White 10:17 Je23 '34. 3929
General utility. PR (Lunt). Alexander Woollcott. 4:25-7 Ap28 '28. 3930
The General's lioness. Prose. Mildred Gilman. 10:42-5 Ag18 '34. 3931
Generous gentleman. Verse. Margaret Widdemer. 6:58 Je14'30. 3932
A generous thought for the wealthy. Verse. Martha Banning Thomas. 6:34 My31'30. 3933
Genesis. Verse. Louis Untermeyer. 13:25*Mr13'37. 3934
Genius. Verse. Alexander K. Laing. 2:89 N13'26. 3935
Genius about town. PR (Heifetz). Helena Huntington Smith. 4:23-5 F25'28. 3936
"Genius always is neurotic." Verse. Clarence Day. 11:63* F23'35. 3937
A genius who made art into big business. PR (Clark). Murdock Pemberton. 1:9-10 Ag1'25. 3938
The gentle Julians. SM. Alexander Woollcott. 5:42 Ap27'29. 3939
A gentle reader speaks. Verse. Baird Leonard. 3:33 D3'27. 3940
The gentle slayer. Prose. Arthur Schmidgall. 7:76 My2'31. 3941
Gentleman about town. Verse. Philip G. Wylie. 2:67 O2'26. 3942
The gentleman downtown. Prose. Arthur Kober. 5:24-5 Mr2'29. 3943
A gentleman from Vienna. PR (Kreisler). Helena Huntington Smith. 4:29-32 N24'28. 3944
The gentleman in politics. PR (Fish). Geoffrey T. Hellman. 9:27-30 O7'33. 3945
The gentleman in the pulpit. PR (Bowie). Richard O. Boyer. 14: 27-33*O22'38. 3946
The gentleman in the tan suit. Prose. John O'Hara. 11:21-2* S7'35. 3947
The gentleman is cold. Prose. James Thurber. 10:18-19*F2 '35. 3948
Gentleman of leisure. Prose. John Chapin Mosher. 7:22-3* Je6'31. 3949
A gentleman phoned. Verse. Marian Storm. 2:35 My29'26. 3950
Gentleman returning from a party. Prose. Marc Connelly. 3:24-5 N19'27. 3951
A gentleman with two cauliflower ears. PR (Craige). Marquis James. 1:9-10 Ap4'25. 3952
Genus homo. Verse. Persis Greely Anderson. 7:36 O10'31. 3953
George. Prose. A. E. Fisher. 9:21-2 S16'33. 3954
George. Prose. Donald Moffat. 15: 85-8*D9'39. 3955
George and the dragon. Verse. George Allen. 12:25*Je27'36. 3956
Georgia vs. the world. Prose. James Thurber. 8:25-9 D31'32. 3957
German in fifteen minutes. Prose. Frederick Packard. 7:67-8 My2 '31. 3958
Geronimo baby. Prose. Max Miller 10:110-12 O13'34. 3959

Gesture. Verse. Scudder Middleton. 8:21 D17'32. 3960
Gesture. Prose. Cuthbert Wright. 3:62 Je25'27. 3961
"Get it up!" RL. Emily Hahn. 9:48-54 My20'33. 3962
Get-rich-quick Callaghan. Prose. Carlton Brown. 12:66-7*Ap25 '36. 3963
Get rid of New Jersey. Prose. E. B. White. 3:15-16 S3'27. 3964
Get up fellows, it's time to go to bed. Verse. Ogden Nash. 15:35*D16'39. 3965
The getaway. Prose. Dorothy Thomas. 15:20-3*My20'39. 3966
Getting a drink. Prose. John O'Hara. 6:60-1 Ja10'31. 3967
Getting a likeness. Prose. Alice Frankforter. 9:48-50 S16'33. 3968
Getting along with women. Prose. E. B. White. 11:35-6*D7'35. 3969
Getting away. Prose. E. B. White. 4:12 Je23'28. 3970
Getting down to work. Verse. Margaret Fishback. 4:65 Je16 '28. 3971
Getting packed. Prose. Alice Frankforter. 5:61-2 Jy13'29. 3972
Getting ready for 1930. Prose. John O'Hara. 5:77-8 N9'29. 3973
Getting settled. Prose. Alice Frankforter. 10:95-6 My26'34. 3974
Getting the ink. MM. Corey Ford. 1:25 S12'25. 3975
Getting their numbers. Prose. John Forbes. 4:79 My12'28. 3976
Getting through the day. Prose. E. B. White. 2:13-14 Ag28'26. 3977
Ghost. Prose. Sally Benson. 7:63-5 O17'31. 3978
Ghost of an opera house. Verse. William Rose Benét. 9:28 Ag5 '33. 3979
Ghost of Bunthorne. Prose. James Reid Parker. 10:46-52 Je16'34. 3980
Ghost of Susie. Prose. Emily Hahn. 11:24-6*Jy6'35. 3981
The ghosting business. PR (Walsh). Alva Johnston. 11:20-5*N23'35. 3982
The ghostly testifier. Verse. Henrietta Fort Holland. 12:44*Je 27'36. 3983
Ghosts. Verse. Margaret McGovern. 14:54*O8'38. 3984
The giant-killer. Prose. T. H. Wenning. 7:16-17*My30'31. 3985
Giant serial's story. Prose. Nate Salisbury. 3:77 Mr26'27. 3986
Gibralter. FP. H. L. Mencken. 10:91-2 Je16'34. 3987
Gide, André. Janet Flanner. 6:86 O4'30. 3988
Gide, André. Janet Flanner. 9:50 Ap29'33. 3989
Gielgud, John. TT. 12:10*O24'36. 3990
Gift. Verse. Louise Bogan. 8:20 My28'32. 3991
A gift of laughter. SM. Alexander Woollcott. 10:40*N17'34. 3992
The gifts. WV. Newman Levy. 5:55 Jy20'29. 3993
Gifts. Verse. Gertrude Curtis Ryan. 3:73 S10'27. 3994
Gil, this is Lola. Prose. Robert M. Coates. 12:15-16*Je13'36. 3995
Gilbert and Sullivan--and Winthrop Ames. Prose. G. M. Hurley. 7:62-3*Je6'31. 3996
The gilded copper. PR (Whalen). Alva Johnston. 4:21-4 Ja12'29. 3997
Ginkgo tree. Verse. William Maxwell. 13:28*My22'37. 3998
Giono, Jean. Janet Flanner. 13:61-3*O23'37. 3999
Gipsy. Prose. Douglass Welch. 14:44-5*Jy23'38. 4000
The gipsy trade. Prose. Helen Woodward. 10:62-3*Ja26'35. 4001
Giradoux, Jean. Janet Flanner. 5:56 D14'29. 4002

God saves the king (and queen). Prose. Henrietta Fort Holland. 9:81 Ja6'34. 4045
God was angry. Prose. Alice Beal Parsons. 15:52-3*Jy15'39. 4046
Godey's lady. Prose. Hazel Hawthorne. 13:16-17*O9'37. 4047
Godfather to Polymnia. PR (Damrosch). Deems Taylor. 5:28-31 N2'29. 4048
Godiva to Tom. Verse. Rosemary Carr Benét. 5:20 Ag3'29. 4049
Godless. Prose. Frances Warfield. 9:83-4 O7'33. 4050
God's country man. Prose. Charles O'Neill. 12:22-3*S26 '36. 4051
Gods in exile. Prose. John Chapin Mosher. 3:84-5 Mr12'27. 4052
Gog and Magog at Forty-second Street. Verse. Ellen McLoughlin. 7:28 Ja16'32. 4053
Gog was a giant. RL. Morris Markey. 1:13 D26'25. 4054
Goin' up, Jack? Prose. Donald Moffat. 6:24-5 My10'30. 4055
Going abroad. Prose. Arthur Kober. 4:36 Ap21'28. 4056
Going home. Prose. Martha Gellhorn. 12:66-8*D12'36. 4057
Going home. Verse. Joseph Moncure March. 2:38 Jy31'26. 4058
Going South. Prose. Alice Frankforter. 5:54-6 N23'29. 4059
Going up! Prose. Carroll Carroll. 3:90-1 O22'27. 4060
Gold. RL. Morris Markey. 7:46-50 S19'31. 4061
Gold, Michael. TT. 10:9 Jy28'34. 4062
The golden age. Prose. David Cort. 6:22-3 My24'30. 4063
The golden age. Verse. Arthur Guiterman. 5:67 Ap27'29. 4064
Golden boy. (Play) TT. 13:13*N 27'37. 4065
The golden rose. Prose. Sylvia Townsend Warner. 13:17-18* Jy24'37. 4066
The golden spoon. PR (Astor). Jack Alexander. 14:20-5*Mr5 '38; 14:23-7*Mr12'38; 14:21-7* Mr19'38. 4067
The goldfish. TA. Will Cuppy. 8: 16 Jy16'32. 4068
Goldfish. Verse. Marjorie Allen Seiffert. 8:48 D3'32. 4069
Golf. NESD. John J. Holzinger. 10:73 Ap28'34. 4070
Golfers. Verse. George Cecil Cowing. 10:78 Je2'34. 4071
Golf's Chevalier Bayard. PR (Jones). Herbert Reed. 2:17-20 Jy17'26. 4072
Goncourt Prize. Janet Flanner. 9: 38 Ja6'34. 4073
Gone with the flood. Prose. Zelda F. Popkin. 12:51-3*O24'36. 4074
Gone with the wind. (Film) TT. 15:16*My6'39. 4075
The good. Verse. Miriam Vedder. 6:42 Ja31'31. 4076
A good address. Prose. Rose C. Feld. 11:60*S28'35. 4077
Good afternoon, dear Mrs. Whale. Prose. Jonathan Harrington. 15: 54*D16'39. 4078
Good and faithful. PR (Kiely). Foster Ware. 3:25-7 D17'27. 4079
Good at games. PR (Vanderbilt). Milton MacKaye. 9:21-5 Mr4 '33. 4080
Good clean fun. Prose. Nunnally Johnson. 2:49-50 My15'26. 4081
The good companions. Verse. Margaret Fishback. 10:87 Mr10'34. 4082
Good company. Verse. Parke Cummings. 6:109 Ap12'30. 4083
Good evening, ladies and gentlemen . . . Prose. John O'Hara. 8:19-20*Ap30'32. 4084
The good fates. Verse. Mark Van Doren. 12:16*Je6'36. 4085
Good Friday. Prose. William Maxwell. 15:17-19*Ap8'39. 4086
Good heavens. Verse. Miriam Vedder. 8:18 Ag6'32. 4087
Good humorist. PR (Young). Max Eastman. 11:21-5*Mr2'35. 4088
"Good hunting." Prose. Corey Ford. 5:16-17 Ag3'29. 4089
A good life. SM. Alexander Wooll-

cott. 7:30-2 F6'32. 4090
The good little saxophoner. Verse. Nate Salisbury. 1:10 Je6'25. 4091
The good long letter. Verse. Mark Van Doren. 13:18*My1'37. 4092
Good loser. Verse. Anon. 2:34 Mr27'26. 4093
Good morning, everybody. Prose. Elspeth O'Halloran. 5:60-1 Mr30'29. 4094
Good morning, friends. Prose. Edwin Corle. 13:28-31*D11'37. 4095
Good morning, judge. PR (Corrigan). Milton MacKaye. 6:22-5 Ag30'30. 4096
Good-night, Dear. Prose. Stephen Leacock. 4:23-4 Ap28'28. 4097
Good old days. WP. Robert Benchley. 4:28-32 Je30'28. 4098
The good old ticker days. Verse. F. P. Adams. 14:25*Mr5'38. 4099
Good old U. S. A. 3's. Prose. Edith Shay. 9:29-32 Ap15'33. 4100
A good parent's garden of vision. Verse. Ogden Nash. 9:16 Mr25'33. 4101
Good party. Prose. John Chapin Mosher. 11:66-7*Mr23'35. 4102
A good play. Prose. Alan Campbell. 9:64-5 Ap8'33. 4103
A good provider. Verse. Margaret Fishback. 11:50*Ja25'36. 4104
A good reporter. Verse. Rollin Kirby. 2:24 O16'26. 4105
A good school for the children. Prose. Zelda F. Popkin. 3:55-8 S10'27. 4106
Good story. Prose. Theodore Dibble. 6:84-5 Ap19'30. 4107
Goodbye, Herman. Prose. John O'Hara. 13:17-18*S4'37. 4108
Goodbye, Jim Zinzinovitch. Prose. Louise Field Cooper. 14:47-8*Ja28'39. 4109
Goodbye, Mr. Jafsie. PR (Condon). St. Clair McKelway. 10:20-6*D29'34. 4110
Goodbye, Mr. O. Charles Meyer! Prose. James Thurber. 12:12-13*Ag1'36. 4111
Goodbye now. Prose. Clifford Orr. 15:56*Mr4'39. 4112
Goodbye, Shirley Temple. Prose. Joseph Mitchell. 15:17-18*S16'39. 4113
Goodbye to palship. Prose. Arthur Kober. 13:52-6*F20'37. 4114
Goose vs. goose. Prose. Joseph Fulling Fishman. 1:11-12 My30'25. 4115
Gordon, Max. TT. 10:18-19 Ap14'34. 4116
The governor. PR (Roosevelt). Milton MacKaye. 7:18-22 Ag15'31; 7:24-9 Ag22'31. 4117
The governor. PR (Lehman). Hickman Powell. 12:21-6*My2'36; 12:25-30*My9'36. 4118
Grace after meat. Verse. Henrietta Fort Holland. 5:109 N23'29. 4119
Grafters, not so gentle. RL. Morris Markey. 3:34-8 N5'27. 4120
Gramercy Park. Verse. E. B. White. 4:27 Mr3'28. 4121
Gramercy section. Verse. Virginia Woods Bellamy. 14:32*Ag20'38. 4122
The grammarian. Prose. Richard Lockridge. 13:26-30*S25'37. 4123
Grand Central. Verse. G. F. Riegel. 3:55 Je4'27. 4124
Grand Central--3 a. m. Verse. Carroll Carroll. 5:58 Mr30'29. 4125
Grand junction. RL. Albert Furth. 9:85-91 D2'33. 4126
The grand passion. Prose. Frank Sullivan. 7:15 S26'31. 4127
Grand sachem. PR (Darlington). Frances Warfield. 8:19-23 Ag6'32. 4128
Grandpa helps at a seance. Prose. Clarence Day. 12:14-16*Jy18'36. 4129
Grandpa keeps his hands off. Prose. Clarence Day. 12:14-16*Ag8'36. 4130
Grandpa makes me a bear pit.

Prose. Clarence Day. 12:15-16*Jy4'36. 4131
The grandson. Prose. Eugene Joffe. 9:18-20 O28'33. 4132
(No entry) 4133
Graph showing fluctuation . . . Prose. E. B. White. 3:19 O22 '27. 4134
The grasshopper. Prose. Frances Crane. 7:51-2 S19'31. 4135
Grasshopper. Prose. Wolcott Gibbs. 9:24-5 Je3'33. 4136
Grasshoppers are very intelligent. Verse. Ogden Nash. 10:24 Jy 28'34. 4137
The grateful notary and the prince. Prose. Frank Sullivan. 9:15-16 Mr11'33. 4138
Gratitood's in the dictionary. Prose. Arthur Kober. 13:17-19*O16'37. 4139
Gratitude. Verse. Arthur Guiterman. 10:40 N10'34. 4140
Gray for psychiatry. Prose. James Reid Parker. 12:55-6* Je6'36. 4141
Gray's. Prose. Bernard Smith. 1:37 N7'25. 4142
The great actor and the witch. Prose. Frank Sullivan. 9:19-20 Ap8'33. 4143
The great and I. Prose. Thomas Beer. 3:28 F26'27. 4144
The great arson plot. TWNY. Kenneth Campbell. 10:55-8 Ag25'34. 4145
Great bottles. Verse. Clarence Day. 10:21 Je9'34. 4146
The great camera mysteries. Prose. Alexander Woollcott. 3:34-6 N12'27. 4147
The great chowder murder. TWNY. Edmund Pearson. 11:53-9*Ap6'35. 4148
Great Dane in summer. Prose. Louis Field Cooper. 15:42-3* O7'39. 4149
The great disappearance movement (1934-1937). Prose. Elmer Rice. 6:23-5 O25'30. 4150
Great events of 1929. Prose. Alvin F. Harlow. 5:50-3 Ja11'30. 4151
The great filibusterer. Prose. Frank Sullivan. 11:15-16*Je29 '35. 4152
The great fire of 1835. TWNY. Herbert Asbury. 6:32-7 Ag2'30. 4153
The great goldfish problem. Prose. Katherine Sproehnle. 3:42-4 Mr19'27. 4154
Great-grandmother. Prose. Alice Frankforter. 10:48-50 Mr10'34. 4155
The great-grandmother. Prose. Nancy Hale. 11:33-5*D7'35. 4156
The great home holiday. Prose. Arthur H. Folwell. 3:120 N19 '27. 4157
The great impersonation. PR (Belasco). Niven Busch, Jr. 6:30-3 O18'30; 6:30-3 O25'30. 4158
The great lady and the gardener. Verse. Helene Mullins. 4:27 O 6'28. 4159
The great linoleum mystery. Prose. T. H. Bliss. 1:25 My16 '25. 4160
The great man. Prose. Alice Frankforter. 9:71-2 Ja13'34. 4161
Great man at home. Prose. Edith Orr. 11:81-2*Ap6'35. 4162
The Great Manta. Prose. Edwin Corle. 10:23-5 My5'34. 4163
Great occasion. Verse. Clarence Day. 11:44*O12'35. 4164
The great peace, or Mr. Thomas V. Smith. Prose. Robert Nathan. 10:16*D22'34. 4165
A great scandal. Verse. Fillmore Hyde. 2:29 N20'26. 4166
The great sheet scandal. Prose. James Thurber. 8:15-16 D17'32. 4167
The great slogan mystery. SM. Alexander Woollcott. 9:30 S30 '33. 4168
The great sophomore. Prose. George Cecil Cowing. 9:63 Je3 '33. 4169
The great spectator. PR (Hayes). Stanley Walker. 8:21-5 S10'32. 4170

Great thoughts. Prose. Morris Bishop. 9:59-60 D9'33. 4171
The great word. Verse. Arthur Guiterman. 14:80*D17'38. 4172
Greater New York. Prose. Theodore Pratt. 10:46 S15'34; 10:64 S22'34; 10:72 S29'34; 10:86 O6'34; 10:60 O20'34. 4173
The greatest accountant in the world. AC. John McCarten. 15:86-95*D16'39. 4174
The greatest man in the world. Prose. James Thurber. 7:20-3 F21'31. 4175
The greatest of these is faith. Prose. Arthur H. Folwell. 3:62-3 F19'27. 4176
The greatest paper-hanger in the world. PR (Stein). Henry Anton Steig. 13:22-6* N6'37. 4177
The greedy ash can. Verse. Anon. 1:10 Ja9'26. 4178
Greek love. Prose. Howard B. Hutchison. 10:57-9 O20'34. 4179
Green baize. RL. Morris Markey. 2:38-43 F12'27. 4180
The green field. Verse. Elizabeth Coatsworth. 10:18 Je16'34. 4181
Green front. PR (Butler). Stanley Walker. 8:20-3 Jy9'32. 4182
Green hill far away. Prose. E. B. White. 14:16-17*Jy2'38. 4183
The Green Pastures. (Play) TT. 6:12 Mr15'30. 4184
The green pastures. SM. Alexander Woollcott. 6:34 Mr22'30. 4185
The green pencil. RL. Jack Alexander 13:42-62*D11'37. 4186
Greenwich Village. Prose. Charles Street. 1:24 Mr21'25. 4187
Greetings, friends. Verse. Frank Sullivan. 8:15-16 D24'32. 4188
Greetings, friends. Verse. Frank Sullivan. 9:13 D23'33. 4189
Greetings, friends. Verse. Frank Sullivan. 11:21-2*D21'35. 4190
Greetings, friends. Verse. Frank Sullivan. 12:19*D26'36. 4191
Greetings, friends. Verse. Frank Sullivan. 13:21*D25'37. 4192
Greetings, friends! Verse. Frank Sullivan. 14:19*D24'38. 4193
Greetings, friends! Verse. Frank Sullivan 15:18*D23'39. 4194
Gregory John. Prose. Clifford Orr. 8:89-92 D3'32. 4195
Grenada. FP. H. L. Mencken. 10:84-5 Je2'34. 4196
Grey, Zane. TT. 15:9-10*N4'39. 4197
Gridiron soliloquies. Verse. J. M. C. 7:35 N21'31. 4198
Grim resolves for 1937. Prose. Hildegarde Dolson. 12:47*Ja2 '37. 4199
Grim-visaged victory. PR (Leader). Herbert Reed. 2:17-18 Je 26'26. 4200
Grist. SM. Alexander Woollcott. 8:28*F27'32. 4201
The grocer's--oh, the grocer's. Prose. C. Knapp. 3:36 D17'27. 4202
Groton, Harvard, and Tahiti. PR (Biddle). Geoffrey T. Hellman. 12:20-6*My30'36. 4203
Groton, Harvard, Wall Street. PR (Whitney). Matthew Josephson. 8:19-22*Ap2'32. 4204
Ground-minded. Prose. Cornelia Otis Skinner. 12:30-2*Je6'36. 4205
Grounds for divorce. Prose. Joseph P. Pollard. 14:54-5*My14 '38. 4206
Grounds of offence. Prose. Oliver La Farge. 14:25-7*Mr26'38. 4207
Group chant against communism. Verse. Morris Bishop. 13:16*S 4'37. 4208
Growing up in New Canaan. Prose. Gil Borg. 8:15-16*Ap23'32. 4209
Grown in Garden City. PR (Doubleday). Foster Ware. 3:21-3 F18 '28. 4210
Guardian angel. Prose. Serena Concord. 11:50-1*Ja18'36. 4211
Guarding the coast. RL. Jack Alexander. 12:49-64*D12'36. 4212
The guardsman. SM. Alexander

Woollcott. 10:38 Ap14'34. 4213
Guerdon. Verse. Peggy Bacon. 14:68*S17'38. 4214
Guessing game. Prose. James Thurber. 8:24-5 S24'32. 4215
The guest. Prose. Marc Connelly. 5:23-4 D21'29. 4216
Guest at the farm. Verse. Martha Banning Thomas. 7:56 Ja 16'32. 4217
Guest, Edgar. (Parody) Franklin P. Adams. 13:33*O30'37. 4218
Guest, Edgar. (Parody). Ogden Nash. 9:16 S23'33. 4219
Guest of honor. Prose. Sally Benson. 15:17-19*S30'39. 4220
The guestroom. WV. Newman Levy. 5:49 Jy27'29. 4221
Guestroom books. Verse. Newman Levy. 6:92 Ap12'30. 4222
Guests of Lady Julia. Prose. James Reid Parker. 11:31-2* Mr2'35. 4223
Guidance. Prose. James Gilbert Shellhase. 11:64*Je8'35. 4224
Guide for motorists. Verse. Margaret Fishback. 2:88 S11'26. 4225
A guide to summer reading. Prose. Newman Levy. 4:22-3 Jy28'28. 4226
A guide to the last of the American bars. Prose. Guy Du Bois. 5:18-19 Jy13'29. 4227
A guide to the pronunciation of words in "Time." Prose. E. B. White. 12:16*Mr14'36. 4228
The Guild. PR (Theatre Guild). Cuthbert Wright. 2:17-20 D25 '26. 4229
Guinea pig. Prose. Ruth McKenney. 13:24-6*Ag7'37. 4230
Gulf Stream lines. Verse. Jean Batchelor. 9:26 Ag26'33. 4231
Gum across the sea. Prose. Mollie Panter-Downes. 15:48-51* Ag19'39. 4232
Guns and game calls. Prose. James Thurber. 11:25-6*D14 '35. 4233
The gyp cab. Prose. Gurney Williams. 8:42-3 Ja21'33. 4234
Gyp. (Gabrielle-Marie-Antoinette De Riquetti). Janet Flanner. 8:29 Jy30'32. 4235

H

The H. J. Winninger girl. Prose. Angelica Gibbs. 9:34-6 My20'33. 4236
H. L. Mencken. Verse. James Norman Hall. 9:73 Ja6'34. 4237
Haberdasher. Verse. Morris Bishop. 12:17*Ap25'36. 4238
The habitual jail breaker. Prose. C. Knapp. 3:42-3 F11'28. 4239
"Had a good time?" Prose. G. B. Stern. 10:96-8 S15'34. 4240
"Hail fellow, thar she blows!" Prose. Robert Benchley. 4:15-16 Ja19'29. 4241
Hail the heroes. RL. Morris Markey. 2:19-20 F27'26. 4242
Hail to Franklin D. Roosevelt. Verse. E. B. White. 11:30*O19 '35. 4243
Hail to October! Verse. Marjorie Allen Seiffert. 8:35 O15'32. 4244
Hail to the chief. OW. Ring Lardner. 9:39-41 My27'33. 4245
Hail to thee blithe spirits. OUWA. St. Clair McKelway. 11:23-31* Je15'35. 4246
Hair scientist. PR (Nessler). Geoffrey T. Hellman. 9:20-4 Ap29'33. 4247
Haldeman-Julius, E. PR. Alexander Woollcott. 1:7-8 Je20'25. 4248
Half a dozen anecdotes about Mr. Hoover. Prose. Wolcott Gibbs. 6:26-7 O18'30. 4249
Half-day. Prose. Sally Benson. 8:20-1 Jy30'32. 4250
Half hours at sea. Prose. David McCord. 2:19 Jy3'26; 2:21 Jy10 '26; 2:18 Jy24'26; 2:20 Ag7'26; 2:21 Ag14'26; 2:21 Ag21'26; 2:24 Ag28'26. 4251
Halfway house. DL. Burke Boyce. 2:44 D25'26. 4252
Hall, Amanda Benjamin. (Parody) EE. 1:16 Mr28'25. 4253
Hall of Science. Verse. Marjorie

Allen Seiffert. 9:42 Ag12'33. 4254

Hall of science wild. Prose. Jerome Barry. 11:56-7*My4'35. 4255

Hallelujah. Prose. James Reid Parker. 7:71-2 S12'31. 4256

Halliburton, Richard. TT. 5:19 D14'29. 4257

Halloween crisis. Prose. Rose C. Feld. 14:54-6*O29'38. 4258

The Hallowe'en party. Prose. John O'Hara. 4:84-5 S22'28. 4259

Halloween party. Prose. John O'Hara. 5:36 O26'29. 4260

The halted man. Verse. Mark Van Doren. 5:32 S14'29. 4261

Hamburg, April. OFC. M. R. C. 10:105-107 My5'34. 4262

Hammam of delicious bathing. Prose. Eunice Tietjens. 11:75-6*O19'35. 4263

The hand. Verse. Persis Greely Anderson. 8:20 Jy2'32. 4264

The hand that feeds you. PR (Childs). Brock Pemberton and Foster Ware. 3:25-8 Ap9'27. 4265

The hand that rocks the cradle. Prose. Henrietta Fort Holland. 9:38-40 Ap15'33. 4266

A handful of little days. Prose. Leane Zugsmith. 10:20-2*N17'34. 4267

Handicap. Verse. Ruth Lambert Jones. 8:19*Ap9'32. 4268

Handin' her a line. Prose. Arthur Kober. 5:77-8 Ap13'29. 4269

Hands. Verse. Scudder Middleton. 5:26 Mr16'29. 4270

Hands across the headlines. Verse. Phyllis McGinley. 15:26*D9'39. 4271

Hands across the sea. Prose. Geoffrey T. Hellman. 15:60*Ap22'39. 4272

Hands across the sea. PR (Corsi). Milton MacKaye. 11:20-5*Mr9'35; 11:28-33*Mr16'35. 4273

Handsome does. Verse. Elspeth O'Halloran. 6:53 Ag2'30. 4274

Handsprings across the sea. PR (Mendl). Janet Flanner. 13:25-9*Ja15'38. 4275

Handy glossary for banquet use. Prose. George Cecil Cowing. 5:24 F1'30. 4276

Handy guide to Florida. Prose. Ponce de Leon. 1:9-10 Ja16'26. 4277

Hanging gardens. Verse. Leslie Nelson Jennings. 10:56 Je2'34. 4278

Hanky-panky. SM. Alexander Woollcott. 5:38 My11'29. 4279

Hanover-on-Hudson. Prose. Wolcott Gibbs. 7:16*Jy4'31. 4280

Hanover Square. DL. Burke Boyce. 2:97 N13'26. 4281

The happiest days. Prose. John Cheever. 15:15-16*N4'39. 4282

Happiest man in the world. Prose. Marc Connelly. 3:15-16 F18'28. 4283

Happiness in a day coach. Prose. Margaret Fishback. 4:60-2 Je9'28. 4284

Happiness in every lease. Verse. Clifton Fadiman. 13:58*Je26'37. 4285

Happy birthday. Prose. Benedict Thielen. 15:51-5*Ap22'39. 4286

A happy day. RC. Fillmore Hyde. 3:14-16 Je18'27. 4287

Happy ending. Prose. Frances Crane. 14:29-32*S10'38. 4288

Happy heart and healthy glands. Verse. Morris Bishop. 15:23*N4'32. 4289

The happy solipsist. Verse. Morris Bishop. 12:18*Ja23'37. 4290

Happy though awake. Prose. John Chapin Mosher. 8:12-13 Jy23'32. 4291

Harbach, Otto. PR. A. J. Liebling. 13:22-7*F27'37. 4292

Harbor hopper. PR (Turner). Rob- M. Coates. 11:25-9*S21'35. 4293

Hard case. Verse. Babette Deutsch. 13:18*Jy24'37. 4294

A hard day with the Ritz Carltons. RC. Fillmore Hyde. 2:13-14 Ag14'26. 4295

Hard lines. Verse. Ogden Nash.

6:23 D20'30. 4296
Hark at this. Prose. G. Schwabe. 4:85-8 F16'29. 4297
Hark! hark! the turncoats. Prose. E. B. White. 7:28 D5'31. 4298
Harlem. NYC. Arthur Gerald Goldberg. 5:82-4 N9'29. 4299
Harlem 1927. Verse. Frances Park. 3:47 D31'27. 4300
"Harlequinade." SM. Alexander Woollcott. 5:40 S7'29. 4301
Harold Olney Pim. Verse. Lee Wilson Dodd. 6:63 O4'30. 4302
The harp lady. PR (Dilling). E. J. Kahn, Jr. 15:25-9 F3'40. 4303
Harper to Mifflin to chance. Verse. E. B. White. 8:21 D10 '32. 4304
Harris, Frank. SM. Alexander Woollcott. 7:32 S26'31. 4305
Harris, Frank. (Parody) Ernest Hemingway. 2:23-4 F12'27. 4306
Harris, Jed. TT. 5:17-18 S21'29. 4307
Harris, Jed. TT. 12:9 S12'36. 4308
A harrowing experience. Prose. G. Schwabe. 2:73 Ja22'27. 4309
Hart, Lorenz. PR. Margaret Case Harriman. 14:19-23*My28 '38; 14:21-5*Je4'38. 4310
Hart, Moss. TT. 6:21 N29'30. 4311
Harte, Bret. TT. 7:8 Ag1'31. 4312
Harvest of half-truths. Verse. E. B. White. 7:20 N28'31. 4313
"A harvest of inventions." PR (Hammond). Gilbert Seldes. 8: 16-20 Jy2'32. 4314
Has photography gone too far? Prose. James Thurber. 10:13-14 Ag11'34. 4315
Has the Sunday paper come yet? WP. Robert Benchley. 14:37-9* My21'38. 4316
Haste makes waste. Prose. Margaret Fishback. 6:68 N22'30. 4317
The hat boy. Verse. Parke Cummings. 2:49 D25'26. 4318
Hat song. Verse. Richard Peckham. 6:64 Mr22'30. 4319
Hats. Prose. Frances Crane. 12: 35-6*Jy25'36. 4320
Haunted. Prose. Frances Crane. 5:69-72 O5'29. 4321
Haunted house. Verse. Frances Park. 4:74 S29'28. 4322
Hauptmann and circumstantial evidence. RL. Edmund Pearson. 11:37-48*Mr9'35. 4323
Hausfrau prima donna. PR (Schumann-Heink). Helena Huntington Smith. 2:17-18 Mr20 '26. 4324
Have a baby. Verse. Joseph Fulling Fishman. 2:49 O2'26. 4325
Have you succeeded as a burglar? Prose. Spud Johnson. 3:31 Mr 5'27. 4326
Hawkshaw in modern clothes. Prose. Émile C. Schnurmacher. 3:57-8 Jy23'27. 4327
Hawthorne Hill. Verse. E. B. White. 12:22*N28'36. 4328
Hay fever. Verse. Ogden Nash. 14: 20*S10'38. 4329
Hay fever lament. Verse. Theodore Roethke. 13:54*Ag14'37. 4330
Hays, Will H. PR. Alva Johnston. 9:18-21 Je10'33; 9:16-19 Je17 '33. 4331
Hays, Will H. PR. Arthur Krock. 2:21-2 My8'26. 4332
Hazards and chases. RL. Geoffrey T. Hellman. 14:28-39*Ap9'38. 4333
Hazards of a trade. RL. Morris Markey. 10:47-54*Ja5'35. 4334
He. Prose. E. B. White. 3:19 F4 '28. 4335
"He also serves--." Prose. Stanley Jones. 5:74-5 Je22'29. 4336
He danced with Mrs. Vanderbilt. Prose. Katherine Lynch. 11:76-7*Ap20'35. 4337
He had a little list. Prose. George Cecil Cowing. 7:20 D19'31. 4338
He looks at us without seeing us. Verse. Edith Franklin Wyatt. 12:55*Ap18'36. 4339
He made a coupla dollars. Prose. Richard Lockridge. 10:21-2 N 10'34. 4340

He saw nothing abroad. Prose. William Rose Benét. 2:52 S 25'26. 4341

He saw what he wanted--. Prose. Donald Thompson. 5:30 My4 '29. 4342

He sensed a spark. Prose. Arthur Kober. 10:24-6*D1'34. 4343

"He skipped from Manhattan..." Verse. Dysart McMullen. 1:22 My23'25. 4344

He takes evvthing sirious. Prose. Emanuel Eisenberg. 14:30-1* Ag27'38. 4345

"He travels fastest--." Prose. Prose. Robert Benchley. 8:12 Je25'32. 4346

He was among friends. Prose. Beverly L. Clarke. 12:38-9* Ag29'36. 4347

He was good to his wife and his kiddies. OSB. C. Knapp. 4:19 Ja5'29. 4348

He was so good to her. Prose. Frank Sullivan. 7:19-20 S12'31. 4349

Head in green bronze. Prose. Hugh Walpole. 14:23*F26'38. 4350

The head waiter. Verse. Anon. 2:53 My8'26. 4351

Headquarters. Verse. George Allen. 14:97*D10'38. 4352

Headquarters. RL. Niven Busch, Jr. 5:26-31 Jy20 '29. 4353

Health and hygiene. Prose. Alva Johnston. 6:13-15 Ag2 '30. 4354

Hear the nightingale sing. Prose. Paul Gallico. 13:29-30*Je26 '37. 4355

Heard in an art gallery. Prose. Martha Banning Thomas. 2:79 S11'26. 4356

Hearing the returns. Prose. Newman Levy. 4:30 N3'28. 4357

Hearst, William Randolph. TT. 1:3-4 Ap18'25. 4358

Hearst, William Randolph. TT. 1:1 Je6'25. 4359

Hearst, William Randolph. PR. John K. Winkler. 3:25-7 Ap23 '27; 3:25-8 Ap30'27; 3:23-6 My 7'27; 3:24-7 My14'27; 3:23-6 My21'27. 4360

Hearst with his own petard. RL. A. J. Liebling. 14:40-7*N19'38. 4361

Heart, be merry! Verse. Elizabeth Coatsworth. 7:21 F28'31. 4362

Heart of gold. Prose. Emily Hahn 9:34-7 Mr25'33. 4363

Heavens! Verse. Mildred Weston. 11:28*D28'35. 4364

Heavier than air. PR (Wright). Eric Hodgins. 6:29-32 D13'30. 4365

Heavy da-dee-dough boys. OW. Ring Lardner. 8:30-5 Je25'32. 4366

The heavy dragoon. (Parody) Ernest Boyd. 9:23 O21'33. 4367

Hecht, Ben. TT. 5:13-14 Je15'29. 4368

Hecht, Ben. TT. 14:11*Mr12'38. 4369

Heeney for champion. Prose. Alva Johnston. 4:25 Je2'28. 4370

Heh-ven as sage. Prose. Emily Hahn. 13:17-19*Jy17'37. 4371

Heh-ven helps me out. Prose. Emily Hahn. 13:43-5*Ja15'38. 4372

The height of liberty. Prose. Berry Fleming. 3:42-4 My14 '27. 4373

Heights and depths. SM. Alexander Woollcott. 10:36 My12'34. 4374

Heil Washington! RL. Russell Maloney. 15:30-2*Mr4'39. 4375

Heil Wilcox! Prose. Frances Warfield. 9:70-1 My6'33. 4376

Heirloom. Verse. Leslie Nelson Jennings. 7:23 Ja30'32. 4377

Heirloom for my daughter. Verse. Alice Corbin. 12:21*O31'36. 4378

Held in trust. Prose. Sally Benson. 7:16-17*Ag1'31. 4379

Helen. Prose. Winifred Willis. 15:31-2*S9'39. 4380

Hell only breaks loose once. Prose. James Thurber. 10:19-20 Mr10'34. 4381

Hello, brother! Prose. Atreus Von Schrader. 10:45-6 O13'34. 4382

Hello everybody! WP. Robert Benchley. 8:34-8*Mr26'32. 4383
Hello, operator? I don't want a policeman. Prose. S. J. Perelman. 15:18-19*Je3'39. 4384
Hell's bells. Verse. Anon. 2:32 S18'26. 4385
Help the younger element. Prose. John O'Hara. 7:75*Je6'31. 4386
Helpful hints for marginaires. Prose. Creighton Peet. 5:64-9 N23'29. 4387
Helpful recipes for the apartment hermit. Prose. Charles Street. 1:23 Jy18'25. 4388
Helping causes. WP. Robert Benchley. 5:32-6 Ap20'29. 4389
Helping Drandma. Prose. Robert Benchley. 8:14-16 Ag27'32. 4390
Helping hand. Prose. Angelica Gibbs. 14:24-6*Ja14'39. 4391
Helping hand. Prose. Donald Thompson. 8:16-18*Ap9'32. 4392
Helping New York grow. Prose. Richard Lockridge. 8:34-6 S10 '32. 4393
The helpmeet. Prose. Helena Huntington Smith. 3:62-4 S17 '27. 4394
Helps for entertaining Count Deterding. Prose. James Thurber. 4:32-6 Ap14'28. 4395
Helth and welth and joliti. RL. Margaret Case Harriman. 14: 44-8*F26'38. 4396
Hemingway, Ernest. Dorothy Parker. 3:76-7 F18'28. 4397
Hemingway, Ernest. PR. Dorothy Parker. 5:28-31 N30'29. 4398
Hemingway, Ernest. (Parody) Clifton Fadiman. 9:75 O28'33. 4399
Hemingway, Ernest. (Parody) TT. 13:7*Ag28'37. 4400
Hemingway, Ernest. (Parody) Verse. E. B. White. 10:31 Ap 14'34. 4401
Hen-party. Verse. Peggy Bacon. 3:36 O8'27. 4402
Henley. Prose. Frances Crane. 11: 41-4*Jy6'35. 4403
Henry, O. TT. 4:20 Mr31'28. 4404
Hens and grammarians. Prose. Clarence Day. 10:17-18 Jy14 '34. 4405
Her debt to literature. Prose. Bessie Breuer. 11:13-14*Jy13 '35. 4406
Her little kingdom. Prose. Frances Woodward Prentice. 9:18-20 F25'33. 4407
Her majesty the Queen. PR (Queen Mary). Janet Flanner. 11:20-4* My4'35; 11:28-32*My11'35. 4408
Her mother was a Singleton. Prose. Angelica Gibbs. 7:31-2 Ag29'31. 4409
Her own things. Prose. Sally Benson. 12:13-15*Je6'36. 4410
Her son. Verse. Martha Banning Thomas. 6:43 Ap26'30. 4411
Heralds of the dawn. Prose. Frederick Packard. 7:50-2 Ap18'31. 4412
Herb and Frank panic 'em. OW. Ring Lardner. 8:58-60 N5'32. 4413
The herbalist. Prose. Frances Crane. 11:61*My4'35. 4414
Herbert Agar's not in our bathroom. Prose. Russell Maloney. 15:51*Ag26'39. 4415
Herbert Pleuthner and son. Prose. Horton Heath. 9:58-9 F3'34. 4416
Herbs and simples. Verse. Leslie Nelson Jennings. 10:70 S22'34. 4417
Here are ladies. SM. Alexander Woollcott. 8:24 Ag20'32. 4418
Here come the clowns. PR (Landolf). A. J. Liebling. 15:25-9* Ap15'39. 4419
Here today and gone tomorrow. Verse. Margaret Fishback. 4:97 My19'28. 4420
Heredity. Verse. Edward W. Barnard. 3:93 S17'27. 4421
The hermit. Verse. Mark Van Doren. 5:24 D21'29. 4422
Hero. Prose. Arthur Kober. 8:16-

18 O22'32. 4423

A hero passes. Prose. A. B. Bernd. 1:9-10 Ja2'26. 4424

Hero, wired for sound. Prose. Frank Sullivan. 10:17-18 F17 '34. 4425

Heroica. Verse. Marya Mannes. 9:27 Ja13'34. 4426

Herr Goebbels gives a music lesson. Prose. Allen Rose. 14:33* Ja28'39. 4427

Herr Scheffel's deadly weapon. Prose. Montgomery Wright. 15: 99-101*D9'39. 4428

The herring. TA. Will Cuppy. 8: 14 Ag13'32. 4429

The herring piece. Prose. Kay Boyle. 13:24-8*Ap10'37. 4430

Hetty Green's son. PR (Green). John K. Winkler. 4:24-7 Ja5 '29. 4431

Heureux Noel. PR (Coward). Alexander Woollcott. 4:21-5 Ja19 '29. 4432

Hewer of stone. PR (Lachaise). Gilbert Seldes. 7:28-31 Ap4'31. 4433

Hey day labor. Prose. E. B. White. 2:21 Ag7'26. 4434

Hey-hey blues. Verse. Langston Hughes. 15:70*N25'39. 4435

Hic jacet-petrel. Verse. Jacqueline Embry. 5:33 O12'29. 4436

Hidden. Verse. Louise Bogan. 11: 20*F15'36. 4437

Hideaways. Prose. James Kevin McGuinness. 3:90-3 Mr12'27. 4438

The hideout. Prose. Stacy V. Jones. 8:52-3 Ja21'33. 4439

The hiding generation. Prose. James Thurber. 12:17-19*My2 '36. 4440

High finance. Prose. Martha Gellhorn. 14:102-104*D3'38. 4441

High finance. Prose. John Chapin Mosher. 3:26 Ag27'27. 4442

The high hat. Prose. Robert Nathan 14:17-18*Mr 26'38. 4443

High noon at City Hall. Prose. Mary Heaton Vorse. 9:46-50 D2'33. 4444

The high sign. Prose. Alexander Laing. 7:13-15*Ag1'31. 4445

High tied. Verse. Margaret Fishback. 8:50 N5'32. 4446

Highball flags. Prose. James Thurber. 12:17*Je13'36. 4447

"Highballs, lowballs . . ." Verse. Arthur Guiterman. 1:26 F13'26. 4448

The higher criticism. Prose. Joseph Fulling Fishman. 2:66 O30 '26. 4449

Higher education. Prose. Berry Fleming. 3:69-71 My21'27. 4450

The higher education. Prose. Emily Hahn. 13:51-4*D18'37. 4451

Higher education. Verse. G. Schwabe. 2:67 N6'26. 4452

The higher-ups. Prose. Ring Lardner. 6:15 N1'30. 4453

Highlights. Prose. Corey Ford. 1: 15 F21'25. 4454

Highlights. Prose. Corey Ford. 1: 23 F28'25. 4455

Highlights. Prose. Corey Ford. 1: 26 Mr21'25. 4456

Hilario. Prose. Theodore Pratt. 9: 32 Ap8'33. 4457

The hillside. Verse. Elizabeth Coatsworth. 10:86 O6'34. 4458

Hillside orchard. Verse. Raymond Holden. 8:16*My7'32. 4459

Him. Verse. Morris Bishop. 13:18* Ja8'38. 4460

Hint. Verse. Parke Cummings. 2: 75 D11'26. 4461

The hint. Verse. Scudder Middleton. 5:26 My11'29. 4462

A hint for the fourteenth of February. Verse. Jean Batchelor. 8: 61 F11'33. 4463

A hint in the park. Prose. John Chapin Mosher. 7:15-16*Ag8'31. 4464

Hint to a scientist. Verse. Hortense Flexner. 11:31*Ja4'36. 4465

Hint to advertisers. Verse. Arthur Guiterman. 5:75 Ap20'29. 4466

A hint to the hopeful. Verse. Jean Batchelor. 15:35*Je24'39. 4467

Hinterlander's dilemma. Verse. Jerome Barry. 15:70*My13

'39. 4468
Hints to a universe. Verse. Arthur Guiterman. 6:50 N8'30. 4469
Hippodrome days. Prose. Murdock Pemberton. 6:81-6 My17 '30; 6:47-53 My24'30; 6:51-6 Je7'30; 6:42-8 Je21'30. 4470
". . . his partner, Henry T. Collins." Prose. John O'Hara. 7: 84-6 N28'31. 4471
His time is my time. Prose. Hildegarde Dolson. 12:40-1*Jy 18'36. 4472
Histoire de France. SM. Alexander Woollcott. 6:32 Mr1'30. 4473
Historical incidents. Verse. Clarence Day. 9:21 O14'33. 4474
Historical incidents. Verse. Clarence Day. 11:19*Ag24'35. 4475
Historical incidents. Verse. Clarence Day. 11:21*S14'35. 4476
Historical record. Verse. Hortense Flexner. 15:47*O21'39. 4477
History lesson. Verse. Mark Van Doren. 13:18*S25'37. 4478
The history of the hansom cab. SM. Alexander Woollcott. 6:36-44 My3'30. 4479
Hit. Prose. Alan Campbell. 9:53-4 N25'33. 4480
Hit on the head with a cow. RL. Joseph Mitchell. 14:21-4*Ag27 '38. 4481
Hit the switch. RL. Morris Markey. 6:46-50 S27'30. 4482
Hith or Smoover--which? Prose. Frank Sullivan. 4:23-5 S15'28. 4483
The Hitler buffoon. Verse. Ernest Boyd. 9:23 O21'33. 4484
Hitler raps party foes. Prose. Reed Johnston. 7:35-6 Ja2'32. 4485
Hizzoner. Prose. Civitas. 1:19 Ag 22'25. 4486
Ho, what is so rare as a day in Sol. Prose. Phyllis Ryan. 4: 101 Ap7'28. 4487
The Hockenputz players. Prose. Burdette Kinne. 6:78-81 O11 '30. 4488
Hockey at the Garden. Verse. Parke Cummings. 2:49 Ja1'27. 4489
Hold 'em, Postal! Prose. Richard Lockridge. 6:66-7 N22'30. 4490
Holdup. Prose. Margaret Ford. 11: 33*Jy27'35. 4491
Holes in stockings. Verse. John O'Hara. 5:52 Je22'29. 4492
The holiday spirit. WP. Robert Benchley. 14:59*Ja14'39. 4493
Holidays are sad days for people who don't have holidays. Verse. E. B. White. 10:22 My26'34. 4494
Hollandaise. Prose. Clifford Orr. 15:60-1*Mr25'39. 4495
Hollywood. Verse. Leslie Nelson Jennings. 7:30*Jy4'31. 4496
Hollywood. Verse. Leslie Nelson Jennings. 7:64 O10'31. 4497
Hollywood. Verse. Leslie Nelson Jennings. 7:54 O17'31. 4498
Hollywood. Verse. R. B. H. 11:32* Je29'35. 4499
Hollywood agent. PR (Hayward). Margaret Case Harriman. 12:20-4*Jy11'36. 4500
A Hollywood diary. Prose. Daniel Fuchs. 14:22-6*Ag6'38. 4501
Hollywood goes to the literary market. Prose. Arthur Caesar. 4:60 Mr3'28. 4502
Hollywood in the home. Prose. Donald Ogden Stewart. 4:27-8 Mr17'28. 4503
Hollywood punch. Prose. Richard Connell. 5:25-6 F8'30. 4504
The Hollywood Zeus. PR (De Mille). R. E. Sherwood. 1:11-12 N28'25. 4505
Hollywood's gain. Prose. Frank Sullivan. 8:15-16*Ap9'32. 4506
The holocaust. Prose. Howard Cushman. 5:26 D21'29. 4507
Holy Hollywood. Prose. Leslie Howard. 3:21 My14'27. 4508
Homage. Verse. Kenneth Fearing. 15:19*D30'39. 4509
Homage to a hero. Prose. Charles

Angoff. 14:37-8*Jy30'38. 4510
Homage to a minor diety. RL. Morris Markey. 10:61-3*N17 '34. 4511
Home again. Prose. John Chapin Mosher. 3:33-5 S3'27. 4512
Home again. Prose. John Chapin Mosher. 5:65-6 Mr16'29. 4513
Home atmosphere. Prose. Sally Benson. 14:17-18*Mr12'38. 4514
Home atmosphere. Verse. Dearing Ward. 4:27 Ag25'28. 4515
Home fires burning. Verse. William Rose Benét. 8:34 D17'32. 4516
Home for the holidays! Prose. Robert Benchley. 9:15-16 Mr 25'33. 4517
Home from school. Verse. Mark Van Doren. 13:25*Mr20'37. 4518
The home front. Prose. Gilbert Seldes. 5:34 O26'29. 4519
Home girl. PR (Smith). Joseph Mitchell. 10:25-9 Mr3'34. 4520
Home is the hunter. Prose. Wolcott Gibbs. 4:22-3 S8'28. 4521
Home, James, home. Verse. Margaret Fishback. 8:34 Ag27'32. 4522
Home life of a Communist. Prose. Frances Park. 10:40-1 Mr31 '34. 4523
Home movies. Prose. Jack Cluett. 3:32 Ag13'27. 4524
Home movies. Prose. Sterling Patterson. 2:47-8 My8'26. 4525
A home on the Avenue. Prose. John Chapin Mosher. 3:30 Ap16 '27. 4526
Home sweet home. Verse. A. C. M. Azoy, Jr. 1:33 O24'25. 4527
Home talent. PR (Tibbett). Robert A. Simon. 8:21-5 Ja21'33. 4528
Home thoughts from abroad. Verse. A. K. Laing. 4:89 S15 '28. 4529
Home thoughts from abroad. Verse. A. K. Laing. 4:113 O13 '28. 4530
Home thoughts from abroad. Verse. A. K. Laing. 5:36 Ap6 '29. 4531
Home thoughts from abroad. Verse. A. K. Laing. 6:100 Ap12'30. 4532
Home thoughts from abroad. Verse. A. K. Laing. 6:71 My31'30. 4533
Home town. Prose. Raymond Holden. 7:15-17*Je20'31. 4534
Home was never like this: or Elmer among the elements. Prose. Elmer Davis. 5:41-3 Ag24'29. 4535
Home coming. Prose. William Maxwell. 13:15-17*Ja1'38. 4536
Homecoming day. RL. John R. Tunis. 7:43-8 N7'31. 4537
Homesick. Verse. Florence S. Small. 6:116 My17'30. 4538
Homeward bound. SM. Alexander Woollcott. 10:35 Mr3'34. 4539
Homework for the statistician. Verse. Margaret Fishback. 3: 109 O15'27. 4540
The homicide squad in action. RL. Jack Alexander. 13:36-43*Ja8 '38. 4541
Homonculus. Verse. Louise Bogan. 6:16 Mr8'30. 4542
Honest confession. Verse. Phyllis McGinley. 10:46*D29'34. 4543
An honest man. WATN. James Thurber. 12:19-20*Je6'36. 4544
The honest sandwich man. WATN. Clarke Sherman. 13:25-9*Mr6 '37. 4545
The honest warrior. Verse. Martha Banning Thomas. 6:25 F7 '31. 4546
A honey, a natural, a smash. Verse. James Reid Parker. 9: 15 D30'33. 4547
"Honey and lemon and gin . . ." Verse. Anon. 3:53 Mr5'27. 4548
Honey boy. Prose. Frances Eisenberg. 15:81-4*D2'39. 4549
Honeycomb for breakfast. Verse. Gerald Raftery. 15:31 F10'40. 4550
Honeymoon, Model 1929. Prose. Elizabeth Crawford. 5:34 O12

'29. 4551
Honk. OFC. Lewis Gannett. 12: 50-2*Je6'36. 4552
Honor to the apple. Prose. Frank Sullivan. 14:18-19*Ap23'38. 4553
Honor to whom honor is due. Verse. Charles N. Lurie. 2:49 Je12'26. 4554
The honorable icebox. Prose. Paul G. Gumbinner. 3:39 S3'27. 4555
Honorary gun moll. Prose. Florence Stone. 8:13-14 Jy9'32. 4556
Honors and awards. Prose. James Reid Parker. 13:59-61*Je12'37. 4557
Honors for New Year's Day. Prose. W. E. Farbstein and Joseph P. Pollard. 8:36-8 D31 '32. 4558
Honors for New Year's day. Prose. W. E. Farbstein and Joseph P. Pollard. 10:17-18*D29 '34. 4559
Honors for New Year's day. Prose. W. E. Farbstein and Joseph P. Pollard. 15:33-4*D30 '39. 4560
Honors for New Year's day. Prose. Joseph P. Pollard. 9: 37-9 D30'33. 4561
Honors for New Year's day. Prose. Joseph P. Pollard. 12: 51-2*Ja2'37. 4562
Honors for New Year's day. Prose. Joseph P. Pollard. 13: 35*Ja1'38. 4563
Honors for New Year's day. Prose. Joseph P. Pollard. 14: 37*D31'38. 4564
Honors for New Year's day. Prose. Joseph P. Pollard and W. E. Farbstein. 11:16-17*D28 '35. 4565
Hook, line, and sinker. PR (Mills). E. J. Kahn, Jr. 14:16-20*Jy9 '38. 4566
The hoosier cyclone. WATN. James Thurber. 14:56-9*S17 '38. 4567
Hope for New York. Prose. Bertram Bloch. 1:22 Mr21'25. 4568
Hope held out to myself. Verse. Frances M. Frost. 5:52 Ja25 '30. 4569
Horatio & tortoise, or the Cinderella. WP. Scudder Middleton. 11:45-9*Je29'35. 4570
Horatio at bridge. Verse. Samuel James. 3:40 Ap30'27. 4571
Horned owl. Verse. Joseph Auslander. 7:17 Ja9'32. 4572
Horoscopes. Verse. Miriam Vedder. 8:36 S17'32. 4573
Horror on the avenue. Prose. Wolcott Gibbs. 5:20-1 Mr23'29. 4574
The horse doctor. RL. Morris Markey. 7:26-34*Ag8'31. 4575
The horse trough. DL. Burke Boyce. 3:34 Ap9'27. 4576
Horses about town. Prose. Margaret Fishback. 3:99-100 D17 '27. 4577
Horsey men. Verse. Anon. 2:36 O 30'26. 4578
Hosanna! RL. Morris Markey. 2: 38-41 O23'26. 4579
Hospital. Verse. Stephen Vincent Benét. 11:18*Je1'35. 4580
Hospital solarium. Verse. Irma Brandeis. 8:28 O1'32. 4581
Hospital song. Verse. Phyllis McGinley. 10:21*Ja5'35. 4582
The hospital was all right. Prose. Joseph Mitchell. 15:59-60*My 27'39. 4583
Hot bottles and cold birds. Prose. Wolcott Gibbs. 9:24 N11'33. 4584
Hot, carnivorous retort to health food menu. Verse. E. B. White. 2:52 Je19'26. 4585
Hot money. RL. Morris Markey. 10:76-83 O13'34. 4586
Hôtel Méditerranée. Prose. Bessie Breur. 13:26*Ag28'37. 4587
Hotel sports. Prose. Anthony Armstrong. 5:14-15 Jy27'29. 4588
Hotspur the swift. Prose. E. B. White. 5:21 Mr16'29. 4589
Houdini's picnic. RL. Joseph

Mitchell. 15:45-55*My6'39. 4590
Hound on the church porch. Verse. Robert P. Tristram Coffin. 14: 24*Ag13'38. 4591
The hounds of Spring. Prose. Elmer Davis. 2:19-20 Mr13'26. 4592
An hour before high noon. Prose. Marc Connelly. 4:23-5 Ap21'28. 4593
Hours Press. Janet Flanner. 6: 36-7 Ap5'30. 4594
The house. Prose. Alice Frankforter. 9:52-3 My13'33. 4595
House blessing. Verse. Arthur Guiterman. 9:22 Ap15'33. 4596
House holder. Verse. Olive Stanton. 12:35*N21'36. 4597
House in Saratoga. Prose. Caroline Slade. 11:31-2*Je29'35. 4598
A house of tone. Prose. John Chapin Mosher. 8:15-17 Je11 '32. 4599
The house organ. Prose. John O'Hara. 5:113-14 Mr23'29. 4600
The house that Jack built. PR (Humphrey). Alexander Woollcott. 12:20-5*D26'36. 4601
The house that love built. Prose. Sally Benson. 14:14-16*My28 '38. 4602
Household note, U. S. S. R. Prose. Robin Kinkead. 7:36-7 Ja30'32. 4603
Household worries. Verse. Clarence Day. 11:18*Mr9'35. 4604
Houseparty. Prose. Walter Bernstein. 14:29*F11'39. 4605
Housewife. Verse. Doris Kirkpatrick. 6:15 Jy12'30. 4606
The housewife saga. Prose. Clinch Calkins. 5:80-1 S7'29. 4607
Housman, A. E. Laurence Housman. 14:64-5*Ap23'38. 4608
Housman, A. E. TT. 9:5 Je17'33. 4609
Housman, A. E. (Parody) E. B. White. 9:29 O14'33. 4610
How a Sunday newspaper is assembled. Prose. Corey Ford. 5:38-40 D14'29. 4611
How brief a thing. Verse. David Morton. 10:27*Ja26'35. 4612
How do you do--that trick with the ring? Prose. Carlton Brown. 11:80-2*O26'35. 4613
How do you Lindbergh? Prose. Oliver Claxton. 3:34-6 Je15'27. 4614
How d'you get what way? Prose. Corey Ford. 1:9-10 Ja9'26. 4615
How hurricanes help. Prose. Clarence Day. 11:34-5*D14'35. 4616
How I am now in Chi. Prose. John O'Hara. 15:19-21*Ap1'39. 4617
How I became a subway excavator. Prose. Frank Sullivan. 1:13-14 Ja23'26. 4618
How I brought society to its senses. Prose. Agnes Rogers Hyde. 2:29-30 N6'26. 4619
How I feel about things. Prose. Charles G. Shaw. 5:24 My18'29. 4620
How I feel about things. Prose. Charles G. Shaw. 5:26-7 Je1'29. 4621
How I feel about things. Prose. Charles G. Shaw. 5:15-17 Jy27 '29. 4622
How I feel about things. Prose. Charles G. Shaw. 5:25-7 S7'29. 4623
How I feel about things. Prose. Charles G. Shaw. 7:31-2 Mr7 '31. 4624
How I founded Pipawah College. Prose. Joseph Alger. 2:68-70 O2'26. 4625
How I got my judgeship for $7. 93. Prose. Alva Johnston. 6:22-4 S 20'30. 4626
How I got my rabbits to lay. Prose. Donald Ogden Stewart. 4:27-8 Ap7'28. 4627
How I happened to buy a phonograph. Prose. M. R. Werner. 10: 110-11 Ap14'34. 4628
How I left the Navy. Prose. Sylvia Townsend Warner. 15:53-4*Ag5 '39. 4629

How I look at things in general. Prose. Charles G. Shaw. 7: 26-7 Ap25'31. 4630

How it feels to be an actor. Prose. Donald Ogden Stewart. 4:23-4 My5'28. 4631

How it feels to kill a man. Prose. James Thurber. 4:27-8 Mr10'28. 4632

How it might have appeared. Verse. Morrie Ryskind. 9:20 Ja27'34. 4633

How like her generation. Verse. Martha Banning Thomas. 6:28 Jy19'30. 4634

How Minnie went wrong. Prose. Harold Norman Denny. 2:48-9 N13'26. 4635

How much a word? Prose. Robert M. Coates. 4:101-103 N17 '28. 4636

How now, Sirrah? oh, anyhow. Verse. Ogden Nash. 11:24*O5 '35. 4637

How one little robin did her duty. Prose. Frank Sullivan. 6:27-8 O11'30. 4638

How paper is made from rags. MM. Corey Ford. 1:1 S5'25. 4639

How Pauline's heart was broken. Prose. Spud Johnson. 2:29-30 N13'26. 4640

How Sheamus Coomara met the banshee. Prose. Robert Benchley. 8:13-14 Ag6'32. 4641

How success came to Bertie Gray. Verse. Stuart Hyde Hawkins. 1:15 Ja16'26. 4642

How the automobile got into Bermuda. Prose. E. B. White. 14: 22-3*Ap9'38. 4643

How the pretzel got bent. Prose. Frank Sullivan. 9:16-18 Ag5 '33. 4644

How the social centre was fixed. Prose. Frank Sullivan. 6:17-19 Mr15'30. 4645

How to achieve success as a writer. Prose. Ruth Suckow. 12:18-19*Ap11'36. 4646

How to acquire animal crackers. Prose. James Thurber. 3:29-30 D24'27. 4647

How to adjust yourself to your work. LYMA. James Thurber. 12:17-19*Ja9'37. 4648

How to appeal to Germany. Prose. Barbara Heggie. 15:69-70*My13 '39. 4649

How to attract the attention of a Schrafft's hostess. Prose. Clifton Fadiman. 13:13-16*S4'37. 4650

How to be elegant. Prose. E. B. White. 3:25 Ag20'27. 4651

How to be obscene. Prose. Upton Sinclair. 3:25-6 Jy2'27. 4652

How to be presented at court. Prose. Donald Ogden Stewart. 4:25-7 My19'28. 4653

How to be professional. Prose. Eve Casanova. 3:59 F11'28. 4654

The "How to" books. Prose. Robert M. Coates and H. H. G. 13:20*F27'37. 4655

How to buy a cat in Manhattan. Prose. Thomas S. Bosworth. 2:56-7 S11'26. 4656

How to cross Columbus Circle. Prose. Carroll Carroll. 1:28 Ap18'25. 4657

How to deal with grommet trouble. Prose. Frank Sullivan. 4:19-20 Jy14'28. 4658

How to drive the new Ford. Prose. E. B. White. 3:17-18 Ja21'28. 4659

How to find a big simple truth in the public library. Prose. L. C. Meyers. 5:69-70 Je22'29. 4660

How to get a customs pass. Prose. A. L. L. 1:21 My16'25. 4661

How to get Reed Smoot. Prose. Stanley Walker. 10:17-18 Jy7'34. 4662

How to increase your bridge scores. Prose. Fairfax Downey. 1:30-1 N21'25. 4663

How to listen to a play. Prose. James Thurber. 11:21-2*O19 '35. 4664

How to make a cat trap. Prose. E. B. White. 6:26 S13'30. 4665

How to make a fortune. Prose.

A. L. L. 1:29 Mr28'25. 4666
How to open a speakeasy. Prose. Thomas L. Stix. 7:64-6 D5'31. 4667
How to pass time at the art gallery. Prose. José Schorr. 2:15 Ag14'26. 4668
How to pass time--at the beach. Prose. José Schorr. 5:46-7 Ag 17'29. 4669
How to pass time at the circus. Prose. José Schorr. 6:52-3 Ap 19'30. 4670
How to pass time at the dance. Prose. José Schorr. 4:30 F16 '29. 4671
How to pass time at the football game. Prose. José Schorr. 2: 36 O23'26. 4672
How to pass time at the race track. Prose. José Schorr. 6: 65-6 Jy12'30. 4673
How to pass time between the acts. Prose. José Schorr. 5:66 Mr9 '29. 4674
How to pass time crossing Broadway at theatre time. Prose. José Schorr. 5:32 Mr2'29. 4675
How to pass time in a subway station. Prose. José Schorr. 4:56 Ja19'29. 4676
How to pass time in bed. Prose. José Schorr. 3:117 Ap9'27. 4677
How to pass the time in New York's waiting places. Prose. José Schorr. 1:34 S12'25. 4678
How to pass time in the bread line. Prose. José Schorr. 6:85-6 D6'30. 4679
How to pass time--in the hotel lobby. Prose. José Schorr. 1: 35 O10'25. 4680
How to pass time in the subway, sitting. Prose. José Schorr. 1: 27 N28'25. 4681
How to pass time in the subway, standing. Prose. José Schorr. 1:8 S19'25. 4682
How to pass time [in] Times Square. Prose. José Schorr. 1:33 N14'25. 4683
How to pass time on the bus top. Prose. José Schorr. 2:24 My15'26. 4684
How to pass time--on the ferry. Prose. José Schorr. 5:39 Jy27 '29. 4685
How to pass time reading the newspaper. Prose. José Schorr. 2:51 D11'26. 4686
How to pass time touring in the country. Prose. José Schorr. 5:45 Ag31'29. 4687
How to pass time while your boss is on his vacation. Prose. José Schorr. 6:48-9 Ag23'30. 4688
How to pass time with a voting machine. Prose. José Schorr. 5:61 N2'29. 4689
How to play telegrams. Prose. Reed Johnston. 6:52-3 Ag2'30. 4690
How to relax while broadcasting. Prose. James Thurber. 10:26-7 My5'34. 4691
How to restore prosperity. Prose. Elmer Davis. 6:15-16 F7'31. 4692
How to see a bad play. Prose. James Thurber. 11:19-20*S14 '35. 4693
How to solve the snow problem. Prose. Corey Ford. 2:13-14 Mr27'26. 4694
How to sustain life on a petit déjeuner. Prose. Fairfax Downey. 3:54 Ag20'27. 4695
How to tell a fine old wine. Prose. James Thurber. 10:17-18 F24'34. 4696
How to tell a major poet from a minor poet. Prose. E. B. White. 6:23-4 N8'30. 4697
How to trace a fish. Prose. James Thurber. 10:15-16 Jy21 '34. 4698
How to use a paper towel. Prose. A. L. L. 1:28 Ap4'25. 4699
How to win profits and influence literature. PR (Simon & Schuster). Geoffrey T. Hellman. 15: 22-8*S30'39; 15:24-30*O7'39; 15:25-9*O14'39. 4700
How to win the Poughkeepsie re-

gatta. Prose. Corey Ford. 6: 34-6 Je21'30. 4701
How to write a long autobiography. Prose. James Thurber. 13:21-2*My15'37. 4702
How wars start. Prose. E. B. White. 3:51 Jy9'27. 4703
How we get that way. Verse. Lee Wilson Dodd. 5:28 Ja25'30. 4704
How we introduced the budget system into our home. Prose. Donald Ogden Stewart. 4:23-4 Je2'28. 4705
How we made both ends meet in the middle. Prose. Donald Ogden Stewart. 4:18-19 Ap28 '28. 4706
How we solved the servant problem. Prose. Donald Ogden Stewart. 4:21-2 Je16'28. 4707
Howard, Sidney. TT. 1:4-5 My30 '25. 4708
Howdy, King; howdy, Queen. Prose. E. B. White. 3:28 Je4 '27. 4709
How's things? Prose. Oliver Claxton. 3:36-8 O29'27. 4710
Huck's warts and notes from "DOS." OUWA. John McNulty. 13:38-42*D25'37. 4711
Hudson Terminal. DL. Burke Boyce. 3:89 Mr12'27. 4712
The Hudson's yonder shore. Prose. John D. McMaster. 5:65 Je29 '29. 4713
The Huey Long boy. Prose. Frances Crane. 11:81*My11'35. 4714
Hughes, Rupert. TT. 1:4-5 S26'25. 4715
Hughie at the inn or, advice from a tapster. Verse. Elinor Wylie. 4:25 N10'28. 4716
The human firecracker. PR (Craig). Geoffrey T. Hellman. 15:23-8* Je17'39. 4717
The human side. PR (Greenspan). St. Clair McKelway. 10:24-7 Ap28'34. 4718
The human touch. Prose. Nunnally Johnson. 3:70-1 Ap30'27. 4719
The humanist. Verse. David McCord. 6:23 Je28 '30. 4720
Humanitarian. Verse. Richard Peckham. 5:24 D28'29. 4721
Humor, American. TT. 15:11*Je 3'39. 4722
Hun-gan. Prose. Ruth McKenney. 14:15-17*Je25'38. 4723
Hunger. Prose. E. B. White. 7:21 Ap4'31. 4724
The hunt. Prose. Fairfax Downey. 1:27 Mr28'25. 4725
The hunt. Verse. Frances M. Frost. 7:27 O31'31. 4726
Hunt-the-cook. Prose. Robert Benchley. 7:13-14*Je20'31. 4727
The hunted. DOL. Lois Long. 7: 21-3 Mr14'31. 4728
Hunter of the snark. PR (Andrews). Helena Huntington Smith. 5:22-5 Je29'29. 4729
Hunter's moon. Verse. Frances Park. 3:30 O22'27. 4730
The huntress. Prose. Wolcott Gibbs. 11:13-14*Ag3'35. 4731
Hurdy-gurdy. Verse. Mildred Weston. 6:45 Jy12'30. 4732
Hurrah for Mrs. Porsena. Prose. Wolcott Gibbs. 5:27 N23'29. 4733
Hurrah for the fun. Verse. Henrietta Fort Holland. 10:83*D1 '34. 4734
Hurricane. RL. John T. Winterich. 14:34-44*D17'38. 4735
Hurst, Fannie. Anon. 1:7 Mr28 '25. 4736
Hurst, Fannie. TT. 2:8-9 Je19 '26. 4737
Hurst, Fannie. TT. 6:8-9 Ag2'30. 4738
Husbands, an appreciation. Prose. Florence Helm. 1:7-8 My23 '25. 4739
Husbands are really annoying. Prose. G. Schwabe. 3:40-3 S24 '27. 4740
The husband's day. Prose. Will H. Greenfield. 1:23 Ag1'25. 4741
Huxley, Aldous. Anthony Gibbs. 5:67 F1'30. 4742

Huxley, Aldous. TT. 2:9-10 My 29'26. 4743
Huxley, Aldous. TT. 2:9-10 Jy17 '26. 4744
Huxley, Aldous. (Parody) Wolcott Gibbs. 12:25-6*Ag15'36. 4745
"Hyar! Tha big flea circus!" Prose. Corey Ford. 2:15 My8 '26. 4746
Hydrotherapy. Prose. Louise Bogan. 7:18-19*Je27'31. 4747
Hylan vs. Craig. Prose. Harpie. 1:23 Je20'25. 4748
Hylidae. Verse. Robert Hillyer. 13:27*My29'37. 4749
H·Y·M·A·N K·A·P·L·A·N, Samaritan. Prose. Leo Rosten. 14:22-4*O29'38. 4750
Hymn for June third. Verse. Ellen McLoughlin. 7:25*My30 '31. 4751
Hymn to memory. Verse. Arthur Guiterman. 9:54 Je17'33. 4752
Hymn to prejudice. Verse. Parke Cummings. 3:55 Mr12'27. 4753
Hymn to the citadel of static. Verse. R. E. Sherwood. 8:13-14 D31'32. 4754
Hymn to the dark. Verse. E. B. White. 11:23*N23'35. 4755
Hymn to the sun and myself. Verse. Ogden Nash. 6:20 Ag16 '30. 4756
Hymns of hate. Prose. Theodore Pratt. 3:59 Jy9'27. 4757
Hyper or hypo? PR (Libman). S. N. Behrman. 15:23-9*Ap8'39. 4758
Hypocrite. Verse. Frances M. Frost. 5:19 Ag10'29. 4759

I

The I. A. G. D. P. W. Prose. Frank Sullivan. 7:17-19 Ap25'31. 4760
I also knew the town. Prose. Herman J. Mankiewicz. 4:91 O6'28. 4761
I am a fugitive from a nation-wide network. OW. Ring Lardner. 9:55-7 Mr18'33. 4762
I am a little world made cunningly. Prose. Emanuel Eisenberg. 10:23-5 Ap21'34. 4763
I am afraid. Verse. Dorothy Dow. 4:69 Mr3'28. 4764
I am the corporal of my soul. Verse. Morris Bishop. 14:25* N12'38. 4765
I am waiting. Prose. Christopher Isherwood. 15:18-22*O21'39. 4766
I and Roosevelt. Prose. Frank Sullivan. 15:22-4*N11'39. 4767
I beg your pardon. Prose. Oliver Claxton. 3:40 Ap30'27. 4768
I blame it all on Mamma. Prose. Joseph Mitchell. 15:19-22*Ja13 '40. 4769
I burn my bridge behind me. Prose. James Thurber. 4:31-2 D1'28. 4770
I confess. Prose. Frances Warfield. 7:22-3 Mr28'31. 4771
I consider the source. SM. Alexander Woollcott. 10:43 Mr31'34. 4772
I could have had a yacht. Prose. John O'Hara. 11:19*Ap6'35. 4773
I could make a futchin. Prose. John Held, Jr. 14:31*Jy2'38. 4774
I could say bella bella. Prose. William Saroyan. 14:20*My14 '38. 4775
I couldn't dope it out. Prose. Joseph Mitchell. 14:78-80*D10'38. 4776
I fear the Greeks. Prose. Henrietta Fort Holland. 7:48-9 O3'31. 4777
I fear the Greeks giving information. Prose. Doris J. Wilson. 9:46-8 S9'33. 4778
I go on a diet, and--. Prose. Charles G. Shaw. 1:19 Mr14 '25. 4779
I hate to mention it. Verse. Fillmore Hyde. 2:23 Ap10'26. 4780
I have used it for years. Verse. Ogden Nash. 9:23 Je24'33. 4781
I hear America singing. Verse. Katharine Dayton. 1:20 My16

I think. Prose. José Schorr. 5:61 N9'29. 4826
I thought about this girl. Prose. Jerome Weidman. 13:54-6*Ja 8'38. 4827
"I thought she was marvelous." Prose. Alan Campbell. 8:42-4 D10'32. 4828
I told you so. Prose. Frank Sullivan. 15:31-2*Ap29'39. 4829
I used to think. Prose. José Schorr. 5:120-1 N23'29. 4830
I want to be insured by Calvin Coolidge. Verse. E. B. White. 5:36 Ap20'29. 4831
I was a wall-flower at a party of morons. Prose. Nunnally Johnson. 3:25-6 Mr19'27. 4832
I was thinking. Verse. Louis Driscoll. 1:29 N28'25. 4833
I went to school with her. Prose. Thyra Samter Winslow. 9:15-16 Ag19'33. 4834
I went to Sullivant. Prose. James Thurber. 11:13-14*Je22'35. 4835
Icarus in the White Mountains. Verse. Dilys Bennett Laing. 15:21*Ja6'40. 4836
Ice cream. Prose. John O'Hara. 11:39-41*Jy20'35. 4837
Ice-cream pants and petticoats. Prose. Mary Doyle. 14:56-8*Ap30'38. 4838
Ice pick, I love you. Prose. Frank Sullivan. 5:18-20 Ap20'29. 4839
Ici, Garçon! Verse. Lois Whitcomb. 1:19 Je13'25. 4840
Iconoclast. Verse. Phyllis McGinley. 12:26*My9'36. 4841
The iconoclast. Prose. T. H. Wenning. 6:70-2 D13'30. 4842
The iconoclast of the courts. PR (Tilden). John K. Winkler. 2:27-9 S18'26. 4843
I'd forgive you if you were in earnest. OSB. C. Knapp. 5:22 F23'29. 4844
"I'd give my shirt for Al." PR (Kenny). Malcolm Ross. 4:19-22 Je23'28. 4845
I'd like to see. Verse. Anon. 2:30 My29'26. 4846
I'd like to see. Verse. Anon. 2:61 O2'26. 4847
I'd like to see. Verse. Anon. 2:63 O9'26. 4848
I'd rather be ragged and dirty. OSB. C. Knapp. 6:26 O11'30. 4849
I'd rather be trite than president. Prose. Corey Ford. 6:26 N22 '30. 4850
The ideal man. Prose. John O'Hara. 15:21-2*Ap29'39. 4851
The ides of February. Prose. Ruth McKenney. 15:19-21 F10'40. 4852
Idle hour man. PR (Bradley). David B. Campbell. 10:21-6*Ja19 '35. 4853
Idyll. Verse. Theodore Roethke. 15:51*Ag26'39. 4854
An idyll of the Greenwood. Prose. Stanley Jones. 5:86-8 N9'29. 4855
If authors trained. Prose. William Weer. 2:54-5 O9'26. 4856
If Grant had been drinking at Appomattox. Prose. James Thurber. 6:24 D6'30. 4857
If humorists wrote our historic incidents. Prose. Nat N. Dorfman. 1:31 O31'25. 4858
If I was brought up a Holy Roller. Prose. John O'Hara. 9:72-3 S16 '33. 4859
If I were king--. Verse. Anon. 1:45 F13'26. 4860
If I were king. Verse. Anon. 2:36 F20'26. 4861
If I were king. Verse. Anon. 2:16 Ap3'26. 4862
If I were king. Verse. Parke Cummings. 2:31 Mr27'26. 4863
If I were king. Verse. Parke Cummings. 2:20 Ap24'26. 4864
If I were king. Verse. Parke Cummings. 2:61 My8'26. 4865
If I were king. Verse. Parke Cummings. 2:63 My22'26. 4866
If I were king. Verse. Parke Cummings. 2:60 Je5'26. 4867
If I were king. Verse. Parke Cummings. 2:73 O23'26. 4868
If I were king. Verse. Parke

Cummings. 2:45 N13'26. 4869
If I were king. Verse. Parke Cummings. 2:56 D18'26. 4870
If we were king. Verse. Parke Cummings. 2:35 Ja1'27. 4871
If I were king. Verse. Parke Cummings. 2:78 Ja29'27. 4872
If I were king. Verse. Parke Cummings. 3:75 Mr12'27. 4873
If I were king. Verse. Parke Cummings. 3:63 Mr26'27. 4874
If I were king. Verse. Elmer Davis. 2:64 N13'26. 4875
If I were king. Verse. F. G. S. 2:64 S25'26. 4876
If I were king. Verse. Spud Johnson. 2:96 D11'26. 4877
If I were king. Verse. L. B. G. 2:14 Ap10'26. 4878
If I were king. Verse. L. W. McL. 2:61 My29'26. 4879
If I were king. Verse. A. K. Laing. 2:53 S18'26. 4880
If I were king. Verse. Katharine S. Angell White. 2:36 My1'26. 4881
If I were king. Verse. Philip G. Wylie. 2:42 D4'26. 4882
If I were king. Verse. Philip G. Wylie. 2:33 D11'26. 4883
If I were queen. Verse. Anon. 2:44 Jy10'26. 4884
If I were queen. Verse. Anon. 2:86 O2'26. 4885
If I were queen. Verse. A. K. Laing. 2:43 Ja29'27. 4886
If I were queen. Verse. Katharine S. Angell White. 2:58 S18'26. 4887
If I were queen. Verse. Katharine S. Angell White. 2:86 O9'26. 4888
If I were queen. Verse. Philip G. Wylie. 2:70 O2'26. 4889
If I were you. Verse. Arthur Guiterman. 14:44*Ja7'39. 4890
If it be not fair--. Verse. Dorothy Parker. 5:14 Ag24'29. 4891
If Summer comes. Prose. Sara Haardt. 9:47-8 Ag19'33. 4892
If these delights. Prose. Sylvia Townsend Warner. 14:57-8*My 28'38. 4893
If these old walls could talk! Prose. Robert Benchley. 5:30-4 My11'29. 4894
If this be treason. Prose. Frank Sullivan. 13:20-1*O16'37. 4895
If wishes were. Verse. Anon. 2:54 Je5'26. 4896
If you have a bachelor complex. Prose. Theodore Pratt. 3:87-8 O8'27. 4897
Il penseroso. Verse. Eleanor W. Koehler. 5:98 My18'29. 4898
Il penserothstein, or: the election. Prose. Frank Sullivan. 5:27-8 O26'29. 4899
"Il reviendra z'à pâques." SM. Alexander Woollcott. 6:40-3 My 17'30. 4900
I'll get one tomorrow. Verse. Ogden Nash. 12:32*D19'36. 4901
I'll know I'm famous. Verse. Harold Wengler. 3:61 Mr12'27. 4902
I'll take mine straight. Verse. Phyllis McGinley. 10:28 My5'34. 4903
I'll take the upper. Prose. Jack Cluett. 5:55-6 O12'29. 4904
Illuminated manuscripts. Prose. Corey Ford. 1:14 S5'25. 4905
Illusion exploders. Verse. W. E. Farbstein. 7:16*Jy18'31. 4906
Illusion of seclusion. Verse. George A. Peck. 1:23 Jy4'25. 4907
The illustrious George. PR (Luks). J. Hansuld. 1:13-14 My9'25. 4908
I'm going to start in writing letters. OSB. C. Knapp. 3:28 D31 '27. 4909
I'm not superstitious. Prose. G. B. Stern. 11:21*S14'35. 4910
I'm not weeping because he is ruined. OSB. C. Knapp. 5:21 Ja 11'30. 4911
I'm proud to admit that I'm blushing. OSB. C. Knapp. 6:20 Ap26 '30. 4912
I'm ready to drop dead. Prose. Kay Boyle. 11:23*Jy6'35. 4913
I'm sorry I'm not like the hero. OSB. C. Knapp. 5:30 O5

'29. 4914
I'm telling you. Verse. Samuel Hoffenstein. 8:21 Jy23'32. 4915
"I'm telling you." Prose. Arthur Kober. 6:102-103 O25'30. 4916
I'm terribly sorry for you, but I can't help laughing. Verse. Ogden Nash. 12:19*Ap11'36. 4917
"Im westen, nichts neues." SM. Alexander Woollcott. 5:32 Jy27 '29. 4918
Image. Verse. Jean Batchelor. 5:40 Ag24'29. 4919
Impasse. Verse. Clarence Day. 11:22*Ap6'35. 4920
Impasse. Verse. Dearing Ward. 5:76 S7'29. 4921
An impecunious lady. Verse. Martha Banning Thomas. 6:20 Mr 22'30. 4922
Imperative address. Verse. Rolfe Humphries. 12:16*Je13'36. 4923
Imperative mood. Verse. Franklin P. Adams. 14:27*Mr12'38. 4924
Imperial Airways. Verse. E. B. White. 4:25 Ag25'28. 4925
The imperturbable spirit. Prose. James Thurber. 5:25-6 D14'29. 4926
Impiety. Verse. David Morton. 12:60*S26'36. 4927
Implored benediction for a new apartment. Verse. Frances M. Frost. 7:77 N28'31. 4928
The importance of being happy. Prose. Winifred Willis. 15:64* Mr18'39. 4929
The importance of cocktails. Prose. Cornelia Otis Skinner. 14:14*Je4'38. 4930
Important, if true. Verse. Arthur Guiterman. 7:17 F28'31. 4931
Important, if true. Verse. Arthur Guiterman. 7:26 Mr7'31. 4932
Important, if true. Verse. Arthur Guiterman. 7:27 Mr21'31. 4933
Impregnable. Verse. Peggy Bacon. 14:23*Je11'38. 4934
Impressions of one who also served. Prose. T. A. Langan, Jr. 2:36-7 My8'26. 4935
Improving the Zodiac. Prose. Corey Ford. 7:16-18 F21'31. 4936
In a bear-market year. Verse. Miriam Vedder. 7:36 Ja2'32. 4937
In a cool tower. Verse. Elspeth O'Halloran. 5:36 Mr23'29. 4938
(No entry) 4939
In a dime-a-ride. Prose. Henry Anton Steig. 12:19-22*N7'36. 4940
In a dull-gold frame. Prose. Richard Lockridge. 11:26-7*Mr 16'35. 4941
In a flop-house. Prose. Stephen Graham. 3:20 Jy30'27. 4942
In a garden. Prose. Oliver Claxton. 2:14 Ag21'26. 4943
In a good cause. Prose. Alice Frankforter. 7:42-3 Ja16'32. 4944
In a later Spring. Verse. Miriam Vedder. 7:52 Ap18'31. 4945
In a lonely garden. Verse. Martha Banning Thomas. 10:59 O20 '34. 4946
In a loud voice with the tongues of angels. Prose. Gilbert Seldes. 5:24-5 S14'29. 4947
In a manner of writing. Verse. Rollin Kirby. 3:67 Mr5'27. 4948
In a receptive mood. Verse. Anon. 3:28 S10'27. 4949
In a Sixth Avenue fruit-shop. Verse. Grace Hazard Conkling. 4:47 D1'28. 4950
In America's image. PR (Lewis). Waldo Frank. 1:10-11 Jy18'25. 4951
In an English tub. Prose. Fairfax Downey. 2:26 Jy31'26. 4952
In back of . . . Prose. Frances Crane. 4:53-5 Je16'28. 4953
In behalf of an absentee. SM. Alexander Woollcott. 8:36-7*Ap9 '32. 4954
In Burgundy. HHT. Donald Moffat. 9:30-3 Jy15'33. 4955

In case of emergency. Prose. Frank Sullivan. 13:17-18*O23 '37. 4956
In case of fire. Prose. Richard Lockridge. 14:57*F19'38. 4957
In Central Park. Verse. Dorothy Dow. 4:98 My5'28. 4958
In conference. Prose. Elizabeth Crawford. 5:84-5 Mr30'29. 4959
In defence of Hollywood. OUWA. S.N. Behrman. 9:38-43 Ja20 '34. 4960
In deference to royalty. Prose. Frances Crane. 15:60-1*Je10 '39. 4961
In far Africa. Verse. Elizabeth Coatsworth. 7:22 Ap11'31. 4962
In Fleet Street. Prose. Frances Crane. 10:44-6*D15'34. 4963
In Gallipolis the bells are tolling. Verse. E.B. White. 14:27*Mr5 '38. 4964
In honor of their daughter. Prose. John Chapin Mosher. 15:27-8* D2'39. 4965
In hospital. Verse. Baird Leonard. 12:39*F13'37. 4966
In hospital. Verse. Baird Leonard. 12:76*My9'36. 4967
In land of an out-door sport--not very athletic either. Verse. Philip G. Wylie. 2:31 D4'26. 4968
In memoriam. Verse. Babette Deutsch. 6:26 Mr29'30. 4969
In memoriam. Verse. Margaret Fishback. 4:29 My26'28. 4970
In memoriam. Verse. Margaret Fishback. 7:14*Ag15'31. 4971
In memoriam. Verse. James Stephens. 5:19 Ap13'29. 4972
In memoriam. Prose. M.R. Werner. 11:40-2*Ag31'35. 4973
In memoriam: Ernst Toller. Verse. W.H. Auden. 15:80*Je 17'39. 4974
In nature's garden. Verse. Morris Bishop. 10:33 My5'34. 4975
In passing. Prose. G. Schwabe. 2:52 My1'26. 4976
In praise of predecessors. Verse. Margaret Widdemer. 1:23 D5 '25. 4977
In re: Christmas. Prose. Agnes Tait. 10:51-2*D22'34. 4978
In re culture. Verse. Anon. 5:78-9 Ap20'29. 4979
In re Goldilocks, et al. Prose. George Cecil Cowing. 4:17-18 Ja19'29. 4980
In re impedimenta. Verse. Harold Willard Gleason. 5:116 My25'29. 4981
In re Miss Mary Wigman. Prose. Frank Sullivan. 6:15-16 Ja24'31. 4982
In re: the sweet restorer. SM. Alexander Woollcott. 8:31 O8'32. 4983
In re women's hotels. Prose. Kay Austin. 11:73-4*N2'35. 4984
In rehearsal. RL. Morris Markey. 2:36-40 S11'26. 4985
In rehearsal. Prose. James Reid Parker. 14:25-6*My28'38. 4986
In scorn of self-protection. Verse. Clinch Calkins. 3:26 D31'27. 4987
In search of Mr. Mencken. Prose. Decla Dunning. 10:113-17 O13 '34. 4988
In that state of life. SM. Alexander Woollcott. 9:32-3 My27'33. 4989
In the beginning. Prose. John Cheever. 13:61-4*N6'37. 4990
In the footsteps of Gutenburg. Prose. H.L. Mencken. 15:30-4*O14'39. 4991
In the harbor. RL. Morris Markey. 4:32-8 Mr24'28. 4992
In the high seats. Prose. Robert S. Winsmore. 2:49-51 N6'26. 4993
In the home of a newspaper headwriter. Prose. Arthur H. Folwell. 2:35 Ja1'27. 4994
In the Italian manner. Prose. Hugo Spie. 9:32-4 Ja20'34. 4995
In the manner of the moth. Verse. Martha Banning Thomas. 3:20 S24'27. 4996
In the menagerie. Prose. Waldo Frank. 1:8 Je6'25. 4997
In the morning sun. Prose. John

O'Hara. 10:15-17 Jy14'34. 4998
In the news. Prose. Morris Markey. 1:12-13 S5'25. 4999
In the news. Prose. Morris Markey. 1:17-18 S12'25. 5000
In the news. Prose. Morris Markey. 1:13 S26'25. 5001
In the news. Prose. Morris Markey. 1:13-14 O3'25. 5002
In the news. Prose. Morris Markey. 1:13-14 O10'25. 5003
In the news. Prose. Morris Markey. 1:13-14 O17'25. 5004
In the original. Prose. Alice Frankforter. 9:51-2 Mr4'33. 5005
In the park. Verse. Charles Henry Ford. 4:100 My26'28. 5006
In the subway. Verse. A. van Steenbergh. 1:27 O24'25. 5007
In this year of rotogravure. Verse. Parke Cummings. 7:66*My30 '31. 5008
In time of civil war. Verse. Harold Lewis Cook. 14:25*My7'38. 5009
In town. Verse. James Kevin McGuinness. 1:20 Ag15'25. 5010
In transit. Verse. Irma Brandeis. 3:33 N5'27. 5011
In tune with the finite. PR (Kahn). Waldo Frank. 2:23-4 F20'26. 5012
In twenty years. Prose. Hannah Lees. 9:51-4 O7'33. 5013
In Washington Square. Verse. A. van Steenbergh. 1:35 S12'25. 5014
In what brief hour. Verse. Helene Mullins. 9:18 Ag26'33. 5015
In Yangtzepoo. Prose. Emily Hahn. 13:21-3*N20'37. 5016
Inadequate notes on a pair of blue eyes. Verse. Martha Banning Thomas. 4:38 Mr17 '28. 5017
Incident at Cannes. Prose. Logan Clendening. 10:54*D8'34. 5018
Incident in the Brown Derby. Prose. Helen Riesenfeld. 10:65-7 S15'34. 5019
Incident of the assessor. Prose. Douglass Welch. 13:98-9*D11 '37. 5020
Incident of the wastebasket. Prose. Douglass Welch. 10:37-8 O20 '34. 5021
Incident on a street corner. Prose. Albert Maltz. 13:22-3*N27'37. 5022
Incident on Madison Avenue. Verse. Phyllis McGinley. 15:51*O28'39. 5023
Incidental music. Verse. Adele Comandini. 7:50*Je6'31. 5024
Including the Scandanavian. Verse. Ogden Nash. 6:21 Ja10'31. 5025
Incompatibility. Verse. Dearing Ward. 4:58 O13'28. 5026
Incomplete automation. Verse. Jean Batchelor. 15:65*Mr25'39. 5027
The incomplete epicure. Verse. Jean Batchelor. 7:73 F28'31. 5028
Inconsiderate Mr. and Mrs. Vance. Prose. Rosemary Carr Benét. 13:36-7*D4'37. 5029
Incredible Mr. Creel. PR (Creel). Harvey O'Higgins. 1:7-8 Jy4'25. 5030
Indecision. Prose. Norman Matson. 10:21-2 Ag25'34. 5031
Independence. Verse. Persis Greely Anderson. 6:75 My3'30. 5032
Independent cop. PR (Valentine). Jack Alexander. 12:21-7*O3'36; 12:24-8*O10'36; 12:28-34*O17 '36. 5033
India house. DL. Burke Boyce. 2:28 N27'26. 5034
Indian country. Verse. Frances M. Frost. 10:25*D8'34. 5035
The Indian sign. Prose. James Thurber. 9:23-5 F18'33. 5036
Indian Summer of a credit man. Prose. John Chapin Mosher. 4:52-6 O13'28. 5037
Indifference. Verse. Arthur Guiterman. 1:27 My9'25. 5038
Indiscreet Spring song. Verse. Jean Batchelor. 10:72 Mr3'34. 5039

Indorsement of illimitability. Verse. Arthur Guiterman. 13: 25*My15'37. 5040
Industrial classicist. PR (Teague). Gilbert Seldes. 10:28-32*D15 '34. 5041
Infallible rule for an interesting life. Verse. Martha Banning Thomas. 7:28 F21'31. 5042
An infant industry? OW. Ring Lardner. 9:57-8 F25'33. 5043
The infant industry. Prose. S. J. Perelman. 13:22*Mr6'37. 5044
Inflation and the poets. Verse. Franklin P. Adams. 9:15 Ag5 '33. 5045
Inflexible logic. Prose. Russell Maloney. 15:19-22 F3'40. 5046
The information booth. Prose. Jack Cluett. 3:32 Jy2'27. 5047
Information gleaned in a dentist's anteroom. Verse. Parke Cummings. 5:52 Mr16'29. 5048
Information straight. Prose. Stanley Jones. 4:72 Mr3'28. 5049
Ingen svups. OFC. Robert Sellmer. 14:59-60*O8'38. 5050
Ingenue. Verse. Oliver Jenkins. 4:46 Ag4'28. 5051
The ingrate. Prose. Leane Zugsmith. 9:49-52 Ja20'34. 5052
Initiate. Verse. Leslie Nelson Jennings. 11:29*Mr23'35. 5053
Inland. Verse. Elspeth O'Halloran. 14:15*S3'38. 5054
Inner fury. Verse. Martha Banning Thomas. 10:36*N24'34. 5055
Innocence astride. Prose. Donald Moffat. 5:31-2 O12'29. 5056
Innocence in a wicked world. Prose. H. L. Mencken. 13:16-18*F20'37. 5057
The innocent man at Sing-Sing. AC. St. Clair McKelway. 15:27-40*N11'39. 5058
The innocents abroad. PR (Hammer). Geoffrey T. Hellman. 9:18-21 D23'33. 5059
Innocents abroad. SM. Alexander Woollcott. 8:32-6 Ja7'33. 5060
The innocents at the theatre. Prose. C. Knapp. 1:22 Mr28 '25. 5061
Inn's comfort. Verse. Clinch Calkins. 3:28 O15'27. 5062
The inquiring reporter. Prose. Ralph Barton. 1:6 Ag29'25. 5063
The inquiring reporter. Prose. Ralph Barton. 1:8 S12'25. 5064
The inquiring reporter. Prose. Ralph Barton. 1:6 S19'25. 5065
The inquiring reporter. Prose. Ralph Barton. 1:6 S26'25. 5066
Inquisitor. PR (Seabury). Richard O. Boyer. 7:20-3*Je27'31. 5067
Insight. Prose. Hannah Lees. 12: 54*Je13'36. 5068
Insignificance. Verse. Martha Banning Thomas. 5:100 N2'29. 5069
Insincerity. Prose. John Collier. 9:13-15 Jy22'33. 5070
The insistent friend. Prose. Francis Steegmuller. 11:22-4*S7'35. 5071
Insolence. Verse. Martha Banning Thomas. 4:77 F2'29. 5072
Inspiration. Prose. Corey Ford. 1:31 Mr28 '25. 5073
Inspiration. Verse. Ruth Lambert Jones. 5:73 Je1'29. 5074
Insubordinate. Verse. Sara Henderson Hay. 10:27*Ja19'35. 5075
The insulted and injured. Prose. Richard Lockridge. 9:19-20 Mr 4'33. 5076
Insurance man. PR (Insurance salesman). St. Clair McKelway. 10: 20-6 Jy7'34. 5077
Insured. Verse. Elspeth O'Halloran. 3:93 Mr5'27. 5078
Intellectual diversions. Verse. David McCord. 5:95 Mr2'29. 5079
Intellectual diversions. Verse. David McCord. 5:24 Mr16'29. 5080
Intellectual diversions. Verse. David McCord. 5:25 Je29'29. 5081
The intellectual pressure. Prose. Gilbert Seldes. 4:22-3 Mr19'27. 5082
Intelligence test. Verse. Martha

Banning Thomas. 3:58 N5'27. 5083
Intercepted conversations. Prose. Kenneth Phillips Britton. 2:57 My22'26. 5084
The interesting cure of introspective Imogen. Verse. Peggy Bacon. 2:34 D4'26. 5085
Interesting discovery. Verse. E. B. White. 3:34 O15'27. 3086
The interesting old fellow. Prose. Anthony Armstrong. 7:57-9 O3 '31. 3087
Interim. Verse. Alfred Hayes. 15: 27 F3'40. 5088
Interim. Verse. Dorothy Leonard. 6:90 Je7'30. 5089
Interlude. Verse. Charles Henri Ford. 3:40 Ag20 '27. 5090
Interlude between dances. Verse. Helene Mullins. 12:42*My2'36. 5091
Intermezzo. Prose. E. L. 2:44 S25 '26. 5092
Intermezzo. Prose. Emily Hahn. 6:76-8 D13'30. 5093
Intermission. WP. Robert Benchly. 6:39-44 Mr8'30. 5094
Intermission--burlesque. Prose. Arthur Kober. 6:18-19 N1'30. 5095
International Mark Twain Society. TT. 12:10-11*Je6'36. 5096
International picnic. Prose. Bettina Sinclair. 11:37-8*Ag3'35. 5097
International plot. Prose. Esther Evarts. 15:68-71 F10'40. 5098
International relations. Verse. Florence Stone. 3:76 O8'27. 5099
The international spy situation. Prose. James Thurber. 10:15-16*Ja19'35. 5100
International Surrealist Exhibition. Conrad Aiken. 12:48-50*Jy25 '36. 5101
The "Interoceanic Magazine" takes after the radio. Prose. Ellis Parker Butler. 6:78-80 S13'30. 5102
Interpretation. Prose. E. B. White. 5:27 Ap13'29. 5103
The interview. Prose. Morris Bishop. 6:108-109 N22'30. 5104
Interview. Prose. George Cecil Cowing. 8:35 Jy2'32. 5105
An interview. Prose. Puysange. 1:7-8 O17'25. 5106
Interview from the zoo. Verse. Anon. 2:17 Je12'26. 5107
Interview with a sparrow. Prose. E. B. White. 3:31 Ap9'27. 5108
Interview with Daisy. Prose. E. B. White. 6:20-1 Ja10'31. 5109
The intimate diary of an opening night. Prose. Leslie Howard. 1:13-14 O31'25. 5110
Intimate glimpses. Prose. Gwynne. 1:37 S12'25. 5111
Intimate photography. Prose. Arthur H. Folwell. 3:40 Mr19'27. 5112
Intimate tour. Verse. A. B. Bernd. 2:39 Mr27'26. 5113
Intimations at Fifty-eighth Street. Verse. E. B. White. 3:23 F11 '28. 5114
Intimations of immortality. Prose. Geoffrey T. Hellman. 14:23*N 12'38. 5115
Into town. Prose. John Chapin Mosher. 3:16 Jy16'27. 5116
The intramural championship. Prose. Berry Fleming. 5:47-9 N30'29. 5117
Introducing Anastasia. Prose. Donald Ogden Stewart. 4:19-20 F25'28. 5118
Introduction to Sally. SM. Alexander Woollcott. 9:40 N18'33. 5119
Invasion. Verse. Anita Grannis. 1:19 Je6'25. 5120
The invasion of the Attilas. Prose. Max Miller. 10:16-18 Jy21'34. 5121
Invention factory. RL. Malcolm Ross. 7:52-9 N28'31. 5122
Inventory. Verse. Margaret Fishback. 5:105 Mr16'29. 5123
Investigation à la française. Prose. Theodore Pratt. 6:27 My3'30. 5124
"An investigation is under way." Prose. Robert Benchley. 6:17-

18 F14'31. 5125
Investment. Verse. Nigel Cauchy. 3:68 My28'27. 5126
Invitation to dinner. WATN. James Thurber. 12:29-33*D5 '36. 5127
Invite. Prose. John O'Hara. 14: 29-30*D10'38. 5128
Invocation. Verse. Ogden Nash. 5:30 Ja11'30. 5129
Invocation. Verse. James Stephens. 5:27 My4'29. 5130
Invocation to Noah. Verse. Miriam Vedder. 6:56 D13'30. 5131
Invocation to various gods. Verse. Lynn Riggs. 2:21 Ja22'27. 5132
The involuntary collector. Verse. Herman Fetzer. 10:29 My19'34. 5133
Inward. Verse. Frances M. Frost. 5:16 Jy13'29. 5134
Inwood. RL. Morris Markey. 9: 112-117 D9'33. 5135
Iolanthe. TT. 2:12-13 My1'26. 5136
Iolanthe. TT. 2:9-10 Jy24'26. 5137
The IPA laws. Prose. Robert M. Coates. 12:62*Mr28'36. 5138
Irasshai. Prose. Holger Lundbergh. 11:98-9*D14'35. 5139
The ire trouble of Chang. Prose. Frank Sullivan. 5:22-3 O5'29. 5140
(No entry) 5141
The iron hand in the velvet whatnot. Prose. Anon. 2:20 Jy31 '26. 5142
Iron-horse men. RL. E. F. K. 12: 34-44*Ja9'37. 5143
The iron man. Verse. E. B. White. 10:22 Mr10'34. 5144
The "iron man of Wall Street." Prose. Frank Sullivan. 2:19-20 S25'26. 5145
Irony to the ironical. Verse. Helene Mullins. 4:73 Mr3'28. 5146
Irrelevant, incompetent, and immaterial. Verse. Ogden Nash. 7:19 O24'31. 5147
Irtnog. Prose. E. B. White. 11:17-18*N30'35. 5148
Irving, Washington. TT. 2:10 Jy3 '26. 5149
Is a train. Verse. E. B. White. 10:26 O27'34. 5150
Is inflation coming? Prose. Frank Sullivan. 13:24-5*My8'37. 5151
Is Shirley insulted? Prose. Arthur Kober. 5:37 D7'29. 5152
Is the allure of glamour cloying? Prose. James Thurber. 9:20 O21'33. 5153
Is the telephone a success? Prose. Corey Ford. 1:15 N21'25. 5154
Is there a Republican Party? Prose. Frank Sullivan. 11:14*D 28'35. 5155
Is there an osteosynchrondroitrician in the house? Prose. S. J. Perelman. 13:69*My15'37. 5156
Is your son an usher? Prose. John Chapin Mosher. 2:23 Ja29 '27. 5157
Isadora. PR (Duncan). Janet Flanner. 2:17-19 Ja1'27. 5158
Isadorian lullaby. Verse. Joseph Moncure March. 1:17 F13'26. 5159
"I'se Ophelia." Prose. Richard Lockridge. 7:20-1 S5'31. 5160
The island. Prose. Alice Frankforter. 7:69-70 My9'31. 5161
The island. RL. Robert Littell. 7:38-46 D12'31. 5162
Island girl. Verse. Grace Hazard Conkling. 5:30 D21'29. 5163
Islander. Verse. Muna Lee. 9:12 Jy8'33. 5164
The isle of God. OFC. Ludwig Bemelmans. 15:46-7*Ag5'39. 5165
Isn't life lovely! Prose. James Thurber. 8:15-16 Je25'32. 5166
The issues at stake. Prose. Jack Cluett. 5:48 N2'29. 5167
Istanbul. FP. H. L. Mencken. 10: 92-3 My19'34. 5168
It all depends on who you are. Verse. Ogden Nash. 10:25 Je16 '34. 5169
It can be done. Prose. Donald Moffat. 5:17-18 Jy6'29. 5170
It can't be done. Prose. Chester T. Crowell. 7:24-5 Ja16'32. 5171

It huffed and it puffed. Prose. Vincent McHugh. 14:39-40* N5'38. 5172
It is easy enough to blame Russia. Prose. John O'Hara. 8:34-6 Ag13'32. 5173
It is rumored Alfonso will visit New York. Verse. Anon. 2:34 Jy24'26. 5174
It might lapse. Prose. Mary Heaton Vorse. 6:44-5 S27'30. 5175
It must be the milk. Verse. Ogden Nash. 12:23*F29'36. 5176
It must have been Spring. Prose. John O'Hara. 10:101-104 Ap21 '34. 5177
It pays to preach. PR (Barton). Richard F. Warner. 6:21-4 N1 '30. 5178
It rolls on. Verse. Morris Bishop. 6:24 N1'30. 5179
It stretches. Prose. Samuel Grafton. 10:65-6 S1'34. 5180
It won't be long now. Prose. Carroll Carroll. 3:28 Je11'27. 5181
Italian in fifteen minutes. Prose. Frederick Packard. 6:55-6 Ja 31'31. 5182
Italian table d'hôte. PR (La Guardia). Henry F. Pringle. 5:26-9 Ag31'29. 5183
Item for a historian. RL. Morris Markey. 10:68-77 Ap7'34. 5184
Item: to the building trade. Verse. A. K. Laing. 3:21 Ag6'27. 5185
Items. Prose. J. F. 5:38 N30'29. 5186
Items for the mayor's committee. Prose. Robert Benchley. 2:13 Jy24'26. 5187
Items from the press in 1776. TWNY. David Boehm. 5:66-70 N16'29. 5188
Items from the press in 1777. TWNY. David Boehm. 5:46-52 N23'29. 5189
Items from the press in 1777. TWNY. David Boehm. 5:50-4 N30'29. 5190
Items from the press in 1778. TWNY. David Boehm. 5:51-3 D14'29. 5191
It'll ruin me to confess it, but. Verse. Harold Wengler. 3:79 Ap30'27. 5192
It's a dirty shame. Prose. Frederick Packard. 15:71-2*My27 '39. 5193
It's a fib. Verse. Elspeth O'Halloran. 3:30 Mr19'27. 5194
It's a move. Prose. Carlton Brown. 12:77-8*Ap4'36. 5195
It's a 'ome. Prose. E. B. White. 4:18-19 Ja5'29. 5196
"It's a scream." Prose. Joseph Fulling Fishman. 2:30-1 O23'26. 5197
It's a wise parent. Prose. Cornelia Otis Skinner. 14:19-20*Mr19'38. 5198
It's about time department. Prose. Editors. 7:26-7 O17'31. 5199
It's all wrong. Prose. Ogden Nash. 7:14*My23'31. 5200
It's always darkest before dawn. Verse. Margaret Fishback. 5:114 O19'29. 5201
It's de-lovely. PR (Wooley). Russell Maloney. 15:25-9 *Ja20'40. 5202
It's fun to be fooled . . . it's more fun to know. Prose. Robert Benchley. 9:16-17 My27'33. 5203
It's fun to know. Prose. George Cecil Cowing. 9:40-2 F10'34. 5204
It's fun to work. DOL. Lois Long. 6:20-3 Ja17'31. 5205
"It's funny how our metropolitan pigeons . . ." Verse. Anon. 1:35 Ja30'26. 5206
It's hot in Egypt. Prose. John Cheever. 15:20-1*Ja6'40. 5207
"It's not too late." Verse. Marjorie Allen Seiffert. 6:30 S6'30. 5208
It's pushcart Spring. Verse. Clinch Calkins. 3:49 Ap23'27. 5209
It's quite an experience. Prose. Sara Haardt. 8:44-6 Je25'32. 5210
It's snug to be smug. Verse. Og-

den Nash. 12:27*My23'36. 5211
It's Spring, Spring in Pittsfield, Mass. Verse. E. B. White. 12: 30*Mr28'36. 5212
It's the heat. Prose. Arthur Kober. 6:38-9 Ag9'30. 5213
It's the humidity. Verse. Ruth Brown. 4:53 Ag4'28. 5214
I've got an anchor on my chest. Prose. R. H. Newman. 14:21-2* N12'38. 5215
"I've never found that being clever . . ." Verse. Arthur Guiterman. 1:18 Ap25'25. 5216
I've still got the stock. Prose. Margaret Fishback. 5:47 N16 '29. 5217
Ivory and apes. RL. Morris Markey. 3:38-44 O8'27. 5218
Izzy and Moe. WATN. James Thurber. 12:18-19*Je6'36. 5219
Izzy cuts in. Prose. Leo Rosten. 13:20-1*O9'37. 5220

J

J. Walter Mendell, M. D. Prose. Arthur Kober. 7:44-6*Je20'31. 5221
Jack ashore. RL. George Weller. 14:33-9*Mr5'38. 5222
Jack pot. Verse. Kenneth Fearing. 15:19*S9'39. 5223
The jacketeer. Verse. Jerome Barry. 5:70 Je22'29. 5224
The Jackson Whites. RL. George Weller. 14:27-36*S17'38. 5225
Jade and gentlemen. Prose. Emily Hahn. 13:16-20*Ja29'38. 5226
J'ai Malraux à la tête. Verse. Clifton Fadiman. 13:56*My29 '37. 5227
Jail. RL. Morris Markey. 2:23-4 My15'26. 5228
Jailbird. Prose. Emily Hahn. 14: 42-4*Je11'38. 5229
(No entry) 5230
(No entry) 5231
Jamaica Inn. (Film) Janet Flanner. 15:53*Je10'39. 5232
James, Henry. James Thurber. 9:11-13 Je17'33. 5233
Jane Peel. Verse. Mildred Weston. 12:63*F22'36. 5234
The janitor's boy. PR (Wagner). Henry F. Pringle. 3:24-6 Mr5 '27. 5235
"Japanese fighting near the Ming tombs." Prose. Elizabeth Link Petrie. 13:71*N6'37. 5236
The Japanese naval situation. Prose. James Thurber. 10:17* Ja12'35. 5237
Jaunt to Coney. Prose. John Chapin Mosher. 10:30-2 Je30'34. 5238
Jaywalker. Verse. Persis Greely Anderson. 8:16 My28'32. 5239
The jazz age blues. Verse. Charles Norman. 2:58 F12'27. 5240
Jazz factory. RL. Morris Markey. 2:42-5 D18'26. 5241
Je suis malade. Prose. Joel Sayre. 12:13-14*Jy4'36. 5242
Jeannine. Prose. Thomas V. Leahy. 11:67-8*N2'35. 5243
Jenkins. Verse. Olive Ward. 3:48 F18'28. 5244
The jenny-cat. Prose. Sylvia Townsend Warner. 12:13-14*Ag29'36. 5245
Jeremiad. Verse. A. K. Laing. 4: 24 D29'28. 5246
Jersey City gendarmerie, je t'aime. Prose. Ring Lardner. 5:24-5 N2'29. 5247
The Jersey lily. TWNY. Russel Crouse. 5:50-4 Ja4'30. 5248
Jerusalem. FP. H. L. Mencken. 10:30-2 Je23'34. 5249
Jerusalem delivered. Verse. Louis Untermeyer. 11:14*Jy6'35. 5250
Jesting at scars. SM. Alexander Woollcott. 10:38 My26'34. 5251
Jeu de paume. RL. Morris Markey. 10:39-40*Ja19'35. 5252
Jew-boy. Prose. Arthur Kober. 7: 52-6 D5'31. 5253
The Jewel box. Prose. Emily Hahn. 13:19-21*Je26'37. 5254
Jig for bassoons. Prose. D. B. Wyndham Lewis. 6:15-16 D27'30. 5255
Jigsaw. Verse. William Rose Benét.

9:53 F25'33. 5256
Jilted. Verse. Mildred Weston. 8:49*F27'32. 5257
Jim. Prose. Emily Hahn. 6:69-71 Ap26'30. 5258
Jim announcing. Prose. H. L. B. 1:20 Ap18'25. 5259
Jimmie Walker. Verse. Fillmore Hyde. 6:20 Mr29'30. 5260
Jimmy comes home. RL. Morris Markey. 11:40-50*N9'35. 5261
Joey on Herta. Prose. John O'Hara. 15:19-22*N25'39. 5262
Joey on the cake line. Prose. John O'Hara. 15:19-20*D23'39. 5263
John. Prose. John O'Hara. 6:28 D27 '30. 5264
John Brown. Verse. Philip G. Wylie. 2:61 N20'26. 5265
John L. Sullivan collects a little bill. TWNY. William Inglis. 14:36-8*Jy9'38. 5266
John Turner Breckenridge. Verse. Lee Wilson Dodd. 6:32 Ja24'31. 5267
Johnson, James Weldon. PR. Robert Wohlforth. 9:22-6 S30 '33. 5268
The jollicum. Prose. Wolcott Gibbs. 11:13*F23'35. 5269
Jolly bear. PR (Smith). Matthew Josephson. 8:22-5*My14'32; 8:21-5*My21'32. 5270
(No entry) 5271
Jolly justice. Prose. Émile C. Schnurmacher. 3:36-40 S10'27. 5272
Jones, Robert Edmond. PR. Gilbert Seldes. 7:25-8 My9'31. 5273
Joseph's colored coat. Verse. Helene Mullins. 5:25 Jy20'29. 5274
A journal. Verse. Garreta Busey. 13:48*O2'37. 5275
Journalism student. Verse. Mary Carolyn Davies. 5:84 S21'29. 5276
Journalistic jingles. Verse. Max Lief. 1:21 Ap4'25. 5277
Journey around my room. Prose. Louise Bogan. 8:16-18 Ja14'33. 5278
Journey toward Olathe. Prose. Richard Lockridge. 12:19-20* Je27'36. 5279
Journeys. Verse. E. B. White. 2:22 Je5'26. 5280
Journey's dead-end. Prose. E. B. White. 9:15-16 F18'33. 5281
Joust. Prose. Jerome Weidman. 15:23-5*Ag26'39. 5282
Joy-riding in the subway. NYC. Elmer Rice. 4:21-3 D29'28. 5283
Joyce, James. Janet Flanner. 11:66-7*F16'35. 5284
Joyce, James. (Parody) James Thurber. 3:69 My7'27. 5285
Joyful wisdom. PR (Brill). Waldo Frank. 1:11-12 O17'25. 5286
Joyous inspection. Verse. Martha Banning Thomas. 8:64 Je4'32. 5287
Juan's song. Verse. Louise Bogan. 6:28 My24'30. 5288
Juarez at one gulp. Prose. Felix Dale. 2:34 Ag7'26. 5289
Jubilate! RL. Morris Markey. 2:21-2 Ap10'26. 5290
Judge flays nic tine orgy. Prose. Spud Johnson. 2:18 Je19'26. 5291
Judgment day. Prose. Louise Field Cooper. 14:28*Jy16'38. 5292
Judicial astrology. Verse. Arthur Guiterman. 9:68 Ja6'34. 5293
Judicial heroes of 1928. Prose. Joseph P. Pollard. 4:109 D1'28. 5294
Judiciary problems. Prose. Joseph P. Pollard. 12:75-6*My9'36. 5295
July. Verse. Anon. 2:15 Jy17'26. 5296
Jumbo. PR (Beery). Alva Johnston. 11:22-7*N9'35. 5297
June. Verse. Richard Armour. 15:65*Je24'39. 5298
Jungle. Verse. Mildred Weston. 6:17 Ag9'30. 5299
Jungle flower. Verse. E. B. White. 9:26 N18'33. 5300

Junior executive. Prose. Frances Warfield. 11:34-8*S7'35. 5301
Junior miss. Prose. Sally Benson. 15:17-20*O28'39. 5302
The jury. RL. Morris Markey. 6:64-9 D6'30. 5303
Jury duty. Prose. Parke Cummings. 6:69-70 My17'30. 5304
Jury duty. Prose. Travis Hoke. 10:41-4 Je23'34. 5305
Jury duty. Prose. Newman Levy. 4:30-1 S15'28. 5306
Just a "bit." Prose. Arthur Kober. 5:32-3 N30'29. 5307
Just a chance. Verse. Franklin P. Adams. 7:16*Je27'31. 5308
Just a day in New York. Verse. William Rose Benét. 2:30 My 8'26. 5309
Just a débutante. PR (Frazier). E. J. Kahn, Jr. 15:23-8*Je10 '39. 5310
Just a little one. Prose. Dorothy Parker. 4:20-1 My12'28. 5311
Just a pal. Prose. Arthur Kober. 4:42-4 Mr31'28. 5312
Just a quiet evening. Prose. Parke Cummings. 5:89-90 F23 '29. 5313
Just about this time. Prose. T. H. Wenning. 3:81-2 N26'27. 5314
Just another soliloquy. Prose. James Barton Zabin. 2:25 Ap 3'26. 5315
Just at midnight. Prose. Frances Warfield. 10:42-6*N17'34. 5316
Just folks. Prose. George Cecil Cowing. 5:38 Ap20'29. 5317
Just for the record. Prose. William McNulty. 12:34-5*Jy11 '36. 5318
Just keep quiet and nobody will notice! Verse. Ogden Nash. 12:20*Ag22'36. 5319
Just looking. Verse. Margaret Fishback. 7:45 S5'31. 5320
Just off the concrete. Verse. Morris Bishop. 9:15 Mr18'33. 5321
Just pals. Prose. Kenneth Fearing. 7:104-105 Ap11'31. 5322
Just suppose. Prose. Richard Lockridge. 7:73-4 My9'31. 5323
Just the image of--. Prose. Rosemary Carr Benét. 3:83-4 My 14'27. 5324
Just the old-time religion. PR (Reisner). Richard O. Boyer. 15:32-8*D16'32. 5325
Just to be free. Prose. John Chapin Mosher. 6:24-6 Mr1'30. 5326
Just walking. Prose. Arthur Kober. 5:24 Ag3'29. 5327
Justice. Prose. Brendan Gill. 15: 58-60*Ag26'39. 5328
Justice. Prose. Theodore Pratt. 7:54-6 S19'31. 5329
Justice labors. RL. Morris Markey. 1:20-1 F13'26. 5330
Justifiable homicide. Prose. Lyon Mearson. 1:10 Ap11'25. 5331

K

K. K. K. Prose. Alice Frankforter. 8:59-60 My28'32. 5332
K. O., middleweight. Prose. Niven Busch, Jr. 6:19-22 Mr1'30; 6:24-6 Mr8'30. 5333
Kahn, Otto. TT. 2:16 S25'26. 5334
Kamp Koolidge nights. Prose. Robert Benchley. 2:25 Je5'26. 5335
K·A·P·L·A·N and Pythias. Prose. Leo Rosten. 13:28-30* Je5'37. 5336
Kaufman, George S. PR. Alexander Woollcott. 5:26-9 My18'29. 5337
Kazooed his bazooka. Prose. Mary Heaton Vorse. 13:17-18*S25'37. 5338
A keen. Verse. Fred G. Steelman. 1:15 Ja2'26. 5339
Keep in a cool dry place. Verse. Margaret Fishback. 3:119 D17 '27. 5340
Keep it clean. Prose. Margaret Fishback. 4:98-9 S15'28. 5341
Keeping fit. Prose. Arthur H. Folwell. 4:79 O27'28. 5342
Keeping fit. Prose. Alice Frankforter. 10:48-50 N10'34. 5343
Keeping quiet. Prose. Frances Crane. 4:30-1 N17'28. 5344
Keeping the crime wave stationery.

Prose. Joseph Fulling Fishman. 2:85-6 O2'26. 5345

Keeping up with Palm Beach. Verse. Leonard Hatch. 1:27 Mr21'25. 5346

Kelly, George. TT. 2:11 My15'26. 5347

Kemp, Harry. PR. Murdock Pemberton. 1:9-10 Ag8'25. 5348

Ken. (Magazine) TT. 14:9-10*Ap 16'38. 5349

Kerb lyric. Verse. Robert Hyde. 5:74 S7'29. 5350

Kern, Jerome. PR. Franklin P. Adams. 5:21-3 F8'30. 5351

A kettle of fish. WP. Robert Benchley. 12:35-8*D19'36. 5352

Kewpie doll. PR (O'Neill). Alexander King. 10:22-6*N24'34. 5353

The key of life. Prose. E. B. White. 7:21-3 O10'31. 5354

The kid from Jersey. Prose. Henry Anton. 12:62-4*Je13'36. 5355

Kid golf. Prose. Henry Anton. 12: 56-7*Ap18'36. 5356

Kiddie's hour at the surrogate's. Prose. James Thurber. 8:20 N19'32. 5357

The kids. RL. E. J. Kahn, Jr. 14:34-40*Ja21'39. 5358

Kilowatt. Verse. John Held, Jr. 6:53 Ap19'30. 5359

Kin defends bard's knuckles. Prose. H. W. Eliot, Jr. 9:51 Mr25'33. 5360

A kind man. PR (Phelps). Waldo Frank. 1:11-12 O24'25. 5361

The kind old blonde. Prose. Joseph Mitchell. 14:26*Je4'38. 5362

Kindergarten. Verse. Margaret Fishback. 5:54 Je1'29. 5363

The king. PR (Macy). Alva Johnston. 7:25-8 S12'31. 5364

King Leer. Verse. Ogden Nash. 9:14 S2'33. 5365

King of Harlem. PR (Robeson). Mildred Gilman. 4:26-9 S29 '28. 5366

The king of spades. Prose. Parke Cummings. 9:32-6 O28 '33. 5367

King of the Bronx. PR (Davies). Robert M. Coates. 5:33-5 D7 '29. 5368

The king of the Philistines. Prose. Kay Boyle. 13:22-5*Mr13'37. 5369

The kingdom and the glory. Verse. Phyllis McGinley. 13:22*My8 '37. 5370

The king's buttons. Prose. Theodore Pratt. 7:99-100 D12'31. 5371

Kings of the talkies. PR (Warner). Alva Johnston. 4:21-4 D22'28. 5372

The Kinnehórrah. Prose. Jerome Weidman. 13:66-8*Ap24'37. 5373

Kinship. Verse. Ruth Lambert Jones. 11:29*My18'35. 5374

Kipling, Rudyard. Conrad Aiken. 11:39*F8'36. 5375

Kipling, Rudyard. John Cowmos. 4:54 O6'28. 5376

Kipling, Rudyard. Daniel Longwell. 2:63 O9'26. 5377

Kit sees the king. Prose. Frances Crane. 4:47-8 Jy7'28. 5378

Kitchen and tableware. NESD. John J. Holzinger. 10:71 Je30 '34. 5379

Kitchen bouquet. Prose. S. J. Perelman. 15:17-18*N4'39. 5380

Kitten in a graveyard. Verse. Selma Robinson. 8:14 Je25'32. 5381

Knew the town. Prose. Charles G. Shaw. 4:86 Je2'28. 5382

Knickerbocker ancestor. Verse. Isabel McLennan McMeekin. 5:92 Ap27'29. 5383

Knickerbocker village. RL. Alva Johnston. 8:26-32 Ag6'32; 8:24-8 Ag13'32. 5384

Knight with the rueful countenance. PR (Stryker). Alexander Woollcott. 14:23-6*Ja21'39. 5385

Knock, knock, knock. Prose. Marshall D. Beuick. 1:10 Jy25'25. 5386

Lady, Lady! Verse. Marjorie Allen Seiffert. 7:40 Ap11'31. 5427
A lady lists additional historical information on London Tower. Verse. Miriam Vedder. 8:36 Ag20'32. 5428
Lady looking over calendar days. Verse. Leslie G. Shaw. 4:87 Mr3'28. 5429
The lady movie critic interviews Beatrice Lillie. Prose. Albert Carroll. 3:34-5 Ja14'28. 5430
Lady of an antique world. PR (Lydig). Margaret K. Leech. 3:28-30 N19'27. 5431
Lady of fashion 1926 model. Prose. Charles G. Shaw. 2:26-7 S25'26. 5432
A lady of fashion sixty years ago. TWNY. Herbert Asbury. 9:34-7 Jy8'33. 5433
Lady of Fourteenth Street. PR (Le Gallienne). Djuna Barnes. 5:29-32 Ap6'29. 5434
Lady of the cats. PR (Ross). Wolcott Gibbs and E. F. Kinkead. 14:21-6*My14'38. 5435
A lady of the chorus watches Dorothy Stone. Prose. E. B. White. 2:29 O30'26. 5436
Lady of the stars. PR (Adams). Alva Johnston. 4:29-32 O27'28. 5437
The Lady of Windsor. Prose. Paul Hyde Bonner. 10:68-72 Ap21'34. 5438
"The lady or the tiger." SM. Alexander Woollcott. 5:41 Je15 '29. 5439
Lady pacifist. Verse. Witter Bynner. 6:63 My17'30. 5440
Lady photographer. Prose. Louise Field Cooper. 11:39-40*D28'35. 5441
The "Lady Regalar" at Saratoga speaks up. Prose. C. Knapp. 3:44-5 Ag20'27. 5442
The Lady Regalar, far from home. Prose. C. Knapp. 5:53-4 Mr2 '29. 5443
The Lady Regalar speaks her mind. Prose. C. Knapp. 4:15-16 Ag4'28. 5444
The Lady Regalar tells a funny one. Prose. C. Knapp. 4:17-18 Ag18'28. 5445
Lady vs. hubcap. Prose. Richard Lockridge. 7:16-17 Jy11'31. 5446
A lady wearing pearls attends a concert. Verse. Ruth Brown. 5:46 F23'29. 5447
Lady with a cause. PR (Achelis). Geoffrey T. Hellman. 15:21-5* D30'39. 5448
Lady with a garden. Verse. Elspeth O'Halloran. 14:24*O29'38. 5449
Lady with a pearl. SM. Alexander Woollcott. 9:29 Jy1'33. 5450
"The lady who lives across the hall . . ." Verse. Anon. 2:25 My29'26. 5451
The lady who was there. Prose. Emily Hahn. 9:41-2 Jy22'33. 5452
A lady who writes. PR (Miller). Harvey O'Higgins. 3:25-7 F19 '27. 5453
Lady with a pretzel. Prose. John Chapin Mosher. 4:32 N10'28. 5454
Lady without an alibi. Prose. Alan Campbell. 10:83-5 Mr17'34. 5455
"A lady (you may well know who) . . ." Verse. Anon. 2:79 Ja22 '27. 5456
A lady's death-bed prayer. Verse. J. L. Sweeney. 5:48 D28'29. 5457
Lady's room. Prose. John Chapin Mosher. 15:14-15*Jy29'39. 5458
L'affaire Jonesy. Prose. Frances Park. 10:68*Ja12'35. 5459
Laird of Woodley. PR (Stimson). Henry F. Pringle. 6:30-3 O4'30. 5460
L'allegro in Flushing. Verse. Will Scarlet. 15:52*Ap1'39. 5461
Lament. Verse. Berton Braley. 8:68 S17'32. 5462
Lament. Verse. Elizabeth Coatsworth. 6:32 N8'30. 5463
Lament. Verse. D'Annunzio Cohen.

The last of the Heath Hens. Prose. Robert Benchley. 9:40-3 My6'33. 5508
Last of the prosecutors. PR (Medalie). Alva Johnston. 9:18-22 Ag19'33. 5509
Last resort. HHT. Donald Moffat. 9:34-8 My27'33. 5510
The last resort. Prose. Gilbert Seldes. 3:29-30 Mr26'27. 5511
The last ride together. Verse. Anon. 4:79 Mr31'28. 5512
Last run of shad. ML. John Strong Newberry. 9:31 Mr25'33. 5513
The last tea. Prose. Dorothy Parker. 2:23-4 S11'26. 5514
The last tear. Prose. Louise Bogan. 9:21-2 Jy22'33. 5515
Last will. Verse. Elspeth O'Halloran. 6:26 F14'31. 5516
Last word. Verse. Elspeth O'Halloran. 3:34 D17'27. 5517
Late afternoon of a patrolman. Prose. Gilbert Seldes. 7: 19-21 Ap11'31. 5518
Late August. Verse. Phyllis McGinley. 10:19 Ag25'34. 5519
Late Autumn. Verse. Raymond Holden. 6:26 N8'30. 5520
Late Autumn note. Verse. Anon. 2:31 N27'26. 5521
Late bird. Verse. Harrison Dowd. 9:55 N18'33. 5522
Late holiday note. Prose. Katherine Sproehnle. 3:54 Ap23'27. 5523
The late Miss Edmunds. SM. Alexander Woollcott. 5:38 Ag 31'29. 5524
Late wakening. Verse. Raymond Holden. 6:23 Ja17'31. 5525
Laud for evensong. Verse. Rolfe Humphries. 11:26*Ag24'35. 5526
The laud will provide. Prose. James Kevin McGuinness. 1:22 F28'25. 5527
Laugh and the world laughs with you. Prose. Oliver Claxton. 2: 18-19 Ag7'26. 5528
Laugh, nurse, laugh. Prose. Patricia Collinge. 13:81*O30 '37. 5529
Laughs from London. Prose. James Thurber. 14:29*Ag27'38. 5530
[Laughter.] Prose. Morris Bishop. 8:19 My28'32. 5531
Launch not your fragile boat. Verse. Marjorie Allen Seiffert. 10:28 Ag25'34. 5532
Laundry art: study in wash. Prose. Corey Ford. 1:22 My16'25. 5533
The laundry list. Prose. Jess Nancy Grice. 3:104-105 Ap16 '27. 5534
Laura. Prose. Emily Hahn. 9:50-4 D9'33. 5535
Laureates of America. OUWA. Morris Bishop. 14:32-8*Ag27'38. 5536
Laurine's pearl. MNL. Thyra Samter Winslow. 10:21-2 My26 '34. 5537
Law. Verse. Newman Levy. 9:72 Je24'33. 5538
The law and the prophets. PR (Townsend). Russell Maloney. 15:21-6*S16'39. 5539
Law-breaking at its source. Prose. Robert Benchley. 5:17-18 Je8'29. 5540
The law of the jungle. Verse. E. B. White. 10:31 Ap14'34. 5541
Lawn dance. Verse. E. B. White. 2:18 S4'26. 5542
Lawndale's fast set. Prose. Marquis James. 1:7-8 D5'25. 5543
Lawndale's winter sports. Prose. Marquis James. 1:15-16 F6'26. 5544
Lawrence, D. H. Clifton Fadiman. 12:82-3*O17'36. 5545
Lawrence, D. H. James Thurber. 12:18-19*Je27'36. 5546
Lawrence, D. H. (Parody) Frank Sullivan. 8:16-18 O29'32. 5547
Lawrence, T. E. TT. 3:18-19 Ap16 '27. 5548
Lawyer. ME. Alfred Kreymborg. 3:22 Ap30'27. 5549
Le dernier cri. Verse. Henrietta Fort Holland. 9:72 Ja13'34. 5550

Le jaseroque. Verse. Frank L. Warrin. 6:52 Ja10'31. 5551
Le point. Prose. Frances Warfield. 8:21-2 O15'32. 5552
Le scandale international. Prose. Ruth McKenney. 13:21-3*Ja15 '38. 5553
Le sport. Prose. Philip G. Wylie. 2:38 Jy31'26. 5554
Le touring. RL. Morris Markey. 7:33-7*Jy25'31. 5555
Le tourisme and the "guide michelin." OUWA. Donald Moffat. 11:44-50*Mr30'35. 5556
Lead all, journalistic candor. Verse. Anon. 1:17 Mr14'25. 5557
Lead from the dummy. Verse. Elspeth O'Halloran. 4:28 Ja5 '29. 5558
The leader. Verse. Persis Greely Anderson. 5:61 N16'29. 5559
Leading ladies. Verse. Ogden Nash. 7:19 O17'31. 5560
The leading man. Prose. Arthur Kober. 5:63-5 S14'29. 5561
Leaf. Verse. Frances M. Frost. 6:94 F22'30. 5562
Leaf, Munro. TT. 13:10*Ja1'38. 5563
Leander bares tale of Hellespont swim in exclusive interview. Prose. Creighton Peet. 1:24 S 5'25. 5564
Leap before you look! Prose. Winifred Willis. 7:24-5 F6'32. 5565
Learned lyricist. PR (Harbach). A. J. Liebling. 13:22-7*F27'37. 5566
Learning to read. Verse. Mark Van Doren. 13:21*Mr6'37. 5567
Leave taking. Verse. Oliver Jenkins. 15:39*S30'39. 5568
Leavetaking. Prose. Robert M. Coates. 10:30-1 O20'34. 5569
Lectures are so broadening. Prose. Elise Jerard. 2:30 N20 '26. 5570
Leda. Verse. Frances M. Frost. 5:83 S21'29. 5571
The left bank. RL. Edmund Pearson. 13:41-5*Ag28'37; 13:32-9*S4'37. 5572
Legal advice. Prose. Richard Lockridge. 11:23-4*N16'35. 5573
Legends of Lizzie. Prose. Edmund Pearson. 9:20-3 Ap22'33. 5574
Legitimate nonchalance. PR (Fields). Alva Johnston. 10:23-6 F2'35; 10:25-8 F9'35; 11:22-6 F16'35. 5575
Lemkau, Pogran, & Blaufox. Prose. Irwin Shaw. 15:17-19*D 30'39. 5576
Lemme tell you why. Prose. Arthur Kober. 8:26-8 Je25'32. 5577
Lengthy symphony. Verse. Persis Greely Anderson. 8:15 O8'32. 5578
Lenludd in the Bronx. Prose. Arthur Kober. 15:21-2*Jy8'39. 5579
Lenten service. Verse. Anon. 4:42 Mr10'28. 5580
Lenten thought. Verse. Elspeth O'Halloran. 3:79 Mr12'27. 5581
L'entente cordiale. Prose. Mary Mulheron. 8:48-50 N5'32. 5582
L'entente cordiale. (Film) Janet Flanner. 15:59 My13'39. 5583
L'envoi. Verse. Paul D. Gesner. 12:56*Mr7'36. 5584
L'envoy at the Waldorf. RL. Charles Merz. 5:30-8 My18'29. 5585
Les amis d'automat. Prose. Frank Sullivan. 13:18-20*Ap24'37. 5586
Less information, please. Verse. Phyllis McGinley. 15:20*Jy29 '39. 5587
Less than the dust. Prose. Sherman Carter. 2:19-20 Ja8'27. 5588
The lesson. Prose. Parke Cummings. 10:57-8 Ag11'34. 5589
The lesson. Prose. Stanley Jones. 3:37-8 Ag6'27. 5590
Lessons learned from the eclipse. Prose. Frank Sullivan. 8:15-16

S10'32. 5591
Let earth go whirling. Verse. Raymond Holden. 7:16 F13'32. 5592
Let freedom ring. PR (Leibowitz). Alva Johnston. 8:21-4 Je4'32; 8:18-23 Je11'32. 5593
Let it be so. Verse. Fillmore Hyde. 7:67 Mr14'31. 5594
Let it go. Prose. Richard O. Boyer. 13:42-3*Jy24'37. 5595
Let it rain. Prose. Oliver Claxton. 4:76 Mr10'28. 5596
Let me help with Christmas. Prose. Marion Sturges-Jones. 14:44*D24'38. 5597
Let there be no more talk. Verse. Mark Van Doren. 9:18 Mr18'33. 5598
Let us go toward home. Verse. Charles Norman. 4:28 F16'29. 5599
Let us hang on to it. Prose. John O'Hara. 7:56-7 N7'31. 5600
"Let us jump." Prose. Ellis Parker Butler. 6:20-1 My3'30. 5601
Let weather enough alone. Prose. Frank Sullivan. 10:19-20 Mr3 '34. 5602
Letdown. Prose. Louise Bogan. 10:22-4 O20'34. 5603
L'été à New York. Prose. Donald Ogden Stewart. 4:17-18 Ag25 '28. 5604
Let's fall in love. Prose. Hildegarde Dolson. 12:24*Ag29'36. 5605
Let's go. Prose. Robert Benchley. 9:15 My13'33. 5606
Let's picnic. Prose. Oliver Claxton. 2:17 Jy31'26. 5607
Let's play Post Office. Prose. Gilbert Seldes. 5:13 Jy27'29. 5608
Let's see your license. Prose. Frederick Packard. 15:56-7* Ag5'39. 5609
"Let's take a ferry-ride and cool off." Prose. Frederick Packard. 5:62-3 Jy6'29. 5610
The letter. Verse. Mark Van Doren. 12:26*Mr7'36. 5611
Letter from a French village. Janet Flanner. 13:35*S18'37. 5612
Letter from a reformed lady. Verse. Mary Brown. 4:38 Je9 '28. 5613
Letter from a Winter resort. Verse. Phyllis McGinley. 12: 18*Ja16'37. 5614
Letter from Barbados. Verse. Arthur Guiterman. 12:55*Mr14'36. 5615
Letter from Bayreuth. Janet Flanner. 14:42-3*S3'38. 5616
Letter from Berlin. Janet Flanner. 12:40-1*Ag1'36; 12:35-7*Ag 15'36; 12:52-5*Ag22'36. 5617
Letter from Berlin. R. T. L. 15: 37-40*D9'39. 5618
Letter from Bordeaux. Janet Flanner. 15:40-1*S30'39. 5619
Letter from Brussels. Janet Flanner. 11:43-4*Je8'35; 12:26*Jy18 '36. 5620
Letter from Budapest. Janet Flanner. 14:45-7*S24'38. 5621
Letter from England. Mollie Panter-Downes. 15:37-9*S30'39. 5622
Letter from France. Janet Flanner. 15:37-8*O7'39; 15:43-6*O 14'39. 5623
Letter from France. A. J. Liebling. 15:62-3*D9'39; 15:40-1*Ja6'40. 5624
(No entry) 5625
Letter from Ghent. Janet Flanner. 14:42*My7'38. 5626
Letter from Glasgow. Janet Flanner. 14:29-32*Je25'38. 5627
Letter from London (London letter). Janet Flanner. 10:69-72 Je16'34; 10:52-3 Je30'34; 12:50*O31'36; 12:67-8*N7'36; 12:110-13*N14 '36; 12:71-2*D12'36; 12:61-3*D 19'36; 12:48-9*Ja2'37; 13:57*F 20'37; 13:41-2*F27'37; 13:76-8* Mr20'37; 13:54-6*My8'37; 13: 37-40*My15'37; 13:62-4*My22 '37; 13:54-5*Je5'37; 13:36*Je 12'37; 13:47-8*Jy3'37; 13:41-3* Jy10'37; 13:48-9*Jy17'37; 13: 48-9*Jy24'37; 13:32-5*N6'37; 13: 45*N27'37; 13:58-64*D4'37; 13:

108*D11'37; 13:79-81*D18'37; 13:36-7*D25'37; 14:42*My28 '38; 14:51-2*Je4'38; 14:31*Je 11'38; 14:32*Jy2'38; 14:45*Jy 9'38; 14:97-9*D3'38; 14:81-3* D10'38; 14:79-80*D17'38; 15: 61-3*My20'39; 15:75-7*My27 '39; 15:69*Je3'39; 15:51-3*Je 10'39; 15:64-6*Je17'39; 15:42- 4*Je24'39. 5628

Letter from London. Mollie Panter-Downes. 15:28-9*S9 '39; 15:30-2*S16'39; 15:34-5* S23'39; 15:34-6*O7'39; 15:40- 2*O14'39; 15:34-6*O21'39; 15: 32-4*N4'39; 15:40-2*N18'39; 15:41-2*D2'39; 15:42-5*D16 '39; 15:28-9*D30'39; 15:46-7* Ja13'40; 15:33-4*Ja20'40; 15: 44-6 F3'40. 5629

Letter from Megève. Janet Flanner. 14:55*Mr5'38. 5629A

A letter from Monaco. Prose. Florence Carroll Atwater. 12: 58-9*Ap18'36. 5629B

Letter from Munich. Janet Flanner. 13:58-9*S11'37. 5629C

Letter from Paris (Paris letter). Janet Flanner. 1:26 O10'25; 1: 28-30 O24'25; 1:26 N7'25; 1:32 N21'25; 1:34-5 D5'25; 1:26 D19 '25; 1:35 Ja2'26; 1:42-3 Ja23 '26; 1:38-9 F6'26; 2:46-8 F20 '26; 2:35-6 Mr6'26; 2:49-50 Mr 20'26; 2:51-2 Ap3'26; 2:60-1 Ap17'26; 2:60-1 My1'26; 2:57- 8 My15'26; 2:42-3 My29'26; 2: 48-9 Je12'26; 2:77-9 S11'26; 2:65-7 S25'26; 2:79-82 O9'26; 2:69-71 O23'26; 2:86-8 N6'26; 2:83-7 N20'26; 2:101-104 D4 '26; 2:88-92 D18'26; 2:65-7 Ja 8'27; 2:39-43 Ja22'27; 2:87-90 F5'27; 2:63-7 F12'27; 3:86-9 Mr5'27; 3:92-6 Mr19'27; 3:75- 9 Ap2'27; 3:95-9 Ap16'27; 3: 105-109 Ap30'27; 3:85-9 My 14'27; 3:60-2 My28'27; 3:53- 5 Je11'27; 3:44-8 Je25'27; 3: 60-3 Jy9'27; 3:41-3 Jy23'27; 3:61-4 Ag6'27; 3:65-8 Ag20'27; 3:36-9 S3'27; 3:84-6 S17'27; 3: 78-80 O1'27; 3:88-90 O15'27; 3:81-4 O29'27; 3:111-15 N19'27; 3:118-21 D3'27; 3:117-20 D10'27; 3:35-7 D24'27; 3:74-6 Ja7'28; 3: 41-3 Ja21'28; 3:70-1 F4'28; 3: 62-5 F18'28; 4:57-9 Mr3'28; 4: 73-6 Mr17'28; 4:85-8 Mr31'28; 4:50-6 Ap14'28; 4:64-7 Ap28'28; 4:98-101 My12'28; 4:60-3 My26 '28; 4:69-71 Je9'28; 4:74-6 Je 23'28; 4:49-51 Jy7'28; 4:34-7 Jy21'28; 4:41-3 Ag4'28; 4:39-41 Ag18'28; 4:62-4 S1'28; 4:83-6 S 15'28; 4:79-81 S29'28; 4:92-5 O 13'28; 4:69-72 O27'28; 4:117-20 N10'28; 4:104-106 N24'28; 4:128- 30 D8'28; 4:57-9 D22'28; 4:55-6 Ja5'29; 4:41-3 Ja19'29; 4:60-2 F9'29; 5:85-8 F23'29; 5:72-3 Mr 9'29; 5:82-4 Mr23'29; 5:56-64 Ap20'29; 5:76-9 My4'29; 5:104- 106 My18'29; 5:55-7 Je1'29; 5: 86 Je15'29; 5:69-70 Je29'29; 5: 43-5 Jy13'29; 5:45 Jy27'29; 5: 48-50 Ag10'29; 5:55-6 Ag24'29; 5:77-9 S7'29; 5:96-8 S21'29; 5: 73-5 O5'29; 5:122-6 O19'29; 5: 79-81 N9'29; 5:54-6 D14'29; 5: 37-8 D28'29; 5:46-9 Ja11'30; 5: 53-5 Ja25'30; 5:44-7 F8'30; 6: 57-8 F22'30; 6:34-6 Mr8 '30; 6: 36-8 Mr22'30; 6:34-7 Ap5'30; 6:86-8 Ap19'30; 6:48-50 My3'30; 6:110-11 My17'30; 6:77-9 My31 '30; 6:60-2 Je14'30; 6:57-9 Je 28'30; 6:46-8 Jy12'30; 6:55-7 Jy26'30; 6:57-9 Ag9'30; 6:52-3 Ag23'30; 6:35-8 S6'30; 6:82-4 S 20'30; 6:84-6 O4'30; 6:79-81 O 18'30; 6:67-8 N1'30; 6:50-2 N15 '30; 6:84-6 N29'30; 6:114-15 D 13'30; 6:37-9 D27'30; 6:63-4 Ja 17'31; 6:41-2 Ja31'31; 6:44-6 F 7'31; 7:30-2 F21'31; 7:79-81 Mr 7'31; 7:65-7 Mr21'31; 7:53-4 Ap 4'31; 7:63-5 Ap18'31; 7:36-8 My 2'31; 7:74-5 My16'31; 7:43-5*My 30'31; 7:40-2*Je13'31; 7:58-60*Je 27'31; 7:49-50*Jy18'31; 7:44*Jy 25'31; 7:46-7 S5'31; 7:53-8 S26 '31; 7:54-6 O10'31; 7:62-3 O24 '31; 7:49-50 N7'31; 7:36-42 N21 '31; 7:57-9 D5'31; 7:75-6 D19 '31; 7:41-2 Ja2'32; 7:57-9 Ja16

ner. 12:29-31*S5'36; 14:36* S10'38. 5634
A letter from the Bronx. Prose. Arthur Kober. 13:23-4*O30'37. 5635
Letter from the bull ring. Janet Flanner. 13:47-8*Ag7'37. 5636
Letter from the Riviera. Janet Flanner. 14:55*Mr12'38. 5637
Letter from Vienna. Janet Flanner. 14:51-3*S17'38. 5638
Letter from Vienna. Florence Stone. 11:43-5*Jy27'35. 5639
Letter home. Prose. Edward L. Gordy. 6:45-6 Ag2'30. 5640
The letter of regret. Prose. Jack Cluett. 6:110-11 N8'30. 5641
Letter to a friend. Prose. Philip Brougham. 14:46-8*Ap9'38. 5642
A letter to Edgar Wallace. Prose. Dorothea Castelhun. 5:62-4 D 28 '29. 5643
Letter to Mr. Bloom. Verse. Arthur Guiterman. 8:23*F27'32. 5644
Letter to Mr. Guiterman. Verse. Ralph Pulitzer. 7:75 My2'31. 5645
Letter to Mr. Morgan. Verse. Arthur Guiterman. 7:76 Ap4'31. 5646
Letter to Mr. Pulitzer. Verse. Arthur Guiterman. 7:72 Ap18 '31. 5647
Letter to Mr. Smith. Verse. Arthur Guiterman. 7:42 Ja30'32. 5648
[Letter to R. M. Coates.] Prose. Ernest Hemingway. 8:86-7 N5 '32. 5649
Letter to the Park Commissioner. Verse. Arthur Guiterman. 10: 40 My12'34. 5650
Letter to the Sixth Avenue Association. Verse. Phyllis McGinley. 15:23*Jy15'39. 5651
Letters from home. Prose. Maddy Vegtel. 9:45-6 O28'33. 5652
The letters of James Thurber. Prose. James Thurber. 14:17 O8'38. 5653
Letters of no consequence. Prose. Margaret Fishback. 7:36-8*My 23'31. 5654
Leviathan: or, whither today and tomorrow. Prose. Robert M. Coates. 6:15-16 Jy26'30. 5655
Lewis, Joseph. PR. Alva Johnston. 8:22-5 O8'32. 5656
Lewis, Sinclair. PR. Waldo Frank. 1:10-11 Jy18'25. 5657
Lewis, Sinclair. Brendan Gill. 12: 42-4 D26'36. 5658
Lewis, Sinclair. TT. 1:4 S12'25. 5659
Lewis, Sinclair. TT. 1:5 N7'25. 5660
Lewis, Sinclair. TT. 2:20-1 N6'26. 5661
Lewis, Sinclair. TT. 5:20 N23'29. 5662
Lewis, Sinclair. TT. 6:17 N22'30. 5663
Lewis, Sinclair. TT. 6:17 N29'30. 5664
Lewis, Sinclair. TT. 12:13-14*N21 '36. 5665
Lewis, Sinclair. PR. W. E. Woodward. 9:24-7 Ja27'34; 9:24-7 F3 '34. 5666
Liberal in a lounge chair. Prose. E. B. White. 14:19-20*F19'38. 5667
Liberal reward. Prose. M. Brooks Howell. 6:93-4 S20'30. 5668
The liberry. Prose. G. M. Hurley. 6:60-1 Ja24'31. 5669
Liberty. Verse. Raymond Holden. 11:44*Ag10'35. 5670
The library. Verse. G. F. Riegel. 3:72 Je4'27. 5671
Library, Embassy Club. TT. 5:13 My11'29. 5672
A library lion. Prose. M. R. Werner. 9:16-20 Ag12'33. 5673
A library lion speaks. Verse. E. B. White. 2:27 Ja8'27. 5674
Licentious soldiery. Prose. Rebecca West. 15:42-3*Ja13'40. 5675
Lid-lifting in lifts. Prose. Ambrose Glutz. 1:31 Mr21'25. 5676
Lie down, lie down. Verse. Raymond Holden. 11:32*O5'35. 5677

Morris Bishop. 12:28*N14'36. 5718
Limericks long after Lear. Verse. Morris Bishop. 12:24*D5'36. 5719
Limericks long after Lear. Verse. Morris Bishop. 12:24*Ja2'37. 5720
Limericks long after Lear. Verse. Morris Bishop. 12:24*F6'37. 5721
Limericks long after Lear. Verse. Morris Bishop. 13:20*Mr6'37. 5722
Limericks long after Lear. Verse. Morris Bishop. 13:23*Ap17'37. 5723
Limericks long after Lear. Verse. Morris Bishop. 13:31*My15'37. 5724
Limericks long after Lear. Verse. Morris Bishop. 13:25*Je19'37. 5725
Limericks long after Lear. Verse. Morris Bishop. 13:20*Ag7'37. 5726
Limericks long after Lear. Verse. Morris Bishop. 13:23*Ag28'37. 5727
Limericks long after Lear. Verse. Morris Bishop. 13:22*S25'37. 5728
Limericks long after Lear. Verse. Morris Bishop. 13:23*N20'37. 5729
Limericks long after Lear. Verse. Morris Bishop. 13:25*Ja1'38. 5730
Limericks long after Lear. Verse. Morris Bishop. 13:17*F5'38. 5731
Limericks long after Lear. Verse. Morris Bishop. 14:27*Mr26'38. 5732
Limericks long after Lear. Verse. Morris Bishop. 14:17*Je25'38. 5733
Limericks long after Lear. Verse. Morris Bishop. 14:19*S24'38. 5734
Limericks long after Lear. Verse. Morris Bishop. 15:19*Ap22'39. 5735
Limericks long after Lear. Verse. Morris Bishop. 15:26*S30'39. 5736
Limitations of intellectuals. Prose. The professor. 1:19-20 Ap11'25. 5737
Lincoln collection. Verse. Edith Franklin Wyatt. 9:21 F10'34. 5738
Lindbergh, Anne Morrow. TT. 11: 14*N2'35. 5739
Lindsay, Howard. TT. 9:8-9 D30 '33. 5740
Lindsay, Vachel. TT. 2:10-11 My1 '26. 5741
Lindsay, Vachel. TT. 1:5 N14'25. 5742
Lindy and Lou. Prose. Joel Sayre. 7:22-3 Ap4'31. 5743
The line. PR (Grenet). A. J. Liebling. 13:20-5*Jy24'37. 5744
Line. Verse. Philip G. Wylie. 4: 34 Mr3'28. 5745
Line of duty. Prose. Robert Wohlforth. 7:77-8 Mr7'31. 5746
Line-up. RL. Morris Markey. 7: 56-62 Ap4'31. 5747
Lines. Verse. Jerome Barry. 5: 27 Je15'29. 5748
Lines. Verse. Kenneth Phillips Britton. 4:30 F2'29. 5749
Lines. Verse. John Cowmos. 4: 115 D15'28. 5750
Lines. Verse. Margaret Fishback. 4:94 O27'28. 5751
Lines. Verse. Margaret Fishback. 5:48 Ap6'29. 5752
Lines. Verse. Nicholas Samstag. 4:73 Mr31'28. 5753
Lines after a motor trip through the South. Verse. Melville Cane. 14:55*My14'38. 5754
Lines coarsely addressed to a Christmas giver. Verse. Martha Banning Thomas. 12:80*D19 '36. 5755
Lines composed while drifting through Lloyd's register of American yachts. Verse. Arthur Bartlett. 14:23*Je4'38. 5756
Lines for an amaryllis keeper. Verse. E. B. White. 5:26 Ja11

'30. 5757
Lines for April 26. Verse. Margaret Fishback. 7:67 Ap25'31. 5758
Lines found in a Brilliantine bottle. Verse. Baird Leonard. 11:24*Mr23'35. 5759
Lines found in a hymnal. Verse. Baird Leonard. 14:83*D10'38. 5760
Lines found in a tack room. Verse. Baird Leonard. 14:26* My28'38. 5761
Lines found on the back of a ballot. Verse. Anon. 3:98 N12 '27. 5762
Lines from a raccoon coat. Verse. Margaret Fishback. 3:62 D17 '27. 5763
Lines from Burns. Prose. Wolcott Gibbs. 10:22-3 My12'34. 5764
Lines in a cocktail bar. Verse. F. B. Gregg. 13:71*Ap17'37. 5765
Lines in anguish. Verse. E. B. White. 2:113 D11'26. 5766
Lines in neither the manner nor the spirit of Thomas A. Kempis. Verse. Baird Leonard. 3: 13 Jy30'27. 5767
Lines inspired by a perusal of the American Kennel Club stud book. Verse. Arthur Bartlett. 14:21*Ap9'38. 5768
Lines inspired by certain misdirected legislation. Verse. Baird Leonard. 2:25 Ja8'27. 5769
Lines instigated by Autumn. Verse. Margaret Fishback. 4:91 O27 '28. 5770
Lines long after Santayana. Verse. E. B. White. 9:21 F3'34. 5771
Lines of envy written on contemplating Mr. Rockefeller's own Fifty-third Street trees. Verse. Margaret Fishback. 3:65 My14 '27. 5772
Lines of worry on Rockefeller Plaza. Verse. Margaret Fishback. 10:34 My12'34. 5773
Lines on a contemplation of labor. Verse. Franklin P. Adams. 13: 56*S4'37. 5774
Lines on a Park Avenue restaurant menu. Verse. Margaret Fishback. 3:101 O22'27. 5775
Lines on a rumble seat. Verse. Margaret Fishback. 4:55 Jy28 '28. 5776
Lines on a St. Regis Roof menu. Verse. Baird Leonard. 4:29 O6 '28. 5777
Lines on declaring an extra dividend or two. Verse. Margaret Fishback. 9:40 My20'33. 5778
Lines on helping a poor blind man. Verse. Margaret Fishback. 4: 124 D8'28. 5779
Lines on "Lay sermons." Verse. Margaretta Manning. 3:113 D17 '27. 5780
Lines on the back of a nurse's chart. Verse. Baird Leonard. 4:32 O27'28. 5781
Lines on the decorating trade. Verse. Parke Cummings. 2:45 Je5'26. 5782
Lines on those who get their claus in early. Verse. Margaret Fishback. 9:117 D9'33. 5783
Lines on watching a mother at her crooning. Verse. Margaret Fishback. 4:24 O20'28. 5784
Lines precipitated by Spring fever caught on Pier 54. Verse. Margaret Fishback. 4:81 Ap14'28. 5785
Lines scribbled on the back of a circular letter. Verse. Baird Leonard. 3:19 My7'27. 5786
Lines to a bad habit. Verse. Margaret Fishback. 4:61 Mr3'28. 5787
Lines to a flippant poet. Verse. Ethel Arnold Tilden. 5:62 Ag17 '29. 5788
Lines to a jilted lady. Verse. Jacqueline Embry. 5:21 Mr16 '29. 5789
Lines to a modern refrigerator. Verse. William Rose Benét. 11: 71*O26'35. 5790
Lines to a puritan. Verse. Marya

Mitchell. 14:37-40*F11'39. 5830
Little Carnegie playhouse. Verse. Parke Cummings. 4:46 D8'28. 5831
The little doctor. Verse. Mark Van Doren. 13:18*F20'37. 5832
A little episode. Prose. James Thurber. 6:20 My24'30. 5833
The little fox-terrier. SM. Alexander Woollcott. 9:26-8 Jy15 '33. 5834
The little Frenchman. Prose. Sally Benson. 8:61-3 My21'32. 5835
A little gent'man. Prose. John Forbes. 11:73*N16'35. 5836
Little giant. PR (Untermyer). Alva Johnston. 6:29-32 My17 '30; 6:24-7 My24'30. 5837
The little girl with talent. Prose. Lillian Day. 6:38-40 Ja17'31. 5838
The little Heinie. PR (Gehrig). Niven Busch, Jr. 5:22-5 Ag10 '29. 5839
The little hours. Prose. Dorothy Parker. 9:13-14 Ag19'33. 5840
Little Janek Wladislaw. Prose. Henry Anton. 12:75-6*Ap4'36. 5841
Little Joe. Prose. James Thurber. 5:24-5 S7'29. 5842
Little Johnny. WATN. James Thurber. 12:19-22*Jy4'36. 5843
Little journeys. Prose. Oliver Claxton. 3:53-4 Jy16'27. 5844
A little knowledge. Verse. Harold Willard Gleason. 6:18 Mr29'30. 5845
A little knowledge is a dangerous thing. Verse. Frances Park. 6:71 Mr1'30. 5846
The little man. Prose. E. B. White. 2:22-3 N6'26. 5847
Little memento. Prose. John Collier. 14:21-3*S17'38. 5848
Little monarch. PR (Prajadhipok). Andrew A. Freeman. 7:24-6 Ap18'31. 5849
The little monkey. Prose. Carroll Carroll. 3:47 Je4'27. 5850
Little Narcissus. PR (Damita). Henry F. Pringle. 5:30-3 O26 '29. 5851
Little Nemo and the cardboard lion. Prose. Wolcott Gibbs. 11: 75*My25'35. 5852
Little newslets. SM. Alexander Woollcott. 8:24 Ag27'32. 5853
The little old New-Yorker. TWNY. Morris Bishop. 11:72-5*Mr16 '35. 5854
Little person. Prose. T. H. Wenning. 7:21-3 S12'31. 5855
Little pitchers. Verse. Philip G. Wylie. 3:44 O29'27. 5856
Little rascal. Prose. Frances Warfield. 12:18-19*Ap18'36. 5857
Little remembrances. Prose. John O'Hara. 6:108-109 Ap12'30. 5858
Little shops on Madison. Verse. Leslie Nelson Jennings. 4:83 Ja 5'29. 5859
A little silent indifference. Prose. Maxwell Bodenheim. 2:63-4 Ja8 '27. 5860
A little something for the scalp. Prose. Corey Ford. 3:24 Jy9'27. 5861
The little tailor. WATN. James Thurber. 12:22*My23'36. 5862
Little Vangie predicts unique year. Prose. Frank Sullivan. 7:15-16 Ja2'32. 5863
Little woman. Prose. Sally Benson. 13:16-18*Ja8'38. 5864
Little words. Verse. Dorothy Parker. 5:14 Ag24'29. 5865
A little yolk about the yegg. Verse. Anon. 1:15 S26'25. 5866
Littoral. Verse. Raymond Holden. 7:24 S26'31. 5867
Liveright, Horace B. PR. Waldo Frank. 1:9-10 O10'25. 5868
Liz. Verse. Dorothy Belle Flanagan. 5:76 O26'29. 5869
Lo, the poor architect. Prose. Archibald Tect. 2:58-9 My1'26. 5870
Loads of fun on snow and ski. Prose. Corey Ford. 4:20-2 F16 '29. 5871
Loaves and fishes? RL. Joel Sayre. 7:35-46 D5'31. 5872

London letter. James C. Oestreicher. 4:77-9 S8'28. 5904
London letter. V. L. Parsons. 3:62-4 N26'27. 5905
London notes. C. B. T. 1:37-9 D 26'25; 1:28-9 Ja30'26; 2:45-6 F27'26; 2:32-4 Mr27'26; 2:55-6 Ap24'26; 2:45-6 Jy3'26; 2:45-6 Jy17'26; 2:47-8 Jy31'26; 2:48-9 Ag7'26; 2:57-9 S4'26; 2:73-5 S18'26; 2:81-4 O2'26; 2:70-3 O16'26; 2:94-7 N13'26; 2:60-2 N27'26; 2:105-107 D11 '26. 5906
London notes. C. B. W. 2:62-3 My 22'26; 2:48-9 Je19'26. 5907
The London story. Prose. Clifford Orr. 15:73*My20'39. 5908
London to Leningrad. RL. Edmund Wilson. 12:36-48*Ap4'36. 5909
The lone prospector: thirty years after. PR (Ochs). Elmer Davis. 1:11-12 N21'25. 5910
The lone wolf. Prose. Ben Ames Williams. 14:21*S3'38. 5911
The lonelier Eve. Prose. Tess Slesinger. 10:32-4 Ap28'34. 5912
The lonely. Verse. Samuel Hoffenstein. 8:15 Jy9'32. 5913
Lonely heart. Prose. Edward Hutchings, Jr. 10:57-8 S8'34. 5914
Lonely women. Verse. Marjorie Allen Seiffert. 7:63 My9'31. 5915
Lonesome man. Prose. Phil Stong. 15:42-4*Je17'39. 5916
Long after Audubon. Prose. Cornelia Otis Skinner. 14:17-18* O1'38. 5917
The long arm. Prose. Mary Heaton Vorse. 8:16-18 My28 '32. 5918
Long distance. Prose. Wolcott Gibbs. 4:19 Je9'28. 5919
The long-distance chess champion. Prose. Jack Cluett. 5:110-11 O5'29. 5920
Long dresses. Prose. Louise S. Cover. 5:65-6 O19'29. 5921
A long epitaph for the short life of any unofficial prime minister. Verse. Ogden Nash. 11: 21*Ja18'36. 5922
The Long Island Railroad. Prose. Elmer Davis. 3:29 S17'27. 5923
Long, Lois. Carl Rose. 3:30-1 Mr 12'27. 5924
Long, long distance. Prose. Philip G. Wylie. 2:47-8 Ja15'27. 5925
A long, long song. RL. Hyman Goldberg. 14:45-51*D10'38. 5926
Long mile. Prose. Alice Frankforter. 10:53-5 Mr31'34. 5927
The long road to Roxy. PR (Deskey). Gilbert Seldes. 9:22-6 F 25'33. 5928
The long run. Prose. Stanley Jones. 7:81-2 My9'31. 5929
The longest way round is the shortest way home. Verse. Margaret Fishback. 9:63 Ap29 '33. 5930
Look for the silver lining. Verse Ogden Nash. 9:14 Ap1'33. 5931
Look out for the Warelians! Prose. James Thurber. 15:17-18*Ap1'39. 5932
Look us over, posterity. Verse. Morris Bishop. 11:20*Ja4'36. 5933
Look what Mr. Liggett found in the boss's waste basket. Prose. William A. Krauss. 13:32-5*Ap 24'37. 5934
Looking backward. Prose. Norman Matson. 8:23 N19'32. 5935
Loos, Anita. PR. Edward E. Paramore, Jr. 2:25-8 N6'26. 5936
Loos, Anita. TT. 2:10 Ap3'26. 5937
L'opéra. Prose. Theodore Pratt. 10:73-4 O13'34. 5938
Lopsided. Prose. E. B. White. 2: 23 Ja22'27. 5939
Lord Fauntleroy in Hollywood. PR (VanDyke). Alva Johnston. 11: 20-4*S28'35. 5940
Lord of Eden. Verse. Marie de L. Welch. 10:59 Je16'34. 5941
Lords of creation. Verse. Margaret Fishback. 7:50 Ja 2

'32. 5942
The lore she brought me. Prose. Franklin P. Adams. 5:31-3 S 21'29. 5943
Los Angeles. OFC. Theodore Pratt. 13:46*F5'38. 5944
Loss to state and nation. Prose. Stanley Walker. 8:34-40 D10 '32. 5945
The lost crusade. Prose. Oliver Claxton. 3:54-6 D17'27. 5946
The lost Dauphin. SM. Alexander Woollcott. 8:44 O29'32. 5947
Lost--eighteen per cent. Verse. John Ogden Whedon. 6:26 S13 '30. 5948
The lost Farragut message. Prose. Frank Sullivan. 10:19-20*F9'35. 5949
A lost headland. Verse. Sylvia Townsend Warner. 15:25*N25 '39. 5950
The lost heart. Verse. Marjorie Allen Seiffert. 10:21 F24'34. 5951
The lost heir. RL. Morris Markey. 6:42-7 N15'30. 5952
Lost lady. Verse. Grace Hazard Conkling. 5:16 F8'30. 5953
A lost lady for Lucifer. Verse. Jacqueline Embry. 4:22 Je16 '28. 5954
The lost leader. Verse. Phyllis McGinley. 9:24 My6'33. 5955
The lost story. SM. Alexander Woollcott. 5:36 Je29'29. 5956
Lost streets. Verse. Kenneth Allan Robinson. 11:29*Ap6'35. 5957
The lost umbrella. Prose. Frances Crane. 7:42-4 Ag29'31. 5958
Lot 777. Prose. Frances Crane. 14:93-5*D3'38. 5959
Lou and her harp. Prose. Maddy Vegtel. 8:49-52 Ja7'33. 5960
"Loud alarums heard offstage." Prose. Joseph Fulling Fishman. 3:87-9 Ap23'27. 5961
The loud laugh that speaks--. Prose. Hedgehog. 1:14 Jy18'25. 5962
A loud sneer for our feathered friends. Prose. Ruth McKenney. 13:31-4*Ag14'37. 5963
Loud speaking in a speakeasy. Prose. Herbert Reed. 3:26-8 Jy30'27. 5964
Louis dot dope. Prose. Robert Benchley. 2:15 Ap3'26. 5965
Love. Verse. E. B. White. 7:58 F13'32. 5966
Love affair. Verse. Dorothy Dow. 7:74 O24'31. 5967
Love among the Ethiopians. Prose. George Sylvester Viereck. 11:41-3*Ja4'36. 5968
Love among the exiles. Prose. James Pelerin. 2:18-19 My22 '26. 5969
Love among the fishes. Prose. Niven Busch, Jr. 3:22 Mr5'27. 5970
Love-ballad of Wall Street. Verse. Fillmore Hyde. 2:29 S18'26. 5971
Love below Tenth Street. Verse. Anon. 2:23 Ap17'26. 5972
The love child. Prose. Hannah Lees. 11:75-6*D21'35. 5973
Love duet. Prose. R. R. 2:30 D11 '26. 5974
Love hear my prayer. Verse. Elise Jerard. 4:87 Mr10'28. 5975
Love in a garden. Verse. E. B. White. 3:24 Jy2'27. 5976
Love in Brooklyn. Prose. Daniel Fuchs. 15:18-22*S2'39. 5977
Love in season--and out. Verse. Ruth Fitch Bartlett. 3:91 Ap16 '27. 5978
Love in the snow. Prose. Joel Sayre. 7:15-17 Ja9'32. 5979
Love letter. Verse. Dorothy Dow. 4:50 Je16'28. 5980
Love letters. Prose. Sally Benson. 8:20-1 D10'32. 5981
Love-lies-bleeding. Prose. Katherine Mansfield. 15:63-5*O14 '39. 5982
Love me, love my dog. Prose. Cuthbert Wright. 11:24*O19'35. 5983
Love on a quantity basis. Prose. Leonard Hall. 1:14 Je13

'25. 5984
Love song. Verse. Frances M. Frost. 6:29 D6'30. 5985
Love song. Verse. Newman Levy. 3:64 D10'27. 5986
Love under the Republicans or Democrats. Verse. Ogden Nash. 6:28 O18'30. 5987
The loved one at home. Prose. J. J. O'Malley. 15:19*Ja27'40. 5988
The loveliest treat. Prose. Marjorie Marks. 11:71-2*O12'35. 5989
Lovely lady. Prose. Emily Hahn. 5:79-80 My25'29. 5990
The lover. Verse. Fillmore Hyde. 4:32 My19'28. 5991
The lovers. Prose. Wolcott Gibbs. 11:20-1*F16'35. 5992
The lovers. Prose. Arthur Kober. 6:25-6 Mr29 '30. 5993
The lovers. Verse. Katharine D. Morse. 4:42 My5'28. 5994
Lovers as guests. Prose. John Chapin Mosher. 8:20-1 Ag13 '32. 5995
Love's encyclopedia. Prose. R. B. Sibley. 5:42 O19'29. 5996
Love's enigma. Verse. Fillmore Hyde. 4:25 Mr10'28. 5997
Lovesick rhymes. Verse. José Schorr. 2:44 F20'26. 5998
Low bridge. Prose. Clifford Orr. 9:21 Ag12'33. 5999
A low whine. Prose. Frank Sullivan. 13:60*Ja8'38. 6000
Lowell, Amy. (Parody) EE. 1:16 Mr28'25. 6001
Lowenfels, Walter. Janet Flanner. 5:75 O5'29. 6002
Lower level. Prose. E. B. White. 2:20 My22'26. 6003
Loyalty at Pook-Wah-Met. Prose. Alan Campbell. 11:61*Je1'35. 6004
Luce, Henry R. PR. Wolcott Gibbs. 12:20-5*N28'36. 6005
Luck charm. Prose. Paul Jones. 15:75-7*Ap15'39. 6006
The luck of Jad Peters. Prose. James Thurber. 10:23-5*D8 '34. 6007
Lucky Cochet. PR (Cochet). John R. Tunis. 4:28-30 S15'28. 6008
The lucky one. Verse. Fanny Heaslip Lea. 6:22 F22 '30. 6009
The lucky stiff. PR (Schwartz). Arthur Krock. 2:15-17 Jy24'26. 6010
Lucrece. Prose. Emily Hahn. 10: 83-5*N24'34. 6011
Lucy Lake. Verse. Ogden Nash. 9:18 F18'33. 6012
Luhan, Mabel Dodge. TT. 15:14-16 F3'40. 6013
Lullaby. Verse. Clinch Calkins. 3:25 N26'27. 6014
Lullaby. Verse. Elizabeth Coatsworth. 7:16 F21'31. 6015
Lullaby. Verse. E. O. 11:72*Ja11 '36. 6016
Lullaby. Verse. Frances M. Frost. 8:25 S24'32. 6017
Lullaby. Verse. Mildred Weston. 15:47*S16'39. 6018
Lullaby. Verse. Philip G. Wylie. 2:14 Je19'26. 6019
Lullaby for a city baby. Verse. E. B. White. 3:35 N19'27. 6020
Lullaby for a movie child. Verse. Sydney King Russell. 5:69 Ja4 '30. 6021
Lullaby for a padlockout. Verse. C. B. E. 1:28 Ap18'25. 6022
Lullaby in an apartment house. Verse. Howard Cushman. 4:67 O6'28. 6023
Lunar moth. Verse. Robert Hillyer. 14:15*Jy30'38. 6024
The lunch. Verse. Arthur Kober. 5:117-18 My25'29. 6025
Lunch counter. Prose. Morley Callaghan. 7:17-19 My2'31. 6026
Lunch hour. Prose. Margaret Ford. 10:86 Mr24'34. 6027
Lunch hour. Prose. Angelica Gibbs. 14:68-9*O22'38. 6028
Lunch hour. Verse. E. B. White. 3:95 My21'27. 6029
Lunch in the financial district. Prose. M. S. 2:34 My29'26. 6030
Lunch in the temple. Prose. Fran-

ces Crane. 12:51*Je20'36. 6031
Lunch Tuesday. Prose. John O'Hara. 13:18-20*Ap3'37. 6032
Lunch with a ripsaw. Prose. Oliver Borden. 8:17-18 F4'33. 6033
The luncheon. Prose. Frances Crane. 14:50-2*S3'38. 6034
Luncheon at sea. Prose. Marc Connelly. 3:18-19 Jy9'27. 6035
Luxury, Inc. PR (Carnegie). Lois Long and Nancy Hardin. 10:23-7 Mr31'34. 6036
The lying-in hospital. RL. Morris Markey. 5:80-3 O19'29. 6037
Lyric of jewelers' windows. Verse. Gretta Palmer. 3:42 Mr12'27. 6038
Lyric to baseball. Verse. Joseph Moncure March. 2:26 My15'26. 6039
Lyric with ambiguous references. Verse. Rolfe Humphries. 11:28 *Je29'35. 6040
Lyricists strike pay dirt. OW. Ring Lardner. 8:53-5 N19'32. 6041
Lyrics from the Pekinese. Verse. Arthur Guiterman. 1:21 F21'25; 1:18F 28'25; 1:21 Mr7'25; 1:20 Mr14'25; 1:17 Mr21'25; 1:18 Mr 28'25; 1:18 Ap4'25; 1:12 Ap11'25; 1:14 Ap25'25; 1:14 My2'25; 1:10 Je13'25; 1:8 S26'25; 1:23 O 17'25; 1:40 O24'25; 1:30 N21 '25; 1:27 N28'25. 6042

M

The M. E. K. NYC. Corinna Reiman. 5:24-7 Je8'29. 6043
The mabelman. Prose. Frank Sullivan. 5:19-20 My4'29. 6044
The McAlpin. SH. Newman Levy. 4:18 Ag18'28. 6045
Mac Arthur, Charles. TT. 5:21 S14'29. 6046
Mac Arthur, Charles. PR. Alexander Woollcott. 5:23-6 Mr9 '29. 6047
Macbeth. TT. 2:20 N20'26. 6048
Macbeth. (Parody) Wolcott Gibbs. 7:19-20 N7'31. 6049
The Macbeth murder mystery. Prose. James Thurber. 13:16-17*O2'37. 6050
McGuire's kitty. Prose. Edwin Corle. 10:15-18 Ag4'34. 6051
Machine age poet. Verse. Louis Untermeyer. 11:25*Mr9'35. 6052
Mc Intyre, John T. TT. 12:16-17* O10'36. 6053
Mac Leish, Archibald. (Parody) Franklin P. Adams. 13:33*O30 '37. 6054
Mac Leish, Archibald. (Parody) Edmund Wilson. 14:23-4*Ja14 '39. 6055
Mac Phee. Verse. Harold Willard Gleason. 4:89 O13'28. 6056
Macy escalator. Verse. William Phillips. 5:109 O19'29. 6057
The mad hatter of Hollywood. PR (Butterworth). Alva Johnston. 11:20-6*Jy27'35. 6058
Madam. Prose. Frances Crane. 8:40-2 N12'32. 6059
Madam Capet. (Play) Janet Flanner. 14:50*Mr19'38. 6060
Madame. Prose. Frances Warfield. 11:27-9*Ag17'35. 6061
Madame Houdin. Prose. Sylvia Townsend Warner. 15:28-9*O21 '39. 6062
Madame la marquise, toujours exquise. Prose. Sally Benson. 15:23-5*N18'39. 6063
Madame president! RL. Richard O. Boyer. 14:35-41*My7'38. 6064
Madame Secretary. PR (Perkins). Russell Lord. 9:16-19 S2'33; 9:20-3 S9'33. 6065
Madame, she is a problem, n'est-ce pas? Prose. Ruth McKenney. 14:15-17*D31'38. 6066
Made in Germany. Prose. Mildred Gilman. 9:34-8 F10'34. 6067
Made in New York. Prose. R. S. W. 1:34 S12'25. 6068
Made to measure. Prose. Paul Hyde Bonner. 9:40-6 N11'33. 6069

Madeira. FP. H. L. Mencken. 10: 61-2 Jy14'34. 6070
Madeline. Prose. Dorothy Belle Flanagan. 7:61-3 Ap25'31. 6071
Madeleine Smith. SM. Alexander Woollcott. 5:28 F1'30. 6072
Mademoiselle. Prose. Maddy Vegtel. 9:34-7 My13'33. 6073
Mademoiselle Napoléon. Prose. Donald Moffat. 13:20-1*Je5'34. 6074
Madness and music. PR (Bloch). Waldo Frank. 2:25-6 S11'26. 6075
The madness of Mr. Bolivar. Prose. Wolcott Gibbs. 8:19-20* F20'32. 6076
Madonna of the chorus. Prose. Hildegarde Angell. 3:24-5 N26 '27. 6077
Madrid to Morata. RL. Martha Gellhorn. 13:31-9*Jy24'37. 6078
The maenads of the muse. Verse. Walter Patter. 2:16 My8'26. 6079
Maestrissimo! PR (Gatti-Casazza). Gilbert W. Gabriel. 1:9-10 F21 '25. 6080
Maestro. Prose. Henry Anton Steig. 12:19-21*Ja9'37. 6081
The maestro of the gong. Prose. Frank Sullivan. 10:23-4 Ap7'34. 6082
The magazine's punctuation farm. MM. Corey Ford. 1:25 O17'25. 6083
Magazines, Ten Cent. TT. 6:17-18 F22'30. 6084
Magic a la mode. Verse. Charles G. Shaw. 1:15 F21'25. 6085
The magic pencil. Prose. George Cecil Cowing. 5:65-6 S14'29. 6086
Magic trick. Verse. Dearing Ward. 4:74 My26'28. 6087
The magician. Prose. Alice Frankforter. 6:70-1 Ja17'31. 6088
The magician. RL. Morris Markey. 2:42-5 N13'26. 6089
Magician. Verse. Mildred Weston. 8:56 O8'32. 6090
Magistrate's court, Bermuda. OFC. Margaret Farrand Thorp. 10: 60-2*F9'35. 6091
The maharajah's ear-rings. SM. Alexander Woollcott. 6:32-4 Je 14'30. 6092
The mahatma. PR (Eilshemius). Milton MacKaye. 11:24-8*S14 '35. 6093
Maid of Salem. WATN. Richard O. Boyer. 13:21-31*S4'37. 6094
Maiden Lane. DL. Burke Boyce. 3:28 D3'27. 6095
Maiden's confession. Verse. Margaret Fishback. 4:60 Mr3'28. 6096
Maiden's pledge. Verse. Margaret Fishback. 3:29 D31'27. 6097
Mail truck. SM. Alexander Woollcott. 9:32 S9'33. 6098
Mailbag. Verse. Henrietta Fort Holland. 8:57*My14'32. 6099
Main currents of American thought. Prose. Irwin Shaw. 15:15-19*Ag 5'39. 6100
Maine. Verse. W. G. Tinckom-Fernandez. 12:101*N14'36. 6101
The majesty of the law. Prose. Philip G. Wylie. 2:76-8 N13'26. 6102
Make it universal. Prose. Leonard Hatch. 1:17 F28'25. 6103
"Make mine a raspberry." TWNY. Beverly Smith. 8:46-54 Je4'32. 6104
Maker of castles. PR (Paterno). Foster Ware. 3:19-20 Jy2'27. 6105
Makes cowards of us all. Verse. Anon. 2:54 Ap24'26. 6106
Making a good impression. Prose. Arthur Kober. 10:84-7 Mr10'34. 6107
Making grammar popular. Prose. Robert Benchley. 9:24 My20'33. 6108
Making it easier for last year's débutante. Prose. Stanley Jones. 4:79 Mr31'28. 6109
Making it easier for the art yearner. Prose. Stanley Jones. 4:46 S15'28. 6110
Making it easier for the bank clerk. Prose. Stanley Jones. 4:

105 My12'28. 6111
Making it easier for the defeated candidate. Prose. Stanley Jones. 4:88 O20'28. 6112
Making it easier for the elevator man. Prose. Stanley Jones. 4: 36 Ap14'28. 6113
Making it easier for the girl who doesn't drink, if such there be. Prose. Stanley Jones. 4:51 D15'28. 6114
Making it easier for the girl with the old fur coat. Prose. Stanley Jones. 4:68 O27'28. 6115
Making it easier for the insurance agent. Prose. Stanley Jones. 4:40 Ap21'28. 6116
Making it easier for the man who decides to keep his old car for another year. Prose. Stanley Jones. 4:46 N24'28. 6117
Making it easier for the man who dropped the punt and lost the game. Prose. Stanley Jones. 4:38 N3'28. 6118
Making it easier for the man who has just been touched by a friend. Prose. Stanley Jones. 4:83 O13'28. 6119
Making it easier for the milliner. Prose. Stanley Jones. 4:111 Ap 7'28. 6120
Making it easier for the perfectly rotten golfer. Prose. Stanley Jones. 4:81 My19'28. 6121
Making it easier for the pretty waitress. Prose. Stanley Jones. 4:83 Ap28'28. 6122
Making it easier for the traffic officer. Prose. Stanley Jones. 4:57 My5'28. 6123
Making it easier for the weekend host and hostess. Prose. Stanley Jones. 4:39 Jy21'28. 6124
Making it easier for the West Sider. Prose. Stanley Jones. 4:68 Je9'28. 6125
Making it unanimous. Verse. Anon. 4:91 N3'28. 6126
Making life easier. Prose. Robert Jay Misch. 3:61 Ja7'28. 6127
The making of the anchovy. Prose. Robert Jay Misch. 1:16 D12'25. 6128
Making the conversation snappy. Prose. Sigmund Spaeth. 3:90 N 19'27. 6129
Making the grade. Prose. Nunnally Johnson. 3:62-5 Ja28'28. 6130
Making the modernistic home. Prose. Joseph Fulling Fishman. 4:84-6 O13'28. 6131
Malcolm. Verse. Raphael McCord. 3:20 F11'28. 6132
Malloy the mighty. RL. Edmund Pearson. 9:52-9 S23'33. 6133
Malvern Festival of Drama. Conrad Aiken. 11:62*S21'35. 6134
Mamie abreast of the times. Prose. Chester T. Crowell. 9: 68-9 Je24'33. 6135
Mammals you ought to know. Prose. Will Cuppy. 7:30-1 O10 '31. 6136
Mammy. Prose. Robert M. Coates. 4:58-9 F9'29. 6137
Man. Verse. Frances M. Frost. 6:75 My17'30. 6138
A man, a museum--and their secret vice. PR (Bach). Murdock Pemberton. 1:12-13 S12'25. 6139
Man-about-town. Prose. Robert Benchley. 8:11-12 Jy23'32. 6140
Man about town. Prose. C. G. Shaw. 2:31 S11'26. 6141
Man-afraid-of-the-cars. Prose. Ida M. Tarbell. 13:45-6*Jy3 '37. 6142
Man against the sky. PR (Hood). Allene Talmey. 7:24-7 Ap11'31. 6143
Man alone. Verse. Louise Bogan. 10:22 N3'34. 6144
Man alone. Prose. Wolcott Gibbs. 8:62-5 D3'32. 6145
The man and the myth. Prose. Wolcott Gibbs. 4:18-19 D22'28. 6146
Man and woman. Prose. Erskine Caldwell. 13:12-13*Jy10'37. 6147
The man behind Prometheus. PR

(Todd). Geoffrey T. Hellman. 12:31-4*N14'36; 12:23-6*N21 '36. 6148
The man behind the buttons. Verse. John Ogden Whedon. 6:36 Je21'30. 6149
A man can't do more than apologize. Prose. Gilbert Seldes. 5:24-5 Jy6'29. 6150
The man from Bucksport, Maine. Prose. R. V. H. 1:24 F21'25. 6151
The man from Chelsea. AC. Hyman Goldberg. 15:32-6*Ja6'40. 6152
The man from Mars. Prose. Daniel Fuchs. 15:20-1*Ap8'39. 6153
The man I am looking for. Prose. Katharine Brush. 3:27 O8'27. 6154
A man I saw. Verse. E. B. White. 6:24 O18'30. 6155
Man in a blue suit. PR (Klem). Niven Busch, Jr. 5:31-3 O5'29. 6156
Man in the aquarium. Verse. Dorothy Dow. 4:56 O13'28. 6157
The man in the corner. PR (Bimstein). A. J. Liebling. 13:28-33* Mr20'37. 6158
The man in the middle. SM. Alexander Woollcott. 6:38 F22 '30. 6159
The man in 32. Prose. E. B. White. 7:18 F13'32. 6160
A man may be down. Prose. Wolcott Gibbs. 9:18-19 S23'33. 6161
Man of ideas. PR (Burgess). H. K. Rigg. 13:20-6*Jy31'37. 6162
A man of letters. SM. Alexander Woollcott. 5:34 Jy20'29. 6163
The man on the train. Prose. James Thurber. 11:19-20*Ap 20'35. 6164
Man on the woman's page. Prose. Ernest Boyd. 10:26-7 Je9'34. 6165
Man, proud man. Verse. John Strong Newberry. 11:23*Ag10 '35. 6166
A man this country needed. PR (Walsh). Sanderson Vanderbilt. 13:24-9*S11'37. 6167
"A man who--." Prose. Robert Benchley. 8:20-1 O8'32. 6168
"A man who--." RL. Morris Markey. 3:36-40 O15'27. 6169
The man who answers telephones. PR (Amsden). Jack Alexander. 15:21-7*Ap22'39. 6170
"A man who drives a bus along . . ." Verse. Anon. 1:19 Ja23'26. 6171
The man who had to talk to somebody. Prose. John O'Hara. 6:60-2 O11'30. 6172
The man who is just-folks. Prose. Ben Hecht. 1:8 Je13'25. 6173
The man who knew too little. Prose. James Thurber. 13:29-30*D4'37. 6174
The man who knew Winchell. Prose. Michael Scully. 8:22-3 Je25'32. 6175
The man who looked like Washington. Prose. Wolcott Gibbs. 8:15-16 My28'32. 6176
The man who made us what we are. PR (Dewey). Waldo Frank. 2:15-16 My22'26. 6177
The man who owed Morgan $150,000. Prose. Kent Winslow. 9:64-5 Je10'33. 6178
The man who reads Dorothy Dix. Prose. Maddy Vegtel. 9:25 N4 '33. 6179
The man who ruined Paris. PR (James). Alexander Woollcott. 2:25-6 O2'26. 6180
The man who stopped smoking. Prose. Morris Bishop. 9:91-2 N18'33. 6181
The man who was wetly. Prose. James Thurber. 6:19 Ja17'31. 6182
The man who wasn't dressed. Prose. John Chapin Mosher. 12:18-20*Ja30'37. 6183
The man with a box. Prose. John Chapin Mosher. 2:18 Mr6'26. 6184
The man with an eight-dollar cheque to cash. Prose. Parke

Cummings. 3:113 Ap23'27. 6185
Man with camera. PR (Cooper). Gilbert Seldes. 7:21-5*My30 '31. 6186
A man with pink cheeks. Verse. A. van Steenbergh. 1:16 N7'25. 6187
The man with the menagerie. Prose. Frances Warfield. 8:26 N5'32. 6188
The man with the squeegee. PR (Norris). Russel Crouse. 8:21-4*My7'32. 6189
Mandates of the heart. Prose. Henrietta Fort Holland. 10:50-6 Ap14'34. 6190
Mangoes. Verse. Grace Hazard Conkling. 6:72 D13'30. 6191
A Manhattan background. Verse. Margaret Fishback. 4:33 Jy21 '28. 6192
Manhattan by-products. Verse. Margaret Fishback. 2:51 O9'26. 6193
Manhattan Christmas. Verse. Jean Batchelor. 5:26 D21'29. 6194
A Manhattan cocktail. Verse. Margaret Fishback. 2:47 O30 '26. 6195
Manhattan cocktail. Verse. Arthur Guiterman. 10:42 Jy7'34. 6196
Manhattan manual. Prose. Robert Jay Misch. 2:16-17 Mr27'26. 6197
Manhattan manual. Prose. Robert Jay Misch. 2:20 Ap3'26. 6198
Manhattan manual. Prose. Robert Jay Misch. 2:19 Ap10'26. 6199
Manhattan manual. Prose. Robert Jay Misch. 2:32-4 Ap17'26. 6200
Manhattan manual. Prose. Robert Jay Misch. 2:19 S4'26. 6201
Manhattan séance. Verse. Margaret Widdemer. 13:20*Ap3'37. 6202
Manhattan transfer. (Novel) TT. 1:5 D19'25. 6203
Manhattan transportation information. Verse. Carroll Carroll. 5:101 Ap6'29. 6204
Manhattan's folly. TWNY. Joseph Harrington. 14:39-45*Ja14'39. 6205
Manifestation. RL. Morris Markey. 9:48-52 S30'33. 6206
The manly art. Prose. Sterling Patterson. 2:28 My22'26. 6207
Mannequin. Verse. Anon. 4:53 Mr 17'28. 6208
Manners and Mr. Louis. Prose. Elizabeth Dickens. 15:53-6*S9 '39. 6209
Manners and morals, 1932. Prose. Gertrude Carver. 8:56-7*Ap30 '32. 6210
Man's limitation. Verse. Clarence Day. 11:15*Mr23'35. 6211
A man's woman. Prose. Sally Benson. 11:16-18*My4'35. 6212
The mantle of Rockne. PR (Meehan). Joel Sayre. 7:23-7 N14'31. 6213
The mantle of Whistler. Prose. Dorothy Parker. 4:15-16 Ag18 '28. 6214
Manuscript found in a beaded bag. Verse. Baird Leonard. 3:27 O 29'27. 6215
Ms. found in a non-refillable bottle. Verse. Baird Leonard. 4: 31 Ap21'28. 6216
Ms. found in East Sixty-eighth Street, folded up into a little paper airplane. Prose. Russell Maloney. 14:16*D17'38. 6217
Many happy returns! Prose. Robert Jay Misch. 3:52-3 N19'27. 6218
Many happy returns, 1929. Prose Robert Jay Misch. 5:98-100 O12 '29. 6219
Map of my country. Verse. John Holmes. 15:24*Ap22'39. 6220
The marble cemeteries. RL. St. Clair McKelway. 10:36-41 Ag4 '34. 6221
Marble halls. Prose. Wolcott Gibbs. 6:19-20 Ag30'30. 6222
Marble-top. Verse. E. B. White. 2: 21 Ja15'27. 6223
March fever. Verse. Helene Mullins. 6:22 Mr8'30. 6224
March, march on down the field. Prose. Irwin Shaw. 14:28-9*N 19'38. 6225

March, with me. Prose. Donald Ogden Stewart. 4:23-5 Mr10 '28. 6226
Marching song. Verse. James Reid Parker. 10:68 Jy14'34. 6227
Marcia in New York town. Prose. Marc Connelly. 2:23-4 O2'26. 6228
Marcia likes me. Prose. Emily Hahn. 12:30-3*Ag1'36. 6229
Marconi started it. RL. Morris Markey. 9:56-61 N4'33. 6230
Marginal notes. Verse. Phyllis McGinley. 10:27 O13'34. 6231
Marie-Antoinette, Axel Fersen, and Eliza Hunter. Prose. Morris Bishop. 11:21-4*Jy20'35. 6232
Marine heraldry. Verse. Jean Batchelor. 9:26 My27'33. 6233
The markee. PR (Madden). Joseph Mitchell. 15:20-7*N4'39. 6234
A market letter. Prose. Leonard Hatch. 2:57-8 S18'26. 6235
The Marlow mystery. RL. Morris Markey. 5:26-34 Ag10'29. 6236
Marlowe, Christopher. (Parody) E. B. White. 13:24*F12'38. 6237
Marooned in Laurel Canyon. Prose. Winifred Willis. 14:58-9*Mr26'38. 6238
Marquand, John P. TT. 15:19*Ap 29'39. 6239
Marquis, Don. TT. 1:3 Ag29'25. 6240
Marquis, Don. TT. 1:4 N28'25. 6241
Marquis, Don. TT. 2:7-8 Ag28'26. 6242
Marriage. Prose. Florence Helm. 2:49-50 My22'26. 6243
Marriage à la mode. Verse. Margaretta Manning. 3:66 Ja28'28. 6244
Marriage à la mode. Verse. Margaretta Manning. 4:119 O13'28. 6245
Marriage-broker. Verse. Phyllis McGinley. 8:31 Jy2'32. 6246
Marriage of convenience. Prose. John Chapin Mosher. 6:16-17 D 27'30. 6247
Mars. Prose. Wolcott Gibbs. 10: 15-17 Je23'34. 6248
Marsupial advantage. Verse. Sylvia Fuller. 2:86 O2'26. 6249
A Martian mistake. Prose. Ralph Barton. 1:8-9 Jy18'25. 6250
Martyrdom of a lady. Prose. Richard Lockridge. 11:15-16*Je22 '35. 6251
Martyred France. Prose. W. E. Farbstein. 7:15 Ja30'32. 6252
Mary. Prose. John O'Hara. 7:40-2 My2'31. 6253
Mary at the fair or, advice from a gypsy. Verse. Elinor Wylie. 4:25 N10'28. 6254
Ma's New York atmosphere. Prose. Edward Hutchings, Jr. 12:47-8*S26'36. 6255
The mascot of the troop. PR (Scheff). Alice Frankforter. 5: 30-3 N16'29. 6256
Masefield, John. TT. 2:17-18 O30 '26. 6257
Masefield, John. TT. 6:11-12 Je7 '30. 6258
Masefield, John. TT. 8:9 Ja7'33. 6259
Mass entertainment. PR (Rose). Alva Johnston. 11:22-9*Ap27 '35. 6260
Mass meetings. RL. Alva Johnston. 4:42-51 D15'28. 6261
Massacree. Prose. Henry Anton. 12:41-2*Jy11'36. 6262
The massooze. Prose. Emily Hahn. 10:15-18 Ag11'34. 6263
A master ditch digger. PR (Rosoff). Russell Owen. 3:19-21 Je4'27. 6264
Master hinter. PR (Copeland). Alva Johnston. 4:21-4 Ag18'28. 6265
The master minds. Prose. Ring Lardner. 7:15-16 Ja16'32. 6266
Master of ceremonies. Prose. John O'Hara. 9:40-3 N25'33. 6267
Master of ceremonies. PR (Herrick). James Thurber. 4:19-22 Jy21'28. 6268
A master of her art. PR (Ryan). John R. Tunis. 1:9-10 Ag22

'25. 6269
Master of masters. PR (Auer). Helena Huntington Smith. 5:24-7 Ap27'29. 6270
Masterpiece!!!! Prose. Oliver Claxton. 4:67 Mr17'28. 6271
Masters of the midway. PR (Dufour & Rogers). A. J. Liebling. 15:22-5*Ag12'39; 15:25-7*Ag19 '39. 6272
The master's touch. Prose. Wolcott Gibbs. 5:23 N9'29. 6273
Matches are made in America. Prose. Gilbert Seldes. 2:22-3 Ja15'27. 6274
Mate-of-the-month club. Prose. E. B. White. 3:30 Ap2'27. 6275
Matinal. Prose. Alice Frankforter. 6:18 Jy19'30. 6276
Matinale. Verse. Marjorie Allen Seiffert. 5:27 N2'29. 6277
Matinee. Prose. L. M. 2:58 My8 '26. 6278
The matron's prayer. Verse. Anon. 3:19 F4'28. 6279
A matter of geography. Prose. Frances Crane. 4:83-5 N10'28. 6280
A matter of perspective. Prose. Patricia Collinge. 6:19-20 Mr 29'30. 6281
A matter of plumbing. Prose. Lynde Denig. 6:98-9 O18'30. 6282
Maunder's biographical treasury. G. B. Stern. 15:43-8*Ap29'39. 6283
Maunk's magic. Prose. Max Miller. 10:36 Jy28'34. 6284
Mausoleum. Verse. Isabel McLennan McMeekin. 4:60 Je16'28. 6285
Mauve starts early grid drill. Prose. John O'Hara. 5:101-102 S21'29. 6286
Max the magnificent. SM. Alexander Woollcott. 6:32 Je21'30. 6287
Maxie, for God's sake! OFC. Stanton L. Catlin. 14:47-8*Jy16 '38. 6288
May. Verse. Peggy Bacon. 9:53 My13'33. 6289
May chant. Prose. Spud Johnson. 2:47-8 My15'26. 6290
May-fly time. Prose. Frances Crane. 5:80-2 My11'29. 6291
May it please your honor. Prose. W. E. Woodward. 9:14-15 My 27'33. 6292
Maya. (Play) TT. 4:17 Mr10'28. 6293
Maybe it was another fellow. Verse. Morris Bishop. 11:49* O19'35. 6294
Mayerling again. Prose. Maddy Vegtel. 13:19-21*N27'37. 6295
Mayerling. (Film) TT. 13:19*D18 '37. 6296
Mayflowerski. Verse. Parke Cummings. 7:93 N14'31. 6297
"The mayor sits in City Hall . . ." Verse. Anon. 2:85 Ja8'27. 6298
The mayoralty dope sheet. RL. Alva Johnston. 5:30-8 F23'29. 6299
The Maypole party. NYC. Bernice Breen. 7:38-46 Ap25'31. 6300
M'baby loves me. Prose. E. B. White. 2:30 F5'27. 6301
Me. PR (Davis). Richard O. Boyer. 15:26-32 Mr11'39. 6302
Me-Mutt! PR (Fisher). Kelly Coombs. 3:27-9 N26'27. 6303
The meadow. Verse. Frances M. Frost. 13:19*Ag14'37. 6304
Meanest man 1,381,456. Prose. Cyril B. Egan. 2:51 S11'26. 6305
The measure. Verse. Hortense Flexner. 9:27 Mr25'33. 6306
Measure for measure. Verse. Mildred Weston. 10:68 O27'34 6307
Measurement. Verse. Frances M. Frost. 5:33 N16'29. 6308
Meaty taste. Prose. Richard Lockridge. 7:19-20 D19'31. 6309
Mechanics of Springtime. Verse. Persis Greely Anderson. 7:20 Mr14'31. 6310
Mechanization. Verse. Hortense Flexner. 15:21 F10'40. 6311
Medals of honor. Verse. Arthur Guiterman. 2:32 Ap10'26. 6312

Medical methods. Verse. Clarence Day. 11:25*F16'35. 6313
Medical methods. Verse. Clarence Day. 11:19*My25'35. 6314
Meditation. Verse. Elspeth O'Halloran. 7:68 D5'31. 6315
Meditation à la russe. Verse. Morris Bishop. 10:27 F17'34. 6316
Meditation in a subway. Verse. Dearing Ward. 2:55 O9'26. 6317
Meditation in hydotherapy. Verse. Theodore Roethke. 13:87*My15'37. 6318
Meditation over cinnamon toast. Verse. Dearing Ward. 5:57 Ag31'29. 6319
Meditations of a housemaid. Verse. Elise Jerard. 3:23 O1'27. 6320
Medusa. HHT. Donald Moffat. 9:48-53 Je24'33. 6321
Meet John Aubrey. SM. Alexander Woollcott. 8:30*Ap16'32. 6322
Meet Mr. Fortune. SM. Alexander Woollcott. 7:32 N21'31. 6323
Meeting at the Pringles. Prose. Mollie Panter-Downes. 15:37-8*Ja6'40. 6324
Meeting in the Bronx. Prose. Arthur Kober. 13:23-5*N13'37. 6325
Meeting of minds. RL. Richard O. Boyer. 13:38-44*F12'38. 6326
A meeting of the Endorsers' Club. Prose. Corey Ford. 5:19-20 My11'29. 6327
Meeting Ring Lardner. Prose. Sherwood Anderson. 9:36-8 N25'33. 6328
Melancholy reflections after a lost argument. Verse. Phyllis McGinley. 9:24 N18'33. 6329
Melissa Anne Carruthers. Verse. Lee Wilson Dodd. 7:36 Mr7'31. 6330
The melody lingers on. WATN. E. J. Kahn, Jr. 15:26-32*F25'39. 6331
Melting pot. Prose. Henry Anton. 12:57*Je27'36. 6332
Memo and another memo. Prose. John O'Hara. 5:89 D14'29. 6333
Memo for an unclaimed pad. Verse. E. B. White. 8:23 Ag27'32. 6334
Memo for March. Verse. Mildred Weston. 14:44*Mr5'38. 6335
Memo to myself on preparing for a Fall weekend. Verse. Margaret Fishback. 7:50 N28'31. 6336
Memoir of deceased pedagogues. Prose. H. L. Mencken. 15:26-31*Je3'39. 6337
Memoirs of a banquet speaker. Prose. James Thurber. 6:17-18 Mr29'30. 6338
Memoirs of a dramatic critic. Prose. E. B. White. 4:23-4 S29'28. 6339
Memoirs of a master. Prose. M. R. A. 15:21-8*D23'39. 6340
Memoirs of a wreath-layer. Prose. James Thurber. 3:32 O15'27. 6341
The memoirs of Santa Claus. Prose. Marc Connelly. 6:19-21 D20'30. 6342
Memoirs of the Jukes family. Prose. Will Cuppy. 7:18-19*Jy18'31. 6343
Memorandum for a lynching. Verse. Phyllis McGinley. 15:27*S2'39. 6344
Memorandum for an infant boy. Verse. E. B. White. 8:18 Ja14'33. 6345
Memorial service. Prose. James Reid Parker. 12:37-42*O17'36. 6346
Memorials of gormandizing. Prose. H. L. Mencken. 15:26-33*Ag26'39. 6347
Memories. Prose. K. S. W. 10:58-9 Mr3'34. 6348
Memories of a census-taker. Prose. G. M. Hurley. 6:69-71 My24'30. 6349
Memories of a criminal. Prose. Joe Taylor. 2:19-20 Mr27'26. 6350
Memories of a criminal. Prose. Joe Taylor. 2:19-20 Ap3'26. 6351
Memories of a criminal. Prose.

Joe Taylor. 2:17-19 Ap10'26. 6352
Memories of a criminal. Prose. Joe Taylor. 2:29-30 Ap17'26. 6353
Memories of a criminal. Prose. Joe Taylor. 2:27-8 Ap24'26. 6354
Memory. Verse. Oriana Atkinson. 14:88*D17'38. 6355
Memory of a journey. Verse. Babette Deutsch. 13:29*S18'37. 6356
Men, after all, are men. Prose. George Cecil Cowing. 9:16 F18 '33. 6357
The men I hate to go out with. Prose. Katharine S. Angell White. 1:33 Ja2'26. 6358
The men I like to go out with. Prose. Katharine S. Angell White. 1:33 Ja2'26. 6359
Men in windows. Prose. S. S. Jones. 5:27 Mr9'29. 6360
Men of affairs. RL. Morris Markey. 3:36-40 F19'27. 6361
Men of Aran. OFC. Elsie McCormick. 12:72-3*O17'36. 6362
Men of principle. Verse. W. E. Farbstein. 14:21*Je11'38. 6363
Men, women, and dogs. Prose. James Thurber. 13:19-20 Ap17 '37. 6364
The menace of moving your bed. Verse. Martha Banning Thomas. 9:29 Mr18'33. 6365
The menace of tap dancing. Prose. Fairfax Downey. 5:33-4 D28'29. 6366
Menaces in May. Prose. James Thurber. 4:30-6 My26'28. 6367
Mencken, H. L. James Norman Hall. 9:73 Ja6'34. 6368
Mencken, H. L. TT. 2:9 Jy3'26. 6369
Mencken, H. L. TT. 9:15 O21'33. 6370
Mencken, H. L. (Parody) Gilbert Seldes. 2:29 Ja29'27. 6371
Mencken, H. L. TT. 1:3-4 My 2'25. 6372
Mencken, H. L. TT. 1:10 Ja 23'26. 6373
A mental mystery. Prose. Arthur H. Folwell. 2:81 Ja8'27. 6374
Mental reservation on accepting an invitation. Verse. Ruth Lambert Jones. 5:47 Jy6'29. 6375
Merchants of glory. RL. Morris Markey. 2:25-6 Ag28'26. 6376
Mercy, the cat's got into the budget. Prose. S. J. Perelman. 13: 69*Mr13'37. 6377
Merely a suggestion. Prose. Arthur H. Folwell. 1:26 Mr21'25. 6378
Merely hearsay. Verse. Miriam Vedder. 7:66 O10'31. 6379
Merrie England. Verse. Leonora Speyer. 12:48*D26'36. 6380
Merrie, merrie, merrie. Prose. John O'Hara. 5:98-100 D7'29. 6381
The merry census. Prose. Donald Moffat. 6:25-7 F22'30. 6382
Merry Christmas. Verse. Grace Hazard Conkling. 4:66 D22'28. 6383
Merry Christmas to all. Prose. James Thurber. 12:16-17*D26 '36. 6384
Merry Christmas to Bennett Cerf. SM. Alexander Woollcott. 10:56* D22'34. 6385
The merry round. Verse. John Ogden Whedon. 5:102 O19'29. 6386
Merrymakers. Prose. John Chapin Mosher. 8:16-18 D17'32. 6387
Merrymakers. Prose. John Chapin Mosher. 10:16-18*Ja19'35. 6388
The Mesecks. Verse. Kenneth Allan Robinson. 4:27 N24'28. 6389
The meshuggah of Manhattan. PR (Straton). Stanley Walker. 3:25-7 Ap16'27. 6390
A mess of clams. RL. Joseph Mitchell. 15:28-36*Jy29'39. 6391
Message. Verse. Peggy Bacon. 14: 23*S10'38. 6392
Messages. Verse. Margaret Fishback. 5:107 Je15'29. 6393

Metamorphic merchant. PR (Schlemmer). Dwight Macdonald. 15:25-31*Jy8'39. 6394
The meteoric rise of little Miss Edna Edna. Verse. Stuart Hyde Hawkins. 2:14 Jy10'26. 6395
Metropolitan blaze. Prose. Theodore Pratt. 9:22-3 D30'33. 6396
Metropolitan monotypes. Verse. Baird Leonard. 1:8 F28'25; 1:10 Ap18'25; 1:8 My2'25; 1:8 Ag8'25; 1:17 Ag15'25; 1:13 Ag22'25; 1:11 Ag29'25; 1:11 S5'25; 1:10 S12'25; 1:13 S19'25; 1:23 O10'25; 1:23 O24'25; 1:10 N21'25; 1:8 D5'25; 1:12 D19'25; 1:28 Ja23'26; 1:20 F6'26; 2:22 F20'26; 2:24 Mr13'26; 2:26 Ap10'26; 2:27 My1'26; 2:14 My22'26; 2:14 My29'26; 2:21 Je19'26; 2:21 Ag28'26; 2:21 Ja1'27; 3:25 Ap2'27; 3:23 My14'27; 3:24 Je4'27; 3:25 S17'27; 4:26 Mr10'28; 4:25 Mr31'28; 4:33 Je2'28; 4:27 S15'28; 4:20 Ja12'29; 5:20 Ja25'30; 6:18 Mr8'30; 6:24 Ap12'30; 6:23 My10'30; 6:21 Je7'30; 7:18 Ja9'32; 8:19*Mr12'32; 8:26 S3'32; 8:16 N12'32; 8:20 D31'32; 9:22 F18'33; 9:28 Ja13'34; 10:24 My12'34. 6397
Metropolitan monotypes. Verse. Murdock Pemberton. 1:12 Mr7'25. 6398
Metropolitan nature fakers. Prose. Nunnally Johnson. 3:24-5 Jy23'27. 6399
Metropolitan nightmare. Verse. Stephen Vincent Benét. 9:15 Jy1'33. 6400
Metropolitan portraits. Verse. Gretta Palmer. 3:55 S24'27. 6401
Metropolitans. Verse. M. M. 2:18 Jy24'26. 6402
The metropolite. Verse. Philip G. Wylie. 3:81 F18'28. 6403
Mexican folksong. Verse. Witter Bynner. 6:73 F14'31. 6404
The Mexican suit. Prose. E. B. White. 3:40-4 Mr26'27. 6405
Mice and men. Prose. Gilbert Seldes. 4:32 Ap21'28. 6406
Mickey-Mouse maker. PR (Disney). Gilbert Seldes. 7:23-7 D19'31. 6407
Midas in the Village. RL. John Mitchell. 5:34-8 S7'29. 6408
Mid-campaign. Prose. Frank Sullivan. 12:15-16*S5'36. 6409
The middle of the month. Verse. Ogden Nash. 11:20*Je15'35. 6410
Middle woman. PR (Rosenberg). Richard O. Boyer. 14:24-9*Ap23'38. 6411
The middle years. Prose. James Thurber. 5:18-19 Ja11'30. 6412
The Midgettes. WATN. Evelyn Miller Crowell. 13:20-3*Ja1'38. 6413
Mid-May song. Verse. Samuel Hoffenstein. 8:16 My21'32. 6414
Midnight-after Sappho. Verse. James Stephens. 5:26 My25'29. 6415
Midnight at Grant's tomb. Verse. Nicholas Samstag. 4:32 Jy7'28. 6416
Midnight blue. Prose. John Collier. 13:18-20*Ja22'38. 6417
Midnight magic. Prose. John Chapin Mosher. 10:28-9 N10'34. 6418
Midnight Mass. Prose. Sally Benson. 7:22-3 D26'31. 6419
Midnight sailing. Verse. Elspeth O'Halloran. 7:24 My2'31. 6420
Midsummer. Prose. Nancy Hale. 10:28-33 S8'34. 6421
Midsummer meditations. Verse. Phyllis McGinley. 12:17*Ag15'36. 6422
Midsummer melancholy. Verse. M. F. 3:28 Jy30'27. 6423
Midsummer misanthropy. Verse. Margaret Fishback. 3:45 Ag20'27. 6424
Midsummer miscellany. SM. Alexander Woollcott. 10:40 Jy21'34. 6425
Midsummer mulligrubs. Verse. M. F. 3:32 Ag27'27. 6426

Midsummer night. Prose. Frances Crane. 10:41-4 Je30'34. 6427
Midsummer night. RL. Morris Markey. 3:28-32 Jy16'27. 6428
Midsummer night's dream. Verse. Mildred Weston. 8:23 Ag20'32. 6429
Mid-town. Prose. Henry Collins Brown. 1:8 S26'25. 6430
The midwife. Prose. Ernest Boyd. 10:43-6 N10'34. 6431
The midwifery of ideas. Prose. Morris Bishop. 10:31-2*D8'34. 6432
Midwinter facial trends. Prose. S. J. Perelman. 12:14-15*Ja16 '37. 6433
Midwinter madness. RL. E. B. White. 8:38-44*F20'32. 6434
Mielziner, Jo. TT. 4:19 Je2'28. 6435
Mighty dealer in dollars. PR (Morgan). John K. Winkler. 4:23-6 F2'29; 4:27-36 F9'29. 6436
Mighty rock. RL. Morris Markey. 11:30-4*Jy6'35. 6437
Migration. Prose. Mary Heaton Vorse. 6:83-5 D6'30. 6438
The Mikado. C. B. T. 2:70-1 O16 '26. 6439
Mikhail and the sabotage. Prose. Leo C. Rosten. 12:62-4*Je27 '36. 6440
Mild surmise. Prose. D. M. 12: 75*Ap11'36. 6441
Military drill. Verse. Clinch Calkins. 3:16 Je18'27. 6442
Milkman. PR (Jeffers). Russell Lord. 8:22-6 D3'32. 6443
Mill Lane. DL. Burke Boyce. 2: 34 O16'26. 6444
Millay, Edna St. Vincent. PR. Griffin Barry. 2:25-7 F12'27. 6445
Millay, Edna St. Vincent. Cora B. Millay. 3:89-90 Ap23'27. 6446
Millay, Edna St. Vincent. TT. 1: 4 Ap25'25. 6447
Millay, Edna St. Vincent. TT. 4: 19-20 N3'28. 6448
Millay, Edna St. Vincent. (Parody) Franklin P. Adams. 13:33*O30 '37. 6449
Miller, Alice Duer. PR. Harvey O'Higgins. 3:25-7 F19'27. 6450
Miller, Caroline. TT. 10:16-17 My 19'34. 6451
Millinery memo. Verse. Phyllis McGinley. 14:43*Ja28'39. 6452
A million dollars. Prose. Arthur Kober. 6:86-7 S27'30. 6453
A million love. Prose. Reed Johnston. 4:54-6 Ag4'28. 6454
Millionaire through the needle's eye. Prose. Wolcott Gibbs. 9:28 Ap8'33. 6455
Millions in prizes. Prose. Joseph Fulling Fishman. 2:13-14 F27 '26. 6456
Millions of strawberries. Verse. Genevieve Taggard. 5:21 Je8'29. 6457
Milne, A. A. St. Clair McKelway. 11:74-9*O26'35. 6458
Mimi starts the Fall term. Verse. Martha Banning Thomas. 4:87 N3'28. 6459
The mind by day. Verse. John Holmes. 13:32*N20'37. 6460
Mind over matter. Prose. Pier Glass. 1:6-7 Ag1'25. 6461
Mind-reader. Prose. Mary F. Watkins. 10:64-6 Ap7'34. 6462
A ministering angel thou. Prose. Frank Sullivan. 10:23*D1'34. 6463
The minnow. TA. Will Cuppy. 8: 18 O1'32. 6464
A minority report. Prose. Waldo Frank. 1:14-15 Ag29'25. 6465
Minotaure. (Magazine) Janet Flanner. 10:67-8 Mr31'34. 6466
A minute with father. Prose. Frank M. O'Brien. 15:47*Ja6'40. 6467
Miracle. Verse. Leon Levy. 3:67 S3'27. 6468
Miracle in stone. AC. Samuel Hopkins Adams. 14:84-6*D10'38. 6469
The mirror. Verse. Grace Hazard Conkling. 4:87 S22'28. 6470
The mirror. Verse. Harold Willard Gleason. 5:52 S7'29. 6471

The mirror. Prose. Henrietta Fort Holland. 14:33*Ja21'39. 6472
The misanthrope. Prose. Alice Frankforter. 10:48-50 S15'34. 6473
Misanthrope. Verse. Ruth Lambert Jones. 5:106 O26'29. 6474
Miscellaneous mentation. LYMA. James Thurber. 13:20-2*My1 '37. 6475
Miscellany. SM. Alexander Woollcott. 6:34 Mr15'30. 6476
Miscreant. Verse. Frances M. Frost. 7:68*Je13'31. 6477
The miserable gardener. Verse. John Holmes. 12:60*Ap25'36. 6478
Misery. Verse. John Holmes. 15:25*S30'39. 6479
Misery loves company. Verse. Margaret Fishback. 6:81 S20 '30. 6480
The misfit. Verse. Persis Greely Anderson. 6:50 Mr8'30. 6481
Misgivings. Verse. Clarence Day. 9:22 S16'33. 6482
Miss Appleby, saloonkeeper. Prose. Richard Lockridge. 9:32-3 N18'33. 6483
Miss Elizabeth Bates. Verse. Milo Ray Phelps. 5:72 D21'29. 6484
Miss Fitch's husband. Verse. Winifred Welles. 14:16*Jy16 '38. 6485
Miss Fixit. PR (Holtzmann). Margaret Case Harriman. 12:21-5* Ja30'37; 12:22-5*F6'37. 6486
Miss Gulp. Prose. Nunnally Johnson. 6:15 Je21'30. 6487
Miss Kanaly's friend. Prose. Agnes Tatt. 11:73-4*Ap27'35. 6488
Miss Keete. Prose. Frances Warfield. 9:20-2 Ja27'34. 6489
Miss Mamie Harris. Prose. Elizabeth Jordan. 11:110-11*D7 '35. 6490
Miss Pettigrew talks. Prose. Anthony Armstrong. 6:21 Jy12'30. 6491
Miss Sawyer, champion. Prose. Ring Lardner. 3:23 S10'27. 6492
Miss Thorpe, take an edict. Prose. Frank Sullivan. 5:19-20 My18 '29. 6493
Miss Travis goes red. Prose. Frances Warfield. 8:19-20*Mr 26'32. 6494
Miss Van Saun and the oracle. Prose. Frances Warfield. 11:63*Je8'35. 6495
Missing. RL. Morris Markey. 10:38-41 Jy28'34. 6496
The missing lynx. SM. Alexander Woollcott. 5:34 Mr16'29. 6497
The missionary. Prose. G. Schwabe. 3:34 Jy16'27. 6498
Missionary's daughter. Prose. John W. Thomason, Jr. 9:18-21 Jy22 '33. 6499
Mississippi Pete vs. the gambling robots. Prose. Donald Thompson. 5:20-2 Ja18'30. 6500
Mr. Ambassador. PR (Bullitt). Janet Flanner. 14:32-5*D10'38; 14:22-7*D17'38. 6501
Mr. and Mrs. Bert Tovey. MNL. Thyra Samter Winslow. 10:31-4 Ag11'34. 6502
Mr. and Mrs. H. Prose. Leane Zugsmith. 14:18-20*Mr26'38. 6503
Mr. App sees it through. RL. Jack Alexander. 12:31-8*O31'36. 6504
Mr. Askew's worm. Prose. Richard Lockridge. 10:95-7 Mr10'34. 6505
Mr. Barbee's terrapin. RL. Joseph Mitchell. 15:46-51*O28'39. 6506
Mr. Blythe asks a simple question. Prose. Robert Coughlan. 13:68-71*N6'37. 6507
Mr. Bonner. Prose. John O'Hara. 5:74-5 My25'29. 6508
Mr. Britton. Prose. Nancy Hale. 9:16-18 Ag26'33. 6509
Mr. Bromley's bed. Prose. Theodore Pratt. 4:20 F2'29. 6510
Mr. Bromley's tonsils. Prose. Nathan Asch. 10:19-20 Ap28'34. 6511
Mr. Buckner explains. Prose.

1:7 N14'25. 6512
Mr. Burr resembles himself. Prose. Richard Lockridge. 10:56-8 My12'34. 6513
Mr. Burr responds. Prose. Richard Lockridge. 11:53-4*D21'35. 6514
Mr. Burr's gold. Prose. Richard Lockridge. 11:71*F16'35. 6515
Mr. Capone dances. Prose. Robert Wilder. 6:61-2 My10'30. 6516
Mr. Carlton crashes through. RC. Fillmore Hyde. 2:13-15 S4'26. 6517
Mr. Cass and the ten thousand dollars. Prose. John O'Hara. 8:53-5 Je25'32. 6518
Mr. Chairman. PR (Battle). Geoffrey T. Hellman. 9:21-5 Mr11 '33. 6519
Mr. Chips and others. SM. Alexander Woollcott. 10:38 Ap21'34. 6520
Mr. Cleary misses a party. Prose. John O'Hara. 6:49-51 F22'30. 6521
Mr. Close's new street. Prose. Agnes Rogers. 14:58-9*Ap2 '38. 6522
Mr. Cowley and the young. Prose. John O'Hara. 9:31-4 Je24'33. 6523
Mr. Dewey goes to town. Verse. J. R. P. 14:61*S17'38. 6524
Mr. Feger. Prose. Raymond Holden. 5:17-19 F15'30. 6525
Mr. Freeman. RL. A. J. Liebling. 13:37-42*My29'37. 6526
Mr. Frown abates a tittle. Prose. Frank Sullivan. 8:20-1 D3'32. 6527
Mr. Gill. Prose. James Reid Parker. 14:41-2*S17'38. 6528
Mr. Granite and Lee Him. OFC. Ik Shuman. 12:53-4*S19'36. 6529
Mr. Grover A. Whalen and the midway. RL. Joseph Mitchell. 13:22-6*Jy3'37. 6530
Mr. Hackett and Mrs. Doane. Prose. Hannah Lees. 9:46-7 Je24'33. 6531
Mr. Heathwin buys a country place. Prose. Frank Sullivan. 7:17-18* Je13'31. 6532
Mr. Higgins' breakdown. Prose. James Thurber. 6:19-20 S20'30. 6533
Mr. Hoover or Mr. Coolidge? Prose. James Thurber. 7:13 Ja 30'32. 6534
Mr. Huxley and Mr. Wilde. Prose. Maddy Vegtel. 10:104-106 My12 '34. 6535
Mr. Jaeckel and a few hides. PR (Jaeckel). S. N. Behrman. 8:22-5*Ap9'32. 6536
Mr. Jenkins goes to church. Prose. Horton Heath. 7:23 F13'32. 6537
Mr. Jonas entertains Wilber. Prose. John McCarten. 11:16-18*Mr9'35. 6538
Mr. Kang on royalty. Prose. Emily Hahn. 12:50-1*F13'37. 6539
Mr. K·A·P·L·A·N almost comes through. Prose. Leo Rosten. 12:15-17*Ag29'36. 6540
Mr. K·A·P·L·A·N and Shakespeare. Prose. Leo Rosten. 13:18-20*Mr27'37. 6541
Mr. K·A·P·L·A·N and the Magi. Prose. Leo Rosten. 12:17-19* D19'36. 6542
Mr. K·A·P·L·A·N and vocabulary. Prose. Leo Rosten. 12:19-20* O17'36. 6543
Mr. K·A·P·L·A·N bares his teeth. Prose. Leo Rosten. 14:36-8*D 10'38. 6544
Mr. K·A·P·L·A·N cuts a Gordian knot. Prose. Leo Rosten. 12:18-21* F6'37. 6545
Mr. K·A·P·L·A·N, the comparative, and the superlative. Prose. Leo Rosten. 12:17-18* S12'36. 6546
Mr. K·A·P·L·A·N the magnificent. Prose. Leo Rosten. 12:35-7* N14'36. 6547
Mr. K·A·P·L·A·N'S dark logic. Prose. Leo Rosten. 13:21-3*Ap 17'37. 6548
Mr. K·A·P·L·A·N'S hobo. Prose. Leo Rosten. 12:17-19* O3

'36. 6549
Mr. K•A•P•L•A•N'S so and so. Prose. Leo Rosten. 13:22-5* My15'37. 6550
Mr. K•A•P•L•A•N'S white banner. Prose. Leo Rosten. 12: 16-18*Ja16'37. 6551
Mr. Laidlaw and Mr. Sage. AC. Edmund Pearson. 13:75-80* My15'37. 6552
Mr. Larousse's Träumerei. Prose. Frederick Packard. 14: 45*Je25'38. 6553
Mr. Louis H. F. Mouquin announces. Verse. Leslie Nelson Jennings. 9:41 O28'33. 6554
Mr. Malone. Prose. Thomas Wolfe. 13:22-7*My29'37. 6555
Mr. Martin and the hotel child. Prose. Sally Benson. 9:44-8 D23'33. 6556
Mr. Maunder's treasury. OUWA. G. B. Stern. 15:43-8*Ap29'39. 6557
Mr. Milliner. Prose. Leane Zugsmith. 12:22-4*Mr28'36. 6558
Mr. Monroe and the moving men. Prose. James Thurber. 6:13-14 Ag2'30. 6559
Mr. Monroe holds the fort. Prose. James Thurber. 5:24-5 N30 '29. 6560
Mr. Monroe outwits a bat. Prose. James Thurber. 5:17-18 Je15 '29. 6561
Mr. Mott essays le tennis. Prose. Donald Moffat. 12:28-30*My2 '36. 6562
Mr. Mott goes to the fire. Prose. Donald Moffat. 11:25-7*F8'36. 6563
Mr. Mowson wakes. Prose. Robert M. Coates. 8:11-13 Jy16'32. 6564
Mister Muggsy. PR (McGraw). William Slavens McNutt. 1: 9 Mr28'25. 6565
Mr. North and the carnivore. Prose. Richard Lockridge. 9: 22 Ag12'33. 6566
Mr. North and the debunkers. Prose. Richard Lockridge. 8: 22-3 N5'32. 6567
Mr. North charges it. Prose. Richard Lockridge. 11:66-8 *My 25'35. 6568
Mr. North, defender. Prose. Richard Lockridge. 9:18 Mr18 '33. 6569
Mr. North does the right thing. Prose. Richard Lockridge. 8: 17-19 S3'32. 6570
Mr. North frogs. Prose. Richard Lockridge. 8:39-40 Ag27'32. 6571
Mr. North helps shop. Prose. Richard Lockridge. 12:55-6*O 10'36. 6572
Mr. North mixes things up. Prose. Richard Lockridge. 12:24*Ap 4'36. 6573
Mr. North sniffs. Prose. Richard Lockridge. 9:14-15 Je17'33. 6574
Mr. North, the pale vegetable. Prose. Richard Lockridge. 8: 17-19 N26'32. 6575
Mr. North's concert. Prose. Richard Lockridge. 9:18-19 Mr11 '33. 6576
Mr. North's ordeal. Prose. Richard Lockridge. 12:60-1*F22'36. 6577
Mr. Palmer's party. Prose. Tess Slesinger. 11:30-2*Ap27'35. 6578
Mr. Pendly and the Poindexter. Prose. James Thurber. 8:13-14*F27'32. 6579
Mr. Perkins passes by. Prose. Lyon Mearson. 6:34-6 N1'30. 6580
Mr. Pierson and the new Messiah TWNY. Christopher Ward. 10: 64-75*D8'34. 6581
Mr. Plenko. Prose. Frances Crane. 7:74-6 Ap4'31. 6582
Mister Poincaray, meet Monsiou Mellon! Prose. Lewis Galantier 2:27-8 O2'26. 6583
Mr. Poppolardo does it on purpose Prose. Jane Douglas. 13:57-8* O16'37. 6584
Mr. Poppolardo tilts with the boss Prose. Jane Douglas. 13:83-5* N20'37. 6585

Mr. Poppolardo's foreign affairs. Prose. Jane Douglas. 13:50-3* Jy24'37. 6586

Mr. Preble gets rid of his wife. Prose. James Thurber. 9:17-18 Mr4'33. 6587

Mr. President. PR (Conant). Henry F. Pringle. 12:20-4 *S12 '36; 12:23-7 *S19'36. 6588

Mr. Purdy keeps his temper. Prose. Horton Heath. 11:51-5*Je15'35. 6589

Mr. Raffles to Mrs. Post. Prose. John Chapin Mosher. 3:85-6 Je18'27. 6590

Mr. Ramage and Mr. Cooper-Shaw. Prose. Victoria Lincoln. 13:16-17*N6'37. 6591

Mr. Rosenthal. Prose. John O'Hara. 5:24-5 Jy20'29. 6592

Mr. Sidney Gainsborough: quality pictures. Prose. John O'Hara. 8:36-40 D17'32. 6593

Mr. Spitzer and the fungus. Prose. Ruth McKenney. 13:38-41*My8 '37. 6594

Mr. Stout's nap. Prose. Frank Sullivan. 6:14-16 Ag9'30. 6595

Mr. Twickham's birthday. Prose. Newman Levy. 8:21-2*Mr5'32. 6596

Mr. Wallace interviews himself. Prose. Edgar Wallace. 5:38 N16 '29. 6597

Mr. Wemble, Wilber, and a brown horse. Prose. John McCarten. 10:23-4*F9'35. 6598

Mr. Wemble, Wilber, and some trouble in the tunnel. Prose. John McCarten. 11:78-9*Ap20 '35. 6599

Mr. Wetherby and the Christmas doll. Prose. John Forbes. 4:42-6 D8'28. 6600

Mr. Whitten, Tawny, and a lover of the cheetah. Prose. John McCarten. 11:71*My25'35. 6601

Mr. Whitten, the shoe men and the weakened metatarsal. Prose. John McCarten. 13:74-5*O30 '37. 6602

Mrs. Andrews. Prose. Gerold Frank. 12:65-6*N7'36. 6603

Mrs. Benson. Prose. G. Schwabe. 5:42-4 Ja18'30. 6604

Mrs. Bigsby. Prose. Alice Frankforter. 8:39-40*Mr26'32. 6605

Mrs. Blum. Verse. Wilfred J. Funk. 7:85 My9'31. 6606

Mrs. Bright and shining star Chibby. Prose. Joseph Mitchell. 14:19-21*N5'38. 6607

Mrs. Brown walks. Verse. Elspeth O'Halloran. 8:36 S3'32. 6608

Mrs. Carlton does it herself. RC. Fillmore Hyde. 2:23-4 N20'26. 6609

Mrs. Carlton errs. RC. Fillmore Hyde. 2:25-6 D18'26. 6610

Mrs. Carrington and Mrs. Crane. Prose. Dorothy Parker. 9:11-12 Jy15'33. 6611

Mrs. Conway stands firm. Prose. P. S. LePoer Trench. 11:35-8* S21'35. 6612

Mrs. Dee and the watering pot. Prose. Hannah Lees. 10:44-8 S22'34. 6613

Mrs. De Payster's parties. Prose. Geoffrey T. Hellman. 12:24*Ag1 '36. 6614

Mrs. Firebrand. PR (Willebrandt). John S. Martin. 4:23-6 F16'29. 6615

Mrs. Galt and Edwin. Prose. John O'Hara. 9:62-5 F18'33. 6616

Mrs. Gittleson. Prose. Arthur Kober. 7:72-4 O24'31. 6617

Mrs. Gross writes to the Bronx. Prose. Arthur Kober. 15:16-17* S9'39. 6618

Mrs. Hemans, in calf. Prose. Richard Lockridge. 9:30-1 O7'33. 6619

Mrs. Hofstadter on Josephine Street. Prose. Dorothy Parker. 10:20-6 Ag4'34. 6620

Mrs. McMorrow. Prose. John O'Hara. 9:48-55 N18'33. 6621

Mrs. Mandelbaum. Prose. Marjorie Marks. 11:73-4*My25'35. 6622

"Mistress Mary, quite contrary. . ." Verse. M. M. 3:87 O15'27. 6623

Mrs. Minnie Pitcher. Verse. Wini-

'33. 6664
Moment musical. Prose. Richard Sherman. 11:69*S7'35. 6665
The moments he remembers. Verse. Mark VanDoren. 13:17* My8'37. 6666
Mona Lisa. Verse. Elizabeth Gunn. 5:47 F8'30. 6667
Monday at nine. Prose. Robert Jay Misch. 2:28 Mr20'26. 6668
Monday is fish day. Verse. Phyllis McGinley. 12:23*S5'36. 6669
Monday, Tuesday, Wednesday--. Verse. William Rose Benét. 9:20 S30'33. 6670
Money in the Bronx. Prose. Arthur Kober. 15:21-3*Mr25'39. 6671
Money moon. Verse. Margaretta Manning. 4:70 Je16'28. 6672
Monkey. Verse. Victor Hill. 4:99 O27'28. 6673
Monkey business. Verse. Mildred Weston. 10:68 Mr31'34. 6674
Monodies of masonry. Verse. A. K. Laing. 2:78 Ja29'27. 6675
Monodies on masonry. Verse. A. K. Laing. 3:40 F19'27. 6676
Monodies on masonry. Verse. A. K. Laing. 2:73 N6'26. 6677
Monograph. Verse. Ruth Lambert Jones. 4:99 Ja5'29. 6678
Monologue at five. Verse. Spud Johnson. 3:80 Mr19'27. 6679
Monologue from a padded cell. Verse. Phyllis McGinley. 11: 23*F1'36. 6680
Monotone. Verse. Martha Banning Thomas. 9:69 Je3'33. 6681
Monotony. Verse. Franklin P. Adams. 14:64*N5'38. 6682
Monroe, Harriet. (Parody) Franklin P. Adams. 13:33*O30'37. 6683
The Monroes find a terminal. Prose. James Thurber. 5:20-1 My25'29. 6684
Monsieur Beaupré. Prose. Theodore Pratt. 7:46-8 Ap18'31. 6685
Monsieur Dupotin. Prose. Theodore Pratt. 7:23 Ag15'31. 6686
Monsieur Gambelle goes to the circus. Prose. Theodore Pratt. 12:69*O10'36. 6687
Monsieur Jourjon. Prose. Theodore Pratt. 6:43-4 Ag30'30. 6688
Monsieur le commissaire. Prose. Theodore Pratt. 6:19-20 My24 '30. 6689
Monsieur le docteur. Prose. Theodore Pratt. 7:30-2 My16'31. 6690
M. Litvinoff writes home. Prose. Leonard Ware, Jr. 9:52-4 N4 '33. 6691
The Monte Carlo gesture. SM. Alexander Woollcott. 5:36 Ag10 '29. 6692
Monterrey, Mexico. OFC. Michael Scully. 8:40-1 My28'32. 6693
Montparnasse. Verse. E. B. White. 4:24 Jy28'28. 6694
Mood from 3000 B. C. Verse. Genevieve Taggard. 9:22 F10'34. 6695
The moon and Mr. North. Prose. Richard Lockridge. 9:23-4 S9'33. 6696
Moon-set. Prose. Spud Johnson. 3:34 Mr26'27. 6697
Moonlight sonata. SM. Alexander Woollcott. 7:36 O3'31. 6698
Moral moments. Verse. Clarence Day. 10:23 Mr3'34. 6699
Moral problems. Verse. Fillmore Hyde. 2:16 Ap24'26. 7000
Moral problems. Verse. Fillmore Hyde. 2:20 My22'26. 7001
Moral reflections. Verse. Arthur Guiterman. 8:63*Ap2'32. 7002
Moral results of a hold-up. Prose. John Chapin Mosher. 3:54-6 Ag 13'27. 7003
The moral tale of Printing-House Square. Verse. Burke Boyce. 4:28 Mr31'28. 7004
Moralistic rhymes. Verse. Philip G. Wylie. 2:76 Ja8'27. 7005
Morality at the aquarium. Verse. J. S. P. 2:19 Ag7'26. 7006
Morand, Paul. Janet Flanner. 4:74 Mr17'28. 7007
Morand, Paul. Janet Flanner. 6:48

Jy12'30. 7008
Morbid reflections induced by unemployment. Verse. Samuel Hoffenstein. 8:16 Je25'32. 7009
More about people. Verse. Ogden Nash. 6:18 D27'30. 7010
More alarms at night. MLHT. James Thurber. 9:13-15 Ag26 '33. 7011
More and worse mammals. Prose. Will Cuppy. 7:20-1 N21'31. 7012
More authors cover the Snyder trial. Prose. James Thurber. 3:69 My7'27. 7013
More blessed. Prose. Alice Frankforter. 7:36 D19'31. 7014
More country life in America. Verse. Martha Banning Thomas. 3:67 Ag6'27. 7015
More country life in America. Verse. Martha Banning Thomas. 3:67 Ag13'27. 7016
More country life in America. Verse. Martha Banning Thomas. 3:98 N19'27. 7017
More epitaphs. Verse. Kenneth Phillips Britton. 2:48 Je5'26. 7018
More foreign letters. Prose. Robert Jay Misch. 1:39 F13'26. 7019
More foreign letters. Prose. Robert Jay Misch. 2:52 F20'26. 7020
More games for the masses. Prose. Flossie Jane Blumberg. 5:73-4 Jy20'29. 7021
More gates, more crashes. Prose. Thomas Longan. 3:53-5 Mr12 '27. 7022
More golden eggs. Prose. Elmer Davis. 10:30-1 Mr24'34. 7023
More ice added to U.S. as thousands cheer. Prose. James Thurber. 10:13-14*D22'34. 7024
More like sisters. Prose. Thyra Samter Winslow. 15:21-3*Mr18 '39. 7025
More like sweethearts. Prose. Sally Benson. 12:15-18*Ap25 '36. 7026
More names. Prose. Stanley Walker. 9:74-6 Ja6'34. 7027
More preyed upon than preying. Verse. Margaret Fishback. 7:18 F28'31. 7028
More slush for Feb. 14. Verse. Margaret Fishback. 13:56*F12 '38. 7029
More songs for Meller. Prose. Robert Benchley. 2:18 My1'26. 7030
More than anything else in the world. Prose. Arthur Kober. 9:49-53 Ag26'33. 7031
More things to come. Verse. Hortense Flexner. 12:38*O3'36. 7032
More truth than prose. Prose. Sidney Skolsky. 3:87 N26'27. 7033
More wine from sour grapes. Verse. Martha Banning Thomas. 4:36 Ag11'28. 7034
Morning. Verse. Frances M. Frost. 5:19 F1'30. 7035
Morning. Verse. Helene Mullins. 6:18 My31'30. 7036
Morning. Verse. Martha Banning Thomas. 3:55 D3'27. 7037
The morning after. Verse. Richard Peckham. 5:61 N23'29. 7038
Morning for a lady. Verse. Richard Viner. 9:18 S9'33. 7039
Morning in December. Verse. Paul M. Saunders. 15:49*D9'39. 7040
The morning mail. Prose. Joseph Fulling Fishman. 3:58-9 O29'27. 7041
Morning of a juryman. Prose. Lyon Mearson. 11:29-30*S14'35. 7042
Morning song. Verse. Price Day. 7:23*Je6'31. 7043
Mornings at eleven. Verse. John Holmes. 11:15*F23'35. 7044
Morningside. NYC. Talbot Faulkner Hamlin. 8:36-9 Ja21'33. 7045
The morose policeman. Prose. Daniel Fuchs. 15:20-2*O14'39. 7046
Morrison. Verse. Florence Kiper Frank. 6:28 Jy5'30. 7047

Much ado about nussing. SM. Alexander Woollcott. 8:38 N5 '32. 7092
Much ado about plenty. Prose. E. B. White. 11:23-4*Ag3'35. 7093
Muenchen im kleinen. RL. Chester L. Morrison. 11:32-41*Jy 13'35. 7094
Mulberry Street. Verse. Mildred Weston. 7:18 F13'32. 7095
Mumford, Lewis. TT. 15:11*Mr4 '39. 7096
Municipal efficiency. Prose. Cornelia Otis Skinner. 9:26-33 Je 3'33. 7097
Municipal lodging house. RL. Emily Hahn. 8:36-40 F4'33. 7098
The municipal sand pile. Prose. Creighton Peet. 2:24 O2'26. 7099
Munsey, the journalist. RL. Morris Markey. 1:13-14 Ja2'26. 7100
Murder. RL. Morris Markey. 2:30-1 F20'26. 7101
Murder as bad art. Prose. Waldo Frank. 1:12-13 S19'25. 7102
Murder by moonlight. Verse. Caroline Duer. 4:31 Mr3'28. 7103
Murder for pleasure. Prose. John Chapin Mosher. 4:40-3 Mr17'28. 7104
Murder for publicity. SM. Alexander Woollcott. 6:31 Jy12'30. 7105
Murder in the family. RL. Morris Markey. 7:28-36*Je27'31. 7106
The murder of Dr. Burdell. TWNY. Edmund Pearson. 11: 62-9*D21'35. 7107
Murder trial talk. Prose. C. P. 2:30 Ag28'26. 7108
Murderers' row. TWNY. Samuel McCoy. 6:48-54 S20'30. 7109
The murderous philologist with but one big toe. AC. Carl Carmer. 12:37-9*Je6'36. 7110
The Murray Hill. SH. Newman Levy. 4:26 Je30'28. 7111
Muses of the frontier. OUWA. Paul Horgan. 10:41-4*F9'34. 7112
The museum guard. Verse. Parke Cummings. 3:59 F26'27. 7113
Music. Verse. Lionel Wiggam. 12: 17*My30'36. 7114
The music dealer. Prose. Sigmund Spaeth. 4:40-1 Je2'28. 7115
The music-haters. Verse. Arthur Guiterman. 11:70*Mr30'35. 7116
Music in the Bronx. Prose. Arthur Kober. 11:58-60*Je29'35. 7117
The music lesson. Prose. Alice Frankforter. 8:68-9*Ap9'32. 7118
Music lessons. Verse. Elise Jerard. 6:71 Je21'30. 7119
Music of the spheres. RL. Morris Markey. 2:44-8 D4'26. 7120
Music with meals. PR (Coleman). Gilbert Seldes. 11:26-30*O19'35. 7121
Musica man. Prose. Henrietta Sperry Ripperger. 9:66-8 O14 '33. 7122
"Musical America" employs an answer man. Prose. Wilella Waldorf. 4:90-1 F16'29. 7123
The musical debut. Prose. Fillmore Hyde. 1:20 Ja23'26. 7124
The musical director. Prose. Arthur Kober. 3:30 O8'27. 7125
Musical mornings. PR (Bagby). Mary Van Rensselaer Thayer. 14:19-25*D31'38. 7126
Musician. Verse. Louise Bogan. 13:20*N20'37. 7127
Music's faithful servant. PR (Schnabel). César Saerchinger. 14:21-5*Ap2'38. 7128
Musings aboard the Stamford local. Verse. Phyllis McGinley. 14:23*N5'38. 7129
Musings of a connoisseur. Prose. Hope Hale. 7:47-8 Mr21'31. 7130
Musings on the moon. Verse. Martha Banning Thomas. 3:29 F19 '27. 7131

Must? WP. Robert Benchley. 13: 37-8*Mr27'37. 7132
A mutinous Sisyphus. Prose. Carroll Carroll. 3:31 Mr19'27. 7133
Mutiny in the offing. Verse. Margaret Fishback. 5:41 S28'29. 7134
Muttering in the ranks. SM. Alexander Woollcott. 8:30 O1'32. 7135
Mutterings from Elba. SM. Alexander Woollcott. 10:34 Je2'34. 7136
Mutton that thinks itself lamb. Verse. Rollin Kirby. 3:101 Mr 26'27. 7137
My affair with an actress. Prose. John Chapin Mosher. 3:34-6 Ja21'28. 7138
My African potentate. Prose. E. J. Kahn, Jr. 13:64-6*Ap3'37. 7139
My aunt from Twelfth Street. Prose. Jerome Weidman. 15: 38-41*Ag12'39. 7140
"My aunt is not inclined to joy. . ." Verse. Anon. 1:31 Ja30 '26. 7141
My boy Herbert. Prose. Dearing Ward. 9:29 Mr18'33. 7142
My brain. Verse. Arthur Guiterman. 7:93 D12'31. 7143
My cabaret confessions. Prose. Nikita Balieff. 5:28-34 Je22'29. 7144
My career as a counterweight. Prose. Richard Lockridge. 14: 19-20*F4'39. 7145
"My child is phlegmatic . . ."-- anxious parent. Verse. Ogden Nash. 7:28 Mr14'31. 7146
My cook is me. Prose. Maddy Vegtel. 11:54-6*D28'35. 7147
My country, right or wrong. Prose. Burdette Kinne. 6:47-9 Je28'30. 7148
My country 'tis of thee. Prose. G. Schwabe. 2:41 Ja15'27. 7149
My cousin. Prose. John C. Emery. 8:44-5*Ap16'32. 7150
My cup runneth over. Prose. Sally Benson. 14:15-17*Je18 '38. 7151
My day. Prose. James Thurber. 11:17*F15'36. 7152
"My dear, they're diving." Prose. Arthur Kober. 9:16 Jy1'33. 7153
My diary. Prose. Frank Sullivan. 7:15-16*Jy4'31. 7154
My dream ship. Prose. Donald Moffat. 7:20-3 My9'31. 7155
My experiences on the American stage. Prose. Victoria Lincoln. 14:28-9*Ja21'39. 7156
My father was a belted earl, etc. Verse. Marian Storm. 2:45 S4 '26. 7157
My friend Harpo. SM. Alexander Woollcott. 7:30-2 Ja23'32. 7158
My friend in Washington. Prose. John O'Hara. 9:20 S23'33. 7159
My friend, the ambassador. Prose. Theodore Pratt. 6:83-4 Je14'30. 7160
My friends. Prose. Elmer Davis. 8:78-80 D10'32. 7161
My girls. Prose. John O'Hara. 13:17-18*My29'37. 7162
My grandma's muff. Prose. Burdette Kinne. 15:53*F25'39. 7163
My husband ain't no bad man. Prose. Jane Douglas. 13:57-9* S4'37. 7164
My interview. Prose. Geoffrey Kerr. 2:21 F27'26. 7165
My investment program for the new year. Prose. Charles W. Morton, Jr. 7:17-18 Ja16'32. 7166
My kisses are all for my husband. Verse. C. Knapp. 3:74-5 Mr12 '27. 7167
My lawyer. PR (Steuer). Alva Johnston. 7:24-7 My16'31; 7:21-4 My23'31. 7168
My life with Clara Bow. Prose. Edward Newhouse. 12:57*O3'36. 7169
My little cabin monoplane. RL. E. B. White. 4:36-42 O6'28. 7170
My lullaby. Verse. C. F. Looms. 3:55 Mr5'27. 7171
My man. Prose. Cuthbert Squire. 10:15 Je16'34. 7172

My memories of D. H. Lawrence. Prose. James Thurber. 12:18-19*Je27'36. 7173
My mother won the war. Prose. Sylvia Townsend Warner. 12: 15-17*My30'36. 7174
My mother's march of time. Prose. Marion Sturges-Jones. 13:39*D4'37. 7175
My only fear. Verse. Paula Lecler. 6:97 My10'30. 7176
My own cherry tree. Prose. John Chapin Mosher. 3:46-8 F18'28. 7177
My own life. Prose. Ernest Hemingway. 2:23-4 F12'27. 7178
My own, my native land. Prose. Thyra Samter Winslow. 10:70-2 Ag18'34. 7179
My own, my native land. Prose. Thyra Samter Winslow. 10:64-8 Ag25'34. 7180
My own, my native land. Prose. Thyra Samter Winslow. 10:41-3 S1'34. 7181
My own, my native land. Prose. Thyra Samter Winslow. 10:60-3 S8'34. 7182
My own, my native land. Prose. Thyra Samter Winslow. 10:68-71 S15'34. 7183
My partner is vulnerable. Verse. Phyllis McGinley. 11:50*Ja4 '36. 7184
My physical handicap, ha ha. Prose. E. B. White. 13:20*Je12 '37. 7185
My plaster cast. Prose. Frances Warfield. 7:29 S12'31. 7186
My political career. Prose. Beverly L. Clarke. 12:18-20*Ag15 '36. 7187
My political crystal ball. Prose. Donald Ogden Stewart. 4:22-3 S22'28. 7188
My poor grandfather. Verse. Herman Fetzer. 7:15*Ag15'31. 7189
My red grouse. Prose. Frances Crane. 4:21-2 O20'28. 7190
My silver dress. Prose. Elinor Wylie. 2:17 My8'26. 7191
My sister Frances. Prose. Emily Hahn. 13:24-7*Mr20'37. 7192
My trip abroad. Prose. James Thurber. 3:25-6 Ag6'27. 7193
My weather cock. Verse. Robert P. Tristram Coffin. 14:12*S3 '38. 7194
Myself. Verse. Charlotte Armstrong. 3:43 D31'27. 7195
Myopia, my own. Prose. Hildegarde Dolson. 14:56-8*F11'39. 7196
The mysteries of Rudolfo. PR (Kommer). Alexander Woollcott. 9:20-3 Mr18'33. 7197
The mysterious death of the typical New Yorker. Prose. John Chapin Mosher. 2:17 Ag28'26. 7198
The mystery. Verse. Fillmore Hyde. 3:30 My14'27. 7199
Mystery at the little church around the corner. Verse. Margaret Fishback. 4:123 D15'28. 7200
The mystery of the hansom cab. SM. Alexander Woollcott. 8:37-8 F11'33. 7201
The mystery revived. RL. Morris Markey. 2:25-6 Ag7'26. 7202

N

"N. B. loves Emma Glotz." Prose. T. H. Bliss. 2:39-40 O16'26. 7203
Naïveté. Verse. M. M. 3:43 N5'27. 7204
A name is made. PR (Talley). Elizabeth Armstrong. 3:18-20 F11'28. 7205
Names. Verse. Zebulon Q. Katzenellenbogen. 2:92 D4'26. 7206
The name's the thing. Prose. Anthony Armstrong. 10:70-2 O13 '34. 7207
Namesake. Verse. Elspeth O'Halloran. 4:14 Jy21'28. 7208
Nan. Prose. Barbara Heggie. 15: 35*O28'39. 7209
Nana. (Film) Janet Flanner. 10:90 Je9'34. 7210
Nancy and Mr. Zinzindorf. Prose. John O'Hara. 7:49-51 S26'31. 7211

Nannie. Prose. Maddy Vegtel. 10:65-8 My5'34. 7212
Napoleon of books. PR (Rosenbach). Avery Strakosh. 4:25-8 Ap14'28. 7213
Narcissa. Verse. Anon. 3:63 Ja 14'28. 7214
The narrative of hard-boiled Nan. Verse. William Rose Benét. 2:68-9 O16'26. 7215
Nassau Street. DL. Burke Boyce. 3:15 Je11'27. 7216
Natasha. Prose. Emily Hahn. 14: 19-21*N19'38. 7217
Nathan, George Jean. Charles G. Shaw. 3:30-1 O15'27. 7218
Nathan, George Jean. TT. 1:1-2 Mr14'25. 7219
Nathan, George Jean. TT. 1:3-4 My2'25. 7220
Nathan, George Jean. TT. 13:16 Mr20'37. 7221
Nathan, George Jean. (Parody) Wolcott Gibbs. 13:14*F12'38. 7222
The national pastime. NESD. John J. Holzinger. 9:46 S30'33. 7223
National Poetry Center. TT. 15: 13*My27'39; 15:10-12*Jy15'39. 7224
Native. Prose. Anon. 2:43 Mr13 '26. 7225
The natives are friendly. Verse. James Reid Parker. 9:48 My6 '33. 7226
Natura in urbe. Verse. E. B. White. 4:26 My26'28. 7227
Natural pictures. Prose. Alan Campbell. 9:85-6 O7'33. 7228
Nature in the raw. Verse. Margaret Fishback. 8:48 O22'32. 7229
Nature knows best. Verse. Ogden Nash. 12:22*Jy11'36. 7230
A nature lover comes to grief. Prose. Margaret Fishback. 3: 58 F18'28. 7231
The nature man. WATN. Richard O. Boyer. 14:21*Je18'38. 7232
Nature note. Verse. Mary Ballard Duryee. 15:59*My13'39. 7233
The nature student. Verse. Persis Greely Anderson. 6:26 Jy 26'30. 7234
Nature study. Verse. Margaret Fishback. 15:35*My27'39. 7235
Nature study. Verse. Philip G. Wylie. 2:59 S4'26. 7236
Naughty mens comed into my playroom. OSB. C. Knapp. 4: 20 F9'29. 7237
Navigation. Verse. E. B. White. 4:21 Jy14'28. 7238
The navigator. PP. Burke Boyce. 6:36 Jy5'30. 7239
The Navy's only mutiny. TWNY. A. J. Liebling. 15:35-8*F18 '39. 7240
Nazi meeting. RL. Richard O. Boyer. 13:39-46*N20'37. 7241
Neanderthal. PR (Loree). Dwight Macdonald. 9:20-3 Je3'33. 7242
Neap-tide. Verse. Gertrude Curtis Ryan. 3:99 O8'27. 7243
Near-and middle-east notes. OFC. John Gunther. 14:45*My21'38. 7244
The near-demise of Mrs. Coe. Prose. E. B. White. 7:15-16 F 21'31. 7245
A near thing. Prose. G. Schwabe. 4:55 D29'28. 7246
Neat. Prose. Theodore Pratt. 14: 37-8*Jy16'38. 7247
A necessary dirge. Verse. Ogden Nash. 11:24*S7'35. 7248
The neediest hundred. Prose. John Chapin Mosher. 2:25 Ja8 '27. 7249
A needle for Central Park. TWNY. Geoffrey T. Hellman. 14:22-8* S3'38. 7250
Negation. Prose. Stanley Jones. 2:55 S11'26. 7251
The neighbor ladies. Prose. Margaret Clark Williams. 11:68* Je8'35. 7252
Neither slumber nor sleep. Prose. Harold Standish Corbin. 1:24 Ag8'25. 7253
Nellie's Rest. RL. Morris Markey. 10:42-5 Jy21'34. 7254
Nephew. Prose. Spud Johnson. 2: 16 S4'26. 7255
The nervous wretch. Prose. Don-

ald Moffat. 5:27-8 D7'29. 7256
The Net. Prose. Robert M. Coates. 15:15-18*Ja27'40. 7257
Net. Verse. Kenneth Fearing. 15: 25*Ag12'39. 7258
Net results of travel. Verse. Elizabeth Wyckoff. 6:71 O11 '30. 7259
Never a dull moment. Prose. John O'Hara. 9:28-30 Jy8'33. 7260
Never a train. Prose. Katherine Sproehnle. 12:43-4*Ja2'37. 7261
Never mind how Mr. Billingsley is! Prose. Russell Maloney. 15:28-9*O28'39. 7262
Never the twain. Verse. A. K. Laing. 2:22 Ap10'26. 7263
Never to hear silence. Prose. William Maxwell. 13:22-3*D18 '37. 7264
Never trust a woman. Prose. Edward Newhouse. 15:56*Jy8'39. 7265
The new American body. Prose. Frank Sullivan. 13:15-16*S25 '37. 7266
A new apparatus. Prose. John O'Hara. 5:61-4 Ap6'29. 7267
New art. Verse. Bob Edwards. 2:20 Mr27'26. 7268
New business. Verse. Margaret Fishback. 5:55 Ag31'29. 7269
New champion. RL. Morris Markey. 10:46-8 Je23'34. 7270
The new conquistadores. Prose. Waldo Frank. 1:7-8 My2'25. 7271
The new crusade. PR (Sabin). Milton MacKaye. 8:20-4 O22 '32. 7272
New day. Prose. John O'Hara. 6:38-9 Ag23'30. 7273
New deal--city style. RL. Morris Markey. 9:53-7 Ja13'34. 7274
The new diplomacy. Prose. Percy Waxman. 3:72 Ja21'28. 7275
The new Earl Carroll Theatre. Prose. Creighton Peet. 7:81-2 S12'31. 7276
New England extract. Verse. Dilys Bennett Laing. 15:24*Ja20 '40. 7277
New England hills. Verse. David Morton. 11:27*Ap20'35. 7278
New England landscape. Verse. Ruth Lambert Jones. 5:21 Je22 '29. 7279
New England meeting house. Verse. Harold Trowbridge Pulsifer. 10:19 Jy28'34. 7280
New England pastoral. Verse. David Morton. 14:28*Ja7'39. 7281
The New England poets see a ghost. Verse. EE. 1:16 Mr28 '25. 7282
New ice. Verse. Olive Ward. 3:77 F11'28. 7283
The new inquisition. Prose. Gilbert Seldes. 1:17 F13'26. 7284
New inventions. Verse. Clarence Day. 10:25*D15'34. 7285
A New Jersey childhood. Verse. Edmund Wilson. 15:65-72*N18 '39. 7286
The new journalism. Prose. Walter Marquiss. 2:73 O9'26. 7287
New light on the Rothstein theory. Prose. Corey Ford. 5:23-4 Mr 2'29. 7288
The new masses. TT. 11:11-12* F8'36. 7289
The new office. Prose. John O'Hara. 6:112-14 My17'30. 7290
The new "old New York." Prose. Arthur H. Folwell. 1:10 Ag8 '25. 7291
New Orleans: Decatur Street. RL. John Peale Bishop. 11:40-4*Ja 11'36. 7292
A new parlor game. Prose. Fairfax Downey. 2:36 N6'26. 7293
The new play. Prose. Arthur Kober. 5:27-9 O5'29. 7294
New plays for old. Prose. Robert Benchley. 6:16 Mr8'30. 7295
New Post Road. RL. Niven Busch, Jr. 5:30-6 My25'29. 7296
A new Red Book. Prose. Arthur Kober. 3:26-7 O22'27. 7297
The new Roxy. RL. Hugh Blake. 8:48-56 D17'32. 7298
New shoes for baby. Prose. Philip

G. Wylie. 3:67-9 F19'27. 7299
The new snobbery. SM. Alexander Woollcott. 5:38 Mr23'29. 7300
The new subway. Verse. Burke Boyce. 4:26 N3'28. 7301
The new suitcase. Prose. Emily Hahn. 14:27*F19'38. 7302
The new telephone cordiality. Prose. Don Herold. 6:36-8 Mr 15'30. 7303
The new wing. Prose. Robert Benchley. 2:15 My15'26. 7304
New woman. PR (Smith). Helena Huntington Smith. 6:28-31 My 10'30. 7305
A new work for New York. Prose. Ruth Richards. 2:38 F27'26. 7306
The new world crisis. Prose. Frank Sullivan. 11:18-19*F16 '35. 7307
The New Yawker. Verse. Fred G. Steelman. 1:31 O24'25. 7308
New York. Prose. T. H. Bliss. 1:17 Mr14'25. 7309
New York--. Prose. Montague Glass. 6:40-4 O18'30. 7310
A New York adolescence. Prose. Lewis Mumford. 13:86-94*D4 '37. 7311
A New York adolescence. Prose. M. R. Werner. 14:43-9*F11 '39. 7312
A New York andante. Prose. Elizabeth Wyckoff. 2:26 F27 '26. 7313
New York as a Summer resort. Prose. C. Knapp. 1:21 S5'25. 7314
New York cats I have known--with one rat. Prose. Ferner Nuhn. 3:40-3 N5'27. 7315
A New York childhood. Prose. Babette Deutsch. 4:31-4 D15 '28. 7316
A New York childhood. Prose. Joseph Gollomb. 5:24-7 Ap13 '29. 7317
A New York childhood. Prose. Ernest Gruening. 5:27-9 Mr16 '29. 7318
A New York childhood. Prose. Elmer Rice. 4:19-21 S8'28; 4: 36-40 S22'28. 7319
New York--December, 1931. Verse. Babette Deutsch. 7:22 D12'31. 7320
New York drama critics. Robert Benchley. 13:26*Mr27'37. 7321
The New York girl. Verse. Anon. 1:31 N21'25; 1:32 N21'25. 7322
The New York girl. Verse. Anon. 1:28 D5'25. 7323
The New York girl. Verse. Anon. 1:42 D12'25. 7324
The New York girl. Verse. Anon. 1:35 Ja9'26. 7325
The New York girl. Verse. Fillmore Hyde. 1:10 N7'25. 7326
The New York girl. Verse. J. H. 1:39 N7'25. 7327
The New York girl. Verse. L. L. B. 1:25 N14'25. 7328
The New York girl. Verse. Fred G. Steelman. 1:35 O31'25. 7329
New York interiors: a broker's office. RL. Morris Markey. 3: 30-3 Ja14'28. 7330
New York interiors: broadcasting. RL. Morris Markey. 4:38-44 Ap14'28. 7331
New York interiors: the dance hall. RL. Morris Markey. 4:46-56 Ap 21'28. 7332
New York interiors: the flop house. RL. Morris Markey. 4:46-52 Mr31'28. 7333
New York interiors: the sale. RL. Morris Markey. 6:47-51 Ap19 '30. 7334
New York interiors: the store. RL. Morris Markey. 4:44-50 Mr17'28. 7335
New York is just a village. Prose. Margaret Case Harriman. 9:78-80 S23'33. 7336
The New York man. Verse. Anon. 1:27 Ja16'26. 7337
New York stuff. Verse. Margaret Searle. 2:35 Jy10'26. 7338
New York Thanksgiving. Verse. Isabel McLennan McMeekin. 4: 48 N24'28. 7339
New York--the perfect host. Prose.

Philip G. Wylie. 2:71-3 O30 '26. 7340
The New York Times Magazine Section. (Parody) James Thurber. 9:19-20 Ag5'23. 7341
New York to Florida. Prose. Theodore Pratt. 10:78-9*Ja5 '35. 7342
New York to Paris, 1908. TWNY. Donald Moffat. 11:37-42*F15 '36. 7343
The New York visit. Prose. Leane Zugsmith. 11:26-8*N16 '35. 7344
New Yorker. ME. Alfred Kreymborg. 3:30 Ap16'27. 7345
A New Yorker. Verse. Richard Peckham. 9:24 Ja20'34. 7346
The New-Yorker (1834). Morris Bishop. 11:72-5*Mr16'35. 7347
New Yorker in Chanak. OFC. Ik Shuman. 12:43*Jy11'36. 7348
A New Yorker in the provinces. Prose. Herman J. Mankiewicz. 1:16 F6'26. 7349
New Yorker, Newarker, or what have you? Prose. A. Amis. 1:28-9 O10'25. 7350
A New Yorker shows New York. Prose. Arthur H. Folwell. 3: 71 O15'27. 7351
A New Yorker shows New York. Prose. Arthur H. Folwell. 3: 115 N19'27. 7352
A New Yorker who sings. PR (Werrenrath). Clare Peeler. 1:9-10 O3'25. 7353
"The New Yorkerette." MM. Corey Ford. 1:25 O24'25. 7354
The New Yorker's chart room. MM. Corey Ford. 1:40 D5'25. 7355
The New Yorker's love. Verse. Joseph Moncure March. 2:38 Ap3'26. 7356
New York's own. DL. Burke Boyce. 2:57 O23'26. 7357
The newest Utopia. Verse. Clarence Day. 10:17*N24'34. 7358
News. Prose. Nunnally Johnson. 3:26 Mr26'27. 7359
News-breeding. WP. Robert Benchley. 6:51-5 Ap12'30. 7360
News flops. WP. Robert Benchley. 7:28-31 Ag29'31. 7361
News from the front. Verse. Rollin Kirby. 3:65 Mr19'27. 7362
News from the front. RL. Morris Markey. 1:18-19 Ja30'26. 7363
News from the seat of war. RL. Stella Benson. 8:34-40*Ap2'32. 7364
News from the wine country. Prose. Frank Schoonmaker. 9: 81-4 N4'33. 7365
News from the wine country. Prose. Frank Schoonmaker. 9: 44-50 D16'33. 7366
News from the wine country. Prose. Frank Schoonmaker. 9: 66-70 Ja13'34. 7367
News from the wine country. Prose. Frank Schoonmaker. 9: 70-5 F10'34. 7368
News from the wine country. Prose. Frank Schoonmaker. 10: 42-8 Ap28'34. 7369
News from the wine country. Prose. Frank Schoonmaker. 10: 66-72 My12'34. 7370
News from the wine country. Prose. Frank Schoonmaker. 10: 46-51 Je30'34. 7371
News galore. WP. Robert Benchley. 8:40-4 Je11'32. 7372
News is stranger than fiction. Prose. James Thurber. 6:21-2 Mr22'30. 7373
News, news, news. WP. Robert Benchley. 7:32-8*Je13'31. 7374
News notes. Verse. Nate Salisbury. 11:69*Ap6'35. 7375
News notes. Verse. Nate Salisbury. 11:34*Ap13'35. 7376
News notes. Verse. Nate Salisbury. 11:75*Ap27'35. 7377
News notes. Verse. Nate Salisbury. 11:65*My11'35. 7378
News notes. Verse. Nate Salisbury. 11:52*Je22'35. 7379
News of the day. Prose. James Thurber. 3:34 Ap2'27. 7380
News outside the door. RL. E. Bagworm Wren. 9:54-60 O28'33. 7381
News photographer. PR (Jackson).

Alva Johnston. 10:28-30*D1 '34; 10:28-31*D8'34. 7382

News pictures. Verse. Martha Banning Thomas. 6:53 Ap5'30. 7383

News-stand man. PP. Burke Boyce. 4:27 Ap28'28. 7384

The news, such as it is. WP. Robert Benchley. 4:30-4 S8'28. 7385

Newspaper crime report, 1950. Prose. Joseph Fulling Fishman. 1:29 F13'26. 7386

The newspaper man. Prose. Leonard Hall. 1:19 S5'25. 7387

Newspapers, movies, crime. Prose. Nate Salisbury. 1:11 Ag1'25. 7388

Newsreel. RL. Morris Markey. 10:88-98 S22'34. 7389

The next revival of "Pinafore." Prose. Corey Ford. 2:20 Je12 '26. 7390

Next to godliness. Prose. W. S.K. 11:73-4*Ap13'35. 7391

The next war. Prose. Frank Sullivan. 7:22-3 O3'31. 7392

Nice baby. Prose. Oliver Claxton. 2:24 Ja8'27. 7393

The nice cool sewer. Prose. Frank Sullivan. 2:21-2 Je5'26. 7394

The nice French people. Prose. Theodore Pratt. 10:18 Je30'34. 7395

Nice girl. Prose. Sherwood Anderson. 12:15-17*Jy25'36. 7396

The nice judge Trowbridge. Prose. Richard Lockridge. 13: 40*Ja29'38. 7397

A nickelodeon childhood. Prose. Robert Wohlforth. 10:42-8 My 12'34. 7398

Nico the baccarat king. Prose. Ferdinand Tuohy. 3:79-83 Ap2 '27. 7399

The nigger of the "Kingsway." RL. Morris Markey. 3:28-32 Ag20'27. 7400

Night and day. (Magazine) Janet Flanner. 13:64*D4'37. 7401

Night club. Verse. Nate Salisbury. 2:73 O30'26. 7402

Night club idyll. Prose. Edward E. Paramore, Jr. 2:53 F20'26. 7403

Night: downtown. RL. Morris Markey. 3:46-50 N19'27. 7404

The night grabber. Verse. Rollin Kirby. 2:78 N27'26. 7405

The night hawk. Verse. Gretta Palmer. 3:83 S17'27. 7406

A night in an inn. Verse. Margaret Fishback. 3:44 O8'27. 7407

A night in Bryant Park. Prose. Gilbert W. Gabriel. 1:18-19 D5 '25. 7408

The night Jean Harlow came to town. Prose. Eugene Joffe. 11: 30-4*Ag24'35. 7409

Night life of Mrs. Brickley. Prose. Wolcott Gibbs. 12:18-19*Je13 '36. 7410

The night my old man came home. Prose. Erskine Caldwell. 13: 24-6*D11'37. 7411

The night nurse. Prose. Babette Deutsch. 3:96-8 D17'27. 7412

Night of San Juan. Verse. Muna Lee. 7:20 S5'31. 7413

Night out. Prose. Robert Henderson. 15:46-7*Ja20'40. 7414

Night piece. Verse. Robert Hillyer. 11:16*Ag3'35. 7415

Night piece. Verse. Lindley Williams Hubbell. 15:24*Je3'39. 7416

Night scene. RL. Morris Markey. 10:31-4*D29'34. 7417

The night the bed fell. MLHT. James Thurber. 9:11-12 Jy8'33. 7418

The night the ghost got in. MLHT. James Thurber. 9:11-12 Ag12 '33. 7419

Night walk. Verse. Martha Banning Thomas. 8:22 O15'32. 7420

Night watchman. PP. Burke Boyce. 3:58 F18'28. 7421

Night, youth, Paris, and the moon. Prose. John Collier. 13:18-19* Ja1'38. 7422

Nightingales in Nassau Street. Verse. Kenneth Allan Robinson. 10:25 Je30'34. 7423

Nightmare. Verse. Martha Banning Thomas. 9:43 D23'33. 7424
Nightmare for future reference. Verse. Stephen Vincent Benét. 14:19-20*Ap2'38. 7425
Nightmare number three. Verse. Stephen Vincent Benét. 11:23* Jy27'35. 7426
Nightmare with angels. Verse. Stephen Vincent Benét. 11:17* My4'35. 7427
Nightmare, with moral. Verse. Lindley Williams Hubbell. 13: 39*D4'37. 7428
Nine days' wonder. Verse. Phyllis McGinley. 10:17 Jy14'34. 7429
The nine muses of Washington. Verse. Morris Bishop. 12:26* My16'36. 7430
Nine needles. Prose. James Thurber. 11:17-18*Ja25'36. 7431
1935. Verse. Stephen Vincent Benét. 11:25*Je29'35. 7432
1939. Verse. Harry Brown. 15: 21*Je24'39. 7433
1937. Verse. Harold Lewis Cook. 13:32*D4'37. 7434
Nineteen-thirty-two-which? Prose. Frank Sullivan. 7:15-16 S5'31. 7435
1923 model. Prose. Gertrude Carver. 7:71-2 S19'31. 7436
Ninety cents for a sardine. Prose. John O'Hara. 7:75*My 23'31. 7437
98¢. Verse. Dorothy Thompson. 9:80 Ja13'34. 7438
Ninety-second and Broadway. Prose. Robert M. Coates. 12: 18-19*My30'36. 7439
Nirvana is near Savannah. OFC. Margaret Case Harriman. 15: 32-9 F3'40. 7440
Nize Sam, ett opp all the G. O. P. PR (Koenig). Oliver H. P. Garrett. 2:15-16 Mr6'26. 7441
No! a thousand times, no! Prose. Frank Sullivan. 8:15-16*My7 '32. 7442
No answer. Verse. Hortense Flexner. 14:51*S10'38. 7443
No boundary. Verse. Frances M. Frost. 12:46*Ja16'37. 7444
No cocktails. Prose. John Chapin Mosher. 5:26-7 S21'29. 7445
No cow. Prose. Frances Warfield. 9:16-17 O28'33. 7446
No duels, drama, or bloodshed to speak of. Verse. Margaret Fishback. 4:30 N3'28. 7447
No hat. Prose. E. B. White. 2:28 N27'26. 7448
No headway at all. Verse. Margaret Fishback. 4:96 Ap21'28. 7449
No hero. PR (Rosendahl). Henry F. Pringle. 8:22-5*Mr26'32. 7450
No hope. Prose. Frances Crane. 8:64-6*F20'32. 7451
No jury would convict. Prose. Irwin Shaw. 13:56-8*O2'37. 7452
No ladies left. Prose. Frances Crane. 11:85-6*N16'35. 7453
No legs. Prose. Theodore Pratt. 6:26 Mr1'30. 7454
No liquor you'll find in our auto. OSB. C. Knapp. 5:20 Ag17'29. 7455
No miosis, please. SM. Alexander Woollcott. 8:34*Ap23'32. 7456
No mistakes. Prose. John O'Hara. 14:18-20*S17'38. 7457
No moral turpitude. RL. Henry F. Pringle. 7:36-43 Ja23'32. 7458
No more biographies. Prose. James Thurber. 8:16*Mr19'32. 7459
No more card tricks. Prose. Richard J. Mayer. 5:100-101 My25'29. 7460
No more lawyers. PR (Olvany). Alva Johnston. 7:22-5 Ja9'32. 7461
No more muzzins. Prose. Reed Johnston. 4:26-7 Ag25'28. 7462
No more rainy Sundays. Prose. Margaret Fishback. 4:91 My12 '28. 7463
No movies then. Prose. Clarence Day. 12:22-4*O31'36. 7464
No news is no news. WP. Robert

Benchley. 4:38-44 O20'28. 7465
No one but Grandma will do. Verse. C. Knapp. 3:34 F19'27. 7466
No pictures, please! Verse. Leslie Nelson Jennings. 8:84 N5 '32. 7467
No questions asked. Prose. Robert A. Simon. 3:96 Mr19'27. 7468
No reply yet. Prose. E. B. White. 2:17 Ja15'27. 7469
No rest for the weary. Verse. Margaret Fishback. 4:26 S8 '28. 7470
No sale. Verse. Richard Armour. 15:42*Ag26'39. 7471
No shampoo today, Louis. Verse. Ogden Nash. 9:15 Ap22'33. 7472
No singe for Mr. Tissock. Prose. Frank Sullivan. 5:17-18 Ja18 '30. 7473
No snow. Verse. Harriett Brownell. 9:25 Mr4'33. 7474
No sooner said. Prose. John O'Hara. 13:13-14*Jy31'37. 7475
No standing room only. Prose. James Thurber. 13:21-2*Mr 20'37. 7476
No star. Verse. Arthur Guiterman. 7:20 Ja9'32. 7477
No starch. Prose. Fleta Campbell Springer. 15:20-2*F18 '39. 7478
No suave inflections. PR (Olsen and Johnson). A. J. Liebling. 14:20-5*Ja28'39. 7479
No tears, no good. Prose. Ruth McKenney. 13:81-4*My15'37. 7480
No traffic tower to guide her. Verse. Margaret Fishback. 4: 85 Ja5'29. 7481
No trouble to show goods. Prose. Frank Sullivan. 7:13-14*Jy18 '31. 7482
No whipped cream. Prose. Frances Crane. 12:34-9*Ja23'37. 7483
No wonder our fathers died. Verse. Ogden Nash. 12:27*D 12'36. 7484
Noah's dove. Verse. Laura Benét. 3:21 My21'27. 7485
Noble merchandise. PR (Duveen). Alva Johnston. 4:29-31 Ap21'28. 7486
Noblesse oblige. Prose. Robert Benchley. 8:45 D24'32. 7487
Noblesse oblige. PR (Roosevelt). Helena Huntington Smith. 6:23-5 Ap5'30. 7488
Noblesse oblige. Verse. Mildred Weston. 15:73*Je3'39. 7489
Nobody goes there. Prose. Frances Crane. 10:57-8 O27'34. 7490
Nobody paid to ride. Prose. Sally Lockwood. 11:27-8*Ag24'35. 7491
Nobody's burden. Prose. Hildegarde Angell. 3:61-2 F19'27. 7492
Nobody's darling. Verse. Margaret Fishback. 5:40 D21'29. 7493
Nocturne. Verse. Persis Greely Anderson. 6:58 S20'30. 7494
Nocturne. Verse. Brownell Carr. 2:54 My1'26. 7495
Nocturne. Verse. Frances M. Frost. 10:115*D15'34. 7496
Nocturne. Prose. Oliver Jenkins. 5:20 Ag10'29. 7497
Nocturne. RL. Morris Markey. 6:32-7 Ag9'30. 7498
Nocturne for April. Verse. Philip G. Wylie. 2:44 Ap3'26. 7499
Nocturne in Beekman Place. Prose. Frank Sullivan. 6:23-4 N22'30. 7500
Noël. Verse. Phyllis McGinley. 11:26*D14'35. 7501
Noel Coward and Mrs. Griffen. Prose. Ruth McKenney. 14:16-18*Ap2'38. 7502
The noise was terrible. Prose. Winifred Willis. 14:52*Ap30'38. 7503
Noises you don't hear any more. Prose. Well known broker. 1: 29 Ap25'25. 7504
Nomination. Verse. M. B. 14:74* O22'38. 7505
Nonchalance. Verse. Richard Ar-

mour. 15:52*Ja13'40. 7506
Nonconformist. Prose. Angelica Gibbs. 9:53 Je17'33. 7507
The nonentity guild. Prose. David Cort. 1:9-10 N21'25. 7508
Nonresistance. Verse. Gustave Lobrano. 11:79*Ap20'35. 7509
Nonsense. Verse. Lee Wilson Dodd. 6:88 Mr29'30. 7510
Non-stop. Prose. Corey Ford. 3:30 N26'27. 7511
The noon telephone operator. Prose. Robert Benchley. 6:22 F22'30. 7512
Nor gloom of night. Prose. Beverly L. Clarke. 12:45-7*Ag8 '36. 7513
Norris, Kathleen. TT. 6:8-9 Ag2 '30. 7514
North America in ferment. Prose. James Thurber. 6:27-8 S27 '30. 7515
North of Boston. PR (Frost). Raymond Holden. 7:24-7*Je6 '31. 7516
A North River crossing. Verse. Carroll Carroll. 5:32 Je1'29. 7517
North Star. Verse. Elizabeth Coatsworth. 9:36 Je10'33. 7518
Northern lights. Verse. Robert Hillyer. 14:18*Jy16'38. 7519
Northern Spring. Verse. Martha Banning Thomas. 10:55 My5'34. 7520
The Norths and the drunk. Prose. Richard Lockridge. 15:90-2*D9 '39. 7521
The Norths go masked. Prose. Richard Lockridge. 14:64-5*O 15'38. 7522
The nose. Verse. Persis Greely Anderson. 8:24 Je18'32. 7523
Nose-gay. Verse. Spud Johnson. 2:71 F5'27. 7524
Nostalgia. Verse. Ruth Lambert Jones. 4:72 F16'29. 7525
Nostalgic note from Dubuque, etc. Verse. Oliver Jenkins. 4:41 Je2'28. 7526
The nostrils of G. B. S. SM. Alexander Woollcott. 9:30 F18 '33. 7527
Not a finger. Prose. Leo Rosten. 15:32-5*Ag19'39. 7528
Not even Ellen Terry. SM. Alexander Woollcott. 7:32 Ja9'32. 7529
Not in forty miles. Prose. Richard Lockridge. 10:21-2 Je2'34. 7530
Not in this valley. Verse. George Allen. 15:15*Jy29'39. 7531
Not more perfect than his fellows. Prose. Dorothea Castelhun. 6:86-8 My24'30. 7532
Not of this world. Prose. James Reid Parker. 11:75*Ap13'35. 7533
Not precisely a book review. Verse. Grace Hazard Conkling. 4:71 D15'28. 7534
Not quite gone are the days. RL. A. J. Liebling. 13:36-40*Jy31 '37. 7535
Not so black. Prose. Henrietta Fort Holland. 10:60-1 Je16'34. 7536
Not so many parades. Verse. Philip G. Wylie. 2:41 Ag14'26. 7537
A not-so-petit chanson. Verse. Sidney Skolsky. 3:64 N26'27. 7538
The not-so-strange story of little Hazel's Xmas. Verse. Stuart Hyde Hawkins. 2:34 D11'26. 7539
Not so very Grimm. Prose. Oliver Claxton. 3:89 N12'27. 7540
Not that. Verse. Anon. 1:16 F6'26. 7541
Not through the iron duke. Prose. Horton Heath. 12:60-2*Mr7'36. 7542
Not to reason why. Prose. Zelda F. Popkin. 13:23-4*Mr6'37. 7543
Not together. Prose. James Thurber. 4:73 Mr3'28. 7544
Note. Verse. Dorothy Dow. 4:107 N17'28. 7545
Note at Fifth Avenue and Twenty-sixth Street. Verse. W. S. K. 8:54 O29'32. 7546
A note for my last testament.

Mary Heaton Vorse. 8:34-6 S17'32. 7585
Notice is hereby given. Verse. Ruth Fitch Bartlett. 3:17 Je4 '27. 7586
Noun quack. Prose. F. Emerson Andrews. 10:104-105*D8'34. 7587
Nous, étrangers à Paris. Prose. H. E. S. 1:20 My9'25. 7588
Nouveau. Verse. Anon. 2:45 S11 '26. 7589
Novel, History of. Robert M. Coates. 8:67-8*F20'32. 7590
Novel, Modern. Robert M. Coates. 7:59-60*Je20'31. 7591
Novel, Modern. Robert M. Coates. 7:61-2*Je27'31. 7592
Novel, Proletarian. James Thurber. 10:17-18 Je9'34. 7593
November. Verse. Herman Fetzer. 9:20 N4'33. 7594
November. Verse. Phyllis McGinley. 10:22 N10'34. 7595
November. Verse. Miriam Vedder. 7:27 N28'31. 7596
November evening. Verse. Grace Hazard Conkling. 4:38 N3'28. 7597
November evening. Verse. Marjorie Allen Seiffert. 8:65 N26 '32. 7598
November portent. Verse. Leslie Nelson Jennings. 7:59 N28'31. 7599
Now for the big stuff. WP. Robert Benchley. 4:40-6 N10'28. 7600
Now go on with the story. Prose. Joseph Fulling Fishman. 3:62-4 Ap16'27. 7601
Now I ask you. SM. Alexander Woollcott. 9:28 Je24'33. 7602
Now I can eat pickles. Prose. Ruth McKenney. 15:25-7*My6 '39. 7603
Now it can be told. Prose. Elmer Davis. 2:23-4 O16'26. 7604
Now kiss your wife. Prose. Leslie Moore. 7:38-40 O24'31. 7605
Now take my case--. Prose. Dorothy Mills Emery. 7:49 N21'31. 7606
Now that I'm organized. Prose. E. B. White. 3:19-20 N5'27. 7607
Now that that's over. WP. Robert Benchley. 5:50-4 N9'29. 7608
Now that there's beer. RL. Morris Markey. 9:46-50 Ap15'33. 7609
Now that you're tanned--what? Prose. Robert Benchley. 5:23 S14'29. 7610
"Now through days . . ." Verse. Anon. 3:77 Mr26'27. 7611
Now with the bloom. Verse. Florence Kiper Frank. 6:55 Ap 12'30. 7612
Nuance. Prose. Patricia Collinge. 6:36-8 O18'30. 7613
Nuit blanche. Prose. Alice Frankforter. 4:48-9 Ja26'29. 7614
Nuit de Noël. Prose. Alice Frankforter. 4:14-15 D22'28. 7615
No. 9 Lexington Avenue. RL. Geoffrey T. Hellman. 14:38-45*O29 '38. 7616
No. 1 Picaroon. PR (Dilley). Richard O. Boyer. 15:24-30*S2'39. 7617
Nunc pro tunc. SM. Alexander Woollcott. 5:48 N16'29. 7618
Nursery cavalcade. Prose. G. B. Stern. 12:16-17*F29'36. 7619
Nursery rhyme. Verse. Clarence Day. 10:17*Ja26'35. 7620
Nursery rhyme. Verse. Phyllis McGinley. 15:20*Je17'39. 7621

O

O. Henry. TT. 4:14 Ap28'28. 7622
O. Henry Award Stories, 1934. Clifton Fadiman. 10:87-8*N24 '34. 7623
O hunting heart! Verse. Marjorie Allen Seiffert. 9:33 N18'33. 7624
O. K., Parnassus. Verse. Phyllis McGinley. 10:20 Mr10'34. 7625
O. K. to go ahead. Prose. E. B. White. 4:18-20 F9'29. 7626
O K·A·P·L·A·N My K·A·P·L·A·N!

Prose. Leo Rosten. 13:17-19* F27'37. 7627

O lovely rain. Verse. Rachel Field. 10:36 My19'34. 7628

O pity poets. Verse. Jacqueline Embry. 4:46 Ap7'28. 7629

O rich content. Verse. Louis Untermeyer. 11:19*Mr2'35. 7630

O tempora, o mores. Verse. Mildred Weston. 10:52 F24'34. 7631

The oak. Verse. Harold Lewis Cook. 12:32*D5'36. 7632

Oath. Verse. Mildred Weston. 7:54 F21'31. 7633

Obit. RL. Morris Markey. 7:40-4 Mr14'31. 7634

Obit on Parnassus. Verse. F. Scott Fitzgerald. 13:27*Je5'37. 7635

Obituary. Prose. E. B. White. 8:16*Mr12'32. 7636

Obituary. SM. Alexander Woollcott. 5:54 S28'29. 7637

Obituary note. Verse. Leslie Nelson Jennings. 3:58 F26'27. 7638

Obituary of a gin mill. RL. Joseph Mitchell. 14:30-7*Ja7 '39. 7639

Objects for common telescopes in the metropolitan district. Prose. Ralph Barton. 4:22-4 My19'28. 7640

Oboes aweigh. Prose. Donald Ogden Stewart. 4:19-20 O20 '28. 7641

O'Brien, Edward J. TT. 15:7* Ag5'39. 7642

Observance. Prose. Stanley Jones. 5:89-90 Ap20'29. 7643

Observation. Verse. Sara Henderson Hay. 7:21 N14'31. 7644

Observation. Verse. E. B. White. 10:16*D29'34. 7645

Observation from a high point. Verse. Thomas Sugrue. 11:28*Mr30'35. 7646

Observation in an Italian restaurant. Verse. Anon. 3:121 D10'27. 7647

"Observe the conventions." Verse. Olive Ward. 4:119 D1 '28. 7648

"Observe the elevatorette . . ." Verse. Fairfax Downey. 1:45 Ja 23'26. 7649

Obsolete. Prose. Frances Crane. 12:83-5*N21'36. 7650

Obstacle race. Verse. Margaret Fishback. 8:36 Jy30'32. 7651

O'Casey, Sean. Anthony Gibbs. 5:72-3 N16'29. 7652

Occupational diseases. Prose. Edith Owen. 11:50*Mr16'35. 7653

Occurance on the six-seventeen. Prose. George Shepherd. 15:31-2*D23'39. 7654

The ocean came over. Prose. John Chapin Mosher. 14:39-40* D24'38. 7655

Ocean swells. Prose. Nancy Hoyt. 4:34 My5'28. 7656

Ochs, Adolph Simon. PR. Elmer Davis. 1:11-12 N21'25. 7657

October madness. Prose. John Chapin Mosher. 9:23-4 O7'33. 7658

October swimming. Verse. Henry Morton Robinson. 8:18 O8'32. 7659

Octogenarians to the front. Prose. John Chapin Mosher. 2:16 Je19 '26. 7660

Odd Mondays and even Tuesdays. Prose. Frank Sullivan. 5:25-6 N23'29. 7661

Odds. Prose. Parke Cummings. 10:88-9 O27'34. 7662

Odds and evens. RL. Morris Markey. 4:32-8 Je9'28. 7663

Odd's bodkins. Prose. Ring Lardner. 9:21-2 O7'33. 7664

Ode for an epoch. Verse. William Rose Benét. 8:23 Ja28'33. 7665

Ode for the poetry society. Verse. Anon. 3:77 Ap9'27. 7666

Ode on a public menace. Verse. D'Annunzio Cohen. 4:66 Mr31 '28. 7667

Ode on the dedication of the new zoo. Verse. Arthur Guiterman. 10:75*D8'34. 7668

Ode, or something, on the opening of the Sheepfold Restaurant

in Central Park. Verse. Arthur Guiterman. 10:36 N3'34. 7669
Ode to a new hotel. Verse. Morris Bishop. 7:27 O24'31. 7670
Ode to a new typewriter. Verse. Martha Banning Thomas. 3:67 N19'27. 7671
Ode to C. B. E. Verse. Ogden Nash. 11:23*Ag31'35. 7672
Ode to Mr. Zimmerman. Verse. Phyllis McGinley. 9:18 Ag5'33. 7673
Ode to Peter Stuyvesant. Verse. Philip G. Wylie. 5:74 N2'29. 7674
Ode to Rockefeller Center. Verse. Arthur Guiterman. 10:51 Je30 '34. 7675
Ode to Summer. Verse. Marjorie Allen Seiffert. 6:49 Ag23'30. 7676
Ode to the amoeba. Verse. Arthur Guiterman. 8:76 N5'32. 7677
Ode to the bath. Verse. Phyllis McGinley. 15:25*Mr4'39. 7678
Ode to the end of Summer. Verse. Phyllis McGinley. 14:27*S24 '38. 7679
Ode to the Hayden Planetarium. Verse. Arthur Guiterman. 14: 55*Je25'38. 7680
Odets, Clifford. PR. John McCarten. 13:21-7*Ja22'38. 7681
Odets, Clifford. TT. 12:15*Mr21 '36. 7682
Odets, Clifford. TT. 13:13*N27 '37. 7683
Odets, Clifford. (Parody) S. J. Perelman. 12:17-18*D26'36. 7684
Odyssey of bus no. 805. Prose. Carroll Carroll. 2:105-107 D4'26. 7685
Oedipus editing. WP. Robert Benchley. 10:42-5 My5'34. 7686
Of a child going to sleep. Verse. Frances M. Frost. 7:23*Ag1 '31. 7687
Of all things difficult to bear. Verse. Helene Mullins. 8:21 D3'32. 7688
Of booze. RL. Morris Markey. 1:13-14 D26'25. 7689
Of course I'm sick of him. Prose. Emily Hahn. 8:26-7 D3'32. 7690
Of Sinclair Lewis and Dr. McGrady. Prose. Brendan Gill. 12:42-4*D26'36. 7691
Of stars one night. Verse. Lenora Speyer. 14:20*Jy9'38. 7692
Of thee I sing. SM. Alexander Woollcott. 8:32*Mr26'32. 7693
Of thee I sing, Baby. PR (Grayce), John O'Hara. 8:23-5 O15'32. 7694
Off balance. Prose. Sherwood Anderson. 9:12-14 Ag5'33. 7695
Offer. Verse. Dearing Ward. 3:53 N5'27. 7696
Office-boy of destiny. PR (Zolotow). Alexander Woollcott. 4:28-30 O 13'28. 7697
The office switchboard. Prose. John O'Hara. 7:79-80 Ap25'31. 7698
Office visitor. Verse. Paul G. Gumbinner. 4:101 Ap7'28. 7699
Office window--February. Verse. Philip G. Wylie. 3:48 F26'27. 7700
The office window washer. Verse. Margaret Fishback. 3:40 Ap16 '27. 7701
An official gentlemen's guide to lawn tennis. Prose. Paul Gould. 3:55-6 Jy9'27. 7702
The official yachting cap. Prose. Robert Benchley. 3:38 Je18'27. 7703
Oft in the stilly night. Prose. Henrietta Fort Holland. 13:50* Mr27'37. 7704
"Oh, Amos Cottle." SM. Alexander Woollcott. 9:34 N4'33. 7705
Oh, burglar! Verse. Ellen McLoughlin. 7:34 S12'31. 7706
"Oh, curses on the landlord's laws . . ." Verse. Anon. 2:70 O30'26. 7707
Oh, Doctor. Verse. Wilfred J.

Funk. 5:33 F1'30. 7708
Oh, fire! Prose. Janet Flanner. 8:19-20 N5'32. 7709
Oh happy day. Verse. Margaret Fishback. 4:62 Je30'28. 7710
Oh, he's charming! Prose. Dorothy Parker. 2:22-3 O9'26. 7711
Oh, I know him. Prose. Oliver Claxton. 3:57 O15'27. 7712
Oh, Mr. Gershwin! Prose. Charles L. Buchanan. 1:23-5 D19'25. 7713
Oh . . . Monday! Verse. Katharine D. Morse. 4:56 Ap21'28. 7714
Oh, no, pioneers. Verse. Phyllis McGinley. 11:21*O12'35. 7715
Oh, pioneers. Prose. Richard Lockridge. 11:35-7*Ag31'35. 7716
Oh pioneers. Prose. John Chapin Mosher. 3:59-61 N26'27. 7717
Oh teacher! Verse. Fillmore Hyde. 1:29 Ja16'26. 7718
Oh, those tropic nights! Prose. Benedict Thielen. 15:18-20* Mr4'39. 7719
Oh, when I was . . . FPI. James Thurber. 15:23*Je3'39. 7720
The old. Verse. Martha Banning Thomas. 6:76 Mr1'30. 7721
Old acquaintance. Prose. T. H. Wenning. 11:51-2*Ja25'36. 7722
Old Adam. Verse. Harold Willard Gleason. 5:18 Ag3'29. 7723
Old age in summer. Verse. Martha Banning Thomas. 15:60*Ag 26'39. 7724
The old bar book. Verse. Arthur Guiterman. 3:63 Jy9'27. 7725
Old bones. Verse. Marjorie Allen Seiffert. 6:25 Je21'30. 7726
Old bottles. Prose. John Chapin Mosher. 2:36 S4'26. 7727
Old boy. Prose. John O'Hara. 6: 28 O18'30. 7728
An old colloquy. Verse. Witter Bynner. 2:52 N6'26. 7729
The old countess. Prose. Frances Crane. 13:102-106*D4'37. 7730
Old couple. ME. Alfred Kreymborg. 3:20 Je11'27. 7731
Old debbil politics. Prose. C. Knapp. 2:31 O23'26. 7732
Old Dick and young Dick. PR (Glendon). Robert F. Kelley. 4: 25-7 Je16'28. 7733
Old divinity. Verse. Louise Bogan. 5:35 D14'29. 7734
The old Dumas market. Prose. Frances Woodward Prentice. 9:67-9 S23'33. 7735
The old familiar places. Verse. Charles Hanson Towne. 4:50 My 19'28. 7736
Old-fashioned dances for an old-fashioned girl. Verse. C. Knapp. 2:73 Ja8'27. 7737
Old-fashioned poem with some sense in it. Verse. Samuel Hoffenstein. 6:18 Ag23'30. 7738
The old friends. Prose. James Thurber. 11:16-18*Mr23'35. 7739
The old gay mare. Prose. Frank Sullivan. 7:17-18*Ag8'31. 7740
Old giant. Verse. Ethel Kelley. 3: 64 Ja21'28. 7741
The old guard. Prose. Stanley Jones. 8:36-7 Je25'32. 7742
The old guard passes. Prose. Etaoin Shrdlu. 1:15 F21'25. 7743
Old Hays. TWNY. Herbert Asbury. 8:36-43*Ap23'32. 7744
Old house. Verse. Virginia Woods Bellamy. 14:33*Jy16'38. 7745
Old house. Verse. Paula Lecler. 6:46 Je14'30. 7746
The old inhabitant laments. Verse. Leslie Nelson Jennings. 3:93 Mr12'27. 7747
Old ladies. Prose. Mary Heaton Vorse. 6:18 D27'30. 7748
The old lady. Prose. Thyra Samter Winslow. 3:14-15 Jy23'27. 7749
Old love. Prose. John Chapin Mosher. 7:21-2 N21'31. 7750
An old love. Prose. Mark Schorer. 15:23-4*Ap15'39. 7751
Old maid. Verse. C. Lee Quong. 6:27 My3'30. 7752
The old man. Prose. A. J. Liebling.

13:21-2*S11'37. 7753
The old man. PR (Football coach). John R. Tunis. 5:30-2 N23'29. 7754
Old man Hoppergrass. Verse. Stephen Vincent Benét. 12:77* My9'36. 7755
Old man liver. Prose. Ring Lardner. 6:17-19 Ja3'31. 7756
Old man March. Prose. Robert M. Coates. 13:15-17*Mr27'37. 7757
Old man on the avenue. Verse. Dearing Ward. 3:58 D3'27. 7758
An old man rides away. Prose. Tom F. Barry. 4:114-15 O13 '28. 7759
The old man shows his air mail. OW. Ring Lardner. 9:75-7 Ap 8'33. 7760
An old man thinks of his first ball. Verse. Martha Banning Thomas. 7:30 N28'31. 7761
The old masters. Verse. Joseph Alger. 10:60 Jy28'34. 7762
Old men and young men. Verse. John Holmes. 10:26 S8'34. 7763
Old Mrs. Pearce. Prose. Horton Heath. 10:59-61*Ja12'35. 7764
Old numbers are best. Prose. Reed Johnston. 4:73-4 N3'28. 7765
The old open busses. Verse. E. B. White. 13:24*My22'37. 7766
The old order. Prose. Weare Holbrook. 2:83-4 Je5'26. 7767
The old order changeth for the better. Verse. Margaret Fishback. 4:40 S29'28. 7768
The old prince. Prose. Stella Benson. 8:18-20 O15'32. 7769
Old rhyme revised. Verse. William T. F. George. 7:21 Ag29 '31. 7770
Old roads of Long Island. Prose. E. B. White. 9:20 Jy15'33. 7771
An old schoolmate. Prose. Carroll Carroll. 5:81-2 My25'29. 7772
The old woman. Prose. Donald Moffat. 13:33-6*Je19'37. 7773
The old woman rests her finger on Matthew 6:20. Verse. Martha Banning Thomas. 9:19 S2 '33. 7774
Old year's night. Verse. Spud Johnson. 2:20 Ja1'27. 7775
Olde Englysshe telephone curse. Verse. Arthur Guiterman. 12: 32*Je6'36. 7776
Olive. Prose. John O'Hara. 11:13-15*Ag17'35. 7777
Oliver shops for Christmas. Verse. Phyllis McGinley. 10:58*D15'34. 7778
Oliver understands women. Verse. Phyllis McGinley. 11:72*N23 '35. 7779
Olympian. Verse. Frances M. Frost. 5:28 O19'29. 7780
The Olympian eye. RL. Ben Hecht. 3:36-8 Ap30'27. 7781
Omar up to date. Verse. E. J. Bruen. 1:16 Je6'25. 7782
The omelet of A. MacLeish. PR (MacLeish). Edmund Wilson. 14: 23-4*Ja14'39. 7783
Omnia vanitas. Verse. Edmund J. Kiefer. 1:27 Mr21'25. 7784
On a certain type of Yuletide fiction. Verse. Sara Henderson Hay. 7:79 D19'31. 7785
On a new leaf. Verse. Margaret Fishback. 3:68 Ja14'28. 7786
On advice of counsel. Prose. Joseph Fulling Fishman. 2:38-40 D18'26. 7787
On argument. Verse. Marjorie Allen Seiffert. 7:23*Je13'31. 7788
On being a lady in Virginia. Prose. Marion Sturges-Jones. 15:57-8* Mr4'39. 7789
On breaking into the doctor's office. Prose. Seymour Barnard. 2:50-2 My1'26. 7790
On Brooklyn Heights. Verse. Seymour Barnard. 7:48 N28'31. 7791
On exchanging confidences. Verse. Marjorie Allen Seiffert. 9:32 D16'33. 7792
On finding a snake, with its head crushed. Verse. Sara Henderson Hay. 6:51 Je28'30. 7793

On finishing some memoirs. Verse. Baird Leonard. 9:22 D2'33. 7794
On going to Potzl. Verse. Sevier Payne. 7:39 D26'31. 7795
On helping a young man select a necktie for a party to which I, unfortunately, am not invited. Verse. Margaret Fishback. 3:92 N26'27. 7796
On high hill. Verse. Sally Benson. 14:12-15*Jy23'38. 7797
On his hands. Prose. John O'Hara. 6:62-4 Mr22'30. 7798
On learning that the reservoir is to be obliterated. Verse. Babette Deutsch. 5:27 N16'29. 7799
On my toes. Verse. Margaret Fishback. 9:51 F3'34. 7800
On Ninth Avenue. Prose. Walter Taegen. 4:66-7 F25'28. 7801
On not being invited to a party. Verse. Mildred Weston. 12:42* N21'36. 7802
On not reading the newspapers. Prose. Elmer Davis. 2:28 Je5 '26. 7803
On quixotic husbands. Verse. Marjorie Allen Seiffert. 9:58 D2'33. 7804
On radio announcers. Prose. John Tasker Howard. 4:68-70 O20 '28. 7805
On reaching years of discretion. Verse. Margaret Fishback. 3: 76 Je4'27. 7806
On reading a new accident policy. Verse. Anon. 2:52 My1'26. 7807
On reading Ovid's Metamorphoses. Verse. Wilfred J. Funk. 8:50* Mr12'32. 7808
On refusing a handsome offer. Verse. Margaret Fishback. 4: 26 S1'28. 7809
On remaining in town over Sunday. Verse. Charles Hanson Towne. 4:48 Ag11'28. 7810
On rudeness. RL. Morris Markey. 3:32-6 O22'27. 7811
On St. Valentine's day. Verse. Irma Brandeis. 7:51 F13 '32. 7812
On saying goodbye to a favorite roadster. Verse. Martha Banning Thomas. 2:65 Ja22'27. 7813
On seeing a grasshopper, beside a monument. Verse. Sara Henderson Hay. 7:18*Jy25'31. 7814
On superstition. Verse. Marjorie Allen Seiffert. 7:57 O24'31. 7815
On taxi drivers. SM. Alexander Woollcott. 5:41 Mr30'29. 7816
On the banks of the Wabash. Prose. Elmer Davis. 2:13-14 Je26'26. 7817
On the beach. Verse. Robert P. Tristram Coffin. 14:16*Je18'38. 7818
On the bridge. Verse. Clinch Calkins. 3:36 D10'27. 7819
On the bus. Prose. Hornet. 1:13 Je20'25. 7820
On the bus. Verse. Philip G. Wylie. 2:39 Je26'26. 7821
On the bus in the Bronx. Prose. Arthur Kober. 11:63-4*Je15'35. 7822
On the edge. Prose. Francis Steegmuller. 10:82-3*D1'34. 7823
On the ineptitude of a simile of Coleridges. Verse. Franklin P. Adams. 14:35*D3'38. 7824
On the other hand. Prose. G. Schwabe. 4:56-7 D15'28. 7825
On the road. Prose. Niven Busch, Jr. 6:23-5 S13'30. 7826
On the sands of time. SM. Alexander Woollcott. 6:32 My24'30. 7827
"On the seat of a cream-colored cabriolet . . ." Verse. M. M. 3:78 O22'27. 7828
On the serious use of troutflies. Prose. Dearing Ward. 3:69-70 D3'27. 7829
On the square. PR (Klein). Milton MacKaye. 8:17-21 Je25'32. 7830
On the sub or unconscious mind. Prose. Jack Cluett. 4:80-1 N3 '28. 7831
On the up. PR (Harvey). Richard F. Warner. 6:24-7 My31

Patricia Collinge. 10:27*D29 '34. 7910
Open-letters department. Prose. Patricia Collinge. 11:71-2*N16 '35. 7911
Open letters department. Verse. Arthur Guiterman. 8:21 Jy16 '32. 7912
Open-letters department. Verse. Arthur Guiterman. 8:38 N26 '32. 7913
Open-letters department. Verse. Arthur Guiterman. 10:87 Ap28 '34. 7914
Open-letters department. Prose. William A. Krauss. 13:68-9* Mr20'37. 7915
Open-letters department. Prose. Richard Lockridge. 9:59-61 F25'33. 7916
Open-letters department. Prose. Richard Lockridge. 9:26 My6 '33. 7917
Open-letters department. Prose. Richard Lockridge. 9:102-104 D9'33. 7918
Open-letters department. Prose. Donald Moffat. 9:24-8 Jy1'33. 7919
Open-letters department. Prose. Frank Sullivan. 9:15-16 Ap29 '33. 7920
Open-letters department. Prose. Ann Terwilliger. 8:34 Ag6'32. 7921
Open letters [to my college]. Prose. Frances Warfield. 8:17 Je18'32. 7922
Open letters to public servants. Prose. Richard Lockridge. 7: 35-8 O31'31. 7923
Open reply to Mrs. Mendelson. Prose. E. B. White. 4:14 D22 '28. 7924
Open sesame. Prose. Alice Frankforter. 6:65-6 My3'30. 7925
Opened by mistake. WP. Robert Benchley. 6:50-4 S6'30. 7926
Opening an account. Prose. John Chapin Mosher. 2:13 Ag7'26. 7927
Opening guns. WP. Robert Benchley. 4:28-34 Ag18'28. 7928
"Opening his case Cyril selected a cigaret." Prose. Fairfax Downey. 1:31 F21'25. 7929
The opening night. Prose. Arthur Kober. 4:29-30 N10'28. 7930
Opening night wires. Prose. Arthur Kober. 3:112-13 Ap9'27. 7931
Opera and the dean. PR (Henderson). Hollister Noble. 2:23-5 O30'26. 7932
Opera box. Prose. Spud Johnson. 2:36-8 Ja22'27. 7933
Opera crashing made easier. Prose. Francis Steegmuller. 4:63-4 Mr31'28. 7934
The opera hat. Prose. John Chapin Mosher. 3:22 N5'27. 7935
Opera hats. Prose. The eskimo. 1:23 F28'25. 7936
Opera hats. Prose. H. A. M. 1:12 Mr7'25. 7937
The opera-house slugger. WATN. A. J. Liebling. 13:28-32*O30 '37. 7938
The opera is here. Prose. W. J. Henderson. 1:7-8 O31'25. 7939
Opera lunch. Prose. Fillmore Hyde. 2:23 N13'26. 7940
Opera season opens. Prose. Newman Levy. 1:30 N14'25. 7941
Opera through glasses. TWNY. Russel Crouse. 4:36-42 N17'28; 4:38-46 N24'28. 7942
Operating the pneumatic air tubes. MM. Corey Ford. 1:1 N21'25. 7943
Operative No. 174 resigns. Verse. Kenneth Fearing. 15:19*Ag26'39. 7944
The opportunists. Verse. Elizabeth Coatsworth. 4:32 N3'28. 7945
Opportunities for ambitious New Yorkers. Prose. Joseph Fulling Fishman. 2:60-1 My22'26. 7946
Opportunities for New Yorkers. Prose. Joseph Fulling Fishman. 2:59-60 Je5'26. 7947
The optimist. Verse. Miriam Vedder. 7:80 Ap25'31. 7948
Or so they say. SM. Alexander Woollcott. 9:34 D2'33. 7949
Or so they tell me. SM. Alexander

Woollcott. 10:28 Je30'34. 7950
Oracle hour speaking. Verse. Horace Gregory. 15:29*N18'39. 7951
Orchard interview. Verse. Henry Morton Robinson. 7:18 N21'31. 7952
Orchard Street. Verse. Philip Pratt. 2:47 Mr27'26. 7953
Orchestra notes. Verse. Melville Cane. 14:50*Mr5'38. 7954
Ordeal by birthday cake. Prose. Robert Benchley. 8:17-18 S17 '32. 7955
Ordeal by family. Verse. Phyllis McGinley. 9:12 Ja20'34. 7956
Ordeal by jury. RL. M. R. Werner. 15:54-9*Je10'39. 7957
Ordeal of a philosopher. Prose. H. L. Mencken. 12:21-4*Ap11 '36. 7958
Ordeal of the opera. Prose. Harry Jameson. 3:28-32 Ag27'27. 7959
Order of the bath. Prose. Rosemary Carr Benét. 7:33-5*Ag15 '31. 7960
Orgy: American style. RL. Morris Markey. 2:34-8 Je5'26. 7961
Originals. Verse. Anon. 3:30 N5 '27. 7962
The orphan. Prose. Brendan Gill. 14:96*D3'38. 7963
'Orrible woman. PR (Lewis). Joseph Bryan, III. 9:25-8 S16'33. 7964
Ostrich. Prose. Theodore Pratt. 10:33-4*Ja12'35. 7965
Othello. Anthony Gibbs. 6:81 Je21 '30. 7966
Other anthems. Verse. Franklin P. Adams. 11:60*D21'35. 7967
Other distinguished visitors. Prose. Anon. 1:22 Je6'25. 7968
The other word. Prose. Oliver Claxton. 3:26 Mr19'27. 7969
The Otter family. Prose. Ambrose Flack. 12:65-6*O10'36. 7970
Otto Kahn, or the new opera season. Prose. Frank Sullivan. 4:22-3 O27'28. 7971
Où sont les neiges? SM. Alexander Woollcott. 6:32 Mr8'30. 7972
Ounces of prevention. Verse. Miriam Vedder. 7:87 S19'31. 7973
Our betters. Verse. Newman Levy. 6:19 Ja17'31. 7974
Our betters. Verse. Newman Levy. 6:24 Ja24'31. 7975
Our betters. Verse. Newman Levy. 6:16 Ja31'31. 7976
Our betters. Verse. Newman Levy. 6:27 F14'31. 7977
Our betters. Verse. Newman Levy. 7:24 F21'31. 7978
Our British benefactors. Verse. Henrietta Fort Holland. 8:20*Mr 19'32. 7979
Our captious readers. Verse. A. J. O. 2:41 Ap10'26. 7980
Our captious readers. Prose. Joseph Fulling Fishman. 2:81-2 N20'26. 7981
Our captious readers. Prose. Zelpha Mitchell. 3:32-4 Je18'27. 7982
Our captious readers. Prose. E. B. White. 1:31 N14'25. 7983
Our collegiate hilltop. Prose. Elmer Davis. 1:9-10 O24'25. 7984
Our disillusioned readers. Prose. Donald Bar Chidsey. 5:90 Je8 '29. 7985
Our fascinating but neglected contributors. Prose. Editors. 14:7*F19'38. 7986
"Our feathered friends." Prose. Stanley Jones. 5:44-6 Je8'29. 7987
Our first "Miss." Prose. Maddy Vegtel. 10:59-62 O6'34. 7988
Our footloose correspondents. Prose. Heywood Broun. 12:36-8*Ag1'36. 7989
Our footloose correspondents. Prose. Emily Z. Friedkin. 10:65-6 Ag18'34. 7990
Our future policy with Japan. Prose. Frank Sullivan. 10:26-7*D8'34. 7991

Our gangs. RL. Morris Markey. 2:36-40 O9'26. 7992
Our gifted readers. Verse. Rose O'Neill. 10:103*D8'34. 7993
Our Gladys at home is just seven. OSB. C. Knapp. 5:23 Ag 31'29. 7994
"Our janitor is not my warmest friend . . ." Verse. Anon. 1:35 Ja16'26. 7995
Our lady of the movie shows. Verse. John McColl. 2:68 S18 '26. 7996
Our little Canadian cousins. Prose. Marion Sturges-Jones. 12:59*Je13'36. 7997
Our little English cousins. Prose. Marion Sturges-Jones. 7:71*Je13'31. 7998
Our little ones. SM. Alexander Woollcott. 9:36 O21'33. 7999
Our Mr. Opper. Prose. Carroll Carroll. 2:73-6 F12'27. 8000
Our nostalgic readers. Prose. Dorothy Walworth Carman. 10:48-50*D22'34. 8001
Our number's in the book. Verse. Ogden Nash. 10:18 Jy7'34. 8002
Our own Lenin. PR (Foster). Alva Johnston. 6:19-22 Je28'30. 8003
Our own Lysistrata. Prose. S. H. Adams. 1:44 Ja23'26. 8004
Our own 100 neediest. SM. Alexander Woollcott. 5:42 D14'29. 8005
Our own perfect state. Prose. Yahoo. 1:24 My16'25. 8006
Our own proscription list. Verse. Anon. 4:24 Mr31'28. 8007
Our pet department. Prose. James Thurber. 6:25 F22'30. 8008
Our pet department. Prose. James Thurber. 6:24 Mr1'30. 8009
Our pet department. Prose. James Thurber. 6:21 Mr15'30. 8010
Our pet department. Prose. James Thurber. 6:20 Ap5'30. 8011
Our pet department. Prose. James Thurber. 6:19 My3'30. 8012
Our pet department. Prose. James Thurber. 6:25 My17'30. 8013
Our pet department. Prose. James Thurber. 6:25 Je7'30. 8014
Our red revolution. Prose. Alva Johnston. 6:21-2 My10'30. 8015
Our sermons on sin. Verse. Hans Stengel. 1:8 S19'25; 1:8 O17'25; 1:23 N21'25; 1:8 N28'25; 1:22 D12'25; 18 D19'25; 1:10 D26'25; 1:10 Ja9'26; 1:26 Ja30'26; 1:14 F13'26; 2:16 Mr20'26. 8016
Our tolerant pigeons. Verse. Arthur Guiterman. 10:32 My26'34. 8017
Our unappreciated statesmen. RL. Hickman Powell. 7:48-57 O31 '31. 8018
Our unbalanced aquariums. Prose. S. J. Perelman. 11:21-2*O26'35. 8019
Our university. Prose. Observant sophomore. 5:30-6 Mr23'29. 8020
Our unmarried readers. Prose. Edna Ferber. 9:54 Je10'33. 8021
Our wooden friends. Prose. Pare Lorentz. 4:38-9 Jy21'28. 8022
Out Etna way. Verse. Morris Bishop. 9:26 Jy29'33. 8023
Out in the sun. Prose. John Chapin Mosher. 15:27-8*S16'39. 8024
Out of season. Prose. Frances Warfield. 8:59-60 O1'32. 8025
Out of the frying pan. Verse. Margaret Fishback. 12:68*F13'37. 8026
Out of the past. PR (McClellan). Milton MacKaye. 8:21-5 My28 '32. 8027
Out of the past. Prose. Russell Maloney. 14:18*D31'38. 8028
Out of the silence. Prose. Dorothy Parker. 4:28-32 S1'28. 8029
Out of the West. Prose. Theodore Pratt. 9:60 N18'33. 8030

Out of town visitors. Prose. Thyra Samter Winslow. 4:25-6 Ag11'28. 8031
Out-of-towner. Prose. Charles G. Shaw. 2:23 N6'26. 8032
Out there. Prose. Frances Crane. 8:58-60 O15'32. 8033
An outline of education. Verse. Elspeth O'Halloran. 4:31 My19 '28. 8034
An outline of scientists. Prose. James Thurber. 12:17-18*S19 '36. 8035
An outline of the Byrd Report. Prose. James Thurber. 6:22-3 Jy26'30. 8036
Outrage. Verse. Hortense Flexner. 7:74*Je6'31. 8037
Outward bound. Verse. Anon. 1:14 Ja2'26. 8038
Outward form and feature. WP. Alexander Woollcott. 7:30-5 D26'31. 8039
Outwitting the lightning. Prose. Amos Andrews. 9:23-4 Ag19 '33. 8040
Over Babel. PR (Bush). Niven Busch, Jr. 3:26-8 Ap2'27. 8041
Over the border. Prose. Alice Frankforter. 7:26-7 N21'31. 8042
Over the neon light. Prose. John Chapin Mosher. 9:19-21 F10 '34. 8043
Over the river and through the wood. Prose. John O'Hara. 10:23-5*D15'34. 8044
Over the waves. Prose. Ring Lardner. 8:30-6 Je18'32. 8045
Overcorrection. Verse. Anne Forbes. 13:27*O23'37. 8046
Overdose. Prose. Frank Sullivan. 7:19-20 My9'31. 8047
Overemphasis again. Prose. Robert J. Misch. 5:110-11 N16'29. 8048
Overheard. Prose. Charles M. Bayer. 3:103 N19'27. 8049
Overheard. Prose. Jack Cluett. 3:52-3 D3'27. 8050
Overheard. Prose. Jack Cluett. 5:96-7 Mr23'29. 8051
Overheard. Prose. Arthur H. Folwell. 3:104 Ap30'27. 8052
Overheard. Prose. Helen Goold. 3:84-5 D17'27. 8053
Overheard. Prose. Paul G. Gumbinner. 3:104 O15'27. 8054
Overheard. Prose. Lewis Harris. 3:28-9 D31'27. 8055
Overheard. Prose. Arthur Kober. 3:52-3 Ap23'27. 8056
Overheard. Prose. Arthur Kober. 3:64-5 Ag3'27. 8057
Overheard. Prose. Arthur Kober. 3:45-7 S3'27. 8058
Overheard. Prose. Theodore Pratt. 3:93 S24'27. 8059
Overheard. Prose. Dorothy Kidder Riggs. 3:42 My28'27. 8060
Overheard. Prose. Florence W. Ross. 3:29 Ap16'27. 8061
Overheard. Prose. Florence W. Ross. 3:28 D24'27. 8062
Overheard. Prose. Stirling Wilson. 4:64 D15'28. 8063
Overheard at a Goldman concert in Central Park. Prose. E. T. Conroy. 4:43 Je23'28. 8064
Overheard at Forest Hills. Prose. Sylvia Fuller. 2:53 S25'26. 8065
Overheard at the guild. Prose. Albert Carroll. 4:56 Ja12'29. 8066
Overheard at Woolworth's. Prose. Al Graham. 4:88 Mr24'28. 8067
Overheard in a telephone booth. Prose. John H. O'Hara. 4:77-8 My19'28. 8068
Overseas. Prose. Emily Hahn. 13:16-18*Jy3'37. 8069
Overset. SM. Alexander Woollcott. 5:32 Ja11'30. 8070
Overset. SM. Alexander Woollcott. 6:32 S6'30. 8071
Oversonnet. Verse. David McCord. 8:17 O8'32. 8072
Owl man. RL. Sanderson Vanderbilt. 12:32-41*N28'36. 8073
The owner of Ben Finney. PR (Egon). Alexander Woollcott. 4:25-8 My12'28. 8074
Oyster's son. Prose. Langston Hughes. 10:51-4*Ja12'35. 8075

P

P. T. Barnum's second wife. Prose. Clara de Morinni. 12: 64-8*Ap11'36. 8076
Packet of letters. Verse. Louise Bogan. 12:21*Ja2'37. 8077
Packs of sealyhams. Prose. Frances Crane. 8:79-80 N19 '32. 8078
Pact. Verse. Kenneth Fearing. 15:25*S23'39. 8079
Pact. Verse. Margaret Fishback. 5:127 O26'29. 8080
Padlocks. Prose. John Chapin Mosher. 4:36-8 Ag4'28. 8081
Paean of self-praise. Verse. Kenneth Phillips Britton. 2:79 Je5 '26. 8082
Paeans of self-praise. Verse. Kenneth Phillips Britton. 2:36 Ag21'26. 8083
The pageant of human progress. Prose. Thomas Much. 1:32 O17'25. 8084
Paging Mr. Webster. Verse. Anon. 2:19 My15'26. 8085
Paging Mr. Webster. Verse. Anon. 2:76 Je5'26. 8086
Paging Mr. Webster. Verse. Lisle Bell. 3:60 Jy2'27. 8087
Paging Mr. Webster. Verse. A. K. Laing. 2:13 Ag7'26. 8088
Paging Mr. Webster. Verse. A. K. Laing. 2:26 Ag21'26. 8089
Paging Mr. Webster. Verse. A. K. Laing. 2:22 S4'26. 8090
Paging Mr. Webster. Verse. A. K. Laing. 2:74 O2'26. 8091
The paid piper. PR (Whiteman). Niven Busch, Jr. 2:25-7 N27 '26. 8092
The pains of poetry. Verse. John Holmes. 11:52*My18'35. 8093
The painted lily. Prose. Charles G. Shaw. 1:14 F21'25. 8094
Painter in the Bronx. Prose. Arthur Kober. 15:19-21*Jy22'39. 8095
A pair of bronzes. Prose. Frances Crane. 10:97-9 O6'34. 8096
Pal, a dog. Prose. Wolcott Gibbs. 5:29 O26'29. 8097
Pal Joey. Prose. John O'Hara. 14:23-4*O22'38. 8098
Pal to millions. RL. Jack Alexander. 13:48-53*Je5'37. 8099
Pale and interesting. Prose. Jess Nancy Grice. 5:76-7 Ap13'29. 8100
Pamphlet. Prose. Spud Johnson. 2:24 D25'26. 8101
Pamphlet on sex war. Prose. Dearing Ward. 5:83-4 Je22'29. 8102
Pandora and the doctor. PR (Erdmann). Niven Busch, Jr. 2:32-4 D4'26. 8103
Panhandler. Prose. Theodore Pratt. 3:48-50 Jy9'27. 8104
A panic in Hollywood. Prose. Marc Connelly. 4:14-15 Jy28 '28. 8105
Panic portraits. Prose. John C. Emery. 8:37*F27'32. 8106
Panic portraits. Prose. John C. Emery. 8:50*Mr12'32. 8107
Panic portraits. Prose. John C. Emery. 8:57*Mr19'32. 8108
Panic portraits. Prose. John C. Emery. 8:28-32*Ap9'32. 8109
Pannickin. Prose. Robert Nathan. 7:17-19 Mr21'31. 8110
The panther. Prose. Alice Frankforter. 7:78-9 Mr21'31. 8111
Paolo and Francesca. Prose. John O'Hara. 7:56-7 O24'31. 8112
Papa and smoking. Prose. John O'Hara. 7:76-7 My16'31. 8113
The paper-match peril. Prose. Robert M. Coates. 4:38-40 O13 '28. 8114
The papers. Verse. Morris Bishop. 10:16 Ag18'34. 8115
Parable for a certain virgin. Verse. Dorothy Parker. 3:27 Ap 23'27. 8116
Parachute jumper. PR (Crane). Geoffrey T. Hellman. 8:16-19 D31'32. 8117
Parade for Fanny Elssler. Verse. Kenneth Allan Robinson. 11:21* Ap27'35. 8118
Parades and terraces. NYC. Grace

Hegger Lewis. 6:22-3 Mr29 '30. 8119
Paradise lost. SM. Alexander Woollcott. 4:40 F16'29. 8120
Paradox. Verse. J. Thorne Smith. 2:48 Mr27'26. 8121
Paradox. Verse. Edith Franklin Wyatt. 9:62 Mr11'33. 8122
Paramount's patriarch. PR (Zukor). Niven Busch, Jr. 5:29-33 S7'29. 8123
Parent life. Prose. Katherine Sproehnle. 11:70-2*D14'35. 8124
The parfit fool. Prose. Lois Long. 14:35-8*N19'38. 8125
Parfum d'amour. Verse. Morris Bishop. 15:33*Ap29'39. 8126
Paris. Prose. Maddy Vegtel. 8:25 O22'32. 8127
Paris. Prose. Maddy Vegtel. 10:57-60 My26'34. 8128
Paris evening. Verse. Margaret Widdemer. 6:53 Jy19'30. 8129
Paris idyll. Prose. Lamar Middleton. 13:60-1*My22'37. 8130
Paris letter. Anon. 1:30 S12'25. 8131
Paris letter. Lois Long. 1:26 S26 '25. 8132
Paris letter. Jo U. Milward. 2:48-9 Je26'26; 2:45-6 Jy10'26; 2:41-2 Jy24'26; 2:47-8 Ag14 '26; 2:51-2 Ag28'26. 8133
Paris—New York—Kansas City. Prose. George Weller. 13:63-5*S18'37. 8134
Paris, 1927 style. Prose. Marc Connelly. 3:60-1 Je4'27. 8135
Paris without embarrassment. Prose. Donald Moffat. 5:54-5 Jy27'29. 8136
Park Avenue. Verse. M. M. 2:26 Jy31'26. 8137
A Park Avenue lodging house. Prose. Alice Hughes. 3:86-9 S24'27. 8138
A Park Avenue person invades our house in the country. Verse. 2:24 Jy24'26. 8139
Park Avenue restaurant. Verse. J. C. Norton. 3:111 Ap9'27. 8140
Park concert. Verse. Jean Batchelor. 6:20 Je21'30. 8141
Parked car. Verse. Ernest E. Sandeen. 14:54*My28'38. 8142
Parnassus--1935. Verse. Robert Hillyer. 11:18*Ap27'35. 8143
Parochial school. Prose. Paul Horgan. 9:14-16 Ap1'33. 8144
Paroled. RL. Morris Markey. 11:38-48*O19'35. 8145
Parrot. Verse. Virginia Woods Bellamy. 13:65*S25'37. 8146
Parrotry, society sport. Prose. Philip Pratt. 1:14 Ag1'25. 8147
Parson Weems, virtue's recruiting-sergeant. Prose. Morris Bishop. 12:20-5*F22'36. 8148
Parsons is prepared. Prose. P. S. LePoer Trench. 11:73*O5'35. 8149
The part-time dog. Prose. Katherine Sproehnle. 3:68-70 O15 '27. 8150
Parting. Verse. Clinch Calkins. 3:25 N19'27. 8151
Partition. Verse. David Morton. 14:50*Je4'38. 8152
Party. Verse. Oliver Jenkins. 5:80 My25'29. 8153
The party. Verse. Ogden Nash. 8:25 Ja21'33. 8154
Party for seven. Verse. Frances M. Frost. 7:42 Ja2'32. 8155
Party linesman. PR (Browder). John McCarten. 14:20-4*S24 '38; 14:22-7*O1'38. 8156
The party spirit. Prose. Gilbert Seldes. 7:17-18 Ja23'32. 8157
Party toward midnight. Verse. Frances Frost. 10:46 S1'34. 8158
Parysatis pauses. Verse. Harold Willard Gleason. 5:42 D7'29. 8159
The passage of animals. Verse. Harry Brown. 15:26*O7'39. 8160
Passengers. Prose. Arthur Kober. 4:84-5 Ja5'29. 8161
The passing of José Perez. OFC. Michael Scully. 15:61-3*Mr18 '39. 8162
The passing of the chief. TWNY.

Elizabeth Jordan. 13:59-61* D18'37. 8163
Passing through. Prose. Robert M. Coates. 14:13-15*Jy9'38. 8164
Passing time at Christmastide. Prose. José Schorr. 1:22 D12 '25. 8165
Passing time at the theatre. Prose. José Schorr. 2:26 Mr 27'26. 8166
The passion in the back yard. Verse. Morris Bishop. 11:32* My11'35. 8167
Passion in 12-C. Prose. Russell Maloney. 13:20*Jy17'37. 8168
The Passion Play. TT. 10:19 Mr 17'34. 8169
Passion vs. passion. Prose. G. Schwabe. 5:56 Ap27'29. 8170
Passionate beyond belief. Verse. Helene Mullins. 12:50*O31'36. 8171
Passionate letters to public utilities. Prose. Katherine Sproehnle. 2:21 Jy24'26. 8172
Passionate letters to public utilities. Prose. Katherine Sproehnle. 2:20 Jy31'26. 8173
Passionate love letter. Prose. T. H. Bliss. 1:43 Ja30'26. 8174
The passionate pagan and the dispassionate public. Verse. Ogden Nash. 8:18*Ap9'32. 8175
The passionate passenger to his love. Verse. E. B. White. 13: 24*F12'38. 8176
The passionate poet to his love. Verse. Berton Braley. 10:64 F17'34. 8177
The passionate professor. PR (Copeland). Heywood Broun. 3:20-2 Ja21'28. 8178
The pastel motif. Verse. Leslie Nelson Jennings. 4:63 Ap7'28. 8179
Pastime. Prose. Theodore Pratt. 3:72-3 Ap23'27. 8180
Pastoral. Verse. Ruth Brown. 4: 52 Ag18'28. 8181
Pastoral. Prose. Louise Owen. 15:44-6*Jy29'39. 8182
Pastoral. Prose. Frances Warfield. 10:19 Ag4'34. 8183
Pastoral at Mr. Piper's. Prose. Mollie Panter-Downes. 14:13-14*Ag6'38. 8184
Pastorale. Verse. Margaretta Byers. 6:56 Je28'30. 8185
Pastorale. Prose. Mark Schorer. 15:61-2*My27'39. 8186
The pastry tray. Verse. Persis Greely Anderson. 7:72 S26'31. 8187
Pastures new. Verse. Richard Armour. 15:94*D9'39. 8188
Pastures not green. Verse. Jean Batchelor. 6:49 Je28'30. 8189
The patchwork heart. Verse. Rachel Field. 6:98 S13'30. 8190
Paterfamilias. Verse. Sydney King Russell. 5:71 Ja25'30. 8191
The pathetic plight of Polly Pecan. Verse. Phyllis McGinley. 9:21 N11'33. 8192
The pathos of Long Island distances. Prose. Henry Tetlow. 4:72-3 S15'28. 8193
Patience. Verse. Dorothy Belle Flanagan. 4:32 N24'28. 8194
Patriot. Prose. Meyer Berger. 14:18-20*D17'38. 8195
Patriotic definition. Verse. Anon. 2:36 Jy24'26. 8196
Patriotism is out. Prose. G. Schwabe. 3:80-1 Ap30'27. 8197
Patriotism, 1917. Prose. Richard Wormser. 12:59-60*S26'36. 8198
The patron and the artist. Verse. Fillmore Hyde. 2:40 Ap10'26. 8199
Patron of letters. Prose. Sally Benson. 15:18-21*Je10'39. 8200
Patron of the preemies. PR (Couney). A. J. Liebling. 15:20-4*Je3'39. 8201
Patrons from the Bronx. Prose. Arthur Kober. 13:15-17*F5'38. 8202
The patsy. Prose. T. H. Wenning. 5:20 Ja11'30. 8203
Paul Revere's ride. Prose. Frederick Lewis Allen. 6:19-21 Ap 19'30. 8204

Pausa. Verse. Babette Deutsch. 6:19 Je14'30. 8205
A pause in the day's occupation. Prose. Ring Lardner. 7:51-2 D26'31. 8206
Pavement pantomine. Verse. Jean Batchelor. 5:47 O26'29. 8207
Pavement pathology. Prose. Frederick Packard. 6:89-90 F22'30. 8208
The pavements of New York. Prose. Fairfax Downey. 2:28 N13'26. 8209
Pawn of fate. Prose. Margaret Ford. 9:68-70 D9'33. 8210
Pay day. Prose. Wolcott Gibbs. 8:19-20 S10'32. 8211
Peace comes to Shanghai. RL. Emily Hahn. 14:76-82*D3'38. 8212
Peace in our time. Verse. Babette Deutsch. 14:29*N19'38. 8213
The peacock-blue Ford. Verse. Anon. 1:39 D19'25. 8214
Peacock parade. Prose. Ferdinand Tuohy. 3:34-6 Ag27'27. 8215
The peanut roaster. Verse. Christopher Morley. 4:17 Je 23'28. 8216
Pearl Street. DL. Burke Boyce. 4:29 Ap14'28. 8217
Peasant by paradox. PR (Sandburg). Waldo Frank. 1:13-14 N14'25. 8218
Peckett's. HHT. Donald Moffat. 9:68-72 N25'33. 8219
Peculiar Christmas spirit. Prose. W. E. Farbstein. 9:22 D16'33. 8220
Pedagogue. PR (Ryan). Helena Huntington Smith. 6:29-32 F22 '30. 8221
A pedant's progress. Prose. Edith Owen. 6:24-6 My17'30. 8222
Pedestrian. Verse. Philip G. Wylie. 2:32 Ja29'27. 8223
Pedestrians. Verse. Mildred Weston. 9:20 S23'33. 8224
Peek a boo! Prose. Mary C. McCall, Jr. 2:74-5 D11'26. 8225
Peep frogs. Verse. Martha Banning Thomas. 8:74 My21'32. 8226
The peepshow season in retrospect. Prose. Wolcott Gibbs. 5:25-6 S21'29. 8227
Peggy. Prose. John O'Hara. 13: 24*Ap17'37. 8228
The pelican's shadow. Prose. Marjorie Kinnan Rawlings. 15: 17-19*Ja6'40. 8229
Pen, paper, and parlor. Prose. Gilbert Seldes. 3:23-4 Ja21'28. 8230
Pen, pencil, and poison. Prose. Gilbert Seldes. 2:23-5 S18'26. 8231
Penalty. Verse. Ruth Lambert Jones. 13:73*O16'37. 8232
Penance. Verse. Mildred Weston. 6:43 S27'30. 8233
Pencil-chewing. Prose. Frank Sullivan. 11:15*My4'35. 8234
Penelope. Verse. Persis Greely Anderson. 6:19 Jy5'30. 8235
Penny arcade. RL. Leo Rosten. 14:31-7*My28'38. 8236
Penny flashback. Prose. Clifford Orr. 9:22 Jy8'33. 8237
Penny-wise. Prose. George Cecil Cowing. 5:88-9 Je8'29. 8238
Penny-wise. Verse. Marjorie Allen Seiffert. 6:28 N1'30. 8239
A penny's worth. TWNY. Henry Anton Steig. 15:42-6*Mr4'39. 8240
The Penguin murder. RL. Morris Markey. 7:51-6 O3'31. 8241
Penguins. Verse. Laura Benét. 6:83 My3'30. 8242
Pensive thoughts on infant prodigies. Verse. Mariana Bonnell. 3:39 F11'28. 8243
People. Verse. Ogden Nash. 6:20 S6'30. 8244
People are fascinating. Prose. Sally Benson. 8:26 S10'32. 8245
People are so careless. Prose. Michael Scully. 14:34-5*Jy9'38. 8246
People in the street. Verse. John

Holmes. 15:25*Mr11'39. 8247
People on a planet. Prose. Daniel Fuchs. 14:25-7*S24'38. 8248
The people who had the house before. Prose. Robert Benchley. 6:17-18 Ap26'30. 8249
People who make news. Prose. John Chamberlain. 3:69 O22 '27. 8250
People who make news. Prose. John Chamberlain. 3:104 N12 '27. 8251
People who make news. Prose. John Chamberlain. 3:73 Ja7 '28. 8252
The people's peace. Verse. John Holmes. 13:13*Jy10'37. 8253
The people's servants. RL. Richard F. Warner. 6:50-5 O18'30; 6:50-8 O25'30. 8254
Pep talk. Prose. Morris Markey. 15:56*Je3'39. 8255
Pepper for the Belgians. Prose. James Thurber. 13:20*D18'37. 8256
Pequeña españa. RL. Morris Markey. 10:48-54*D1'34. 8257
Percy on babies and baby-talk. Verse. Richard Butler Glaenzer. 2:69 D18'26. 8258
Pere Lachaise and the legion. Prose. Mildred Gilman. 3:38 O1'27. 8259
Peregrine's Sunday song. Verse. Elinor Wylie. 2:29 F12'27. 8260
The perennial freshman. PR (Lloyd). R. E. Sherwood. 1:15-16 Ja30'26. 8261
The perfect audience. Prose. Robert Benchley. 6:16 My31'30. 8262
The perfect egg. Prose. John Chapin Mosher. 6:81-3 O4'30. 8263
The perfect hostess. Prose. Sally Benson. 8:23-4*Mr5'32. 8264
The perfect infinitive. OMEU. James Thurber. 5:27 Je22'29. 8265
Perfect ladies. Prose. C. Knapp. 9:36-8 N4'33. 8266
The perfect man. Prose. Laura Mount. 8:19-21*Ap23'32. 8267
The perfect man. Prose. Thyra Samter Winslow. 3:22 Jy30'27. 8268
Perfect murder. Prose. John Collier. 10:17-18 Mr24'34. 8269
The perfect radio program. OW. Ring Lardner. 9:35-6 Ag26'33. 8270
Perfect 36. RL. Nancy Hale. 10:76-82 Ap21'34. 8271
Perfume and politics. PR (Coty). Janet Flanner. 6:22-5 My3'30. 8272
Perhaps. Prose. Frank Sullivan. 11:30*Ap6'35. 8273
Peril at sea. Prose. Theodore Pratt. 11:78-9*N2'35. 8274
Peril by night. Prose. Allen Saalburg. 9:20-1 S2'33. 8275
The perils of electricity. Prose. Robert Wohlforth. 14:42-3*Ag20 '38. 8276
The perils of peace. Verse. Jean Batchelor. 10:84 Ap14'34. 8277
Perils of poverty. Prose. Clinch Calkins. 3:20-1 Ag27'27. 8278
Perils of poverty. Prose. Clinch Calkins. 3:25 S10'27. 8279
Perils of poverty. Prose. Clinch Calkins. 3:27 S24'27. 8280
Perils of poverty. Prose. Clinch Calkins. 3:23-4 O22'27. 8281
Perils of the sea. Prose. Nelson Lansdale. 12:69-70*S19'36. 8282
Permanent investment. Verse. Henry Morton Robinson. 8:60 My21'32. 8283
Permit an anthropologist. Prose. Pliny Earle Goddard. 1:20 Ja30 '26. 8284
Permutating pies. ML. John Strong Newberry. 9:33 Je3'33. 8285
Perpetual emotion. Prose. Hildegarde Dolson. 14:44-6*S10'38. 8286
Perquisite. Verse. Ruth Lambert Jones. 5:82 Je15'29. 8287
Persephone. Verse. Audrey Wurdemann. 4:86 My26'28. 8288

mour. 15:51*Mr18'39. 8332
Pianist. Verse. Frances M. Frost. 8:17*F27'32. 8333
Piano. Prose. Theodore Pratt. 3:34 Ap23'27. 8334
Piano recital. Prose. Alice Frankforter. 10:43-4 Mr3'34. 8335
Pianola d'amore. Verse. David McCord. 9:29 Ap8'33. 8336
Piccolo. Verse. Rollin Kirby. 2:20 Ag7'26. 8337
The pick-up. Prose. Arthur Kober. 4:36-8 F25'28. 8338
Pick-ups here and there. Prose. Charles G. Shaw. 1:28 Ap4'25. 8339
Pick-ups here and there. Prose Charles G. Shaw. 1:19 S5'25. 8340
Picking on Charlie Chaplin. Prose. Ralph Barton. 3:17-19 Jy23'27. 8341
Pickles and trading stamps. NYC. Bernice Breen. 5:28-30 D21 '29. 8342
Picnic with the Quicks. Prose. Hannah Lees. 10:96-8 S8'34. 8343
The picture. Prose. Dorothy Thomas. 11:26-8*Je29'35. 8344
Picture for a Christmas card. Verse. Martha Banning Thomas. 11:72*D14'35. 8345
Pier watchman. Verse. James Kevin McGuinness. 1:29 S26 '25. 8346
Pigeon English. Verse. Sara Henderson Hay. 13:30*Ja22'38. 8347
Pigeon man's progress. PR (Jacobs). G. F. T. Ryall. 15: 20-4*Ag5'39. 8348
Pigeon, sing cuccu! Verse. E. B. White. 13:27*Ap10'37. 8349
The pike. TA. Will Cuppy. 8:23 Je25'32. 8350
Pilgrim. Verse. Dearing Ward. 4:87 O6'28. 8351
Pilgrimage. Verse. Anon. 2:25 S18'26. 8352
Pines after snow. Verse. Robert P. Tristram Coffin. 13:56*Ja8 '38. 8353
Ping-pong. Prose. St. Clair McKelway. 12:47-50*S12'36. 8354
Pins and needles. (Revue) TT. 13:11-12*D25'37. 8355
Pioneer. PR (Bocher). Janet Flanner. 15:24-8*Ja13'40. 8356
Pioneer bologna. Prose. Frances Warfield. 4:24 N3'28. 8357
The pipe prevails. Prose. Agnes Scott Yost. 2:41-2 My1'26. 8358
The pirate's knife. Verse. Brownell Carr. 2:43 Ap17'26. 8359
Piscatorial. NESD. John J. Holzinger. 10:34 Mr10'34. 8360
Piscina, sine piscibus. Verse. Rolfe Humphries. 13:30*Je5'37. 8361
Pish to wives. Verse. Marjorie Allen Seiffert. 7:43*Ag15'31. 8362
Pitnick in the Bronx. Prose. Arthur Kober. 11:16-18*Je1'35. 8363
Pity the blind. Verse. Marion Sturges-Jones. 11:38*S21'35. 8364
Place and leave with. PR (Grossman). St. Clair McKelway. 11: 23-6*Ag24'35; 11:21-4*Ag31'35. 8365
Place-cards. Prose. Niven Busch, Jr. 2:23 D25'26. 8366
Place cards. Prose. Niven Busch, Jr. 3:22-3 Ap23'27. 8367
Place-cards. Prose. Niven Busch, Jr. 3:14 O1'27. 8368
The Place du Terte. Prose. Anthony Armstrong. 7:73-4*Je6 '31. 8369
Place in the sun. Prose. Frances Warfield. 7:28-32*My23'31. 8370
Placecards. Prose. Clifford Orr. 9:38-42 Ap22'33. 8371
Places. Prose. Louise Field Cooper. 12:37-9*Jy4'36. 8372
Plagiarism. Prose. Burton Rascoe. 6:24-6 O18'30. 8373
Plagiarism. (Drama) TT. 1:3-4 Jy 11'25. 8374
The plain princess. Prose. Oliver Claxton. 2:34-6 F12'27. 8375
Plaint. Verse. Frances M. Frost.

6:38 Mr15'30. 8376
Planetarium. Verse. Florence S. Edsall. 11:28*Ja25'36. 8377
Plans for a horrid old age. Verse. John Ogden Whedon. 5:64 My25 '29. 8378
Plans for May Day. Verse. Margaret Fishback. 3:90 Ap30'27. 8379
Plans, plans, plans! Prose. Robert Benchley. 5:16-17 Je29'29. 8380
Plastic. Verse. Jerome Barry. 6:26 D27'30. 8381
Platform conversation. Prose. Carroll Carroll. 3:39-40 Ag13 '27. 8382
Platitudes. Verse. Olive Ward. 4:70 My5'28. 8383
Platt Street. DL. Burke Boyce. 3:63 Je18'27. 8384
Play a march. Prose. John Cheever. 12:20-1*Je20'36. 8385
Play school. Prose. Sally Benson. 7:26-7 O17'31. 8386
A play we want to see. Prose. Newman Levy. 1:18 Mr14'25. 8387
The playboy of politics. PR (Longworth). John K. Winkler. 2:15-16 Ap10'26. 8388
Playfair, Nigel. Anthony Gibbs. 6:43 Ag2'30. 8389
Playing ball with Mr. Reinman. Prose. Alan Campbell. 9:95-6 D16'33. 8390
The playing fields of Bedlam. Prose. Wolcott Gibbs. 9:20-1 Ja20'34. 8391
Plays, Current, London. Janet Flanner. 15:43*Je24'39. 8392
Plays, Current, Paris. Janet Flanner. 15:54*Jy8'39. 8393
A plea for bad fiction. Prose. Anon. 5:18-19 Ag10'29. 8394
A plea for bad plays. Prose. Ben Hecht. 4:25-6 S22'28. 8395
A plea for better manners. SM. Alexander Woollcott. 5:32 Ag 24'29. 8396
A plea for disarmament. Verse. Margaret Fishback. 3:68 O29 '27. 8397
A plea for less malice toward none. Verse. Ogden Nash. 9:14 Ap15'33. 8398
A plea to heaven. Verse. Marjorie Allen Seiffert. 7:30*My30 '31. 8399
Plea to the Theatre Guild. Verse. Arthur Guiterman. 6:30 Mr8'30. 8400
"Please do not flout natural laws." Prose. Robert Benchley. 6:23 My17'30. 8401
Please mention--. Verse. Philip G. Wylie. 2:69 N20'26. 8402
Please omit flowers. Prose. Elizabeth Dickens. 15:52-3*Mr18 '39. 8403
Pleasure. Prose. John O'Hara. 10:70-3 Mr10'34. 8404
Pleasure cruise. Prose. William A. Krauss. 11:66*S14'35. 8405
The pleasure of your company. Prose. Marc Connelly. 8:16-18 Ja7'33. 8406
The pliocene god. Prose. Clarence Day. 9:26 Ja13'34. 8407
A plot for Mr. Dreiser. SM. Alexander Woollcott. 9:32-4 O14'33. 8408
A plot of land. Prose. Kenneth Rosenheck. 11:71-2*N9'35. 8409
Plots. Prose. Patricia Collinge. 1:22 Ap4'25. 8410
Plumes. DL. Burke Boyce. 3:89 O22'27. 8411
Plush and gaslight. PR (Bates). Joseph Gollomb. 5:23-6 Je15'29. 8412
Pnyxie of Pnyx Hill. Prose. Cora McAlbert. 15:80-4*Ap29'39. 8413
Pocahontas. Verse. Phyllis McGinley. 11:18*Ag10'35. 8414
Poco agitato. Prose. E. B. White. 2:57-8 My29'26. 8415
Poem. Verse. Anon. 2:46 Ap3'26. 8416
Poem about acting. Verse. Philip G. Wylie. 1:20 F6'26. 8417
Poem about bond-selling. Verse. Philip G. Wylie. 1:45 Ja30'26. 8418
Poem about dining out. Verse. Philip G. Wylie. 2:34 F20

'26. 8419
Poem about dogs. Verse. Philip G. Wylie. 2:60 F20'26. 8420
Poem about hockey. Verse. Philip G. Wylie. 2:45 Mr6'26. 8421
Poem about the tropics. Verse. Philip G. Wylie. 1:5 Ja23'26. 8422
Poem for Mother's Day. Verse. Anon. 4:107 My12'28. 8423
Poem for the body. Verse. Frances M. Frost. 7:23*Ag15'31. 8424
Poem for youth. Verse. Frances M. Frost. 6:27 My24'30. 8425
Poem of pain and passion. Verse. Leslie S. Pearl. 4:63 Jy21'28. 8426
Poem of praise. Verse. Elizabeth Coatsworth. 10:26 Ag4'34. 8427
Poesy department. Verse. Laura McGuffey Helser. 8:28*Ap2'32. 8428
Poet. Verse. E. B. White. 5:26 Ap6'29. 8429
The poet as farmer. Verse. Genevieve Taggard. 5:28 S21'29. 8430
The poet commutes. Verse. Anon. 2:32 My1'26. 8431
The poet cornered. Prose. Frank Sullivan. 7:19-20 Mr14'31. 8432
Poet deranged. Verse. Anon. 2:20 Jy3'26. 8433
Poet in steel. PR (Ammann). Milton MacKaye. 10:23-7 Je2'34. 8434
Poet-laureate, American. TT. 9:5 Ja20'34. 8435
Poet reduced to the cliché. Verse. Martha Banning Thomas. 2:17 Mr13'26. 8436
Poetic headlines. Prose. Don Gray. 3:105-107 Ap9'27. 8437
The poetic pedestrian. Verse. Anon. 3:59 N19'27. 8438
Poetry By children. Dorothy Mills and Morris Bishop. 13:32-7*N13'37. 8439
Poetry, Dream. Edmund Wilson. 13:50-2*Jy31'37. 8440
Poets. Verse. Emily Hahn. 6:57 S27'30. 8441
Poets are being watched. Prose. E. B. White. 4:22 F25'28. 8442
Poet's meter. Verse. Mildred Weston. 9:63 O7'33. 8443
Poets must expound. Verse. Martha Banning Thomas. 6:17 My3 '30. 8444
Poet's pedigree. Verse. Jerome Barry. 5:27 S7'29. 8445
Poet's progress. ML. John Strong Newberry. 9:56 Ap15'33. 8446
Poet's progress. PR (Kemp). Murdock Pemberton. 1:9-10 Ag8'25. 8447
Poison. RL. Beverly L. Clarke. 4:34-40 Ja19'29. 8448
Poisonous mushrooms--are we at the crossroads? Prose. S. J. Perelman. 9:24-5 S23'33. 8449
Poisson d'avril. Prose. Donald Moffat. 9:12 Ap1'33. 8450
Polar serenade. Verse. Arthur Guiterman. 7:53*Ag8'31. 8451
The pole at last. Prose. Corey Ford. 2:13 My22'26. 8452
Police! Prose. Theodore Pratt. 3:30-2 Je25'27. 8453
Police are baffled. Prose. Wolcott Gibbs. 5:22-3 Ja25'30. 8454
Police Gazette. Donald Thompson. 5:26-7 N30'29. 8455
Policeman on horseback. PP. Burke Boyce. 3:33 F11'28. 8456
Policy. Verse. Carolyn Wells. 4:25 Ag11'28. 8457
Polite drinking. Prose. E. M. Cody. 3:69-70 Je18'27. 8458
Political assault. Prose. Hugh O'Connor. 3:34-8 F11'28. 8459
The political outlook. Prose. Frank Sullivan. 4:23-4 Mr31'28. 8460
The political situation. Prose. Frank Sullivan. 13:30-2*Ag7'37. 8461
Political strategy. Verse. John Holmes. 12:29*O10'36. 8462
The politician. Verse. Ogden Nash. 12:23*Jy4'36. 8463
Politics. Prose. Loring M. Black, Jr. 1:19 Ja23'26. 8464
Pollock, Channing. PR. Percy Ham-

Portrait of a financier. SM. Alexander Woollcott. 7:30 Ja 30'32. 8511
Portrait of a floor-walker. Verse. Charles Norman. 4:92 S15'28. 8512
Portrait of a gentleman. Verse. Herbert Gerhard Bruncken. 5: 38 Mr30'29. 8513
Portrait of a gilded male lily. Prose. Nancy Hardin. 5:128-9 D14'29. 8514
Portrait of a lady. Verse. Frances M. Frost. 6:16 Jy5'30. 8515
Portrait of a lady. Verse. Frances Park. 3:57 O8'27. 8516
Portrait of a lady. Verse. Selma Robinson. 5:74 O12'29. 8517
Portrait of a lady. Prose. James Thurber. 3:99 Ap9'27. 8518
Portrait of a lady bathing. Prose. Alice Frankforter. 4:51-2 Ag18 '28. 8519
"Portrait of a man with red hair." PR (Marx). Alexander Woollcott. 4:33-6 D1'28. 8520
Portrait of a poet at the Dome. Verse. E. B. White. 2:64 S11 '26. 8521
Portrait of a referee. Prose. John O'Hara. 6:88-90 N15'30. 8522
Portrait of a wife. Prose. Myra M. Waterman. 8:36-7 Ja14'33. 8523
Portrait of an American author. Prose. Elmer Davis. 1:24 F6 '26. 8524
A portrait of Aunt Ida. Prose. James Thurber. 10:19-20 N10 '34. 8525
Portrait of ladies. Prose. Mark Schorer. 14:26-7*Ja14'39. 8526
Portrait of my brother. Prose. Alice Frankforter. 5:45-6 S21 '29. 8527
Portrait of two. Verse. Oliver Jenkins. 5:92 Ap13'29. 8528
Portraits on thumbnails. Verse. Irma Brandeis. 4:92 Mr3'28. 8529
Portraits on thumbnails. Verse. Irma Brandeis. 4:81 Mr24'28. 8530
Post Road impression. Verse. Anon. 2:53 My15'26. 8531
A Post-Road pickup. Prose. Emile C. Schnurmacher. 5:45-6 S14'29. 8532
The post-card addict takes the stand. Prose. Frank Sullivan. 6:14-15 Je28'30. 8533
Postcard to R. N. Verse. Stephen Vincent Benét. 14:75*D3'38. 8534
Post-election forecast. Prose. Frank Sullivan. 12:38-42*N21 '36. 8535
The post-election slump. WP. Robert Benchley. 4:42-7 D1'28. 8536
Postscript. SM. Alexander Woollcott. 7:35 O17'31. 8537
Postscript to a profile. SM. Alexander Woollcott. 9:30 O28'33. 8538
Postscript to publicity. Verse. Hortense Flexner. 14:28*Ap16 '38. 8539
Postscripts. SM. Alexander Woollcott. 10:116*D8'34. 8540
Post time. RL. Morris Markey. 11:34-40*Mr2'35. 8541
Postwar generation. Verse. Helene Mullins. 7:27 N14'31. 8542
Post-war morals. Prose. Stanley Walker. 1:12 Ag8'25. 8543
Pot luck at a Fifth Avenue florist's. Verse. Margaret Fishback. 8:54 S17'32. 8544
Potemkin. (Film) TT. 2:20 S11'26. 8545
The Potts case. Prose. Frances Crane. 6:24-6 Jy26'30. 8546
Pound, Ezra. (Parody) Lee Wilson Dodd. 9:69 My20'33. 8547
Pour la patrie. Prose. Rose Feld. 15:96-9*D16'39. 8548
Pour la patrie. Prose. John K. Hutchens. 10:66-8 Ap14'34. 8549
Pour le sport. Prose. Sally Benson. 7:44-6 N14'31. 8550
Pour le sport. RL. Morris Markey. 6:46-52 N22'30. 8551
Pour prendre congé. Verse. Doro-

Chapin Mosher. 7:15-16*Jy4 '31. 8599
Prelude to reunion. Prose. Oliver LaFarge. 15:73-4*Ap15'39. 8600
Prelude to Winter. Verse. William Carlos Williams. 15:24*O14'39. 8601
Premature epitaph. Verse. Fairfax Downey. 3:53 S3'27. 8602
Premonition. Verse. Frances M. Frost. 8:14 Ag27'32. 8603
Preparatory questions for income tax blanks. Prose. C. T. Greenwood. 3:56 Mr12'27. 8604
Preposterous parables. Prose. E. B. White. 13:17*Jy10'37; 13:26*Jy17'37; 13:17-18*Jy31'37; 15:18*Jy22'39. 8605
Prescription for a suffering friend. Verse. Margaret Fishback. 5:34 F8'30. 8606
Presenting the Belmont bar. Prose. E. B. White. 6:23 Je28 '30. 8607
Presently--a modern Achilles. Prose. A. G. Lockhart. 1:16 F13'26. 8608
Preserving the peace. Prose. T.H. Wenning. 7:43-5 S5'31. 8609
The president. PR (Hoover). Henry F. Pringle. 6:20-3 D27'30; 6:22-5 Ja3'31; 6:22-5 Ja10'31. 8610
The president. PR (Roosevelt). Henry F. Pringle. 10:20-5 Je 16'34; 10:20-4 Je23'34; 10:20-4 Je30'34. 8611
Presidential year. RL. Morris Markey. 4:36-42 Mr10'28. 8612
Presidents in the Bronx. Prose. Arthur Kober. 14:16-18*Je4 '38. 8613
The President's son. Prose. Donald Ogden Stewart. 3:24-5 D10 '27. 8614
Press agents I have known. Prose. Groucho Marx. 5:52-5 Mr9'29. 8615
The press announcement. Prose. Arthur Kober. 6:59-60 S13'30. 8616
The press in review. Prose. Robert Benchley. 3:28-32 Jy23'27. 8617
The press in review. Prose. Robert Benchley. 3:28-30 Ag13'27. 8618
The press in review. Prose. Robert Benchley. 3:25-6 S3'27. 8619
The press in review. Prose. Robert Benchley. 3:33-4 O8'27. 8620
The press in review. Prose. Robert Benchley. 3:26-8 N5'27. 8621
The press in review. Prose. Robert Benchley. 3:48-52 D3'27. 8622
The press in review. Prose. Philip G. Wylie. 3:28-30 Jy2'27. 8623
Presto! Fame! RL. Morris Markey. 2:23-4 S4'26. 8624
Presumption. Verse. Miriam Vedder. 6:75 F14'31. 8625
The pretenders. RL. Morris Markey. 2:26-31 Je12'26. 8626
A pretty girl. Prose. Beth Wendel. 12:63*My23'36. 8627
A pretty pass. Prose. Robert Benchley. 3:14-16 O1'27. 8628
Pretty poems. Verse. W. E. Farbstein. 11:30*O26'35. 8629
Pretty poems. Verse. W. E. Farbstein. 12:17*O24'36. 8630
Pretty thanks. Verse. Hortense Flexner. 14:53*S24'38. 8631
Pretzel peddler. PP. Burke Boyce. 4:29 S29'28. 8632
Prewar era. NYC. Ralph McAllister Ingersoll. 10:41-8 Ap14'34. 8633
Prey. Verse. Mildred Weston. 10:66 S8'34. 8634
The price of liquor. RL. Edward Angly. 9:62-7 O21'33. 8635
The price of Prohibition. Prose. Fairfax Downey. 3:38-9 Jy2'27. 8636
Price's--always open. Prose. John O'Hara. 13:15-17*Ag14'37. 8637
Prima donna. Prose. Henry Anton. 12:18-20*O24'36. 8638

Loon. 3:27 My7'27. 8680
The program-note writer deals with a new tone poem. Prose. Creighton Peet. 3:44-6 D10 '27. 8681
Program notes. Prose. Elmer Rice. 7:20-2 Mr28'31. 8682
Program notes. Prose. Robert A. Simon. 2:34-6 Ap24'26. 8683
Progress. Verse. Fillmore Hyde. 2:21 My29'26. 8684
Progress. Prose. Marion Sturges-Jones. 9:72-3 S30'33. 8685
Progress in Boston. Verse. Trench. 12:59*S12'36. 8686
Progress of science. Verse. Arthur Guiterman. 11:30*My25 '35. 8687
Progress of science. Verse. Arthur Guiterman. 11:25*Je1'35. 8688
Progress on the lakes. OFC. E. F. K. 12:44-6*S26'36. 8689
Prokosch, Frederic. TT. 12:13*O 10'36. 8690
Prologue to anything. Verse. Arthur Guiterman. 6:79 My3'30. 8691
Promenade. Verse. Anon. 2:84 N6'26. 8692
Prometheus bound. PR (Day). Geoffrey T. Hellman. 9:18-22 My27'33. 8693
Prominent New Yorkers. Prose. Marc Connelly. 4:21-2 Ap28 '28. 8694
Promise. Verse. Elspeth O'Halloran. 8:28 Je4'32. 8695
The promised land. Prose. Emily Hahn. 14:57-9*My21'38. 8696
Promising lad. WATN. James Thurber. 12:21-3*Ap25'36. 8697
The promoter. Verse. Persis Greely Anderson. 7:68 My2'31. 8698
The promoter. Prose. Arthur Kober. 4:30-1 My12'28. 8699
The promotion. Prose. Arthur Kober. 5:44-7 Mr16'29. 8700
Promotion. Prose. Harold Wengler. 5:57-8 O26'29. 8701
Propaganda and such. WP. Robert Benchley. 5:53-9 O5'29. 8702
Prophecy. Verse. Frances M. Frost. 5:102 Je8'29. 8703
Prophecy. Verse. Philip G. Wylie. 2:51 Ja15'27. 8704
Prophet, 1931. PR (Wise). Geoffrey T. Hellman. 7:22-5 N7'31. 8705
Prophet of doom. PR (Babson). Henry F. Pringle. 5:23-5 F15 '30. 8706
The prophets. RL. Morris Markey. 6:37-41 Ja24'31. 8707
Prosit New Year. Prose. Alice Frankforter. 6:60-1 Ja3'31. 8708
Prospectus. Verse. Lee Wilson Dodd. 8:20*Mr19'32. 8709
Prospectus. Prose. Robert Sellmer. 12:62-3*F22'36. 8710
Prospectus of Pandemonium Court. Prose. Elmer Davis. 5:18-20 Je22'29. 8711
Protected. Prose. Frances Crane. 8:63-4 Je4'32. 8712
Protest. Prose. Owen P. White. 1:8 Ag8'25. 8713
Protest along vegetarian lines. Verse. Margaret Fishback. 9: 23 S16'33. 8714
Protest of a man about town. Verse. Margaret Fishback. 7: 73 D19'31. 8715
The proud. Verse. Charles Norman. 6:17 Je7'30. 8716
Proust, Marcel. Janet Flanner. 3: 37 D24'27. 8717
Proven field. Verse. Frances M. Frost. 5:34 O26'29. 8718
Provençal. Prose. Theodore Pratt. 7:47-8*Je20'31. 8719
Proverbs from a younger Solomon. Prose. Isabelle Stewart Way. 1:24 S5'25. 8720
Proverbs from a younger Solomon. Prose. Isabelle Stewart Way. 1:25 S19'25. 8721
Provincetown night. Verse. Frances Park. 3:40 Jy23'27. 8722
Provincial. Verse. Ethel Arnold Tilden. 5:126 O19'29. 8723
The prudent man's guide to profligacy. Verse. Ogden Nash. 12: 18*My2'36. 8724

'35. 8768
Putting it mildly. SM. Alexander Woollcott. 9:36 Ap22'33. 8769
Puzzled parent. Verse. John Holmes. 14:29*Ja28'39. 8770
Pythagoras and the ladder. LYMA. James Thurber. 12:15-17*N28'36. 8771

Q

Q. E. D. Prose. Eleanor Gilchrist. 15:62-4*My13'39. 8772
Q's and A's. RL. Meyer Berger. 15:39-40*Ja27'40. 8773
Quadroon. Prose. Ring Lardner. 7:17-18 D19'31. 8774
Quake well before losing. Verse. Margaret Fishback. 5:91 D7 '29. 8775
Quandary. Verse. Leslie Nelson Jennings. 4:101 My5'28. 8776
Quarrel. Verse. Philip G. Wylie. 3:97 F19'27. 8777
Quatrain by a chorine. Verse. Anon. 2:52 Mr13'26. 8778
A quatrain of quotations. Prose. W. E. Farbstein. 9:24 Jy15'33. 8779
Quatrain on Spring. Verse. Anon. 2:36 Ap24'26. 8780
The queen of Hackensack. TWNY. Herbert Asbury. 7:19-22 F13 '32. 8781
The Queen's ghost. Verse. Margaret Widdener. 13:34*D11'37. 8782
Queens, up-to-date. Verse. Edith Franklin Wyatt. 13:29* My1'37. 8783
Queens weep. Verse. Clinch Calkins. 3:15 Ag20'27. 8784
Queer birds I have known. Prose. William Rose Benét. 4:14-15 Je30'28. 8785
Query. Verse. Anon. 4:52 Mr31 '28. 8786
Query. Verse. Mildred Weston. 6:120 D6'30. 8787
Query for April 24th. Verse. Margaret Fishback. 8:31*Ap23'32. 8788
Quest. Verse. Persis Greely Anderson. 7:36 Mr21'31. 8789
Quest. Verse. Clinch Calkins. 3:17 F11'28. 8790
Quest metropolitan. Verse. Philip G. Wylie. 2:47 S25'26. 8791
Question in a field. Verse. Louise Bogan. 13:19*Jy31'37. 8792
The question mark. Verse. Persis Greely Anderson. 6:85 O11'30. 8793
? Prose. Joseph Fulling Fishman. 2:52-3 N13'26. 8794
Question mark. RL. Morris Markey. 6:42-9 S13'30. 8795
Question, more or less direct. Verse. E. B. White. 9:14 Jy22 '33. 8796
A question of taste. Prose. Lois Long and Nancy Hardin. 1:22 F28'25. 8797
Questionnaire. Prose. Robert M. Coates. 9:32-6 S30'33. 8798
Questionnaire. SM. Alexander Woollcott. 6:28 Ag23'30. 8799
Questionnaire for a lightning bug operating in East Fiftieth Street. Verse. Margaret Fishback. 8:34 Jy16'32. 8800
Questionnaires. Prose. Elmer Rice. 7:18-21*Je6'31. 8801
Quick curtain. Verse. Elspeth O'Halloran. 5:38 My18'29. 8802
Quick lunch. Prose. Spud Johnson. 3:44-6 Mr26'27. 8803
Quiet at home. Prose. George Shepherd. 14:47-51*S10'38. 8804
A quiet evening with the phone book. Prose. Philip G. Wylie. 3:102-103 Ap30'27. 8805
Quiet old Gramercy. Prose. Jess Nancy Grice. 6:40-2 F7'31. 8806
Quiet places. Verse. Babette Deutsch. 13:26*Jy17'37. 8807
Quiet, please. Verse. Anon. 1:17 D26'25. 8808
Quiet please! WP. Robert Benchley. 6:32-8 Ja10'31. 8809
Quiet please. Verse. James Thurber. 4:79 F9'29. 8810
Quiet zone. Verse. Margaret Fish-

back. 5:87 Mr30'29. 8811

Quite true, partner, quite true. Verse. Parke Cummings. 7:69*Je13'31. 8812

Quito. OFC. Ludwig Bemelmans. 13:88*O30'37. 8813

Quo vadimus? Prose. E. B. White. 6:17-18 My24'30. 8814

R

Râbat. FP. H. L. Mencken. 10:32-4 Jy21'34. 8815

R. F. Tweedle D. Prose. E. B. White. 14:18*My14'38. 8816

Rabbit season. Verse. Frances M. Frost. 8:27 N5'32. 8817

The rabbit that bit the bulldog. PR (Broun). Heywood Broun. 3:18-22 O1'27. 8818

The rabbits conquer fear. Prose. Clarence Day. 9:25-6 D9'33. 8819

The race. Verse. Robert P. Tristram Coffin. 14:23*Ag20'38. 8820

The racket racket. Prose. Frederick Packard. 5:65-6 Ja11'30. 8821

Radio blues. Verse. Kenneth Fearing. 14:24*N26'38. 8822

Radio bridge. Verse. Parke Cummings. 3:38 D3'27. 8823

Radio clinic. Verse. Leslie Nelson Jennings. 12:49*F13'37. 8824

Radio football. Prose. John R. Tunis. 1:27-8 D5'25. 8825

Radio patrol. RL. Morris Markey. 10:49-52 Mr3'34. 8826

Radio sans static. Prose. Clara Janson. 1:10 Je20'25. 8827

Radio's all-America team for 1932-1933. OW. Ring Lardner. 9:43-4 Je17'33. 8828

Rafter and feast. Verse. Frances M. Frost. 6:22 Ap5'30. 8829

"Rain." OFC. Beatrice Wels. 13:64*O9'37. 8830

Rain. (Film) TT. 4:18 Mr17'28. 8831

Rain in an evil world. Verse. Raymond Holden. 9:31 O21 '33. 8832

Rain in New Hampshire. Verse. Frances M. Frost. 12:47*Jy25 '36. 8833

Rain in the Bronx. Prose. Arthur Kober. 10:53-6 Je2'34. 8834

Rain song. Verse. Frances M. Frost. 6:66 Jy12'30. 8835

The rainbow man. (Film) TT. 5:15 Ap27'29. 8836

Raincoats. Verse. Arthur Guiterman. 14:62*Mr19'38. 8837

Rainy day taxi blues. Verse. Joseph Moncure March. 3:54 Ap9 '27. 8838

Rainy night. Verse. Dorothy Parker. 1:10 S26'25. 8839

Rainy Sunday. Verse. Dudley Fitts. 15:36*D30'39. 8840

Rainy woods. Verse. Frances M. Frost. 6:25 Jy19'30. 8841

A raise in salary. Prose. St. Clair McKelway. 10:20-2 O27 '34. 8842

Raise the flag. Verse. Margaret Fishback. 4:56 S1'28. 8843

Ramon. Prose. Frances Crane. 15:67-8*Ap15'39. 8844

Rampant but respectable. PR (Wald). Helena Huntington Smith. 5:32-5 D14'29. 8845

Random reflections. Verse. Ogden Nash. 6:16 Jy12'30. 8846

Random reflections. Verse. Ogden Nash. 6:22 Ag9'30. 8847

Random reflections. Verse. Ogden Nash. 6:24 S20'30. 8848

Random reflections. Verse. Ogden Nash. 6:28 O25'30. 8849

Random reflections. Verse. Ogden Nash. 6:18 N1'30. 8850

Random reflections on a passé Feb. Verse. Ogden Nash. 8:22* Mr5'32. 8851

Rare as music. PR (Ornstein). Waldo Frank. 1:9-10 D19'25. 8852

Rascoe, Burton. (Parody) Jack Alexander. 13:38-40 Je12'37. 8853

The rather difficult case of Mr. K·A·P·L·A·N. Prose. Leo Rosten. 12:18-20*Ag22'36. 8854

A rather unusual essay. Prose. Marc Connelly. 2:29-30 D11 '26. 8855
Rational history. Verse. Parke Cummings. 7:52 S12'31. 8856
Rattling a skeleton. SM. Alexander Woollcott. 10:38-40 N10 '34. 8857
Raze New York as moral blot, church may beg Congress. Verse. Howard Cushman. 1:32 O17'25. 8858
Reaction. Verse. Florence Stone. 3:48 Je25'27. 8859
Reactions of a reactionary. Prose. H. L. Mencken. 15:56-60*N4 '39. 8860
The reader writes. Verse. Carl Crane. 15:22*Jy8'39. 8861
The Reader's Digest discovers the Bible. Prose. E. B. White. 12:20*Ja30'37. 8862
Readers Digest. (Parody) E. B. White. 12:20*Ja30'37. 8863
Readers to the sea. Verse. Richard Armour. 15:46*Jy29'39. 8864
Reading and writhing. Prose. S. J. Perelman. 11:18-19*Ja11'36. 8865
Reading the sports. Prose. Waldo Frank. 2:21 My8'26. 8866
Reading time: eternity. Prose. Wolcott Gibbs. 13:14*F12'38. 8867
Readings, forecasts, personal guidance. Verse. Kenneth Fearing. 15:23*My20'39. 8868
The ready-made house. OUWA. Lewis Mumford. 12:61-4*N7 '36. 8869
Real estate. Verse. E. B. White. 2:26 Ja22'27. 8870
A real need. Prose. W. G. H. 1: 21 My16'25. 8871
Real news. WP. Robert Benchley. 10:40-4 Mr10'34. 8872
A real nice story. Prose. Carlton Brown. 11:74-6*Ap6'35. 8873
The real real Louis McHenry Howe. Prose. Frank Sullivan. 9:20-1 F18'33. 8874
Realism, French and American. Janet Flanner. 6:44 F7'31. 8875
Realistic review. Verse. Dearing Ward. 8:22*F20'32. 8876
Really a blessing. Prose. Horton Heath. 11:63*O19'35. 8877
Really living. Prose. Sally Benson. 11:18-20*F8'36. 8878
Realtor. PR (French). Robert M. Coates. 5:22-5 Je1'29. 8879
Reasonableness. Verse. Anon. 1: 27 Ja16'26. 8880
Rebuke. SM. Alexander Woollcott. 9:31 S23'33. 8881
Rebuttal. Prose. Baird Leonard. 3:20 Jy9'27. 8882
Recalling O. Henry. Prose. Art Young. 6:22-5 Jy12'30. 8883
Recapitulation. Verse. Leslie Nelson Jennings. 3:73 D10'27. 8884
The receiving line. Prose. E. B. White. 2:21 S25'26. 8885
Recessional. Verse. Margaretta Manning. 4:32 S1'28. 8886
Recipe for an evening musicale. Verse. Phyllis McGinley. 12:69* Mr21'36. 8887
Recipe for anger. Verse. Mildred Weston. 9:76 S16'33. 8888
Reciprocity in sports. Prose. Stanley Jones. 1:32 S19'25. 8889
Recital. Verse. Philip G. Wylie. 2:58 O2'26. 8890
Recitation piece. Verse. David McCord. 15:18*F25'39. 8891
Reclamation. SM. Alexander Woollcott. 5:36 Je8'29. 8892
A recluse contemplates vagabondia. Verse. Rollin Kirby. 3:27 My14 '27. 8893
Recollections of academic orgies. Prose. H. L. Mencken. 15:29-34*Je17'39. 8894
Recollections of Henry James. Prose. James Thurber. 9:11-13 Je17'33. 8895
Recollections of my mother. Prose. Victoria Sackville-West. 13:19-20*S11'37; 13:19-21*S18 '37; 13:19-20*O2'37; 13:19*O16 '37; 13:25-6*O30'37. 8896

The recommendation. Prose. Charlton Andrews. 4:69-70 My5'28. 8897
Recommendation. Verse. Parke Cummings. 5:64 D28'29. 8898
Recompense. Verse. Oriana Atkinson. 13:39*Jy17'37. 8899
Reconstruction of the crime. Prose. Margaret Ford. 9:38 S2'33. 8900
The record. RL. Hugh Blake. 8:42-8 O8'32. 8901
Record by Yvette Guilbert. Verse. Babette Deutsch. 14:18*My28 '38. 8902
Record of a crusade. Prose. James Kevin McGuinness. 1:24 Jy25'25. 8903
Record of the self-effacement of a rank outsider. Verse. A. K. Laing. 3:50 Je25'27. 8904
Recreation. Prose. A. C. M. Azoy. 3:60 Ag27'27. 8905
Red berries. Verse. James Stephens. 5:26 My25'29. 8906
Red dress. Verse. Mildred Weston. 4:34 Je16'28. 8907
The red hat. Prose. Morley Callaghan. 7:18-20 O31'31. 8908
Red hot. PR (Stevens). Niven Busch, Jr. 4:23-5 Ag11'28. 8909
Red-hot Summer news. WP. Robert Benchley. 4:28-33 Jy21'28. 8910
The red house. RL. Matthew Josephson. 8:39-44 S17'32. 8911
The red-ink day. Prose. Richard Lockridge. 15:64-5*Ap22'39. 8912
The red-light district. Prose. Rube Goldberg. 4:22-4 N3'28. 8913
Red Sea sacrifice. Prose. Wolcott Gibbs. 13:19-20*Ja15'38. 8914
Red spectacles. Verse. Elise Jerard. 14:41*S3'38. 8915
Red star at evening. Prose. Robert Buckner. 11:28-30*My25 '35. 8916
Red thirst. Prose. Bettina Sinclair. 11:63*F23'35. 8917
Red, white, and blue. PR (Bowlby). Henry F. Pringle. 5:30-3 S28'29. 8918
Redecoration day. Verse. Frances Lockridge. 11:60*S28'35. 8919
Redemption. Prose. Ted Patrick. 4:68-9 N17'28. 8920
References satisfactory. Prose. Elmer Davis. 5:19-20 Je15'29. 8921
Referred to Pontius Pilate. SM. Alexander Woollcott. 5:30 F8 '30. 8922
Reflection. Verse. Tristram Livingstone. 13:54*S4'37. 8923
Reflection. Verse. Sydney King Russell. 7:14*My30'31. 8924
Reflection becomes the morning after "Mourning becomes Electra." Verse. Arthur Guiterman. 7:28 D5'31. 8925
Reflections (in all senses) on my friends. Verse. Hortense Flexner. 9:54 Mr18'33. 8926
Reflections of a young lady about to be married. Verse. Charlotte Armstrong. 4:51 Mr10'28. 8927
Reflections of an aging juror. Prose. McAlister Coleman. 8:44-50 N12'32. 8928
Reflections of more or less silent New Yorkers. Prose. Zelda F. Popkin. 2:103-104 D11'26. 8929
Reflections of silent citizens. Prose. Zelda F. Popkin. 2:81 F12'27. 8930
Reflections of silent citizens. Prose. Zelda F. Popkin. 3:69 F26'27. 8931
Reflections of silent New Yorkers. Prose. Zelda F. Popkin. 2:38-9 O30'26. 8932
Reflections on Douglas Fairbanks. Verse. James Norman Hall. 9:21 Jy1'33. 8933
Reflections on living practically next door to the Metropolitan Tower chimes. Verse. Margaret Fishback. 3:47 Jy30'27. 8934
Reflections on seeing a young couple depart on their honey-

moon. Verse. Margaret Fishback. 4:55 Je23'28. 8935
Reform. Verse. Rosemary Carr Benét. 5:78 F15'30. 8936
Reform. Verse. Parke Cummings. 4:79 O27'28. 8937
Reform. Prose. Morris Markey. 6:23-5 N29'30. 8938
Reformed spellbinder. PR (Littleton). Alva Johnston. 8:18-22 Ag20'32. 8939
Reformed witches. Verse. Elizabeth Coatsworth. 13:47*S18 '37. 8940
Refrain from the Palisades. Verse. Sylvia Fuller. 4:68 Je 23'28. 8941
Refuge. Verse. Frances M. Frost. 5:27 Je22'29. 8942
Regina vs. Wilde. SM. Alexander Woollcott. 8:34 N12'32. 8943
Rehearsal. Prose. T. H. Wenning. 6:23-4 Ja17'31. 8944
Reigen. (Play) TT. 6:9 N1'30. 8945
Reincarnations. Verse. Clarence Day. 10:29 Ap28'34. 8946
Reinhardt and revolution. Prose. Mary Heaton Vorse. 7:37-9 D26'31. 8947
The rejected one. Prose. Morley Callaghan. 9:23-5 D9'33. 8948
Relativity. Verse. Lenore G. Marshall. 11:27*My25'35. 8949
Relic. Verse. Peggy Bacon. 10:50 F24'34. 8950
Relic. Verse. Isabel McLennan McMeekin. 5:78 Mr2'29. 8951
Relief. RL. Morris Markey. 11:40-6*Ap20'35. 8952
Relief ahead. Prose. Margaret Fishback. 5:92-4 S28'29. 8953
Religion. Verse. Arthur Guiterman. 1:14 Je13'25. 8954
Remaining adventure. Verse. Alice Corbin. 13:52*Jy17'37. 8955
The remarkable case of Mr. Bruhl. Prose. James Thurber. 6:23-5 N15'30. 8956
Remarks on the proposed abandonment of the Rutland Railroad. Verse. Morris Bishop. 14:19*O8'38. 8957
Remarque, Erich-Maria. Janet Flanner. 6:50-1 N15'30. 8958
Remembrance of things past. Verse. Baird Leonard. 6:109 My17'30. 8959
Remembrance of things past. Prose. James Thurber. 12:25-6*S12'36. 8960
Reminiscences of my career on the operatic stage. Prose. Margaret Fishback. 3:49-51 F 26'27. 8961
Remnant of Attica. RL. Morris Markey. 11:47-50*Ap13'35. 8962
Remorse under the "L." Verse. Margaret Fishback. 8:19 Ag13 '32. 8963
Rendevous. Verse. Arthur Guiterman. 1:8 Mr28'25. 8964
Renegade. Verse. Marjorie Allen Seiffert. 12:54*S19'36. 8965
Renfrew Mudge. Verse. Lee Wilson Dodd. 6:26 Ap26'30. 8966
Rent-collector. TWNY. M. R. Werner. 11:97-102*D7'35. 8967
The renting agent muses. Prose. James Kevin McGuinness. 1:15 O31'25. 8968
Renting the Leviathan. Prose. E. B. White. 2:50-1 O2'26. 8969
The repatriation of the minstrel. Prose. Stephen Leacock. 4:28 O6'28. 8970
The repertorial dance marathon. WP. Robert Benchley. 8:28-32 Jy23'32. 8971
Reply, in kind. Verse. George Henry Payne. 8:79 N19'32. 8972
Reply to an invitation to drive to Sea Bright and back next Sunday. Verse. Margaret Fishback 6:54 Ag16'30. 8973
Reply to petition to the mayor. Verse. Joseph V. McKee. 8:23 D24'32. 8974
Replying to your favor. Prose. George Cecil Cowing. 5:42-6 Je15'29. 8975
Report from the field. Prose. P. T. L. Putnam. 7:38-9 F28

Prose. Robert Benchley. 3:24 Ag20'27. 9058
Revolution. RL. Morris Markey. 11:49-54*My25'35. 9059
Revolution's number one boy. PR (Odets). John McCarten. 13:21-7*Ja22'38. 9060
Reward. Verse. Brownell Carr. 3:31 Ap16'27. 9061
The reward of virtue. Prose. James B. Clark. 6:32-4 My3 '30. 9062
Rewards and fairies. Verse. Arthur Guiterman. 6:56 O4'30. 9063
Rex redivivus. Verse. David McCord. 9:57 Mr11'33. 9064
Rhapsody in blue. Verse. James Reid Parker. 7:17*Jy4'31. 9065
Rhapsody in cochineal-pink. Prose. Geoffrey T. Hellman. 15:71-2*Je17'39. 9066
Rhyme. Verse. Louise Bogan. 11:26*Je8'35. 9067
Rhyme after vacation. Verse. Grace Hazard Conkling. 5:23 O5'29. 9068
Rhyme of an involuntary violet. Verse. Dorothy Parker. 2:16 My15'26. 9069
A rhyme of contrast. Verse. Grace Hazard Conkling. 5:13 Jy27'29. 9070
Rhyme to jingle in the purse. Verse. Martha Banning Thomas. 5:67 D7'29. 9071
Rhymes for budding bards. Prose. Robert M. Coates. 14:44*D31 '38. 9072
Rhymes from a coquette's diary. Verse. Maxwell Bodenheim. 1:30 Ja23'26. 9073
Rhymes from out of town. Verse. Elizabeth Coatsworth. 7:77 My 16'31. 9074
Rhymes from out of town. Verse. Elizabeth Coatsworth. 7:23 Ag 22'31. 9075
Rhymes from out of town. Verse. Elizabeth Coatsworth. 7:25 Ag 29'31. 9076
Rhymes from out of town. Verse. Elizabeth Coatsworth. 7:25 S5 '31. 9077
Rhymes from out of town. Verse. Elizabeth Coatsworth. 7:29 S12 '31. 9078
Rhymes from out of town. Verse. Elizabeth Coatsworth. 7:78 Ja9 '32. 9079
Rhymes from out of town. Verse. Elizabeth Coatsworth. 8:15 Ag20 '32. 9080
Rhymes from out of town. Verse. Elizabeth Coatsworth. 8:17 Ag 27'32. 9081
Rhymes from out of town. Verse. Elizabeth Coatsworth. 8:21 S3 '32. 9082
Rhymes from out of town. Verse. Elizabeth Coatsworth. 8:16 S17 '32. 9083
Rice, Elmer. Janet Flanner. 5:54-6 D14'29. 9084
Rice, Elmer. TT. 5:14-15 F23'29. 9085
Richard Wagner: public domain. Prose. John O'Hara. 14:12*S3 '38. 9086
Richelieu in Shanghai. Prose. Emily Hahn. 12:22-3*Ap4'36. 9087
A richer life for parents. Prose. Elmer Davis. 14:16-18*Ap16'38. 9088
Rickard rounds up the rubes. PR (Rickard). W. O. McGeehan. 1:17-18 D12'25. 9089
Ricordi to the rescue. OW. Ring Lardner. 9:43-4 Ag5'33. 9090
Ride with Judith. Prose. Richard Lockridge. 8:46-7 F11'33. 9091
A ride with Olympy. Prose. James Thurber. 14:17-20*Ap30'38. 9092
A ride with Ralph. Prose. Francis Steegmuller. 10:19-21 Ap21'34. 9093
Rien à déclarer. Verse. Henrietta Fort Holland. 4:26 Ag18'28. 9094
Rien ne va plus. SM. Alexander Woollcott. 8:36*Mr5'32. 9095
The Riggs-Van Plank correspondence. Prose. Joseph Alger. 2:

15:41*N4'39. 9183
Rotary Club celebrates. Prose. Anon. 1:19 Mr21'25. 9184
Rotogravure. Verse. Carol Phyllis Schmid. 5:121 My25'29. 9185
Rotten--and not in Denmark. Prose. Don Herold. 6:30-2 F 14'31. 9186
Rouge on the brain. Prose. Hildegarde Dolson. 13:36-7*Ja 1'38. 9187
Roughneck and romancer. PR (O'Neill). Maxwell Bodenheim. 1:17-18 F6'26. 9188
Roumania's royal saleslady. PR (Queen Marie). John K. Winkler. 2:26-7 O23'26. 9189
Round trip to Nanking. RL. Emily Hahn. 13:52-62*S18'37. 9190
Route salesman. PR (Reiselin). Robert M. Coates. 11:18-22*Je 22'35. 9191
Royal love matches. Prose. Frank Sullivan. 10:22-4*S22 '34. 9192
A royal visit. RL. Morris Markey. 2:26-30 Je19'26. 9193
The royal visitor. RL. Morris Markey. 2:34-6 O30'26. 9194
Royce, William H. PR. Alva Johnston. 9:18-21 Ap1'33. 9195
Roycroft revisited. RL. Morris Bishop. 14:48-52*O8'38. 9196
The royil plan. Prose. Robert M. Coates. 11:59-60*Mr2'35. 9197
Rubbing elbows. Prose. E. B. White. 3:23-4 Je11'27. 9198
Rubia. Prose. Arthur Kober. 10: 82-4*N17'34. 9199
Ruby Moon. MNL. Thyra Samter Winslow. 10:52-6 Jy28'34. 9200
Rudy in irate mood. OW. Ring Lardner. 8:49-50 F4'33. 9201
The rueful rhyme of a robin. Verse. Martha Banning Thomas. 3:30 My21'27. 9202
Rueful rhymes. Verse. Martha Banning Thomas. 3:46 Ap9'27. 9203
The ruin of an artist. Prose. H. L. Mencken. 15:23-6*My27 '39. 9204
Ruins. Verse. E. B. White. 2:18 Ag28'26. 9205
Rule by commission. RL. Alva Johnston. 4:28-36 Jy28'28. 9206
Rules of the game. Verse. Margaret Fishback. 7:20 N7'31. 9207
Rum runners must live. Prose. Emile C. Schnurmacher. 2:25-6 Mr6'26. 9208
Rumba. Prose. Frances Crane. 15:62-5*Mr25'39. 9209
Rumpelstiltzkin. Verse. Helene Mullins. 4:22 Je23'28. 9210
The run-around. Prose. Arthur Kober. 5:111-13 Ap20'29. 9211
Runes of increase. ML. John Strong Newberry. 9:24 Je17'33. 9212
Runyon, Damon. Janet Flanner. 13: 63-4*D4'37. 9213
Runyon, Damon. TT. 15:12*F18 '39; 15:13-14*My27'39. 9214
Rural New Yorker. PR (Dillon). Arthur Bartlett. 14:25-9*My21 '38. 9215
Rural New-Yorker. PR (Tugwell). Russell Lord. 11:20-4*Mr23 '35; 11:22-6*Mr30'35. 9216
Rural reminiscence. Verse. Gertrude Curtis Ryan. 7:74 Ap18 '31. 9217
A rural rout. Prose. Berry Fleming. 3:63-5 Je25'27. 9218
Rus in urbe. Prose. Elmer Davis. 3:21-2 Ag13'27. 9219
The rush of world events. WP. Robert Benchley. 5:30-8 Mr30 '29. 9220
Rus-sia. Prose. Freudy. 1:11 Ag 29'25. 9221
Russia Resartus. Verse. Margaretta Manning. 3:26 F18'28. 9222
Russia, third class. Prose. Hannah Lees. 12:46-9*O17'36. 9223
Russian: child's size. Prose. Emily Hahn. 15:46-9 *D9'39. 9224
Russian firebird. PR (Stravinsky). Janet Flanner. 10:23-8*Ja5'35. 9225
The Russian soul. Prose. John

Chapin Mosher. 6:20 Jy5'30. 9226

S

S for snuggly. Prose. Alan Campbell. 9:66-8 S9'33. 9227
The S. P. C. A. TWNY. Robert Curry. 5:57-60 S21'29. 9228
S. S. Log Chateau. HHT. Donald Moffat. 8:37-9 Ja28'33. 9229
S. S. Vaterland. RL. Jack Alexander. 13:29-35*Ag21'37. 9230
Sabbath in Westchester. Prose. John Chapin Mosher. 3:36 Jy 30'27. 9231
Sabbath morning subway. Verse. Ferner Nuhn. 3:55 Ja21'28. 9232
Sabbatical Summer. Prose. Louise Bogan. 7:18-21*Jy4'31. 9233
Sachem and totem at Pook-Wah-Met. Prose. Alan Campbell. 10:34-6 Ag25'34. 9234
Sackcloth and ashes. Verse. Sonia Ruthèle Novák. 6:105 Mr 8'30. 9235
Saco legends. Prose. Dane Yorke. 8:50-1 S3'32. 9236
Sacre du Printemps. RL. Morris Markey. 2:23 Jy17'26. 9237
The sacred grove. SM. Alexander Woollcott. 9:36-7 Ap1'33. 9238
The sacred white cow. Prose. Ben Hecht. 1:8 Ap18'25. 9239
Sacrilege. Verse. Gertrude Curtis Ryan. 3:103 O22'27. 9240
A sad song about Greenwich Village. Verse. Frances Park. 3:73 S17'27. 9241
Sad song from sanctuary. Verse. Phyllis McGinley. 13:26*O2'37. 9242
Sad song from the Gaelic. Verse. Arthur Guiterman. 8:25*Mr26 '32. 9243
Sad sounds. Verse. Theodore Shane. 1:35 O10'25. 9244
"The sad young women." Prose. M. Wilsey. 2:47 My29'26. 9245
A safe and sane Fourth. Prose. John O'Hara. 4:79-82 S15'28. 9246
Safety match. Verse. Margaret Fishback. 5:42 Jy13'29. 9247
Saffercisco. Prose. John O'Hara. 12:14*Ap11'36. 9248
Said with flowers. Prose. Katharine Brush. 4:55 Je16'28. 9249
Sailor off the Bremen. Prose. Irwin Shaw. 15:15-18*F25'39. 9250
Sailor, take warning. Verse. Margaret Fishback. 7:57 F21'31. 9251
Sailors' Snug Harbor. RL. Geoffrey T. Hellman. 10:67-73 My 26'34. 9252
Saint Al. PR (Woods). Percy Hammond. 3:25-7 F26'27. 9253
St. Elite. Prose. T. H. Bliss. 1:30-1 S19'25. 9254
St. George of Manhattan. PR (Jerome). Milton MacKaye. 7: 19-23 Ja30'32. 9255
Saint in politics. PR (Tuttle). Alva Johnston. 5:23-6 Mr23'29. 9256
St. Nicholas blues. Verse. Will Scarlet. 13:37*D25'37. 9257
The St. Nicholas League--a postscript. Prose. Albert Bigelow Paine. 10:84*Ja5'35. 9258
St. Valentine's. Prose. John Forbes. 3:76-7 F11'28. 9259
Saint's day in Elizabeth Street. Prose. Alice Frankforter. 6:24-6 Ag2'30. 9260
Saints in bed. Prose. John Chapin Mosher. 9:13-14 Jy29'33. 9261
Sale today. Verse. Phyllis McGinley. 15:45*Ja20'40. 9262
Salem-town. Verse. Dorothy Belle Flanagan. 4:18 D29'28. 9263
Sales promotion at the Brevoort. Verse. Margaret Fishback. 8:29* Ap30'32. 9264
Sales resistance. Verse. Margaret Fishback. 6:64 My17'30. 9265
Saleslady's Spring song. Verse. Margaret Fishback. 4:59 Ap7'28. 9266
Salesmanship. Prose. Winifred Willis. 7:75-6 S12'31. 9267
Salesmanship in the Champs-Elysées. Prose. F. Scott Fitz-

Schoolmarm. ME. Alfred Kreymborg. 3:20 S3'27. 9350
Schools. Verse. Anon. 2:24 Jy31 '26. 9351
Schuster, M. Lincoln. PR. Geoffrey T. Hellman. 15:22-8*S30 '39; 15:24-30*O7'39; 15:25-9* O14'39. 9352
Science. Verse. Clarence Day. 11:33*My11'35. 9353
Scientific evenings in New York. No. 1. RL. Morris Markey. 2:26-30 Jy3'26. 9354
Scientific evenings in New York. No. 2. RL. Morris Markey. 2:25-6 Jy24'26. 9355
The scientific mind. Prose. Brendan Gill. 13:16-19*My22 '37. 9356
A scientific Santa Claus. PR (Rockefeller). John K. Winkler. 4:27-31 Je2'28; 4:20-4 Je 9'28. 9357
Scientist and mob idol. PR (Einstein). Alva Johnston. 9:23-6 D2'33; 9:29-32 D9'33. 9358
Scissors-grinder. PP. Burke Boyce. 3:17 Ja7'28. 9359
"Scoop." WP. Robert Benchley. 6:43-50 O4'30. 9360
Scoops and denials. WP. E. B. White. 5:26-31 Jy6'29. 9361
Scotch in fifteen minutes. Prose. Frederick Packard. 7:55-8 Ap 11'31. 9362
Scotland in August. Prose. Francis Crane. 14:44-6*Ag20'38. 9363
Scout boy. Prose. Henry Anton. 12:74*My9'36. 9364
Scrambled eggs. Prose. Homer McCoy. 15:69*Ap15'39. 9365
Scrap-metal reporter. Prose. Richard Lockridge. 12:25-7* D12'36. 9366
A scrap of grammar. Prose. Richard Lockridge. 10:26-7 Ap7'34. 9367
Scratched brass. Prose. Jerome Barry. 10:62-4 My5'34. 9368
Screen test. Prose. Alan Handley. 10:46-8 O20'34. 9369
Screen test. Prose. John O'Hara. 8:44-8 D3'32. 9370
The sculptor of Minetta Lane. Verse. A. K. Laing. 3:47 Jy16 '27. 9371
Sculptors are different. PR (Davidson). Ferdinand Tuohy. 3:27-9 Mr26'27. 9372
The sculpture game. Verse. Price Day. 8:53*Mr26'32. 9373
Sculpture, not machinery. PR (Barnard). Babette Deutsch. 6: 26-9 Ja17'31. 9374
Sea beacon. RL. E. B. White. 4: 48-55 D1'28. 9375
Sea change. Prose. Alice Frankforter. 13:49-50*Ja29'38. 9376
Sea change. Prose. Wolcott Gibbs. 5:17-19 Je29'29. 9377
Sea change. SM. Alexander Woollcott. 10:40-3*D1'34. 9378
Sea-chill. Verse. Arthur Guiterman. 8:51 Ja21'33. 9379
Sea-dog. Prose. John Chapin Mosher. 4:20 Ag11'28. 9380
Sea of the South. Verse. Grace Hazard Conkling. 5:26 F1'30. 9381
Sea pasture. Verse. Olive Ward. 9:24 Ag19'33. 9382
Sea town. Verse. Frances M. Frost. 12:63*My9'36. 9383
Sea voyage. Prose. Harold Johnsrud. 7:36-40 Ap4'31. 9384
The seal. Verse. Laura Benét. 6:27 My31'30. 9385
Sealing wax. Prose. James M. Cain. 7:25 My2'31. 9386
The seamstress. Prose. Lillian Day. 7:86-9 Ap11'31. 9387
Search for civilization. Prose. Dwight Kasson Tripp. 1:24 Ag8 '25. 9388
Searcher. Verse. Frances M. Frost. 6:43 My17'30. 9389
Seashore song. Verse. Margaret Fishback. 3:40 Ag13'27. 9390
The season at Newport. Prose. Frank Sullivan. 5:20-2 Ag31'29. 9391
The season at Saratoga. Prose. Frank Sullivan. 5:15-17 Ag17 '29. 9392
Seasonable. Verse. Miriam Vedder

Sex ex machina. LYMA. James Thurber. 13:16-19*Mr13'37. 9477
Sex is out. Prose. Robert Benchley. 1:16 D26'25. 9478
Shadowland. Prose. Niven Busch, Jr. 6:24-6 O11'30. 9479
Shadows. Verse. Jean Batchelor. 6:18 Ap26'30. 9480
Shakespeare, here's your hat. Prose. Wolcott Gibbs. 15:17-18*Ja13'40. 9481
Shakespeare in fifteen minutes. Prose. Frederick Packard. 8:46-7 Jy9'32. 9482
Shall we finish the "unfinished"? Prose. Frank Sullivan. 4:13-15 Ag4'28. 9483
Shame the devil. Prose. Margaret Ford. 10:53 Ag25'34. 9484
Shanghai racket. Prose. John W. Thomason, Jr. 11:15-16*Jy27 '35. 9485
Shanghai refugee. Prose. Emily Hahn. 13:19-21*O23'37. 9486
The shark's-fin soup. Prose. John Chapin Mosher. 9:52-3 D23'33. 9487
Shattered glass. Prose. Corey Ford. 1:16 Je6'25. 9488
Shave. Prose. John O'Hara. 13: 22-3*Mr20'37. 9489
Shaw, Charles G. (Parody) Hope Hale. 7:47-8 Mr21'31. 9490
Shaw, George Bernard. Anthony Gibbs. 5:73 N16'29. 9491
Shaw, George Bernard. Charles Graves. 4:101 Ap21'28. 9492
Shaw, George Bernard. Charles Graves. 4:61 Je16'28. 9493
Shaw, George Bernard. TT. 1:3 Je13'25. 9494
Shaw, George Bernard. TT. 1:6-7 Ja9'26. 9495
Shaw, George Bernard. TT. 2:19-20 S18'26. 9496
Shaw, George Bernard. TT. 4:14 S22'28. 9497
Shaw, George Bernard. TT. 5:17-18 Mr16'29. 9498
Shaw, George Bernard. TT. 9:13 Ap8'33. 9499
Shaw, George Bernard. TT. 9:9 Jy1'33. 9500
Shaw, George Bernard. Alexander Woollcott. 7:32 S26'31. 9501
Shaw, George Bernard. Alexander Woollcott. 9:30 F18'33. 9502
Shaw plays. Anthony Gibbs. 6:115 Ap12'30. 9503
She is not satisfied. Verse. Grace Hazard Conkling. 5:28 Mr30'29. 9504
She makes a suggestion to herself. Verse. Muna Lee. 6:22 S20'30. 9505
She meets a friend of her son. Verse. Martha Banning Thomas. 5:67 F8'30. 9506
She presents the flock. Prose. C. Knapp. 1:19 F21'25. 9507
She reports no progress. Verse. Martha Banning Thomas. 7:60 S19'31. 9508
She speaks across a decade. Verse. Marjorie Allen Seiffert. 6:90 F22'30. 9509
A sheer case of something or other. Prose. Corey Ford. 4: 34-6 D8'28. 9510
The shell. Verse. Harold Lewis Cook. 13:20*Ap17'37. 9511
She'll get your number. Prose. Jack Cluett. 3:52-3 Ja28'28. 9512
Shepherd. Prose. Rachel Biggs. 9:44-5 Ag12'33. 9513
Sherlock Holmes in pictures. Prose. Frederic Dorr Steele. 13:35-42*My22'37. 9514
Sherriff, R. C. TT. 5:18-19 Ap6 '29. 9515
Sherriff, R. C. TT. 6:10 Ag23'30. 9516
The Sherry-Netherland. SH. Newman Levy. 4:27 O13'28. 9517
"She's boy-crazy." Prose. Margaret Ford. 10:45-6 Mr3'34. 9518
She's in the "mo'om pitcher game." Prose. Arthur Kober. 3:26 Jy23'27. 9519
Shilling. Prose. Theodore Pratt. 3:30 My7'27. 9520

10:29*Ja5'35. 9565
Sic semper cinema. Prose. Laurence Reid. 1:17 Je6'25. 9566
The sick man of politics. RL. Alva Johnston. 9:32-7 Ag5'33. 9567
Sickroom visitors. Prose. Patricia Collinge. 5:43-4 S14'29. 9568
Side street tragedies. Verse. William Weer. 1:12 Ap18'25. 9569
Sidesaddle. Prose. John O'Hara. 14:21-2*N5'38. 9570
Sideshow people. Prose. Alva Johnston. 10:27-30 Ap14'34; 10:30-6 Ap21'34; 10:90-7 Ap 28'34. 9571
Sidewalk fisherman. PR (Schultz). Meyer Berger. 14:16-20*Jy23 '38. 9572
Siege perilous. Prose. Alice Frankforter. 9:64-5 Ap29'33. 9573
Significant lawsuits of 1932. Prose. Joseph P. Pollard. 8: 84-5 Ja7'33. 9574
Significant omission. Verse. Hortense Flexner. 15:27*Mr4'39. 9575
Signifying nothing. Prose. Edward Acheson. 10:41-2 Jy7'34. 9576
The Sikirevtzima system. Prose. Gilbert Seldes. 12:18*F29'36. 9577
The silence of the gears. Verse. E. B. White. 10:23 My19'34. 9578
The silent enemies. Prose. Willard Cooper. 1:7-8 S5'25. 9579
Silhouette of a lady disappointed in love. Verse. Dearing Ward. 4:24 Mr3'28. 9580
Silk and leather. PR (Sande). Niven Busch, Jr. 3:15-18 Jy30 '27. 9581
Silk stockings. Prose. Morley Callaghan. 8:16-19*Ap16'32. 9582
The silver car. Verse. James Stephens. 5:21 Ap20'29. 9583
Silver fishes. Prose. Frances Warfield. 8:59*Mr5'32. 9584
Silver liners. Prose. Elmer Davis. 6:25-6 D13'30. 9585
Silver sties for authors. Prose. David Cort. 2:50-1 Je12'26. 9586
Silver-tongue. PR (Bryan). Charles Willis Thompson. 1:9-10 Je13'25. 9587
Similarity. Verse. Frances M. Frost. 7:48 Ag22'31. 9588
Similes of New York, N. Y. Prose. Fairfax Downey. 1:17 F28'25. 9589
Simon & Schuster. PR. Geoffrey T. Hellman. 15:22-8*S30'39; 15:24-30*O7'39; 15:25-9*O14'39. 9590
Simon, Richard L. PR. Geoffrey T. Hellman. 15:22-8*S30'39; 15:24-30*O7'39; 15:25-9*O14 '39. 9591
Simonetta at the glove counter. Verse. Katharine D. Morse. 4:38 Je2'28. 9592
Simple anatomy. NESD. John J. Holzinger. 9:51 N11'33. 9593
Simple and effective. Prose. Kathleen Cannell. 1:21 My23 '25. 9594
Simple foreign Christmas. Prose. Frances Woodward Prentice. 8:17-18 D24'32. 9595
Simple household remedies. Verse. Margaret Fishback. 7:42*Je13 '31. 9596
Simple lines from an American in Bagdad. Verse. Irma Brandeis. 7:30 D5'31. 9597
Simples. Verse. Mildred Weston. 9:30 F25'33. 9598
Simples for cabinet members. Verse. E. B. White. 9:19 Mr4 '33. 9599
Simply appalling. Prose. John Collier. 9:15-16 N4'33. 9600
Simpson. Prose. Wolcott Gibbs. 8:15-16 Ag20'32. 9601
Since 1818. PR (Brooks Brothers). Russell Maloney. 14:20-3*My7 '38. 9602
Since other fruits are late. Verse.

Mullins. 6:16 N1'30. 9645
Sleep lady, sleep. Prose. Franklin P. Adams. 12:53*My2'36. 9646
Sleep, reader, sleep. Prose. Franklin P. Adams. 11:18*Ja 4'36. 9647
Sleep that knits up the ravell'd sleave of care. Prose. Robert Wohlforth. 5:26 F15'30. 9648
Sleeping beauty. Prose. T. H. Wenning. 11:61*S21'35. 9649
The Sleepy Hollow massacre. TWNY. Edmund Pearson. 11: 41-5*S21'35. 9650
A slight alteration. Prose. Edward Longstreth. 7:66-7 Mr14 '31. 9651
A slight case of woe in the Bronx. Prose. Arthur Kober. 15:19-20*Je17'39. 9652
Slight resemblance. Verse. Hortense Flexner. 14:42*Ag27'38. 9653
Slighted obituaries of 1939. Prose. W. E. Farbstein. 15:48*Ja6'40. 9654
Slightly worried thoughts. Verse. Ruth Brown. 4:39 Ag11'28. 9655
Slipcovers. Prose. John Chapin Mosher. 10:81-4 Je16'34. 9656
Slogan with a belt. Prose. Edward Horton. 13:62-5*O16'37. 9657
Slow—dangerous foibles ahead! Prose. S. J. Perelman. 15:17-18*Mr4'39. 9658
Slow freights. Prose. E. B. White. 6:23 My31'30. 9659
Sludge. Verse. Morris Bishop. 7:44 Mr7'31. 9660
The sluggard. Verse. Harrison Dowd. 5:48 My4'29. 9661
Small change. Prose. Thomas S. Bosworth. 4:27-8 Jy14'28. 9662
Small claims. RL. Richard O. Boyer. 14:28*Jy30'38. 9663
A small day. Prose. Erskine Caldwell. 12:22-5*Ag22'36. 9664
Small favor. Prose. George Cecil Cowing. 7:72-4 O3'31. 9665
Small hours in Times Square. RL. Morris Markey. 10:58-66 Je2'34. 9666
A small package. PR (Huggins). Henry F. Pringle. 3:25-7 O8 '27. 9667
Small song with repeated chorus. Verse. Genevieve Taggard. 15: 65*S16'39. 9668
Small thanks to you. Prose. E. B. White. 13:21*D27'37. 9669
Smart-aleck. Prose. Leane Zugsmith. 10:73-6 S29'34. 9670
Smashup. Prose. James Thurber. 11:23-5*O5'35. 9671
The smith. Verse. Mark Van Doren. 5:23 Ja4'30. 9672
Smoking-room. Prose. A. Schaeffer, Jr. 8:40-4 N19'32. 9673
The smuggling boom. RL. Alva Johnston. 4:48-58 N10'28. 9674
The snail. Verse. Sara Henderson Hay. 7:44 Ag29'31. 9675
Snake. Verse. Robert Hillyer. 12: 41*Ap18'36. 9676
The snake man. Prose. Francis Steegmuller. 11:62-3*O26'35. 9677
Snakes' supper. RL. E. B. White. 6:41-8 Mr22'30. 9678
Snappers. Prose. Frances Warfield. 8:15 D31'32. 9679
Snappy little Sadie. Verse. Elias Lieberman. 3:97 S24'27. 9680
Snapshot of a dog. Prose. James Thurber. 11:15-16*Mr9'35. 9681
The snob. Prose. Morley Callaghan. 10:15-17 Jy7'34. 9682
Snobbery of the vine and tablecloth. OUWA. Raymond Postgate. 13:69-73*N20'37. 9683
Snow. Verse. Virginia Woods Bellamy. 9:34 Ja20'34. 9684
Snow effect. Verse. Henry Morton Robinson. 13:27*Ja22'38. 9685
Snow man. PR (Ledoux). Niven Busch, Jr. 2:27-9 F5'27. 9686
Snow scene. Verse. Mildred Weston. 10:81 F17'34. 9687
The snow situation. Prose. Frank Sullivan. 8:15-16*Mr26'32. 9688

Snow White and Red Rose. Prose. Spud Johnson. 3:88-9 F19'27. 9689
Snow White and the seven dwarfs. (Parody) Wolcott Gibbs. 13:30* F5'38. 9690
Snowcroft. Prose. James Reid Parker. 11:54*F15'36. 9691
Snowy day. Verse. Harriett Brownell. 8:21 Ja28'33. 9692
Snubbing time for Hiram Johnson. Prose. Frank Sullivan. 4:22-3 O6'28. 9693
So I ups to Morgan. Verse. E. B. White. 9:25 Ap29'33. 9694
So many mothers. Prose. John Chapin Mosher. 3:42-6 D17'27. 9695
So then Mutt says to Jute . . . Prose. Russell Maloney. 15: 21-2*Je17'39. 9696
So this is Paris! Verse. R. R. 2: 61 My15'26. 9697
So what? RL. Chester T. Crowell. 8:40-4 Jy9'32. 9698
So you won't talk, eh? Prose. Frank Sullivan. 8:11-12 D31 '32. 9699
So you're going to a hotel! Prose. James Thurber. 6:16-18 N1'30. 9700
So you're going to Europe. Prose. Robert Jay Misch. 2: 80-2 Je5'26. 9701
So you're going to New York. Prose. Robert Benchley. 5:22 S7'29. 9702
Soap. Prose. John Chapin Mosher. 6:42-5 D20'30. 9703
The sob-sisters arise. Prose. Edmund Pearson. 9:25-8 N11 '33. 9704
Sob stuff. Prose. Elspeth O'Halloran. 7:79-80 Ap18'31. 9705
The social bridge game. Prose. Beatrice Kaufman. 4:60-4 N24 '28. 9706
Social contrasts. Verse. Arthur Guiterman. 11:21*S21'35. 9707
The social cut. Prose. A. van Steenbergh. 1:19 S12'25. 9708
The social director. Prose. Arthur Kober. 5:60-1 Ag10 '29. 9709
Social director. Prose. Charles O'Neill. 11:63-5*S7'35. 9710
Social economy. Verse. Arthur Guiterman. 15:37*S23'39. 9711
Social evasions. Prose. Stanley Jones. 3:70 O15'27. 9712
Social evasions. Prose. Stanley Jones. 3:85 O22'27. 9713
Social evasions. Prose. Stanley Jones. 3:73 O29'27. 9714
Social evasions. Prose. Stanley Jones. 3:96 N5'27. 9715
Social evasions. Prose. Stanley Jones. 3:119 N12'27. 9716
Social evasions. Prose. Stanley Jones. 3:110 N19'27. 9717
Social evasions. Prose. Stanley Jones. 3:93 N26'27. 9718
Social evasions. Prose. Stanley Jones. 3:75 D3'27. 9719
Social evasions. Prose. Stanley Jones. 3:98 D17'27. 9720
Social evasions. Prose. Stanley Jones. 3:35 D31'27. 9721
Social evasions. Prose. Stanley Jones. 3:54-5 Ja7'28. 9722
Social evasions. Prose. Stanley Jones. 3:67 Ja14'28. 9723
Social evasions. Prose. Stanley Jones. 3:47 Ja21'28. 9724
Social hints for ambitious dreamers. Prose. Maddy Vegtel. 10: 35-7*D29'34. 9725
Social invasions. Prose. Jack Cluett. 3:114 D10'27. 9726
Social obligations. Verse. Arthur Guiterman. 10:27*N24'34. 9727
Social paleontology. Prose. Willard Cooper. 3:30 F26'27. 9728
Sociologist. Verse. Doris Kirkpatrick. 7:29 Mr28'31. 9729
Soc. 2B. Prose. Harold Bergman. 5:94-6 O5'29. 9730
Soda-counter lunch. Verse. John Ogden Whedon. 4:99 N3'28. 9731
The soft heart. Verse. Fillmore Hyde. 3:18 F18'28. 9732
"Soir." Prose. Noël Scott. 1:7 Je 6'25. 9733
Solace for spinsters. Verse. Jean Batchelor. 9:32 My20'33. 9734

Winifred Willis. 14:70-1*My14 '38. 9771
Something serious. Prose. Edith Owen. 11:67*Mr9'35. 9772
Something to read. Prose. Alice Frankforter. 5:71-2 Je29'29. 9773
Something to say. PR (Vereker). James Thurber. 8:17-19 Jy30 '32. 9774
Somewhere a Roscoe. Prose. S.J. Perelman. 14:17-18*O15'38. 9775
Sonata. Verse. M. M. 4:26 Jy7'28. 9776
Sonata-municipale. Verse. E.C.S. 1:12 S26'25. 9777
Song. Verse. W. H. Auden. 15:21* Ap15'39. 9778
Song. Verse. Parke Cummings. 3:87 Ap2'27. 9779
Song. Verse. Ogden Nash. 8:18 Ja 7'33. 9780
Song. Verse. Frederic Prokosch. 14:23*My21'38; 15:30*D16'39. 9781
Song and dance man. PR (Cohan). Gilbert Seldes. 10:27-31 Mr17 '34; 10:23-7 Mr24'34. 9782
Song and sentiment. PR (Lehmann). Marcia Davenport. 11: 18-22*F23'35. 9783
Song at twilight. Verse. Henrietta Fort Holland. 11:78*Mr16'35. 9784
Song before matrimony. Verse. Ruth Brown. 4:93 F16'29. 9785
Song before Spring. Verse. Sara Henderson Hay. 14:46*Mr5'38. 9786
Song de luxe. Verse. A. B. Bernd. 2:30 S11'26. 9787
Song for a back-porch campaign. Verse. Phyllis McGinley. 15: 28*S16'39. 9788
Song for a furnished house. Verse. Rachael Field. 15:59* O21'39. 9789
Song for a late hour. Verse. Raymond Holden. 6:20 Jy5'30. 9790
Song for a reference library. Verse. Phyllis McGinley. 9:16 Ap29'33. 9791
Song for an alley cat. Verse. Philip G. Wylie. 5:42 N23'29. 9792
Song for before breakfast. Verse. E. B. White. 4:32 My5'28. 9793
Song for government. Verse. Raymond Holden. 11:23*Je22'35. 9794
Song for heroes. Verse. Ellis Parker Butler. 6:44 N22'30. 9795
Song for insomnia. Verse. Martha Banning Thomas. 9:51 Ja6 '34. 9796
Song for Summer. Verse. Richard Armour. 14:42*Je18'38. 9797
Song for the delegates. Verse. E. B. White. 7:18 Ja23'32. 9798
Song for the morning bath. Verse. Nate Salisbury. 4:59 Ja26'29. 9799
Song for the nearest rivetting machine. Verse. Newman Levy. 4: 82 Je2'28. 9800
Song for the undone. Verse. Harold Lewis Cook. 12:25*Ja30'37. 9801
Song for thrift week. Verse. Mildred Weston. 10:42*Ja19'35. 9802
Song for two. Verse. Frances M. Frost. 6:77 N8'30. 9803
A song for wives. Verse. Kathleen Cotter Gross. 5:79 Je22'29 9804
Song from an x-ray table. Verse. E. B. White. 8:13 Ag13'32. 9805
Song from New Rochelle. Verse. Phyllis McGinley. 10:18 Mr24 '34. 9806
Song in time of pestilence. Verse. Baird Leonard. 15:44*S2'39. 9807
A song is written. Prose. George D. Lottman. 4:28-30 Je9'28. 9808
Song of a jaded appetite. Verse. Clinch Calkins. 8:25*Ap9'32. 9809
Song of a lady of little if any importance. Verse. Martha L. Wilchinski. 3:46 D3'27. 9810
Song of Americans resident in

France. Verse. Dorothy Parker. 2:18 My1'26. 9811
The song of business. Verse. Richard Armour. 13:68*Mr6 '37. 9812
Song of change. Verse. Price Day. 8:44*F27'32. 9813
Song of honor students. Verse. Elias Lieberman. 2:84 N13'26. 9814
Song of mitigated sorrow. Verse. Ruth West. 6:40 Ja10'31. 9815
Song of self. Verse. Price Day. 7:101 Ap11'31. 9816
Song of tears. Verse. Margaret Widdemer. 2:43 F12'27. 9817
Song of the bus top rider. Verse. Anon. 1:16 F6'26. 9818
Song of the lowbrow. Verse. Ruth Richards. 2:38 Ap17'26. 9819
The song of the machine. OUWA. Daniel Sayre. 10:41-4 Mr17 '34. 9820
Song of the New York immigrants. Verse. Carroll Carroll. 4:62 F16'29. 9821
Song of the not so open road. Verse. Phyllis McGinley. 10:22*F9'35. 9822
Song of the open road. Verse. Ogden Nash. 8:18 O15'32. 9823
Song of the pushcart. DL. Burke Boyce. 2:85 N6'26. 9824
The song of the tabloid. Verse. Charles Street. 1:22 My30'25. 9825
Song out of a rainy night. Verse. Frances M. Frost. 5:25 N30 '29. 9826
Song to a babe. Verse. Marjorie Allen Seiffert. 6:30 Je7'30. 9827
Song to be disregarded. Verse. E. B. White. 4:31 Je2'28. 9828
Song (to be strummed on a lute). Verse. Mildred Weston. 6:51 Jy19'30. 9829
Song to the Empire State Building. Verse. Price Day. 7:34 Ap4'31. 9830
Songs and sentiments. Verse. John J. Holzinger. 11:76*N16 '35. 9831
Songs for the nearest harmonica. Verse. Dorothy Parker. 3:21 Ja7'27. 9832
Songs for the nearest harmonica. Verse. Dorothy Parker. 3:28 N12'27. 9833
Songs for the nearest harmonica. Verse. Dorothy Parker. 4:20 My26'28. 9834
Songs not encumbered by reticence. Verse. Dorothy Parker. 3:28 F19'27. 9835
Songs not encumbered by reticence. Verse. Dorothy Parker. 3:26 Mr5'27. 9836
Songs not encumbered by reticence. Verse. Dorothy Parker. 3:28 Mr12'27. 9837
Songs not encumbered by reticence. Verse. Dorothy Parker. 3:28 Mr19'27. 9838
Songs not encumbered by reticence. Verse. Dorothy Parker. 3:26 Mr26'27. 9839
Songs of a markedly personal nature. Verse. Dorothy Parker. 2:21 S25'26. 9840
Songs of crime. Verse. Joseph Fulling Fishman. 1:20 Ja23'26. 9841
Songs of firms. Verse. Newman Levy. 4:24 S1'28. 9842
Songs of innocence. OUWA. Dorothy Mills and Morris Bishop. 13:32-7*N13'37. 9843
Songs they do not sing. Verse. Anon. 3:59 Ja7'28. 9844
Sonnet. Verse. David McCord. 5:31 O12'29. 9845
Sonnet. Verse. Marya Mannes. 6:18 Ag9'30. 9846
Sonnet. Verse. Helene Mullins. 5:22 Mr9'29. 9847
Sonnet. Verse. E. B. White. 4:19 F2'29. 9848
Sonnet and limerick. Verse. Morris Bishop. 13:21*O23'37. 9849
Sonnet for a candle-lighter. Verse. Miriam Vedder. 7:23 D26'31. 9850
Sonnet for an exceptional apple pie. Verse. Sara Henderson

Hay. 8:14 Jy30'32. 9851
A sonnet in attack of Winter. Verse. Philip G. Wylie. 2:79 Ja22'27. 9852
Sonnet in dimeter. Verse. Arthur Guiterman. 15:56*Jy15 '39. 9853
Sonnet 965. Verse. David McCord. 10:26*D1'34. 9854
Sonnet sequins. Verse. David McCord. 7:20 S12'31. 9855
Sonnet to dining in foreign restaurants. Verse. Philip G. Wylie. 2:44 Mr27'26. 9856
Sonnet to sky-writing. Verse. Philip G. Wylie. 2:49 O16'26. 9857
Sonnet to subways. Verse. Philip G. Wylie. 2:17 Ap24'26. 9858
Sonnets from the Finnish. Verse. Fillmore Hyde. 2:25 O23'26. 9859
Sonnets to Baedeker. Verse. David McCord. 8:21*Ap23'32. 9860
Sonnets to Baedeker. Verse. David McCord. 10:21 F17'34. 9861
Sonny boy. Prose. Arthur Kober. 8:74-6 Ja7'33. 9862
Sonny boy's diary. Prose. Nunnally Johnson. 5:26 N9'29. 9863
Soon the opera. Prose. W. Perceval-Monger. 1:7-8 O10'25. 9864
Soprano. Verse. Anon. 3:57 Ag6 '27. 9865
A sort of genius. WATN. James Thurber. 12:21-7*Ja23'37. 9866
Sotto voce. Prose. Alexander Clark, Jr. 7:31-41 F13'32. 9867
Soufflée. Prose. Katherine Sproenhle. 4:69-70 S22'28. 9868
Soul surgeon. PR (Buehman). Alva Johnston. 8:22-5*Ap23'32. 9869
Souls in torment. Verse. Clarence Day. 9:15 Ag26'33. 9870
The sound and the fury. WP. Robert Benchley. 13:40-2*Mr13 '37. 9871
Sounds. Prose. Martha Banning Thomas. 9:28 Ap1'33. 9872
Sounds suburban. Verse. Martha Banning Thomas. 6:65 Je21'30. 9873
Sour grapes for October 1. Verse. Margaret Fishback. 6:45 S27 '30. 9874
Sour note on folk-dancing. Prose. Frances Warfield. 5:20-1 Je29 '29. 9875
South Pole Charlie. PR (Bob). Alva Johnston. 7:22-5*Jy4'31. 9876
South Street. DL. Burke Boyce. 2:23 Ja29'27. 9877
South Street, Prose. Kenneth Campbell. 4:32-4 Ap28'28. 9878
The Southern girl. Prose. Nancy Hoyt. 5:18-19 Ap13'29. 9879
Southern tour. Prose. Emily Hahn. 15:65-7 F3'40. 9880
Souvenir. Prose. John Forbes. 3:71-2 O15'27. 9881
Souvenir of Malta. Prose. Oriana Atkinson. 15:59-61*My6'39. 9882
The sovereign voice. Prose. Morris Markey. 1:15-16 N7'25. 9883
Space champions. Prose. George Cecil Cowing. 7:22 D12'31. 9884
Space-chasing. Prose. Fillmore Hyde. 3:18-19 My14'27. 9885
Spain in Fifty-ninth Street. Verse. E. B. White. 11:14*Je15'35. 9886
Spanish in fifteen minutes. Prose. Frederick Packard. 6:32-4 S20 '30. 9887
Spanish in fifteen minutes--viva Hemingway. Prose. Frederick Packard. 7:47-8 S12'31. 9888
The Spanish mackerel. TA. Will Cuppy. 8:22 O15'32. 9889
A Spanish shawl for Miss Garbo. OFC. E. W. Selsey. 14:61-2* Ap23'38. 9890
Sparring partner. PR (Nicholson). A. J. Liebling. 15:25-8*Je24 '39. 9891
Sparrows among dry leaves. Verse. William Carlos Williams. 15:

72*N18'39. 9892
Spartacus in Westchester. PR (Muldoon). Stanley Walker. 3:18-21 Jy16'27. 9893
Spasm at a luncheon. Prose. John Chapin Mosher. 7:22-3 Ag22'31. 9894
The speakeasy. Verse. A. van Steenbergh. 1:32 S19'25. 9895
Speakeasy. Verse. John Ogden Whedon. 4:127 N10'28. 9896
Speakeasy. Verse. Philip G. Wylie. 2:86 D4'26. 9897
Speakeasy cats. Prose. Edmund S. Whitman. 5:62 S14'29. 9898
Speakeasy cats. Prose. Edmund S. Whitman. 5:72 O5'29. 9899
Speakeasy cats. Prose. Edmund S. Whitman. 5:67 O12'29. 9900
Speakeasy cats. Prose. Edmund S. Whitman. 5:121 O19'29. 9901
The speakeasy hostess does her stuff. Prose. C. Knapp. 5:94-6 Mr23'29. 9902
A speakeasy life. Prose. Louise Bogan. 7:15-16 Ag29'31. 9903
Speakeasy nights. Prose. Niven Busch, Jr. 3:18-19 My7'27. 9904
Speakeasy nights. Prose. Niven Busch, Jr. 3:16-17 Je4'27. 9905
Speakeasy nights. Prose. Niven Busch, Jr. 3:14-15 Jy2'27. 9906
Speakeasy nights. Prose. Niven Busch, Jr. 3:14-15 Ag6'27. 9907
Speakeasy nights. Prose. Niven Busch, Jr. 3:17-18 F18'28. 9908
Speakeasy nights. Prose. Niven Busch, Jr. 4:23-4 Mr17'28. 9909
Speakeasy nights. Prose. Niven Busch, Jr. 4:23-4 Je16'28. 9910
Speakeasy nights. Prose. Niven Busch, Jr. 4:18 Jy7'28. 9911
Speakeasy nights. Prose. Niven Busch, Jr. 4:24 Ag18'28. 9912
Speakeasy nights. Prose. Niven Busch, Jr. 4:32 S15'28. 9913
Speakeasy nights. Prose. Niven Busch, Jr. 4:30 S29'28. 9914
Speakeasy nights. Prose. Niven Busch, Jr. 4:66-7 O6'28. 9915
Speakeasy nights. Prose. Niven Busch, Jr. 4:32 N3'28. 9916
Speakeasy nights. Prose. Niven Busch, Jr. 4:67-8 N17'28. 9917
Speakeasy nights. Prose. Niven Busch, Jr. 4:34-6 D15'28. 9918
Speakeasy nights. Prose. Niven Busch, Jr. 4:23 D29'28. 9919
Speakeasy nights. Prose. Niven Busch, Jr. 4:22 F2'29. 9920
Speakeasy nights. Prose. Niven Busch, Jr. 5:30 Mr16'29. 9921
Speaking of counterweights. Prose. E. B. White. 15:19-22*F25'39. 9922
Speaking of Europe. Prose. Charles G. Shaw. 1:28 Ap25'25. 9923
Speaking of Florida real estate. Prose. C. Knapp. 2:64 F20'26. 9924
"Speaking of India--." Prose. Stephen Leacock. 3:19-20 F18 '28. 9925
Speaking of prohibition. Prose. Charles G. Shaw. 1:19 Jy4'25. 9926
Speaking of skirts. Verse. Richard Peckham. 6:79 Mr1'30. 9927
Speaking of the theatre. Prose. Charles G. Shaw. 1:28 F28'25. 9928
Speaking on streets. Prose. McAlister Coleman. 7:75-8 O31 '31. 9929
Special added attraction. Prose. Lionel M. Kaufman. 11:43-5* Ag3'35. 9930
The special checking account. Prose. Beverly L. Clarke. 14:51-2*Ap9'38. 9931
The special luncheon. Prose. E. B. White. 10:23-4 Ag11'34. 9932
Special nurse. Prose. Edith Owen. 7:72-3*My23'31. 9933

Carroll. 4:30-2 Ap14'28. 10020
Stagecoach--new style. RL. Morris Markey. 10:62-8 O20'34. 10021
Stagger. Prose. Mary Heaton Vorse. 6:18-20 S6'30. 10022
Stalactite. Verse. Muna Lee. 10:24 Je23'34. 10023
Stallings, Laurence. Dr. Winkle. 1:26 Mr7'25. 10024
Stallings, Laurence. TT. 1:3-4 Jy4'25. 10025
Stallings, Laurence. TT. 1:10-11 Ja23'26. 10026
Stalwart Guss Minff. Prose. James Kevin McGuinness. 1:13 Jy11'25. 10027
Stamford sees the light. Prose. Fillmore Hyde. 3:14-15 Ag20 '27. 10028
Stamp out schistosomiasis! Prose. Robert Benchley. 9:15 Je3'33. 10029
A stand against war. Prose. Raymond Holden. 10:47-8*D29'34. 10030
Standards for Elise. Prose. Elizabeth Jordan. 9:29-30 Je17'33. 10031
Standing room only. Verse. Margaret Fishback. 7:52 Ja16'32. 10032
Stanley Sherwood. Prose. Sylvia Townsend Warner. 13:19-20* N20'37. 10033
Star. Prose. Alan Hynd. 9:35-6 Mr4'33. 10034
Star bright. Prose. Jan Spiess. 13:56*My15'37. 10035
The "star dust" set. Prose. George Cecil Cowing. 11:28* Ag31'35. 10036
Star of today. Verse. W. E. Farbstein. 6:56 O11'30. 10037
Star-spangled ode. Verse. Phyllis McGinley. 14:18*Jy2'38. 10038
Starlight, star bright. Verse. Frances Park. 4:109 My26'28. 10039
The stars. Verse. Marjorie Allen Seiffert. 6:58 D6'30. 10040
The stars and stripes forever. Prose. Stanley Jones. 11:71*Ap 27'35. 10041
Star's chauffeur. Prose. John F. DeVine. 10:38*Ja5'35. 10042
The stars, dear Brutus. Prose. Pier Glass. 1:6 Jy4'25. 10043
Stars in my eyes. Verse. John O'Hara. 15:61*My6'39. 10044
The stars in their courses. Prose. Wolcott Gibbs. 11:13*Ja18'36. 10045
Stars over Peekskill. RL. E. J. Kahn, Jr. 14:35-41*S3'38. 10046
Starting fresh. WP. Robert Benchley. 5:38-42 Ja11'30. 10047
Starving princes. Prose. Florence Helm. 3:104-105 Ap9'27. 10048
The state of Bontana. Prose. James Thurber. 9:17-18 F3'34. 10049
States of bliss. Verse. Clarence Day. 9:24 N4'33. 10050
Static. Verse. Rolfe Humphries. 12:16*F13'37. 10051
The static quo. Verse. Margaret Fishback. 11:30*Ap6'35. 10052
Stationery salesman. Prose. Gerold Frank. 13:40*Mr27'37. 10053
Statue in the park. Prose. Frances Warfield. 10:58-60 My19'34. 10054
Statues. DL. Burke Boyce. 3:26 O1 '27. 10055
Stature. Verse. Frances M. Frost. 6:20 F14'31. 10056
Steam. Verse. Fillmore Hyde. 2:54 D11'26. 10057
Steam song. RL. Eric Hodgins. 6:32-40 Jy19'30. 10058
Steamer-chair. Verse. Marion Canby. 6:65 Je14'30. 10059
Steamer letter. Verse. Brownell Carr. 2:33 Ag7'26. 10060
Steel. RL. Morris Markey. 12:42-7*My30'36. 10061
Steel. PR (Schwab). John K. Winkler. 7:23-6 Ap25'31; 7:26-35 My 2'31. 10062
Steel gables. Prose. Marcy Johnson. 3:28 Mr12'27. 10063
Steer joints. BR. Jack Wynn. 3:

101-103 N26'27. 10064
Steffens plays the game. Prose. Arthur Bartlett. 14:46*Jy9 '38. 10065
Stein, Gertrude. Janet Flanner. 11:51*F15'36. 10066
Stein, Gertrude. Janet Flanner. 13:45*Ja29'38. 10067
Stein, Gertrude. Janet Flanner. 14:56*Ap16'38. 10068
Stein, Gertrude. TT. 10:22-3 O13 '34. 10069
Stein, Gertrude. TT. 10:12-13*N 24'34. 10070
Stein, Gertrude. (Parody) Frank Sullivan. 9:13-14 Jy1'33. 10071
Stein, Gertrude. (Parody) James Thurber. 3:69 My7'27. 10072
Stenographic study Monday a. m. Verse. M. Wilsey. 2:16 Je19 '26. 10073
Stentor. PR (Humphreys). Meyer Berger. 9:24-7 O14'33; 9:27-30 O21'33. 10074
A step forward. Prose. E. B. White. 1:21 Ap18'25. 10075
A step forward in sermons. OUWA. Dean S. Jennings. 12:48-51*Ap25'36. 10076
Stepfathers of art. RL. Forbes Watson. 3:32-8 My14'27. 10077
The sterile warfare. Verse. Herman Fetzer. 9:23 D30'33. 10078
Stewart's on the Square. RL. Sherwood Anderson. 10:77-80 Je9'34. 10079
Stick to hogs. Prose. Philip Monk. 2:28 My29'26. 10080
The stickleback. TA. Will Cuppy. 8:14 Jy2'32. 10081
Stiff isn't absolute. Prose. Richard Lockridge. 9:49-51 Je3'33. 10082
Still life. Verse. Peggy Bacon. 14:57*O1'38. 10083
Still life. Verse. Phyllis McGinley. 14:86*D3'38. 10084
Still more poems. Verse. Rolfe Humphries. 12:20*N21'36. 10085
Still to be neat. ML. John Strong Newberry. 9:48 Ag19'33. 10086
The sting of death. Prose. Joseph P. Pollard. 4:80 O6'28. 10087
Stirrup and leather. PR (Clark). Margaret Case Harriman. 10:20-4 S29'34. 10088
Stock. Verse. Elizabeth Coatsworth. 5:32 Mr9'29. 10089
A stockholder's plaint. Verse. Smoff. 7:45*My30'31. 10090
The stocking industry. Verse. Margaret Fishback. 5:55 Ja25 '30. 10091
Stone walls. Verse. Frances M. Frost. 9:19 Jy29'33. 10092
Stony acre. Verse. Frances M. Frost. 9:15 Je17'33. 10093
Stop and go. Verse. Marjorie Allen Seiffert. 6:36 S13'30. 10094
Stop-off at Essen. Prose. Mollie Craig. 15:50-2*S9'39. 10095
Stop-watch art. Prose. Hamilton Eames. 3:103-104 D3'27. 10096
Stopover. Prose. Rachel Biggs. 9:22 Jy29'33. 10097
Stories of the great. Prose. Herbert Crooker. 1:30 Mr7 '25. 10098
Stories of today. Verse. W. E. Farbstein. 6:69 Mr8'30; 6:64 Mr15'30; 6:56 Mr22'30; 6:28 Mr 29'30; 6:30 Ap5'30; 6:66 Ap12 '30; 6:32 Ap19'30; 6:80 My3'30; 6:66 My24'30; 6:30 My31'30; 6:68 Je28'30; 6:55 Jy19'30; 6:44 Ag9'30; 6:57 Ag16'30; 6:62 Ag23 '30; 6:102 S13'30; 6:47 S20'30; 6:38 O4'30; 6:46 N1'30; 6:36 N8 '30; 6:48 N15'30; 6:49 Ja31'31; 7:53 Mr14'31; 7:42 Mr21'31; 7:68 Mr28'31; 7:60 Ap18'31; 7:54 Ap25'31; 7:46 My2'31; 7:71*My 23'31; 7:50*My30'31; 7:37*Je20 '31; 7:60*Je27'31; 7:31*Jy4'31; 7:32 O24'31; 7:32 N7'31; 7:80 N 14'31; 8:51*F27'32; 8:33*Mr26 '32; 8:35*Ap9'32; 8:46 Jy23'32; 8:61 S17'32; 8:28 S24'32; 8:28 O29'32; 8:64 N12'32; 8:73 D17 '32; 8:43 Ja14'33; 9:29 Mr11'33; 9:63 My20'33; 9:37 Je17'33; 9:49 Jy8'33; 9:44 Ag26'33; 9:63 O14 '33; 9:84 O21'33; 9:40 Ja27'34; 9:81 F10'34; 10:36 Mr3'34; 10:55

Mr31'34; 10:83 Ap21'34; 10:45 Je23'34; 10:60 Jy21'34; 10:44 S1'34; 10:40 S15'34; 10:42 O13 '34; 10:84*D8'34; 10:51*D22'34; 10:54*Ja19'35; 10:55*Ja26'35; 11:30*F16'35; 11:30*Ap20'35; 11:60*My4'35; 11:68*My18'35; 11:28*Je1'35; 11:55*Je15'35; 11:53*Je29'35; 11:26*Jy13'35; 11:26*Ag10'35; 11:35*Ag24'35; 11:76*O19'35; 11:80*N9'35; 11: 55*N23'35; 11:111*D7'35; 11: 69*D14'35; 11:40*Ja4'36; 11: 39*F1'36; 12:59*F22'36; 12: 62*Mr7'36; 12:42*Mr14'36; 12: 57*Ap4'36; 12:59*Ap18'36; 12: 31*My2'36; 12:73*My16'36; 12: 52*Je6'36; 12:60*Je13'36; 12: 32*Je27'36; 12:42*Jy11'36; 12: 47*Ag8'36; 12:73*S12'36; 12: 28*S26'36; 12:50*O24'36; 12: 58*N21'36. 10099

The storm. Prose. Sally Benson. 13:20-2*N13'37. 10100

The storm. Verse. Elizabeth Coatsworth. 11:35*Jy27'35. 10101

Storm at sea. Prose. John Chapin Mosher. 7:20-1 Ag29'31. 10102

Storm over the Bronx. Prose. Arthur Kober. 10:50-6 O6'34. 10103

A story I'm going to tell you. OSB. C. Knapp. 4:19 S1'28. 10104

Story of a life. RL. Morris Markey. 3:28-32 O1'27. 10105

Story of Manhattankind. Prose. Anon. 1:12 Ap4'25. 10106

The story of Manhattankind. Prose. Sawdust. 1:6 F21'25. 10107

The story of Manhattankind. Prose. Sawdust. 1:8 F28'25. 10108

The story of Manhattankind. Prose. Sawdust. 1:6 Mr7'25. 10109

Story of Manhattankind. Prose. Sawdust. 1:14 Mr14'25. 10110

Story of Manhattankind. Prose. Sawdust. 1:12 Mr21'25. 10111

Story of Manhattankind. Prose. Sawdust. 1:8 My9'25. 10112

The story of Samson and Delilah. Prose. Tracy Hammond Lewis. 1:28 My23'25. 10113

Story of the Bible in tabloid. Prose. Wolcott Gibbs. 1:39 F13 '26. 10114

Story-teller's holiday. SM. Alexander Woollcott. 9:26 Ap15'33. 10115

Stoves in country places. Prose. John Forbes. 11:32-4*F8'36. 10116

A stowaway on the night boat. Prose. John Chapin Mosher. 2: 26 S4'26. 10117

Straight pool. Prose. John O'Hara. 9:38-42 D16'33. 10118

A strange adventure. Prose. Herbert Asbury. 1:9-10 Ag15'25. 10119

The strange case of Mr. Dreggs. Prose. Kent Smith. 3:111-13 Ap23'27. 10120

The strange case of XX. Prose. Robert Jay Misch. 1:30 Ja23'26. 10121

Strange interborough. Verse. Carroll Carroll. 4:69 F9'29. 10122

Strange interlude blues. Verse. Tom Powers. 4:18 Ja19'29. 10123

Strange interlude. (Play) TT. 4:17 My5'28. 10124

Strange interlude. (Play) TT. 4: 18-19 Je2'28. 10125

Strange interlude. (Play) TT. 5:19 Mr16'29. 10126

Strange, Michael. TT. 7:12 Ag29 '31. 10127

Strange mind. Verse. Miriam Vedder. 8:25 S3'32. 10128

The stranger. Prose. Emily Hahn. 5:15 Ag3'29. 10129

A strangers version. Prose. Edmund S. Whitman. 2:46-8 Je5'26. 10130

The strategists. Prose. James Reid Parker. 13:56-7*S25'37. 10131

Strauss. Prose. Maddy Vegtel. 9: 58-9 Mr18'33. 10132

The straw hat salesman. Prose. C. Knapp. 1:20 My23'25. 10133

Straws. Prose. Frances Warfield. 8:17-18 N12'32. 10134
The stream of legend. SM. Alexander Woollcott. 10:41 My5 '34. 10135
Stream of unconsciousness. Verse. Hortense Flexner. 14: 55*O15'38. 10136
Street cries of New York. Prose. Frank Sullivan. 10:22-3 My19 '34. 10137
Street digger. PP. Burke Boyce. 6:59 Ag9'30. 10138
Street floor. Verse. Margaret Fishback. 4:29 N10'28. 10139
Street in St. Louis. Prose. Frances Warfield. 10:55*Ja12'35. 10140
The street of the dead. Prose. Elliot Senior. 10:16*F2'35. 10141
Street scene. Verse. Jean Batchelor. 5:56 D28'29. 10142
Street scene. Prose. G. Schwabe. 5:52-3 Ag17'29. 10143
Street song. Verse. James Thurber. 3:81 F26'27. 10144
The street washer. Verse. Stuart Hyde Hawkins. 3:71 Mr5'27. 10145
Streets and carpets. Verse. Alfred Kreymborg. 4:16 D29'28. 10146
The stricken. Verse. Samuel Hoffenstein. 4:29 D15'28.10147
Strictly homelike. Prose. J. P. Grover. 4:44-6 Mr24'28. 10148
Strictly personal. SM. Alexander Woollcott. 7:32 O31'31. 10149
Strictly sex. NESD. John J. Holzinger. 9:32 N25'33. 10150
Strike. RL. Hyman Goldberg. 14: 42-9*O15'38. 10151
Strike me pink. Verse. Marion Sturges-Jones. 11:61*Je1'35. 10152
Strikes à l'Italienne. Prose. Anthony Armstrong. 5:38-9 O26'29. 10153
Strive not for fame. Verse. Arthur Guiterman. 10:27 Mr24 '34. 10154
The stroller. Verse. Robert Hilyer. 13:21*N27'37. 10155
Strong silent men. Verse. Anon. 2:62 O2'26. 10156
Studio breakfast. Verse. Persis Greely Anderson. 8:52*My7'32. 10157
A studio tea. Verse. Martha Banning Thomas. 2:15 Ja1'27. 10158
Study for a portrait. Prose. Alice Frankforter. 5:36-8 Je22'29. 10159
Study in black and white. Verse. Babette Deutsch. 13:18*O2'37. 10160
Study in color. Verse. Joyce Lacey. 3:108 D17'27. 10161
A study in dazzling anatomy. Verse. Margaret Fishback. 4: 94 O6'28. 10162
A study in fractions. Prose. Marshall D. Beuick. 1:11-12 My23 '25. 10163
Study in indigo. Prose. Wolcott Gibbs. 10:20-2*F9'35. 10164
A study in scarlet. Prose. Henrietta Fort Holland. 7:55-6 Ja 16'32. 10165
Study in sentiment. Prose. John Chapin Mosher. 7:20-1 N14'31. 10166
A study in vituperation. Prose. Sterling Wilson. 1:21 Je6'25. 10167
A study of the clinical "we." Prose. E. B. White. 9:13 Je10 '33. 10168
Style centre. Verse. Winifred Willis. 14:45*Ja14'39. 10169
Style note. Verse. Henrietta Fort Holland. 7:40 N7'31. 10170
Style note. Verse. Marjorie Allen Seiffert. 7:29 O10'31. 10171
The subjunctive mood. OMEU. James Thurber. 5:25 Ag17'29. 10172
Subscriber's nightmare. Prose. James Thurber. 6:19 Ja3'31. 10173
Suburban community centre. Verse. Morris Bishop. 12:68* Mr7'36. 10174
Suburbanite's Spring. Verse. Anon. 2:40 My1'26. 10175

Suburbaphobia. Verse. Margaret Fishback. 10:56 Ap14'34. 10176
Suburbia. Verse. Anon. 2:54 O2 '26. 10177
Suburbia. Prose. Thomas Langan. 2:53 S18'26. 10178
Subway change man. PP. Burke Boyce. 4:22 Jy21'28. 10179
The subway circuit. Prose. Robert M. Coates. 3:30-3 F11'28. 10180
Subway dementia. Prose. Charles W. MacGregor. 2:77-8 O2'26. 10181
The subway guard. Verse. Anon. 2:41 My8'26. 10182
Subway intimacies. Verse. Maxwell Bodenheim. 1:35 Ja9'26. 10183
Subway people. Verse. E. B. White. 1:30 D5'25. 10184
Subway salesmanship. Prose. Sterling Wilson. 2:31 D4'26. 10185
Subway Sam. Verse. Paul G. Gumbinner. 4:58 Ap28'28. 10186
The subway sun. Prose. Van D. 1:28 Ap25'25. 10187
The subway trouble explained. Prose. E. B. White. 4:25 Ap7 '28. 10188
Subway windows. Prose. Corey Ford. 1:10 O31'25. 10189
Success. RL. Morris Markey. 7:36-42*My30'31. 10190
Success story. RL. Morris Markey. 12:31-41*F22'36. 10191
"Such a lovely game!" Prose. G. Schwabe. 2:36 N20'26. 10192
Such a pretty day. Prose. Dawn Powell. 15:17-21*Je24'39. 10193
Such is fame. Prose. Leslie Howard. 1:16-17 N14'25. 10194
Suffocation. Verse. Clinch Calkins. 3:24 D17'27. 10195
The sugar-lump scourge. Verse. Margaret Fishback. 7:34 O3'31. 10196
Suggested telegrams. Prose. E. B. White. 3:26 Je18'27. 10197
A suggestion. Verse. Anon. 2:32 Jy3'26. 10198
Suggestions. Prose. William Rose Benét. 4:26-7 Mr31'28. 10199
Suggestions for visiting authors. Prose. Ruth Suckow. 3:27-8 O15'27. 10200
Suite 2049. Prose. Sally Benson. 12:18-21*Mr14'36. 10201
Suitor rejected. Verse. Helene Mullins. 4:32 S15'28. 10202
Suitors. Prose. Arthur Kober. 7:72-4 Ap18'31. 10203
Suits pressed. Prose. John O'Hara. 5:28 F8'30. 10204
Suki. Verse. Martha Banning Thomas. 4:88 F16'29. 10205
Suli suli. Prose. James Thurber. 12:17-19*My16'36. 10206
Sullen retort against a Sunday serman. Verse. Martha Banning Thomas. 6:51 F22'30. 10207
A summary. Verse. Samuel Hoffenstein. 8:20 Jy30'32. 10208
Summer. DL. Burke Boyce. 3:67 Jy16'27. 10209
A summer camp for adults. Prose. Arthur Kober. 4:19 Ag 25'28. 10210
Summer clothes. Prose. John Chapin Mosher. 3:40-2 Je4'27. 10211
Summer evening. Prose. Sally Benson. 6:26 Ag16'30. 10212
Summer friendship. Verse. Helene Mullins. 4:21 Ag4'28. 10213
Summer heat. WP. Robert Benchley. 6:36-40 Je14'30. 10214
Summer in the city of light. Prose Ralph Barton. 1:12-13 Jy4'25. 10215
Summer is lovely. Prose. Sally Benson. 10:25-7 O13'34. 10216
The summer labor problem. Prose. Wolcott Gibbs. 5:17-18 Jy13'29. 10217
Summer night. RL. Morris Markey. 11:44-9*S7'35. 10218
Summer of 1937: a memorandum. Prose. Katharine Brush. 13:58-9*S25'37. 10219

Summer plans. RC. Fillmore Hyde. 3:22-4 Mr26'27. 10220
The Summer resort. NYC. Gilbert Seldes. 5:21-3 Ag17'29. 10221
(No entry) 10222
A Summer romance. Prose. Velma Carson. 5:42 Ag10'29. 10223
The Summer show. Prose. Stanley Jones. 3:58 Jy16'27. 10224
Summer sloth. Verse. Mildred Weston. 7:57*Jy25'31. 10225
Summer-sports forecasts. Prose. John C. Emery. 6:59 Ap12'30. 10226
Summer storm. Verse. Frances M. Frost. 9:53 Ag26'33. 10227
Summer Sundays in New York. Verse. Margaret Fishback. 3:75 S3'27. 10228
Summer wind. Verse. Theodore Roethke. 15:58*Jy22'39. 10229
Summergreen for president. Verse. Ogden Nash. 12:29*Mr 7'36. 10230
Summing up. Verse. Margaret Fishback. 10:66 Je2'34. 10231
Sumner, John S. PR. Alva Johnston. 13:22-7 F20'37. 10232
Sundae school. Prose. Elinor Wylie. 2:29 F20'26. 10233
Sunday. Prose. Sally Benson. 7:29 My9'31. 10234
Sunday. Verse. Elizabeth Coatsworth. 15:49*Mr25'39. 10235
Sunday at five. Prose. Louise Bogan. 7:19 D12'31. 10236
Sunday broadcast: transcribed. Verse. Christopher LaFarge. 15:21*O14'39. 10237
Sunday company. Prose. Arthur Kober. 10:50-5 My5'34. 10238
The Sunday game of auction. Prose. Byron Steel. 4:92 Mr 24'28. 10239
The Sunday hike. Prose. Arthur Kober. 6:47-8 Ag2'30. 10240
Sunday morning. RL. Morris Markey. 2:19-20 Mr6'26. 10241
Sunday night thoughts. Verse. Katharine Day Little. 3:72 F18 '28. 10242
Sunday night was a dangerous night. Prose. Joseph Mitchell. 15:29-31*D2'39. 10243
Sunday services. Prose. Myra M. Waterman. 8:80-1 Ja7'33. 10244
The Sunday shiny sheet. Prose. Thomas S. Bosworth. 2:37-9 Ag21'26. 10245
Sunday visit. Prose. Robert M. Coates. 11:23-4*My11'35. 10246
The sundial of tomorrow. Verse. David McCord. 15:69*O14'39. 10247
Sunlight. Verse. Elspeth O'Halloran. 4:99 Mr3'28. 10248
The sunny side. Verse. Edward W. Barnard. 3:69 N5'27. 10249
Sunset. Verse. Witter Bynner. 10:29 Mr3'34. 10250
Sunshine biscuit sign versus Stuyvesant Park. Verse. Margaret Fishback. 6:103 My17'30. 10251
Sunshine, strip tease, and astrology. OFC. Theodore Pratt. 15:41*F18'39. 10252
Superfluous woman. Prose. Anthony Armstrong. 6:18-19 My3 '30. 10253
Superman. Verse. Clarence Day. 10:29*F9'35. 10254
Supper club lights. Verse. James Kevin McGuinness. 1:6 My23 '25. 10255
The supper restaurant. Verse. Anon. 1:29 Mr7'25. 10256
Supply hunting for the carte de jour. Prose. Clifford Pangburn. 2:53-4 My1'26. 10257
Suppressing the Sunday supplement. Prose. Joseph Fulling Fishman. 3:99-101 Mr26'27. 10258
The supremacy of Uruguay. Prose. E. B. White. 9:18-19 N25'33. 10259
Sure, come on and give thanks! Verse. Ogden Nash. 10:20*N24 '34. 10260
The surgeon. RL. Morris Markey.

9:42-6 F3'34. 10261
Surprise! Prose. John Chapin Mosher. 3:35-6 O8'27. 10262
Surprise! Prose. Frank Sullivan. 12:13-14*Jy11'36. 10263
Surrender. Verse. David McCord. 5:25 S28'29. 10264
The survey. Prose. Marc Connelly. 10:18-19 My12'34. 10265
A survey of the political situation. Prose. Newman Levy. 4:20-2 Jy7'28. 10266
Survival of Wilcox. Prose. Frances Warfield. 8:18-19 My28 '32. 10267
Susan and Father Christmas. Prose. Mollie Panter-Downes. 14:20*D24'38. 10268
Susanna passes. Verse. Sydney King Russell. 6:75 Je21'30. 10269
Suspicion. Prose. Elizabeth Jordan. 9:32-8 Ap29'33. 10270
Sustenance. Verse. Jerome Barry. 5:22 My11'29. 10271
Susy is marriageable. Prose. Margaret Widdemer. 8:32-5 N 26'32. 10272
Suum cuique. Verse. David McCord. 9:27 N25'33. 10273
Suzanne. Verse. Nate Salisbury. 2:24 O16'26. 10274
Swallow penthouse. Verse. Martha Banning Thomas. 8:44 Jy23 '32. 10275
Swampscott correspondence. Prose. Marquis James. 1:23 Jy18'25. 10276
The swan. Verse. Persis Greely Anderson. 8:16 O29'32. 10277
The swan of the heart. Verse. Raymond Holden. 6:24 N22'30. 10278
Swan song. Verse. Dorothy Parker. 3:23 Ap2'27. 10279
Swan-upping indeed. Prose. Will Cuppy. 11:15*S28'35. 10280
Swastika. Verse. William Rose Benét. 9:23 Ap15'33. 10281
Swearing off. Verse. Arthur Guiterman. 8:18 O29'32. 10282
Sweet age of something or other. Prose. The New Yorker. 6:32-4 My31'30. 10283
Sweet and hot. Prose. S. J. Perelman. 12:15-16*F22'36. 10284
Sweet child but stupid. Prose. G. Schwabe. 4:54 S29'28. 10285
Sweet Maggie Moncrieff. TWNY. Morris Bishop. 10:60-8 N3'34. 10286
Sweet revenge. Prose. W. Peter Schramm. 1:35 S19'25. 10287
Sweet time is still a-flying. Verse. Henrietta Fort Holland. 13:56*Je5'37. 10288
Sweetest li'l husbands. Prose. C. Knapp. 1:22 Ap25'25. 10289
Sweetheart. PR (Pickford). Margaret Case Harriman. 10:29-33 Ap7'34. 10290
Sweetly solemn thought. Verse. John Holmes. 11:16*Ag31'35. 10291
Sweetness and light. Prose. Katharine S. Angell White. 2:17 Mr 13'26. 10292
Swell art. Prose. Marc Connelly. 2:23 N27'26. 10293
The swell steerage. Prose. E. B. White. 2:20 Ag14'26. 10294
The swift completion of their appointed round. Verse. Margaret Fishback. 7:50 Ja9'32. 10295
Swig of pins. Prose. Richard Lockridge. 10:26-7*Ja12'35. 10296
Swimming Elm Avenue. Verse. Genevieve Taggard. 4:26 O6'28. 10297
The swindling presidente. AC. Janet Flanner. 15:38-42*Ag26 '39; 15:31-4*S2'39. 10298
The swing of the pendulum. DOL. Lois Long. 6:18-20 Ja31'31. 10299
Swiss letter. Janet Flanner. 9:45-6 Ag5'33. 10300
Sylvia in heaven. Verse. Florence Kiper Frank. 4:47 Ja19'29. 10301
A symbol in pugilism. PR (Dempsey). James Kevin McGuinness. 1:15-16 Mr14'25. 10302
A symbol of justice. PR (Steuer). Alva Johnston. 1:13-14 My16

The tat racket. BR. Jack Wynn. 3:105-107 N12'27. 10346

Tattletale. Verse. Martha Banning Thomas. 10:60 Ag18'34. 10347

The tattooed man versus Sir Mordred. Prose. Alva Johnston. 12:21-5 O24'36. 10348

Taxi-dance. RL. Leo Rosten. 14: 31-6*D31'38. 10349

Taxi-driver. Verse. Sydney King Russell. 5:111 N30'29. 10350

A taxi driver comments on the Whalen Plan. Prose. Alice Harvey. 4:36 F9'29. 10351

Taxi driver philosophy. Prose. G. Schwabe. 3:98 N12'27. 10352

Taxi driver philosophy. Prose. Katharine S. Angell White. 3: 32 O8'27. 10353

Taxi-driver philosophy. Prose. Katharine S. Angell White. 3: 65 O29'27. 10354

Taxi-driver philosophy. Prose. H. E. Yates. 3:46 D10'27. 10355

Taxi loves. Robert Hyde. 3:79 Ja28'28. 10356

Taxidermy: its cause and cure. Prose. S. J. Perelman. 9:20-1 Je17'33. 10357

The taxpayers get their money's worth. Prose. E. F. H. 1:33 S19'25. 10358

Tchatzu. Prose. Janet Flanner. 8:18-20*Mr19'32. 10359

Tchekov and Edison. Prose. Anton Chekov. 5:48-50 O19'29. 10360

Tea at Mrs. Armsby's. Prose. James Thurber. 4:15 D29'28. 10361

Tea for a viper. RL. Meyer Berger. 14:47-50 Mr12'38. 10362

Tea for two. Verse. Susanna Valentine Mitchell. 10:58 Mr 31'34. 10363

Tea room etiquette. Prose. F. B. M. 1:15 O17'25. 10364

Tea with the grownups. Prose. Beatrice Kaufman. 5:83-5 Ap 27'29. 10365

Teacher of dramatics. Verse. Edward J. Fitzgerald. 11:30* S21'35. 10366

Teaneck express or, blood will tell. Prose. Frank Sullivan. 8: 17-19 N19'32. 10367

Tears on St. Valentine's Eve. Verse. Spud Johnson. 2:36 F12 '27. 10368

The technician. Prose. Jack Cluett. 3:68-9 S24'27. 10369

Technicolor. John Chapin Mosher. 13:75*Mr20'37. 10370

Technicolor. TT. 13:19*D11'37. 10371

Technique. RL. Morris Markey. 10:67-70 O6'34. 10372

Technique. Prose. T. H. Wenning. 5:76-7 Mr30'29. 10373

Technocracy and Wilcox. Prose. Frances Warfield. 8:25 Ja14 '33. 10374

Teddy and Ann. Prose. John O'Hara. 10:102-105 S15'34. 10375

The teeth. Prose. Wolcott Gibbs. 6:28 N29'30. 10376

Telephone booths. Prose. Clara Janson. 1:13 Je27'25. 10377

Telephonetics. Verse. Arthur Guiterman. 8:28 My28'32. 10378

"Tell him you're a friend of mine." Prose. Gertrude Carver. 7:63-5 My16'31. 10379

Tell me about my daddy, or, the bootlegger's son. Verse. C. Knapp. 2:53 F12'27. 10380

Tell me all about Europe. Prose. Mildred Harris. 6:73-4 S6'30. 10381

Tell me, pretty Gipsy. Prose. Vera Caspary. 6:81-2 D20'30. 10382

Tell Mother I died for my country. Verse. C. Knapp. 3:45 My14 '27. 10383

The telltale heart. Verse. Marjorie Allen Seiffert. 12:26*Ag 15'36. 10384

Tema con variazione. Prose. James Reid Parker. 7:16-17 Ja16'32. 10385

The temperamental Suzanne. PR

Testimonial to G. B. S. Verse. Arthur Guiterman. 8:45*Ap16 '32. 10426
Testimony. Verse. Ruth Fitch Bartlett. 5:53 Ag31'29. 10427
Text. Verse. Audrey Wurdemann. 8:15 Je18'32. 10428
Text for a sampler. Verse. Ellen McLoughlin. 9:19 N25'33. 10429
Text for today. Verse. Phyllis McGinley. 10:16*F2'35. 10430
The Thanatopsis Murder Case. SM. Alexander Woollcott. 6:28 Ag2'30. 10431
Thank you. Verse. Morris Bishop. 6:16 Ja10'31. 10432
Thank you, New York telephone company. Prose. Frances Warfield. 7:54-7 Mr7'31. 10433
Thankfully received. SM. Alexander Woollcott. 7:34 N14'31. 10434
Thanks-for-strange-presents department. Prose. Wolcott Gibbs. 6:25 F7'31. 10435
Thanks for the buggy ride. Prose. Oliver Claxton. 3:28 My28'27. 10436
Thanks to cash. Prose. Frances Warfield. 8:33-4 Jy16'32. 10437
Thanksgiving. Prose. W. E. Farbstein. 6:25 N22'30. 10438
Thanksgiving. Prose. W. E. Farbstein. 8:19 N26'32. 10439
Thanksgiving. Prose. W. E. Farbstein. 9:23 N25'33. 10440
Thanksgiving. Prose. W. E. Farbstein. 11:22*N30'35. 10441
Thanksgiving on the Equator. Prose. Donald Ogden Stewart. 4:26-7 N24'28. 10442
That affair at Penge. SM. Alexander Woollcott. 10:32-4 Mr 24'34. 10443
That awful Seeley dinner. TWNY. Lucius Beebe. 7:34-8 Ja16'32. 10444
That certainly was New York. Prose. Christopher Ward. 6: 19-20 Ja3'31. 10445
That French musical comedy. Prose. Frederick Packard. 5:28 Mr23'29. 10446
That goes for you, Siegfried. Verse. E. B. White. 11:25*Ja25 '36. 10447
"That is now..." Prose. Agnes McKay. 7:45 Mr28'31. 10448
"That old New York..." Verse. Herman W. Albert. 2:50 Jy17 '26. 10449
That past condition contrary to the fact. Verse. Marjorie Allen Seiffert. 6:32 Mr22'30. 10450
That sad young man. PR (Fitzgerald). John Chapin Mosher. 2: 20-1 Ap17'26. 10451
That sound is a busy signal. Prose. A. N. Bass. 3:123 N19'27. 10452
That strange poltroonery. SM. Alexander Woollcott. 8:30*Ap30 '32. 10453
That summer. Prose. Nancy Hale. 13:19-21*Mr6'37. 10454
That was college life! Prose. Morris Bishop. 9:58-63 S16'33. 10455
That was New York. Prose. Russel Crouse. 4:34-8 O13'28. 10456
That was New York. Prose. Russel Crouse. 4:40-4 O27'28. 10457
That was New York. Prose. Russel Crouse. 4:49-56 D8'28. 10458
That was New York. Prose. Russel Crouse. 4:32-4 Ja12'29. 10459
That was New York. Prose. Russel Crouse. 5:40-6 Ap6'29. 10460
That was New York. Prose. Russel Crouse. 5:28-34 Je15'29. 10461
That's for you. Verse. Fanny Heaslip Lea. 6:19 My24'30. 10462
That's New York. Prose. T. H. Bliss. 1:7-8 My9'25. 10463
Theatre. Prose. John O'Hara. 4: 70 Ja5'29. 10464
Theatre business. NESD. John J.

Holzinger. 10:83 F24'34. 10465
Theatre gabble. Prose. C. Knapp. 2:28 Ap24'26. 10466
A theatre-goer's reflections. Verse. Herbert J. Mangham. 1:23 Ag8'25. 10467
Theatre Guild. PR. Cuthbert Wright. 2:17-20 D25'26. 10468
Theatre season, New York, 1928-29. Alexander Woollcott. 5:40 My25'29. 10469
Theatre season, New York, 1929-30. Robert Benchley. 6:26-30 Je7'30. 10470
Theatre season, New York, 1930-31. Robert Benchley. 7:24-6 Je27'31. 10471
Theatre season, New York, 1931-32. Robert Benchley. 8:24-6 Je 25'32. 10472
Theatre season, New York, 1932-33. Robert Benchley. 9:24-6 My27'33. 10473
Theatre season, New York, 1935-36. Robert Benchley. 12:36-8 My2'36. 10474
Theatre season, New York, 1937-38. Robert Benchley. 14:26* Ap16'38. 10475
Theatre tickets and periodicals. Prose. Jack Cluett. 3:34 Ag20 '27. 10476
Their country right, but not wrong. RL. St. Clair McKelway. 15:42-6*S30'39. 10477
Their mother's purse. Prose. Morley Callaghan. 12:15-16* S12'36. 10478
Theme song. Verse. Frances Park. 6:62 Mr29'30. 10479
Theme song for a movie. Verse. John Ogden Whedon. 4:57 S22 '28. 10480
Themis. Verse. David McCord. 5:28 Ap20'29. 10481
Then and now. Verse. Babette Deutsch. 8:25*Mr12'32. 10482
There and here. Verse. Philip G. Wylie. 2:65 Ja29'27. 10483
There is in this room... Verse. Harriett Brownell. 8:25 My21 '32. 10484
There is no Marion Davies. Prose. E. B. White. 3:38 N12 '27. 10485
There is no opera like "Lohengrin." Verse. John Wheelwright. 15:27*My6'39. 10486
There is this about sleep... Verse. Elspeth O'Halloran. 5: 25 Mr2'29. 10487
There should be music. Verse. Elspeth O'Halloran. 5:103 Mr16 '29. 10488
There was a time. Verse. Leslie Nelson Jennings. 5:111 O12'29. 10489
"There's a tower in the sky..." Verse. E. B. White. 2:17 Jy31 '26. 10490
There's an owl in my room. Prose. James Thurber. 10:19-20*N17'34. 10491
There's no place like home. Prose. James Thurber. 13:18-20*Ag14'37. 10492
There's nothing like an egg shampoo. Prose. Elizabeth Wilder. 13:58-9*My1'37. 10493
"There's nothing worse." Prose. Stanley Jones. 4:56 D22'28. 10494
These balmy days. Prose. David Cort. 2:16 Ag14'26. 10495
These crisp Autumn nights. Prose. James Reid Parker. 8:81-4 N5 '32. 10496
These exoduses. Prose. Frances Crane. 5:68-70 N30'29. 10497
These movie heroes. Prose. Don Ryan. 1:12 O3'25. 10498
These trivial accomplishments. Prose. Richard Lockridge. 6: 64-5 N15'30. 10499
These vanities. Verse. Nancy Hoyt. 3:34 Mr12'27. 10500
They call it burlesque. Prose. Gilbert W. Gabriel. 1:12-13 Ag 22'25. 10501
They catch a lion. RC. Fillmore Hyde. 2:24-6 F5'27. 10502
They come and go. Prose. Isabel Currier. 14:54-5*Je25'38. 10503
They come with joyous song. RL. E. B. White. 15:25-8*My13

'39. 10504

They defend themselves. RL. A. J. Liebling. 15:34-46 F10'40. 10505

They get a bad scare and Ritza learns a lesson. RC. Fillmore Hyde. 2:23-4 O23'26. 10506

They got married at Elkton. RL. Joseph Mitchell. 9:52-9 N11'33. 10507

They have never kept a secret from us yet. Verse. E. B. White. 6:24 O4'30. 10508

They have to be careful. Prose. Angelica Gibbs. 15:38-40*Ag19 '39. 10509

They live, they breathe. Verse. Ogden Nash. 7:25 Ap4'31. 10510

They live, they breathe. Verse. Ogden Nash. 7:21 Ap11'31. 10511

They meet cute. Prose. Alan Campbell. 13:56*My22'37. 10512

They meet on the subway. Prose. Theodore Shane. 1:14 Je20'25. 10513

They never will be slaves. Verse. Henrietta Fort Holland. 8:18*Ap2'32. 10514

They shall not pass. Verse. Richard Armour. 15:79*Ap29 '39. 10515

They speak it in Tiflis. Prose. John Chapin Mosher. 9:16-17 D30'33. 10516

They used to have yachts. Prose. John Chapin Mosher. 10:54-8 Je9'34. 10517

They were eleven. PR (Sanger). Helena Hungtington Smith. 6: 22-5 Jy5'30. 10518

They were good fortune's. Verse. Mark Van Doren. 9:15 My13'33. 10519

They were New Yorkers. Prose. Herbert Asbury. 5:34-44 Mr9 '29. 10520

They were New Yorkers. Prose. Russel Crouse. 3:22-3 Mr12 '27. 10521

They were New Yorkers. Prose. Russel Crouse. 3:22-3 Ap2'27. 10522

They were New Yorkers. Prose. Russel Crouse. 3:28-9 Ap16'27. 10523

They were New Yorkers. Prose. Russel Crouse. 3:20-1 My21'27. 10524

They were New Yorkers. Prose. Russel Crouse. 3:15-16 Jy16'27. 10525

They were New Yorkers. Prose. Russel Crouse. 3:23-4 S17'27. 10526

They were New Yorkers. Prose. Russel Crouse. 3:19-20 O22'27. 10527

They're in the Army now. RL. Richard O. Boyer. 14:32-45*Mr 26'38. 10528

They've come to caviar. Prose. S. J. Perelman. 7:30-2 O17'31. 10529

Thin pickings. WP. Robert Benchley. 6:49-53 F7'31. 10530

The thin rain. Verse. Charles Norman. 5:19 F23'29. 10531

The thin red leash. Prose. James Thurber. 3:60-1 Ag13'27.10531A

Things are not as they seem. Prose. Maddy Vegtel. 2:14 Ag7 '26. 19532

Things I have never done. Prose. Morris Markey. 7:24-31*Ag15 '31. 10533

Things I have never liked. Prose. Charles G. Shaw. 7:23 D5'31. 10534

Things I have never liked. Prose. Charles G. Shaw. 7:42 Ja30'32. 10535

Things I have never liked. Prose. Charles G. Shaw. 7:28 F6'32. 10536

Things I have observed. Verse. Martha Banning Thomas. 5:95 O19'29. 10537

Things I shall never understand about New York. Prose. Katharine Brush. 12:39-40*Mr28'36. 10538

Things temporal. Prose. Edward L. Gordy. 6:44-5 Jy19'30.10539

Things that bother me. Prose. E. B. White. 3:19 My21'27. 10540
Things that will depress me if my husband gets them for Christmas, though they will enchant him. Prose. Sarah Addington. 14:89*D17'38. 10541
Things to come, baby. Prose. Al Graham. 12:60*Ap25'36. 10542
Think of a number. Prose. Margaret Ford. 10:32-4 My12'34. 10543
The thinker. Verse. Persis Greely Anderson. 7:85 Mr7'31. 10544
Thinker in bed. Verse. John Holmes. 13:32*Ja15'38. 10545
The third-and-a-half estate. WP. Robert Benchley. 8:41-6*My7 '32. 10546
Third-class local. Prose. Olive Ward. 10:42-3 Ag4'34. 10547
Thirteen. Prose. Gertrude Carver. 7:77-9 D19'31. 10548
Thirteen keys. Prose. James Thurber. 10:23-4 S8'34. 10549
Thirty. Verse. Frances Park. 4:34 Ap7'28. 10550
Thirty-five-cent special. Prose. Margaret Ford. 10:65-6 S8'34. 10551
Thirty-five years of Balzac. PR (Royce). Alva Johnston. 9:18-21 Ap1'33. 10552
31, Rue Cambon. PR (Chanel). Janet Flanner. 7:25-8 Mr14 '31. 10553
Thirty-seven. Prose. Patricia Collinge. 5:17-19 F1'30. 10554
This chap what's-'is-name. Verse. Paul G. Gumbinner. 5:79 Mr2 '29. 10555
This child knows the answer--do you? Prose. Jack Cluett. 3:62 Je4'27. 10556
This-cool-eve. Verse. Martha Banning Thomas. 4:45 Ag25'28. 10557
This Fall. Prose. Maddy Vegtel. 10:69-70 S22'34. 10558
This girl of the channel. PR (Ederle). Lurton Blassingame. 2:15-16 Ag28'26. 10559
"This is marriage, . . . " Verse. Dorothy Dow. 4:24 D29'28. 10560
This is my house... Verse. Harriett Brownell. 8:23 Je11'32. 10561
This is the boy. Verse. Mark Van Doren. 11:19*F8'36. 10562
"This is the girl I'm going to marry." Prose. E. B. White. 5:28 O 19'29. 10563
This is the mail for which you sent postage. Prose. Elmer Davis. 14:37*O1'38. 10564
This is the root. Verse. Robert Nathan. 14:21*Ap16'38. 10565
This little kitty stayed cool. Prose. James Thurber. 8:17-18 S10'32. 10566
This, now, education. Prose. Owen P. White. 1:23 Jy25'25. 10567
This one is Father. Verse. John Holmes. 14:33*D3'38. 10568
This one is on me. Verse. Ogden Nash. 11:18*Je29'35. 10569
This passion for Paris frocks and rest. Verse. Richard Butler Glaenzer. 3:35 D3'27. 10570
This prize problem. Prose. John Chapin Mosher. 2:15 My29'26. 10571
This science. RL. Morris Markey. 7:50-8 My9'31. 10572
This side of Summer. Verse. Raymond Holden. 8:25*Ap30'32. 10573
This strange secretiveness. SM. Alexander Woollcott. 8:30-4 Ja 21'33. 10574
This sweet adversity. Prose. Dorothey Mills Emery. 8:48-9*F20 '32. 10575
This thing called they. SM. Alexander Woollcott. 8:32*My7'32. 10576
This Vassar business. Prose. Creighton Peet. 3:43-4 Ag20'27. 10577
This way out. Prose. Hildegarde Dolson. 13:60-1*Je19'37. 10578
This way out. Verse. Margaret Fishback. 6:86 O25'30. 10579

This way out. Prose. Joseph Fulling Fishman. 6:116-17 D 13'30. 10580
This way to the Fair. SM. Alexander Woollcott. 9:32 Jy8'33. 10581
This week's award. Prose. Marquis James. 1:21 Ap18'25. 10582
This week's horoscope. Prose. Robert Benchley. 8:15 Ag13'32. 10583
This week's miracle. Prose. James Thurber. 5:25-6 Ap6'29. 10584
Thompson, Dorothy. TT. 15:11* Mr4'39. 10585
Thompson, Dorothy. TT. 15:13* Ja20'40. 10586
Thompson, Dorothy. E. B. White. 15:19-20*My27'39. 10587
Thor plays polo. PR (Milburn). Herbert Reed. 2:23-4 Je5'26. 10588
Thoreau, Henry D. (Parody) Edmund Wilson. 10:21 Mr17'34. 10589
The thorn in friendship's garland. Verse. Morris Bishop. 12:38*D19'36. 10590
Those boys in Chicago. Prose. Frances Park. 9:59-60 O21'33. 10591
Those Fifth Avenue girls. Prose. Frederick Lewis Allen. 5:19-20 F8'30. 10592
Those intellectual chorus girls. Verse. Fillmore Hyde. 2:14 Je26'26. 10593
Those little theatres. Prose. Laura Benét. 2:32 F27'26. 10594
Those radio talks. Prose. Stark Childe. 1:23 N21'25. 10595
Those were consumers. Prose. Richard Lockridge. 11:20-2* Ap6'35. 10596
Those were the days. PR (Worth et Cie). Janet Flanner. 9:17-20 Ja20'34. 10597
"Those who claim to be esthetic." Verse. Anon. 2:15 My15'26. 10598
Those who read in bed. Verse. Persis Greely Anderson. 6:40 Ja31'31. 10599
Though Winter sunsets widen. Verse. Harry Kemp. 5:54 Ja4 '30. 10600
Thought for a sunshiny morning. Verse. Dorothy Parker. 3:31 Ap9'27. 10601
A thought in preface. Prose. Warner Fabian. 2:23 Mr13'26. 10602
Thoughtful Mrs. Bennett. Prose. Jo Pennington. 11:58*Je22'35. 10603
Thoughts. Verse. Ruth Brown. 5:75 Mr9'29. 10604
Thoughts. Prose. E. B. White. 3:16 Je18'27. 10605
Thoughts. Prose. E. B. White. 3:15-16 D24'27. 10606
Thoughts at a radio. Verse. Charles Norman. 15:23*My13 '39. 10607
Thoughts from Mr. Tierney. Prose. James Thurber. 7:13-14 F13'32. 10608
Thoughts in the subway. Verse. Viola Paradise. 2:41 Ja1'27. 10609
Thoughts obscure, concise, metaphysical, and seasonal. Verse. Parke Cummings. 7:74*My23 '31. 10610
Thoughts of loved ones. Verse. Margaret Fishback. 4:37 D22 '28. 10611
Thoughts on a train. Verse. Ruth Lambert Jones. 5:91 Mr30'29. 10612
Thoughts on human intercourse. Verse. Margaret Widdemer. 11:42*F1'36. 10613
Thoughts on the cavalier poets. Verse. Parke Cummings. 7:40 S26'31. 10614
Thoughts on the ermine. Prose. Will Cuppy. 12:24*Ap25'36. 10615
Thoughts on the United States census. Verse. Ellen McLoughlin. 7:30 O24'31. 10616
Thoughts on where to live. Verse.

E. B. White. 11:25*My4'35. 10617
Thoughts while waiting for five o'clock. Prose. Florence W. Ross. 3:48 D10'27. 10618
The thousand-dollar bill. Prose. John Chapin Mosher. 6:26-7 F14'31. 10619
A thousand pounds a minute. RL. Edmund Pearson. 9:44-8 Je3 '33. 10620
Threat to a fickle lady. Verse. Dorothy Parker. 14:20*Mr26 '38. 10621
Three at tea. Prose. Frances Crane. 4:89-90 F16'29. 10622
Three bells and a jingle. RL. Morris Markey. 6:36-40 Ag16 '30. 10623
A three dimensional person. PR (White). Edna Ferber. 1:9-10 My30'25. 10624
Three dollars a ticket. Verse. Roswell J. Powers. 1:35 N7 '25. 10625
The three little Christmas carols. Verse. Ogden Nash. 10:15-16* D22'34. 10626
Three methods of acquiring loam. Prose. Frank Sullivan. 4:21-2 My26'28. 10627
Three more sisters. Prose. Oliver Claxton. 2:46-7 N13'26. 10628
Three poems. Verse. Charles Norman. 5:40 S21'29. 10629
Three rings and a ruse. Verse. Paul G. Gumbinner. 3:99 Ap16 '27. 10630
Three soliloquies. Verse. Nancy Byrd Turner. 5:51-2 Ag17'29. 10631
The three veterans. Prose. Leane Zugsmith. 11:24-5*Mr16'35. 10632
Three-volume novel. Verse. William Rose Benét. 8:19 N12'32. 10633
The threefold problem of world economic coöperation. Prose. James Thurber. 9:19-20 Ag5'33. 10634
Thrift. Prose. Anon. 2:65-6 F20 '26. 10635
Thrift. Verse. Ruth Lambert Jones. 13:30*O23'37. 10636
The thrilling Thirties. NYC. Joel Sayre. 8:40-3 N26'32. 10637
Through a glass darkly. Prose. Arthur H. Folwell. 3:28-9 F19 '27. 10638
Through a glass darkly. Prose. Burdette Kinne. 8:51-2 O29'32. 10639
Through the magnifying glass. Prose. Charles G. Shaw. 3:25 Jy9'27. 10640
Through the magnifying glass. Prose. Charles G. Shaw. 3:30-1 O15'27. 10641
Through the magnifying glass. Prose. Charles G. Shaw. 3:21-2 N5'27. 10642
Through the magnifying glass. Prose. Charles G. Shaw. 3:36-8 D3'27. 10643
Through the microscope. Prose. John Peter Toohey. 3:102-103 N19'27. 10644
Through the walls. Prose. Julia Cobb. 5:97-8 My18'29. 10645
Thumb of a plumber. Prose. Charlcie Hedge. 10:83 My12'34. 10646
Thunder on the left. Verse. Anon. 2:55 My1'26. 10647
Thurber, James. Janet Flanner. 13:36*Je12'37. 10648
Thy rocks and rills. Verse. Elizabeth Coatsworth. 9:32 Ap22 '33. 10649
Tick-tock and bong! Prose. Frederick Packard. 14:66*Ap9'38. 10650
The ticket graft. RL. Morris Markey. 3:34-40 S24'27. 10651
Tickets, please. Prose. Anon. 1:22 Mr28'25. 10652
The ticking titantic struggle. Prose. A. L. L. 1:28 Ap4'25. 10653
Tidbits. Prose. James Thurber. 3:88-9 Mr12'27. 10654
Tide. Verse. Frances M. Frost. 6:15 Je28'30. 10655
Tidings. Prose. Douglass Welch. 12:68*S19'36. 10656

The tie that blinds. Prose. Corey Ford. 1:29 My16'25. 10657
Tiger, tiger. RL. Morris Markey. 1:11-12 Ja9'26. 10658
Tiger, tiger, tiger! Prose. Jack Cluett. 7:19 O24'31. 10659
The tiger's skin. Prose. Edward John Dunsany. 7:22-3 Je20'31. 10660
Tightrope-walker. Verse. Marion Strobel. 15:47*Ap15'39. 10661
Tiller traditions. Prose. Frank Sullivan. 3:22-3 F19'27. 10662
Time dozes. Verse. Babette Deutsch. 7:19 N7'31. 10663
Time... Fortune... Life... Luce. PR (Luce). Wolcott Gibbs. 12: 20-5*N28'36. 10664
Time, gentlemen, time! Verse. Oliver St. John Gogarty. 13:22* Ap3'37. 10665
The time I couldn't see Mrs. Fiske. Prose. Paul Horgan. 13: 31-2*D4'37. 10666
The time I ran away. Prose. Anna Mary Wells. 15:54-8*Ja 20'40. 10667
Time in its flight. Prose. Robert M. Coates. 13:27-8*Je12 '37. 10668
Time is money. Prose. John C. Emery. 8:30*My14'32. 10669
Time magazine. (Parody). Wolcott Gibbs. 12:20-5 *N28'36. 10670
Time magazine. (Parody) E. B. White. 12:16 Mr14'36. 10671
Time out. Verse. Margaret Fishback. 4:103 Ap21'28. 10672
Time out. Verse. Oliver Jenkins. 15:38*Ja27'40. 10673
The time-saver. Verse. Ted Robinson, Jr. 5:72 O12'29. 10674
The time savers. Prose. Sigmund Spaeth. 2:27 N27'26. 10675
The time will come. Prose. Sally Benson. 12:14-16*Jy11 '36. 10676
Time will kiss and tell. Verse. Ogden Nash. 12:26*Ja9'37. 10677
A timely suggestion. Prose. Frank Sullivan. 11:18*O12'35. 10678
Timely warning. Prose. Joseph P. Pollard. 4:32 Jy7'28. 10679
Timely warning. Prose. Joseph P. Pollard. 4:50 Ag18'28. 10680
Timely warning. Prose. Joseph P. Pollard. 4:56 S1'28. 10681
Timely warning. Prose. Joseph P. Pollard. 4:71 S15'28. 10682
Timely warning. Prose. Joseph P. Pollard. 4:68 S29'28. 10683
Times change. Prose. Wayne G. Haisley. 1:17 Je6'25. 10684
Time's winged chariot. Prose. Mollie Panter-Downes. 15:18-20*Ag26'39. 10685
A timid little man. PR (Hopkins). R. Hale. 1:9-10 Mr21'25. 10686
The timid nautilus. Verse. E. B. White. 7:24 Mr28'31. 10687
Timid plea to a great big aviation company advertising "sleep while you fly." Verse. Martha Banning Thomas. 12:28*D26'36. 10688
The timid soul. Prose. Sigmund Spaeth. 2:42-3 My8'26. 10689
Timothy Harshaw's flute. Prose. Morley Callaghan. 9:17-19 F10 '34. 10690
Tirade against wisdom. Verse. William Rose Benét. 12:18*F22 '36. 10691
A tired ballad of travel. Verse. Phyllis McGinley. 9:21 Jy8'33. 10692
Tit for tat. Prose. Leane Zugsmith. 11:15-16*Ag3'35. 10693
The Titans. Verse. Fillmore Hyde 4:21 F25'28. 10694
The title. Prose. Arthur Kober. 5:90-2 Ap27'29. 10695
Titles mean nothing. Prose. Frances Crane. 6:35-6 Jy5'30. 10696
The tittering taxi. Verse. Morris Bishop. 9:24 O28'33. 10697
To--. Prose. Frederick Packard. 13:80*D11'37. 10698
To a baby in Longacre Square. Verse. Lee Wilson Dodd. 7:92

Ap11'31. 10699
To a baby one day old. Verse. Margaret Fishback. 9:12 Ag12 '33. 10700
To a bee in a bonnet. Verse. Margaret Fishback. 10:66 Je9 '34. 10701
To a born cook. Verse. Sara Henderson Hay. 6:44 Mr8'30. 10702
To a broker promising much. Verse. Grace Hazard Conkling. 5:53 D14'29. 10703
To a cat. Verse. Samuel Hoffenstein. 6:27 S27'30. 10704
To a cat loitering at Twenty-eighth Street and Sixth Avenue. Verse. Margaret Fishback. 5:113 Ap20'29. 10705
To a clergyman. Verse. Carroll Carroll. 2:66 D11'26. 10706
To a Connecticut hostess. Verse. Carroll Carroll. 5:88 Je15'29. 10707
To a constant nymph. Verse. Helen Rockwell. 1:29 D26'25. 10708
To a coquette. Verse. Franklin P. Adams. 14:32*My7'38. 10709
To a fir tree. Verse. Frances Park. 4:131 D15'28. 10710
To a flapper. Verse. Anon. 2:41 Je26'26. 10711
To a fly in an amber bead. Verse. Julia Gilcrest. 4:120 N10'28. 10712
To a friend. Verse. Margaret Fishback. 6:49 S6'30. 10713
To a gallant spinster. Verse. Frances M. Frost. 7:32 Mr7 '31. 10714
To a garter snake. Verse. Mildred Weston. 12:59*Ap25'36. 10715
To a ghost facing a busy winter. Verse. S. A. T. 11:46*Jy20'35. 10716
To a guest. Verse. Witter Bynner. 6:30 Mr1'30. 10717
To a hot water bottle named Jonathan. Verse. E. B. White. 3:28 F18'28. 10718
To a household pet. Verse. Marjorie Allen Seiffert. 10:62 Mr 31'34. 10719
To a lady. Verse. Franklin P. Adams. 13:46*Ja1'38. 10720
To a lady. Verse. Ruth McClellan. 3:99 N5'27. 10721
To a lady holding the floor. Verse. Mildred Weston. 15:48*Ap29'39. 10722
To a lady reaching a ripe old age. Verse. Haniel Long. 15:40*D2 '39. 10723
To a lady, who must write verse. Verse. Dorothy Parker. 3:22 Je18'27. 10724
To a lady who was once a freshman. Verse. E. B. White. 4:25 O13'28. 10725
To a little tenement child. Verse. Baird Leonard. 4:22 Ag4'28. 10726
To a maid dusting the furniture in Sloane's window. Verse. Margaret Fishback. 7:20 S19 '31. 10727
To a Manhattan canary. Verse. Parke Cummings. 5:77 Je8'29. 10728
To a metropolitan. Verse. Fillmore Hyde. 6:87 N15'30. 10729
To a minor corporation. Verse. Persis Greely Anderson. 8:55* Mr26'32. 10730
To a modernistic Christmas tree. Verse. Phyllis McGinley. 8:41 D24'32. 10731
To a new fiancé/fiancée. Verse. Elspeth O'Halloran. 4:19 Jy28 '28. 10732
To a patient in St. Luke's Hospital. Verse. Howard Cushman. 6:95 N8'30. 10733
To a perfumed lady at the concert. Verse. E. B. White. 8:23*Mr19 '32. 10734
To a perhaps unavoidably late rose. Verse. E. B. White. 6:28 O11'30. 10735
To a poet. Verse. Richard Eberhart. 15:52*S9'39. 10736
To a president returned from fishing. Verse. Ora Stark. 2:53 S25

'26. 10737

To a reckless lady's ghost. Verse. Phyllis McGinley. 7:32 Ja23'32. 10738

To a scarecrow. Verse. Mildred Weston. 8:12 Jy30'32. 10739

To a small boy standing on my shoes while I am wearing them. Verse. Ogden Nash. 7:23 My9'31. 10740

To a sophisticate. Verse. Le Baron Cooke. 1:33 N14'25. 10741

To a taxi-driver intent on having the island to himself. Verse. Margaret Fishback. 8:72 O15 '32. 10742

To a timetable. Verse. Arthur L. Lippmann. 3:73 Ap16'27. 10743

To a very literary lady. Verse. Vincent Starrett. 6:81 My31 '30. 10744

To a very quiet guest at a party. Verse. Martha Banning Thomas. 6:26 Je28'30. 10745

To a wine-(in a manner of speaking) cork. Verse. Brownell Carr. 3:78 Mr19'27. 10746

To a worm. Verse. John Ogden Whedon. 4:24 Ja12'29. 10747

To a young girl. Verse. Marjorie Allen Seiffert. 8:55 Je18 '32. 10748

To a young man going to hell. Verse. Elizabeth Gunn. 4:70 D8'28. 10749

To a young man selecting six orchids. Verse. Margaret Fishback. 6:127 D6'30. 10750

To a young man who is afraid he is polygamous. Verse. Elspeth O'Halloran. 3:36 D17 '27. 10751

To a young sailor. Verse. Elspeth O'Halloran. 4:45 Ag11 '28. 10752

To a young suicide. Verse. Elspeth O'Halloran. 4:20 Mr24 '28. 10753

To a young tennis star. Verse. Parke Cummings. 4:103 Ap14 '28. 10754

To all men that they be virtuous. Verse. Herman Fetzer. 6:32 N29'30. 10755

To an adding machine. Verse. Arthur Guiterman. 6:70 S6'30. 10756

To an ailanthus tree. Verse. Harry Kemp. 4:34 My19'28. 10757

To an artist, to take heart. Verse Louise Bogan. 13:15*Jy3'37. 10758

To an insect, flying about in church. Verse. Sara Henderson Hay. 8:55 S10'32. 10759

To an insurance solicitor. Verse. Margaret Fishback. 8:42 Ag6 '32. 10760

To an iris, a caterpillar, and a wren. Verse. Martha Banning Thomas. 9:67 My6'33. 10761

To an old woman on the subway. Verse. Sara Henderson Hay. 5:40 N2'29. 10762

To an over-cultured jazz band leader. Verse. Parke Cummings. 2:104 D11'26. 10763

To an unfinished cathedral. Verse. Clinch Calkins. 3:20 Jy30'27. 10764

To an uninteresting man who was once a suitor. Verse. Martha Banning Thomas. 5:24 Mr2'29. 10765

To another sad young man. Verse Lee Wilson Dodd. 7:31 S5'31. 10766

To Autumn bluebirds. Verse. Elizabeth Coatsworth. 9:72 N11 '33. 10767

To be continued. Verse. Margaret Fishback. 3:59 Ja14'28. 10768

To be sung on the water. Verse. Louise Bogan. 13:26*Ap21'37. 10769

To be whistled in April. Verse. Olive Ward. 4:28 Ap7'28. 10770

To bellman, tramway and councillor. Verse. Ruth Lambert Jones 4:71 D1'28. 10771

To C--. Verse. Persis Greely Anderson. 6:16 Ag2'30. 10772

To Cab Calloway. Verse. Vincent McHugh. 9:27 F3'34. 10773

To certain fellow-poets. Verse. Arthur Guiterman. 1:14 O17 '25. 10774
To Chicot, a very French bulldog. Verse. Kenneth Allan Robinson. 10:104 Ap21'34. 10775
To cool the air. Prose. Sylvia Townsend Warner. 15:19-20*S 16'39. 10776
To genius, dying young. Verse. Samuel Hoffenstein. 6:33 S13 '30. 10777
To going abroad. Verse. L. B. G. 2:47 Ap24'26. 10778
To have its fun. Verse. Marjorie Allen Seiffert. 7:40 S12'31. 10779
To Helen on her second birthday. Verse. Jean Batchelor. 6:18 Jy26'30. 10780
To her Ladyship. Verse. Margaret Fishback. 12:56*O3'36. 10781
To hold up its stocking. Verse. Martha Banning Thomas. 2:22 My22'26. 10782
To live dangerously--. Prose. Angelica Gibbs. 7:63-4 Ap11'31. 10783
To Lucasta on dropping her flat. Verse. José Schorr. 2:65 N20 '26. 10784
To mail a letter. Prose. Robert M. Coates. 13:64-5*My1'37. 10785
To meet Edwina. Prose. Angelica Gibbs. 14:63-4*F11'39. 10786
To meet the Wrights. Prose. James Reid Parker. 12:58-60* O3'36. 10787
To Miss Manhattan. Verse. Arthur H. Folwell. 1:17 O24'25. 10788
To my brother. Verse. Louise Bogan. 11:31*O26'35. 10789
To my country. Verse. Raymond Holden. 5:28 N23'29. 10790
To my father. Verse. Clinch Calkins. 3:21 Je4'27. 10791
To my heroes. Prose. Eugene Kinkead. 14:55*Ja14'39. 10792
To my Irish wolfhound upon parting. Clinch Calkins. 3:24 F18 '28. 10793
To my mother. Verse. Garreta Busey. 13:16*S25'37. 10794
To my nose with love. Verse. Jacqueline Embry. 6:25 Ja24 '31. 10795
To my small son at the seashore. Verse. Sara Henderson Hay. 5: 45 Ag31'29. 10796
To my small son, at the zoo. Verse. Sara Henderson Hay. 12: 32*O10'36. 10797
To my small son busy in the backyard. Verse. Sara Henderson Hay. 5:72 Je29'29. 10798
To my small son, in church. Verse. Sara Henderson Hay. 6:66 My3'30. 10799
To my small son, inclined to warfare. Verse. Sara Henderson Hay. 5:56 O12'29. 10800
To my small son on certain occasions. Verse. Sara Henderson Hay. 6:50 O4'30. 10801
To my small son, skating. Verse. Sara Henderson Hay. 6:75 Je7 '30. 10802
To my small son, wading. Verse. Sara Henderson Hay. 5:73 Jy20 '29. 10803
To my wife. Verse. Clarence Day. 9:19 F10'34. 10804
To my young sister. Verse. Sara Henderson Hay. 7:26 N21'31. 10805
To one unseen. Verse. Elizabeth Coatsworth. 8:20 Je4'32. 10806
To one who reads all the literary supplements. Verse. Parke Cummings. 2:48 Ja15'27. 10807
To our great economists. Verse. Ralph Pulitzer. 7:96 D5'31. 10808
To resume. WP. Robert Benchley. 7:48-54 My2'31. 10809
To Robin. Verse. Lee Wilson Dodd. 9:16 Ap1'33. 10810
To sad young women who bewail in verse the sameness of the male. Verse. Henry Morton Robinson. 7:56 D5'31. 10811
To sublet, furnished. Prose. Wolcott Gibbs. 10:17-19 S29

'34. 10812
To Summer. Verse. Philip G. Wylie. 2:19 Ag21'26. 10813
To take leave. Prose. Louise Bogan. 10:26-7*Ja26'35. 10814
To the ant, thou sluggard. Verse. Ruth Lambert Jones. 13:64*My 8'37. 10815
To the colors. Prose. Frank Sullivan. 14:23-4*My21'38. 10816
To the crocus--with my love. Verse. Marion Sturges-Jones. 11:20*Mr30'31. 10817
To the employment agencies. Verse. Anon. 3:90 N19'27. 10818
To the king over the water. Prose. E. F. K. 12:39-40*Ja2 '37. 10819
To the ladies. Verse. Anne Forbes. 13:30 O16'37. 10820
To the ladies! Prose. Baird Leonard. 3:19 Ja28'28. 10821
To the ladies. Prose. Maddy Vegtel. 11:19-20*N9'35. 10822
To the love-lorn editor. Verse. Catherine Girdler. 4:71 S29'28. 10823
To the planet Venus. Verse. Elizabeth Coatsworth. 9:16 Mr 11'33. 10824
To the pure--. Prose. Patricia Collinge. 6:30 My24'30. 10825
To the returner. Verse. Price Day. 7:38 S26'31. 10826
To the roast turkey. Verse. Mildred Weston. 10:78*D1'34. 10827
To the tiresome friend. Verse. Genevieve Taggard. 13:29*N 27'37. 10828
To the top of the New York Central Building--illuminated. Verse. Sigmund Spaeth. 5:80 Mr16'29. 10829
To the women. Verse. Hortense Flexner. 14:56*Je11'38. 10830
To them that hath. RL. Geoffrey T. Hellman. 9:42-7 Mr4'33. 10831
To time--for a baby. Verse. Elizabeth Coatsworth. 8:79 Ja 7'33. 10832
To Tosti. Verse. Elias Lieberman. 1:12 O10'25. 10833
To waiters and a chef. PR (Cerutti and Cavallero). Margaret Case Harriman. 11:20-4*Je1'35; 11:22-6*Je8'35. 10834
To whom it may concern. Prose. Donald Moffat. 8:22-3 Ag27'32. 10835
To William Shakespeare. Verse. D. M. 13:58*Ap10'37. 10836
To your corner. Verse. Margaret Fishback. 3:47 Ja14'28. 10837
Toast. Verse. Witter Bynner. 11: 25*Mr16'35. 10838
Toast. Verse. Frances M. Frost. 14:32*Ja28'39. 10839
A toast. Prose. James Reid Parker. 8:39-41 Ag20'32. 10840
Toast to a great reformer. Verse. Phyllis McGinley. 10:27 F24'34. 10841
A toast to Captain Jerk. Prose. J. J. O'Malley. 15:47-8*S30'39. 10842
Toast to your smile. Verse. Martha Banning Thomas. 3:25 D10 '27. 10843
Tobacco Road. (Play) TT. 12:12* My16'36. 10844
Together with orioles. Prose. John Chapin Mosher. 11:24-6*Ag31 '35. 10845
Toiler's return (1980 A. D.). Verse. Persis Greely Anderson. 6:45 Jy19'30. 10846
Tolstoy, Alexandra Lvovna. TT. 15:11-12*Jy22'39. 10847
Tom the young kidnapper, or, pay up and live. Prose. James Thurber. 9:14-16 Je10'33. 10848
The tombs. TWNY. Samuel McCoy. 6:42-6 F22'30. 10849
Tombs are best. Prose. E. B. White. 3:14-15 Ag13'27. 10850
Tombstones in the starlight. Verse. Dorothy Parker. 5:22 My4'29. 10851
Tomorrow: fairly cloudy. Prose. S. J. Perelman. 14:12-13*Ag20 '38. 10852
Tong leader. PR (Wing). St. Clair

McKelway. 9:18-22 D30'33. 10853

Tong war. Verse. Henry F. Pringle. 1:32 S26'25. 10854

Tongue-tister. Verse. Mildred Weston. 10:52*D29'34. 10855

Tongues of angels. Prose. Wolcott Gibbs. 6:26-7 D6'30. 10856

The tonic. Prose. John Chapin Mosher. 6:26-7 My10'30.10857

Tonight of a village I'm dreaming. OSB. C. Knapp. 5:22 Je15 '29. 10858

The tonsils of the gift horse. Prose. John Chapman Hilder. 1:8 Mr14'25. 10859

Too bad. Prose. Marcia Clarke. 4:86-7 S22'28. 10860

Too bad. Verse. Clarence Day. 10:29*N17'34. 10861

Too bad! Prose. William Slavens McNutt. 1:20-1 Ap25'25. 10862

Too good for the morons. Prose. Plutarch. 1:19-20 My30'25. 10863

Too much talk. Verse. Marjorie Allen Seiffert. 6:48 N29'30. 10864

Too temperamental. Prose. Parke Cummings. 12:52-4*Ja23'37. 10865

Too, too beautiful. Prose. Burdette Kinne. 10:53-6 F17'34. 10866

Too young. Prose. John O'Hara. 15:15-16*S9'39. 10867

The tool chest. NESD. John J. Holzinger. 10:26 Ag11'34. 10868

The topaz cufflinks mystery. Prose. James Thurber. 8:14 Jy23'32. 10869

Topics of the day. Prose. James Thurber. 4:25 N24'28. 10870

Topless in Ilium. Prose. Wolcott Gibbs. 12:25-6*Ag15'36. 10871

Topsy-turvy. Verse. Jerome Barry. 5:86 Mr23'29. 10872

A tory's night thought. Verse. Clarence Day. 11:25*N30'35. 10873

Toscanini. Prose. Baird Leonard. 6:62 Ap19'30. 10874

The touch of greatness. Prose. Oliver LaFarge. 14:18-20*Je4 '38. 10875

The touching romance of Patience and Jobab. Verse. Stuart Hyde Hawkins. 2:31 N6'26. 10876

The touchstone. Prose. Jean Batchelor. 9:24-6 Jy29'33. 10877

Tough customers. RL. Morris Markey. 6:36-40 Ja31'31.10878

Tough spot. Prose. George Cronyn. 9:40-5 F25'33. 10879

The toughest dump in town. Prose. Gilbert W. Gabriel. 1: 14-15 S12'25. 10880

Toujours femme. Verse. Margaretta Manning. 4:52 Je23'28. 10881

Tour number seventy-six. Prose. Robert Benchley. 2:17 Ap24'26. 10882

A tour of Minskyville. RL. Alva Johnston. 8:34-40 My28'32. 10883

Tourist cabin. Prose. George Cecil Cowing. 5:22-3 Mr16'29. 10884

Tourist home. Prose. Benedict Thielen. 14:19-21*F11'39. 10885

The tourist--third language. Prose. George Cecil Cowing. 5:53 S28'29. 10886

The tournament. Prose. John O'Hara. 5:81-3 Je8'29. 10887

Tout à fait française. Prose. Alice Frankforter. 6:71-2 N8 '30. 10888

Toward the air. RL. Morris Markey. 4:42-9 Je2'28. 10889

The tower apartment. Prose. Arthur H. Folwell. 1:17 S19'25. 10890

Towers of dullness. RL. Morris Markey. 1:15-16 Ja23'26. 10891

Town triolets. Verse. Irma Brandeis. 2:87 D18'26. 10892

Toys for sleep. Verse. George Allen. 14:53*N5'38. 10893

Tracks in the snow. Verse. David

McCord. 8:15 F11'33. 10894
Trade in. Prose. Richard Lockridge. 13:30*S18'37. 10895
Trade last. Prose. T. H. Wenning. 11:67-9*Mr16'35. 10896
The trade of law. RL. Morris Markey. 3:36-40 Ap16'27. 10897
Tradition. Verse. Ruth Lambert Jones. 7:23*Je27'31. 10898
Traffic. RL. Morris Markey. 3: 42-5 N26'27. 10899
Traffic. RL. Morris Markey. 6: 44-8 N29'30. 10900
Traffic. Verse. C. Lee Quong. 9:23 Je3'33. 10901
A traffic dialogue. Prose. Arthur H. Folwell. 2:36 D25'26. 10902
Traffic lights. Verse. Ellen McLoughlin. 7:25*Jy4'31. 10903
Traffic tremens. Verse. Jean Batchelor. 15:57*Je17'39. 10904
Traffics and annoyances. Prose. Gilbert Seldes. 6:24-5 Mr29'30. 10905
Tragedy at the beach. Prose. Ambrose Flack. 13:27-8*Ag28 '37. 10906
Tragedy of a practical woman. Verse. Helene Mullins. 6:22 My24'30. 10907
The tragedy of Mr. Barr. Prose. Theodore Pratt. 5:62-3 Jy20 '29. 10908
A train. RL. Morris Markey. 3:36-8 Mr19'27. 10909
Training a radio announcer. Prose. Arthur Chapman. 1:33 O31'25. 10910
Training for leadership. Prose. Leonard Ware, Jr. 8:52-7 Mr19'32. 10911
Transatlantic broadcast. Verse. Martha Banning Thomas. 15: 21*Je10'39. 10912
The transatlantic season. Prose. Morris Markey. 6:33-8 Jy12 '30. 10913
Transfer of reality. Verse. Rolfe Humphries. 11:40*Jy6 '35. 10914
The transient public. Prose. Howard Cushman. 1:8 D19'25. 10915
Transient's impressions. Prose. Stephen Graham. 3:16 Jy23'27. 10916
Transit. RL. Morris Markey. 3: 40-6 N12'27. 10917
The transit situation. Prose. Newman Levy. 1:16 F28'25. 10918
Translations from the Calvinese. Verse. E. B. White. 6:22 Ap19 '30. 10919
The translator. Verse. Persis Greely Anderson. 5:80 D14'29. 10920
Trap shooters. Verse. Margaret Fishback. 13:64*Je19'37. 10921
Travel. Verse. Margaret Fishback. 3:51 O1'27. 10922
Travel is broadening. Prose. Julian R. Meade. 14:98-101*D 10'38. 10923
Travel is really broadening. Prose. G. Schwabe. 2:37 Jy17 '26. 10924
Travel notes. Verse. Christopher Ward. 10:27 Je2'34. 10925
Traveler's aid, China division. Prose. Douglass Welch. 12:80* D19'36. 10926
Traveler's rest. Verse. Ogden Nash. 11:19*Jy20'35. 10927
The traveller. Prose. Marc Connelly. 2:17-19 Ap17'26. 10928
The traveller. Prose. Theodore Pratt. 9:54 F25'33. 10929
Travelogue. Verse. Paul G. Gumbinner. 3:83 Mr5'27. 10930
Travelogue. Verse. Leslie Nelson Jennings. 4:24 Ja26'29. 10931
Travelogue. Prose. Dorothy Parker. 2:20-1 O30'26. 10932
Travelogue. SM. Alexander Woollcott. 7:32 D5'31. 10933
Treading where the saints have trod. Prose. Edith Neisser. 5: 20-1 Je1'29. 10934
Treason. Verse. Harold Lewis Cook. 9:18 My13'33. 10935
Treasure hunt. Verse. Dorothy Dow. 3:55 Ja14'28. 10936
Treasure Island in the Sound. RL.

Jack Alexander. 15:37-42*S9 '39. 10937

Treasures upon Earth. Prose. E. B. White. 4:22 My12'28. 10938

Treatise on trailers. Verse. David McCord. 13:23*Je26'37. 10939

Trees about town. Prose. Margaret Fishback. 3:56-7 S24 '27. 10940

Trees fall gently. Verse. Ruth Lambert Jones. 15:55*Mr4'39. 10941

Trench episode. Prose. R. L. 1: 26 S19'25. 10942

Trend. Verse. Richard Armour. 14:32*F11'39. 10943

A trend in dogs. Prose. James Reid Parker. 12:32*F13'37. 10944

The trend to refinement. Prose. W. E. Farbstein. 7:26 F13'32. 10945

The trend toward trends. Prose. David Cort. 2:22 My15'26. 10946

The trepid man. Verse. F. Emerson Andrews. 10:66 N10'34. 10947

Trepidation of a scientist. Verse. Martha Banning Thomas. 4:90 My12'28. 10948

The trial. RL. Morris Markey. 10:39-42*Ja26'35. 10949

Trial and error. Verse. Phyllis McGinley. 10:54 S29'34. 10950

Trial flight. RL. Morris Markey. 3:30-6 Ja7'28. 10951

Trial of a Führer. RL. M. R. Werner. 15:51-61*D9'39. 10952

Trials and tribulations. SM. Alexander Woollcott. 5:42 O5 '29. 10953

Tribal union. Prose. Paul Horgan. 10:30-3 Je2'34. 10954

Triborough Bridge. RL. Morris Markey. 10:77-84 N10'34. 10955

Tribute. Verse. Ruth Lambert Jones. 12:79*S19'36. 10956

Tribute. Verse. Fanny Heaslip Lea. 5:18 D28'29. 10957

The trinity--and a dog. PR (Knopf). Lurton Blassingame. 2:15-17 Ag21'26. 10958

Trinity in midsummer. RL. St. Clair McKelway. 12:32-5*Ag29 '36. 10959

Triolet after due reflection. Verse. Margaret Fishback. 5:90 My18 '29. 10960

Triolet for a charming young man. Verse. Margaret Fishback. 4:17 Ja26'29. 10961

Triolet for a snowy day. Verse. Margaret Fishback. 4:62 Mr10 '28. 10962

Triolet in a minor strain. Verse. Margaret Fishback. 5:22 S7'29. 10963

Triolet in a rash moment. Verse. Margaret Fishback. 8:54*Mr12 '32. 10964

Triolet in re Spring and a young girl's fancies. Verse. Margaret Fishback. 5:25 Ap6'29. 10965

Triolet on a domestic product. Verse. Margaret Fishback. 7: 23 Ap4'31. 10966

Triolet on a fragrant manifestation of Spring. Verse. Margaret Fishback. 3:43 My7'27. 10967

Triolet on a home truth. Verse. Margaret Fishback. 4:34 D29'28. 10968

Triolet on a Manhattan garden. Verse. Margaret Fishback. 4:46 My12'28. 10969

Triolet on a Volstead Act. Verse. Margaret Fishback. 7:13 Ja30 '32. 10970

Triolet on a warm bench. Verse. Margaret Fishback. 3:89 Mr26 '27. 10971

Triolet on an enviable existence. Verse. Margaret Fishback. 4:16 Ag18'28. 10972

Triolet on half a dozen urns. Verse. Margaret Fishback. 7:81 My2'31. 10973

Triolet on the appearance of Spring in Twenty-seventh Street. Verse. Margaret Fishback. 3:40

Ap2'27. 10974
Triolet on the deplorable lack of reliability of a certain season. Verse. Margaret Fishback. 3: 100 Ap9'27. 10975
Triolet on the disadvantages of suffering in silence. Verse. Margaret Fishback. 3:95 D17 '27. 10976
Triolet on the joys of Autumn. Verse. Margaret Fishback. 3: 97 O8'27. 10977
Triolet on the pigeon surplus. Verse. Margaret Fishback. 3: 58 S17'27. 10978
Triolet to Pegasus. Verse. Anon. 2:32 Jy10'26. 10979
A trip for this Summer. Prose. John Chapin Mosher. 15:23-4* Jy8'39. 10980
A trip in a taxi. Prose. George D. Lottman. 2:55-6 My22'26. 10981
Trip to the moon. Prose. John Chapin Mosher. 9:23-4 O28'33. 10982
Trip to the stars. RL. Morris Markey. 11:35-8*S28'35. 10983
The tripes. Prose. Frank Sullivan. 10:15-16 Ag18'34. 10984
The triple warning. SM. Alexander Woollcott. 7:36 S19'31. 10985
Tristan. Prose. Frances Crane. 13:46*Jy31'37. 10986
Triumph of a shadow. RL. Morris Markey. 6:34-8 Je28'30. 10987
The triumph of the egg. Prose. Joseph Fulling Fishman. 2:14 Ap10'26. 10988
Trochaic tribute to idleness. Verse. Philip G. Wylie. 2:54 My22'26. 10989
Trolley ride. Prose. Paul G. Gumbinner. 4:103-104 N17'28. 10990
Trolloping in Hoboken. Prose. Christopher Morley. 5:52-3 Jy 13'29. 10991
Trombonist extraceptional. Prose. Henry Anton. 12:14-17*S26'36. 10992
Troopers. RL. Morris Markey. 11: 33-40*Je8'35. 10993
Tropical fish in the aquarium. Verse. Lindley Williams Hubbell. 12:66*O10'36. 10994
The Trotskyists. RL. Geoffrey T. Hellman. 15:60-8*D16'39. 10995
Troubadour. PR (Gershwin). S. N. Behrman. 5:27-9 My25'29. 10996
Troubadour transplanted. Prose. John K. Hutchens. 10:19-20 S1 '34. 10997
Trouble in the Bronx. Prose. Arthur Kober. 13:32-3*D18'37. 10998
Trouble with the French is--. Prose. Helen Simson. 14:49-50* N5'38. 10999
Troublemaker. PR (Tresca). Max Eastman. 10:31-6 S15'34; 10:26-9 S22'34. 11000
Trowel couchant on a field of sugar. Verse. Nicholas Samstag. 3:49 O1'27. 11001
Truce. Verse. Babette Deutsch. 5:20 Je1'29. 11002
(No entry) 11003
A truculent stockholder speaks her mind. Verse. Margaret Fishback. 8:27*F27'32. 11004
A true confession. Prose. Ann Honeycutt. 5:32 N30'29. 11005
"True confession." Verse. Martha Banning Thomas. 5:34 Je8'29. 11006
A true fairy tale. Verse. Dearing Ward. 2:54 O16'26. 11007
True news. ME. Alfred Kreymborg. 3:23 Ag6'27. 11008
True, simple poem. Verse. Samuel Hoffenstein. 6:18 S6'30. 11009
True stories. Verse. W. E. Farbstein. 5:36 D28'29. 11010
True stories. Verse. W. E. Farbstein. 5:30 F1'30. 11011
True story magazine. (Parody) Ann Honeycutt. 5:32 N30'29. 11012
The true story of Rapunzel. Prose. Spud Johnson. 3:69 Ap2

'27. 11013
Trunk-room. Prose. Raymond Holden. 11:28-30*Ap13'35. 11014
Trust fund. Prose. John Chapin Mosher. 7:25-6 O3'31. 11015
Trust-gobbler. PR (Odlum). Geoffrey T. Hellman. 9:20-4 Ag26 '33. 11016
The truth about Ruth. OW. Ring Lardner. 8:26-8 Jy2'32. 11017
The truth about the Lindbergh case. RL. Meyer Berger. 14: 45-9 *Mr19'38. 11018
Truth and print. RL. Morris Markey. 1:21 F13'26. 11019
Truth, beauty, and efficiency. Prose. Nathan Asch. 11:71-2* N2'35. 11020
Try again. Prose. Heywood Broun. 5:17 Ja4'30. 11021
Tsiang, H. T. TT. 11:10-11 Jy6 '35. 11022
Tu ne quaesieris. Verse. Clinch Calkins. 3:18 My21'27. 11023
Tubes. Verse. E. B. White. 2:81 F5'27. 11024
Tugboat. Verse. Anon. 2:58 My15 '26. 11025
Tummler. PR (Night-club owner). A. J. Liebling. 14:24-9*F26'28. 11026
Tunnel talk. Prose. Creighton Peet. 3:40 N26'27. 11027
Tunney's little man. Prose. E. B. White. 4:20 Ag11'28. 11028
Turf and gridiron. PR (Mara). A. J. Liebling. 13:25-9*S18'37. 11029
Turn about. Prose. Theodore Pratt. 9:108-109 D9'33. 11030
The turn-arounder. Prose. Arthur Kober. 5:62-4 D14'29. 11031
Turncoat. ML. John Strong Newberry. 9:53 My6'33. 11032
Turnstile power. Prose. Howard Cushman. 4:66 N17'28. 11033
The turtle. Verse. Laura Benét. 6:31 My10'30. 11034
The tuxedos. Prose. Jerome Weidman. 14:65-8*S17'38. 11035
'Twas the month after Christmas. Verse. Baird Leonard. 4:18 Ja 26'29. 11036
'Twas the night before Christmas. Prose. Marion Sturges-Jones. 5:67 D21'29. 11037
'Twas the week before Christmas. Verse. Margaret Fishback. 6:24 D20'30. 11038
Twelfth night. (Play) TT. 6:19 S27 '30. 11039
Twelfth night. (Play) TT. 6:20-1 O25'30. 11040
Twelve good men and true. Verse. Parke Cummings. 6:88 Ap26 '30. 11041
Twelve questions in search of an answer. Verse. Parke Cummings. 7:57 Mr7'31. 11042
Twelve-thirty, sharp. Prose. Elspeth O'Halloran. 4:85-6 Ap7 '28. 11043
Twelve years after. Prose. Thomas S. Bosworth. 3:74-5 D10'27. 11044
A twentieth century puritan. PR (Fosdick). Lurton Blassingame. 3:18-20 Je18'27. 11045
Twenty-five thousand dollars. RL. J. B. C. 13:36-42*N6'37. 11046
"24-hour service." Prose. George Dock, Jr. 5:85-6 Mr23'29. 11047
Twenty-one stevedores. RL. Alva Johnston. 7:49-51*Jy4'31. 11048
Twenty questions. Prose. Emily Hahn. 10:40-4 O27'34. 11049
Twenty thousand wheels. Verse. Fillmore Hyde. 2:30 D11'26. 11050
Twenty years' passion. Prose. A. K. Laing. 12:51-3*S12'36. 11051
Twice blest. Prose. Jerome Weidman. 12:26*Ag29'36. 11052
The twig and the tablecloth. Prose. Frances Warfield. 9:22-3 Ap1 '33. 11053
The twilight beauty. Verse. Marjorie Allen Seiffert. 8:18*My14 '32. 11054
Twilight of the gods. Verse. Mildred Weston. 9:51 Je3'33. 11055

The twist of tongues. Prose. Robert M. Coates. 13:62-4*S25 '37. 11056
Two by the window. Prose. Reed Johnston. 5:78-9 Je22'29. 11057
Two courts. RL. Niven Busch, Jr. 5:36-42 Ap13'29. 11058
The two deeps. Verse. William Rose Benét. 9:24 Jy22'33. 11059
Two-eyed Connelly. PR (Connelly). Alexander Woollcott. 6:29-32 Ap12'30. 11060
Two famous fire engines. TWNY. Herbert Asbury. 6:45-54 Mr15 '30. 11061
The two friends. Prose. Vincent McHugh. 11:16*Jy13'35. 11062
Two gardens. Verse. Elizabeth Corse. 6:40 Je28'30. 11063
Two-gun. RL. Morris Markey. 7: 34-40*Je6'31. 11064
Two in the orchestra. Prose. Sterling Wilson. 2:53-4 My29 '26. 11065
Two minutes silence. Prose. Sylvia Townsend Warner. 12: 27*N21'36. 11066
291. PR (Stieglitz). Waldo Frank. 1:9-10 Ap18'25. 11067
Two of them. Prose. Irma Brandeis. 11:69-70*S14'35. 11068
Two on the aisle. PR (McBride). Kenneth Macgowan. 3:18-21 Ag 6'27. 11069
A two-Ringling circus. PR (Ringling). Helena Huntington Smith. 2:19-20 My1'26. 11070
Two rooms, bath and kitchenette. Prose. Charles G. Shaw. 2: 15-16 Mr20'26. 11071
Two schools of thought. Verse. John Holmes. 10:58 S1'34. 11072
Two ships bring Americans of note and English author. Prose. James Thurber. 5:18 Je8'29. 11073
Two small songs. Verse. Mary Ballard Duryee. 14:23*Ag27'38. 11074
Two songwriters at work. Prose. Sidney Skolsky. 3:71-2 Ja21 '28. 11075
220 East 42nd. Prose. Mary Heaton Vorse. 6:21-2 S20'30. 11076
Type model. PR (Chrysler). Lurton Blassingame. 2:21-4 Ja8'27. 11077
The typewriter blues. Verse. Frances Park. 3:101 Ap2'27. 11078
Typhoid carrier No. 36. PR (Mallon). Stanley Walker. 10:21-5* Ja26'35. 11079
The typical old New Yorker. Prose. Mary Heaton Vorse. 7: 76-8 Ja9'32. 11080

U

Über alles. RL. Janet Flanner. 7: 36-50 Ja9'32. 11081
The uglification movement. Prose. Katherine Sproehnle. 2:24 Mr20 '26. 11082
Ugly duckling. PR (Swanson). Helena Huntington Smith. 5:24-7 Ja18'30. 11083
Ulysses. (Novel) Janet Flanner. 1: 27 O10'25. 11084
Ulysses. (Novel) Janet Flanner. 5: 45 Jy27'29. 11085
Ulysses ashore--for a while. PR (Baruch). Arthur Krock. 2:15-16 Ag7'26. 11086
Unanswered by request. Verse. Ogden Nash. 10:18*Ja19'35. 11087
The unbalanced budgeteer. Verse. Jean Batchelor. 8:41*Ap30'32. 11088
The unbearable hush. Prose. Wolcott Gibbs. 5:24 Ag31'29. 11089
The unbeliever. Verse. Philip G. Wylie. 3:55 Ja7'28. 11090
Uncalled-for epitaphs. Verse. Ogden Nash. 8:25 Ja14'33. 11091
Uncensored. OFC. David Sandler. 13:46-7*Mr27'37. 11092
The uncensored diary of an elevator attendant. Prose. Donald Ogden Stewart. 3:14-15 Ja14'28. 11093
Unclassified. Prose. Charles G. Shaw. 2:88-9 N13'26. 11094

Uncle Calvin's no-waste games. Prose. Robert Benchley. 1:17 Ja9'26. 11095

Uncle Dockery and the independent bull. Prose. Joseph Mitchell. 15:41-3*My13'39. 11096

Uncle Don. PR (Carney). Margaret Case Harriman. 9:24-9 D16'33. 11097

Uncle Wiggily. Prose. George Cecil Cowing. 8:41-2 Ag13'32. 11098

Unconditioned reflexes. Prose. John O'Hara. 5:58-61 Ag31'29. 11099

Undefeated. Verse. Dorothy Dow. 3:62 D10'27. 11100

Under a beach umbrella. Verse. Martha Banning Thomas. 3:39 Jy2'27. 11101

Under Orion. Verse. Harold Lewis Cook. 13:18*D25'39. 11102

Under Sirius. Verse. Rolfe Humphries. 15:27*Ag19'39. 11103

Under the "L." RL. Jack Alexander. 14:32-9*F19'38. 11104

Undergraduate fraternity meeting. Prose. Morris Bishop. 8:67-8 D17'32. 11105

Underground. RL. Robert M. Coates. 6:33-6 D27'30. 11106

Underground. RL. Eric Hodgins. 8:38-46*Mr5'32; 8:34-40*Mr12 '32. 11107

Underground resistances. Verse. E. B. White. 10:27 Je9'34. 11108

Underground wireless. Verse. Sylvia Townsend Warner. 15: 19*Ag5'39. 11109

Undressing the bishop. Prose. Sylvia Townsend Warner. 15: 30*Ap15'39. 11110

The unearthly Mr. Bottle. Prose. Wolcott Gibbs. 8:20*My7'32. 11111

Uneasy city. OFC. Ruth McKenney. 12:83-7*D19'36. 11112

Uneasy nights. Prose. Joseph Fulling Fishman. 3:38-40 O22 '27. 11113

Uneasy ought to lie the head... Verse. Hortense Flexner. 15: 41*Ag5'39. 11114

Unencumbered. Verse. Marjorie Allen Seiffert. 6:28 N22'30. 11115

Unfamiliar misquotations. Prose. James Thurber. 15:18*My20'39. 11116

Unfinished business. SM. Alexander Woollcott. 8:28 D10'32. 11117

An unfinished history. Verse. Archibald MacLeish. 8:16 Ja21 '31. 11118

An unfinished story. SM. Alexander Woollcott. 5:36 Ja18'30. 11119

Unhappy ladies. Verse. William Rose Benét. 7:27*Je6'31. 11120

An unidentified man... Prose. Thomas Sugrue. 11:13-14*Jy6 '35. 11121

Uniforms and liquor kegs. TWNY. Herbert Asbury. 5:36-42 F15'30. 11122

Unimportant. SM. Alexander Woollcott. 7:34 N28'31. 11123

Unimportant observation. Verse. Josiah Titzell. 6:48 Ap12'30. 11124

Union Square: the sixth walk. RL. Leo Rosten. 12:55-8*O17'36. 11125

Unique verse. Verse. Philip G. Wylie. 2:27 D18'26. 11126

Universe of glass. Verse. Martha Banning Thomas. 15:68*Je24'39. 11127

The unknown citizen. Verse. W. H. Auden. 15:19*Ja6'40. 11128

Unknown soldier. Verse. V. Valerie Gates. 4:104 O13'28. 11129

An unlikely tale. Verse. Arthur Guiterman. 1:12 N28'25. 11130

"Unmanly whimpering." SM. Alexander Woollcott. 5:40 N30'29. 11131

Unnatural history. Verse. Arthur Guiterman. 10:102*D15'34. 11132

Unofficial document. Prose. Edward Hope. 5:28-30 D14'29. 11133

The unregenerate takes a stand at New Year's. Verse. Martha Banning Thomas. 3:33 D31 '27. 11134
Unseen. Verse. Peggy Bacon. 15: 47*Ja13'40. 11135
The unspeakables. RL. Jean-Jacques. 5:32-8 Je1'29. 11136
The unsung heroes. Prose. Robert Benchley. 3:22 Je18'27. 11137
The untainted sport. RL. John R. Tunis. 7:32-5*Jy4'31. 11138
Unter dem Hakenkreuz. Prose. Mary Heaton Vorse. 9:35-7 Jy1'33. 11139
Until called for. Prose. Alice Frankforter. 11:80*Mr16'35. 11140
Until they get out. RL. Sanderson Vanderbilt. 14:35-42*S24'38. 11141
Until vacated. Prose. Don Wharton. 10:108-109 S15'34. 11142
Unto us. Prose. Emily Hahn. 13: 32-5*D11'37. 11143
The unusual affair. Verse. Fillmore Hyde. 4:24 Je16'28. 11144
Unwelcome host. Prose. Bettina Sinclair. 11:70*Mr30'35. 11145
The unwelcome obelisk. Prose. Oliver Claxton. 3:26 Mr5'27. 11146
Unwilling advice to a child. Verse. Witter Bynner. 11:23* O19'35. 11147
Up from Amherst. PR (Meredith). Wolcott Gibbs. 13:24-30*Ap3 '37. 11148
Up from Fifth Avenue. PR (Whitney). Carl Brandt. 1:8-9 Jy25 '25. 11149
Up from Harvard. PR (Mills). Robert S. Allen. 7:25-8 D12'31. 11150
Up from Hell's Kitchen. PR (Kelly). Charles Robbins. 6:22-5 Ap26'30. 11151
Up from lethargy. Prose. George Flemming. 11:32-6*S14'35. 11152
Up in the hills. Prose. Dorothy Thomas. 11:18-22*Ag3'35. 11153
Up stage. Verse. M. M. 3:84 N5'27. 11154
"Up the dark stairs--." Prose. Robert Benchley. 1:7-8 D19'25. 11155
Upon a midnight clear. Prose. Sally Benson. 13:15-18*D25'37. 11156
Upon due consideration. Verse. Martha Banning Thomas. 3:46 D31'27. 11157
Upon facing the fact that it will be necessary to go into reverse to see forty again. Verse. Martha Banning Thomas. 7:72 Mr14'31. 11158
Upon finishing the latest thrillers. Verse. Baird Leonard. 4:28 My 12'28. 11159
Upon looking at an advertisement for women's sport wear. Verse. Martha Banning Thomas. 5:17 Je1'29. 11160
Upon receiving a letter. Verse. Martha Banning Thomas. 3:22 Ja21'28. 11161
Upon receiving checks for one's pet charity. Verse. M. M. 4:41 D29'28. 11162
Upon re-reading "The mauve decade." Verse. Margaretta Manning. 2:57 Ja29'27. 11163
Upon Washington Bridge, 1936. Verse. Louis Untermeyer. 11: 24*Ja11'36. 11164
The upper berth. Prose. Alice Frankforter. 4:96-7 Ja5'29. 11165
The ups and downs of Vinland the Good. OUWA. Frank Schoonmaker. 12:32-9*S5'36. 11166
Upside down. Prose. E. B. White. 2:19-20 Ja1'27. 11167
Urban lullaby. Verse. Leslie G. Shaw. 7:56 O3'31. 11168
The urge to merge. Prose. Margaret Fishback. 5:84 S21'29. 11169
Urgent, Doctor! Verse. Hortense Flexner. 14:48*O22'38. 11170
The U. S. A. blues. Verse. David

Cort. 6:18 Ag30'30. 11171
U. S. A. 1927. (Book) Janet Flanner. 4:74 Mr17'28. 11172
US 1 (Southern division). Prose. Theodore Pratt. 13:42*Jy17'37. 11173
The useful gift--why not? Prose. Elinor Wylie. 1:9-10 D26'25. 11174
The uses of adversity. RL. Morris Markey. 11:38-44*Ap27'35. 11175
The uses of heredity. Verse. Anon. 3:111 O15'27. 11176
Utilities. Verse. Herman Fetzer. 7:16*Jy25'31. 11177

V

V. A. PR (Van Anda). Alexander Woollcott. 1:7-8 Mr7'25. 11178
Vacancy. Prose. James Reid Parker. 8:59-60*My14'32. 11179
Vacant lot. Prose. Richard Lockridge. 11:68*F23'35. 11180
Vacation pin money. Prose. Joe W. Savage. 5:67-8 Je1'29. 11181
Vacation thoughts, from home. Verse. Will Scarlet. 15:47* Ag19'39. 11182
Vacation time. Prose. Martha Banning Thomas. 4:20 Ag18'28. 11183
Vagabond cruise. Prose. Hannah Lees. 9:38-40 F3'34. 11184
The vagabonds. RL. Morris Markey. 6:42-8 Ja17'31. 11185
Vagrancy. SM. Alexander Woollcott. 9:44 My20'33. 11186
Vain longings. Verse. Lee Wilson Dodd. 6:86 My17'30. 11187
Valentine. Verse. Franklin P. Adams. 13:28*F12'38. 11188
Valentine. Verse. Margaret Fishback. 3:43 F11'28. 11189
Valentine. Verse. Margaret Fishback. 4:17 F9'29. 11190
The Valentine. Prose. Hannah Lees. 11:52-3*F15'36. 11191
A Valentine. Verse. Miriam Vedder. 7:14 F13'32. 11192
Valentine. Verse. Mildred Weston. 6:40 F14'31. 11193
Valentine: A. D. '34. Verse. Mildred Weston. 9:38 F10'34. 11194
Valentine for a charge account. Verse. Phyllis McGinley. 9:27 F10'34. 11195
A valentine for Sydney Kingsley. Prose. William Maxwell. 13:21-2*Ap10'37. 11196
Valentine to end all Valentines. Verse. Arthur Guiterman. 12:51*F13'37. 11197
Valentines by wire. Prose. Bernice Breen. 5:72 F15'30. 11198
"A valet is a little guy..." Verse. Anon. 1:32 D12'25. 11199
Valse. Prose. Carroll Carroll. 4:33-4 D29'28. 11200
Vamp in violet. PR (Kayshus). Sinclair Lewis. 12:20-5*Ja16'37. 11201
Van Anda, Carr Vatell. PR. Alexander Woollcott. 1:7-8 Mr7'25. 11202
The Vanderbilt convention. Prose. Frank Sullivan. 6:13-14 Jy26'30. 11203
Van Dine, S. S. (Parody) Alexander Woollcott. 6:28 Ag2'30. 11204
Van Doren, Mark. (Parody) EE. 1:16 Mr28'25. 11205
The vanished judge. RL. Morris Markey. 6:43-6 O11'30. 11206
Vanishing American. PR (Beard). Joel Sayre. 8:17-20 Jy23'32. 11207
The vanishing lady. SM. Alexander Woollcott. 5:32 Jy6'29; 5:36 Jy13 '29. 11208
The vanishing lady. SM. Alexander Woollcott. 8:22 Ag13'32. 11209
Vanishing news. WP. Robert Benchley. 14:26-7*D24'38. 11210
Van Loon, Hendrik Willem. PR. Waldo Frank. 2:19-20 Je19'26. 11211
Van Vechten, Carl. TT. 1:2 Jy11 '25. 11212
Van Vechten, Carl. TT. 1:4 N7

'25. 11213
Variation. Verse. Elizabeth Coatsworth. 6:44 O18'30. 11214
Variation on a sentence. Verse. Louise Bogan. 12:16*S12'36. 11215
Variation on an old theme. Verse. Anon. 3:83 O15'27. 11216
Variations on a theme. Verse. Elspeth O'Halloran. 3:75 My7 '27. 11217
Variations on a theme of Gilman. Prose. Wolcott D. Street. 8: 60-1*Ap23'32. 11218
Varsity manager. Prose. John O'Hara. 6:62-4 O25'30. 11219
The vaudeville doctor. Prose. John Forbes. 3:54-7 N5'27. 11220
The vaudeville doctor. Prose. John Forbes. 3:86-9 N19'27. 11221
The vaudeville doctor. Prose. John Forbes. 4:73-5 Mr10'28. 11222
Vaudeville talk. Prose. Julius Marx. 1:14 Je20'25. 11223
Vault trouble. Prose. Cornelia Otis Skinner. 14:16-17*Ag27'38. 11224
Vegetable luncheon. Prose. Grace Hegger Lewis. 6:30 Mr15'30. 11225
Venetian perspective. Prose. Janet Flanner. 10:17-19 Ag25 '34. 11226
"Vengeance is mine--." Verse. Helene Mullins. 6:25 Ag16'30. 11227
The vengeance of 3902090. Prose. James Thurber. 15:16-17*Je10 '39. 11228
Veni, vidi, vicky. PR (Hayes). Margaret Case Harriman. 15: 24-30*My20'39; 15:28-35*My 27'39. 11229
Venice. FP. H. L. Mencken. 10: 37-8 Je30'34. 11230
Verge. Verse. Frances M. Frost. 7:19 Ap25'31. 11231
Vernal anticlimax. Verse. Jean Batchelor. 8:44 My21'32. 11232
Vernal equinox. Verse. Leslie Nelson Jennings. 8:58*Ap2'32. 11233
Veronica's veil. (Play) TT. 10:19 Mr17'34. 11234
Versatility personified. PR (Taylor). Newman Levy. 1:9-10 Je 6'25. 11235
Verse, with colors. Verse. Rolfe Humphries. 15:55*Jy8'39. 11236
Verses. Verse. Phyllis McGinley. 10:20 Ap28'34. 11237
Verses of Mr. Chesterfield to his son. Verse. Franklin P. Adams. 12:19*Mr14'36; 12:23*Mr21'36; 12:31*Ap4'36; 12:24*Ap25'36; 12:23*My16'36. 11238
Vs. descendants. Verse. Ogden Nash. 7:31 O10'31. 11239
The very golden apple. Prose. E. A. Tosbell. 3:28-33 S3'27. 11240
Very low. Prose. Frances Warfield. 9:81-3 Ja13'34. 11241
The very thing. Prose. Sally Benson. 10:89-92 O20'34. 11242
A very young lady. Verse. Philip G. Wylie. 2:37 My8'26. 11243
The veteran. DL. Burke Boyce. 2:34 S11'26. 11244
Via America. Prose. St. Clair McKelway. 10:52-3 Ag18'34. 11245
Vicious circle. Verse. Persis Greely Anderson. 8:16 O22'32. 11246
Victoria changes for a local. Prose. Marjorie Damsey Wilson. 12:17-19*N21'36. 11247
Victoria has nothing to do. Prose. Marjorie Damsey Wilson. 12: 17-19*My23'36. 11248
Victoria looks into politics. Prose. Marjorie Damsey Wilson. 12: 17-18*O31'36. 11249
Victoria seeks an award. Prose. Marjorie Damsey Wilson. 12: 18-20*F13'37. 11250
Victoria Theatre. Loney Haskell. 6:38-47 D13'30; 6:50-6 D20'30. 11251
Victoria's first orchid. Prose. Marjorie Damsey Wilson. 12:

16-18*Ja2'37. 11252
Viennese tomboy. PR (Jeritza). Pitts Sanborn. 6:21-4 Ja24'31. 11253
Viennese visitor. PR (Adler). Lola Jean Simpson. 4:29-31 My5'28. 11254
View from a fifth-floor fire escape. Verse. Margaret Fishback. 5: 102 S14'29. 11255
A villa in Brittany. Prose. Donald Moffat. 6:15-17 Je7'30. 11256
A villa in Brittany. Prose. Donald Moffat. 6:16-18 Je14'30. 11257
A villa in Brittany. Prose. Donald Moffat. 6:16-18 Je28'30. 11258
A villa in Brittany. Prose. Donald Moffat. 6:17-19 Jy5'30. 11259
A villa in Brittany. Prose. Donald Moffat. 6:19-21 Jy12'30. 11260
A villa in Brittany. Prose. Donald Moffat. 6:19-20 Ag16'30. 11261
The village green. RL. Morris Markey. 3:36-8 Mr5'27. 11262
Village Sunday. Verse. Frances Park. 3:36 Ja7'28. 11263
Villain of villains. PR (Scotti). George White Garland. 1:15-16 F13'26. 11264
Villanelle. Verse. Irma Brandeis. 2:81 D18'26. 11265
Villanelle of Horatio Street, Manhattan. Verse. James Thurber. 3:74 F26'27. 11266
"Vincent." PR (Millay). Griffin Barry. 2:25-7 F12'27. 11267
Vinous. Verse. Dorothy Leonard. 5:46 O26'29. 11268
Virago with garlic. Prose. Edith Owen. 5:84-7 Ap13'29. 11269
Virginibus puerisque. Prose. Emily Hahn. 7:52-4 My16'31. 11270
Virginibus puerisque. Prose. Frances Warfield. 7:79 Ja9'32. 11271
Virtue is its own reward. Verse. Margaret Fishback. 4:103 O20 '28. 11272
Virtuoso. Prose. Wolcott Gibbs. 4:27-8 N17'28. 11273
The virtuous New Yorker. Verse. Franklin P. Adams. 15:69*Je10 '39. 11274
Visionary. Verse. William Rose Benét. 4:30 Ap28'28. 11275
A visit from Saint Nicholas. Prose. James Thurber. 3:17-18 D24'27. 11276
Visit in the Bronx. Prose. Arthur Kober. 14:56-8*Mr5'38. 11277
Visitant. Verse. Muna Lee. 9:13 Mr18'33. 11278
Visiting Englishman. Prose. John Chapin Mosher. 6:32-4 Ja 31'31. 11279
Visitor. Prose. Theodore Pratt. 7:26 Ag29'31. 11280
Visitors allowed. Prose. Robert Wohlforth. 6:47-50 N8'30. 11281
Visitors from the South. TWNY. Kemp P. Battle. 11:46-52*My 18'35. 11282
Vissi d'arte, vissi d'amour. Prose. Vandy Cape. 13:56*F12'38. 11283
Vistas visited. Prose. Theodore Pratt. 2:53-4 My22'26. 11284
The visualization of Vivienne. Prose. Anon. 1:23 Mr14'25. 11285
Vital statistics. Prose. Raymond Holden. 12:53-4*F6'37. 11286
Vive la France! Prose. Sally Benson. 9:14-15 Jy8'33. 11287
Vive la France! Prose. William C. White. 11:83-5*D14'35. 11288
Vive l'impératrice! Prose. Alice Frankforter. 7:26-7 S19'31. 11289
Vixen. Verse. Isabel McLennan McMeekin. 4:22 My26'28. 11290
Vixen. Verse. Marjorie Allen Seiffert. 8:25 O22'32. 11291
Vocal. Prose. Burton Davis. 2:49-50 Mr13'26. 11292
The voice. Prose. Robert M. Coates. 11:20-2*Ag24'35. 11293

The voice. PR (Taylor). Margaret Case Harriman. 11:26-9*O26'35; 11:24-8*N2'35. 11294
The voice. Prose. Sigmund Spaeth. 2:27 N13'26. 11295
Voice culture. Prose. Margaret Halsey. 13:68-9*O9'37. 11296
Voice teacher. Prose. Lillian Day. 7:73-6 Mr14'31. 11297
Voices. Prose. E. B. White. 6:32 N15'30. 11298
Voices from a box. Prose. James Thurber. 8:20-1*F20'32. 11299
Voices through the trumpet. RL. Carl Carmer. 12:27-34*My16'36; 12:35-9*My23'36. 11300
Volunteer. Prose. Kay Boyle. 12:25-6*My16'36. 11301
The volunteer. Prose. Elizabeth B. Sayre. 6:78-81 Ap12'30. 11302
Von Freytag-Loringhoven, Elsa. Janet Flanner. 3:76 Ja7'28. 11303
The Vorarlberg. OFC. Donald Moffat. 10:64-72 F24'34. 11304
Votarist. Verse. Ruth Lambert Jones. 7:16 Ag29'31. 11305
Votes from contented precincts. Prose. Frank Sullivan. 4:28-30 D1'28. 11306
Vox populi. PR (Patterson). Jack Alexander. 14:16-21*Ag6'38; 14:19-24*Ag13'38; 14:19-23*Ag20'38. 11307
Vox populi. Prose. Anon. 1:18 Mr7'25. 11308
The voyage out. Prose. Morley Callaghan. 12:15-17*Je27'36. 11309
A voyage to Purilia. Prose. Elmer Rice. 5:25-9 O12'29; 5:34-5, 46-8 O19'29; 5:37-8, 113-19 O26'29; 5:33, 109-17 N2'29; 5:32, 116-23 N9'29; 5:36, 112-15 N16'29; 5:35, 117-19 N23'29; 5:97-9 N30'29; 5:68-76 D7'29; 5:130-3 D14'29; 5:79-83 D21'29. 11310

W

Wading. Verse. Mildred Weston. 10:56 Jy28'34. 11311
Wafers are exploded. Prose. Wolcott Gibbs. 12:15-16*F29'36. 11312
Wage slave. Verse. James Reid Parker. 12:26*Ag22'36. 11313
Wagnerian note. Verse. Marc Connelly. 13:42*Mr13'37. 11314
The wahoo boy. PR (Zanuck). Alva Johnston. 10:24-8 N10'34; 10:24-9*N17'34. 11315
(No entry) 11316
Waifs in the city. RL. Morris Markey. 9:30-4 D30'33. 11317
The waiter. Prose. Forks. 1:19 Jy11'25. 11318
Waiter no. 327, 549. Prose. Charles G. Shaw. 4:61-2 Mr10'28. 11319
Waiter, please ask all those respectable people to go away. Verse. Ogden Nash. 9:22 Ja6'34. 11320
Waiting. RL. Morris Markey. 11:66*N16'35. 11321
Waiting for Lawrence. Prose. Victoria Lincoln. 11:20-1*N9'35. 11322
Waiting for Santy. Prose. S. J. Perelman. 12:17-18*D26'36. 11323
Waiting for the train. Verse. Martha Banning Thomas. 7:31 N21'31. 11324
A waitress. Verse. LeBaron Cooke. 2:50 Mr13'26. 11325
A waitress in Childs's. Verse. Anon. 1:31 Mr28'25. 11326
Wake up and live, eh? Prose. James Thurber. 12:17-18*Ap18'36. 11327
Wake up, you're forty. Prose. John Chapin Mosher. 8:17-18*Ap30'32. 11328
Waken in the night. Verse. Louise Townsend Nicholl. 13:97*D11'37. 11329
The Waldorf-Astoria. TWNY. Russel Crouse. 4:32-8 F16'29. 11330
A walk on Sunday. Prose. Robert

M. Coates. 12:104-106*D5'36. 11331
A walk on the aqueduct. RL. Robert M. Coates. 13:34-8*O 23'37. 11332
Wall Street. Verse. Anon. 1:35 D5'25. 11333
The Wall Street bard. Verse. John McColl. 1:27 O17'25. 11334
Wall Street mystery. Prose. Leonard Hatch. 2:24 Ag14'26. 11335
A Wall Street mystery. Prose. Etaoin Shrdlu. 1:25 Mr21'25. 11336
The wallaby. Prose. Frances Crane. 7:78-80 S12'31. 11337
Wallace, Edgar. Alexander Woollcott. 5:38 Mr23'29. 11338
The wallflower's friend. PR (Murray). Milton Mackaye. 9:27-30 Ja6'34. 11339
Walpole, Hugh. TT. 2:18 O16'26. 11340
Walsh, Christy. PR. Alva Johnston. 11:20-5*N23'35. 11341
Walter saw a red tree. Prose. Richard Lockridge. 14:47-8*O 22'38. 11342
The waltz. Prose. Dorothy Parker. 9:11-12 S2'33. 11343
Wanderlust. Prose. Spud Johnson. 3:85-7 Ap16'27. 11344
Wanted--an Arcadia. Prose. Dorothy Homans. 4:62-3 My19 '28. 11345
"Wanted dead or alive." Prose. Corey Ford. 4:18-19 Jy28'28. 11346
War in Paris. Prose. Kay Boyle. 14:18-20*N26'38. 11347
The war in Westchester. Prose. Theodore Pratt. 15:49*O7'39. 11348
Ward McAllister. Verse. Kenneth Allan Robinson. 9:26 D9'33. 11349
The wardrobe. NESD. John J. Holzinger. 9:36 Ja6'34. 11350
The wardrobe mistress. Prose. Albert Carroll. 4:69-71 Ja26 '29. 11351
Warm days in February. Verse. Sara Henderson Hay. 14:54* F26'38. 11352
Warm weather lyrics. Verse. Eleanor Bachman. 3:98 Mr26 '27. 11353
A warning. Prose. Robert Benchley. 8:13-14 Jy2'32. 11354
The warning. Verse. Harold Lewis Cook. 13:21*Ag14'37. 11355
Warning. Verse. Frances M. Frost. 5:17 Ja4'30. 11356
Warning. Verse. Phyllis McGinley. 8:52 O22'32. 11357
Warning. Verse. Miriam Vedder. 7:25 My23'31. 11358
Warning before storm. Verse. Phyllis McGinley. 13:29*S11'37. 11359
The wary collaborators. Verse. Margaret Fishback. 7:21 D5'31. 11360
Washing up. Prose. E. B. White. 7:17 D26'31. 11361
Washington in a sack suit. Prose. Marc Connelly. 3:28 Mr5'27. 11362
Washington market. DL. Burke Boyce. 2:40 F5'27. 11363
Washington racket. Prose. John W. Thomason, Jr. 12:62-3*Ap11'36. 11364
Washington Square. Verse. Anon. 2:26 My8'26. 11365
Washington weekend. RL. Morris Markey. 9:44-8 Mr18'33. 11366
Washington's Birthday. TWNY. Russel Crouse. 6:46-7 F22'30. 11367
Washington's Birthday Eve. Verse. Ogden Nash. 11:23*F23'35. 11368
The waste land. Verse. Betty Morrow. 13:27*O16'37. 11369
The waste land. (Parody) Betty Morrow. 13:27*O16'37. 11370
Waste not, want not. Prose. Katharine Brush. 3:52-4 Ja7'28. 11371
Watch. Prose. Theodore Pratt. 3:27 F19'27. 11372
Watch the leaf. Verse. Harrison Dowd. 8:22 N19'32. 11373

Watch your weight. Prose. Evelyn Seeley. 5:80-2 Mr2'29. 11374
Watches for Malidadi. Prose. Ferdinand Czernin. 11:69-70* N30'35. 11375
Watching the comic strip. Prose. Joseph Fulling Fishman. 3:73-5 F19'27. 11376
Water poor. Prose. Frank Sullivan. 7:17*Je6'31. 11377
Waterfront: Sunday. Verse. Ruth Lechlitner. 15:19*O28'39. 11378
The water's house. Verse. Sylvia Townsend Warner. 15:18*Jy22 '39. 11379
Watkins, Maurine. TT. 2:18 Ja 29'27. 11380
Wavy sasparilla. Prose. Frances Warfield. 7:22 O31'31. 11381
Way for the mounted. RL. Morris Markey. 11:42-8*O26'35. 11382
'Way South. Prose. Berry Fleming. 6:19-20 Mr8'30. 11383
The way Spring affects me. Verse. Ruth Brown. 4:63 Ap 28'28. 11384
The way things happen. Verse. Ruth Brown. 4:51 S22'28. 11385
The way you talk. Verse. Grace Hazard Conkling. 4:15 Ag4'28. 11386
Wayfarer. Verse. Muna Lee. 7:18 D19'31. 11387
The wayward encyclopedias. Prose. Titus Oates. 12:41-2*Mr21'36. 11388
The wayward encyclopedias. Prose. Frank M. O'Brien. 12:55-8*My 2'36. 11389
We are, roughly speaking, seven. Prose. G. B. Stern. 11:21-2* N2'35. 11390
We don't know you. Prose. George Weller. 14:43-4*Ag13 '38. 11391
We don't want any trouble. RL. William H. Toumey. 15:31-42* Jy22'39. 11392
We have been here before. Verse. Morris Bishop. 14:28*O29'38. 11393
We meet J. P. Morgan's gateman. Prose. Eugene Kinkead. 15:48-9*Jy1'39. 11394
We might let you be our playmate. OSB. C. Knapp. 6:15 Ag2'30. 11395
We move enchanted. Verse. Marjorie Allen Seiffert. 6:17 Ja24 '31. 11396
We must see a lot of you this Winter. Prose. Frances Woodward Prentice. 8:16-17 Ag27'32. 11397
We of the physics department. Prose. James Reid Parker. 12: 42-4*Mr14'36. 11398
We photograph Alice. Prose. Mildred Gilman. 10:37-8 Je9'34. 11399
We stand corrected. Prose. Robert Benchley. 6:50 D13'30. 11400
We want Central Park West dug up again. Prose. Frank Sullivan. 4:17-18 D29'28. 11401
The weather. Prose. John Goldstrom. 5:77-8 Ja4'30. 11402
The weather-vain. Prose. Araminta. 1:25 Mr21'25. 11403
(No entry) 11404
The weather wit takes the stand. Prose. Frank Sullivan. 6:19-20 Mr22'30. 11405
"The weather's hot--or cold as ice..." Verse. Anon. 2:50 Jy3 '26. 11406
The weaver. Prose. Francis Steegmuller. 10:42-6 S29'34. 11407
Webster Hall. Verse. Anon. 1:14 D26'25. 11408
Webster's new international, second edition. TT. 10:17-18 O6 '34. 11409
A wedded pair, in oils. Verse. Dorothea Kingsland. 15:46 F3 '40. 11410
Wedding. Prose. Dorothy Belle Flanagan. 7:55-7 F21'31. 11411
Wedding breakfast. Prose. Hannah Lees. 10:62-4 Mr17'34. 11412

What I give my kiddies to read. Prose. Sylvia Fuller. 4:67-8 S29'28. 11490
What is a merchant? PR (Heckscher). Babette Deutsch. 6:20-3 Ag2'30. 11491
What is the bleakest job in New York? Prose. Corey Ford. 2:66-8 Je5'26. 11492
What is the bleakest job in New York? Prose. Corey Ford. 2:17 Jy3'26. 11493
What is the bleakest job in New York? Prose. Corey Ford. 2:24 Jy10'26. 11494
What is the bleakest job in New York? Prose. Corey Ford. 2:21 Jy17'26. 11495
What life did to us. Prose. James Thurber. 5:16-17 F1'30. 11496
What, Ma, no jam? Prose. E. B. White. 2:35 D11'26. 11497
What number, please? Prose. Oliver Claxton. 2:30-1 N13'26. 11498
What numerology has done for 'em. Prose. Marion Sturges-Jones. 6:52-4 S13'30. 11499
What price a farewell to designs? Prose. James Thurber. 9:13 Mr18'33. 11500
What price glory. (Play) TT. 1:3-4 Jy4'25. 11501
What price ideas? Prose. Lois Long and Nancy Hardin. 1:26 Mr7'25. 11502
What shall I serve next? Prose. Charles W. Morton, Jr. 8:43-4 My21'32. 11503
What shall we do about the calendar? Prose. Corey Ford. 2:33-4 S18'26. 11504
"What shall we say?" Prose. Robert Benchley. 6:18-19 Je7 '30. 11505
What songs the sirens sang. Prose. Gilbert Seldes. 5:50-4 O12'29. 11506
What the Hoovers had to learn. Prose. Parke Cummings. 5:104 Mr23'29. 11507
What the well-dressed Yosian will wear. Prose. Sylvia Fuller. 4:61-2 Ag18'28. 11508
What they did with the rope. Prose. W. G. H. 1:23 My30'25. 11509
What they want. Prose. John Forbes. 4:24 F9'29. 11510
What to do when the weekends come. Prose. Thyra Samter Winslow. 3:22-3 Je11'27. 11511
What to play up. WP. Robert Benchley. 10:60-6 Je9'34. 11512
What to talk about. Prose. T. H. Bliss. 1:24 My30'25. 11513
"What women do?"--say. Verse. Raymond Lewis. 1:24 Ag1'25. 11514
What would you do? Prose. Joseph Fulling Fishman. 1:31-2 D12 '25. 11515
Whatever became of flaming youth? Prose. Marc Connelly. 2:35-6 D4'26. 11516
The whatnot. Verse. Persis Greely Anderson. 6:99 O18'30. 11517
What's in a name? Prose. C. Knapp. 3:96-7 Ap23'27. 11518
"What's in a name?" Verse. Charles G. Shaw. 1:29 Mr21'25. 11519
What's to prevent? Prose. Margaret Fishback. 3:42-4 O29'27. 11520
Wheels in his head. PR (Hedley). Henry F. Pringle. 3:17-19 D31 '27. 11521
When Boyton twisted the lion's tail. TWNY. William Inglis. 15:53-7*Mr25'39. 11522
When broomsticks ride. Verse. Henrietta Fort Holland. 10:60 Mr17'34. 11523
When East is West. Prose. Eugene P. F. Wright. 2:18-19 Ag21'26. 11524
(No entry) 11525
When Greek meets Greek. Prose. Milton Grunauer. 6:87-8 Mr29 '30. 11526
When in Rome. Verse. Phyllis McGinley. 12:23*Ja23'37. 11527
When New York was really wicked. Prose. Herbert Asbury. 3:25-8 D3'27. 11528

When New York was really wicked. Prose. Herbert Asbury. 3:30-2 D10'27. 11529
When New York was really wicked. Prose. Herbert Asbury. 3:29-31 D17'27. 11530
When New York was really wicked. Prose. Herbert Asbury. 3:20-2 D31'27. 11531
When New York was really wicked. Prose. Herbert Asbury. 3:22-4 Ja7'28. 11532
When New York was really wicked. Prose. Herbert Asbury. 3:21-3 Ja14'28. 11533
When Spring was late. Verse. Scudder Middleton. 5:26 Mr30 '29. 11534
When the moon comes over the Raymond Fosdick mountains. Prose. Geoffrey T. Hellman. 15:63-4*Mr11'39. 11535
When the moon shines over and over. Verse. Ogden Nash. 8:27 O1'32. 11536
When we were rather young. Prose. Willa Kay Smith. 5:58-9 Ag10'29. 11537
When witches ride. Prose. Sally Benson. 6:27-8 O25'30. 11538
Where are the beauties of New York? Prose. Willa Kay Smith. 3:40-1 O29'27. 11539
"Where are you going, my pretty maid?" Verse. Margaret Mochrie. 2:79 S18'26. 11540
Where credit is due. Prose. Anon. 1:22 My2'25. 11541
Where is my wandering mind tonight? Verse. Ogden Nash. 13:20*Ap24'37. 11542
Where, oh! where is fair Harvard? Prose. Charles A. Bickford. 3:91-2 Ap9'27. 11543
Where the blue songs come from. Prose. Arthur Chapman. 1:19 Je6'25. 11544
Where the champions come from. RL. Morris Markey. 11:29-32* D28'35. 11545
Where the sun never sets. Verse. Henrietta Fort Holland. 9:28 My13'33. 11546
Where West End meets Death Avenoo. Verse. Elise Jerard. 4:20 O20'28. 11547
Whether. OMEU. James Thurber. 5:28 Ap13'29. 11548
Which. OMEU. James Thurber. 5:28 My4'29. 11549
While you wait. Prose. Theodore Pratt. 6:30-2 Mr29'30. 11550
Whiskey rebellion, 1939. Prose. S. J. Perelman. 15:16*Ap22'39. 11551
Whispering hope. Verse. Elspeth O'Halloran. 6:57 My24'30. 11552
White as snow. Prose. Kay Boyle. 9:20-8 Ag5'33. 11553
White-collar man in Spring. Verse. Raymond Holden. 11:73* My18'35. 11554
White-collar neighbors. RL. Alberta Williams. 10:48-61*N24 '34. 11555
A white hot tamale. PR (Maxim). Joseph T. Scarry. 2:25-7 O16 '26. 11556
White lies. Verse. Arthur Guiterman. 8:40*Ap9'32. 11557
White-light silhouettes. Prose. Niven Busch, Jr. 4:76-7 Ap7'28. 11558
White-light silhouettes. Prose. Niven Busch, Jr. 4:32 My12'28. 11559
White man's Harlem. Verse. M. McL. L. 14:41*Ap16'38. 11560
White mice. Prose. Don Herold. 9:27-8 Ap8'33. 11561
The white poodle. Prose. John Chapin Mosher. 8:16-18 Ja28 '33. 11562
The white pony. Prose. Morley Callaghan. 14:18-19*Ag27'38. 11563
White, William Allen. PR. Edna Ferber. 1:9-10 My30'25. 11564
White, William Allen. TT. 1:4 F21 '25. 11565
Whither are we puffing? Prose. Frank Sullivan. 15:54-5 F10'40. 11566
Whitman, Walt. TT. 7:11-12*My30 '31. 11567

Whitman, Walt. (Parody) Morris Bishop. 11:17*F23'35. 11568
Whitman, Walt. (Parody) Katharine Dayton. 1:20 My16'25. 11569
The whizz of infinity. Prose. Wolcott Gibbs. 7:15-16 F6'32. 11570
Who am I, Jessie? Prose. Angelica Gibbs. 14:22-3*O15'38. 11571
Who and whom. OMEU. James Thurber. 4:22-3 Ja5'29. 11572
Who is this king of glory? PR (Father Divine). St. Clair McKelway and A. J. Liebling. 12: 21-8*Je13'36; 12:22-8*Je20'36; 12:22-32*Je27'36. 11573
Who steals my purse--. Verse. Eleanor Graham. 15:48 F10'40. 11574
Who understands who anyhow? Verse. Ogden Nash. 12:21*O10 '36. 11575
Who was Robb de Peyster Tytus? Prose. Stanley Walker. 9:19-20 D2'33. 11576
Who weeps for strangers? OUWA. Annemarie Ewing and Morris Bishop. 15:35-40*Mr18'39. 11577
Who won? WP. Robert Benchley. 8:48-50 N19'32. 11578
Who won the repeal? RL. Alva Johnston. 9:52-6 S9'33. 11579
Who wrote Cock Robin? Prose. Robert Benchley. 8:17-18 O1 '32. 11580
A whole house. Prose. Gilbert Seldes. 7:18-19*My23'31. 11581
Who'll buy my violets? Prose. Heywood Broun. 3:29-31 D3'27. 11582
Who'll kill Cock Robin? Prose. Jack Cluett. 6:39-40 Je28'30. 11583
Who's afraid of Walt Disney? Prose. Frank Sullivan. 9:15-16 O28'33. 11584
Who's conducting this course? Prose. Paul Horgan. 6:96-8 O18'30. 11585
Who's who at the circus. Verse. Virginia Woods Bellamy. 13: 46*Ap17'37. 11586
Who's who in American poetry. TT. 12:7*Je6'36. 11587
Whose are you wearing? Prose. Marjorie Gane Harkness. 15: 83-4*N18'39. 11588
Why Albert Ferncroft is a bitter man. Prose. E. B. White. 3:28 F19'27. 11589
Why doesn't somebody... ? OFC. Ludwig Bemelmans. 14:91-3* D10'38. 11590
Why druggists look that way. Verse. E. T. Conroy. 4:81 S22 '28. 11591
Why go to Rome for ruins? Prose. Elmer Davis. 3:28-32 F4'28. 11592
Why I am moving to 204th Street. Prose. Frances Warfield. 2: 83-4 N6'26. 11593
Why I like Berlin. Prose. William B. Powell. 7:77 O3'31. 11594
Why I like New York. Prose. E. B. White. 1:10 Ag22'25. 11595
Why I like New York. Prose. E. B. White. 1:31 O10'25. 11596
Why I like New York. Prose. Katharine S. Angell White. 1:37 D19'25. 11597
Why is it when I plan to pass a quiet evening alone that--. Prose. Charles G. Shaw. 1:28 My2'25. 11598
Why men leave jail. Prose. C. Knapp. 2:45 O16'26. 11599
Why Mr. Walker went to California. Prose. James Thurber. 7:23 D5 '31. 11600
Why neglect the poets? Prose. Ruth Suckow. 4:58-9 My12'28. 11601
Why not die? Prose. James Thurber. 11:21*S21'35. 11602
Why not in minds as well as houses? Verse. Martha Banning Thomas. 3:62 Ag20'27. 11603
Why not she-friends? Prose. Dorothy Parker. 1:35 S19'25. 11604
The why of genius. Prose. Ben Hecht. 1:12 Je20'25. 11605
Why, Papa? Verse. Herbert As-

bury. 2:27-8 F12'27. 11606
Why pick on the opera? Prose. W. J. Henderson. 5:66-72 O26 '29. 11607
Why struggle? Verse. Marjorie Allen Seiffert. 7:27 Ja30'32. 11608
Why the flowers are wild. Prose. William Rose Benét. 8:58-60 O22'32. 11609
Why they waged war. Verse. John Peale Bishop. 15:19*N25'39. 11610
Why we go to cabarets. Prose. Ellin Mackay. 1:7-8 N28'25. 11611
Why we laugh--or do we? Prose. Robert Benchley. 12: 14*Ja2'37. 11612
Why, you reckon. Prose. Langston Hughes. 10:22-5 Mr17'34. 11613
A wide place in the road. OFC. James Finan. 10:87-91 My19 '34. 11614
The width of the Atlantic. Prose. Edward Acheson. 10:28-9 Ap28 '34. 11615
The wife beating wave. Prose. Ben Hecht. 1:9-10 Je27'25. 11616
A wife's secret. Verse. Anon. 1:28 Ja23'26. 11617
The wife's song. Verse. Elizabeth Coatsworth. 7:24 O17'31. 11618
Wilcox, Ella Wheeler. Jenny Ballou. 15:68-70 F3'40. 11619
Wild! RL. Morris Markey. 3:30-6 O29'27. 11620
Wild animal. Prose. Sally Benson. 11:18-20*Jy20'35. 11621
Wild bird. Prose. Robert M. Coates. 10:29-31 O6'34. 11622
Wild bird Hickok and his friends. Prose. James Thurber. 13:18-20*My29'37. 11623
Wild geese. Verse. Frances M. Frost. 9:21 Mr25'33. 11624
Wild Irish. Verse. Margaretta Manning. 4:43 Mr17'28. 11625
Wild oats. Prose. Emily Hahn. 6:14-15 Ag23'30. 11626
Wilde, Oscar. Anthony Gibbs. 6: 43 Ag2'30. 11627
Wilder, Thornton. TT. 4:14-15 My 26'28. 11628
Wilder, Thornton. TT. 4:8 Ag4'28. 11629
Wildfire. Verse. Margaret Fishback. 6:41 Ja24'31. 11630
Will and testament. Verse. Persis Greely Anderson. 8:29 N26'32. 11631
Will-o'-the-wisp in town. Verse. Harold Willard Gleason. 5:98 S21'29. 11632
Will ransom. Verse. Mark Van Doren. 13:25*Ag21'37. 11633
The will to believe. Prose. Parke Cummings. 5:87-8 O5'29. 11634
Will you be my perisphere? Prose. Geoffrey T. Hellman. 14:34-5*F4'39. 11635
Willa the weeper. Prose. Frank Sullivan. 8:15-16 N26'32. 11636
The willingness. Verse. Mark Van Doren. 9:12 Ap22'33. 11637
Willow River. Verse. Marjorie Allen Seiffert. 11:36*Mr30'35. 11638
Wilson's night thoughts. Verse. Edmund Wilson. 10:21 Mr17'34. 11639
Wimbledon. RL. John R. Tunis. 6:38-43 Jy5'30. 11640
Winchell in Newton Center. Prose. Russell Maloney. 14:17*N26'38. 11641
A window in Spain. Prose. George Weller. 12:55-7*O31'36. 11642
The window model. Verse. Anon. 1:55 D12'25. 11643
Window shopping. Verse. Frances Park. 3:75 Ja14'28. 11644
Windowbox. Verse. Marion Sturges-Jones. 8:24*My7'32. 11645
Wine from sour grapes. Verse. Martha Banning Thomas. 4:42 Jy21'28. 11646
Wine when it is read. Verse. Mildred Weston. 9:16 D23'33. 11647
The wings of Orville. Prose. E. B. White. 7:13-14*Ag8'31. 11648

Wings over America. PR (Bellanca). William Weimar. 5:22-5 Mr30'29. 11649
Wings over Hollywood. Prose. S. J. Perelman. 13:48-9*Ap17'37. 11650
Wings over Mugbourne. Prose. Mollie Panter-Downes. 14:41-2*O22'38. 11651
Wings over the elevated. RL. George Weller. 13:42-54*My 15'37. 11652
Winning against time. PR (Lacoste). John R. Tunis. 1:10-11 S5'25. 11653
Winnowing the débutantes. Prose. Frank Sullivan. 7:15-16 Ja23 '32. 11654
Winter. DL. Burke Boyce. 2:30 Ja8'27. 11655
Winter afternoon. Verse. Florence Kiper Frank. 4:18 Ja12 '29. 11656
Winter afternoon. Prose. Raymond Holden. 8:17-18*Mr12 '32. 11657
Winter comes to Nantucket. Prose. Geoffrey T. Hellman. 14:46-50*F19'38. 11658
Winter in Italy. Prose. Kay Boyle. 11:15-16*N23'35. 11659
Winter in Quebec. RL. Donald Moffat. 7:32-5 Ja30'32. 11660
Winter set. Verse. Will Scarlet. 11:25*F15'36. 11661
Winter-sports note. Verse. Franklin P. Adams. 14:20*F19'38. 11662
Wisdom. Verse. Frances M. Frost. 7:27 My16'31. 11663
Wisdom. Verse. Winifred Welles. 14:54*Mr12'38. 11664
The wise rise of Reginald Koff. Verse. Stuart Hyde Hawkins. 3:23 Ap16'27. 11665
Wish you were here, Queen. Prose. Frank Sullivan. 5:16-18 Ag10'29. 11666
Wisteria. SM. Alexander Woollcott. 6:30 Ag30'30. 11667
Wistful wail. Verse. Mary Carolyn Davies. 5:121 O19'29. 11668
Witch and spider. Verse. Grace Hazard Conkling. 5:25 Ag31'29. 11669
Witch in the forest. Verse. Grace Hazard Conkling. 5:33 S21'29. 11670
The witch, inland. Verse. Grace Hazard Conkling. 5:18 Jy13'29. 11671
Witch's money. Prose. John Collier. 15:19-24*My6'39. 11672
With Aunt Annabelle in her phaeton. Prose. Charles W. MacGregor. 2:39 Ag14'26. 11673
With cat. Prose. Margaret Widdemer. 6:22-3 Ag23'30. 11674
With collar. Prose. Wolcott Gibbs. 5:19 Ja18'30. 11675
With Episcopal sanction. Prose. Marc Connelly. 9:16-17 Ap15 '33. 11676
With expression. Prose. Alice Frankforter. 6:28-9 N15'30. 11677
With greater fortitude. Verse. Marjorie Allen Seiffert. 8:20 S10'32. 11678
With malice. Prose. Geoffrey T. Hellman. 14:63-4*N5'38. 11679
With mallets toward none. SM. Alexander Woollcott. 6:30 Ag9 '30. 11680
With reference to romance. Prose. John Chapin Mosher. 14:61-4* My14'38. 11681
Within the empire. Verse. Henrietta Fort Holland. 8:52 D3'32. 11682
Without a doubt! Prose. Herman J. Mankiewicz. 1:21 My9'25. 11683
Without a past. Prose. Frank Sullivan. 6:16-17 Ja3'31. 11684
Without all due respect. Verse. Ogden Nash. 6:16 Jy26'30. 11685
Without all due respect. Verse. Ogden Nash. 6:25 N8'30. 11686
Without all due respect. Verse. Ogden Nash. 6:32 N22'30. 11687
Without all due respect. Verse. Ogden Nash. 7:20 Ap25'31. 11688

Without benefit of Galsworthy. Prose. John Collier. 15:21-2* Mr11'39. 11689
Without benefit of tin foil. PR (Shattuck). Oliver H. P. Garrett. 4:29-31 My19'28. 11690
The witness. Prose. Sally Benson. 11:21-4*Ap13'35. 11691
Wit's end. Prose. Wolcott Gibbs. 9:22-3 O21'33. 11692
The wizard. PR (Edison). Alva Johnston. 5:21-4 D28'29; 5:24-6 Ja4'30; 5:22-5 Ja11'30. 11693
"Woe to the tabloids..." Verse. Philip G. Wylie. 3:91 Mr19'27. 11694
Wolfe, Thomas. TT. 13:16 Mr6 '37. 11694A
Woman. Verse. Frances M. Frost. 5:32 D7'29. 11695
The woman across the street. Prose. Tom F. Barry. 3:120-1 D10'27. 11696
Woman among women. Prose. Richard Lockridge. 12:62*Ap 18'36. 11697
Woman and the saloon. Prose. Paul Palmer. 6:38-42 N29'30. 11698
Woman out of taxi. Verse. Marjorie Allen Seiffert. 8:28*My 7'32. 11699
The woman pays. Verse. Anon. 3:24 O8'27. 11700
Woman pulls the wires. Verse. Ogden Nash. 12:13*Ag1'36. 11701
The woman who died twice. RL. Carl Carmer. 12:45-50*My9 '36. 11702
The woman who goes abroad to forget. Prose. Djuna Barnes. 4:28 D8'28. 11703
Woman wish. Verse. Sonia Ruthèle Novák. 5:67 Ja18'30. 11704
The woman with an apartment to sublet. Prose. Frances Warfield. 3:58-9 Jy23'27. 11705
Woman's place. Prose. Sally Benson. 11:57-60*Je8'35. 11706
The women. RL. Jack Alexander. 13:52-9*F27'37. 11707
Women. Verse. Sydney King Russell. 6:94 O25'30. 11708
Women and children first. Verse. Anon. 2:76 O23'26. 11709
Women without men. Prose. Mollie Panter-Downes. 15:63-4*Ap 1'39. 11710
The wonder book. SM. Alexander Woollcott. 9:34 Ap8'33. 11711
Wonderful institution, our schools. Prose. Zelda F. Popkin. 7:52-4 N14'31. 11712
Wonderful response. Prose. James Reid Parker. 12:102-106*N14 '36. 11713
The wood duck. Prose. James Thurber. 12:19-22*N21'36. 11714
Wood haul. Verse. Frances M. Frost. 13:38*F27'37. 11715
Wood mouse. Verse. Arthur Guiterman. 12:36*D5'36. 11716
Wooden shoes. Prose. Maddy Vegtel. 9:58 Je3'33. 11717
Wooing and winning through the ages. Prose. Donald Thompson. 8:64-6 O15'32. 11718
The "wooing" of Mr. Monroe. Prose. James Thurber. 5:17-18 My11'29. 11719
Wooing song for Sir Toby. Verse. Christopher Morley. 3:14 F18 '28. 11720
Woollcott, Alexander. PR. Wolcott Gibbs. 15:24-9*Mr18'39; 15:24-9*Mr25'39; 15:22-7*Ap1'39. 11721
Woollcott, Alexander. TT. 7:9 Ja 16'32. 11722
Woolworth Tower. DL. Burke Boyce. 3:79 My7'27. 11723
A word for the red book. Prose. H. J. Littlefield. 5:47-8 F1'30. 11724
A word for "who's who." Prose. Alvin F. Harlow. 6:102-106 My 10'30. 11725
The word not spoken. Verse. Grace Hazard Conkling. 5:19 Je29'29. 11726
A word on wind. Verse. Ogden Nash. 13:19*Mr13'37. 11727

A word to Dionysus. Verse. Mildred Weston. 9:68 O14'33. 11728
A word to rabbits. Verse. Mildred Weston. 10:116*D15'34. 11729
A word to the wilful. Verse. Martha Banning Thomas. 3:100 N26'27. 11730
A word to the young! Prose. John Chapin Mosher. 4:30-1 Je16'28. 11731
A word with Collette. Prose. T. H. Bliss. 1:25 My23'25. 11732
Words. Verse. Frances M. Frost. 6:21 S20'30. 11733
Words. Verse. E. B. White. 3:23 Mr19'27. 11734
Words across the sea. Prose. Andrée L. Eilert. 11:74-5*O5 '35. 11735
Words and music. PR (Kern). Franklin P. Adams. 5:21-3 F 8'30. 11736
Words and music. PR (Rodgers and Hart). Margaret Case Harriman. 14:19-23*My28'38; 14:21-5*Je4'38. 11737
Words around the world. Prose. Stuart Hyde Hawkins. 4:85-8 N24'28. 11738
Words to be spoken on an Autumn night. Verse. Frances M. Frost. 6:58 O25'30. 11739
Words to be spoken on the last night of the year. Verse. Frances M. Frost. 6:16 D27 '30. 11740
Words to the unwise. Verse. James Reid Parker. 13:83*D 18'37. 11741
Work. Verse. Mildred Weston. 8:28 N12'32. 11742
Work for the censor. Verse. Arthur Guiterman. 5:109 O26'29. 11743
Work in progress. Verse. John Holmes. 12:20*My23'36. 11744
The work of printing presses. MM. Corey Ford. 1:1 N7'25. 11745
The worker. Verse. Mark Van Doren. 14:29*Ja21'39. 11746
The world about us. Verse. Marc Connelly. 11:32*S28'35. 11747
The World Almanac 1932. Verse. Arthur Guiterman. 7:61 Ja23 '32. 11748
The world and Sauk Center. PR (Lewis). W. E. Woodward. 9:24-7 Ja27'34; 9:24-7 F3'34. 11749
World cruise. Verse. Rollin Kirby. 2:44 N20'26. 11750
World cruise: new style. RL. Morris Markey. 7:50-4 Mr21'31. 11751
World-cruise notes. OFC. Ann Gordon. 11:32-4*O12'35; 11:34* O26'35; 11:65*N16'35; 11:84*N 23'35. 11752
World events. WP. Robert Benchley. 4:30-4 Ja26'29. 11753
World of five-cent hot dogs. RL. A. J. Liebling. 15:33-41*Ag5 '39. 11754
The world of tomorrow. Verse. Morris Bishop. 15:20*Mr18'39. 11755
World of tomorrow, or next day. RL. Richard O. Boyer. 14:43-6*Ap30'38. 11756
World première. SM. Alexander Woollcott. 8:32*Mr12'32. 11757
The world rocks. Prose. Frances Crane. 9:46-7 Ap1'33. 11758
The World War as seen through German spectacles. (Film) Charles Graves. 4:103 Ap21 '28. 11759
The world we live in. SM. Alexander Woollcott. 9:35 D16'33. 11760
The worldling. Prose. Alice Frankforter. 9:28 D9'33. 11761
World's fair ode. Verse. Franklin P. Adams. 13:33*O30'37. 11762
World's series. Verse. Margaret Fishback. 4:107 O13'28. 11763
The world-swallowers. Prose. Creighton Peet. 1:26-7 N21'25. 11764
Worm turning. Prose. E. B. White. 3:16 O1'27. 11765
The worm turns--too late. WP. Robert Benchley. 9:64-6 Ap15

'33. 11766
Worm's eye view. Verse. Jean Batchelor. 11:70*Ap13'35. 11767
Worry? Nonsense! Prose. Katherine Sproehnle. 2:30 My15 '26. 11768
The worst thing about love. Verse. Herman Fetzer. 9:27 Ja27'34. 11769
Worthies on a carrousel. Prose. John Chapin Mosher. 2:52-3 S11'26. 11770
Wouldn't those ideals work today? Prose. Alvin F. Harlow. 6:76-7 N29'30. 11771
Wrap securely--mark plainly--and mail early. Prose. Donald Ogden Stewart. 3:15-16 Ja21'28. 11772
The wrath of the Annamite. OFC. Mona Gardner. 14:45*F4'39. 11773
A wreath for Mr. Flaherty. Verse. Phyllis McGinley. 12:21*Mr14'36. 11774
A wreath for Mrs. Roosevelt. Verse. Phyllis McGinley. 14:19*Ap30'38. 11775
Wright, Willard Huntington. Alexander Woollcott. 5:40 F23'29. 11776
Writers, amateur and professional. TT. 5:11-12 My11'29. 11777
Writer's digest. E. B. White. 10:49-56 My26'34. 11778
Writing man. Prose. Horton Heath. 8:15-16*Ap2'32. 11779
Wrong numbers. Prose. Katharine Brush. 3:31-2 D3'27. 11780
A wrong Wendel. Prose. Beth Wendel. 8:35-6*My7'32. 11781

X

The XYZ of politics. Prose. Fillmore Hyde. 3:24 Je11'27. 11782
X-ray. Prose. Ring Lardner. 6:15 Jy5'30. 11783

Y

The yacht complex. Prose. Katherine Sproehnle. 3:15 Ag13'27. 11784
Yale Bowl. Verse. Martha Banning Thomas. 3:85 N12'27. 11785
The Yale hour. Prose. Parke Cummings. 12:49-52*S19'36. 11786
The Yankee clippers. Prose. S. J. Perelman. 11:15*Je1'35. 11787
A Yankee holdiay. RL. Morris Markey. 1:21-2 My22'26. 11788
Yankee horse trader. PR (Cox). Arthur Bartlett. 11:19-24*Ag10 '35. 11789
Yankee kingdom come. RL. Brendan Gill. 15:28-31*N4'39. 11790
The yard. RL. A. J. Liebling. 14:23-6*Jy2'38. 11791
Yardstick. Verse. Jerome Barry. 5:104 O12'29. 11792
Ye antique market. Prose. A. van Steenbergh. 1:15 S26'25. 11793
Ye gods! Prose. Sterling Patterson. 1:43 F13'26. 11794
Ye olde Englyshe inne. Prose. Thomas Burke. 1:7-8 Je13'25. 11795
Ye olde ivory tower. Prose. S. J. Perelman. 15:60-1*Mr18'39. 11796
The yellow Bowery. RL. Niven Busch, Jr. 5:26-35 Ag3'29. 11797
Yellow chartreuse. Verse. David McCord. 15:60*N4'39. 11798
A yellow primrose was to him. Prose. John McNamara. 12:48-50*Jy11'36. 11799
Yellow signal received. RL. Mollie Panter-Downes. 15:34-40* N25'39. 11800
Yes--and no. Prose. G. Schwabe. 4:60 S8'28. 11801
The ye's have it. Prose. Martin Marten. 2:29 N20'26. 11802
Yes, Mr. Mayer. PR (Mayer). Henry F. Pringle. 12:26-31*Mr28

'36; 12:26-30*Ap4'36. 11803

Yes, sir. Prose. Sigmund Spaeth. 3:59 D3'27. 11804

Yes, the serial will be continued. Verse. Kenneth Fearing. 15: 30*D2'39. 11805

Yes--yes! Verse. D. D. P. 1:20 My23'25. 11806

Yo! ho! a bottle of rum! Prose. Yahoo. 1:23 My23'25. 11807

Yo-ho-ho, and thirteen black cats. Verse. Jerome Barry. 15:36* O21'39. 11808

Yoga. Prose. Nancy Wilson Ross. 10:36-8 O6'34. 11809

Yoga attempted. Prose. Cornelia Otis Skinner. 14:58-9*Je18'38. 11810

Yoo-hoo, Mr. Ectoplasm! Prose. S. J. Perelman. 13:15*Ag7'37. 11811

You and your rapids. Prose. Frank Sullivan. 7:48-50*Je13 '31. 11812

You cad, why don't you cringe? Verse. Ogden Nash. 15:20*O7 '39. 11813

You can always tell--. Prose. Watkins Eppes Wright. 2:24 My8'26. 11814

You can't afford to do that. Prose. George Cecil Cowing. 7:34-5* Jy18'31. 11815

You can't kill a bull in France. Prose. Theodore Pratt. 6:43 Jy 19'30. 11816

You Can't lose. Prose. Paul Gould. 4:53-4 D22'28. 11817

You can't take it with you. (Play) TT. 12:11 F13'37. 11818

You can't tell the players. Prose. Heywood Broun. 12:15-16*Ag22 '36. 11819

You can't vote if you own bricks. Prose. Theodore Pratt. 4:36-8 O27'28. 11820

"You don't know the hat of it, Dearie." Prose. Charles G. Shaw. 1:23 Je27'25. 11821

You don't want to miss anything. Prose. Elmer Davis. 4:30-4 F 25'28. 11822

You have only yourself to blame. Verse. Margaret Fishback. 5: 85 Ap27'29. 11823

You know how the French are. Prose. James Thurber. 13:15- 16*Jy17'37. 11824

You know how to live. Prose. John O'Hara. 10:20-1*F2'35. 11825

You know Irma, don't you? Prose. Robert M. Coates. 15:25-6*O21 '39. 11826

You made your bed, Ena. Prose. Frank Sullivan. 7:19-20 My2 '31. 11827

You make better time by walking. Prose. Carl Rose. 3:30-1 Mr12 '27. 11828

"You make the best time up Fifth." Prose. Lois Long. 2: 30-1 F12'27. 11829

You must come up and see us sometime. Prose. Thyra Samter Winslow. 8:20-1 D17'32. 11830

You need a rest. Prose. John O'Hara. 8:57-8 Ja14'33. 11831

You never know the people next door. Prose. Theodore Pratt. 4:40-4 My12'28. 11832

You never used to be like this. Prose. Edward Newhouse. 15: 45-6*Je3'39. 11833

You should have heard them last week. Prose. Charles W. Morton, Jr. 8:66-8 O8'32. 11834

You should live so, Walden Pond. Prose. S. J. Perelman. 15:20* S30'39. 11835

You tell 'em, Mr. Ambassador. Prose. Frank Sullivan. 7:16-17* Jy25'31. 11836

You, too, can have a merry Christmas. Prose. Elizabeth Crawford. 5:25-6 D21'29. 11837

You were perfectly fine. Prose. Dorothy Parker. 5:17-18 F23'29. 11838

You wouldn't know I was in it. Prose. Alan Campbell. 9:77-8 O21'33. 11839

You'd never know it was the same place. Prose. Parke Cummings. 13:45*S25'37. 11840

You'll love it up there. Prose. R. E. S. Thompson. 15:64-5*Ap 8'39. 11841
Young Arrowsmith. RL. Morris Markey. 2:38-43 Ja29'27. 11842
The young artist. Prose. Alice Frankforter. 6:102-103 My24'30. 11843
Young England. Prose. Morrison Fitch. 11:49-50*Jy20'35. 11844
The young Knick. SM. Alexander Woollcott. 9:44-6 My6'33. 11845
A young man-about-town. Verse. Charles G. Shaw. 1:24 Mr21 '25. 11846
Young man from Dubuque. PR (Josephs). Jo Swerling. 1:9-10 S26'25. 11847
(No entry) 11848
Young man of affairs. PR (Lindbergh). Morris Markey. 6:26-9 S20'30; 6:30-3 S27'30. 11849
Young man of Manhattan. Prose. Alice Frankforter. 11:64*S21 '35. 11850
Young man with a viola. PR (Hammond). E. J. Kahn, Jr. 15:19-24*Jy29'39. 11851
Young man's darling. Prose. Elspeth O'Halloran. 4:50-2 Ap 28'28. 11852
A young man's fancy. Prose. Alice Frankforter. 7:72*Je13 '31. 11853
The young monk of Siberia. PR (MacArthur). Alexander Woollcott. 5:23-6 Mr9'29. 11854
The young priest. Prose. Morley Callaghan. 6:24-7 S27'30. 11855
The young Shelley. Prose. Morris Bishop. 10:41-4*Ja5'35. 11856
Young Spring. Verse. Robert P. Tristram Coffin. 15:22*Ap29 '39. 11857
Young tropicals. Verse. David McCord. 11:71*Mr30'35. 11858
Young woman at a window. Verse. Mark Van Doren. 11:28*N16 '35. 11859
A young woman in green lace. Prose. Dorothy Parker. 8:15-17 S24'32. 11860
Younger brother. Prose. Morley Callaghan. 7:16-18*My23'31. 11861
The younger generation. Verse. Anon. 2:73 O16'26. 11862
The younger generation. Verse. Margaret Fishback. 9:45 F25 '33. 11863
The youngsters as critics. Prose. James Thurber. 3:31 Ap30'27. 11864
Your correspondent. SM. Alexande Woollcott. 7:28 F13'32. 11865
Your hat, sir? RL. A. J. Liebling. 14:42-50*Ap16'38. 11866
"Your honor--." RL. Morris Markey. 6:34-8 D20'30. 11867
Your letter today made me cry. OSB. C. Knapp. 4:28 Jy14'28. 11868
You're a vert. Prose. Thyra Samter Winslow. 3:23-4 S10'27. 11869
You're to ride for the honor of Dixie. OSB. C. Knapp. 6:28 My 17'30. 11870
Yours for the revolution. Prose. Norman Matson. 8:19-21 Ja28 '33. 11871
The Yule in retrospect. Prose. John O'Hara. 4:40-1 D29'28. 11872
Yule-tied. Verse. Will Scarlet. 12:53*D26'36. 11873
Yutang, Lin. TT. 12:12-13 Ja16'37. 11874
Yvonne. Prose. Frank Sullivan. 8:13-14 F4'33. 11875
Yvonnesong. Prose. Patricia Collinge. 9:54-5 F18'33. 11876

Z

Zeal. Verse. Peggy Bacon. 3:81 S 24'27. 11877
The Zeppelin passenger returns. Prose. Robert J. Misch. 5:85-6 S7'29. 11878
Zero. Verse. Raymond Holden. 5:34 D21'29. 11879
Zero. Verse. Mildred Weston. 11:

50*F15'36. 11880
Zero hour. Verse. Margaret Fishback. 4:88 Mr17'28. 11881
Zero hour. Verse. Ruth Lambert Jones. 13:82*Mr13'37. 11882
Zest. Prose. Louise Bogan. 7:16-19 O24'31. 11883
Ziegfeld hits evils of pulpit. Prose. Ogden Nash. 6:28-9 D6 '30. 11884
Zip Melloy and the peanut-brittle racket. Prose. Henry Anton. 12:54-5*My30'36. 11885
Zola, Emile. Janet Flanner. 3: 83-4 O29'27. 11886
The zoo. NESD. John J. Holzinger. 10:36 Ap7'34. 11887
The zoo. Verse. G. F. Riegel. 3:63 Je11'27. 11888
Zoological notes from further Asia. OFC. Mona Gardner. 15: 53-5*Ap1'39. 11889

-- & Co. by Jean-Richard Bloch. (Smith) 5:80-1 Ja25'30. B 11890

A la carte. by George Kelly, et al. (Long) 3:49 Ag27'27. T 11891

À nous la liberté. (Mosher) 8:52 My28'32. CC 11892

Aaron Burr. by Samuel H. Wandell and Meade Minnigerode. (Dounce) 1:22 N14'25. B 11893

Abe Lincoln in Illinois. by Robert E. Sherwood. (Gibbs) 14:34*O22'38. T 11894

Abe Martin's town pump. by Frank McKinney Hubbard. (Smith) 5:117 O5'29. B 11895

Abide with me. by Clare Boothe. (Benchley) 11:24*N30'35. T 11896

Abie's Irish Rose. (Claxton) 4:89 Ap28'28. CC 11897

Abie's Irish Rose. by Anne Nichols. (Brackett) 3:38 My28'27. T 11898
(White) 3:32 Ag6'27. T 11899
(Gibbs) 13:28 My22'37. T 11900

Abraham Lincoln. by Albert J. Beveridge. (Leonard) 4:88-9 S29'28. B 11901

Abraham Lincoln. by Raymond Holden. (Smith) 5:80-1 Ja4'30. B 11902

Abraham Lincoln: the prairie years. by Carl Sandburg. (Dounce) 1:45 F6'26. B 11903

Abraham Lincoln: the war years. by Carl Sandburg. (Fadiman) 15:94*D2'39. B 11903A

Abroad with Mayor Walker. by Hector Fuller. (Leonard) 4:64 Je30'28. B 11904

Absalom, Absalom! by William Faulkner. (Fadiman) 12:62-4*O31'36. B 11905

Accent on youth. (Mosher) 11:46*Ag17'35. CC 11906

Accent on youth. by Samson Raphaelson. (Benchley) 10:34† Ja5'35. T 11907

Accident. by Arnold Bennett. (Lowrie) 4:88 F2'29. B 11908

According to the flesh. by Fleta Campbell Springer. (Coates) 6:135-6 D6'30. B 11909

Accused. by Eugene Brieux. (Mankiewicz) 1:17-18 O10'25. T 11910

The ace of cads. (Claxton) 2:66-8 O23'26. CC 11911

Achilles had a heel. by Martin Flavin. (Benchley) 11:32*O26'35. T 11912

Across Spoon River: an autobiography. by Edgar Lee Masters. (Anon.) 12:118-19*N14'36. B 11913

Across the world with Mr. & Mrs. Martin Johnson. (Mosher) 5:62 F1'30. CC 11914

Across to Singapore. (Claxton) 4:86 My5'28. CC 11915

Action at Acquila. by Hervey Allen. (Fadiman) 14:59*Mr5'38. B 11916

Ada beats the drum. by John Kirkpatrick. (Benchley) 6:38 My17'30. T 11917

Adam and Eve. by John Erskine. (Parker) 3:116-17 N19'27. B 11918

The Adams family. by James Truslow Adams. (Smith) 6:85 Je14'30. B 11919

The admirable Crichton. by James M. Barrie. (Parker) 7:28-30 Mr21'31. T 11920

The adorable liar. by Roy Briant and Harry Durant. (Brackett) 2:33-4 S11'26. T 11921

Adventure girl. (Mosher) 10:64 Ag18'34. CC 11922

Adventures in pygmy land. (Claxton) 4:64 Mr10'28. CC 11923

Adventures of a novelist. by Gertrude Atherton. (Coates) 8:64-5*Ap16'32. B 11924

Adventures of a young man. by John Dos Passos. (Fadiman) 15:74*Je3'39. B 11925

The adventures of Huckleberry Finn. (Mosher) 15:64-5* Mr4 '39. CC 11926
The adventures of Robin Hood. (Mosher) 14:55-6*My21'38. CC 11927
The adventures of the black girl in her search for God. by George Bernard Shaw. (Coates) 9:62-3 F25'33. B 11928
The adventures of Tom Sawyer. (Mosher) 14:52*F26'38. CC 11929
The adventurous age. by Frederick Witney. (Brackett) 3:33 F19'27. T 11930
Affair. by Emily Hahn. (Fadiman) 11:76-7*Ap13'35. B 11931
An affair of the Follies. (Claxton) 3:78-9 Mr5'27. CC 11932
The affairs of Cellini. (McKelway) 10:80 S15'34. CC 11933
Africa dances. by Geoffrey Gorer. (Fadiman) 11:73*O12'35. B 11934
Africa speaks. (Mosher) 6:75-6 S27'30. CC 11935
The African witch. by Joyce Cary. (Anon.) 12:72*S26'36. B 11936
Africana. by Donald Heyward. (White) 3:36 Jy23'27. T 11937
After all. by John Van Druten. (White) 7:30-2 D12'31. T 11938
After dark. by Dion Boucicault. (Brackett) 4:28 D29'28. T 11939
After leaving Mr. Mackenzie. by Jean Rhys. (Coates) 7:53*Jy4 '31. B 11940
After many a Summer dies the swan. by Aldous Huxley. (Fadiman) 15:50-1*Ja27'40. B 11941
After the death of Don Juan. by Sylvia Townsend Warner. (Fadiman) 14:45*Ja7'39. B 11942
After the thin man. (Mosher) 12: 50*Ja2'37. CC 11943
After tomorrow. by John Golden and Hugh Stanislaus Stange. (Benchley) 7:30-1 S5'31. T 11944
After tonight. (Mosher) 9:74 N11 '33. CC 11945
Age of innocence. (Mosher) 10:85 O27'34. CC 11946
The age of innocence. by Margaret Ayer Barnes. (Brackett) 4:38 D8'28. T 11947
Ah king. by W. Somerset Maughan (Fadiman) 9:81 N11'33. B 11948
Ah, wilderness! (Mosher) 11:49* Ja4'36. CC 11949
Ah, wilderness! by Eugene O'Neill. (Gibbs) 9:30 O14'33. (Benchley) 9:24 D23'33. T 11950
The air circus. (Claxton) 4:90 S15 '28. CC 11951
Airways, Inc. by John Dos Passos (Brackett) 5:30-2 Mr9'29. T 11952
Alaskan adventures. (Claxton) 3:93 My14'27. CC 11953
Alcestis. by Euripides; Dudley Fitts, trans., and Robert Fitzgerald, trans. (Bogan) 12:61-2*Ag22'36. B 11954
Alexander Hamilton. (Mosher) 7: 73-4 S26'31. CC 11955
Alexander Nevsky. (Mosher) 15: 67*Ap1'39. CC 11956
Alexander's ragtime band. (Maloney) 14:39*Ag13'38. CC 11957
Alfred E. Smith: a critical study. by Henry F. Pringle. (Parker) 3:88-9 O1'27. B 11958
Algiers. (Mosher) 14:44*Jy16'38. CC 11959
Ali Baba goes to town. (Mosher) 13:89*O30'37. CC 11960
Alias Jimmy Valentine. (Mosher) 4:92 N24'28. CC 11961
Alias the deacon. (Claxton) 3:51 Je25'27. CC 11962
Alibi. (Mosher) 5:76-7 Ap20'29. CC 11963
Alice Adams. (Mosher) 11:45*Ag 24'35. CC 11964
Alice in Wonderland. (Mosher) 9:46 D30'33. CC 11965
Alice in Wonderland. Eva Le Gallienne, adapt. and Florida Friebus, adapt. (Benchley) 8:2 F11'33. T 11966
Alice sit-by-the-fire. by James M. Barrie. (Woollcott) 8:34*F 20'32. T 11967
Alien corn. by Sidney Howard. (Benchley) 9:26 Mr4'33. T 11968
Alison's house. by Susan Glaspell (Benchley) 6:34 D13'30; 7:26 M

23'31. T 11969

All at sea. by Osbert Sitwell and Sacheverell Sitwell. (Markey) 4:107-108 My26'28. B 11970

All brides are beautiful. by Thomas Bell. (Anon.) 12:66* O31'36. B 11971

All for one. by Ernest Cortis and Louise Cortis. (Brackett) 3:36 My28'27. T 11972

All good Americans. by S. J. Perelman and Laura Perelman. (Benchley) 9:30-2 D16'33. T 11973

All kneeling. by Anne Parrish. (Parker) 4:102-103 S15'28. B 11974

All men are brothers. Pearl S. Buck. (Fadiman) 9:75 S30'33. B 11975

All men are enemies. by Richard Aldington. (Fadiman) 9:47 Jy29'33. B 11976

All our yesterdays. by H. M. Tomlinson. (Smith) 5:81-2 Ja18 '30. B 11977

All quiet on the Western Front. (Mosher) 6:98-9 My10'30. CC 11978

All quiet on the Western Front. by Erich-Maria Remarque. (Smith) 5:103-104 Je8'29. B 11979

All rights reserved. by Irving Kaye Davis. (Benchley) 10:30-2†N17'34. T 11980

All that glitters. by John Baragwanath and Kenneth Simpson. (Benchley) 13:23*Ja29'38. T 11981

All the king's horses. by Frederick Herendeen. (Benchley) 9:30-2 F10'34. T 11982

All the king's men. by Fulton Oursler. (Brackett) 4:28 F16 '29. T 11983

All the living. by Hardie Albright. (Benchley) 14:30*Ap2 '38. T 11984

All the sad young men. by F. Scott Fitzgerald. (Dounce) 2: 51 Mr13'26. B 11985

All this and Heaven too. by Rachel Field. (Fadiman) 14: 63*O29'38. B 11986

Allez-oop. by J. P. McEvoy, et al. (Long) 3:47 Ag27'27. T 11987

Allure. by Leigh Burton Wells. (Benchley) 10:32 N10'34. T 11988

An almanac for moderns. by Donald Culross Peattie. (Fadiman) 11:73*Mr30'35; 11:66-7*S21'35. B 11989

Almost pagan. by J. D. Beresford. (Dounce) 2:82 S18'26. B 11990

The almost perfect state. by Don Marquis. (Boyd) 3:99-100 My21 '27. B 11991

Aloma of the South Seas. (Claxton) 2:58 My22'26. CC 11992

Aloma of the South Seas. by John B. Hymer and LeRoy Clemens. (Anon.) 1:11-12 My2'25. T 11993

Alone. (Mosher) 8:60 Je4'32. CC 11994

Alone. by William Byrd. (Fadiman) 14:68-9*N5'38. B 11995

An altar in the fields. by Ludwig Lewisohn. (Fadiman) 10:86 F17 '34. B 11996

The amateur gentleman. (Claxton) 2:36 Ag21'26. CC 11997

The amazing Dr. Clitterhouse. (Mosher) 14:53*Jy23'38; 14:44* S3'38. CC 11998

(No entry) 11999

The amazing Dr. Clitterhouse. by Barré Lyndon. (Benchley) 13:32*Mr13'37. T 12000

Ambrose Bierce. by Carey McWilliams. (Smith) 5:65-6 D28 '29. B 12001

Ambrose Holt and family. by Susan Glaspell. (Coates) 7:90-2 Ap18'31. B 12002

America and Alfred Stieglitz. by Waldo Frank, ed. (Fadiman) 10:108-10*D8'34. B 12003

America in midpassage. by Charles A. Beard. (Fadiman) 15:78*My20'39. B 12004

America set free. by Hermann Alexander Keyserling. (Smith) 5:116 N16'29. B 12005

America was promises. by Archibald MacLeish. (Bogan) 15: 100*D16'39. B 12006
The American caravan. by Alfred Kreymborg, ed.; Lewis Mumford, ed. and Paul Rosenfeld, ed.
(Smith) 5:123 O26'29 B 12007
(Coates) 7:93 Ap18'31 B 12008
American colony. by Charles Brackett. (Smith) 5:58 Ag24'29. B 12009
The American diplomatic game. by Drew Pearson and Constantine Brown. (Fadiman) 10:65-7*Ja19'35. B 12010
An American doctor's odyssey. by Victor Heiser. (Fadiman) 12: 49-50*Ag29'36. B 12011
American dream. by Michael Foster. (Fadiman) 13:66*Je19 '37. B 12012
American dream. by George O'Neil. (Benchley) 9:26-8 Mr4 '33. T 12013
American earth. by Carleton Beals. (Anon.) 15:71*Ap1'39. B 12014
An American girl. by Tiffany Thayer. (Parker) 9:64-5 Mr18 '33. B 12015
American girl. by John R. Tunis. (Smith) 6:63 Ag16'30. B 12016
American inquisitors. by Walter Lippmann. (Markey) 4:85 Je16 '28. B 12017
The American jitters. by Edmund Wilson. (Coates) 8:65* Ap23'32. B 12018
American landscape. by Elmer Rice. (Benchley) 14:40*D10'38. T 12019
The American language. by H. L. Mencken. (Fadiman) 12:74-7* My16'36. B 12020
The American Leviathan. by Charles A. Beard and William Beard. (Coates) 6:122 D13'30. B 12021
American madness. (Mosher) 8: 37 Ag13'32. CC 12022
American outpost. by Upton Sinclair. (Coates) 8:65-6*Ap23 '32. B 12023
American parade (quarterly). (Dounce) 1:27 Ja23'26. B 12024
The American procession. by Frederick Lewis Allen and Agnes Rogers. (Fadiman) 9:93 4 O21'33. B 12025
The American testament: a narrative of rebels and romantics. by Joseph Freeman. (Anon.) 12:65 O24'36. B 12026
An American tragedy. (Mosher) 7:42*Ag15'31. CC 12027
An American tragedy. by Theodore Dreiser. (Dounce) 1:23 Ja9'26. B 12028
An American tragedy. by Patrick Kearney. (Brackett) 2:33-4 O2 '26. T 12029
The American Venus. (Shane) 1: 40 Ja30'26. CC 12030
The American way. by George S Kaufman and Moss Hart. (Benchley) 14:26-8*Ja28'39. T 12031
Americana. by J. P. Mc Evoy, et al. (Brackett) 2:40-1 Ag7'26; 4:35 N10'28. (Mosher) 8:28-30 O15'32. T 12032
(No entry) 12033
America's sweetheart. by Herbe Fields; Richard Rodgers and Lorenz Hart. (Parker) 7:26-8 F21'31. T 12034
Amok. by Stefan Zweig. (Coates) 7:63*Je27'31. B 12035
Among the lost people. by Conrad Aiken. (Fadiman) 10:69 Mr31'34. B 12036
Among the married. by Vincent Lawrence. (Benchley) 5:40 O1 '29. T 12037
Among the nudists. by Frances Merrill and Mason Merrill. (Coates) 7:94-5 Ap25'31. B 120
The amorous antic. by Ernest Pascal. (Benchley) 5:36 D14 '29. T 1203
Amphitryon. (Mosher) 13:71-2*A 3'37. CC 1204
Amphitryon 38. by Jean Giraud and S. N. Behrman, adapt. (Benchley) 13:30-1*N13

'37. 12041
Anabase. by St. John Perse and T. S. Eliot, trans. (Bogan) 14: 63-4*Mr12'38. B 12042
Anatol. by Arthur Schnitzler and Harley Granville-Barker. (Benchley) 6:26-8 Ja31'31. T 12043
Anatole France abroad. Jean Jacques Brousson. 4:106-107 Ap21'28. B 12044
Anatole France himself. Jean Jacques Brousson. (Markey) 4: 106-107 Ap21'28. B 12045
Ancestor Jorico. by William J. Locke. (Smith) 5:134-6 D14 '29. B 12046
The ancient hunger. by Edwin Granberry. (Boyd) 3:103-104 Mr26'27. B 12047
. . . and be my love. Lewis Galantiere and John Houseman. (Benchley) 9:28 Ja27'34. T 12048
And no birds sing. by Pauline Leader. (Coates) 7:52*Jy4'31. B 12049
And now good-bye. by Philip Howard. (Benchley) 12:28*F13 '37. T 12050
And quiet flows the Don. by Mikhail Sholokhov. (Fadiman) 10: 69-70 Jy7'34. B 12051
And so to bed. by James B. Fagan. (Brackett) 3:35 N19'27. T 12052
And so--Victoria. by Vaughn Wilkins. (Fadiman) 13:50-1* Ag7'37. B 12053
And stars remain. by Julius J. Epstein and Philip Epstein. (Benchley) 12:28-30*O24'36. T 12054
And sudden death. (Mosher) 12:57* Jy25'36. CC 12055
Andrée's story--the complete record of his polar flight. by J. G. Andersson, ed. (Coates) 6:73 Ja3'31. B 12056
Andrew Jackson: the border captain. by Marquis James. (Coates) 9:55-6 Ap1'33. B 12057
Androcles and the lion. by George Bernard Shaw. (Mankiewicz) 1:14 D5'25. T 12058
Andy Brandt's ark. by Edna Bryner. (Boyd) 3:112-13 Ap30'27. B 12059
Angel. (Mosher) 13:75*N6'37. CC 12060
Angel. by DuBose Heyward. (Dounce) 2:76-7 O16'26. B 12061
Angel child. by Grace Perkins. (Leonard) 4:123 N10'28. B 12062
Angel Island. by Bernie Angus. (Gibbs) 13:34*O30'37. T 12063
The angel of Broadway. (Claxton) 3:87 N5'27. CC 12064
Angel pavement. by J.B. Priestley. (Smith) 6:76-7 S6'30. B 12065
The angel that troubled the waters. Thornton Wilder. (Leonard) 4: 112 N17'28. B 12066
Angels in undress. by Mark Benney. (Fadiman) 13:83-4*Mr20 '37. B 12067
Animal crackers. (Mosher) 6:66-7 S6'30. CC 12068
Animal crackers. by George S. Kaufman and Morrie Ryskind. (Brackett) 4:33 N3'28. T 12069
The animal in me. (Mosher) 11: 59-60*S21'35. CC 12070
The animal kingdom. (Mosher) 8:40 D31'32. CC 12071
The animal kingdom. by Philip Barry. (Benchley) 7:26-8 Ja23 '32. T 12072
Animal treasure. Ivan T. Sanderson. (Fadiman) 13:72-3*S11'37. B 12073
Animula vagula. by Leonard Bacon. (Boyd) 2:83-4 Ja8'27. B 12074
Ann Vickers. (White) 9:77 O7'33. CC 12075
Ann Vickers. by Sinclair Lewis. (Coates) 8:51-2 Ja28'33. B 12076
Anna. by Rudolph Lothar. (Brackett) 4:50-1 My26'28. T 12077
Anna Christie. (Mosher) 6:60-1 Mr22'30. CC 12078
Anna Karenina. (Mosher) 11:61-2* S7'35. CC 12079
Annie Laurie. (Claxton) 3:89 My21 '27. CC 12080
Annie Oakley. (Mosher) 11:49*Ja4

'36. CC 12081
Another Caesar. by Alfred Neumann. (Fadiman) 10:64-5*Ja26 '35. B 12082
Another language. by Rose Franken. (Benchley) 8:26-8*My7'32. T 12083
Another language. (Mosher) 9:43 Ag12'33. CC 12084
Another thin man. (Mosher) 15: 93*D2'39. CC 12085
The ant heap. by Edward Knoblock. (Smith) 6:92-4 Ap26'30. B 12086
Anthology for the enjoyment of poetry. by Max Eastman. (Bogan) 15:68-9*O28 '39. B 12087
An anthology of the younger poets. Oliver Wells, ed. (Bogan) 9:66 F18'33. B 12088
An anthology of world poetry. by Mark Van Doren, ed. (Lowrie) 4:69 Ja12'29. B 12089
Anthony Adverse. by Hervey Allen. (Fadiman) 9:49-50 Jy1'33. B 12090
Anthony Adverse. (Mosher) 12:46* Ag29'36. CC 12091
Anthony Comstock. by Margaret Leech and Heywood Broun. (Boyd) 3:97-8 Mr19'27.B 12092
Antonia. by Melchior Lengyel. (Mankiewicz) 1:20 N7'25. T 12093
Antony and Cleopatra. by William Shakespeare. (Benchley) 13: 30-2*N20'37. T 12094
Anybody's woman. (Mosher) 6:59 Ag23'30. CC 12095
Anything goes. by Guy Bolton; P. G. Wodehouse; Howard Lindsay; Russel Crouse and Cole Porter. (Benchley) 10:36-8†D1 '34. T 12096
Apes, men, and morons. by Earnest Albert Hooton. (Fadiman) 13:93-4*O30'37. B 12097
Apocalypse. by D. H. Lawrence. (Coates) 8:61*Mr12'32.B 12098
Appassionata. by Fannie Hurst. (Dounce) 2:59 Ap24'26.B 12099
Appendicitis. by Thew Wright. (Parker) 4:93 Mr24'28.B 12100
Applause. by Beth Brown. (Leonard) 4:96 O27'28. B 12101
Applause. (Mosher) 5:110-13 O19 '29. CC 12102
The apple cart. by George Bernard Shaw. (Benchley) 6:27-8 Mr8'30. T 12103
Apples be ripe. by Llewelyn Pow (Smith) 6:92 Je7'30. B 12104
Appointment in Samarra. by John O'Hara. (Fadiman) 10:68-9 S1 '34. B 12105
Apron strings. by Dorrance Davis (Benchley) 6:28 Mr1'30. T 12106
Apron strings. by May Freud Dickenson. (Leonard) 4:61-2 A 4'28. B 12107
Arabesque. by Cloyd Head; Euni Tietjens and Ruth White Warfield. (Mankiewicz) 1:19-20 N 'Y25. T 12108
Arabia Felix. by Bertram Thom (Coates) 8:83-4*Mr19'32. B 121
Ararat. by Elgin Groseclose. (Fadiman)15:53-4*S2'39. B 121
The arches of the years. by Hal day Sutherland. (Fadiman) 9:5 Je17'33. B 12111
Architects of ideas. by Ernest Tattner. (Fadiman) 14:72*My '38. B 12112
Arctic adventure. by Peter Freu en. (Fadiman) 12:68-9*Mr28' B 12113
The Arcturus adventure. by Wil liam Beebe. (Dounce) 2:89 Je '26. B 12114
Are parents people? (Anon.) 1:1 Je20'25. CC 12115
Are they the same at home? by Beverley Nichols. (Hoyt) 3:96 O29'27. B 1211
Are we civilized? (Mosher) 10: 2 Je23'34. CC 1211
Aren't we all? (Mosher) 8:48-9 9'32. CC 1211
The Argyle case. (Mosher) 5:76 S7'29. CC 1211
Ariadne. by A. A. Milne. (Anon. 1:11 Mr7'25. T 1212
Ariane. (Mosher) 10:86 Mr17'34 CC 1212
Aricie Brun. by Émile Henriot. (Dounce) 1:44 F13'26.B 1212

The aristocratic West. by Katharine Fullerton Gerould. (Dounce) 1:23 Ja16'26. B 12123

The Arizonian. (Mosher) 11:41* Ag3'35. CC 12124

Armageddon. by Eugene Löhrke, ed. (Smith) 6:93 Je7'30. B 12125

Arms and the man. by George Bernard Shaw. (Mankiewicz) 1:17-18 S26'25. T 12126

Arms for Venus. by Randolph Carter. (Benchley) 13:34-6* Mr20'37. T 12127

Around the corner. by Martin Flavin. (Benchley) 12:28-32* Ja9'37. T 12128

Around the world in eighty minutes. (Mosher) 7:78-9 N28'31. CC 12129

Arouse and beware. by MacKinlay Kantor. (Fadiman) 12: 114-15*N14'36. B 12130

Arrest that woman. by Maxine Alton. (Gibbs) 12:26*S26'36. T 12131

The arrow. by Christopher Morley. (Boyd) 3:110 Ap30'27. B 12132

Arrowsmith. by Sinclair Lewis. (Anon.) 1:28 Mr21'25. B 12133

Arrowsmith. (Mosher) 7:74 D19 '31. CC 12134

Arsène Lupin. (Mosher) 8:63*Mr 5'32. CC 12135

Art and Mrs. Bottle. by Benn W. Levy. (Benchley) 6:34 N29'30. T 12136

Art et phynance. by Paul Poiret. (Flanner) 11:67*F16'35. 12137

The art of bundling. by Dana Doten. (Fadiman) 14:78-9*N26 '38. B 12138

The art of successful bidding. George Reith. (Parker) 4:102-103 Mr17'28. B 12139

The art of the American Indian. by Paul Radin. (Hoyt) 3:53-4 D31'27. B 12140

Art of the night. by George Jean Nathan. (Parker) 4:93-4 Mr24 '28. B 12141

Artist among the bankers. by Will Dyson. (Fadiman) 9:50 D30 '33. B 12142

An artist in America. by Tom Benton. (Fadiman) 13:69*O23 '37. B 12143

An artist in the family. by Sarah Gertrude Millin. (Hoyt) 4:94-5 Mr24'28. B 12144

Artists and models. (Maloney) 13: 33*Ag7'37. CC 12145

Artists and models. by Harold Atteridge and Harry Wagstaff Gribble. (Mankiewicz) 1:15 Jy4 '25. T 12146

Artists and models. by Harold Stern and Ernie Golden. (Benchley) 6:26-30 Je21'30. T 12147

Arundel. by Kenneth Roberts. (Smith) 5:82-3 Ja18'30.B 12148

As far as Jane's grandmother's. by Edith Olivier. (Lowrie) 5: 109 Ap27'29. B 12149

As good as new. by Thompson Buchanan. (Benchley) 6:30-1 N 15'30. T 12150

As husbands go. by Rachel Crothers. (Parker) 7:34-6 Mr21'31. T 12151

As I lay dying. by William Faulkner. (Coates) 6:109 O25'30; 7:86 Mr7'31. B 12152

As I saw it. by Alden Brooks. (Smith) 6:96-7 S20'30.B 12153

As I was going down Sackville Street. by Oliver St. John Gogarty. (Fadiman) 13:77-8* Ap10'37. B 12154

As it was. by Helen Noble Thomas. (Boyd) 3:92 Mr5'27. B 12155

As the earth turns. by Gladys Hasty Carroll. (Coates) 9:74 My6'33. B 12156

As thousands cheer. by Irving Berlin and Moss Hart. (Gibbs) 9:32-4 O7'33. T 12157

As we were. by E. F. Benson. (Coates) 6:108-109 O25'30. B 12158

As you desire me. (Mosher) 8:61 Je11'32. CC 12159

As you desire me. by Luigi Pirandello and Dmitri Ostrow, adapt. (Benchley) 6:30 F7'31.T 12160

As you like it. (Mosher) 12:96-7*

N14'36. CC 12161
As you like it. by William Shakespeare. (Gibbs) 13:30*N6'37. T 12162
The ascent of F6. by W. H. Auden and Christopher Isherwood. (Bogan) 12:64-5*F13'37. B 12163
Ash Wednesday. by T. S. Eliot. (Smith) 6:115 My17'30. B 12164
Ashes of rings. by Mary Butts. (Dounce) 2:60 My15'26. B 12165
The Asiatics. by Frederic Prokosch. (Fadiman) 11:80*N2 '35. B 12166
Ask me another! by Justin Spafford and Lucien Esty. (Boyd) 2:85 F12'27. B 12167
Asphalt. (Mosher) 6:99-101 My10 '30. CC 12168
The assassins. by Frederic Prokosch. (Bogan) 12:67*O3'36. B 12169
Asylum. by William Seabrook. (Fadiman) 11:45-6*Ag10'35. B 12170
At home abroad. by Howard Dietz and Arthur Schwartz. (Gibbs) 11:26-8*S28'35. T 12171
At Mrs. Beam's. by C. K. Munro. (Gabriel) 2:26 My8'26. T 12172
At the circus. (Mosher) 15:71*N 25'39. CC 12173
At the sign of the goat and compasses. by Martin Armstrong. (Dounce) 1:18-19 O10'25. B 12174
At the South Pole. (Mosher) 5: 85-6 Mr2'29. CC 12175
At Yale. (Claxton) 4:59 Ag4'28. CC 12176
Attorney for the defense. (Mosher) 8:60 Je4'32. CC 12177
The auction block. (Shane) 2:54 F 20'26. CC 12178
Audubon. by Constance Rourke. (Anon.) 12:66-7*O31'36. B 12179
August. by Eugene Gay-Tifft. (Coates) 7:80-1 O31'31. B 12180
August Strindberg: the bedeviled Viking. by V. J. McGill. (Hellman) 6:103-104 Ap19'30. B 12181
Australia Felix. by Henry Handel Richardson. (Smith) 6:99 F22 '30. B 12182
Autobiographies. by William Butler Yeats. (Boyd) 3:91-2 Mr5 '27. B 12183
Autobiography. by Juan Belmonte. (Fadiman) 13:67-9*F27'37. B 12184
Autobiography. by Gilbert Keith Chesterton. (Fadiman) 12:78-80*N7'36. B 12185
The autobiography and memoirs of Robert Haydon. by Robert Haydon. (Boyd) 2:81 Ja29'27. B 12186
The autobiography of Alice B. Toklas. by Gertrude Stein. (Flanner) 9:37 M4'33. B 12187
(Fadiman) 9:50-1 S2'33. B 12188
An autobiography of America. by Mark Van Doren. (Gannett) 5: 138 D14'29. B 12189
The autobiography of an ex-colored man. by James Weldon Johnson. (Boyd) 3:72 S3'27. B 12190
The autobiography of John Middleton Murry: between two worlds. by John Middleton Murry. (Fadiman) 12:66*Je6'36. B 12191
The autocracy of Mr. Parham. by H. G. Wells. (Smith) 6:62 Jy5 '30. B 12192
Autumn crocus. (Mosher) 11:64* S14'35. CC 12193
Autumn crocus. by C. L. Anthony. (Lockridge) 8:36 D3'32. T 12194
Autumn love. (Claxton) 3:56 Jy23 '27. CC 12195
Avarice House. by Julian Green. (Hoyt) 3:124-5 D10'27. B 12196
The Avon flows. by George Jean Nathan. (Fadiman) 12:63*F6'37. B 12197
Awake and rehearse. by Louis Bromfield. (Smith) 5:119 My25 '29. B 12198
Awake and sing! by Clifford Odet (Benchley) 11:26†Mr2'35; 15:30 1*Mr18'39. T 12199
The awakening. (Mosher) 4:60-1 J 12'29. CC 12200
The awakening college. by Clarence C. Little. (Smith) 6:107 My10'30. B 12201

The awful truth. (Mosher) 13:77-8*N13'37. CC 12202
Axel's castle. by Edmund Wilson. (Coates) 7:86-8 Mr7'31. B 12203

B

The Babbitt warren. by Cyril Michinson Joad. (Boyd) 3:90-1 Mr5'27. B 12204
Babe comes home. (Claxton) 3:50 Ag6'27. CC 12205
Babes in arms. (Mosher) 15:63-4*O28'39. CC 12206
Babes in arms. by Richard Rodgers and Lorenz Hart. (Benchley) 13:30*Ap24'37. T 12207
Babes in toyland. (Mosher) 10:34*D22'34. CC 12208
Babes in toyland. by Glen Macdonough and Victor Herbert. (Benchley) 6:26 Ja3'31.T 12209
Babies à la carte. by Seaman Lewis. (Long) 3:48 Ag27'27. T 12210
The baby cyclone. by George M. Cohan. (Brackett) 3:31 S24'27. T 12211
The Babylons. by Clemence Dane. (Leonard) 4:99 O6'28. B 12212
Bachelor born. by Ian Hay. (Benchley) 13:26-30*F5'38. T 12213
Bachelor mother. (Mosher) 15:56*Jy1'39. CC 12214
The bachelor father. by Edward Childs Carpenter. (Brackett) 4:33 Mr10'28. T 12215
Bachelor's affairs. (Mosher) 8:34 Jy2'32. CC 12216
Bachelor's brides. by Charles Horace Malcolm. (Mankiewicz) 1:13 Je6'25. T 12217
Back door to heaven. (Mosher) 15:67*Ap22'39. CC 12218
Back in circulation. (Mosher) 13:60*O2'37. CC 12219
Back to God's country. (Claxton) 3:91 O29'27. CC 12220
Back to stay. by Jonathan Leonard. (Lowrie) 5:94-5 Mr30'29. B 12221
Background. by Mabel Dodge Luhan. (Parker) 9:65-6 Mr18'33. B 12222
A backward glance. by Edith Wharton. (Fadiman) 10:101-102 Ap28'34. B 12223
Backwater. by T. S. Stribling. (Smith) 5:88 F15'30. B 12224
Bad girl. (Mosher) 7:44 Ag22'31. CC 12225
Bad girl. by Viña Delmar. (Markey) 4:98-9 Ap14'28. B 12226
Bad girl. by Brian Marlow and Viña Delmar. (Benchley) 6:36 O11'30. T 12227
Bad habits of 1926. by Arthur Herzog. (Gabriel) 2:26 My15'26. T 12228
The bad man of Brimstone. Mosher) 13:54*F5'38. CC 12229
The bad one. (Mosher) 6:80 Je21'30. CC 12230
Bagatelles pour un massacre. by Louis-Ferdinand Céline. (Flanner) 13:55*F5'38. B 12231
The balconinny. by J. B. Priestley. (Coates) 7:76-7*My23'31. B 12232
Bali and Angkor, or looking at life and death. by Geoffry Gorer. (Anon.) 12:50*Ag15'36. B 12233
Ballads and poems--1915-1930. by Stephen Vincent Benét. (Bogan) 7:83 Mr21'31. B 12234
Ballyhoo. by Harry Ruskin and Leighton K. Brill. (Benchley) 6:27-8 Ja3'31. T 12235
Ballyhoo! by Kate Horton. (Brackett) 2:25 Ja15'27. T 12236
Ballyhoo of 1932. by Norman B. Anthony. (White) 8:30 S17'32. T 12237
Baltic deputy. (Mosher) 13:63*S11'37. CC 12238
Balzac. by Francis Gribble. (Smith) 6:80 Mr1'30. B 12239
Bamboola. by D. Frank Marcus, et al. (Brackett) 5:47 Jy13'29. T 12240
Band concert. (Mosher) 11:55*Mr2'35. CC 12241
The band plays Dixie. by Morris

Markey. (Boyd) 3:96-7 Mr12 '27. B 12242

The band wagon. by George S. Kaufman and Howard Dietz. (Benchley) 7:28*Je13'31; 7:24* Jy25'31. T 12243

Banjo. by Claude McKay. (Smith) 5:119-20 My25'29. B 12244

Banjo on my knee. (Mosher) 12: 88*D19'36. CC 12245

Barbary coast. (Mosher) 11:72-3*O26'35. CC 12246

Barbed wire. (Mosher) 3:63-4 Ag 20'27. CC 12247

Barchester Towers. by Thomas Job. (Benchley) 13:44*D11'37. T 12248

Bardelys the magnificent. (Claxton) 2:77 N6'26. CC 12249

The barker. (Mosher) 4:117 D15 '28. CC 12250

The barker. by Kenyon Nicholson. (Brackett) 2:33 Ja29'27. T 12251

Barnum's own story. by Waldo R. Browne, ed. (Boyd) 3:87-8 Je18'27. B 12252

Baron Fritz. by Karl Federn. (Smith) 6:54-5 Ag30'30. B 12253

Barren ground. by Ellen Glasgow. (Anon.) 1:26 My2'25. B 12254

The Barretts of Wimpole Street. (McKelway) 10:87 O6'34. CC 12255

The Barretts of Wimpole Street. by Rudolf Besier.
(Parker) 7:25-6 F21'31. T 12256
(White) 7:24-6 D26'31. T 12257
(Flanner) 10:54 O27'34. T 12258
(Benchley) 11:26-8 Mr9'35. T 12259

Barricade. (Mosher) 15:59*D16 '39. CC 12260

The barrier. (Shane) 2:49 Mr27 '26. CC 12261

The bat. by Mary Roberts Rinehart and Avery Hopwood. (Gibbs) 13:39*Je12'37. T 12262

The bat whispers. (Mosher) 6:59 Ja24'31. CC 12263

The battle. (Mosher) 10:57*D1'34. CC 12264

The battle of Gallipoli. (Mosher) 7:95 D12'31. CC 12265

The battle of the horizons. by Sylvia Thompson. (Markey) 4: 84 Je23'28. B 12266

The battle of the sexes. (Mosher) 4:93 O20'28. CC 12267

The battle to the weak. by Hilda Vaughan. (Dounce) 2:47-8 F27 '26. B 12268

The battles of Coronel and Falkland Islands. (Claxton) 4:69-70 F25'28. CC 12269

Battleship Gertie. by Frederick Hazlett Brennan. (Benchley) 10: 30†Ja26'35. T 12270

Battling butler. (Claxton) 2:36 Ag 28'26. CC 12271

The beachcomber. (Mosher) 14: 48*D31'38. CC 12272

The beadle. by Pauline Smith. (Boyd) 3:103 Mr26'27. B 12273

Beale Street. by George Washington Lee. (Fadiman) 10:61-2 Jy 21'34. B 12274

Beasts called wild. by André Demaison. (Smith) 6:106 O4'30. B 12275

Beasts of Berlin. (Mosher) 15:71* N25'39. CC 12276

The beaten track. by Elbert Hubbard and J. O. Francis. (Gabriel) 2:34 F20'26. T 12277

Beatrice. by Arthur Schnitzler. (Dounce) 2:60 My8'26. B 12278

Beau Broadway. (Claxton) 4:59 Ag 4'28. CC 12279

Beau Gallant. by Stuart Olivier. (Gabriel) 2:28 Ap17'26. T 12280

Beau geste. (Claxton) 2:39-41 S4 '26. CC 12281

Beau geste. (Mosher) 15:59-60* Ag5'39. CC 12282

Beau-strings. by C. K. Munro. (Gabriel) 2:26 My8'26. T 12283

The beauties and furies. by Chri tina Stead. (Fadiman) 12:68-70 Ap25'36. B 12284

The beautiful years. by Henry Wi liamson. (Smith) 5:104-105 S14 '29. B 12285

Beauty and the beast. by Kathlee Norris. (Parker) 4:97-8 Ap14 '28. B 12286

Becky Sharp. (Mosher) 11:53*Je2 '35. CC 12287

A bedtime story. (Mosher) 9:56 Ap29'33. CC 12288
Beethoven: his spiritual development. by J.W.N. Sullivan. (Fadiman) 11:67*Ja11'36. B 12289
Before I forget. by Burton Rascoe. (Fadiman) 13:64*My29 '37. B 12290
Before the bombardment. by Osbert Sitwell. (Dounce) 2:90 N20 '26. B 12291
Before you're 25. by Kenyon Nicholson. (Brackett) 5:30 Ap 27'29. T 12292
Beggar on horseback. (F. J. S.) 1:14 Je6'25. CC 12293
Beggar on horseback. (Shane) 1:17 Jy18'25. CC 12294
Beggars abroad. by Jim Tully. (Smith) 6:108-109 O4'30. B 12295
Beggars of life. by Jim Tully. (Anon.) 1:26 My9'25. B 12296
The beggar's opera. by John Gay. (Brackett) 4:34 Ap7'28. T 12297
Begin no day. by Wellington Roe. (Fadiman) 14:75*My14'38. B 12298
The beginning of a mortal. by Max Miller. (Fadiman) 9:96 N18'33. B 12299
The beginnings of critical realism in America. by Vernon Louis Parrington. (Coates) 6: 113-14 N22'30. B 12300
The behavior of Mrs. Crane. by Harry Segall. (Brackett) 4:33-4 Mr31'28. T 12301
Behind red lights. by Samuel Shipman. (Benchley) 12:28*Ja 23'37. T 12302
Behind the ballots. by James Farley. (Fadiman) 14:105*D3 '38. B 12303
Behind the curtains of the Broadway Beauty Trust. by Will A. Page. (Boyd) 2:84 F12 '27. B 12304
Behind the doctor. by Logan Clendening. (Fadiman) 9:83 O14'33. B 12305
Behind the front. (Shane) 2:54 F 20'26. CC 12306
Behind the German lines. (Mosher) 4:125 D8'28. CC 12307
Behind the green lights. by Cornelius W. Willemse. (Coates) 6:78-80 F14'31. B 12308
Behind your front. by James Oppenheim. (Leonard) 4:110-11 N17'28. B 12309
Behold, the bridegroom. by George Kelly. (Brackett) 3:25 Ja7'28. T 12310
Behold, this dreamer. by Walter de la Mare. (Fadiman) 15:65* S9'39. B 12311
Behold this dreamer. by Fulton Oursler and Aubrey Kennedy. (Brackett) 3:32 N12'27. T 12312
Bella. by Jean Giraudoux. (Boyd) 3:89 Je4'27. B 12313
Bella-vista. by Sidonie Gabrielle Colette. (Flanner) 13:45*Ja29 '38. B 12314
The Bellamy trial. by Frances Noyes Hart and Frank E. Carstarphen. (Benchley) 7:24 My2 '31. T 12315
The bells of Basel. by Louis Aragon and Haakon M. Chevalier, trans. (Fadiman) 12:71-2*S26'36. B 12316
The beloved brat. (Maloney) 14: 66-7*My7'38. CC 12317
Beloved enemy. (Mosher) 12:50* Ja2'37. CC 12318
The beloved rogue. (Claxton) 3: 81-2 Mr19'27. CC 12319
Below the line. (Shane) 1:20 S26 '25. CC 12320
Below the sea. (Mosher) 9:61 Je 10'33. CC 12321
The belt. by Paul Sifton. (Brackett) 3:29 O29'27. T 12322
Ben-Hur. (Shane) 1:30 Ja9'26. CC 12323
Benjamin Franklin. by Carl Van Doren. (Fadiman) 14:67-8*O8 '38. B 12324
Benjamin Franklin: the first civilized American. by Phillips Russell. (Boyd) 2:95 D18'26. B 12325
Berkeley Square. by John L. Balderston. (Benchley) 5:34-5 N16

'29. T 12326
Berkeley Square. (Mosher) 9:74-5 S23'33. CC 12327
Berlin. by Valentine Williams and Alice Crawford. (Benchley) 7:26-8 Ja9'32. T 12328
Bernard Quesnay. by André Maurois. (Boyd) 3:113 Ap30 '27. B 12329
Bernard Shaw. by Frank Harris. (Coates) 7:101-102 D12'31. B 12330
Bernard Shaw, Frank Harris, and Oscar Wilde. by Robert Harborough Sherard. (Anon.) 12:66*Ja23'37. B 12331
The best butter. by Elinor Rice. (Fadiman)14:61*F19'38. B 12332
Best man wins. (Mosher) 10:58* Ja12'35. CC 12333
The best plays of 1925-1926. by Burns Mantle. (Boyd) 2:116 D11'26. B 12334
Best sellers. by Dorothy Bennett. (Benchley) 9:26 My13'33. T 12335
The best short stories of 1927. by Edward O'Brien, ed. (Parker) 3:110-11 D17'27. B 12336
Best years. by Raymond Van Sickle. (White) 8:30 S17'32. T 12337
Betrayal. (Mosher) 5:96 My11'29. CC 12338
Betrayal. (Mosher) 15:57*S30'39. CC 12339
The better 'ole. (Claxton) 2:41 O 16'26. CC 12340
Better think twice about it. by Luigi Pirandello. (Fadiman) 10:64-5*Ja12'35. B 12341
Betty, be careful. by Willis Maxwell Goodhue. (Benchley) 7:30 My9'31. T 12342
Between the devil. by Howard Dietz and Arthur Schwartz. (Benchley) 13:28*Ja1'38. T 12343
Between two worlds. by Elmer Rice. (Benchley) 10:30-2 N3 '34. T 12344
Beverly of Graustark. (Shane) 2:51 Ap24'26. CC 12345
Beware of pity. by Stefan Zweig. (Anon.) 15:69*Mr18'39. B 12346
Beyond Bengal. (Mosher) 10:89 My26'34. CC 12347
Beyond evil. by David Thorne. (Brackett) 2:31 Je19'26. T 12348
Beyond sing the woods. by Trygve Gulbranssen. (Fadiman) 12:67-8*My2'36. B 12349
Beyond the Bund. by Philip Kerby. (Hoyt) 3:107 N26'27. B 12350
Beyond the horizon. by Eugene O'Neill. (Brackett) 2:44 D11'26. T 12351
Beyond the street. by Edgar Calmer. (Fadiman) 10:70 Mr31'34. B 12352
Beyond the wall. (Claxton) 2:75-6 F5'27. CC 12353
The Bible: designed to be read as living literature. by Ernest Sutherland Bates, ed. (Anon.) 12:85*O17'36. B 12354
Big blow. by Theodore Pratt. (Anon.) 12:82*S12'36. B 12355
The big blow. by Theodore Pratt. (Gibbs) 14:26-8*O8'38. T 12356
The big broadcast of 1938. (Mosher) 14:56*Mr12'38. 12357
Big business. by A. S. M. Hutchinson. (Coates) 8:43 Ag13'32. B 12358
Big business girl. (Mosher) 7:55* Je20'31. CC 12359
The big city. (Claxton) 4:83-4 Mr 31'28. CC 12360
Big city. (Mosher) 13:65*S25'37. CC 12361
The big drive. (Mosher) 8:48 Ja 28'33. CC 12362
The big fight. by Milton Herbert Gropper and Max Marcin. (Brackett) 4:31-2 S29'28. T 12363
Big hearted Herbert. by Sophie Kerr and Anna Steese Richardson. (Benchley) 9:25 Ja13'34. T 12364
The big house. (Mosher) 6:50 Jy5 '30. CC 12365
The big killing. (Claxton) 4:70 Jy 14'28. CC 12366
Big lake. by Lynn Riggs. (Brackett) 3:33 Ap23'27. T 12367
The big money. by John Dos Pas-

sos. (Fadiman) 12:52-3*Ag8 '36. B 12368

Big night. by Dawn Powell. (Benchley) 8:24-6 Ja28'33. T 12369

The big noise. (Claxton) 4:94 My 12'28. CC 12370

The big parade. (Shane) 1:26 N28 '25. CC 12371

The big pond. by George Middleton and A. E. Thomas. (White) 4:36-41 S1'28. T 12372

The big shot. by John McGowan. (Benchley) 5:41 S28'29. T 12373

Big show. by Charles Cooke. (Fadiman) 14:72-4*S24'38. B 12374

Big time. (Mosher) 5:91 S14'29. CC 12375

The big trail. (Mosher) 6:78 N1 '30. CC 12376

Bill Nye: his own life story. by Edgar Wilson Nye. (Dounce) 2: 92-3 N20'26. B 12377

A bill of divorcement. (Mosher) 8:61-2 O8'32. CC 12378

Billie. by George M. Cohan. (Brackett) 4:33 O13'28. T 12379

Billy draws a horse. by Lesley Storm. (Benchley) 15:26*D30 '39. T 12380

Bill Rose's crazy quilt. by Billy Rose. (Benchley) 7:26-8 My30 '31. T 12381

Billy the kid. (Mosher) 6:93 O25 '30. CC 12382

Biography. by S. N. Behrman. (Benchley) 8:24-6 D24'32. T 12383

Biography of a bachelor girl. (Maloney) 11:61*Mr9'35. CC 12384

The biography of President von Hindenburg. by Rudolph Weterstetten and A. M. K. Watson. (Smith) 6:104 My24'30. B 12385

Bird in hand. by John Drinkwater. (Brackett) 5:30 Ap13'29. T 12386
(Benchley) 6:28 Ap19'30. T 12387

Bird life at the Pole. by Wolcott Gibbs. (Coates) 7:89 Mr7'31. B 12388

Bird of paradise. (Gibbs) 8:52-3 S24'32. CC 12389

Birthday. by Aimée Stuart and Philip Stuart. (Benchley) 10: 34†Ja5'35. T 12390

Birthright. by Richard Maibaum. (Benchley) 9:30-2 D2'33. T 12391

The Bishop misbehaves. by Frederick Jackson. (Benchley) 11: 28*Mr2'35. T 12392

The Bishop's wife. by Robert Nathan. (Leonard) 4:104-105 S15'28. B 12393

Bison of clay. by Max Begouën. (Boyd) 2:80-1 Ja29'27. 12394

Bitter Creek. by James Boyd. (Anon.) 15:69-70*Mr25'39. B 12395

Bitter oleander. by Federico Garcia Lorca. (Benchley) 11: 28†F23'35. T 12396

Bitter sweet. by Noel Coward. (Benchley) 5:34 N16'29. T 12397

The bitter tea of General Yen. (Mosher) 8:47 Ja21'33. CC 12398

Bitter victory. by Louis Guilloux. (Fadiman) 12:114*N14'36. B 12399

Bitter waters. by Heinrich Hauser. (Smith) 6:99 F22'30. B 12400

The black bird. (Shane) 1:35 F6 '26. CC 12401

Black boy. by Jim Tully and Jack Dazy. (Brackett) 2:33 O16'26. T 12402

The black crook. by Charles M. Barras. (Brackett) 5:27-8 Mr 23'29. T 12403

Black cyclone. (Anon.) 1:31 My30 '25. CC 12404

Black Fury. (Mosher) 11:72*Ap20 '35. CC 12405

Black God. by D. Manners-Sutton. (Fadiman) 10:101-102 S8'34. B 12406

Black is my true love's hair. by Elizabeth Madox Roberts. (Fadiman) 14:69-70*O15'38. B 12407

Black legion. (Mosher) 12:61*Ja23 '37. CC 12408

Black limelight. by Gordon Sherry. (Benchley) 12:28*N21'36. T 12409

Black Manhattan. by James Weldon Johnson. (Smith) 6:70-1 Jy 12'30. B 12410

Black mischief. by Evelyn Waugh. (Coates) 8:63 O1'32. B 12411

Black monastery. by Aladar Kuncz.

(Fadiman) 10:110-12 S15'34. B 12412
The black mountain. by Alan Hillgarth. (Fadiman) 9:84-6 Ja13'34. B 12413
Black narcissus. by Rumer Godden. (Fadiman) 15:59*Jy15'39. B 12414
The black pirate. (Shane) 2:51 Mr20'26. CC 12415
Black pit. by Albert Maltz. (Gibbs) 11:28*Mr30'35. T 12416
Black roses. Francis Brett Young. (Smith) 5:123 O12'29. B 12417
Black stream. by Nathalie Colby. (Parker) 3:94-5 O8'27. B 12418
Black valley. by Raymond Weaver. (Dounce) 1:27 Ja23'26. B 12419
The black watch. (Mosher) 5:75 Je1'29. CC 12420
Black widow. by Samuel John Park. (Benchley) 12:28*F22 '36. T 12421
Blackbirds. by Lew Leslie. (Benchley) 6:25-6 N1'30. T 12422
Blackbirds of 1926. by Lew Leslie. (Gabriel) 2:28 Ap17'26. T 12423
Blackbirds of 1928. by Dorothy Fields and Jimmy McHugh. (Brackett) 4:34 My19'28. T 12424
The blacker the berry. by Wallace Thurman. (Lowrie) 5:84 Mr9'29. B 12425
Blackmail. (Mosher) 15:58*S23 '39. CC 12426
Bless you, Sister. by John Meehan and Robert Riskin. (Brackett) 3:26 Ja7'28. T 12427
Blessed event. (Mosher) 8:54-5 S10'32. CC 12428
Blessed event. Manuel Seff and Forrest Wilson. (Benchley) 8: 32*F20'32. T 12429
Blind alley. (Mosher) 15:73*Je3 '39. CC 12430
Blind alley. by James Warwick. (Gibbs) 11:38*O5'35. T 12431
Blind alleys. (Claxton) 3:78 Mr5 '27. CC 12432
Blockade. (Mosher) 14:53*Je18 '38. CC 12433
The blonde captive. (Mosher) 8: 63*Mr5'32. CC 12434
Blonde or brunette. (Claxton) 2:61 Ja15'27. CC 12435
Blonde Venus. (Gibbs) 8:54-5 O1 '32. CC 12436
Blood money. by George Middleton. (Long) 3:55 S3'27. T 12437
Blood on the moon. by Jim Tully. (Coates) 7:76*My23'31. B 12438
The blood ship. (Claxton) 3:34 Jy 30'27. CC 12439
Bloodstream. by Frederick Schlick. (Benchley) 8:26-7*Ap9 '32. T 12440
Bloody laughter. by Ernst Toller. (White) 7:34 D12'31. T 12441
Blow ye winds. by Valentine Davies. (Gibbs) 13:28-30*O2 '37. T 12442
The blue angel. (Gibbs) 6:109 D13 '30. CC 12443
The blue angel. (Mosher) 6:79 D 20'30. CC 12444
The blue bird. (Mosher) 15:49*Ja 27'40. CC 12445
The blue Danube. (Claxton) 4:87 My5'28. CC 12446
The blue eagle from egg to earth. by Hugh S. Johnson. (Anon.) 11:75*Mr30'35. B 12447
The blue ghost. by Bernard J. McOwen and J. P. Riewerts. (Brackett) 6:30-2 Mr22'30. T 12448
The blue light. (Mosher) 10:85-6 My19'34. CC 12449
Blue Monday. by Benson Inge. (Benchley) 8:24-6 Je11'32. T 12450
The blue peter. by E. Temple Thurston. (Anon.) 1:13-14 Ap4 '25. T 12451
Blue voyage. by Conrad Aiken. (Boyd) 3:62-3 Ag27'27. B 12452
The blue widow. by Marianne Brown Waters. (Gibbs) 9:26 S9 '33. T 12453
Bluebeard's eighth wife. (Mosher) 14:60*Mr26'38. CC 12454
Bluebeard's seven wives. (Shane) 1:31 Ja9'26. CC 12455

Blushing brides. (Gibbs) 6:56 Ag 9'30. CC 12456
Body and soul. (Mosher) 7:75-7 Mr21'31. CC 12457
The boiling point. by H. R. Knickerbocker. (Fadiman) 10:100-102 My26'34. B 12458
Bolivar: the passionate warrior. by Thomas R. Ybarra. (Gannett) 5:104-105 N30'29. B 12459
Bombay Mail. (Mosher) 9:79 Ja13 '34. CC 12460
Bombshell. (Mosher) 9:65-6 O28 '33. CC 12461
The bon vivant's companion, or how to mix drinks. by Jerry Thomas. (Leonard) 4:95 O27 '28. B 12462
Bondage. (Mosher) 9:56-7 Ap29 '33. CC 12463
Boojum. by Charles Wertenbaker. (Markey) 4:99-100 My5'28. B 12464
The book of Catherine Wells. by Catherine Wells. (Leonard) 4: 73 S1'28. B 12465
The book of charm. by John Kirkpatrick. (Mankiewicz) 1:21 S12'25. T 12466
The book of gallant vagabonds. by Henry Beston Sheahan. (Dounce) 1:44 Ja30'26. B 12467
A book of hours. by Donald Culross Peattie. (Fadiman) 13:75-7*Ap17'37. B 12468
The book of inns. by Thomas Burke. (Hoyt) 3:61 D24'27. B 12469
The book of living verse. by Louis Untermeyer, ed. (Bogan) 7:62 F13'32. B 12470
A book of miracles. by Ben Hecht. (Fadiman) 15:77-8*Je17 '39. B 12471
A book of other wines than French. by P. Morton Shand. (Smith) 5:59 Ag24'29. B 12472
The book of Talbot. by Violet Clifton. (Fadiman) 9:81-2 S23 '33. B 12473
Boom boom. by Fanny Todd Mitchell. (Brackett) 4:23 F9 '29. T 12474
The border legion. (Mosher) 6:50 Jy5'30. CC 12475
Bordertown. (Mosher) 10:57*F2 '35. CC 12476
Borgia. by Zona Gale. (Smith) 5:120 N2'29. B 12477
Born reckless. (Mosher) 6:79 Je 14'30. CC 12478
Born to be. by Taylor Gordon. (Smith) 5:120-2 O26'29. B 12479
Born to be bad. (Mosher) 10:84 Je9'34. CC 12480
Born to dance. (Mosher) 12:97* D12'36. CC 12481
Borrowed love. by Bide Dudley. (Brackett) 5:46-8 Je29'29. T 12482
Borrowed reputations. by J. Wesley Putnam. (Leonard) 4:63 Ag 25'28. B 12483
The Borzoi, 1925. by Knopf, publ. (Dounce) 1:44 Ja30'26.B 12484
"Boss" Tweed. by Denis Lynch. (Hoyt) 3:117-18 N19'27. B 12485
Boswell's journal of a tour to the Hebrides with Samuel Johnson, LL. D. by Frederick A. Pottle, ed. and Charles A. Bennett, ed. (Anon.) 12:81*N7'36. B 12486
Both your houses. by Maxwell Anderson. (Benchley) 9:26 Mr18 '33. T 12487
Bottled. by Anne Collins and Alice Timoney. (Brackett) 4:30 Ap28 '28. T 12488
Bottom dogs. by Edward Dahlberg. (Smith) 6:101-102 Mr29'30. B 12489
Bottomland. by Clarence Williams. (Wright) 3:40-1 Jy9'27. T 12490
Bought. (Mosher) 7:44 Ag22'31. CC 12491
Boundary against night. by Edmund Gilligan. (Fadiman) 13: 51-2*Ja29'38. B 12492
Bouquet. by G. B. Stern. (Boyd) 3:55 Jy30'27. B 12493
Bow down to wood and stone. by Josephine Lawrence. (Fadiman) 13:57*F5'38. B 12494
Boy meets girl. (Mosher) 14:44* S3'38. CC 12495
Boy meets girl. by Samuel Spe-

wack and Bella Spewack.
(Benchley) 11:44*D7'35.T 12496
(Fadiman) 11:53-4*F1'36. 12497
Boy of the streets. (Mosher) 13:56*Ja22'38. CC 12498
Boy slaves. (Mosher) 14:70*F11'39. CC 12499
The boys from Syracuse. by George Abbott; Richard Rodgers and Lorenz Hart. (Benchley) 14:36-8*D3'38. T 12500
Boys town. (Mosher) 14:59*S10'38. CC 12501
Brain guy. by Benjamin Appel. (Fadiman) 10:57-8 Jy28'34. B 12502
Brain sweat. by John Charles Brownell. (Benchley) 10:34 Ap14'34. T 12503
The Brandons. by Angela Thirkell. (Fadiman) 15:58*Jy1'39.B 12504
Brass ankle. by Du Bose Heyward. (Benchley) 7:24 My2'31. T 12505
A brass hat in no man's land. by F. P. Crozier. (Smith) 6:63 Ag16'30. B 12506
Brave new world. by Aldous Huxley. (Coates) 8:52-3*F27'32. B 12507
Brawnyman. by James Stevens. (Dounce) 2:53-5 Je19'26.B 12508
Brazilian adventure. by Peter Fleming. (Fadiman) 9:85-6 Ja6'34. B 12509
Bread and circuses. by W. E. Woodward. (Dounce) 1:17 D5'25. B 12510
Bread and fire. by Charles R. Walker. (Boyd) 3:88-9 Je4'27. B 12511
Bread and wine. by Ignazio Silone. (Fadiman)13:73-5*Ap3'37.B 12512
The breadwinner. by W. Somerset Maugham. (Benchley) 7:34 O3'31. T 12513
Break o' day. by Con O'Leary. (Boyd) 3:107-108 Ap16'27.B 12514
Break of hearts. (Mosher) 11:69-70*My25'35. CC 12515
Break the heart's anger. by Paul Engle. (Bogan) 12:80*My23'36. B 12516
The breaks. by J. C. Nugent and Elliott Nugent. (Brackett) 4:29 Ap28'28. T 12517
Breathe upon these slain. by Evelyn Scott. (Fadiman) 10:100 My26'34. B 12518
The breathless moment. by Philip Van Doren Stern and Herbert Asbury. (Fadiman) 10:65-6*Ja26'35. B 12519
Bridal wise. by Albert Hackett and Frances Goodrich. (Benchley) 8:24 Je11'32. T 12520
Bride of the lamb. by William Hurlburt. (Gabriel) 2:25 Ap10'26. T 12521
Bride of the regiment. (Brackett) 6:73-4 My31'30. CC 12522
The bride of Torozko. by Ruth Langner. (Gibbs) 10:32 S22'34. T 12523
The bride walks out. (Mosher) 12:45*Jy18'36. CC 12524
The bride wore red. (Mosher) 13:73*O16'37. CC 12525
The bridegroom cometh. by Waldo Frank. (Fadiman) 15:78-9*My20'39. B 12526
The bridge of San Luis Rey. (Mosher) 5:55-6 My25'29. CC 12527
The bridge of San Luis Rey. by Thornton Wilder. (Hoyt) 3:124-5 D3'27. B 12528
Brief candles. by Aldous Huxley. (Smith) 6:115 My17'30.B 12529
Brief moment. by S. N. Behrman. (Benchley) 7:28 N21'31. T 12530
Bright eyes. (Mosher) 10:49-50*D29'34. CC 12531
Bright honor. by Henry R. Misrock. (Gibbs) 12:28*O3'36. T 12532
Bright intervals. by Nancy Hoyt. (Smith) 5:65 Ag31'29. B 12533
The bright land. by Janet Ayer Fairbank. (Coates) 8:43-4 D31'32. B 12534
Bright rebel. by Stanley Young. (Benchley) 14:26-8*Ja7'39. T 12535
Bright skin. by Julia Peterkin. (Coates) 8:64*Ap16'32.B 12536

Bright star. by Philip Barry. (Benchley) 11:32*O26'35.T 12537
Brighton rock. by Graham Greene. (Kronenberger) 14: 56*Je25'38. B 12538
Bring! bring! by Conrad Aiken. (Anon.) 1:26 My16'25. B 12539
Bring 'em back alive. (Mosher) 8:49 Je25'32. CC 12540
Bringing up baby. (Mosher) 14:47-8*Mr5'38. CC 12541
Bringing up Father. by Nat Leroy. (Anon.) 1:13-14 Ap11'25. T 12542
British agent. (Mc Kelway) 10:56 S29'34. CC 12543
Brittle heaven. by Vincent York and Frederick J. Pohl. (Benchley) 10:28†N24'34. T 12544
Broadway. (Mosher) 5:97 Je8'29. CC 12545
Broadway. by Philip Dunning and George Abbott. (Brackett) 2:30 S25'26. T 12546
The Broadway melody. (Mosher) 4:83 F16'29. CC 12547
Broadway melody. (Mosher) 11: 63-4*S28'35. CC 12548
Broadway racketeers. by John O'Connor. (Leonard) 4:107-108 N24'28. B 12549
Broadway scandal. (Mosher) 5: 112-13 N9'29. CC 12550
Broadway to Hollywood. (Mosher) 9:70 S9'33. CC 12551
Broken blossoms. (Mosher) 12: 63*Ja23'37. CC 12552
Broken dishes. by Martin Flavin. (Benchley) 5:35 N16'29. T 12553
Broken necks. by Ben Hecht. (Boyd) 2:108 D4'26. B 12554
Bronx ballads. by Robert A. Simon. (Boyd) 3:88-9 Je18'27. B 12555
A brood of ducklings. by Frank Swinnerton. (Leonard) 4:111 N 17'28. B 12556
Brook Evans. by Susan Glaspell. (Leonard) 4:60 Jy7'28. B 12557
Broomsticks, amen! by Elmer Greensfelder. (Benchley) 10:28 F17'34. T 12558
Brother rat. (Mosher) 15:49*Ja27 '40. CC 12559
Brother rat. by John Monks, Jr. and Fred F. Finklehoffe. (Benchley) 12:26-8*D26'36. T 12560
Brothers. by Herbert Ashton, Jr. (Brackett) 4:26 Ja12'29.T 12561
The brothers Ashkenazi. by I. J. Singer. (Fadiman) 12:80*S12'36. B 12562
Brothers in the West. by Robert Raynolds. (Coates) 7:60 S5'31. B 12563
The brothers Karamazov. by Jacques Copeau and Jean Croué. (Brackett) 2:25 Ja15 '27. T 12564
The brothers Karamazov. (Mosher) 7:73 S26'31. CC 12565
Brown buddies. by Carl Rickman. (Benchley) 6:36 O18'30. T 12566
The brown Danube. by Burnet Hershey. (Gibbs) 15:50*My27 '39. T 12567
The brown decades. by Lewis Mumford. (Coates) 7:91-2 O10 '31. B 12568
The brown derby. (Shane) 2:37 Je 19'26. CC 12569
Brown of Harvard. (Shane) 2:52-3 My8'26. CC 12570
Brown women and white. by Andrew A. Freeman. (Coates) 8:60*Ap2'32. B 12571
Bryan. by M. R. Werner. (Lowrie) 5:88-9 My4'29. B 12572
Bryan, the great commoner. by J. C. Long. (Leonard) 4:61 Jy7 '28. B 12573
The buccaneer. by Maxwell Anderson and Laurence Stallings. (Mankiewicz) 1:17 O10'25. T 12574
The buccaneer. (Mosher) 14:53*F 26'38. CC 12575
The buck in the snow. by Edna St. Vincent Millay. (Leonard) 4:116 O13'28. B 12576
Bula matari. by Jacob Wassermann. (Coates) 8:59 Ja14'33. B 12577
Bulldog Drummond. (Mosher) 5:96-7 My11'29. CC 12578

Bulldog Drummond strikes back. (Mosher) 10:44 Ag25'34. CC 12579
Bullets or ballots. (Mosher) 12: 58-9*My30'36. CC 12580
The bullfighters. by Henry de Montherlant. (Hoyt) 3:118-19 N19'27. B 12581
Bulls, bears, and asses. by Milton Herbert Gropper. (Benchley) 8:26*My14'32. T 12582
The Bulpington of Blup. by H. G. Wells. (Coates) 8:54-5 Ja21 '33. B 12583
Bunk of 1926. by Gene Lockhart and Percy Waxman. (Gabriel) 2:23 My22'26. T 12584
Burlesque. George Manker Watters and Arthur Hopkins. (Long) 3:71-2 S10'27. T 12585
The burning bush. by Sigrid Undset and Arthur G. Chater, trans. (Coates) 8:66-7 S10'32. B 12586
Burning city. by Stephen Vincent Benét. (Bogan) 12:60-1*Je20 '36. B 12587
The burning fountain. by Eleanor Carroll Chilton. (Lowrie) 5:105 Ap13'29. B 12588
Burning up. (Mosher) 5:83-4 F15 '30. CC 12589
Bury the dead. by Irwin Shaw. (Gibbs) 12:26*Ap25'36. T 12590
Burton. by Fairfax Downey. (Coates) 7:95-6 Ap25'31. B 12591
But beauty vanishes. by Richard Blaker. (Anon.) 12:74*O10'36. B 12592
But for the grace of God. by Leopold Atlas. (Benchley) 12: 28*Ja23'37. T 12593
But--gentlemen marry brunettes. by Anita Loos. (Markey) 4:86 Je9'28. B 12594
But it still goes on. by Robert Graves. (Coates) 6:78 F14'31. B 12595
The butter and egg man. by George S. Kaufman. (Mankiewicz) 1:19 O3'25. T 12596
Butterfield 8. by John O'Hara. (Fadiman) 11:77-8*O19'35. B 12597
Button, button. by Maurice Clark. (Benchley) 5:38 N2'29. T 12598
Button Hill. by Gordon Stowell. (Smith) 6:69-70 Je28'30. B 12599
Buy, buy, baby. by Russell Medcraft and Norma Mitchell. (Brackett) 2:34 O16'26. T 12600
The buzzard. by Courtenay Savage. (Brackett) 4:30 Mr24'28. T 12601
By request. by J. C. Nugent and Elliott Nugent. (Brackett) 4:33 O6'28. T 12602
By the way. by Ronald Jeans and Harold Simpson. (Mankiewicz) 1:19 Ja9'26. T 12603
By your leave. by Gladys Hurlbut and Emma Wells. (Benchley) 9:30-2 F3'34. T 12604
Bye bye Bonnie. by Bide Dudley and Louis Simon. (Brackett) 2:36 Ja29'27. T 12605
Byrd at the South Pole. (Mosher) 6:43-4 Je28'30. CC 12606
Byron. by André Maurois. (Smith) 6:101 Mr29'30. B 12607
Bystander. by Maxim Gorki. (Smith) 6:120 Ap12'30. B 12608

C

Cabaret. (Claxton) 3:85 My7'27. CC 12609
The cabinet of Dr. Caligari. (Claxton) 2:77 N6'26. CC 12610
Caesar and Cleopatra. by George Bernard Shaw. (Anon.) 1:11 My 2'25. T 12611
Café: a play of the boulevards. by Marya Mannes. (Benchley) 6:28 S6'30. T 12612
Cafe society. (Mosher) 15:58*F25 '39. CC 12613
Cakes and ale. by W. Somerset Maugham. (Smith) 6:98 O11'30. B 12614
Calamity Jane and the Lady Wildcats. by Duncan Aikman. (Hoyt) 3:60-1 D24'27. B 12615
Caleb Catlum's America. by Vincent McHugh. (Fadiman) 12:62-4*O24'36. B 12616
The caliph of Bagdad. by Robert Hobart Davis and Arthur B. Maurice. (Coates) 7:74*Je13

'31. B 12617
Call her savage. (Mosher) 8:84 D3'32. CC 12618
Call it a day. by Dodie Smith. (Benchley) 11:28*F8'36. T 12619
The call of life. by Arthur Schnitzler. (Mankiewicz) 1:19 O17'25. T 12620
The call of the wild. (Mosher) 11:46*Ag24'35. CC 12621
Calling all stars. by Lew Brown. (Benchley) 10:30*D29'34. T 12622
Calling Western Union. by Genevieve Taggard. (Bogan) 12:67* O3'36. B 12623
Cambric tea. by Rebecca Lowrie. (Markey) 4:99-100 Ap14'28. B 12624
The camel through the needle's eye. by Frantisek Langer. (Brackett) 5:29 Ap27'29. T 12625
Camille. (Claxton) 3:99 Ap30'27. CC 12626
Camille. (Mosher) 12:49-51*Ja16 '37. CC 12627
Canaries sometimes sing. by Frederick Lonsdale. (Benchley) 6:25 N1'30. T 12628
The canary murder case. (Mosher) 5:95 Mr16'29. CC 12629
Candelabra. by John Galsworthy. (Coates) 9:62 Mr4'33. B 12630
Candida. by George Bernard Shaw. (Benchley) 13:36*Mr20 '37. T 12631
Candle-light. by P. G. Wodehouse. (Benchley) 5:36-8 O12'29. T 12632
Canfield. by Alexander Gardiner. (Smith) 6:80 Mr1'30. B 12633
Cantos. by Ezra Pound. (Bogan) 8:39 Jy30'32; 9:47-8 Jy15'33. B 12634
Cape smoke. by Walter Frost. (Parker) 1:13 F28'25. T 12635
Capital city. by Mari Sandoz. (Fadiman) 15:94-6*D2'39. B 12636
Caponsacchi. by Arthur Goodrich and Rose A. Palmer. (Brackett) 2:33-4 N6'26. T 12637
Caprice. by Geza Silberer and Philip Moeller, trans. (Brackett) 4:42 Ja12'29. T 12638
Captain Fury. (Mosher) 15:81*My 27'39. CC 12639
Captain Horatio Hornblower. by C. S. Forester. (Fadiman) 15: 96-7*Ap29'39. B 12640
Captain of the guard. (Mosher) 6: 99 Ap5'30. CC 12641
Captain Salvation. (Claxton) 3:61 Jy2'27. CC 12642
Captains Courageous. (Mosher) 13:85*My15'37. CC 12643
Captains outrageous. by Gill Clark. (Fadiman) 14:62-3*My 28'38. B 12644
The captive. by Edouard Bourdet and Arthur Hornblow, Jr. (Brackett) 2:33 O9'26. T 12645
The captive of the Sahara. by E. M. Hull. (Coates) 7:46*Ag1'31. B 12646
Caravan. (McKelway) 10:87-8 O6 '34. CC 12647
Caravan. by John Galsworthy. (Dounce) 1:17 Ag8'25. B 12648
Caravan. by Clifford Pember and Ralph Cullinan. (White) 4:26 S8'28. T 12649
The Cardinal's mistress. by Benito Mussolini. (Parker) 4: 100-102 S15'28. B 12650
Career. by Phillip D. Stong. (Fadiman) 11:57*Ja18'36. B 12651
The careless age. (Gibbs) 5:79 S28'29. CC 12652
Caribbean treasure. by Ivan T. Sanderson. (Fadiman) 15:71-3* N11'39. B 12653
Carl Akeley's Africa. by Mary L. Jobe Akeley. (Smith) 5:84 D21 '29. B 12654
Carmen. (Claxton) 4:83 My19'28. CC 12655
Carnival. by William R. Doyle. (Brackett) 5:29 My4'29. T 12656
The Carolinian. by Rafael Sabatini. (Anon.) 1:26 My2'25. B 12657
Carry Nation. by Herbert Asbury. (Smith) 5:124-5 O12'29. B 12658
Carry Nation. by Frank McGrath. (Benchley) 8:22 N12'32. T 12659
Casanova, his known and unknown life. by S. Guy Endore. (Gannett) 5:105-106 N30'29. B 12660
The case against Mrs. Ames.

(Mosher) 12:62*Je6'36. CC 12661

The case for India. by Will Durant. (Coates) 6:91 N29'30. B 12662

Case of Clyde Griffiths. by Erwin Piscator and Lena Goldschmidt. (Benchley) 12:24-5* Mr21'36. T 12663

The case of Lena Smith. (Mosher) 4:70-1 Ja19'29. CC 12664

The case of Mr. Crump. by Ludwig Lewisohn. (Flanner) 2:40-1 Ja22'27. B 12665

The case of Sergeant Grischa. (Mosher) 6:93-5 Mr15'30. CC 12666

The case of Sergeant Grischa. by Arnold Zweig. (Lowrie) 4:67 D22'28. B 12667

The case of the curious bride. (Mosher) 11:64*Ap13'35. CC 12668

Casey at the bat. (Claxton) 3:103 Ap9'27. CC 12669

Casey Jones. by Robert Ardrey. (Benchley) 14:30-1*F26'38. T 12670

Cast down the laurel. by Arnold Gingrich. (Fadiman) 11:72-4* F16'35. B 12671

Castaway. by James Gould Cozzens. (Fadiman) 10:86-7*N17 '34. B 12672

Caste. by Cosmo Hamilton. (Parker) 3:86-8 O1'27. B 12673

The castle. by Franz Kafka. (Smith) 6:95-6 S20'30. B 12674

Castle Island. by R. H. Mottram. (Coates) 7:58*Jy25'31. B 12675

Castles in the air. by Raymond W. Peck and Percy Wenrich. (Brackett) 2:31 S18'26. T 12676

The casuarina tree. by W. Somerset Maugham. (Dounce) 2:88 O2'26. B 12677

The cat and the canary. (Claxton) 3:77-9 S17'27. CC 12678

The cat and the canary. (Mosher) 15:71*N25'39. CC 12679

The cat and the fiddle. by Jerome Kern and Otto Harbach. (Benchley) 7:28-30 O24'31. T 12680

The cat creeps. (Mosher) 6:85-7 N15'30. CC 12681

Catalogue. by George Milburn. (Fadiman) 12:80-1*S12'36. B 12682

Catherine de' Medici and the los revolution. by Ralph Roeder. (Fadiman) 12:71-4*Ja9'37. B 12683

Catherine-Paris. by Marthe Bibesco. (Markey) 4:106-107 26'28. B 12684

Catherine: the portrait of an empress. by Gina Kaus. (Fadim 11:62*Je1'35. B 12685

Cat's cradle. by Maurice Baring (Dounce) 2:51-2 Mr13'26. B 12686

Cats in the Isle of Man. by Dais Fellowes. (Smith) 5:104 N30'2 B 12687

The cat's paw. (Mosher) 10:42 A 25'34. CC 12688

Cavalcade. (Mosher) 8:52 Ja14'3 CC 12689

The cave man. (Shane) 2:37 Mr6 '26. CC 12690

Cavender's house. by Edwin Arlington Robinson. (Lowrie) 5: 115-16 My18'29. B 12691

Caviar. by Leo Randole. (Benchley) 10:26 Je16'34. T 12692

Ceiling zero. (Mosher) 11:46*F1 '36. CC 12693

Ceiling zero. by Frank Wead. (Gibbs) 11:28*Ap20'35. T 12694

Celebrity. by Willard Keefe. (Brackett) 3:24 Ja14'28. T 1269

Célestine: being the diary of a chambermaid. by Octave Mirbeau. (Parker) 6:59 Ja31'3 B 12696

The centuries. by Em Jo Bassh (Brackett) 3:34-5 D10'27. T 12697

A century of ocean travel. by Frank C. Bowen. (Coates) 6:5 D27'30. B 12698

Certain people. by Edith Wharto (Smith) 6:113 N8'30. B 12699

A certain young man. (Claxton) 4 76 Je16'28. CC 12700

Chained. (Mosher) 10:87-8 S8'34. CC 12701

Chains: lesser novels and storie

by Theodore Dreiser. (Boyd) 3:88 My28'27. B 12702
Chalk dust. by Harold Clarke and Maxwell Nurnberg. (Benchley) 12:32-4*Mr28'36. T 12703
Chalked out. by Lewis E. Lawes and Jonathan Finn. (Benchley) 13:25*Ap3'37. T 12704
The challenge. (Mosher) 15:63-4* O7'39. CC 12705
Challenge to defeat. by William Harlan Hale. (Coates) 8:76-7 My21'32. B 12706
The champ. (Mosher) 7:78-9 N21 '31. CC 12707
Champagne, sec. by Alan Child and Robert A. Simon. (Gibbs) 9:32-4 O21'33. T 12708
Champagne waltz. (Mosher) 12: 60-1*F13'37. CC 12709
Champs-Elysees. (Mosher) 15:65* Mr4'39. CC 12710
Chances. (Mosher) 7:54*Je20'31. CC 12711
Chances. by Arthur Hamilton Gibbs. (Smith) 6:70 Je28'30. B 12712
Chang. (Claxton) 3:98 Ap30'27. CC 12713
Change of heart. (Mosher) 10:86 My19'34. CC 12714
Change your luck. by Garland Howard. (Benchley) 6:30 Je21'30. T 12715
Changing New York. by Berenice Abbott. (Anon.) 15:71*Ap22'39. B 12716
The channel road. by Alexander Woollcott and George S. Kaufman. (Benchley) 5:42-6 O26'29. T 12717
Chapayev. (Mosher) 11:58*My4 '35. CC 12718
Chariot wheels. by Sylvia Thompson. (Smith) 5:162-4 D7'29. B 12719
Charlemagne, first of the moderns. by Charles Edward Russell. (Smith) 6:92-3 Je7'30. B 12720
Charlot revue, 1926. by Arch Selwyn. (Mankiewicz) 1:18 N21 '25. T 12721
The charmer. (Anon.) 1:31 Ap18 '25. CC 12722
Charming sinners. (Mosher) 5:59 Jy13'29. CC 12723
The charwoman's shadow. by Edward John Dunsany. (Dounce) 2:54 Ag21'26. T 12724
Chauve-souris. by F. Ray Comstock, prod. (Brackett) 3:30 O 22'27; 4:28 F9'29. T 12725
Cheapjack. by Philip Allingham. (Fadiman) 10:99 S8'34. B 12726
Check and double check. (Mosher) 6:101 N8'30. CC 12727
Chee-chee. by Herbert Fields; Richard Rodgers and Lorenz Hart. (Brackett) 4:33 O6'28. T 12728
The cheerful fraud. (Claxton) 2:48 Ja1'27. CC 12729
Chéri. by Sidonie Gabrielle Colette. (Smith) 5:95 S28'29. B 12730
The cherry orchard. by Anton Chekhov. (Benchley) 9:26-7 Mr 25'33. T 12730A
Chevrons. by Leonard Nason. (Dounce) 2:89-90 O2'26. B 12731
Chicago. (Claxton) 3:67 Ja7'28. CC 12732
Chicago. by Maurine Watkins. (Brackett) 2:29 Ja8'27. T 12733
Chicago surrenders. by Edward Dean Sullivan. (Smith) 6:82 N1 '30. B 12734
Chicago: the history of its reputation. by Lloyd Lewis and Henry Justin Smith. (Smith) 5:105 S14 '29. B 12735
Chicken à la king. (Claxton) 4:76 Je16'28. CC 12736
Chickie. (Anon.) 1:31 My9'25. CC 12737
The chief thing. by Nicholas Evreinoff. (Gabriel) 2:27 Ap3 '26. T 12738
Child of Manhattan. by Preston Sturges. (Benchley) 8:28-9*Mr 12'32. T 12739
The childhood of Maxim Gorky. (Mosher) 14:55*O8'38. CC 12740
Children of darkness. by Edwin Justus Mayer. (Benchley) 5:28-30 Ja18'30. T 12741

Children of divorce. by Owen Johnson. (Boyd) 3:105 Ap2'27. B 12742
Children of God. by Vardis Fisher. (Fadiman) 15:53*S2'39. B 12743
The children of Mu. by James Churchward. (Coates) 7:78*My 23'31. B 12744
The children's hour. (Mosher) 12:55-6*Mr28'36. CC 12745
The children's hour. by Lillian Hellman. (Benchley) 10:34-6† D1'34. T 12746
China express. (Mosher) 6:93 Mr 15'30. CC 12747
China seas. (Mosher) 11:41*Ag10 '35. CC 12748
The Chinese are like that. by Carl Crow. (Fadiman) 15:61* S23'39. B 12749
"Chinese" O'Neill. by Cushing Donnell. (Brackett) 5:30 Je1 '29. T 12750
The chip and the block. by E. M. Delafield. (Dounce) 2:58 Mr20 '26. B 12751
Christina Alberta's father. by H. G. Wells. (Dounce) 1:21 O3'25. B 12752
Christina of Sweden. by Margaret Goldsmith. (Fadiman) 9: 52 D30'33. B 12753
Christine and other stories. by Julian Green. (Hellman) 6:103 Mr29'30. B 12754
A Christmas carol. (Mosher) 14: 45-6*D24'38. CC 12755
Christmas Eve. by Gustav Eckstein. (Benchley) 15:28*Ja6'40. T 12756
Christmas holiday. by W. Somerset Maugham. (Fadiman) 15: 75-6*O21'39. B 12757
Christopher Bean. (Mosher) 9:80-1 D2'33. CC 12758
Christopher Strong. (Mosher) 9: 62-3 Mr18'33. CC 12759
A church mouse. by Ladilaus Fodor. (Benchley) 7:28 O24'31. T 12760
The chute. by Albert Halper. (Fadiman) 13:76-7*N6'37. B 12761
Cimarron. by Edna Ferber. (Smith) 6:101 Mr29'30. B 12762
Cimarron. (Mosher) 6:67 F7'31. CC 12763
Cinderella's daughter. by John Erskine. (Smith) 6:112 N22'30. B 12764
Cindy. by Rose Wilder Lane. (Leonard) 4:65-6 Ag18'28. B 12765
The circle. (Shane) 1:19-20 S26 '25. CC 12766
The circle. by W. Somerset Maugham. (Gibbs) 14:28*Ap30 '38. T 12767
The circus. (Claxton) 3:60-1 F18 '28. CC 12768
The circus kid. (Mosher) 4:63-4 D22'28. CC 12769
Circus of Dr. Lao. by Charles G. Finney. (Fadiman) 11:52-4* Jy20'35. BB 12770
Circus parade. by Jim Tully. (Boyd) 3:66-7 Ag13'27. B 12771
The circus princess. by Harry B. Smith; Julius Brammer and Alfred Grunwald. (Brackett) 3:29 My7'27. T 12772
The citadel. (Mosher) 14:57*N5 '38. CC 12773
The citadel. by A. J. Cronin. (Fadiman) 13:71-2*S11'37. B 12774
The citadel of silence. (Mosher) 15:51*Ja6'40. CC 12775
The city. (Mosher) 15:80*My27 '39. CC 12776
The city chap. by Jerome Kern; James Montgomery and Anne Caldwell. (Mankiewicz) 1:20 N 14'25. T 12777
City editor. by Stanley Walker. (Fadiman) 10:118-20 O13'34. B 12778
The city gone wild. (Claxton) 3:103 D17'27. CC 12779
City lights. (Mosher) 7:60-1 F21 '31. CC 12780
City streets. (Mosher) 7:79-81 Ap25'31. CC 12781
Civilization. by Clive Bell. (Leonard) 4:100 O6'28. B 12782
Claire Adams. by Daniel N. Rubi

(Benchley) 5:34 N30'29. T 12783
Claire Ambler. by Booth Tarkington. (Parker) 3:77 Ja28'28. B 12784
Clamoring self. by Leonhard Frank. (Coates) 6:116 N8'30. B 12785
Classified. (Shane) 1:23 N7'25. CC 12786
Claudine at school. by Sidonie Gabrielle Colette. (Smith) 6:96-8 N15'30. B 12787
Claudius the god. by Robert Graves. (Fadiman) 11:87-8*Ap 6'35. B 12788
Clear all wires! (Mosher) 9:57 Mr11'33. CC 12789
Clear all wires. by Samuel Spewack and Bella Spewack. (White) 8:26-8 S24'32. T 12790
Cleopatra. (Mosher) 10:42-4 Ag25 '34. CC 12791
Cleopatra: the story of a queen. by Emil Ludwig. (Fadiman) 13:118-19*D4'37. B 12792
The climax. by Edward Locke. (White) 9:24-6 Je24'33. T 12793
Cloistered. (Mosher) 12:59*My30 '36. CC 12794
The closed garden. by Julian Green. (Markey) 4:95-7 My19 '28. B 12795
Closing hour. by Norah Hoult. (Hellman) 6:103-104 Mr29'30. B 12796
Clothes make the man. (Shane) 1:29-30 D5'25. CC 12797
Cloud cuckoo land. by Naomi Mitchison. (Dounce) 1:44 F13 '26. B 12798
Cloudy with showers. by Floyd Dell and Thomas Mitchell. (Benchley) 7:32-4 S12'31. T 12799
Club de femmes. (Mosher) 13:66-7*O23'37. CC 12800
The clutching claw. by Ralph Thomas Kettering. (Brackett) 4:27-8 F25'28. T 12801
The coast of folly. (Shane) 1:17 S5'25. CC 12802
Cobwebs and cosmos. by Paul Eldridge. (Parker) 7:84 Ap4 '31. B 12803
The cock eyed world. (Mosher) 5:53-4 Ag10'29. CC 12804
Cock robin. by Philip Barry and Elmer Rice. (Brackett) 3:25 Ja 28'28. T 12805
Cocktail hour. (Mosher) 9:61 Je10 '33. CC 12806
Cocoanut Grove. (Mosher) 14:53* Je25'38. CC 12807
The cocoanuts. (Mosher) 5:74-5 Je1'29. CC 12808
The cocoanuts. by George S. Kaufman and Irving Berlin. (Mankiewicz) 1:17-18 D19'25. T 12809
(Brackett) 3:36-8 My28'27. 12810
The cold journey. by Grace Zaring Stone. (Fadiman) 10:112-13 S15'34. B 12811
Collected poems. by Hart Crane. (Bogan) 9:46-7 Jy15'33. B 12812
Collected poems. by T. S. Eliot. (Bogan) 12:78*My23'36. B 12813
Collected poems. by Robert Frost. (Hawthorne) 6:116 N22'30. B 12814
Collected poems. by James Joyce. (Bogan) 13:73*S25'37. B 12815
Collected poems. by Laura Riding. (Bogan) 14:51-2*D24'38. B 12816
Collected poems. by James Stephens. (Boyd) 2:85 Ja8'27. B 12817
Collected poems. by Sara Teasdale. (Bogan) 13:73*S25'37. B 12818
Collected poems. by Elinor Wylie. (Bogan) 8:39-40 Jy30'32. B 12819
Collected poems. by William Butler Yeats. (Bogan) 10:112-13 Ap7'34. B 12820
Collected poems: 1939. by Robert Frost. (Bogan) 15:69-70*Mr4 '39. B 12821
The collected poems of Ezra Pound. by Ezra Pound. (Boyd) 2:82-3 Ja8'27. B 12822
Colleen. (Mosher) 12:63*Mr14'36. CC 12823
College. (Claxton) 3:79-80 S17'27. CC 12824
College holiday. (Mosher) 12:50*

Ja2'37. CC 12825

College sinners. See First episode. T 12826

College swing. (Mosher) 14:53-4* Ap30'38. CC 12827

Collegiate. (Mosher) 11:47*F1'36. CC 12828

Colonel Bob Ingersoll. by Cameron Rogers. (Boyd) 3:118-19 Ap9'27. B 12829

Colonel Lawrence: the man behind the legend. by Liddell Hart. (Fadiman) 10:110-11 Ap7'34. B 12830

The colonel's daughter. by Richard Aldington. (Coates) 7:85 S12'31. B 12831

Come and get it. (Mosher) 12:69-70*N7'36. CC 12832

Come and get it. by Edna Ferber. (Fadiman) 11:65-6*F23'35. B 12833

Come easy. by Felicia Metcalfe. (Gibbs) 9:26 S9'33. T 12834

Come in at the door. by William March. (Fadiman) 10:84 F24 '34. B 12835

Come of age. by Clemence Dane. (Benchley) 9:22 Ja20'34. T 12836

Come to Harlem. by Claude McKay. (Parker) 4:103 Mr17'28. B 12837

Come to my house. (Claxton) 3:65 Ja21'28. CC 12838

Come what may. by Richard F. Flournoy. (Benchley) 10:32 My 26'34. T 12839

The comic. by Lajos Luria. (Brackett) 3:34 Ap30'27. T 12840

The comic artist. by Susan Glaspell and Norman Matson. (Benchley) 9:26-8 Ap29'33. T 12841

The coming forth by day of Osiris Jones. by Conrad Aiken. (Bogan) 7:62-4 F13'32. B 12842

Coming of age in Samoa. by Margaret Mead. (Leonard) 4:72 S1 '28. B 12843

The coming of the Lord. by Sarah Gertrude Millin. (Leonard) 4:99 O6'28. B 12844

The coming victory of democracy. by Thomas Mann. (Fadiman) 14:43-4*Jy2'38. B 12845

The command to love. by Rudol Lothar and Fritz Gottwald. (Brackett) 3:25 O1'27. T 12846

The Commodore marries. by Ka Parsons. (Benchley) 5:34-8 S1 '29. T 12847

Common clay. (Gibbs) 6:55-6 Ag '30. CC 12848

The common sin. by Willard Ma (Brackett) 4:36 O27'28. T 12849

The company. by Edwin Seaver. (Hellman) 6:104 Ap5'30. B 12850

Company's coming. by Alma Wilson. (Benchley) 7:24 My2'31. T 12851

The compleat angler. by Izaak Walton. (Coates) 7:68-9 F21'3 B 12852

Complete novels and plays. by Hector H. Monro. (Fadiman) 9:45 Jy15'33. B 12853

The complete ski-runner. by Arnold Lunn. (Coates) 6:67 Ja10 '31. B 12854

The complete works of François Villon. by François Villon anc J. V. Nicholson, trans. (Leonard) 4:75 Jy14'28. B 12855

The complete works of Thomas Otway. by Thomas Otway and Montague Summers, ed. (Boyc 3:119-20 Ap9'27. B 12856

Compromise. (Shane) 1:23 O31'25 CC 12857

Concert pitch. by Elliot Paul. (Anon.) 14:68*Mr26'38. B 12858

Condemned. (Mosher) 5:103 N16'2 CC 12859

Confession. by Cosmo Hamilton. (Boyd) 2:56 Ja1'27. B 12860

Confessions. by Arthur Symons. (Smith) 6:63 Ag16'30. B 12861

Confessions of a Nazi spy. (Mosher) 15:70-1*My6'39. CC 12862

Confessions of a rum runner. by James Barbican. (Hoyt) 4:104-105 Mr17'28. B 12863

Confessions of an actor. by John Barrymore. (Dounce) 2:50 Jy1 '26. B 12864

Conflict. by Warren F. Lawrence (Brackett) 5:31 Mr16'29. T 12865

Congaï. by Harry Hervey and Carlton Hildreth. (Brackett) 4:38 D15'28. T 12866

Congorilla. (Mosher) 8:36 Jy30 '32. CC 12867

Congratulations. by Morgan Wallace. (Brackett) 5:28 My11'29. T 12868

Congress dances. (Mosher) 8:70-1 My21'32. CC 12869

A Connecticut yankee. (Mosher) 7:83-5 Ap18'31. CC 12870

A Connecticut yankee. by Herbert Fields; Richard Rodgers and Lorenz Hart. (Brackett) 3:33 N12'27. T 12871

The conning tower book. by Franklin P. Adams. (Dounce) 2:48 F27'26. B 12872

Conqueror of the seas. by Stefan Zweig. (Fadiman) 13:57-8*F5 '38. B 12873

The conquerors. (Mosher) 8:58 N26'32. CC 12874

Conquest. (Mosher) 4:83 F16'29. CC 12875

Conquest. (Mosher) 13:74-5*N6 '37. CC 12876

The conquests of Peter the Great. (Mosher) 15:52*S2'39. CC 12877

Conquistador. by Archibald MacLeish. (Bogan) 8:39 Jy30'32. B 12878

The Constant nymph. (Mosher) 10:96 Ap14'34. 12879

The constant nymph. by Margaret Kennedy. (Dounce) 1:26 F28'25. B 12880

The constant nymph. by Margaret Kennedy and Basil Dean. (Brackett) 2:35 D18'26. T 12881

The constant sinner. by Mae West. (Benchley) 7:26 S26'31. T 12882

The constant wife. by W. Somerset Maugham. (Brackett) 2:39 D11'26. T 12883

Consultation room. by Frederic Loomis. (Fadiman) 14:53-4*Ja 28'39. BB 12884

Continental varieties. Anon. (Benchley) 10:36-8 O13'34. T 12885

The contracting circle. by E. L. Grant Watson. (Dounce) 1:19 Ag 29'25. B 12886

Conversation at midnight. by Edna St. Vincent Millay. (Bogan) 13:51-3*Ag7'37. B 12887

Conversation piece. by Noel Coward. (Benchley) 10:30 N3'34. T 12888

Convoy. (Claxton) 3:91 My14'27. CC 12889

Coonardoo. by Katharine Susannah Prichard. (Smith) 6:94 Ap 26'30. B 12890

Coquetry for men. by Horace Coon. (Coates) 8:44 Ag13'32. B 12891

Coquette. (Mosher) 5:91 Ap13'29. CC 12892

Coquette. by George Abbott and Ann Preston Bridgers. (Brackett) 3:34 N19'27. T 12893

Cora. by Ruth Suckow. (Smith) 5:121-2 O12'29. B 12894

Cordelia Chantrell. by Meade Minnigerode. (Dounce) 2:87-8 S11'26. B 12895

Co-respondent unknown. by Mildred Harris and Harold Goldman. (Benchley) 12:26-8*F22 '36. T 12896

Coronation commentary. by Geoffrey Dennis. (Fadiman) 13:69-70*My8'37. B 12897

Coronet. by Manuel Komroff. (Smith) 5:79-80 Ja4'30.B 12898

Correspondence of Gerard Manley Hopkins and Richard Watson Dickson. by Gerard Manley Hopkins and C. C. Abbott, ed. (Bogan) 11:66*My4'35. B 12899

The corsair. (Mosher) 7:79 N28 '31. CC 12900

Cosmic religion. by Albert Einstein. (Coates) 7:88-9 Mr28'31. B 12901

The cosmological eye. by Henry W. Miller. (Fadiman) 15:89*N 18'39. B 12902

Costumes by Eros. by Conrad Aiken. (Leonard) 4:100 O6'28. B 12903

Counsellor-at-law. (Mosher) 9:89-90 D16'33. CC 12904

Counsellor-at-law. by Elmer Rice. (Benchley) 7:30-2 N14 '31. T 12905
Count Belisarius. by Robert Graves. (Fadiman) 14:75*N26 '38. B 12906
The Count of Monte Cristo. (McKelway) 10:88 O6'34. CC 12907
Counter-statement. by Kenneth Burke. (Coates) 7:84-5 O17'31. B 12908
Countess Maritza. by Harry B. Smith and Emmerich Kalman. (Brackett) 2:33-4 O2'26. T 12909
The country doctor. (Mosher) 12: 63*Mr21'36. CC 12910
Country lawyer. by Bellamy Partridge. (Fadiman) 15:54*S2 '39. B 12911
The country wife. by William Wycherley. (Benchley) 12:52* D12'36. T 12912
Courage. (Brackett) 6:74 My31'30. CC 12913
The court of fair maidens. by William Speyer. (Anon.) 12:67-8*O3'36. B 12914
Courtesan. by Irving Kaye Davis. (Benchley) 6:34 My10'30. T 12915
Cracked nuts. (Mosher) 7:99-101 Ap11'31. CC 12916
Cradle of life. by Louis Adamic. (Fadiman) 12:82-4*S19'36. B 12917
The cradle of the deep. by Joan Lowell. (Lowrie) 5:107-108 Mr 16'29. B 12918
Cradle snatchers. (Claxton) 3:70 Je11'27. CC 12919
Cradle snatchers. by Russell Medcraft and Norma Mitchell. (Mankiewicz) 1:19-20 S19'25. T 12920
The cradle song. by Gregorio Martinez Sierra and Marie Martinez Sierra. (Brackett) 2:33 F5'27. T 12921
The cradle will rock. by Marc Blitzstein. (Benchley) 13:34-6*D18'37. T 12922
Craig's wife. (Mosher) 4:117 D15 '28. CC 12923
(Mosher) 12:70-1 O10'36. 12924
Craig's wife. by George Kelly. (Mankiewicz) 1:20 O31'25. T 12925
Crazy pavements. by Beverley Nichols. (Boyd) 3:111 Ap30'27. B 12926
The creaking chair. by Allene Tupper Wilkes. (Gabriel) 2:23 Mr6'26. T 12927
Creoles. by Samuel Shipman and Kenneth Perkins. (Brackett) 3: 26 O1'27. T 12928
Crescendo. by Henry Bellamann. (Leonard) 4:89 S29'28. B 12929
Crescendo. by Ethel Mannin. (Smith) 5:96 Je22'29. B 12930
Crime and punishment. by Fyodor Dostoievsky. (Benchley) 10:30† F2'35. T 12931
The crime doctor. (Mosher) 10: 86 My19'34. CC 12932
Crime et châtiment. (Mosher) 11: 79-80*N23'35. CC 12933
Crime marches on. by Bertrand Robinson and Maxwell Hawkins. (Benchley) 11:30-2*N2'35. T 12934
The crime of Cuba. by Carleton Beals. (Fadiman) 9:51 S2'33. B 12935
Crime without passion. (Mosher) 10:48 S1'34. CC 12936
Criminal at large. by Edgar Wallace. (Benchley) 8:26-7 O22'32. T 12937
The criminal code. (Mosher) 6:57 Ja10'31. CC 12938
The criminal code. by Martin Flavin. (Benchley) 5:38-40 O12 '29. T 12939
Criminal obscenity. by John Ford (Boyd) 3:78-81 F26'27. B 12940
Crisis. (Mosher) 15:65*Mr18'39. CC 12941
Critical woodcuts. by Stuart P. Sherman. (Dounce) 2:55 Ap3 '26. B 12942
Critique of love. by Fritz Wittels. (Smith) 5:164 D7'29. B 12943
The croquet player. by H.G. Wells. (Fadiman) 13:69*F27'37. B 12944
Cross my heart. by Daniel Kusell (Brackett) 4:32 S29'28. T 12945

Cross roads. by Martin Flavin. (Benchley) 5:36 N23'29. T 12946
The crowd. (Claxton) 4:77-9 Mr3 '28. CC 12947
The crowd roars. (Mosher) 8:56* Ap2'32. CC 12948
The crowd roars. (Maloney) 14: 39-40*Ag13'38. CC 12949
The crown of lies. (Shane) 2:47 Ap3'26. CC 12950
The crown prince. by Zoë Akins and Ernest Vajda. (Brackett) 3:33 Ap2'27. T 12951
The crowning of a king. by Arnold Zweig. (Fadiman) 14:61* My28'38. B 12952
The Crow's Inn tragedy. by Annie Haynes. (Boyd) 3:80 Je25'27. B 12953
Crucibles. by Bernard Jaffe. (Smith) 6:84-5 Je21'30. B 12954
Crude. by Robert Hyde. (Parker) 3:101-102 O22'27. B 12955
Cruel fellowship. by Cyril Hume. (Dounce) 1:17 Je13'25. B 12956
Crusade. by Donn Byrne. (Markey) 4:100 Ap14'28. B 12957
The crusades. (Mosher) 11:43*Ag 31'35. CC 12958
The crusades. by Harold Lamb. (Smith) 6:99-100 Mr22'30. B 12959
The cry of the world. (Mosher) 8:51*My14'32. CC 12960
The crystal cup. (Claxton) 3:89-91 O29'27. CC 12961
The culture of cities. by Lewis Mumford. (Fadiman) 14:59-60* Ap16'38. B 12962
Cups, wands and swords. by Helen Simpson. (Hoyt) 3:79-80 Ja7'28. B 12963
Curious trials and criminal cases. by Edward Hale Bierstadt. (Leonard) 4:89 S22'28. B 12964
Curly top. (Mosher) 11:42*Ag10 '35. CC 12965
Curtain call. by LeRoy Bailey. (Gibbs) 13:30*My1'37. T 12966
The curtain falls. by Joseph Verner Reed. (Fadiman) 11:61-2* Mr2'35. B 12967
Custody children. by Everett Young. (Boyd) 2:95-6 D18 '26. B 12968
Cynara. (Mosher) 8:40 D31'32. CC 12969
Cynara. by H. M. Harwood and R. F. Gore-Browne. (Benchley) 7:28 N14'31. T 12970
Cyrano de Bergerac. (Shane) 1: 16-17 Jy11'25. CC 12971
Cyrano de Bergerac. by Edmond Rostand. (Gabriel) 2:23-4 Mr6 '26. T 12972
Czar Ivan the terrible. (Claxton) 4:89 Mr17'28. CC 12973
Czardas. by Jeno Heltai. (Coates) 8:60*Ap2'32. B 12974

D

Daddy Long Legs. (Mosher) 7:64* Je13'31. CC 12975
Daisy Mayme. by George Kelly. (Brackett) 2:33 N6'26. T 12976
Dame nature. by André Birabeau. (Gibbs) 14:26*O8'38. T 12977
Damn the tears. by William Gaston. (Brackett) 2:34 F5'27. T 12978
Damned little fool. by Cosmo Hamilton. (Parker) 7:84 Ap4'31. B 12979
A damsel in distress. (Mosher) 13:73*N27'37. CC 12980
Dance, little gentlemen. by Gilbert Frankau. (Smith) 5:81 Ja25 '30. B 12981
Dance night. by Kenyon Nicholson. (Gibbs) 14:36*O22'38. T 12982
The dance of life. (Mosher) 5:53 Ag24'29. CC 12983
The dance of life. (Mosher) 5:75-6 S7'29. CC 12984
Dance with your gods. by Kenneth Perkins. (Benchley) 10:38 O13 '34. T 12985
The dancer of Paris. (Shane) 2:47 Ap3'26. CC 12986
Dancers in the dark. (Mosher) 8:52-3* Mr19'32. CC 12987
Dancing lady. (Mosher) 9:110-11 D9'33. CC 12988
Dancing mothers. (Shane) 2:54 F20 '26. CC 12989
Dancing partner. by Alexander

Engel; Alfred Grunwald; Frederic Hatton, adapt. and Fanny Hatton, adapt. (Brackett) 6:24 Ag23'30. T 12990
Dandelion days. by Henry Williamson. (Hellman) 6:102-103 Ap19'30. B 12991
Dangerous. (Mosher) 11:49*Ja4 '36. CC 12992
Dangerous corner. by J. B. Priestley. (Benchley) 8:26 N5 '32. T 12993
Dangerous curves. (Mosher) 5:69 Jy20'29. CC 12994
The dangerous woman. (Mosher) 5:56 My25'29. CC 12995
D'Annunzio. by Tom Antongini. (Fadiman) 14:57-8*Je11'38. B 12996
Dante's inferno. (Mosher) 11:42* Ag10'35. CC 12997
Danton's death. by Georg Buchner and Geoffrey Dunlop, trans. (Gibbs) 14:32*N12'38. T 12998
Danton's Tod. by Georg Buchner. (Brackett) 3:23 D31'27. T 12999
The Danube. by Emil Lengyel. (Fadiman) 15:92*O14'39. B 13000
Daphne Bruno. by Ernest Raymond. (Dounce) 2:50-1 Ag7'26. B 13001
Daphne's in love. by Negley Farson. (Boyd) 3:97 S10'27. B 13002
The dark. by Martin Brown. (Brackett) 2:33 F12'27. T 13003
The dark angel. (Shane) 1:23 O17 '25. CC 13004
The dark angel. by H. B. Trevelyan. (Parker) 1:13 F21'25. T 13005
The dark dawn. by Martha Ostenso. (Boyd) 2:60-1 D25'26. B 13006
Dark duel. by Marguerite Steen. (Smith) 5:64 Jy6'29. B 13007
Dark hazard. by William Riley Burnett. (Fadiman) 9:51 S2'33. B 13008
Dark Hester. by Anne Douglas Sedgwick. (Lowrie) 5:104 Ap13 '29. B 13009
The dark horse. (Mosher) 8:52-3 Je18'32. CC 13010
The dark hours. by Don Marquis. (Benchley) 8:22 N26'32. T 13011
Dark laughter. by Sherwood Anderson. (Dounce) 1:22 O17'25. B 13012
Dark moon of March. By Emmett Gowen. (Fadiman) 9:82-3 S23 '33. B 13013
Dark rapture. (Mosher) 14:56*O 22'38. CC 13014
Dark star. by Lorna Moon. (Lowrie) 5:17 My18'29. B 13015
The dark tower. by Alexander Woollcott and George S. Kaufman. (Benchley) 9:34 D9'33. T 13016
The dark tower. by Francis Brett Young. (Dounce) 1:44 F13'26. B 13017
Dark victory. (Mosher) 15:66-7*Ap 22'39. CC 13018
Dark victory. by George Brewer, Jr. and Bertram Bloch. (Benchley) 10:28-30†N24'34. T 13019
Darkened rooms. by Philip Gibbs. (Lowrie) 5:92 F23'29. B 13020
Darkness to dawn. by Alexei Tolstoi. (Fadiman) 12:68*Mr28'36. B 13021
Das lied vom leben. (Mosher) 7:73 O31'31. CC 13022
Das lockende ziel. (Mosher) 9:45 Jy1'33. CC 13023
Daughter of Earth. by Agnes Smedley. (Lowrie) 5:96 Mr30 '29. B 13024
A daughter of the Medici. by Jean H. Mariéjol. (Gannett) 5:86 D21'29. B 13025
Daughters and sons. by Ivy Compton-Burnett. (Fadiman) 14:63-4*Ap23'38. B 13026
Daughters courageous. (Mosher) 15:64-5*Je24'39. CC 13027
Daughters of Atreus. by Robert Turney. (Benchley) 12:30*O24 '36. T 13028
David Copperfield. (Mosher) 10:56-7*Ja26'35. CC 13029
David Golder. by Irene Nemirovsky. (Smith) 6:106 O25'30. B 13030
David Harum. (Mosher) 10:88-9

Mr10'34. CC 13031
Dawn. (Claxton) 4:62-3 Je2'28. CC 13032
Dawn. by Theodore Dreiser. (Parker) 7:64-6*My30'31. B 13033
The dawn patrol. (Mosher) 6:54 Jy19'30. CC 13034
The dawn patrol. (Mosher) 14: 46*D24'38. CC 13035
A day at the races. (Mosher) 13: 63*Je19'37. CC 13036
The day before. by H. L. Tomlinson. (Fadiman) 15:68*N4'39. B 13037
A day of battle. by Vincent Sheean. (Fadiman) 14:56*Jy23'38. B 13038
The day of the locust. by Nathanael West. (Fadiman) 15:79-80* My20'39. B 13039
Daybreak. by Arthur Schnitzler. (Hoyt) 3:72-3 Ja14'28. B 13040
Day's end. by H. E. Bates. (Leonard) 4:89 S22'28. B 13041
Days of our years. by Pierre van Paassen. (Fadiman) 14:54-8* F4'39. B 13042
Days of wrath. by André Malraux and Haakon M. Chevalier, trans. (Fadiman) 12:65-6*Je6 '36. B 13043
Dead end. (Mosher) 13:46*Ag28 '37. CC 13044
Dead end. (Mosher) 14:72-3*My14 '38. CC 13045
Dead end. by Sidney Kingsley. (Benchley) 11:28*N9'35. T 13046
Dead lovers are faithful lovers. by Frances Newman. (Parker) 4:92-4 My19'28. B 13047
A dead man dies. by Percy Marks. (Lowrie) 5:96 Mr2'29. B 13048
Dead men tell no tales. (Mosher) 15:57*Jy29'39. CC 13049
Dealers in death. (Mosher) 10:99* D15'34. CC 13050
Dear octopus. by Dodie Smith. (Benchley) 14:30*Ja21'39. T 13051
Dear old darling. by George M. Cohan. (Benchley) 12:28*Mr14 '36. T 13052
Dear old England. by H. F. Maltby. (Benchley) 6:28 Ap5'30. T 13053
Dearest enemy. by Herbert Fields; Lorenz Hart and Richard Rodgers. (Mankiewicz) 1:20 O3'25. T 13054
The death and birth of David Markand. by Waldo Frank. (Fadiman) 10:120 O13'34. B 13055
Death comes for the Archbishop. by Willa Cather. (Boyd) 3:93 S17'27. B 13056
Death in the afternoon. by Ernest Hemingway. (Coates) 8:61-3 O1 '32. B 13057
Death in the woods, and other stories. by Sherwood Anderson. (Coates) 9:67-8 Ap22'33. B 13058
Death of a hero. by Richard Aldington. (Smith) 5:95-6 S28'29. B 13059
Death of a man. by Kay Boyle. (Anon.) 12:73*O10'36. B 13060
Death of a world. by Jules Romains. (Fadiman) 14:62-3*O1 '38. B 13061
The death of Christopher. by John Sommerfield. (Coates) 6:66-7 Ja10'31. B 13062
The death of society. by Romer Wilson. (Leonard) 4:60 Jy7'28. B 13063
The death of the heart. by Elizabeth Bowen. (Fadiman) 14:52-3*Ja28'39. B 13064
Death of the swan. (Mosher) 14: 86-7*N19'38. CC 13065
Death on the installment plan. by Louis-Ferdinand Céline. (Fadiman) 14:56-8*Ag27'38. B 13066
The death ship. by B. Traven. (Fadiman) 11:66*Je15'35. B 13067
Death takes a holiday. by Alberto Casella. (Benchley) 5:30 Ja4'30. T 13068
Death takes a holiday. (Mosher) 10:66-7 Mr3'34. CC 13069
Debits and credits. by Rudyard Kipling. (Dounce) 2:87-8 O2'26. B 13070
Debonair. by G. B. Stern. (Parker) 4:104-106 Ap21'28. B 13071
Decadence. by Maxim Gorky. (Boyd) 3:97 Mr12'27. B 13072

Deep dark river. by Robert Rylee. (Fadiman) 11:61-2*Je29 '35. B 13073
Deep evening. by Eugene Löhrke. (Coates) 7:77-8*My23'31. B 13074
The deepening stream. by Dorothy Canfield. (Smith) 6:100 O 18'30. B 13075
Delay in the sun. by Anthony Thorne. (Fadiman) 10:54*D29 '34. B 13076
The delectable mountains. by Struthers Burt. (Boyd) 2:79 Ja 29'27. B 13077
Deluge. by S. Fowler Wright. (Parker) 4:83 Mr10'28. B 13078
De luxe. by Louis Bromfield and John Gearon. (Benchley) 11: 34-6†Mr16'35. T 13079
The depths and the heights. by Jules Romains. (Fadiman) 13: 70-1*S25'37. B 13080
Der Hauptmann von Koepenick. (Mosher) 8:47 Ja28'33. CC 13081
Der Kampf. (Mosher) 12:78*S19 '36. CC 13082
Der raub der Mona Lisa. (Mosher) 8:67-7*Ap9'32. CC 13083
Derelict. (Mosher) 6:75 N29'30. CC 13084
The derelict boat. by Franz Molnar. (Dounce) 2:61 My29'26. B 13085
The desert flower. (F. J. S.) 1:15 Je13'25. CC 13086
Desert nights. (Mosher) 5:97 My 11'29. CC 13087
The desert of love. by François Mauriac. (Smith) 5:122-4 N23 '29. B 13088
The desert song. (Mosher) 5:97 My11'29. CC 13089
The desert song. by Sigmund Romberg; Otto Harbach; Oscar Hammerstein, II and Frank Mandel. (Brackett) 2:42 D11'26. T 13090
Design for living. by Noel Coward. (Benchley) 8:24-8 F4'33. T 13091
Desire. by Jean Fayard and Warre B. Wells, trans. (Coates) 8:61 S24'32. B 13092
Desire under the elms. by Eugene O'Neill. (Mankiewicz) 1: 15 Jy18'25. T 13093
The desk drawer anthology. by Alice Roosevelt Longworth an Theodore Roosevelt. (Bogan) 13:50-2*D25'37. B 13094
Destination unknown. (Mosher) 9:62-3 Ap15'33. CC 13095
Destinies. by François Mauriac. (Lowrie) 5:89 My4'29. B 13096
Destiny Bay. by Donn Byrne. (Leonard) 4:88-9 S22'28. B 13097
Destry rides again. (Mosher) 15 97*D9'39. CC 13098
The devil. by Maurice Garçon a Jean Vinchon. (Smith) 6:80 M '30. B 13099
Devil and the deep. (Mosher) 8: 8 Ag27'32. CC 13100
The devil doll. (Maloney) 12:49* 8'36. CC 13101
The devil horse. (Claxton) 2:35 Jy17'26. CC 13102
The devil in the cheese. by Tor Cushing. (Brackett) 2:25-6 Ja 15'27. T 13103
Devil in the mind. by William I Laurence. (Benchley) 7:30-2 I 9'31. T 13104
The devil is a sissy. (Mosher) 1 59*O24'36. CC 13105
The devil is a woman. (Mosher) 11:67*My11'35. CC 13106
The devil is driving. (Mosher) 8:42 D24'32. CC 13107
Devil may care. (Mosher) 5:48 Ja4'30. CC 13108
The Devil passes. by Benn W. Levy. (Benchley) 7:26-8 Ja16 '32. T 13109
The devil takes a bride. by Joe Bates Smith. (Gibbs) 14:28*O '38. T 13110
The devil to pay. (Mosher) 6:29 30 D27'30. CC 13111
The devil to pay. by Herman Heijermans. (Mankiewicz) 1:2 4 D12'25. T 13112
The devil within. by Charles Horan. (Anon.) 1:13 Mr28'25. T 13113
Devils. by Daniel N. Rubin.

(Gabriel) 2:25 Ap10'26. T 13114
The devil's circus. (Shane) 2:47 Ap3'26. CC 13115
The devil's holiday. (Mosher) 6:101 My17'30. CC 13116
Devil's Island. (Claxton) 2:35 Ag 7'26. CC 13117
Devil's lottery. (Mosher) 8:67*Ap 9'32. CC 13118
The devil's wheel. (Claxton) 3:59 Je4'27. CC 13119
Devotion. (Mosher) 7:81 O10'31. CC 13120
Diamond Jim. (Mosher) 11:43*Ag 31'35. CC 13121
Diamond Lil. by Mae West. (Brackett) 4:33-4 Ap21'28.T 13122
Diana. by Irving Kaye Davis. (Benchley) 5:33-4 D21'29. T 13123
Diana. by Emil Ludwig. (Smith) 5:84 D21'29. B 13124
The diary and letters of Madame d'Arblay. by Muriel Masefield, ed. (Coates) 7:51 Ap29 '31. B 13125
The diary of a rum-runner. by Alastair Mornay. (Smith) 5:78-9 Jy20'29. B 13126
The diary of a young lady of fashion in the year 1764-1765. by Magdalen King-Hall. (Dounce) 1:44-5 F6'26. B 13127
The diary of Dostoyevsky's wife. by Anna Grigorevna Dostoyevsky. (Lowrie) 4:100 Ja5'29. B 13128
The diary of our own Samuel Pepys. by Franklin P. Adams. (Fadiman) 11:81-2*N9'35. B 13129
The diary of Philip Hone. by Philip Hone. (Hoyt) 3:60 D24 '27. B 13130
The diary of Tolstoy's wife. by Sophie Tolstoy. (Smith) 6:80-1 Mr1'30. B 13131
Die dreigroschenoper. (Mosher) 7:69*My23'31. CC 13132
Dimples. (Mosher) 12:77*O17'36. CC 13133
Dinner at eight. (Mosher) 9:46-7 S2'33. CC 13134
Dinner at eight. by George S. Kaufman and Edna Ferber. (Benchley) 8:26 O29'32. T 13135
Dinners long and short. by A. H. Adair. (Lowrie) 4:75 F9'29. B 13136
Diplomacy. (Claxton) 2:50 S18'26. CC 13137
Diplomacy. by Victorien Sardou. (Long) 4:41 Je9'28. T 13138
Dirigible. (Mosher) 7:99 Ap11'31. CC 13139
Discovery. by Richard E. Byrd. (Anon.) 11:113-14*D7'35. B 13140
A dish for the gods. by Cyril Hume. (Middleton) 5:115-16 Ap 20'29. B 13141
Dishonored. (Mosher) 7:79 Mr14 '31. CC 13142
Dishonored lady. by Margaret Ayer Barnes and Edward Sheldon. (Benchley) 5:28 F15'30. T 13143
Disillusioned India. by Dhan Gopal Mukerji. (Coates) 6:90 N29'30. B 13144
The disinherited. by Jack Conroy. (Fadiman) 9:96 N18'33. B 13144A
Disraeli. (Mosher) 5:60 O12'29. CC 13145
Disraeli. by André Maurois. (Parker) 3:78-9 F18'28. B 13146
Disraeli. by D. L. Murray. (Boyd) 3:78-9 Je11'27. B 13147
The distaff side. by John van Druten. (Gibbs) 10:32-4 O6'34. T 13148
A distant drum. by Vincent Lawrence. (Brackett) 3:25 F4'28. T 13149
Distant drums. by Dan Totheroh. (Benchley) 7:24 Ja30'32. T 13150
The distant shore. by Donald Blackwell and Theodore St. John. (Benchley) 11:28†Mr2'35. T 13151
District nurse. by Faith Baldwin. (Coates) 8:61 My28'32. B 13152
Diversey. by MacKinlay Kantor. (Leonard) 4:66 Ag18'28. B 13153
Diversion. by John van Druten. (Brackett) 3:25 Ja21'28. T 13154
Divided by three. by Beatrice Kaufman and Margaret Leech. (Gibbs) 10:38-40 O13'34. T 13155

A divine drudge. by Vicki Baum and John Golden. (Benchley) 9:28 N4'33. T 13156
The divine lady. (Mosher) 5:86 Mr30'29. CC 13157
The divorcee. (Mosher) 6:100-101 My17'30. CC 13158
Do what you will. by Aldous Huxley. (Gannett) 5:107-108 N30 '29. B 13159
Doctor Addams. by Irving Fineman. (Fadiman) 15:76-7*Mr11 '39. B 13160
Doctor Faustus. by Christopher Marlowe. (Benchley) 12:26*F6 '37. T 13161
Dr. Jekyll and Mr. Hyde. (Mosher) 7:75 Ja9'32. CC 13162
Doctor Kerkhoven. by Jacob Wasserman and Cyrus Brooks, trans. (Coates) 7:64 F6'32. B 13163
The doctor looks at biography. by Joseph Collins. (Dounce) 1:20 D19'25. B 13164
A doctor looks at doctors. by Joseph Collins. (Hoyt) 3:96-7 O29'27. B 13165
The doctor looks at love and life. by Joseph Collins. (Dounce) 2:84-5 O9'26. B 13166
The doctor looks at marriage and medicine. by Joseph Collins. (Leonard) 4:95 N3'28. B 13167
Dr. Martino and other stories. by William Faulkner. (Fadiman) 10:105-106 Ap21'34. B 13168
Dr. Monica. (Mosher) 10:64 Je30 '34. CC 13169
Doctor Monica. by Marja M. Szczepkowska. (Benchley) 9:36 N18'33. T 13170
Dr. Norton's wife. by Mildred Walker. (Fadiman) 14:45-6*Ja 7'39. B 13171
Doctor Rhythm. (Mosher) 14:59-60*My28'38. CC 13172
Doctor Serocold. by Helen Ashton. (Smith) 6:58 Jy26'30. B 13173
Doctor Syn. (Mosher) 13:88*N20 '37. CC 13174
Dr. Traprock's memory book. by George S. Chappell, ed. (Coates) 7:81 My2'31. B 13175
Doctor X. (Mosher) 8:37 Ag13'32. CC 13176
A doctor's diary. (Maloney) 13:60 F27'37. CC 13177
The doctor's dilemma. by George Bernard Shaw. (Brackett) 3:34 D3'27. T 13178
The doctor's secret. (Mosher) 4:72 F9'29. CC 13179
Dodsworth. (Mosher) 12:61*O3'36. CC 13180
Dodsworth. by Sidney Howard. (Benchley) 10:30-2 Mr3'34. T 13181
Dodsworth. by Sinclair Lewis. (Parker) 5:106-107 Mr16'29. B 13182
Dollars only. by Edward Bok. (Dounce) 2:60 Mr20'26. B 13183
A doll's house. by Henrik Ibsen. (Benchley) 13:32*Ja8'38. T 13184
Domestic manners of the Americans. by Frances Trollope. (Boyd) 3:71-2 S3'27. B 13185
The dominant sex. by Michael Egan. (Gibbs) 11:32*Ap13'35. T 13186
Domino. by Marcel Achard. (Flanner) 8:50*F27'32. T 13187
Don Fernando. by W. Somerset Maugham. (Fadiman) 11:51-2* Jy20'35. B 13188
Don Juan. (Claxton) 2:33 Ag14'26 CC 13189
Don Juan. by Joseph Delteil and Kay Boyle, trans. (Coates) 7: 80 My2'31. B 13190
Don Juan. by André Maurois. (Flanner) 6:57 F22'30. B 13191
Don Juan and the wheelbarrow. by L. A. G. Strong. (Coates) 9: 62 F25'33. B 1319[illegible]
Don Q. (Anon.) 1:15 Je20'25. CC 1319[illegible]
Don Quichotte. (Flanner) 9:33-6 Ap15'33. CC 1319[illegible]
Don Quixote of the seas. by Jac Wassermann. (Smith) 6:98-9 22'30. B 1319[illegible]
Doña Maria la Brava. by Walte O. Lindsey, prod. (Gabriel) 25 My29'26. T 1319[illegible]

The donkey of God. by Louis Untermeyer. (K. White) 8:95 D10'32. B 13197
Donogoo. by Jules Romains. (Flanner) 6:85 N29'30. T 13198
The Donovan affair. by Owen Davis. (Brackett) 2:33 S11'26. T 13199
Don't tell the wife. (Claxton) 3:79 Mr5'27. CC 13200
The doomed battalion. (Mosher) 8:52 Je18'32. CC 13201
Doomsday. (Claxton) 4:95 Ap7 '28. CC 13202
The doomsday men. by J. B. Priestley. (Fadiman) 14:43-4* Jy30'38. B 13203
The door of life. by Enid Bagnold. (Fadiman) 14:63*O1'38. B 13204
The doorway to hell. (Mosher) 6:104 N8'30. CC 13205
Dorian Gray. by David Thorne. (Brackett) 4:53 Je2'28. T 13206
Dostoevsky. by Julius Meier-Graefe. (Leonard) 4:62 Ag25 '28. B 13207
Double door. (Mosher) 10:94 My12 '34. CC 13208
Double door. by Elizabeth McFadden. (Gibbs) 9:28 S30'33. T 13209
Double dummy. by Tom McKnight and Doty Hobart. (Benchley) 12:28-35*N21'36. T 13210
Double or nothing. (Mosher) 13:66-7*S11'37. CC 13211
Doubting Thomas. (Mosher) 11:47-8*Jy20'35. CC 13212
The dove. (Claxton) 3:65-7 Ja14 '28. CC 13213
Down in the valley. by H. W. Freeman. (Smith) 6:98 Mr15 '30. B 13214
Down stream. by Alexander C. Herman and Leslie P. Eichel. (Mankiewicz) 1:23 Ja23'26. T 13215
Down under the sea. (Mosher) 12:44*Ag15'36. CC 13216
Downfall. by Harold Brecht. (Lowrie) 5:105 My11'29. B 13217
Downstairs. (Mosher) 8:67-8 O15 '32. CC 13218
Dracula. (Mosher) 7:63 F21'31. CC 13219
Dracula. by Hamilton Deane and John L. Balderston. (Brackett) 3:33 O15'27. T 13220
The drag net. (Claxton) 4:80 Je9 '28. CC 13221
The dreadful decade. by Don Seitz. (Dounce) 2:55 Je19'26. B 13222
Dream child. by J. C. Nugent. (Gibbs) 10:34 O6'34. T 13223
Dream of destiny. by Arnold Bennett. (Coates) 8:65-6 Je4'32. B 13224
The dream of love. (Mosher) 4:50 D29'28. CC 13225
The dream play. by August Strindberg. (Gabriel) 1:23 Ja30 '26. T 13226
Dreaming lips. (Mosher) 13:57* My29'37. CC 13227
Dreamy rivers. by Henry Baerlein. (Coates) 6:54-5 D27'30. B 13228
Dreiser looks at Russia. by Theodore Dreiser. (Gibbs) 4:115 D1 '28. B 13229
Dress parade. (Claxton) 3:85-7 N5 '27. CC 13230
Dressed to kill. (Claxton) 4:90-1 Mr17'28. CC 13231
The Dreyfus case. (Gibbs) 7:55 S5'31. CC 13232
Drôle de voyage. by Drieu La Rochelle. (Flanner) 9:35-8 Je 24'33. B 13233
Drums. (Mosher) 14:49*O1'38. CC 13234
Drums. by James Boyd. (Anon.) 1:26 My23'25. B 13235
Drums along the Mohawk. (Mosher) 15:69*N11'39. CC 13236
Drums along the Mohawk. by Walter D. Edmonds. (Fadiman) 12:42-4*Ag1'36. B 13237
Drums of love. (Claxton) 3:65 F4 '28. CC 13238
The drunkard. by H. S. Smith. (Benchley) 10:34-6 Ap7'34; 11:28*F15'36. T 13239
Drusilla with a million. (F. J. S.) 1:14 Je6'25. CC 13240
The dry decade. by Charles Merz.

(Coates) 6:81 F14'31. B 13241

Dry martini: a gentleman turns to love. by John Thomas. (Dounce) 2:81-2 S18'26. B 13242

The DuBarry. by Rowland Leigh and Desmond Carter. (Lockridge) 8:36-8 D3'32. T 13243

DuBarry was a lady. by B. G. De Sylva; Herbert Fields and Cole Porter. (Benchley) 15:40* D16'39. T 13244

DuBarry, woman of passion. (Mosher) 6:101-103 N8'30. CC 13245

The Duchess of Buffalo. (Claxton) 2:34 Ag14'26. CC 13246

Duck soup. (Mosher) 9:81 D2'33. CC 13247

Duel. by Ronald Fangen. (Fadiman) 10:70-1 Je23'34. B 13248

Duino elegies. by Rainer Maria Rilke. (Bogan) 15:70-1*Je24 '39. B 13249

Duke Herring. by Maxwell Bodenheim. (Coates) 7:46-7*Ag1'31. B 13250

The duMauriers. by Daphne du Maurier. (Fadiman) 13:72*Ap 24'37. B 13251

The dunce boy. by Lula Vollmer. (Anon.) 1:11 Ap18'25. T 13252

Duranty reports Russia. by Gustavus Tuckerman, ed. (Fadiman) 10:84-6 F24'34. B 13253

Dusk at the grove. by Samuel Rogers. (Fadiman) 10:100-101 S8'34. B 13254

Dust be my destiny. (Mosher) 15: 60-1*S9'39. CC 13255

Dust over the ruins. by Helen Ashton. (Anon.) 11:58*Ja18'36. B 13256

Dusty answer. by Rosamond Lehmann. (Boyd) 3:73 S3'27.B13257

Dwarf's blood. by Edith Olivier. (Coates) 7:54*Jy4'31. B 13258

Dwell in the wilderness. by Alvah C. Bessie. (Fadiman) 11:53-4*Ag24'35. B 13259

The dybbuk. by S. Ansky. (Mankiewicz) 1:19 D26'25. T 13260
(Brackett) 2:25 D25'26. T 13261

Dynamite. by Louis Adamic. (Coates) 7:87-8 Mr28'31.B 13262

Dynamo. by Eugene O'Neill. (Brackett) 5:27-8 F23'29. T 13263

Dynasty of death. by Taylor Caldwell. (Fadiman) 14:73-4*S17'38 B 13264

E

"E & O E." by Eliot Crawshay. (Gibbs) 11:32*Jy20'35. T 13265

Each dawn I die. (Mosher) 15:57* Jy29'39. CC 13266

Each to the other. by Christophe La Farge. (Fadiman) 15:71*Ap '39. B 13267

The eagle. (Shane) 1:23 N14'25. CC 13268

The eagle and the hawk. (Moshe 9:61-2 My20'33. CC 13269

Eagle forgotten. by Harry Barna (Fadiman) 14:65-6*My21'38. B 13270

The eagle of the sea. (Claxton) 2 78 N20'26. CC 13271

The eagles gather. by Taylor Caldwell. (Fadiman) 15:52-3*J 6'40. B 13272

Earl Carroll's sketch book. by Earl Carroll. (Brackett) 5:46- Jy13'29. T 13273

Earl Carroll's sketch book. by Eugene Conrad and Charles Sherman. (Gibbs) 11:21*Je15'3 T 13274

Earl Carroll's vanities. by Earl Carroll, et al. (Mankiewicz) 1:15 Jy18'25; 1:15 Ag8'25. T 13275

Earl Carroll's vanities. by Clarence Gaskill and William A. Grew. (Mankiewicz) 1:20 Ja9 '26. T 1327

Earl Carroll's vanities. by Earl Carroll. (Brackett) 2:25-6 Ja 22'27. T 1327

Earl Carroll's vanities. by Ear Carroll, et al. (White) 4:36 18'28. T 1327
(Benchley) 6:26-30 Jy12'30; 15:30-2*Ja20'40. T 1327

Earl Carroll's vanities. by Joh McGowan, et al. (White) 8:2

O8'32. T 13280
Earl Carroll's vanities. by Ralph Spence and Eddie Welch. (Benchley) 7:26-8 S5'31. T 13281
Early Autumn. by Louis Bromfield. (Dounce) 2:77-8 O16'26. B 13282
The early life of Thomas Hardy. by Florence Emily Hardy. (Lowrie) 4:59-60 D29'28. B 13283
Early to bed. (Mosher) 12:56*Jy25'36. CC 13284
Early to bed. by Wood Kahler. (Leonard) 4:75-6 Jy14'28. B 13285
The early worm. by Robert Benchley. (Boyd) 3:98-9 My21 '27. B 13286
Earth. by Em Jo Basshe. (Brackett) 3:34 Mr19'27. T 13287
The earth between. by Virgil Geddes. (Brackett) 5:32 Mr16 '29. T 13288
The earth trembles. by Jules Romains. (Fadiman) 12:50-1* Jy18'36. B 13289
The easiest way. (Mosher) 7:73 Mr7'31. CC 13290
East Lynne. (Mosher) 7:67 F28 '31. CC 13291
East Lynne. by Ellen Price Wood. (Gabriel) 2:27 Mr20'26. T 13292
East of Borneo. (Mosher) 7:79 O3'31. CC 13293
East of the Hudson. by J. Brooks Atkinson. (Coates) 6:73 Ja3'31. B 13294
East side, West side. (Claxton) 3:87-9 O22'27. CC 13295
East side, West side. by Felix Riesenberg. (Boyd) 3:95-7 F19 '27. B 13296
East wind. by Oscar Hammerstein, II; Frank Mandel and Sigmund Romberg. (Benchley) 7:32 N14'31. T 13297
Easter. by August Strindberg. (Gabriel) 2:27 Ap3'26. T 13298
Easy living. (Mosher) 13:56*Jy17 '37. CC 13299
Easy virtue. by Noel Coward. (Mankiewicz) 1:20 D26'25. T 13300
The eater of darkness. by Robert M. Coates. (Smith) 5:68-9 Ag17'29. B 13301
Ebb tide. by Harry Chapman Ford. (Benchley) 7:24-6*Je20'31. T 13302
The economy of abundance. by Stuart Chase. (Fadiman) 10:99-101 Mr24'34. B 13303
Eden end. by J. B. Priestley. (Benchley) 11:30*N2'35. T 13304
Edgar Allen Poe. by Joseph Wood Krutch. (Dounce) 2:54-5 Mr27 '26. B 13305
Edge of Taos desert. by Mabel Dodge Luhan. (Fadiman) 13:72-3*S18'37. B 13306
The edge of the world. (Mosher) 14:63*S17'38. CC 13307
Edmund Kean, prince among lovers. (Claxton) 3:69-70 Je11'27. CC 13308
Edna his wife. by Cornelia Otis Skinner. (Benchley) 13:36*D18 '37. T 13309
Education before Verdun. by Arnold Zweig and Eric Sutton, trans. (Fadiman) 12:67*My2'36. B 13310
Education of a princess. by Marĭia, grand duchess of Russia and Russell Lord, trans. (Coates) 6:67 Ja24'31. B 13311
The Edwardian era. by André Maurois and Hamish Miles, trans. (Fadiman) 9:85 N4'33. B 13312
The Edwardians. by Victoria Sackville-West. (Smith) 6:75-6 S6'30. B 13313
Eight bells. by Percy G. Mandley. (Benchley) 9:28-31 N4'33. T 13314
Eight girls in a boat. (Mosher) 9:58-9 Ja20'34. CC 13315
An Eighteenth Century miscellany. by Louis Kronenberger, ed. (Fadiman) 12:72-3*Mr14'36. B 13316
Eimi. by E. E. Cummings. (Coates) 9:78-9 Ap8'33. B 13317
Ein mädel von der Reeperbahn. (Mosher) 6:69 F7'31. CC 13318
El Indio. by Gregorio Lopez y Fuentes. (Fadiman) 13:63-4*

F20'37. B 13319
Electra. by Sophocles. (Brackett) 3:29 My14'27. T 13320
Electric love. by Victoria Cross. (Smith) 5:134 D14'29. B 13321
Elegant infidelities of Madame Li Pei Fou. by Charles Pettit. (Parker) 4:98-9 O20'28. B 13322
Elephant Boy. (Mosher) 13:71*Ap 3'37. CC 13323
Elizabeth and Essex. by Lytton Strachey. (Lowrie) 4:130-1 D15 '28. B 13324
Elizabeth Barrett Browning. by Louise Schutz Boas. (Smith) 6:101 Mr22'30. B 13325
Elizabeth, the Queen. by Maxwell Anderson. (Benchley) 6:30 N15 '30. T 13326
Ella Cinders. (Shane) 2:36 Je12 '26. CC 13327
Ellen Adair. by Frederick Niven. (Dounce) 1:19 Ag29'25. B 13328
Elmer Gantry. by Patrick Kearney. (White) 4:36-8 Ag18'28. T 13329
Elmer Gantry. by Sinclair Lewis. (Boyd) 3:98-100 Mr19'27. B 13330
Elmer the Great. by Ring Lardner. (Brackett) 4:33 O6'28. T 13331
Emak Bakia. (Claxton) 3:81 Mr12 '27. CC 13332
Embers. by A. E. Thomas. (Gabriel) 2:24-5 F27'26. T 13333
The embezzlers. by Valentine Kataev. (Smith) 5:116 N16'29. B 13334
Emerson: the enraptured Yankee. by Régis Michaud. (Smith) 6: 6:91-2 Je7'30. B 13335
Emerson, the wisest American. by Phillips Russell. (Smith) 5:120-1 N2'29. B 13336
The emigrants. by Johan Bojer. (Dounce) 1:23 O17'25. B 13337
Emily Dickinson. by Josephine Pollitt. (Smith) 6:99-100 Mr15 '30. B 13338
Emily Dickinson face to face. by Martha Dickinson Bianchi. (Coates) 8:78-9 D17'32. B 13339
Emma. (Mosher) 7:57-8 F13 '32. CC 13340
The Emperor Jones. (Mosher) 9: 75 S23'33. CC 13341
The Emperor's candlesticks. (Mosher) 13:51*Jy10'37. CC 13342
The Empress Elizabeth of Austria. by Karl Tschuppik. (Hellman) 6:104 Mr29'30. B 13343
The enchanted April. by Kane Campbell. (Mankiewicz) 1:15 S5'25. T 13344
Enchanted vagabonds. by Dana Lamb. (Fadiman) 14:62*My28 '38. B 13345
Enchantment. by Joseph Jefferson Farjeon. (Brackett) 3:30 My7 '27. T 13346
The end of a childhood. by Henry Handel Richardson. (Fadiman) 10:95-6 N3'34. B 13347
The end of desire. by Robert Herrick. (Coates) 7:60 Ja23'32. B 13348
The end of St. Petersburg. (Claxton) 4:79 Je9'28. CC 13349
End of Summer. by S. N. Behrman. (Benchley) 12:26-8*F29 '36. T 13350
The end of the world. by Geoffrey Dennis. (Smith) 6:100 O11'30. B 13351
Ends and means. by Aldous Huxley. (Fadiman) 13:91*N20'37. B 13352
The enemy. (Claxton) 3:65 Ja14 '28. CC 13353
The enemy. by Channing Pollock. (Mankiewicz) 1:19-20 N14'25. T 13354
An enemy of the people. by Henrik Ibsen. (Brackett) 3:34 O15 '27. T 13355
Enfants terribles. by Jean Cocteau (Smith) 6:85 Je21'30. B 13356
Engaged. by William S. Gilbert. (Mankiewicz) 1:15 Je27'25. T 13357
England speaks. by Philip Gibbs. (Anon.) 11:81-2*D21'35. B 13358
English journey. by J. B. Priestley. (Fadiman) 10:61-2 Ag11'34. B 13359
English years. by James Whitall.

(Fadiman) 11:73*S14'35. B 13360
Enjoyment of laughter. by Max Eastman. (Anon.) 12:118*N14 '36. B 13361
Enter the Greek. by Anthony Gibbs. (Leonard) 4:89 S22'28. B 13362
Erie water. by Walter D. Edmonds. (Coates) 8:59 F4'33. B 13363
Eroica. by Samuel Chotzinoff. (Smith) 6:101 Mr22'30. B 13364
Escapade. (Mosher) 11:51-2*Jy13 '35. CC 13365
Escape. by John Galsworthy. (Brackett) 3:24 N5'27. T 13366
Escape. by Francesco Nitti. (Smith) 6:100-101 F22'30. B 13367
Escape. by Ethel Vance. (Fadiman) 15:60*S23'39. B 13368
Escape me never. (Mosher) 11: 55-6*Je1'35. CC 13369
Escape me never! by Margaret Kennedy. (Benchley) 10:28-30† F2'35. T 13370
Escape this night. by Robert Steiner and Harry Horner. (Gibbs) 14:28*Ap30'38. T 13371
Eskimo. (Mosher) 9:73 N25'33. CC 13372
Eskimo. by Peter Freuchen. (Fadiman) 14:43*Jy2'38. B 13373
Espionage! by H. R. Berndorff. (Hellman) 6:96 Ap26'30. B 13374
Espionage agent. (Mosher) 15:57* S30'39. CC 13375
Eternal love. (Mosher) 5:107 My 18'29. CC 13376
The eternal mask. (Mosher) 12: 65*Ja9'37. CC 13377
The eternal moment. by E. M. Forster. (Markey) 4:97 My19 '28. B 13378
The eternal road. by Franz Werfel and William A. Drake, adapt. (Benchley) 12:26*Ja16 '37. T 13379
Ethan Frome. by Owen Davis and Donald Davis. (Benchley) 11: 28*F1'36. T 13380
Etiquette. by Emily Post. (Parker) 3:51-3 D31'27. B 13381
Etruscan places. by D. H. Lawrence. (Coates) 8:66 N26'32. B 13382
Eugene V. Debs. by McAlister Coleman. (Smith) 6:82-3 My31 '30. B 13383
Europa. by Robert Briffault. (Fadiman) 11:73*S7'35. B 13384
Europa in limbo. by Robert Briffault. (Fadiman) 13:71-2*S25 '37. B 13385
Europe on the eve. by Frederick Schuman. (Anon.) 15:70*Mr18 '39. B 13386
Eva. by Jacques Chardonne. (Coates) 6:72-3 Ja17'31. B 13387
Evangeline. (Mosher) 5:38 Ag3'29. CC 13388
Evelyn Prentice. (Mosher) 10:78* N17'34. CC 13389
Evensong. by Beverley Nichols and Edward Knoblock. (Benchley) 8:26-8 F11'33. T 13390
Evergreen. (Mosher) 10:59*Ja19 '35. CC 13391
Every day a holiday. (Mosher) 13:48*Ja29'38. CC 13392
Every man a king. by Huey P. Long. (Fadiman) 9:88-9 N25'33. B 13393
Every mother's son. by Norman Lindsay. (Smith) 6:81-2 N1'30. B 13394
Every Thursday. by Doty Hobart. (Benchley) 10:30 My19'34. T 13395
Everybody's acting. (Claxton) 2: 85 N13'26. CC 13396
Everybody's autobiography. by Gertrude Stein. (Fadiman) 13: 115-18*D4'37. B 13397
Everybody's Boswell. by F. V. Morley, ed. (Coates) 6:53-4 D 27'30. B 13398
Everybody's old man. (Mosher) 12:71-2*Ap4'36. CC 13399
Everybody's welcome. by Harold Atteridge. (Benchley) 7:28 O31'31; 8:22 Jy2'32. T 13400
Everything's jake. by Don Marquis. (Benchley) 5:28 Ja25'30. T 13401
Everywhere I roam. by Arnold Sundgaard and Marc Connelly.

(Benchley) 14:26*Ja7'39.T 13402
Eve's leaves. by Harry Chapman Ford. (Anon.) 1:11-12 Ap18 '25. T 13403
Evidence. (Mosher) 5:62-4 O12'29. CC 13404
Ex-husband. by Anon. (Smith) 5: 103-104 N30'29. B 13405
The ex-Mrs. Bradford. (Mosher) 12:62-3*Je6'36. CC 13406
Ex-wife. by Ursula Parrott. (Smith) 5:58 Ag24'29. B 13407
Excavations. by Carl Van Vechten. (Dounce) 1:44 Ja30'26. B 13408
Excess baggage. (Mosher) 4:78 S29'28. CC 13409
Excess baggage. by John Mc Gowan. (Brackett) 3:25 Ja14 '28. T 13410
Exclusive. (Maloney) 13:49*Jy31 '37. CC 13411
Exclusive story. (Mosher) 11:56* Ja25'36. CC 13412
Excursion. by Victor Wolfson. (Benchley)13:30*Ap17'37. T 13413
The exile. by Pearl S. Buck. (Fadiman) 11:65*F15'36.B 13414
Exile's return. by Malcolm Cowley. (Fadiman) 10:89-90 Je2 '34. B 13415
Experiment in autobiography. by H. G. Wells. (Fadiman) 10:90 O27'34. B 13416
Expiation. by Mary Annette Russell. (Lowrie) 5:85 Mr9'29. B 13417
Explorers of the world. (Mosher) 7:49-50 D26'31. CC 13418
Expression in America. by Ludwig Lewisohn. (Coates) 8:59* Mr26'32. B 13419
The extraordinary adventures of Julio Jurenito and his disciples. by Ilya Ehrenburg. (Smith) 6:62 Jy5'30. B 13420
Extraordinary women. by Compton Mackenzie. (Leonard) 4: 104 S15'28. B 13421
Eyeless in Gaza. by Aldous Huxley. (Kronenberger) 12:52-4* Jy11'36. B 13422
Eyes of the world. (Mosher) 6:58-9 Ag23'30. CC 13423

F

Faber. by Jacob Wassermann. (Dounce) 1:20-1 N21'25.B13424
A fable for wives. by Robert E. McClure. (Coates) 8:62-3 My 28'32. B 13425
The fabulous invalid. by George S. Kaufman and Moss Hart. (Gibbs) 14:36*O22'38. T 13426
Façade. by Douglas Goldring. (Hoyt) 4:96-7 Mr3'28. B 13427
Face the music. by Irving Berlin and Moss Hart. (Benchley) 8: 24-6*F27'32. T 13428
Face value. by J. L. Campbell. (Boyd) 3:63 Ag27'27. B 13429
Fads, frauds and physicians. by T. Swann Harding. (Smith) 6:88-9 N29'30. B 13430
The fair co-ed. (Claxton) 3:91 O 29'27. CC 13431
Fair winds and foul. by Heinrich Hauser. (Coates) 8:84*Mr19 '32. B 13432
The fall guy. by James Gleason and George Abbott. (Anon.) 1: 13-14 Mr28'25. T 13433
Fallen angels. by Noel Coward. (Brackett) 3:32 D17'27. T 13434
False dreams, farewell. by Hugh Stanislaus Stange. (Benchley) 9:30 Ja27'34. T 13435
False youth. by Lawrence Rising (Smith) 5:122-3 O26'29.B 13436
Falstaff. by James Plaisted Webber; Porter Steele and Brian Hooker. (Brackett) 4:29 Ja5'2 T 13437
Family affairs. by Earle Crooke and Lowell Brentano. (Benchley) 5:34 D21'29. T 13438
The family circle. by André Maurois and Hamish Miles, trans. (Coates) 8:43-4 Ag13'3 B 13439
Family history. by Victoria Sackville-West. (Coates) 8:85-6 N '32. B 13440
The family picnic. (Claxton) 4:5 Jy7'28. CC 13441

Family portrait. by Lenore Coffee and William Joyce Cowen. (Benchley) 15:30*Mr18'39. T 13442
The family reunion. by T. S. Eliot. (Bogan) 15:83-5*Ap15'39. B 13443
Famine. by Liam O'Flaherty. (Fadiman) 13:64*O2'37. B 13444
The fanatics. by Miles Malleson. (Brackett) 3:35 N19'27. T 13445
Fanny. by Willard Mack and David Belasco. (Brackett) 2:33 O2'26. T 13446
Fanny Kemble: a passionate Victorian. by Margaret Armstrong. (Fadiman) 14:43*Jy2'38. B 13447
Far-away bride. by Stella Benson. (Smith) 6:110 N22'30. B 13448
Far away horses. by Michael Birmingham and Gilbert Emery. (Benchley) 9:24-6 Ap1'33. T 13449
Far end. by May Sinclair. (Dounce) 2:86-7 S11'26. B 13450
The far-off hills. by Lennox Robinson. (Gibbs) 13:28-30*O23 '37. T 13451
Faraway. by J. B. Priestley. (Coates) 8:46-7 Ag6'32. B 13452
Farewell Miss Julie Logan. by James M. Barrie. (Coates) 8: 66 N26'32. B 13453
A farewell to arms. (Mosher) 8: 69-70 D17'32. CC 13454
A farewell to arms. by Ernest Hemingway. (Smith) 5:120 O12 '29. B 13455
(Coates) 8:61 S24'32. 13456
A farewell to arms. by Laurence Stallings. (Benchley) 6:34 O4'30. T 13457
A farewell to India. by Edward Thompson. (Coates) 7:55*Jy4 '31. B 13458
Farewell to reform. by John Chamberlain. (Coates) 8:94-5 D3'32. B 13459
Farewell to sport. by Paul Gallico. (Anon.) 14:64*Ap16'38. B 13460
Farewell to youth. by Storm Jameson. (Leonard) 4:64-5 Jy 21'28. B 13461
The farm. by Louis Bromfield. (Fadiman) 9:54 Ag19'33. B 13462
Farm of three echoes. by Noel Langley. (Benchley) 15:34*D9 '39. T 13463
The farmer in the dell. (Mosher) 12:64*Mr14'36. CC 13464
The farmer takes a wife. (Mosher) 11:47*Ag17'35. CC 13465
The farmer takes a wife. by Frank B. Elser and Marc Connelly. (Benchley) 10:30 N10 '34. T 13466
Fascinating youth. (Shane) 2:52 My15'26. CC 13467
Fashions for women. (Claxton) 3:89-90 Ap2'27. CC 13468
Fast life. (Mosher) 5:54 Ag24'29. CC 13469
Fast life. by Samuel Shipman and John B. Hymer. (Brackett) 4: 33 O13'28. T 13470
The fatal alibi. by Michael Morton. (Benchley) 8:28-30*F20'32. T 13471
The fate of the jury. by Edgar Lee Masters. (Lowrie) 5:116-17 My18'29. B 13472
The father. by Katharine Holland Brown. (Lowrie) 4:114-15 D1 '28. B 13473
The father. by August Strindberg. (Brackett) 4:51 My26'28. T 13474
(Benchley) 7:28 O17'31. 13475
Father Goose. by Gene Fowler. (Fadiman) 10:97-8 N3'34. B 13476
Father Malachy's miracle. by Brian Doherty. (Benchley) 13: 30-2*N27'37. T 13477
Fathers of the revolution. by Philip Guedalla. (Dounce) 2:50 Jy10'26. B 13478
The fault of angels. by Paul Horgan. (Fadiman) 9:54-5 Ag26'33. B 13479
Faust. (Claxton) 2:94-5 D11'26. CC 13480
Faust. by Johann Wolfgang von Goethe. (Brackett) 4:26 O20'28. T 13481

Favorite jokes of famous people. by Frank Nicholson. (Parker) 4:108-109 N17'28. B 13482
Fazil. (Claxton) 4:75 Je16'28. CC 13483
Fear and trembling. by Glenway Wescott. (Coates) 8:75-6 My21 '32. B 13484
A feather in her hat. (Mosher) 11:76*N2'35. CC 13485
The feathered nest. by Margaret Leech. (Leonard) 4:123-4 N10 '28. B 13486
Feet first. (Mosher) 6:101 N8'30. CC 13487
Feliciana. by Stark Young. (Fadiman) 11:50-1*Jy27'35. B 13488
Female. (Mosher) 9:74-5 N11'33. CC 13489
Ferment. by John T. McIntyre. (Fadiman) 13:54-5*Jy10'37. B 13490
A few foolish ones. by Gladys Hasty Carroll. (Fadiman) 11: 79*Ap27'35. B 13490A
The fiddler. by Sarah Gertrude Millin. (Smith) 5:70 Ag17'29. B 13491
Fiddlers' green. by Albert R. Wetjen. (Coates) 7:78*Je6'31. B 13492
The fields beyond. by Francis Bosworth. (Benchley) 12:28-30*Mr14'36. T 13493
Fiesta. by Michael Gold. (Benchley) 5:38-41 S28'29. T 13494
Fifth Avenue girl. (Mosher) 15:55-6*Ag26'39. CC 13495
The fifth column and the first forty-nine stories. by Ernest Hemingway. (Fadiman) 14: 82-3*O22'38. B 13496
The fifth decad of cantos. by Ezra Pound. (Bogan) 13:94*D 18'37. B 13497
The fifty-fifty girl. (Claxton) 4:84 My19'28. CC 13498
Fifty million Frenchmen. (Mosher) 7:77-9 Ap4'31. CC 13499
Fifty million Frenchmen. by Herbert Fields and Cole Porter. (Benchley) 5:39-40 D7'29. T 13500
Fifty roads to town. (Mosher) 13: 62*Je5'37. CC 13501
Fifty roads to town. by Frederick Nebel. (Fadiman) 11:60-1*Ja25 '36. B 13502
The fight for life. by Paul De Kruif. (Fadiman) 14:60*Ap30'38. B 13503
Fighting angel. by Pearl S. Buck. (Fadiman) 12:115-16*D5'36. B 13504
Fighting caravans. (Mosher) 6:51 Ja31'31. CC 13505
Fighting love. (Claxton) 3:79 My 28'27. CC 13506
The fighting 69th. (Mosher) 15: 49*Ja27'40. CC 13507
Fighting years. by Oswald Garrison Villard. (Fadiman) 15:72-3*Ap8'39. B 13508
Find Daddy. by Tadema Bussiere. (Gabriel) 2:27 Mr20'26. T 13509
Fine and dandy. by Donald Ogden Stewart. (Benchley) 6:34 O4'30. T 13510
Fine clothes. (Shane) 1:23 O24'25. CC 13511
Fine manners. (Claxton) 2:41 S4 '26. CC 13512
The finger points. (Mosher) 7:77 Ap4'31. CC 13513
Finn and Hattie. (Mosher) 6:67-9 F7'31. CC 13514
Finnegan's wake. by James Joyce. (Fadiman) 15:72-5*My6'39. B 13515
Fioretta. by Earl Carroll; George Bagby and G. Romilli. (Brackett) 4:27 F16'29. T 13516
The fire brigade. (Claxton) 2:48 Ja1'27. CC 13517
Fire over England. (Mosher) 13: 61*Mr6'37. CC 13518
Fire under the Andes. by Elizabeth Shepley Sergeant. (Boyd) 3:106-107 Ap16'27. B 13519
Firebird. by Lajos Zilahy. (Lockridge) 8:36 D3'32. T 13520
The firefly. (Mosher) 13:60*S4'37. CC 13521
The firefly. by Otto Harbach and Rudolph Friml. (White) 7:32-4 D12'31. T 13522

First a girl. (Mosher) 11:63-4* Ja11'36. CC 13523
First and last. by Ring W. Lardner. (Fadiman) 10:91 Je9'34. B 13524
First episode (College sinners). by Terence Rattigan and Philip Heimann. (Gibbs) 10:26-8 S29 '34. T 13525
The first hundred years. (Mosher) 14:54*Ap16'38. CC 13526
First lady. (Mosher) 13:45*D25 '37. CC 13527
First lady. by Katherine Dayton and George S. Kaufman. (Benchley) 11:44-6*D7'35. T 13528
First love. (Mosher) 15:69*N11 '39. CC 13529
First love. by Zoë Akins. (Brackett) 2:33 N20'26. T 13530
First love. by E. M. Delafield. (Lowrie) 4:72 Ja26'29. B 13531
The first Mrs. Fraser. by St. John Ervine. (Benchley) 5:27 Ja11'30. T 13532
First night. by Frederick Rath. (Benchley) 6:36 D6'30. T 13533
The First World War. (Mosher) 10:105-106 N10'34. CC 13534
The First World War. by Laurence Stallings, ed. (Fadiman) 9:47-8 Ag5'33. B 13535
Fish preferred. by P. G. Wodehouse. (Smith) 5:65 Jy13'29. B 13536
Fishes, their journeys and migrations. by Louis Roule. (Fadiman) 11:63*Je1'35. B 13537
The Fishmans. by H.W. Katz. (Fadiman) 14:50-1*Jy9'38. B 13538
Five and ten. (Mosher) 7:48*Jy18 '31. CC 13539
Five came back. (Mosher) 15:69-70*Jy8'39. CC 13540
Five cities. by George R. Leighton. (Fadiman) 15:82-3*Ap15 '39. B 13541
Five generations. by Margaret Armstrong. (Smith) 6:120 Ap12 '30. B 13542
Five masters. by Joseph Wood Krutch. (Coates) 6:122-3 D13 '30. B 13543
Five of a kind. (Mosher) 14:58* O29'38. CC 13544
Five silver daughters. by Louis Golding. (Fadiman) 10:108-109 My5'34. B 13545
Five star final. (Mosher) 7:80 S19 '31. CC 13546
Five star final. by Louis Weitzenkorn. (Benchley) 6:26 Ja10'31. T 13547
Fix bayonets! by John W. Thomason, Jr. (Dounce) 2:62 Ap17 '26. B 13548
Flames coming out of the top. by Norman Collins. (Fadiman) 14:74-5*My14'38. B 13549
The flaming frontier. (Shane) 2:45 Ap10'26. CC 13550
The flashing stream. by Charles Morgan. (Gibbs) 15:30*Ap22'39. T 13551
Flaubert and Madame Bovary. by Francis Steegmuller. (Fadiman) 15:68*F18'39. B 13552
The fleeting. by Walter de la Mare. (Bogan) 9:48 Jy15'33. B 13553
The fleet's in. (Mosher) 4:85 O6 '28. CC 13554
Flesh. by A. J. Lamb. (Anon.) 1:15 My23'25. T 13555
Flesh and the devil. (Claxton) 2: 59-61 Ja15'27. CC 13556
Flight. by Susan Meriwether and Victor Victor. (Brackett) 5:30 Mr2'29. T 13557
A flock of birds. by Kathleen Coyle. (Smith) 6:85-6 Je14'30. B 13558
Flood. by Robert Neumann. (Hellman) 6:122-3 Ap12'30. B 13559
The florodora girl. (Mosher) 6:87 Je7'30. CC 13560
The flowering of New England. by Van Wyck Brooks. (Fadiman) 12:59*Ag22'36. B 13561
Flowering wilderness. by John Galsworthy. (Coates) 8:82 N19 '32. B 13562
Flowers and trees. (Mosher) 8:54 S10'32. CC 13563
Flowers of evil. by Charles Bau-

delaire; George Dillon, trans. and Edna St. Vincent Millay, trans. (Bogan) 12:78-9*My23 '36. B 13564

Flowers of the forest. by John van Druten. (Gibbs) 11:28*Ap 20'35. T 13565

Flush. by Virginia Woolf. (Fadiman) 9:89 O7'33. B 13566

Fly away blackbird. by Jerrard Tickell. (Fadiman) 12:78*My9 '36. B 13567

Fly away home. by Dorothy Bennett and Irving White. (Benchley) 10:28-30†Ja26'35. T 13568

The flying carpet. by Richard Halliburton. (Coates) 8:82-3 N19'32. B 13569

Flying colors. by Howard Dietz and Arthur Schwartz. (White) 8:26 S24'34. T 13570

Flying down to Rio. (Mosher) 9: 46 D30'33. CC 13571

The flying Dutchman. by Michael Arlen. (Fadiman) 15:59-60*Jy 15'39. B 13572

The flying fleet. (Mosher) 4:83-4 F16'29. CC 13573

Flying high. by B. G. DeSylva; Lew Brown and John McGowan. (Brackett) 6:27 Mr15'30. T 13574

The flying Irishman. (Mosher) 15: 80*Ap15'39. CC 13575

The flying mouse. (Mosher) 10: 56 Jy21'34. CC 13576

The flying Yorkshireman. by Whit Burnett, ed. and Martha Foley, ed. (Fadiman) 14:59-60* Ap30'38. B 13577

Foch speaks. by Charles Bugnet. (Smith) 5:73 Je29'29. B 13578

Fog. by John Willard. (Brackett) 3:34 F19'27. T 13579

Fog-bound. by Hugh Stanislaus Stange. (Brackett) 3:34 Ap9'27. T 13580

Folies Bergère. (Maloney) 11:61* Mr9'35. CC 13581

The folklore of capitalism. by Thurman W. Arnold. (Fadiman) 13:61-2*Ja15'38. B 13582

The folks. by Ruth Suckow. (Fadiman) 10:100-101 O6'34. B 13583

Follow the fleet. (Mosher) 12:5 F29'36. CC 1358

Follow the furies. by Eleanor Carroll Chilton. (Anon.) 11: 63*Mr2'35. B 1358

Follow thru. (Mosher) 6:90 S20 CC 1358

Follow thru. by Laurence Schwa and B. G. DeSylva. (Brackett) 4:31-2 Ja19'29. T 1358

Fontamara. by Ignazio Silone an Michael Wharf, trans. (Fadiman) 10:101 S22'34. B 1358

The fool of the family. by Margaret Kennedy. (Smith) 6:104 O25'30. B 1358

The fool of Venus. by George Cronyn. (Fadiman) 10:98-100 Mr10'34. B 1359

Fools rush in. by Norman Zeno et al. (Benchley) 10:34†Ja5'35. T 13591

Foolscap. by Gennaro Mario Cu ci and Eduardo Cianelli. (Bench ley) 8:26 Ja21'33. T 13592

Foot-loose in India. by Gordon Sinclair. (Coates) 8:60 Ja14'3 B 13593

Footlight parade. (White) 9:77-8 O7'33. CC 13594

Footlights. by Roland Oliver. (Long) 3:54 S3'27. T 13595

Footlights across America. by Kenneth Macgowan. (Smith) 5:67 D28'29. B 13596

Footloose widows. (Shane) 2:40- Je26'26. CC 13597

A footnote to folly. by Mary Heaton Vorse. (Anon.) 11:55* Ja4'36. B 13598

For alimony only. (Claxton) 2:7 O2'26. CC 13599

For better or worse. by Allen De Lano. (Brackett) 2:34 F12 '27. T 13600

For dear life. by Belinda Jellif (Anon.) 12:52*Ag29'36. B 13601

For heaven's sake. (Shane) 2:45 Ap10'26. CC 13602

For services rendered. by W. Somerset Maugham. (Benchle 9:25-6 Ap22'33. T 13603

For the defense. (Mosher) 6:53-

Jy26'30. CC 13604

For the defense. by Edward Majoribanks. (Smith) 5:65 D28'29. B 13605

Forbidden. (Mosher) 7:53-4 Ja16 '32. CC 13606

Forbidden love. (Mosher) 4:71 Ja 19'29. CC 13607

Forbidden melody. by Otto Harbach and Sigmund Romberg. (Benchley) 12:42*N14'36.T 13608

The forbidden woman. (Claxton) 3:85 N5'27. CC 13609

Foreign affairs. by Paul Hervey Fox and George Tilton. (Benchley) 8:28-30*Ap23'32. T 13610

Forever after. (Claxton) 2:86 N13 '26. CC 13611

Forgotten faces. (Claxton) 4:55 Ag11'28. CC 13612

Forgotten faces. (Mosher) 12:47* Jy11'36. CC 13613

Forgotten men. (Mosher) 9:62 My20'33. CC 13614

Forsaking all others. by Edward Roberts and Frank Cavett. (Benchley) 9:26 Mr11'33. T 13615

The fortress. by Hugh Walpole. (Coates) 8:66 S17'32. B 13616

Forty days of Musa Dagh. by Franz Werfel. (Fadiman) 10: 84-6*D1'34. B 13617

45 fathers. (Mosher) 13:84-5*D18 '37. CC 13618

The forty-second parallel. by John Dos Passos. (Smith) 6: 102 Mr8'30. B 13619

42nd Street. (Mosher) 9:62 Mr18 '33. CC 13620

40,000 against the Arctic. by H. P. Smolka. (Fadiman) 13:51*Ag28 '37. B 13621

Forty thousand sublime and beautiful thoughts. by Charles Noel Douglas, ed. (Parker) 6:62-4 Ja24'31. B 13622

Forty-two years in the White House. by Irwin Hood Hoover. (Fadiman) 10:100 S22'34. B 13623

Forty years of Scotland Yard. by Frederick Porter Wensley. (Coates) 7:58-60 S5'31. B 13624

The forward pass. (Mosher) 5:96 D7'29. CC 13625

The foundry. by Albert Halper. (Fadiman) 10:99-100 S8'34. B 13626

The fountain. (Mosher) 10:48 S1 '34. CC 13627

The fountain. by Eugene O'Neill. (Mankiewicz) 1:17 D19'25. T 13628

Four daughters. (Mosher) 14:52* Ag27'38. CC 13629

(Mosher) 14:50-1*Ja28'39 13630

Four days' wonder. by A. A. Milne. (Fadiman) 9:82 O14'33. B 13631

Four devils. (Mosher) 4:103-104 O13'28. CC 13632

Four feathers. (Maloney) 15:47* Ag12'39. CC 13633

The four feathers. (Mosher) 5:88 Je22'29. CC 13634

Four frightened people. (Mosher) 9:61-2 F3'34. CC 13635

Four hours to kill. (Mosher) 11: 71*Ap20'35. CC 13636

The 400,000,000. (Mosher) 15: 65-6*Mr18'39. CC 13637

Four infantrymen. by Ernst Johannsen. (Hellman) 6:96 Ap 26'30. B 13638

Four men and a prayer. (Mosher) 14:73*My14'38. CC 13639

Four sons. (Claxton) 4:69 F25'28. CC 13640

Four walls. by Dana Burnet and George Abbott. (Brackett) 3:25 O1'27. T 13641

Four wives. (Mosher) 15:52-3*D 23'39. CC 13642

The fourth commandment. (Claxton) 3:91 Ap2'27. CC 13643

Framed. (Claxton) 3:52 Je25'27. CC 13644

France. by Sisley Huddleston. (Boyd) 3:95-6 Mr12'27.B 13645

Francis Joseph. by Eugene Bagger. (Hoyt) 3:93-4 N5'27. B 13646

Francis Joseph I. by Karl Tschuppik. (Smith) 6:93 Je7'30. B 13647

Francis Rabelais. by Albert Jay Nock and Catherine Rose Wilson. (Smith) 5:103 N30'29. B 13648

Francis the First. by Francis Hackett. (Fadiman) 11:61*Mr 2'35. B 13649
François Villon. by D. B. Wyndham Lewis. (Parker) 4:86-7 S29'28. B 13650
Frank Fay vaudeville. by Frank Fay. (Benchley) 15:32*Mr11'39. T 13651
Frankenstein. (Mosher) 7:95-6 D 12'31. CC 13652
Franklin, the apostle of modern times. by Bernard Fay. (Gannett) 5:137 D14'29. B 13653
The frantic Atlantic. by Basil Woon. (Boyd) 3:55 Jy30'27. B 13654
Fräulein Else. by Arthur Schnitzler. (Dounce) 1:21 N21'25. B 13655
Freaks. (Mosher) 8:45-6 Jy16'32. CC 13656
Frederika. by Franz Lehar and Edward Eliscu, adapt. (Benchley) 12:28*F13'37. T 13657
Free. by Blair Niles. (Smith) 5: 88 F15'30. B 13658
Free and equal. (Anon.) 1:31 My2 '25. CC 13659
Free for all. by Oscar Hammerstein, II and Laurence Schwab. (Benchley) 7:28-30 S 19'31. T 13660
A free soul. (Mosher) 7:61-3*Je13 '31. CC 13661
A free soul. by Willard Mack. (Brackett) 3:25 Ja28'28. T 13662
Freedom, farewell! by Phyllis Bentley. (Fadiman) 12:52*F29 '36. B 13663
The Freiburg passion play. (Brackett) 5:28 My11'29. T 13664
The French quarter. by Herbert Asbury. (Anon.) 12:75*O10'36. B 13665
French without tears. by Terence Rattigan. (Gibbs) 13:28-30*O9 '37. T 13666
Fresh fields. by Ivor Novello. (Benchley) 12:26*F22'36. T 13667
The freshman. (Shane) 1:19 S26 '25. CC 13668
Friday's business. by Maurice Baring. (Coates) 9:66-8 Mr18 '33. B 13669
Friends of Mr. Sweeney. by Elmer Davis. (Dounce) 1:17 D5 '25. B 13670
Friendship. by George M. Cohan. (Benchley) 7:30-2 S12'31. T 13671
Frisco Sally Levy. (Claxton) 3:93-4 Ap16'27. CC 13672
From day to day. by Ferdynand Goetel. (Coates) 7:89 My16'31. B 13673
From death to morning. by Thomas Wolfe. (Fadiman) 11:87*N16 '35. B 13674
From Vienna. by Lothar Metzl, et al. (Gibbs) 15:28*Jy1'39. T 13675
The front page. (Mosher) 7:79 Mr 28'31. CC 13676
The front page. by Ben Hecht and Charles MacArthur. (White) 4: 32 Ag25'28. T 13677
Front page woman. (Mosher) 11: 47*Jy20'35. CC 13678
Frontier. (Mosher) 11:64*Ja11'36. CC 13679
Frozen justice. (Mosher) 5:105-107 N2'29. CC 13680
The fruit of the family tree. by Albert Edward Wiggam. (Dounce) 1:28 Mr7'25. B 13681
A fugitive crosses his tracks. by Aksel Sandemose and Eugene Gay-Tifft, trans. (Anon.) 12: 51-2*Jy18'36. B 13682
Fugitive lovers. (Mosher) 9:58 Ja 20'34. CC 13683
Fugitive's return. by Susan Glaspell. (Smith) 5:124 N9'29. B 13684
Full circle. by John Collier. (Coates) 9:73 My13'33. B 13685
Full flavour. by Doris Leslie. (Fadiman) 10:69-70 S1'34. B 13686
Fully dressed and in his right mind. by Michael Fessier. (Fadiman) 11:78-9*My25'35. B 13687
Fulton of Oak Falls. by George M. Cohan. (Benchley) 13:30*F20'37. T 13688
Funny face. by Fred Thompson;

Paul Gerard Smith; George Gershwin and Ira Gershwin. (Brackett) 3:35 D3'27. T 13689

The furies. by Zoë Akins. (Brackett) 4:31 Mr17'28. T 13690

Furnished rooms. by Ragnhilde Brúland. (Benchley) 10:28 Je9 '34. T 13691

Fury. (Mosher) 12:66-7*Je13'36. CC 13692

G

G-men. (Mosher) 11:59*My4'35; 11:61-2*Je8'35. CC 13693

Gabriel over the White House. (Mosher) 9:68-9 Ap8'33. CC 13694

Galahad. by John Erskine. (Dounce) 2:89 N20'26. B 13695

Galatea. by Margaret Rivers Larminie. (Leonard) 4:65 Ag18 '28. B 13696

The galaxy. by Susan Ertz. (Smith) 5:69-70 Ag17'29. B 13697

The gallant came late. by Marian Storm. (Lowrie) 4:74 Ja19'29. B 13698

A gallery of women. by Theodore Dreiser. (Smith) 5:134 D14'29. B 13699

Gallions Reach. by H. M. Tomlinson. (Hoyt) 3:97 O29'27. B 13700

Gallows' orchard. by Claire Spencer. (Smith) 6:102 Ap5'30. B 13701

Gambling lady. (Mosher) 10:95-6 Ap14'34. CC 13702

The game of love and death. by Romain Rolland. (Benchley) 5:40-2 D7'29. T 13703

Gang war. by Willard Mack. (White) 4:36 S1'28. T 13704

The gang's all here. by Russel Crouse; Oscar Hammerstein, II and Morrie Ryskind. (Parker) 7:23 F28'31. T 13705

Gangs of New York. (Mosher) 14:60*My28'35. CC 13706

The gangs of New York. by Herbert Asbury. (Markey) 4:94-5 My19'28. B 13707

Gangster's boy. (Mosher) 14:95* N12'38. CC 13708

The garden. by L. A. G. Strong. (Coates) 7:54*Jy4'31. B 13709

The garden of Adonis. by Caroline Gordon. (Fadiman) 13:93* O30'37. B 13710

The garden of Allah. (Claxton) 3:87 S10'27. CC 13711

The garden of Allah. (Mosher) 12:79*N21'36. CC 13712

The garden of disorder. by Charles Henri Ford. (Bogan) 14:83-4*O22'38. B 13713

The garden of Eden. by Avery Hopwood. (Brackett) 3:31-2 O8 '27. T 13714

Garrick gaieties. by Allen Boretz, et al. (Benchley) 6:26-8 Je14 '30. T 13715

Garrick gaieties. by Richard Rodgers and Lorenz Hart. (Gabriel) 2:23 My22'26. T 13716

Gasoline gypsies. by Charles Conger Stewart. (Benchley) 7: 24*Je20'31. T 13717

The Gaucho. (Claxton) 3:111 D3'27. CC 13718

The gaudy empire. by Alfred Neumann. (Fadiman) 13:72-3*Ap24 '37. B 13719

Gay agony. by H. A. Manhood. (Parker) 7:86 Ap4'31. B 13720

The gay defender. (Claxton) 3:67 Ja7'28. CC 13721

The gay desperado. (Mosher) 12: 70*O10'36. CC 13722

The gay diplomat. (Mosher) 7:76 O17'31. CC 13723

The gay divorcée. (Mosher) 10: 79-80*N24'34. CC 13724

Gay divorce. by Dwight Taylor and Cole Porter. (Lockridge) 8:30-3 D10'32. T 13725

Gay Paree. by Harold Atteridge. (Mankiewicz) 1:17 Ag29'25. T 13726

The gay retreat. (Claxton) 3:93 O15'27. CC 13727

The general. (Claxton) 2:51-2 F12 '27. CC 13728

The general. by C. S. Forester. (Anon.) 12:53*F29'36. B 13729

General Crack. (Mosher) 5:74 D14 '29. CC 13730

The general died at dawn. (Mosher) 12:74-5*S12'36. CC 13731
Generals without buttons. (Mosher) 14:57*Mr12'38. CC 13732
Geneva. by George Bernard Shaw. (Gibbs) 15:28-31 F10'40.T 13733
Genitrix. by François Mauriac. (Smith) 6:54 Ag30'30. B 13734
The gentle libertine. by Sidonie Gabrielle Colette. (Coates) 6:77 F7'31. B 13735
The gentle people. by Irwin Shaw. (Benchley) 14:28-30*Ja14'39. T 13736
The gentle savage. by Richard Wyndham. (Anon.) 12:85-6*O17'36. B 13737
The gentleman from America. by Polan Banks. (Smith) 6:77 S6'30. B 13738
Gentleman Johnny Burgoyne. by Francis Josiah Hudleston. (Hoyt) 3:95-6 O29'27. B 13739
A gentleman of Paris. (Claxton) 3:83 O8'27. CC 13740
Gentlemen are born. (Mosher) 10:57*D1'34. CC 13741
Gentlemen, I address you privately. by Kay Boyle. (Fadiman) 9:86-7 N4'33. B 13742
Gentlemen of the press. (Mosher) 5:107-108 My18'29. CC 13743
Gentlemen of the press. by Ward Morehouse. (White) 4:25 S8'28. T 13744
Gentlemen prefer blondes. (Claxton) 3:65 Ja21'28. CC 13745
Gentlemen prefer blondes. by Anita Loos and John Emerson. (Brackett) 2:33 O9'26. T 13746
Gentlewoman. by John Howard Lawson. (Benchley) 10:28-30 Mr31'34. T 13747
Geography. by Hendrik Willem van Loon. (Coates) 8:66 S17'32. B 13748
George and Margaret. by Gerald Savory. (Gibbs) 13:28*O2'37. T 13749
The George and the crown. by Sheila Kaye-Smith. (Dounce) 1:17 Je20'25. B 13750
George IV. by Shane Leslie. (Boyd) 2:115 D11'26. B 13751
George Washington. by W. E. Woodward. (Dounce) 2:74-8 O30'26. B 13752
George Washington 1777-1781 (Vol. III). by Robert Hughes. (Smith) 5:83-4 F8'30. B 13753
George White's Music Hall varieties. by George White and William K. Wells. (Lockridge) 8:38-40 D3'32. T 13754
George White's scandals. (Mosher) 10:89-90 Mr24'34. CC 13755
George White's scandals. by William K. Wells and George White. (Mankiewicz) 1:15 Jy4'25. T 13756
(Long) 4:42 Jy14'25. T 13757
(Benchley) 5:34-6 O5'29. 13758
George White's scandals. by George White. (Brackett) 2:25 Je26'26. T 13759
George White's scandals. by George White; Matt Brooks and Eddie Davis. (Gibbs) 15:26*S9'39. T 13760
George White's scandals. by George White; Lew Brown and Irving Caesar. (Benchley) 7:26 S26'31. T 13761
Georgie May. by Maxwell Bodenheim. (Leonard) 4:64-5 Je30'28. B 13762
Gerald: a portrait. by Daphne du Maurier. (Fadiman) 11:86-7*Ap6'35. B 13763
Geronimo. (Mosher) 15:75-6 F10'40. CC 13764
Get me in the movies. by Charlton Andrews and Philip Dunning. (Brackett) 4:52-3 Je2'28. T 13765
Gettin' in society. by George Blake. (Leonard) 4:61 Ag4'28. B 13766
Getting married. by George Bernard Shaw. (Parker) 7:32-4 Ap11'31. T 13767
The ghost goes West. (Mosher) 11:52*Ja18'36; 12:62-3*My16'36. CC 13768
The ghost of Yankee Doodle. by Sidney Howard. (Benchley) 13:38*D4'37. T 13769

The ghost parade. by Hadley Waters. (Benchley) 5:34 N9 '29. T 13770
The ghost train. by Arnold Ridley. (Brackett) 2:52 S4'26. T 13771
Ghosts. by Henrik Ibsen. (Gabriel) 2:25 Mr27'26. T 13772
(Brackett) 2:25 Ja22'27. 13773
(Benchley) 11:24-5*D21'35. 13774
(Gibbs) 12:31*My23'36. 13775
Giant killer. by Elmer Davis. (Leonard) 4:100 O20'28. B 13776
The giant swing. by William Riley Burnett. (Coates) 8:67 S10'32. B 13777
Giants in the Earth. by O. E. Rölvaag. (Boyd) 3:79 Je11'27. B 13778
Gigolo. (Claxton) 2:70 O9'26. CC 13779
Gilbert and Sullivan. by A. H. Godwin. (Boyd) 2:68-9 Ja15'27. B 13780
The gilded lily. (Mosher) 11:64-5*F16'35. CC 13781
"Gimme," or how politicians get rich. by Emanuel H. Lavine. (Coates) 7:73-4*Je13'31. B 13782
Ginger. (Mosher) 11:41-2*Jy27 '35. CC 13783
The ginger griffin. by Ann Bridge. (Fadiman) 10:107-109 My12'34. B 13784
Girl crazy. by Guy Bolton; John McGowan; George Gershwin and Ira Gershwin. (Benchley) 6:36 O25'30. T 13785
The girl everybody knew. by James T. Farrell. (Parker) 4:83 Mr10'28. B 13786
The girl friend. by Herbert Fields; Richard Rodgers and Lorenz Hart. (Gabriel) 2:26 Mr27'26. T 13787
The girl from Coney Island. (Claxton) 2:83 D18'26. CC 13788
The girl from Missouri. (Mosher) 10:56 Ag11'34. CC 13789
The girl from Rector's. by George Rector. (Boyd) 3:98-100 My14'27. B 13790
The girl of the golden West. (Mosher) 6:78-9 N1'30. CC 13791
The girl of the golden West. (Mosher) 14:61*Mr26'38. CC 13792
The girl said no. (Mosher) 6:111 Ap16'30. CC 13793
The girl said no. (Mosher) 13:67*O23'37. CC 13794
Girl trouble. by Barry Conners. (Brackett) 4:36 N3'28. T 13795
The girl was young. (Mosher) 13:60*F12'38. CC 13796
Girls' dormitory. (Mosher) 12:59*S5'36. CC 13797
Girls' school. (Mosher) 14:94-5*N12'38. CC 13798
Give me yesterday. by A. A. Milne. (Parker) 7:30-8 Mr14 '31. T 13799
A glad day. by Kay Boyle. (Bogan) 14:83-4*O22'38. B 13800
The glass key. (Mosher) 11:53*Je22'35. CC 13801
The glass key. by Dashiell Hammett. (Parker) 7:91 Ap25'31. B 13802
The glass slipper. by Ferenc Molnar. (Mankiewicz) 1:19 O31 '25. T 13803
Glorifying the American girl. (Mosher) 5:73-5 Ja18'30. CC 13804
Glorious Apollo. by Lily Adams Beck. (Dounce) 2:49-50 Jy31'26. B 13805
Glorious Betsy. (Claxton) 4:87 My 5'28. CC 13806
Glorious morning. by Norman MacOwen. (Benchley) 14:38-40*D3'38. T 13807
Glory hallelujah. by Thomas Mitchell and Bertram Bloch. (Gabriel) 2:28 Ap17'26. T 13808
The go-getter. (Mosher) 13:62*Je 5'37. CC 13809
Go she must. by David Garnett. (Boyd) 2:76-7 Ja22'27. B 13810
Go West. (Shane) 1:22-3 O31'25. CC 13811
Go West, young man. (Mosher) 12:79-81*N21'36. CC 13812
Goat song. by Franz Werfel. (Gabriel) 1:26 F6'26. T 13813
God head. by Leonard Cline. (Anon.) 1:26 D12'25. B 13814
God loves us. by J. P. McEvoy.

(Brackett) 2:31-2 O30'26. T 13815
God's country. by Ralph Barton. (Lowrie) 5:109 Mr16'29.B 13816
Gods' country and the woman. (Mosher) 12:51*Ja16'37. CC 13817
God's gold. by John T. Flynn. (Coates) 8:70-1O8'32. B 13818
Gods of the lightning. by Maxwell Anderson and Harold Hickerson. (Brackett) 4:34 N3'28. T 13819
Goethe. by Emil Ludwig. (Leonard) 4:81 S8'28. B 13820
Goin' home. by Ransom Rideout. (White) 4:41 S1'28. T 13821
Goin' to town. (Mosher) 11:67*My 18'35. CC 13822
Going Hollywood. (Mosher) 9:46 D30'33. CC 13823
Going places. (Mosher) 14:44*Ja 7'39. CC 13824
Gold braid. by Ann Shelby. (Benchley) 6:28 My24'30.T13825
Gold diggers in Paris. (Maloney) 14:50*Je4'38. CC 13826
Gold diggers of Broadway. (Mosher) 5:75 S7'29. CC 13827
Gold diggers of 1935. (Maloney) 11:61*Mr23'35. CC 13828
Gold diggers of 1937. (Mosher) 12:51*D26'36. CC 13829
Gold eagle guy. by Melvin Levy. (Benchley) 10:36†D8'34. T 13830
Gold is where you find it. (Mosher) 13:59-60*F12'38. CC 13831
The gold rush. (Shane) 1:17 Ag22 '25. CC 13832
Gold rush days with Mark Twain. by William R. Gillis. (Smith) 6:105 My24'30. B 13833
Golden boy. (Mosher) 15:60*S9 '39. CC 13834
Golden boy. by Clifford Odets. (Benchley) 13:31*N13'37. T13835
The golden dancer. by Cyril Hume. (Dounce) 2:85-6 S11'26. B 13836
Golden dawn. by Otto Harbach and Oscar Hammerstein, II. (Brackett) 3:34 D10'27. T 13837
The golden fleece. by John Gunther. (Middleton) 5:116 Ap 20'29. B 13838
The golden journey. by Edwin Gilbert. (Gibbs) 12:24-5*S26'36. T 13839
The golden touch. (Maloney) 11: 78*Ap6'35. CC 13840
The Goldwyn follies. (Mosher) 14: 58*F19'38. CC 13841
The golem. (Mosher) 13:55*Mr27 '37. CC 13842
The gondoliers. by William S. Gilbert and Arthur Sullivan. (Simon) 10:38-40 S15'34. T 13843
Gone with the wind. (Mosher) 15: 47*D30'39. CC 13844
Gone with the wind. by Margaret Mitchell. (Kronenberger) 12:48* Jy4'36. B 13845
The good. by Chester Erskin. (Gibbs) 14:28*O15'38. T 13846
Good and naughty. (Shane) 2:36-7 Je19'26. CC 13847
Good boy. by Otto Harbach; Oscar Hammerstein, II and Henry Myers. (Brackett) 4:34-5 S15 '28. T 13848
The good companions. by J. B. Priestley. (Smith) 5:120 O26 '29. B 13849
The good companions. by J. B. Priestley and Edward Knoblock. (Benchley) 7:34-6 O10'31. T 13850
Good dame. (Mosher) 10:90 Mr24 '34. CC 13851
The good earth. (Mosher) 12:59-60*F6'37. CC 13852
The good earth. by Owen Davis and Donald Davis. (Benchley) 8:24 O29'32. T 13853
The good fairy. by Ferenc Molnar. (White) 7:29 D5'31. T 13854
The good fellow. by George S. Kaufman and Herman J. Mankiewicz. (Brackett) 2:33 O16 '26. T 13855
Good girls go to Paris. (Mosher) 15:56-7*Jy1'39. CC 13856
The Good Hope. by Hermann Heijermans. (Brackett) 3:33 N 12'27. T 13857
Good men and true. by Brian Marlow and Frank Merlin. (Benchley) 11:32*N2'35. T 13858

Good morning, America. by Carl Sandburg. (Leonard) 4:124 N 10'28. B 13859
Good news. by Laurence Schwab and B. G. DeSylva. (Brackett) 3:61-2 S17'27. T 13860
The good soldier Schweik. by Jaroslav Hasek. (Smith) 5:85 F8'30. B 13861
Good time Charley. (Claxton) 3: 65-6 N26'27. CC 13862
A good woman. by Louis Bromfield. (Boyd) 3:65-6 Ag13'27. B 13863
A good woman, poor thing. by Dillard Long. (Benchley) 8:28 Ja21'33. T 13864
Good-bye to all that. by Robert Graves. (Smith) 5:81 Ja18'30. B 13865
Good-bye to western culture. by Norman Douglas. (Smith) 6: 106 O4'30. B 13866
Good-bye, Wisconsin. by Glenway Wescott. (Leonard) 4:88 S29 '28. B 13867
Goodbye again. by Allan Scott and George Haight. (Benchley) 8:26 Ja7'33. T 13868
Goodbye, Mr. Chips. (Mosher) 15:76-7*My20'39. CC 13869
Goodbye to the past. by William Riley Burnett. (Fadiman) 10: 101 S8'34. B 13870
Goona-goona. (Gibbs) 8:52 S24'32. CC 13871
The goose and the gander. (Mosher) 11:60*S21'35. CC 13872
The gorgeous hussy. (Mosher) 12: 75*S12'36. CC 13873
The gorilla. (Claxton) 3:65 N26'27. CC 13874
The gorilla. by Ralph Spence. (Anon.) 1:11 My9'25. T 13875
The gossipy sex. by Lawrence Grattan. (Brackett) 3:34 Ap30 '27. T 13876
Gotobedde Lane. by Marian Bower. (Leonard) 4:99-100 O20'28. B 13877
The gourmets' almanac. by Allan Ross Macdougall. (Smith) 5:81-2 Ja25'30. B 13878
Gow, the head hunter. (Mosher) 4:92 Ja5'29. CC 13879
Goya. by Charles Poore. (Fadiman) 14:63-6*O29'38. B 13880
Graft in business. by John T. Flynn. (Coates) 7:88 O3'31. B 13881
Grand Canary. (Mosher) 10:51 Jy 28'34. CC 13882
The grand duchess and the waiter. (Shane) 1:36 F13'26. CC 13883
The grand duchess and the waiter. by Arthur Richman and Alfred Savoir. (Mankiewicz) 1:19 O24 '25. T 13884
Grand Hotel. (Mosher) 8:56*Ap16 '32; 8:56-7*Ap23'32. CC 13885
Grand Hotel. by Vicki Baum and William A. Drake, trans. (Benchley) 6:34 N22'30. T 13886
Grand illusion. (Mosher) 14:66* S24'38. CC 13887
Grand Street follies. by Agnes Morgan, et al. (Mankiewicz) 1:15 Jy4'25. T 13888
(Brackett) 2:25 Je26'26. 13889
(Long) 4:40-1 Je9'28. 13890
Grand Street follies. by Agnes Morgan and Max Ewing. (Brackett) 3:36 My28'27. T 13891
Grand Street follies of 1929. by Agnes Morgan, et al. (Brackett) 5:27-8 My11'29. T 13892
Grandeur and misery of victory. by Georges Clemenceau. (Smith) 6:100 Ap19'30. B 13893
(Coates) 7:89-90 Ap4'31. 13894
The grandmothers. by Glenway Wescott. (Boyd) 3:61-2 Ag27 '27. B 13895
Grandsons. by Louis Adamic. (Fadiman) 11:69-70*Mr23'35. B 13896
Granite. by Clemence Dane. (Brackett) 3:33-4 Mr12'27. T 13897
The grapes of wrath. (Mosher) 15: 61 F3'40. CC 13898
The grapes of wrath. by John Steinbeck. (Fadiman) 15:81-2*Ap15 '39. B 13899
Grass. (Anon.) 1:31 Ap11'25. CC 13900
The grasshoppers come. by David

Garnett. (Coates) 7:61*Je20 '31. B 13901

Graustark. (Shane) 1:24 S12'25. CC 13902

Gray shadow. by Roger Wheeler. (Parker) 7:30-2 Mr21'31.T13903

The great adventure. by Arnold Bennett. (Brackett) 2:23-4 Ja1 '27. T 13904

The great American ass. by Charles Leroy Edson. (Dounce) 2:85-6 O9'26. B 13905

The great American band wagon. by Charles Merz. (Parker) 3: 77-8 F18'28. B 13906

The great American novel. by Brion Davis. (Fadiman) 14:60-1*Je4'38. B 13907

The great Barrington. by Franklin Russell. (Parker) 7:23 F28 '31. T 13908

Great circle. by Conrad Aiken. (Coates) 9:74-5 My6'33.B 13909

The great day. by Georgette Carneal. (Coates) 8:71-2*Ap9'32. B 13910

Great day. by William Cary Duncan; John Wells and Vincent Youmans. (Benchley) 5:46 O26 '29. T 13911

The great flirtation. (Mosher) 10: 64 Je30'34. CC 13912

The great Gabbo. (Mosher) 5:92 S21'29. CC 13913

The great Garrick. (Mosher) 13: 89-90*O30'37. CC 13914

The great Gatsby. by Owen Davis. (Gabriel) 1:23 F13'26. T 13915

The great Gatsby. by F. Scott Fitzgerald. (Anon.) 1:26 My23 '25. B 13916

The great god Brown. by Eugene O'Neill. (Gabriel) 1:26-7 F6 '26. T 13917

Great guy. (Mosher) 12:64-5*Ja 9'37. CC 13918

The great Jasper. (Mosher) 9:55-6 F25'33. CC 13919

The great John Ericsson. (Mosher) 14:60*My28'38. CC 13920

Great lady. by Earle Crooker and Lowell Brentano. (Benchley) 14:40-2*D10'38. T 13921

A great man. by Walter Vogdes (Lowrie) 5:97 Mr2'29.B 1392

The great Magoo. by Ben Hecht and Gene Fowler. (Lockridge 8:33 D10'32. T 1392

The great man votes. (Mosher) 14:59*Ja21'39. CC 1392

The great Mary Celeste hoax. b Laurence J. Keating. (Smith) 5:62-3 Ag10'29. B 1392

The great meadow. (Mosher) 7: Mr21'31. CC 1392

The great meadow. by Elizabeth Madox Roberts. (Smith) 6:10 104 Mr8'30. B 1392

The great mouthpiece. by Gene Fowler. (Coates) 7:84 O17'31. B 1392

The great necker. by Elmer Ha ris. (Brackett) 4:31-2 Mr17'2 T 1392

The great offensive. by Maurice Hindus. (Fadiman) 9:85-6 N4' B 1393

The great O'Malley. (Mosher) 1 78*Mr13'39. CC 1393

The great one. by Henry Hart. (Fadiman) 10:100 My19'34. B 1393

The great power. (Mosher) 5:86 7 Mr30'29. CC 1393

A great rich man. by Louise Schnutz Boas. (Smith) 5:104 S '29. B 1393

The great temptations. by Haro Atteridge, et al. (Gabriel) 2:2 My29'26. T 1393

The great tradition. by Granvill Hicks. (Fadiman) 9:83 S23'33. B 1393

The great waltz. (Mosher) 14:73 N26'38. CC 1393

The great waltz. by A. M. Willn et al. (Gibbs) 10:26 S29'34. T 1393

Great winds. by Ernest Poole. (Coates) 9:70-1 My20'33.B 1393

The great Ziegfeld. (Mosher) 12 63-4*Ap18'36. CC 1394

The greater glory. (Shane) 2:53 My8'26. CC 13941

The greatest show on earth. by Vincent Duffey and Irene Alex

ander. (Benchley) 13:30*Ja15 '38. T 13942
The Greeks had a word for it. by Zoë Akins. (Benchley) 6:34 O4'30. T 13943
The Greeks had a word for them. (Mosher) 7:58 F13'32. CC 13944
The green bay tree. by Mordaunt Shairp. (Gibbs) 9:26 O28'33. T 13945
(Benchley) 9:24 D23'33. 13946
Green forest. by Nathalie Colby. (Boyd) 2:79 Ja29'27. B 13947
The green goddess. (Mosher) 6: 88 F22'30. CC 13948
Green grow the lilacs. by Lynn Riggs. (Benchley) 6:26-8 F7 '31. T 13949
The green hat. by Michael Arlen. (Mankiewicz) 1:17 S26'25. T 13950
Green hell. (Mosher) 15:76*F10 '40. CC 13951
Green hills of Africa. by Ernest Hemingway. (Fadiman) 11:80-2*N2'35. B 13952
Green isle. by Alice Duer Miller. (Smith) 6:108 O4'30. B 13953
Green laurels. by Donald Culross Peattie. (Fadiman) 12:51*Jy18 '36. B 13954
Green light. (Maloney) 13:60-1* F20'37. CC 13955
Green margins. by E. P. O'Donnell. (Fadiman) 12:64-6*O3'36. B 13956
The green parrot. by Marthe Bibesco. (Smith) 5:79-80 Je1 '29. B 13957
The green pastures. (Mosher) 12: 44-5*Jy18'36. CC 13958
The green pastures. by Marc Connelly. (Benchley) 6:28 Mr8 '30; 7:24*Je27'31; 11:28†Mr9 '35. T 13959
Green waters. by Max Catto. (Benchley) 12:38-42*N14'36. T 13960
The Greene murder case. (Mosher) 5:64 Ag17'29. CC 13961
Greenwich Village follies. by Harold Atteridge, et al. (Brackett) 4:34 Ap21'28.T 13962
Greenwich Village follies. by Harold Levey and Owen Murphy. (Mankiewicz) 1:19 Ja2'26. T 13963
The grey fox. by Lemist Esler. (Brackett) 4:34-6 N3'28. T 13964
Growing pains. by Aurania Rouverol. (Benchley) 9:32 D2'33. T 13965
Growing up in New Guinea. by Margaret Mead. (Smith) 6:89 S27'30. B 13966
Grumpy. (Gibbs) 6:55 Ag9'30. CC 13967
The guardsman. (Mosher) 7:79 S 19'31. CC 13968
The guest room. by Arthur Wilmurt. (Benchley) 7:28 O17'31. T 13969
Guilty. (Mosher) 6:112 Ap12'30. CC 13970
Guilty as hell. (Mosher) 8:37 Ag 13'32. CC 13971
Guinea fowl and other poultry. by Leonard Bacon. (Boyd) 3:96 S10'27. B 13972
The guinea pig. by Preston Sturges. (Brackett) 4:24 F9'29. T 13973
Gulliver's travels. (Mosher) 15: 52*D23'39. CC 13974
The gun. by C. S. Forester. (Fadiman) 9:46-7 Ag12'33.B 13975
Gunga Din. (Mosher) 14:52-3*F4 '39. CC 13976
Guns. by James Hagan. (White) 4:38 Ag18'28. T 13977
Gypsy. by Maxwell Anderson. (Brackett) 4:25-6 Ja26'29. T 13978

H

H. M. S. Pinafore. by Arthur Sullivan and William S. Gilbert. (Gabriel) 2:28 Ap17'26.T13979
Haiti. by William DuBois. (Benchley) 14:28*Mr12'38. T 13980
Half a widow. by Harry B. Smith and Frank Dupree. (Brackett) 3:32 S24'27. T 13981
Half gods. by Sidney Howard. (Benchley) 5:27 Ja4'30.T13982

Half mile down. by William Beebe. (Fadiman) 10:110*D8'34. B 13983
The half-naked truth. by N. Brewster Morse. (Brackett) 2:31-2 Je19'26. T 13984
Hallelujah. (Mosher) 5:56-7 Ag31 '29. CC 13985
Hallelujah, I'm a bum! (Mosher) 9:59 F18'33. CC 13986
Hamlet. by William Shakespeare. (Mankiewicz) 1:19-20 O24'25; 1:17 N21'25. T 13987
Hamlet. by William Shakespeare. (Benchley) 7:28 N14'31; 12:28* O17'36; 12:28*N21'36. T 13988
A handbook to Pickwick papers. by Logan Clendening. (Fadiman) 12:83*Ap4'36. B 13989
Hands of Orlac. (Claxton) 4:75-6 Je16'28. CC 13990
Hands up. (Shane) 1:38-9 Ja23'26. CC 13991
The handy man. by Fred Wall and Ralph Murphy. (Anon.) 1:13 Mr21'25. T 13992
Hangman's house. by Donn Byrne. (Dounce) 2:53 Je12'26. B 13993
Hangman's house. by Willard Mack. (Brackett) 2:26 D25'26. T 13994
Hanna. by Thomas Beer. (Smith) 5:126-7 N23'29. B 13995
Hannibal Hooker. by William Harlan Hale. (Fadiman) 15:68*F18 '39. B 13996
Hans Frost. by Hugh Walpole. (Smith) 5:116 O5'29. B 13997
Happiness. by William Lyon Phelps. (Parker) 3:90-1 N5'27. B 13998
Happiness ahead. (Claxton) 4:77-9 Je23'28. CC 13999
The happiest days. by Charlotte Armstrong. (Gibbs) 15:28*Ap22 '39. T 14000
Happy days, 1880-1892. by H. L. Mencken. (Fadiman) 15:51-2* Ja27'40. B 14001
Happy-go-lucky. by Ian Hay Beith. (Gabriel) 2:26 My15'26. T 14002
The happy husband. by Harrison Owen. (Brackett) 4:33-4 My19 '28. T 14003
Happy landing. by John B. Hymer and William E. Barry. (Benchley) 8:26*Ap2'32. T 14004
The happy mountain. by Maristan Chapman. (Leonard) 4:62-3 Ag 11'28. T 14005
The happy warrior. (Shane) 1:17 Jy18'25. CC 14006
The harbourmaster. by William McFee. (Coates) 7:51-3 Ja2 '32. B 14007
Hard boiled Haggerty. (Claxton) 3:57 S3'27. CC 14008
The hard-boiled virgin. by Frances Newman. (Boyd) 2:90 N27 '26. B 14009
Hard to get. (Mosher) 5:68 O5'29. CC 14010
Hard to handle. (Mosher) 8:53 F11'33. CC 14011
The Hardys ride high. (Mosher) 15:66*Ap22'39. CC 14012
Harlan miners speak. by Dreiser Committee. (Coates) 8:61*Ap30 '32. B 14013
Harlem. by William Jourdan Rapp and Wallace Thurman. (Brackett) 5:29 Mr2'29. T 14014
Harlequin house. by Margery Sharp. (Anon.) 15:85*Ap15'39. B 14015
Harmer John. by Hugh Walpole. (Dounce) 2:79-80 O16'26. B 14016
Harriet. by Elizabeth Jenkins. (Fadiman) 10:99 Mr24'34. B 14017
Harriet Hume. by Rebecca West. (Smith) 5:124 N9'29. B 14018
Hart Crane: the life of an American poet. by Philip Horton. (Fadiman) 13:64-6*My29'37. B 14019
Harvest. (Mosher) 15:57*S30'39. CC 14020
Harvest. by Jean Giono. (Fadiman) 15:80*My20'39. B 14021
Harvest comedy. by Frank Swinnerton. (Fadiman) 13:62*F12'38. B 14022
Hat check girl. (Mosher) 8:68 O15

(Benchley) 8:26-8 Je4'32.T 14064
Helen of Troy. (Claxton) 3:101-103 D17'27. CC 14065
Hell below. (Mosher) 9:62 My6 '33. CC 14066
Hell bent fer heaven. (Shane) 2:53 My8'26. CC 14067
Hell bound. (Mosher) 7:81-2 My 16'31. CC 14068
Hell divers. (Mosher) 7:47 Ja2 '32. CC 14069
Hell freezes over. by John Patrick. (Benchley) 11:26*Ja11 '36. T 14070
Hell on earth. (Mosher) 9:61 F3 '34. CC 14071
Hell on ice: the saga of the "Jeanette." by Edward Ellsberg. (Fadiman) 13:61-2*F12 '38. B 14072
Hello, Daddy. by Herbert Fields. (Brackett) 4:29-30 Ja5'29. T 14073
Hello, Lola! by Dorothy Donnelly. (Mankiewicz) 1:23-4 Ja23'26. T 14074
Hello towns. by Sherwood Anderson. (Smith) 5:120 My25'29. B 14075
Hell's angels. (Mosher) 6:57-8 Ag23'30. CC 14076
Hell's highway. (Gibbs) 8:55 O1 '32. CC 14077
Hell's house. (Mosher) 8:62*F20 '32. CC 14078
Hell's Island. (Mosher) 6:54 Jy26 '30. CC 14079
Hell's kitchen. (Mosher) 15:70*Jy 8'39. CC 14080
Hellz-a-poppin. by Ole Olsen and Chic Johnson. (Gibbs) 14:30* O1'38. T 14081
Heloise and Abelard. by George Moore. (Dounce) 2:58-9 Mr20 '26. B 14082
Henry—behave! by Lawrence Langner. (Brackett) 2:52-3 S4'26. T 14083
Henry IV, part I. by William Shakespeare. (Benchley) 14:30*F11'39. T 14084
Henry VIII. (Mosher) 10:74-5 F24 '34. CC 14085
Henry Hudson. by Llewelyn Powys. (Hoyt) 4:100 Mr31'28. B 14086
Henry, King of France. by Heinrich Mann. (Kronenberger) 15:61-3*Ag5'39. B 14087
Henry of Navarre. by Henry Dwight Sedgwick. (Smith) 6:88 S27'30. B 14088
Henry the VIIIth. by Francis Hackett. (Lowrie) 5:87-8 My4'29. B 14089
Henry Ward Beecher: An American portrait. by Paxton Hibben. (Parker) 3:108-109 O15 '27. B 14090
Her cardboard lover. by Jacques Deval; Valerie Wyngate and P. G. Wodehouse. (Brackett) 3:33 Ap2'27. T 14091
Her father's house. by Hilda Vaughan. (Smith) 6:104-105 S13 '30. B 14092
Her first affaire. by Merrill Rogers. (Long) 3:54-5 S3'27. T 14093
Her jungle love. (Mosher) 14:54-5*Ap16'38. CC 14094
Her knight comes riding. by John V. A. Weaver. (Leonard) 4:58-9 Jy28'28. B 14095
Her man of wax. by Walter Hasenclever. (Gibbs) 9:34-5 O21'33. T 14096
Her master's voice. by Clare Kummer. (Benchley) 9:26 N4'33. T 14097
Her privates we. by Frederic Manning. (Smith) 6:62 Jy5'30. B 14098
Her supporting cast. by Harold Sherman. (Benchley) 7:30 My16 '31. T 14099
Her wedding night. (Mosher) 6:95 O4'30. CC 14100
Her wild oat. (Claxton) 3:67 F11 '28. CC 14101
Here and beyond. by Edith Wharton. (Dounce) 2:60 My15'26. B 14102
Here come the clowns. by Philip Barry. (Benchley) 14:28*D17 '38. T 14103
Here comes Cookie. (Mosher) 11:

68*O19'35. CC 14104
Here comes the king. by Philip Lindsay. (Fadiman) 9:46 Ag12 '33. B 14105
Here comes the Navy. (Mosher) 10:51 Jy28'34. CC 14106
Here goes the bride. by Curtis Arnoux Peters. (Benchley) 7: 32 N14'31. T 14107
Here is my heart. (Mosher) 10: 69*Ja5'35. CC 14108
Here lies. by Dorothy Parker. (Fadiman) 15:97*Ap29'39. B 14109
Here lies a most beautiful lady. by Richard Blaker. (Fadiman) 12:52-3*F29'36. B 14110
Here today. by George S. Oppenheimer. (White) 8:26 S17'32. T 14111
Here's audacity! by Frank Shay. (Coates) 6:104-105 O18'30. B 14112
Here's Howe! by Fred Thompson and Paul Gerard Smith. (Brackett) 4:34 My19'28. T 14113
Here's luck! by Hugh Wiley. (Leonard) 4:80 S8'28. B 14114
Here's to romance. (Mosher) 11: 67*O12'35. CC 14115
Heritage. by George F. Hummel. (Fadiman) 11:80-1*Ap20'35. B 14116
Herman Melville. by Lewis Mumford. (Lowrie) 5:94 Mr30'29. B 14117
The herne's egg. by William Butler Yeats. (Bogan) 14:61-2*Ap 16'38. B 14118
The heroes. by Millen Brand. (Anon.) 15:69*Ap22'39. B 14119
Hetty Green. by Boyden Sparkes and Samuel Taylor Moore. (Smith) 6:92 Ap26'30. B 14120
Hey Nonny Nonny! by Max Lief and Nathaniel Lief. (Benchley) 8:24 Je18'32. T 14121
Hidden. by William Hurlbut. (Brackett) 3:33 O15'27. T 14122
The hidden city. by Philip Gibbs. (Smith) 5:74 F1'30. B 14123
Hide in the dark. by Frances Noyes Hart. (Smith) 5:58-9 Ag 24'29. B 14124
Hide-out. (Mosher) 10:48 S1'34. CC 14125
High pressure. (Mosher) 7:59 F6 '32. CC 14126
The high road. by Frederick Lonsdale. (Brackett) 4:27 S22 '28. T 14127
High society blues. (Mosher) 6: 89-91 Ap26'30. CC 14128
High Tor. by Maxwell Anderson. (Benchley) 12:26*Ja16'37. T 14129
High, wide, and handsome. (Maloney) 13:49*Jy31'37. CC 14130
A high wind in Jamaica. by Richard Hughes. (Fadiman) 14:68-9*O8'38. B 14131
Hilda Cassidy. by Henry Lieferant and Sylvia Lieferant. (Benchley) 9:26-8 My13'33. T 14132
The hill between. by Lula Vollmer. (Benchley) 14:28*Mr19 '38. T 14133
him. by e. e. cummings. (Brackett) 4:29-30 Ap28'28. T 14134
Hindoo holiday. by J. R. Ackerley. (Coates) 8:47 Jy16'32. B 14135
Hipper's holiday. by John Crump. (Benchley) 10:30 O27'34. T 14136
His brother's wife. (Mosher) 12: 38*Ag22'36. CC 14137
His captive woman. (Mosher) 5: 91-2 Ap13'29. CC 14138
His double life. (Mosher) 9:49-50 D23'33. CC 14139
His girl Friday. (Mosher) 15:51-2* Ja13'40. CC 14140
His greatest gamble. (Mosher) 10: 51 Jy28'34. CC 14141
His majesty Bunker Bean. (Shane) 1:22 S19'25. CC 14142
His majesty's car. by Attila von Orbok. (Benchley) 6:26 N1'30. T 14143
His private life. (Mosher) 4:97 N17'28. CC 14144
His queen. by John Hastings Turner. (Anon.) 1:15 My23'25. T 14145
His secretary. (Shane) 1:23 Ja2 '26. CC 14146
His supreme moment. (Anon.) 1:

31 Ap25'25. CC 14147
History of Anthony Waring. by May Sinclair. (Parker) 3:89 O1'27. B 14148
A history of caricature. by Bohun Lynch. (Boyd) 3:100 Mr19 '27. B 14149
The history of Egg Pandervil. by Gerald Bullett. (Smith) 5:65 Ag31'29. B 14150
The history of piracy. by Philip Gosse. (Coates) 8:61-2 O22'32. B 14151
Hit the deck. (Mosher) 5:72 Ja25 '30. CC 14152
Hit the deck! by Herbert Fields and Vincent Youmans. (Brackett) 3:29 My7'27. T 14153
Hit the snow. (Claxton) 4:69-70 Jy14'28. CC 14154
Hitch your wagon. by Bernard C. Schoenfeld. (Benchley) 13:26* Ap17'37. T 14155
Hitler's reign of terror. (Mosher) 10:96 My5'34. CC 14156
Hitting a new high. (Mosher) 13: 45*D25'37. CC 14157
Hizzoner Big Bill Thompson. by John Bright. (Smith) 6:102 My 3'30. B 14158
Hizzoner the mayor. by Joel Sayre. (Coates) 9:66 Mr11'33. B 14159
Hobby house. by Russell Neale. (Lowrie) 5:95-6 Mr30'29.B14160
Hobo. by Frank Merlin. (Parker) 7:28 F21'31. T 14161
The Hohenzollerns. by Herbert Eulenberg. (Smith) 5:121 My25 '29. B 14162
Hold everything. by B. G. DeSylva and John McGowan. (Brackett) 4:27-8 O20'28. T 14163
Hold that lion. (Claxton) 2:52 S18 '26. CC 14164
Hold your horses. by Russel Crouse and Corey Ford. (Gibbs) 9:34 O7'33. T 14165
Hold your man. (Mosher) 9:46 Jy 8'33. CC 14166
Holiday. (Mosher) 6:60-1 Jy12'30. CC 14167
Holiday. (Mosher) 14:42-3*Jy2 '38. CC 14168
Holiday. by Philip Barry. (Brackett) 4:37-8 D8'28. T 14169
Holiday party. (Mosher) 10:79 Je 2'34. CC 14170
The holiday round. by A. A. Milne. (Dounce) 1:17 Ag1'25. B 14171
Holka polka. by Bert Kalmar and Harry Ruby. (Mankiewicz) 1:20 O24'25. T 14172
Hollywood cavalcade. (Mosher) 15: 74*O21'39. CC 14173
The Hollywood revue. (Mosher) 5:53-4 Ag24'29. CC 14174
Holy deadlock. by A. P. Herbert. (Fadiman) 10:54 Ag4'34.B 14175
Holy Ireland. by Norah Hoult. (Anon.) 11:65-6*F15'36.B 14176
The holy lover. by Marie Conway Oemler. (Boyd) 3:66-7 Jy16'27. B 14177
The home place. by Dorothy Thomas. (Fadiman) 12:62*Jy25 '36. B 14178
The home towners. (Mosher) 4:83-4 N3'28. CC 14179
The home towners. by George M. Cohan. (Brackett) 2:51 S4'26. T 14180
Homecoming. (Mosher) 4:93 N24 '28. CC 14181
Homeplace. by Maristan Chapman. (Smith) 5:68 Ag17'29. B 14182
Honest liars. by Robert Weenolsen and Sherrill Webb. (Brackett) 2:36-7 Jy31'26. T 14183
Honey in the horn. by Harold Davis. (Fadiman) 11:52-3*Ag24 '35. B 14184
Honeymoon. by Samuel Chotzinoff and George Backer. (Benchley) 8:26-30 Ja7'33. T 14185
Honeymoon hate. (Claxton) 3:103-104 D17'27. CC 14186
Honeymoon lane. by Eddie Dowling. (Brackett) 2:34 O2'26. T 14187
Honor among lovers. (Mosher) 7: 75 Mr7'31. CC 14188
Honor be damned. by Willard Mack. (Brackett) 2:34 F12'27. T 14189
The honorable picnic. by Thomas

Raucat. (Boyd) 3:78-9 Je25'27. B 14190
Honourable estate. by Vera Brittain. (Anon.) 12:117*N14'36. B 14191
The hook-up. by Jack Lait and Stephen Gross. (Gibbs) 11:30* My18'35. T 14192
Hooray for what! by Howard Lindsay and Russel Crouse. (Benchley) 13:46*D11'37. T 14193
Hope of heaven. by John O'Hara. (Fadiman) 14:63*Mr19'38. B 14194
The Hopkins manuscript. by R. C. Sherriff. (Fadiman) 15:71*Jy8 '39. B 14195
Horatio Alger. by Herbert R. Mayes. (Hoyt) 4:108 Ap7'28. B 14196
The horror of it. by Frederick Barber. (Coates) 8:64*Ap16'32. B 14197
Horse and buggy doctor. by Arthur E. Hertzler. (Fadiman) 14:42-3*Jy30'38. B 14198
Horse feathers. (Mosher) 8:37-8 Ag20'32. CC 14199
Hospital. by Rhoda Truax. (Coates) 8:67-8*Mr5'32. B 14200
Hostages to fortune. by Elizabeth Cambridge. (Fadiman) 9:45 Jy 15'33. B 14201
Hot chocolates. by Andy Razaf, et al. (Brackett) 5:48 Je29'29. T 14202
Hot countries. by Alec Waugh. (Smith) 6:107-108 My10'30. B 14203
Hot for Paris. (Mosher) 5:72 Ja 11'30. CC 14204
The hot Mikado. by Charles L. Cooke, et al. (Gibbs) 15:28*Ap 1'39. T 14205
Hot news. (Claxton) 4:51 Jy28'28. CC 14206
Hot news. by Emile Gauvreau. (Coates) 7:52*Jy18'31. B 14207
Hot pan. by Michael Swift. (Brackett) 4:28 F25'28. T 14208
Hot Saturday. by Harvey Fergusson. (Dounce) 2:86 S11'26. B 14209
Hot water. by P. G. Wodehouse. (Coates) 8:42 Ag20'32. B 14210
Hotbed. by Paul Osborn. (Brackett) 4:34 N24'28. T 14211
Hot-cha! by Lew Brown, et al. (Benchley) 8:28-30*Mr19'32. T 14212
Hotel for women. (Mosher) 15:51-2*S2'39. CC 14213
Hotel Imperial. (Claxton) 2:79 Ja 8'27. CC 14214
Hotel in Spain. by Nancy Johnstone. (Fadiman) 14:62*Mr12 '38. B 14215
Hotel Universe. by Philip Barry. (Benchley) 6:27-8 Ap26'30. T 14216
Houdini. by Harold Kellock. (Markey) 4:83 Je23'28. B 14217
The hound of Florence. by Felix Salten. (Smith) 6:86 Je14'30. B 14218
The hound of the Baskervilles. (Mosher) 15:67-8*Ap1'39. CC 14219
The hounds of Spring. by Sylvia Thompson. (Dounce) 2:50 Ap10 '26. B 14220
The hour of decision. by Oswald Spengler. (Fadiman) 10:84-5 F 17'34. B 14221
House afire. by Mann Page. (Benchley) 6:33 Ap12'30. T 14222
The house at Pooh Corner. by A. A. Milne. (Parker) 4:98 O20 '28. B 14223
A house divided. by Pearl S. Buck. (Fadiman) 10:65*Ja19'35. B 14224
The house in Paris. by Elizabeth Bowen. (Anon.) 12:76*Mr7'36. B 14225
The house of a thousand candles. (Mosher) 12:70*Ap11'36. CC 14226
The house of Connelly. by Paul Green. (Benchley) 7:32-4 O10 '31. T 14227
House of exile. by Nora Waln. (Woollcott) 9:28-30 Jy29'33. B 14228
The house of lost identity. by Donald Corley. (Boyd) 3:54 Jy 30'27. B 14229
House of Remsen. by Nicholas Soussanin and William J. Perl-

man. (Benchley) 10:32-4 Ap14 '34. T 14230

House of Rothschild. (Mosher) 10:86-7 Mr17'34. CC 14231

The house of shadows. by Leigh Hutty. (Brackett) 3:29-30 My7 '27. T 14232

The house of Travelinck. by Jo van Ammers-Küller. (Fadiman) 14:63-4*O1'38. B 14233

The house of Ussher. by H. V. Esmond. (Mankiewicz) 1:24 Ja 23'26. T 14234

The house of women. by Louis Bromfield. (Brackett) 3:33-4 O15'27. T 14235

The house on 56th Street. (Mosher) 9:111 D9'33. CC 14236

Houseboat on the Styx. by Kenneth Webb and John E. Hazzard. (Brackett) 4:32 Ja5'29. T 14237

Houseparty. by Kenneth Britton and Roy Hargrave. (Benchley) 5:36-8 S21'29. T 14238

How beautiful with shoes. by Wilber Daniel Steele and Anthony Brown. (Benchley) 11:46-8*D7 '35. T 14239

How green was my valley. by Richard Llewellyn. (Fadiman) 15:77-8 F10'40. B 14240

How he lied to her husband. by George Bernard Shaw. (Benchley) 6:28 Ja31'31. T 14241

How to commit a murder. by Danny Ahearn. (Hellman) 6:95-6 Ap26'30. B 14242

How to get tough about it. by Robert Ardrey. (Benchley) 14:30*F19'38. T 14243

How to run a war. by Bruce Winton Knight. (Anon.) 12:66*O24 '36. B 14244

Howdy king. by Mark Swan. (Brackett) 2:24-6 D25'26. T 14245

How's your health? by Booth Tarkington and Harry Leon Wilson. (Benchley) 5:38 D14 '29. T 14246

The Hudson. by Carl Carmer. (Fadiman) 15:58-9*Jy1'39. B 14247

Hudson River bracketed. by Edith Wharton. (Smith) 5:103 N30'29. B 14248

Hula. (Claxton) 3:89 S10'27. CC 14249

The human adventure. (Mosher) 12:77*O17'36. CC 14250

Humanism and America. by Norman Foerster, ed. (A. T.) 6:104-105 Mr8'30. B 14251

The humble. by Lawrence Irving. (Brackett) 2:34 O23'26. T 15252

The hunchback of Notre Dame. (Mosher) 15:47*D30'39. CC 15253

The hundred years. by Philip Guedalla. (Fadiman) 12:56-8* Ja30'37. B 14254

A hundred years old. by Joaquin Alvarez Quintero and Serafin Quintero. (Benchley) 5:38 O12 '29. T 14255

Hungarian rhapsody. (Mosher) 5:54 Ag10'29. CC 14256

Hunky. by Thames Williamson. (Smith) 5:57 Jy27'29. B 14257

Huntsman in the sky. by Granville Toogood. (Smith) 6:102-103 Ap5'30. B 14258

Huntsman, what quarry? by Edna St. Vincent Millay. (Bogan) 15:80-2*My20'39. B 14259

The hurricane. (Mosher) 13:87-8* N20'37. CC 14260

The hurricane. by Charles Nordhoff and James Norman Hall. (Anon.) 12:70*F22'36. B 14261

I

I am a fugitive from a chain gang. (Mosher) 8:73-4 N19'32. CC 14262

I am my youth. by Ernest Pascal and Edwin Blum. (Benchley) 14:28*Mr19'38. T 14263

I am still alive. by Dick Grace. (Coates) 7:52-3*Jy18'31. B 14264

I am Suzanne. (Mosher) 9:61 Ja27 '34. CC 14265

I am the fox. by Winifred Van Etten. (Fadiman) 12:50-1*Ag29'36. B 14266

I believe. by Clifton Fadiman, ed. (Kronenberger) 15:53-4*Ag12'39. B 14267

I change worlds. by Anna Louise Strong. (Fadiman) 11:81-2*Ap 20'35. B 14268

I cover the waterfront. by Max Miller. (Coates) 8:58 Je18'32. B 14269

I dream too much. (Mosher) 11: 93-4*D7'35. CC 14270

I have no regrets. by Hans Bringolf and Blaise Cendrars, ed. (Coates) 8:44 Ag13'32. B 14271

I have this to say. by Violet Hunt. (Boyd) 2:110-12 D4'26. B 14272

I knock at the door. by Sean O'Casey. (Kronenberger) 15: 65-7*Jy22'39. B 14273

I know a secret. by Christopher Morley. (Parker) 3:112 N12'27. B 14274

I live my life. (Mosher) 11:67*O 19'35. CC 14275

I love an actress. by Chester Erskin, adapt. (Benchley) 7: 26-8 S26'31. T 14276

I love that man. (Mosher) 9:42 Jy15'33. CC 14277

I loved you Wednesday. (Mosher) 9:63 Je24'33. CC 14278

I loved you Wednesday. by Molly Ricardel and William DuBois. (Benchley) 8:26 O22'32. T 14279

I married an angel. by Richard Rodgers and Lorenz Hart. (Gibbs) 14:30*My21'38. T 14280

I met him in Paris. (Mosher) 13: 61-2*Je5'37. CC 14281

I, myself. by Adelyn Bushnell. (Benchley) 10:30 My19'34. T 14282

I saw it myself. by Henri Barbusse. (Lowrie) 4:67-8 D22'28. B 14283

I see a wondrous land. by Gudmundur Kamban. (Fadiman) 14:67*Mr26'38. B 14284

I stand condemned. (Mosher) 12: 47*Jy11'36. CC 14285

I swear by Apollo. by William E. Aughinbaugh. (Fadiman) 14:54-5*S3'38. B 14286

I think I remember. by Magdalen King-Hall. (Boyd) 3:80-1 Je25 '27. B 14287

I want a policeman! by Rufus King and Milton Lazarus. (Benchley) 11:26*Ja25'36. T 14288

I want my wife. by B. M. Kaye. (Benchley) 6:28 Mr29'30. T 14289

I went to Russia. by Liam O'Flaherty. (Coates) 7:89 O3'31. B 14290

I write as I please. by Walter Duranty. (Fadiman) 11:87*N16 '35. B 14291

Iceland fisherman. (Mosher) 11:70* O5'35. CC 14292

I'd rather be right. by George S. Kaufman; Richard Rodgers and Lorenz Hart. (Benchley) 13:30* N13'37. T 14293

Ida Elizabeth. by Sigrid Undset. (Fadiman) 9:74-5 S30'33. B 14294

Idiot's delight. (Mosher) 14:70*F 11'39. CC 14295

Idiot's delight. by Robert E. Sherwood. (Benchley) 12:32-4*Ap4 '36. T 14296

The idle rich. (Mosher) 5:89 Je 22'29. CC 14297

Idle women. by Dorothy Black. (Leonard) 4:96 N3'28. B 14298

If. by Edward John Dunsany. (Brackett) 3:25 N5'27. T 14299

If. by John Collings Squire, ed. (Coates) 7:90-1 Ap4'31. B 14300

If Booth had missed. by Arthur Goodman. (Benchley) 7:24 F13 '32. T 14301

If I had a million. (Mosher) 8:85 D10'32. CC 14302

If I was rich. by William Anthony McGuire. (Brackett) 2:34 S11 '26. T 14303

If I were free. (Mosher) 9:79-80 Ja13'34. CC 14304

If I were king. (Mosher) 14:48-9*O1'38. CC 14305

If I were single. (Claxton) 4:63-4 Mr10'28. CC 14306

If I were you. by Sholem Aleichem. (Benchley) 7:34 O3'31. T 14307

If it die. by André Gide. (Fadiman) 11:82*N2'35. B 14308

If memory serves. by Anatole France. (Fadiman) 11:73-4*O

12'35. B 14309
If this be treason. by John Haynes Holmes and Reginald Lawrence. (Gibbs) 11:36*O5'35. T 14310
Igloo. (Mosher) 8:36 Jy30'32. CC 14311
Il Trovatore. (Mosher) 11:93*D14 '35. CC 14312
I'll take romance. (Mosher) 13: 84*D18'37. CC 14313
Illusion. by Arthur Train. (Smith) 5:104 Je15'29. B 14314
I'm no angel. (Mosher) 9:69-70 O14'33. CC 14315
Immoral Isabella? by Lawton Campbell. (Brackett) 3:25 N5 '27. T 14316
Immortal lyrics. by Hudson Strode. (Bogan) 14:84*O22'38. B 14317
Impassioned pygmies. by Keith Winter. (Fadiman) 12:70-1*Mr 21'36. B 14318
Impatient maiden. (Mosher) 8:56* Mr12'32. CC 14319
An imperfect lover. by Robert Gore Browne. (Smith) 5:60-1 Ag3'29. B 14320
Imperial city. by Elmer Rice. (Fadiman)13:81-2*N13'37.B 14321
Imperial palace. by Arnold Bennett.(Smith) 6:87 N29'30. B 14322
The importance of being earnest. by Oscar Wilde. (Gabriel) 2: 26 My15'26. T 14323
(Benchley) 14:32*Ja21'39. 14324
The impregnable women. by Eric Linklater. (Fadiman) 14:45-6* Ag6'38. B 14325
Improvisations in June. by Max Mohr. (Brackett) 4:33-4 Mr10 '28. T 14326
In a garden. by Philip Barry. (Mankiewicz) 1:15 N28'25.T 14327
In Abraham's bosom. by Paul Green. (Brackett) 3:33 F26'27. T 14328
In all countries. by John Dos Passos. (Fadiman) 10:106 Ap 21'34. B 14329
In coldest Africa. by Carveth Wells. (Smith) 5:84-5 D21'29. B 14330
In my end is my beginning. by Maurice Baring. (Coates) 7:92-3 N14'31. B 14331
In old Arizona. (Mosher) 4:65 Ja 26'29. CC 14332
In old Chicago. (Mosher) 13:52-3*Ja15'38. CC 14333
In old Kentucky. (Claxton) 3:66 N26'27. CC 14334
In our time. by Ernest Hemingway. (Coates) 6:116 N22'30. B 14335
In person. (Mosher) 11:73-4*D21 '35. CC 14336
In Princeton town. by Day Edgar. (Smith) 5:124 O26'29. B 14337
In search of peace. by Neville Chamberlain. (Fadiman) 15:58* Jy1'39. B 14338
In such a night. by Babette Deutsch. (Boyd) 3:107 Ap16'27. B 14339
In the beginning. by Norman Douglas. (Markey) 4:102-103 My12'28. B 14340
In the days of bicycles and bustles by R. D. Blumenfield. (Smith) 6:88-9 S27'30. B 14341
In the Golden Nineties. by Henry Collins Brown. (Hoyt) 3:60 D24 '27. B 14342
In the next room. (Mosher) 6:112 Ap12'30. CC 14343
In the reign of Rothstein. by Donald Henderson Clarke. (Lowrie 5:92 F23'29. B 14344
In the service of the king. by Aimee Semple McPherson. (Parker)4:79-81 F25'28. B 14345
In the worst possible taste. by John Riddell. (Coates) 8:61*My 14'32. B 14346
In their own image. by Hamilton Basso. (Fadiman) 11:74*Mr30 '35. B 14347
In Times Square. by Dodson L. Mitchell and Clyde North. (White) 7:29-30 D5'31. T 14348
The incredible Marquis. by Herbert Gorman. (Smith) 5:115-16 O5'29. B 14349
Indeed this flesh. by Grace Flandrau. (Fadiman) 10:100-

102 My19'34. B 14350
Indian air. by Paul Morand. (Fadiman) 9:47 Ag12'33. B 14351
Indian stories from the Pueblos. by Frank G. Applegate. (Smith) 5:128-9 N23'29. B 14352
Indiscreet. (Mosher) 7:81 My16 '31. CC 14353
Indiscretion. by Myron C. Fagan. (Brackett)5:31-2 Mr16'29. T 14354
An infamous army. by Georgette Heyer. (Anon.) 14:76*Ap9'38. B 14355
Infatuation. (Shane) 1:31 Ja9'26. CC 14356
The infinite shoeblack. by Norman Mac Owen. (Benchley) 6:28 Mr1'30. T 14357
The informer. (Mosher) 11:67*My 18'35. CC 14358
Inhale and exhale. by William Saroyan. (Fadiman) 12:67-9*F 22'36. B 14359
Inheritance. by John Drinkwater. (Coates) 7:88 N28'31. B 14360
Inheritors. by Susan Glaspell. (Brackett) 3:33 Mr19'27. T 14361
Ink. by Dana Watterson Greeley. (Brackett) 3:32 N12'27. T 14362
Innocent Summer. by Frances Frost. (Anon.) 11:54-5*F1'36. B 14363
The innocent voyage. by Richard Hughes. (Middleton) 5:117 Ap 20'29. B 14364
The innocents of Paris. by C. E. Andrews. (Markey) 4:100 My5 '28. B 14365
The inquisitor. by Francis Brett Young. (Fadiman) 11:73-4*S7 '35. B 14366
Insanity fair. by Douglas Reed. (Fadiman) 14:64-5*My21'38. B 14367
The insect menace. by L. O. Howard. (Coates) 7:55 D26'31. B 14368
Inside Asia. by John Gunther. (Fadiman) 15:76-8*Je10'39. B 14369
Inside Europe. by John Gunther. (Fadiman) 11:68-9*F8'36. B 14370
Inside Nazi Germany—1938. (Mosher) 13:48*Ja29'38. CC 14371
The inside story. by George Bryant and Francis M. Verdi. (Benchley) 8:34*Mr5'32. T 14372
The inspector general. by Nikolai Gogol. (Benchley) 6:30 Ja3'31; 11:28†F23'35. T 14373
Inspector Kennedy. by Milton Herbert Gropper and Edna Sherry. (Benchley) 5:27 Ja4'30. T 14374
Inspiration. (Mosher) 6:71-3 F14 '31. CC 14375
Insult. by Jan Fabricius. (Benchley) 6:34 S27'30. T 14376
The intelligent man's guide to marriage and celibacy. by Juanita Tanner. (Smith) 5:64-5 Jy13'29. B 14377
The intelligent woman's guide to socialism and capitalism. by George Bernard Shaw. (Markey) 4:84 Je16'28. B 14378
Interference. (Mosher) 4:93 N24 '28. CC 14379
Interference. by Roland Pertwee and Harold Dearden. (Brackett) 3:28 O29'27. T 14380
Intermezzo: a love story. (Mosher) 15:63*O7'39. CC 14381
The international. by John Howard Lawson. (Brackett) 3:26 Ja28'28. T 14382
International House. (Mosher) 9: 64 Je3'33. CC 14383
International review. by Lew Leslie. (Benchley) 6:28-9 Mr8'30. T 14384
Intimate acrobatics. by Donald Stites Fairchild. (Boyd) 3:121 Ap9'27. B 14385
The intimate journal of Rudolph Valentino. (Coates) 7:80-1 Ja9 '32. B 14386
The intriguing duchess. by Dorothy de Brissac Campbell. (Coates) 6:84 N1'30. B 14387
Introduction to Sally. by Mary Annette Russell. (Dounce) 2:84 O9'26. B 14388
The invader. by Hilda Vaughan. (Leonard) 4:60-1 Ag4'28. B 14389
Invasion. by Maxence van der Meersch. (Flanner) 11:51*F15 '36. B 14390

J

(Dounce) 1:26 F28'25. B 14433
Jail break. (Mosher) 12:44*Ag15 '36. CC 14434
Jake Lingle. by John Boettiger. (Coates) 7:84 O17'31. B 14435
Jalna. (Mosher) 11:45-6*Ag24'35. CC 14436
Jamaica Inn. (Flanner) 14:52*Je 10'39. CC 14437
Jamaica Inn. (Mosher) 15:88-9*O 14'39. CC 14438
Jamaica Inn. by Daphne du Maurier. (Fadiman) 12:68-9*My2 '36. CC 14439
James Branch Cabell. by Carl Van Doren. (Coates) 8:70-1* F20'32. B 14440
Jarnegan. by Charles Beahan and Garrett Fort. (Brackett) 4:33-4 O6'28. T 14441
Jarnegan. by Jim Tully. (Dounce) 2:69 S25'26. B 14442
The jay walker. by Olga Printzlau. (Gabriel) 2:34 F20'26. T 14443
Jayhawker. by Sinclair Lewis and Lloyd Lewis. (Benchley) 10:32†N17'34. T 14444
Jazz heaven. (Mosher) 5:112-13 N9'29. CC 14445
The jazz singer. (Claxton) 3:91-3 O15'27. CC 14446
The jazz singer. by Samson Raphaelson. (Mankiewicz) 1:16 N28'25. T 14447
The jealous moon. by Theodore Charles and Jane Cowl. (Brackett) 4:38 D1'28. T 14448
Jealousy. (Mosher) 5:91-2 S21'29. CC 14449
Jealousy. by Eugene Walter. (Brackett) 4:33-4 N3'28. T 14450
Jean Clarambaux. by Jean Tousseul. (Fadiman) 15:68*N4'39. B 14451
Jean-Jacques Rousseau. by Matthew Josephson. (Coates) 7:53 Ja30'32. B 14452
Jeb Stuart. by John W. Thomason, Jr. (Coates) 6:116 N8'30. B 14453
Jedermann. by Hugo von Hofmannsthal. (Brackett) 3:32 D17 '27. T 14454
Jefferson and Hamilton. by Claude G. Bowers. (Dounce) 1:22 D26 '25. B 14455
Jehol, city of emperors. by Sven Hedin. (Coates) 8:60 Ja14'33. B 14456
Jennie Gerhardt. (Mosher) 9:51-2 Je17'33. CC 14457
Jenny. by Margaret Ayer Barnes and Edward Sheldon. (Benchley) 5:36 O19'29. T 14458
Jenny Heysten's career. by Jo van Ammers-Küller. (Smith) 6:104 S13'30. B 14459
Jeremiah. by Stefan Zweig. (Benchley) 14:30-2*F11'39. T 14460
Jerome, or the latitude of love. by Maurice Bedel. (Leonard) 4:60 Ag4'28. B 14461
Jerry for short. by William A. Grew. (Brackett) 5:39-40 Ag24 '29. T 14462
Jessie James. (Mosher) 14:59*Ja 21'39. CC 14463
The jest. by Sam Bennelli. (Gabriel) 2:33-4 F20'26. T 14464
Jesting Pilate. by Aldous Huxley. (Boyd) 2:93 N27'26. B 14465
A Jew at war. (Mosher) 7:45*Ag1 '31. CC 14466
A Jew in love. by Ben Hecht. (Coates) 6:75-7 F7'31. B 14467
The Jew of Rome. by Lion Feuchtwanger. (Fadiman) 11:52*Ja4 '36. B 14468
The jewel. by Claire Goll. (Coates) 7:74*Je13'31. B 14469
Jewel robbery. by Bertram Bloch. (Benchley) 7:28 Ja23'32. T 14470
Jews without money. by Michael Gold. (Hellman) 6:104 Mr29'30. B 14471
Jezebel. (Mosher) 14:57-8*Mr19 '38. CC 14472
Jezebel. by Owen Davis. (Benchley) 9:24 D30'33. T 14473
Jig saw. by Dawn Powell. (Benchley) 10:30 My12'34. T 14474
Jill. by E. M. Delafield. (Boyd) 3:97 F19'27. B 14475
Jimmy the gent. (Mosher) 10:61 Mr31'34. CC 14476
Joan of Arc. by Joseph Delteil.

(Dounce) 2:49 Jy17'26. B 14477
Joe and Ethel Turp call on the President. (Mosher) 15:52*Ja 13'40. CC 14478
Joe Pete. by Florence E. McClinchey. (Gannett) 5:166-8 D7 '29. B 14479
John. by Philip Barry. (Brackett) 3:34 N19'27. T 14480
John Brown's body. by Stephen Vincent Benét. (Leonard) 4:63 Ag11'28. B 14481
John D.; a portrait in oils. by John K. Winkler. (Smith) 5:73 Je29'29. B 14482
John Deth, and other poems. by Conrad Aiken. (Bogan) 7:83-4 Mr21'31. B 14483
John Ferguson. by St. John Ervine. (White) 9:24 Jy22'33. T 14484
John Gabriel Borkman. by Henrik Ibsen. (Gabriel) 1:22 F13'26. T 14485
John Henry. by Roark Bradford. (Benchley) 15:30*Ja20'40. T 14486
John Jay Chapman and his letters. by M. A. De Wolfe Howe. (Fadiman) 13:63*O2'37. B 14487
John L. Sullivan. by R. F. Dibble. (Anon.) 1:26 Ap25'25. B 14488
John Meade's woman. (Maloney) 13:61*F20'37. CC 14489
John Paul Jones. by Phillips Russell. (Boyd) 3:94-5 S24'27. B 14490
John Reed: the making of a revolutionary. by Granville Hicks. (Anon.) 12:73-4*Ap18'36. B 14491
Johnny Johnson. by Paul Green (Benchley) 12:26*N28'36. T 14492
Jonesy. by Anne Morrison and John Peter Toohey. (Brackett) 5:29-30 Ap20'29. T 14493
Joseph. by Bertram Bloch. (Benchley) 6:34 F22'30. T 14494
Joseph and his brethren. by H. W. Freeman. (Lowrie) 4:69 Ja 12'29. B 14495
Joseph and his brothers. by Thomas Mann. (Fadiman) 10:91-2 Je9'34; 14:58-62*F26'38. B 14496
Joseph Fouche. by Stefan Zweig. (Smith) 6:63 Ag23'30. B 14497
Joseph Suss. by Ashley Dukes. (Benchley) 5:25 F1'30. T 14498
Josephus. by Lion Feuchtwanger. (Coates) 8:74-5 O15'32. B 14499
Joshua's vision. by William J. Locke. (Lowrie) 4:142-3 D8'28. B 14500
Journal of a crime. (Mosher) 10: 97 My5'34. CC 14501
The journal of Arnold Bennett. by Arnold Bennett. (Coates) 8:66 N 26'32; 8:66-7 Je4'32. B 14502
(Fadiman) 9:71 Je3'33. 14503
The journal of Gamaliel Bradford by Gamaliel Bradford and Van Wyck Brooks, ed. (Fadiman) 9:77-8 S9'33. B 14504
Journal of Katherine Mansfield. by Katherine Mansfield. (Parker) 3:95-6 O8'27. B 14505
A journal of these days. by Albert Jay Nock. (Fadiman) 10: 102 Mr17'34. B 14506
Journal of things old and new. by Arnold Bennett. (Smith) 6:96 S 20'30. B 14507
The journey down. by Aline Bernstein. (Fadiman) 14:61*F19'38 B 14508
The journey inward. by Kurt Heuser; Willa Muir, trans. and Edwin Muir, trans. (Coates) 8: 43 Ag13'32. B 14509
Journey to a war. by W. H. Auden and Christopher Isherwood. (Kronenberger) 15:53*Ag12'39. B 14510
Journey to the end of the night. by Louis-Ferdinand Céline. (Fadiman) 10:99-100 Ap28'34. B 14511
Journeyman. by Erskine Caldwell (Fadiman) 10:64*F2'35. B 14512
Journey's end. (Mosher) 6:56-7 A 19'30. CC 14513
Journey's end. by R. C. Sherriff (Brackett) 5:27 Mr30'29. T 1451
(Gibbs) 15:30-2 S30'39. 14515
The joy girl. (Claxton) 3:87-9 S1 '27. CC 14516
Joy of living. (Maloney) 14:66*M

7'38. CC 14517
The joyous season. by Philip Barry. (Benchley) 9:28 F10'34. T 14518
Juan in America. by Eric Linklater. (Coates) 7:108-109 Ap11 '31. B 14519
Juarez. (Mosher) 15:94-5*Ap29 '39. CC 14520
Juarez and Maximilian. by Franz Werfel. (Brackett) 2:33 O23'26. T 14521
Jubilee. by Cole Porter and Moss Hart. (Benchley) 11:32-4*O19 '35. T 14522
Judas. by Walter Ferris and Basil Rathbone. (Brackett) 4:28 F2'29. T 14523
Judge and fool. by Vladimir Zhabotinskii. (Smith) 6:74 Mr1 '30. B 14524
Judge Priest. (Mosher) 10:88 O 20'34. CC 14525
Judgment day. by Elmer Rice. (Gibbs) 10:32 S22'34. T 14526
The judge's husband. by William Hodge. (Brackett) 2:34 O9'26. T 14527
Judith. by Jean Giradoux. (Flanner) 7:58-9 D5'31. T 14528
Judith. by Gladys Unger. (Anon.) 1:11 Mr7'25. T 14529
Julie. by Corning White. (Brackett) 3:30 My21'27. T 14530
Julius Caesar. by William Shakespeare. (Benchley) 13:30-2*N20 '37. T 14531
July '14. by Emil Ludwig. (Smith) 5:116 N16'29. B 14532
Jumbo. by Ben Hecht and Charles MacArthur. (Benchley) 11:26-30*N23'35. T 14533
June days. by Cyrus Wood and Clifford Grey. (Mankiewicz) 1:13-14 Ag15'25. T 14534
June moon. by Ring Lardner and George S. Kaufman. (Benchley) 5:38-40 O19'29. T 14535
Jungle days. by William Beebe. (Dounce) 1:17 Jy18'25. B 14536
Jungle ways. by William Seabrook. (Coates) 7:93 Ap18'31. B 14537
Juno and the paycock. by Sean O'Casey. (Gabriel) 2:25 Mr27 '26. T 14538
(Brackett) 3:23 D31'27. 14539
(Benchley) 15:26*Ja27'40. 14540
Just around the corner. (Mosher) 14:96-7*D10'38. CC 14541
Just imagine. (Mosher) 6:75 N29 '30. CC 14542
Just life. by John Bowie. (Brackett) 2:29-30 S25'26. T 14543
Just suppose. (Shane) 1:39 Ja23 '26. CC 14544
Just the other day, an informal history of Great Britain since the war. by John Collier and Iain Lang. (Coates) 8:93-4 D3 '32. B 14545
Just to remind you. by Owen Davis. (Benchley) 7:30 S19'31. T 14546

K

Kai Lung unrolls his mat. by Ernest Bramah. (Markey) 4:89 Je2'28. B 14547
Kameradschaft. (Mosher) 8:74 N19 '32. CC 14548
Karl and Anna. by Leonhard Frank. (Benchley) 5:36-8 O19 '29. T 14549
Katerina. by Leonid Andreyev. (Brackett) 5:29-30 Mr9'29. T 14550
Katia. (Mosher) 15:53*D23'39. CC 14551
Katja, the dancer. by Frederick Lonsdale. (Brackett) 2:31 O30 '26. T 14552
Katy did. by Willis Maxwell Goodhue. (Brackett) 3:30 My21'27. T 14553
Keep moving. by Newman Levy and Jack School. (Gibbs) 10:46 S1'34. T 14554
Keep shufflin'. by Flourney E. Miller and Aubrey Lyles. (Brackett) 4:33 Mr10'28. T 14555
The keeper of the keys. by Valentine Davies. (Gibbs) 9:28 O28 '33. T 14556
Kempy. by J. C. Nugent and El-

liott Nugent. (Brackett) 3:36 My28'27. T 14557
The kennel murder case. (Mosher) 9:79 N4'33. CC 14558
Kentucky moonshine. (Mosher) 14: 72*My14'38. CC 14559
The key. (Mosher) 10:80 Je2'34. CC 14560
Key Largo. by Maxwell Anderson. (Benchley) 15:34*D9'39. T 14561
Kid boots. (Claxton) 2:41 O16'26. CC 14562
The kid brother. (Claxton) 2:68 Ja29'27. CC 14563
The kid from Kokomo. (Mosher) 15:81*My27'39. CC 14564
The kid from Spain. (Mosher) 8: 59 N26'32. CC 14565
Kid Galahad. (Mosher) 13:57-8* My29'37. CC 14566
Kid millions. (Mosher) 10:80*N24 '34. CC 14567
Kidnapped. (Maloney) 14:49-50*Je 4'38. CC 14568
Kiki. (Shane) 2:45 Ap10'26. CC 14569
Kiki's memoirs. by Alice Prin. (Smith) 6:62-3 Ag16'30. B 14570
Kill that story. by George Abbott and Philip Dunning. (Gibbs) 10: 34 S8'34. T 14571
The killers. by Louis E. Bisch and Howard Merling. (Brackett) 4:33 Mr31'28. T 14572
Kimiko. (Mosher) 13:69-70*Ap10 '37. CC 14573
Kind lady. by Edward Chodorov. (Gibbs) 11:26*My4'35. T 14574
Kindred. by Paul Vincent Carroll. (Benchley) 15:28*Ja6'40. T 14575
The king and the chorus girl. (Mosher) 13:72*Ap3'37. CC 14576
King Edward VII. by Sidney Lee. (Anon.) 1:26 Ap18'25. B 14577
King Edward VIII. by Hector Bolitho. (Fadiman) 13:68-9*My 8'37. B 14578
King for a night. (Mosher) 9:90 D16'33. CC 14579
King Haber. by Alfred Neumann. (Smith) 6:122 Ap12'30. B 14580
King Henry V. by William Shakespeare. (Brackett) 4:29-30 Mr 24'28. T 14581
King Kong. (Mosher) 9:56-7 Mr 11'33. CC 14582
King Mob. by Frank K. Notch. (Smith) 6:91 Je7'30. B 14583
King of burlesque. (Mosher) 11: 55-6*Ja25'36. CC 14584
The king of kings. (Claxton) 3: 97-8 Ap30'27. CC 14585
The king on Main Street. (Shane) 1:23 O31'25. CC 14586
King Richard II. by William Shakespeare. (Benchley) 12:28* F13'37. T 14587
King Solomon's mines. (Mosher) 11:41*Ag3'35. CC 14588
King Spider: some aspects of Louis XI of France and his companions. by D. B. Wyndham Lewis. (Gannett) 5:165-6 D7'29. B 14589
The king steps out. (Mosher) 12: 63*Je6'36. CC 14590
The king who was a king. by H. G. Wells. (Smith) 5:79 Je1'29. B 14591
The kingdom of God. by Gregorio Martinez Sierra. (Brackett) 4: 25-6 D29'28. T 14592
The king's people. (Mosher) 13: 70*My22'37. CC 14593
King's pleasure. by Ida Zeitlin. (Smith) 5:164 D7'29. B 14594
The king's vacation. (Mosher) 8: 47 Ja28'33. CC 14595
The kink. by Lynn Brock. (Boyd) 3:79-80 Je25'27. B 14596
Kismet. (Mosher) 6:103-104 N8'30. CC 14597
The kiss. (Mosher) 5:110 N23'29. CC 14598
A kiss for Cinderella. (Shane) 1:22-3 Ja2'26. CC 14599
A kiss in a taxi. (Claxton) 3:83 Mr19'27. CC 14600
A kiss in the taxi. by Clifford Grey. (Mankiewicz) 1:15 S5'25. T 14601
Kiss me. by Derick Wulff and Max Simon. (White) 3:32-3 Ag6 '27. T 14602
Kiss me again. (Anon.) 1:31 My9 '25. CC 14603

Kiss me again. (Shane) 1:17 Ag1 '25. CC 14604
Kiss me again. (Mosher) 6:67 Ja 17'31. CC 14605
A kiss of importance. by Arthur Hornblow, Jr.; André Picard and H. M. Harwood. (Benchley) 6:33-4 D13'30. T 14606
Kiss the boys goodbye. by Clare Boothe. (Gibbs) 14:26*O8'38. T 14607
The kiss to the leper. by François Mauriac. (Smith) 6:54 Ag30'30. B 14608
Kit Brandon: a portrait. by Sherwood Anderson. (Fadiman) 12: 72-3*O10'36. B 14609
Kitchen prelude. by Pierre Hamp. (Fadiman) 9:51 Jy8'33. B 14610
Kitty Foyle. by Christopher Morley. (Fadiman) 15:67*O28'39. B 14611
Kitty's kisses. by Philip Bartholomae and Otto Harbach. (Gabriel) 2:23 My22'26. T 14612
Kivalina of the icelands. (Shane) 1:17 Jy4'25. CC 14613
Klondike Annie. (Mosher) 12:63-4*Mr21'36. CC 14614
Knickerbocker holiday. by Maxwell Anderson and Kurt Weill. (Gibbs) 14:30*O29'38. T 14615
Knight at arms. by H. C. Bailey. (Dounce) 1:17 Ag8'25. B 14616
Knight without armor. (Mosher) 13:50-1*Jy10'37. CC 14617
Knights of song. by Glendon Allvine. (Gibbs) 14:30-2*O29'38. T 14618
Kongo. (Mosher) 8:58-9 N26'32. CC 14619
Kosher Kitty Kelly. (Claxton) 2: 75 O2'26. CC 14620
Kosher Kitty Kelly. by Leon De Costa. (Mankiewicz) 1:15 Je27 '25. T 14621
Krakatit. by Karel Capek. (Dounce) 1:18 N28'25. B 14622
The Kramer girls. by Ruth Suckow. (Hellman) 6:103-104 Ap5'30. B 14623
The Krassin. by Maurice Parijanine. (Lowrie) 4:75 F9 '29. B 14624

L

La Boheme. (Shane) 2:37 Mr6'26. CC 14625
La dame aux Camélias. (Maloney) 11:63-4*Mr30'35. CC 14626
La fleur des pois. by Edouard Bourdet. (Flanner) 8:44 O22'32. T 14627
La gringa. by Tom Cushing. (Brackett) 3:25 F11'28. T 14628
La Kermesse héroique. (Mosher) 12:61*O3'36. CC 14629
La machine infernale. by Jean Cocteau. (Flanner) 10:50-2 My 12'34. T 14630
La Marseillaise. (Flanner) 13:59* O2'37. CC 14631
(Flanner) 14:50*Mr19'38. 14632
La pettite Catherine. by Alfred Savoir. (Flanner) 6:52 N15'30. T 14633
La sang noir. by Louis Guilloux. (Flanner) 11:51*F15'36. B 14634
La Savelli. (Flanner) 9:71 S30'33. CC 14635
La voix humaine. by Jean Cocteau. (Flanner) 6:36 Mr8'30. T 14636
Laburnum Grove. by J. B. Priestley. (Benchley) 10:30†Ja26'35. T 14637
Lace petticoat. by Stewart St. Clair. (Brackett) 2:26 Ja22'27. T 14638
Ladies all. by Prince Bibesco and Elmer Harris, adapt. (Brackett) 6:24 Ag23'30. T 14639
Ladies and gentlemen. by Ben Hecht and Charles MacArthur. (Gibbs) 15:30*O28'39. T 14640
Ladies love brutes. (Mosher) 6:97 My24'30. CC 14641
Ladies' man. by Rupert Hughes. (Smith) 6:107 My10'30. B 14642
Ladies' money. by George Abbott. (Benchley) 10:32 N10'34. T 14643
Ladies' night in a Turkish bath. (Claxton) 4:92 Ap14'28. CC 14644
Ladies of the jury. (Mosher) 8: 67*Ap9'32. CC 14645

Ladies of the jury. by Fred Ballard. (Benchley) 5:38-40 N2 '29. T 14646

Ladies should listen. (Mosher) 10:51 Ag4'34. CC 14647

Lady alone. by Laetitia McDonald. (Brackett) 2:33-4 Ja29'27. T 14648

Lady beyond the moon. by William R. Doyle. (Parker) 7:34-8 Ap11'31. T 14649

Lady Chatterley's lover. by D. H. Lawrence. (Coates) 8:66 S10 '32. B 14650

Lady Dedlock. by Paul Kester. (Brackett) 4:25-6 Ja12'29. T 14651

Lady do. by Jack McClellan and Albert Cowles. (Brackett) 3:34 Ap30'27. T 14652

Lady fingers. by Eddie Buzzell, adapt. (Brackett) 4:27-8 F16 '29. T 14653

Lady for a day. (Mosher) 9:74 S16'33. CC 14654

A lady for a night. by Hutcheson Boyd. (Brackett) 4:29 Ap28'28. T 14655

The lady from the sea. by Henrik Ibsen. (Brackett) 5:27-8 Mr30 '29. T 14656

(Benchley) 10:30 My12'34. 14657

The lady in ermine. (Claxton) 2:80 Ja8'27. CC 14658

A lady in love. by Dorrance Davis. (Brackett) 3:34 Mr5'27. T 14659

Lady in marble. by Robert E. McClure. (Leonard) 4:59 Jy28'28. B 14660

Lady Jane. by H. M. Harwood. (Gibbs) 10:32-4 S22'34. T 14661

The lady of laws. by Susanne Trautwein. (Smith) 5:96 Je22 '29. B 14662

Lady of letters. by Turner Bullock. (Gibbs) 11:32-4*Ap6'35. T 14663

A lady of scandal. (Mosher) 6:79 Je21'30. CC 14664

The lady of stainless raiment. by Mathilde Eiker. (Leonard) 4:101 O20'28. B 14665

Lady of the night. (Hays) 1:27 Mr14'25. CC 14666

The lady of the orchids. by E. Ray Goetz. (Brackett) 4:26-8 D29'28. T 14667

Lady of the pavements. (Mosher) 5:94-5 Mr16'29. CC 14668

Lady of the rose. by Martin Flavin. (Anon.) 1:15 My30'25. T 14669

Lady of the tropics. (Mosher) 15:62*S2'39. CC 14670

Lady precious stream. by S. I. Hsiung. (Benchley) 11:30*F8'36. T 14671

The lady remembers. (Benchley) 8:26 My21'32. T 14672

A lady to love. (Mosher) 6:97-9 Mr8'30. CC 14673

The lady vanishes. (Mosher) 14:45*D24'38. CC 14674

Lady, what of life? by Lesley Storm. (Hoyt) 3:95-6 N5'27. B 14675

The lady who lied. (Shane) 1:17 Jy11'25. CC 14676

Lady Windermere's fan. (Shane) 1:48-9 D12'25. CC 14677

The lady's from Kentucky. (Mosher) 15:71*My6'39. CC 14678

A lady's morals. (Mosher) 6:84 N 15'30. CC 14679

A lady's virtue. by Rachel Crothers. (Mankiewicz) 1:24 D 12'25. T 14680

LaFayette. by Brand Whitlock. (Smith) 5:120-1 O12'29. B 14681

Lafayette. by W. E. Woodward. (Fadiman) 14:75*N26'38. B 14682

Lafayette: a life. by Andreas Latzko. (Fadiman) 11:69-70* F8'36. B 14683

L'age d'or. (Flanner) 6:38-9 D27 '30. CC 14684

L'age d'or. (Mosher) 9:53-4 Ap1 '33. CC 14685

L'aiglon. by Edmond Rostand and Clemence Dane. (Benchley) 10:32†N17'34. T 14686

The lake. by Dorothy Massingham and Murray MacDonald. (Benchley) 9:32-4 Ja6'34. T 14687

Lally. by Henry Stillman. (Brackett) 3:33 F19'27. T 14688

L'âme d'un poète. (Flanner) 6:39

D27'30. CC 14689

Lament for the death of a bull-fighter and other poems. by Federico Garcia Lorca. (Bogan) 13:72-3*S25'37. B 14690

Laments for the living. by Dorothy Parker. (Smith) 6:84 Je21 '30. B 14691

Lancer at large. by Francis Yeats-Brown. (Fadiman) 12:65* Ja23'37. B 14692

Lancer spy. (Mosher) 13:77*N13 '37. CC 14693

Land below the wind. by Agnes Newton Keith. (Fadiman) 15:71* N11'39. B 14694

Land of liberty. (Mosher) 15:63-4*Jy22'39. CC 14695

The land of plenty. by Robert Cantwell. (Fadiman) 10:99-101 Ap28'34. B 14696

The land of the children. by Sergiei Ivanovich Gusev. (Hoyt) 4:104 Mr17'28. B 14697

Land of the free. by Archibald MacLeish. (Bogan) 14:61-2*Ap 2'38. B 14698

Land of the Pilgrims' pride. by George Jean Nathan. (Boyd) 3: 94-5 S10'27. B 14699

The larger view. by Benjamin Kaverin. (Fadiman) 14:61-2* Mr12'38. B 14700

The last Adam. by James Gould Cozzens. (Coates) 8:86-7 Ja7 '33. B 14701

The last command. (Claxton) 3:67 Ja28'28. CC 14702

The last days of Pompeii. (Mosher) 11:73*O26'35. CC 14703

The last enemy. by Iris Barry. (Smith) 5:122 O26'29. B 14704

The last enemy. by Frank Harvey. (Benchley) 6:34-6 N8'30. T 14705

The last enemy. by L. A. G. Strong. (Anon.) 12:73-4*O10 '36. B 14706

The last flight. (Mosher) 7:47 Ag 29'31. CC 14707

The last gangster. (Mosher) 13: 101-102*D11'37. CC 14708

The last gentleman. (Mosher) 10: 85 O27'34. CC 14709

The last laugh. (Hays) 1:28 F21 '25. CC 14710

The last mile. by John Wexley. (Benchley) 6:27-8 Mr1'30. T 14711

The last moment. (Claxton) 4:77 Mr24'28. CC 14712

The last of Mr. Norris. by Christopher Isherwood. (Fadiman) 11:82-3*My11'35. B 14713

The last of Mrs. Cheyney. (Mosher) 5:63-4 Ag17'29. CC 14714

The last of Mrs. Cheyney. (Maloney) 13:61*F27'37. CC 14715

The last of Mrs. Cheyney. by Frederick Lonsdale. (Mankiewicz) 1:17 N21'25. T 14716

The last outpost. (Mosher) 11:67-8*O12'35. CC 14717

The last parade. (Mosher) 7:75-6 Mr7'31. CC 14718

The last paradise. by Hickman Powell. (Smith) 6:86-7 Je14'30. B 14719

Last poems. by D. H. Lawrence. (Bogan) 9:47 Jy15'33. B 14720

The last post. by Ford Madox Ford. (Parker) 3:74-7 F4'28. B 14721

The last puritan. by George Santayana. (Fadiman) 11:51-3*F1 '36. B 14722

The last salon: Anatole France and his Muse. by Jeanne Simone Pouquet. (Boyd) 3:114-15 Ap23'27. B 14723

The last trail. (Claxton) 2:76 F5 '27. CC 14724

The last waltz. (Claxton) 3:101 N19'27. CC 14725

The late Christopher Bean. by René Fauchois and Sidney Howard. (Benchley) 8:22 N12'32. T 14726

The late George Apley. by John P. Marquand and George S. Kaufman. (Benchley) 14:34*O17 '38. T 14727

Late one evening. by Audrey Carten and Waveney Carten. (Benchley) 8:26-8 Ja21'33. T 14728

The later years of Thomas Hardy. by Florence Emily Hardy. (Smith) 6:87 Je14'30. B 14729
Laugh and lie down. by Robert Cantwell. (Coates) 7:75-6 O24 '31. B 14730
Laughing boy. by Oliver La Farge. (Smith) 5:128 N23'29. B 14731
The laughing lady. (Mosher) 5:71-2 Ja11'30. CC 14732
Laughter. (Mosher) 6:103 N22'30. CC 14733
Laughter in the dark. by Vladimir Nabokov. (Fadiman) 14:72-3* My7'38. B 14734
Lawrence and the Arabian adventure. by Robert Graves. (Markey) 4:94-5 Ap28'28. B 14735
A lawyer tells the truth. by Morris Gisnet. (Coates) 7:88-9 O3 '31. B 14736
Lay sermons. by Margot Asquith. (Parker) 3:98-100 O22'27. B 14737
Le bonheur. by Henri Bernstein. (Flanner) 9:51 Ap29'33. T 14738
Le corsaire. by Marcel Achard. (Flanner) 14:56*Ap16'38. T 14739
Le feu follet. by Drieu LaRochelle. (Flanner) 7:41*Je13'31. B 14740
Le jour. by Henri Bernstein. (Flanner) 6:41 Ja31'31. T 14741
Le messager. by Henri Bernstein. (Flanner) 9:35 D23'33. T 14742
Le million. (Mosher) 7:59*My30 '31. CC 14743
Le nouveau testament. by Sacha Guitry. (Flanner) 10:54 O27 '34. T 14744
Le souverain captif. by André Tardieu. (Flanner) 12:36-8*My 9'36. B 14745
Le temps de Mépris. by André Malraux. (Flanner) 11:47*Jy6 '35. B 14746
The leaf is green. by John V. Craven. (Coates) 7:88-9 My16 '31. B 14747
Lean harvest. by Ronald Jeans. (Benchley) 7:28 O24'31. T 14748
Lean men. by Ralph Bates. (Fadiman) 10:69-70*F9'35. B 14749
Leave it to me. by Samuel Spewack; Bella Spewack and Cole Porter. (Benchley) 14:30*N19 '38. T 14750
Leave me with a smile. by Elliott White Springs. (Hoyt) 4:83-5 Mr10'28. B 14751
The Left Bank. by Elmer Rice. (Benchley) 7:28 O17'31. T 14752
The legend of Leonora. by James M. Barrie. (Brackett) 3:33 Ap9 '27. T 14753
The legend of the bear's wedding. (Claxton) 3:77-9 My28'27. CC 14754
The legion of the condemned. (Claxton) 4:77 Mr24'28. CC 14755
Lenin in October. (Mosher) 14:69*Ap9'38. CC 14756
Lenin's dowry. by David Vardi. (Benchley) 8:26-8 My21'32. T 14757
Leopold of the Belgians. by Louis de Lichtervelde. (Smith) 5:120-1 My25'29. B 14758
Les adventures du Roi Pausole. by Pierre Louÿs. (Flanner) 6:41-2 Ja31'31. T 14759
Les cloches de Bâle. by Louis Aragon. (Flanner) 11:57*Mr2 '35. B 14760
Les filles du Diable. by Daisy Fellowes. (Flanner) 9:38 Je24 '33. B 14761
Les misérables. (Claxton) 3:56 S3 '27. CC 14762
Les misérables. (Mosher) 11:69-70*Ap27'35; 12:60-1*O31'36. CC 14763
L'espoir. by André Malraux. (Flanner) 13:45-6*Ja29'38. B 14764
Let and sub-let. by Martha Stanley. (Benchley) 6:28-30 My31 '30. T 14765
Let 'em eat cake. by George S. Kaufman and Morrie Ryskind. (Gibbs) 9:26 O28'33. T 14766
Let freedom ring! by Albert Bein. (Benchley) 11:32*N16'35. T 14767
Let it rain. (Claxton) 3:81-3 Mr12 '27. CC 14768
Let the people sing. by J. B. Priestley. (Fadiman) 15:52*Ja6

'40. B 14769
Let there be beer! by Bob Brown. (Coates) 8:43-4 Ag27'32.B 14770
Let us be gay. (Mosher) 6:54 Jy 19'30. CC 14771
Lethargy. by Roger Dilworthy. (Coates) 7:54*Ag8'31. B 14772
Let's go native. (Mosher) 6:67 S6 '30. CC 14773
The letter. (Mosher) 5:94 Mr16 '29. CC 14774
The letter. by W. Somerset Maugham. (Brackett) 3:31 O8 '27. T 14775
A letter from Pontus. by John Masefield. (Bogan) 12:61*Je20 '36. B 14776
Letter of introduction. (Mosher) 14:44*S3'38. CC 14777
Letters from Joseph Conrad. by Joseph Conrad and Edward Garnett, ed. (Markey) 4:103-104 My12'28. B 14778
The letters of Gerard Manley Hopkins to Robert Bridges. by Gerard Manley Hopkins and C. C. Abbott, ed. (Bogan) 11: 66*My4'35. B 14779
Letters of Henry Adams. by Henry Adams and Worthington Chauncey Ford, ed. (Smith) 6: 106-108 O4'30. B 14780
The letters of Sacco and Vanzetti. by Nicola Sacco; Bartolomeo Vanzetti; Marion D. Frankfurter, ed., and Gardner Jackson, ed. (Lowrie) 4: 68 D22'28. B 14781
The letters of T. E. Lawrence. by T. E. Lawrence and David Garnett, ed. (Fadiman) 15:76* Mr11'39. B 14782
Letters to an artist: from Vincent van Gogh to Anton Rider van Rappard. by Vincent van Gogh and Rela van Messel, trans. (Anon.) 12:86*S19'36. B 14783
Letty Lynton. (Mosher) 8:64*My7 '32. CC 14784
Lew Leslie's blackbirds of 1939. by Lew Leslie, et al. (Benchley) 15:28-30*F18'39. T 14785
Lew Tyler and the ladies. by Wallace Irwin. (Leonard) 4:62-3 Ag25'28. B 14786
Libel! by Edward Wooll. (Benchley) 11:26-8*D28'35. T 14787
Libeled lady. (Mosher) 12:58-9*O 24'36. CC 14788
Liberty. by Everett Dean Martin. (Smith) 6:91 Je7'30. B 14789
The lie of Nina Petrovna. (Mosher) 14:69*Ap9'38. CC 14790
Liebe im Ring. (Mosher) 6:56 Ag 16'30. CC 14791
Life. by Robert Esmonde Sencourt. (Smith) 5:120 N16'29. B 14792
Life among the lowbrows. by Eleanor Rowland Wembridge. (Coates) 7:79-80 My2'31.B 14793
The life and death of a Spanish town. by Elliot Paul. (Fadiman) 13:49-50*Ag7'37.B 14794
Life and death of an American. by George Sklar. (Gibbs) 15: 50*My20'39. T 14795
Life and letters of Jefferson. by Francis W. Hirst. (Dounce) 2: 52 Ap10'26. B 14796
The life and mind of Emily Dickinson. by Genevieve Taggard. (Smith) 6:62-3 Jy5'30. B 14797
The life and private history of Emily Jane Brontë. by Romer Wilson. (Markey) 4:85 Je23'28. B 14798
The life and strange and surprising adventures of Daniel De Foe. by Paul Dottin. (Smith) 5:122 N2'29. B 14799
The life and times of Lydia E. Pinkham. by Robert Collyer Washburn. (Coates) 7:83-4 My 9'31. B 14800
The life and times of William Howard Taft. by Henry F. Pringle. (Fadiman) 15:68*O28'39.B 14801
Life begins. by Mary Macdougal Axelson. (Benchley) 8:26*Ap9 '32. T 14802
Life begins at 8:40. by David Freedman; Harold Arlen and Ira Gershwin. (Gibbs) 10:34 S8 '34. T 14803
Life begins at 40. (Mosher) 11:

63*Ap13'35. CC 14804

Life dances on. (Mosher) 14:50* Ap2'38. CC 14805

Life goes on. by W. G. Rogers. (Smith) 5:88-9 S7'29. B 14806

Life in letters of William Dean Howells. by William Dean Howells and Mildred Howells, ed. (Lowrie) 4:129 D15'28. B 14807

The life of Emerson. by Van Wyck Brooks. (Coates) 8:70-1*Ap9'32. B 14808

The life of Emile Zola. (Mosher) 13:58-9*Ag14'37. CC 14809

The life of Giovanni Boccaccio. by Thomas Caldecot Chubb. (Smith) 6:115 My17'30. B 14810

The life of Greece. by Will Durant. (Fadiman) 15:68*O28'39. B 14811

The life of Jimmy Dolan. (Mosher) 9:62 Je24'33. CC 14812

The life of Lady Byron. by Ethel Colburn Mayne. (Smith) 5:104 S21'29. B 14813

The life of Madame Roland. by Madeleine Clemenceau-Jacquemaire. (Smith) 6:55 Ag30'30. B 14814

The life of the party. (Mosher) 6:85 N15'30. CC 14815

The life of the party. (Mosher) 13:67*O9'37. CC 14816

The life of Vergie Winters. (Mosher) 10:61 Je23'34. CC 14817

The life of Vice-Admiral William Bligh, R. N., F. R. S. by George Mackaness. (Anon.) 12:65*S5'36. B 14818

Life with father. by Howard Lindsay and Russel Crouse. (Gibbs) 15:32*N18'39. T 14819

Life's ebb and flow. by Frances Evelyn Warwick. (Smith) 5:104 S21'29. B 14820

Life's too short. by John O. Whedon and Arthur Caplan. (Gibbs) 11:28*S28'35. T 14821

Light in August. by William Faulkner. (Coates) 8:73 O15 '32. B 14822

The light of Asia. by Georgina Jones Walton. (Brackett) 4:26-7 O20'28. T 14823

The light of western stars. (Mosher) 6:98 My3'30. CC 14824

The light shines through. by Octavus Roy Cohen. (Leonard) 4:72-3 S1'28. B 14825

Lightnin'. (Shane) 1:16-17 Jy25'25. CC 14826

Lightnin'. (Mosher) 6:119-20 D6 '30. CC 14827

Lightnin'. by Winchell Smith and Frank Bacon. (Gibbs) 14:28*S24 '38. T 14828

The lights of New York. (Claxton) 4:69 Jy14'28. CC 14829

Lights of old Broadway. (Shane) 1:23 N7'25. CC 14830

Lightship. by Archie Binns. (Fadiman) 10:70 S1'34; 13:77-8*Ap 17'37. B 14831

Liliom. (Mosher) 6:88 O11'30. CC 14832

Liliom. by Ferenc Molnar. (Benchley) 8:26 N5'32. T 14833

L'Illusioniste. by Sacha Guitry. (Brackett) 2:25 Ja22'27. T 14834

Lilly Turner. (Mosher) 9:62-3 Je 24'33. CC 14835

Lilly Turner. by Philip Dunning and George Abbott. (White) 8:28 O1'32. T 14836

The lily. (Claxton) 2:80 N20'26. CC 14837

Lily Christine. by Michael Arlen. (Lowrie) 4:142 D8'28. B 14838

Lily Sue. by Willard Mack. (Brackett) 2:34 N27'26. T 14839

Limehouse blues. (Mosher) 10:34* D22'34. CC 14840

The limestone tree. by Joseph Hergesheimer. (Coates) 6:67 Ja10'31. B 14841

Limits and renewals. by Rudyard Kipling. (Coates) 8:58-60*Ap30 '32. B 14842

Lincoln. (Mosher) 6:65-6 S6'30. CC 14843

Lincoln. by Emil Ludwig. (Smith) 5:84 F8'30. B 14844

The links. by Robert Hunter. (Dounce) 2:60-1 My15'26. B 14845

L'invitation au voyage. by Jean-

Jacques Bernard and Ernest Boyd, trans. (Brackett) 4:38 N10'28. T 14846
Lion. by Martin Johnson. (Middleton) 5:116-17 Ap20'29.B14847
The lion and the mouse. (Claxton) 4:77 Je23'28. CC 14848
The lion tamer. by E. M. Hull. (Parker) 4:60-2 Ag25'28.B14849
The lion tamer. by Alfred Savoir. (Brackett) 2:33 O23'26.T 14850
Liquor, loot and ladies. by Chester T. Crowell. (Hellman) 6: 123-4 Ap12'30. B 14851
Listen for a lonesome drum. by Carl Carmer. (Anon.) 12:52* Jy4'36. B 14852
Listen to the wind. by Anne Morrow Lindbergh. (Fadiman) 14: 68-9*O15'38. B 14853
The literary mind. by Max Eastman. (Coates) 7:111-12 D5'31. B 14854
Little accident. (Gibbs) 6:56 Ag9 '30. CC 14855
Little accident. by Floyd Dell and Thomas Mitchell. (Brackett) 4:34-6 O27'28. T 14856
Little America. by Richard E. Byrd. (Smith) 6:118-20 D13'30. B 14857
Little Caesar. (Mosher) 6:65-7 Ja17'31. CC 14858
Little Caesar. by William Riley Burnett. (Smith) 5:97 Je22'29. B 14859
The little colonel. (Maloney) 11: 62*Mr23'35. CC 14860
The little dog laughed. by Leonard Merrick. (Smith) 6:105 S 13'30. B 14861
Little Eyolf. by Henrik Ibsen. (Gabriel) 1:22-3 F13'26.T 14862
The little foxes. by Lillian Hellman. (Benchley) 15:25*F25'39. T 14863
Little friend. (Mosher) 10:84-5 O27'34. CC 14864
The little giant. (Mosher) 9:64 Je 3'33. CC 14865
The little Irish girl. (Shane) 2:53 My15'26. CC 14866
A little journey. (Claxton) 2:80 Ja8'27. CC 14867
Little Lord Fauntleroy. (Mosher) 12:69*Ap11'36. CC 14868
Little man, what now? (Mosher) 10:83-4 Je9'34. CC 14869
Little man, what now? by Hans Fallada. (Fadiman) 9:70-1 Je3 '33; 14:96*N12'38. B 14870
Little men. (Mosher) 11:62*F23 '35. CC 14871
The little minister. (Mosher) 10: 49*D29'34. CC 14872
The little minister. by James M. Barrie. (Anon.) 1:13 Ap4'25. T 14873
Little Miss Broadway. (Mosher) 14:53*Jy23'38. CC 14874
Little ol' boy. by Albert Bein. (Benchley) 9:34 My6'33.T 14875
Little orchid Annie. by Hadley Waters and Charles Beahan. (Benchley) 6:28 My3'30.T 14876
Little pitchers. by Isa Glenn. (Boyd) 2:55 Ja1'27. B 14877
The little poor man. by Harry Lee. (Mankiewicz) 1:13 Ag15 '25. T 14878
The little princess. (Shane) 1:24 S12'25. CC 14879
The little princess. (Mosher) 15: 74-5*Mr11'39. CC 14880
Little ships. by Kathleen Norris. (Dounce) 1:19 O10'25. B 14881
The little show. by Howard Dietz and Arthur Schwartz. (Brackett) 5:27 My11'29. T 14882
The little spitfire. by Myron C. Fagan. (Brackett) 2:38-9 Ag28 '26. T 14883
Little tough guy. (Mosher) 14:41* Ag20'38. CC 14884
Little women. (Mosher) 9:83-4 N 18'33. CC 14885
Little women. by Marian de Forest. (White) 7:32 D19'31.T 14886
The littlest rebel. (Mosher) 11:50* D28'35. CC 14887
Live, love, and learn. (Mosher) 13:73*N27'37. CC 14888
Lives. by Gustav Eckstein. (Coates) 8:70*My7'32. B 14889
Lives and times. by Meade Minnegerode. (Anon.) 1:28 Mr28

'25. B 14890
The lives of a Bengal lancer. (Mosher) 10:58-9*Ja19'35. CC 14891
The lives of a Bengal lancer. by Francis Yeats-Brown. (Smith) 6:112 N8'30. B 14892
Living dangerously. by Reginald Simpson and Frank Gregory. (Benchley) 10:30†Ja19'35. T 14893
The living dead man. (Claxton) 3:81 Mr12'27. CC 14894
The living Jefferson. by James Truslow Adams. (Fadiman) 12:76*Ap11'36. B 14895
Living on velvet. (Maloney) 11:71*Mr16'35. CC 14896
Lloyd's of London. (Mosher) 12:102-103*D5'36. CC 14897
The locked door. (Mosher) 5:72-3 Ja25'30. CC 14898
Logical nonsense. by Lewis Carroll; Philip C. Blackburn, ed. and Lionel White, ed. (Fadiman) 10:109-10 N10'34. B 14899
Lolly. by Fanny Heaslip Lea. (Benchley) 5:40-2 O26'29. T 14900
Lolly Willowes. by Sylvia Townsend Warner. (Dounce) 1:44 F13'26. B 14901
Lombardi, ltd. by Frederic Hatton and Fanny Hatton. (Wright) 3:66-7 Je25'27. T 14902
London. (Claxton) 2:43 O30'26. CC 14903
London after midnight. (Claxton) 3:103 D17'27. CC 14904
London promenade. by William Gaunt. (Coates) 6:107 O25'30. B 14905
Lone cowboy. by Will James. (Smith) 6:62 Ag16'30. B 14906
Lonesome. (Mosher) 4:103 O13'28. CC 14907
Lonesome ladies. (Mosher) 3:51 Ag13'27. CC 14908
Long hunt. by James Boyd. (Smith) 6:100-102 My3'30. B 14909
Long Island's story. by Jacqueline Overton. (Smith) 5:62 Ag3 '29. B 14910
Long pants. (Claxton) 3:89 Ap2 '27. CC 14911
Long pennant. by Oliver La Farge. (Fadiman) 9:82 O14'33. B 14912
Long remember. by MacKinlay Kantor. (Fadiman) 10:106-10 Ap7'34. B 14913
The long road. by Hugh Stanislaus Stange. (Benchley) 6:30 S20'30. T 14914
The long valley. by John Steinbeck. (Fadiman) 14:72*S24'38. B 14915
Look homeward, Angel. by Thomas Wolfe. (Smith) 5:118 N16'29. B 14916
Looking back. by Norman Douglas. (Coates) 9:73-4 My13'33. B 14917
Loose ankles. by Sam Janney. (Brackett) 2:38 Ag28'26. T 14918
Lord of himself. by Percy Marks. (Boyd) 2:93 F5'27. B 14919
Lord Jeff. (Mosher) 14:42*Jy2'38. CC 14920
Lord Jim. (Shane) 1:21 N21'25. CC 14921
The Lorenzo bunch. by Booth Tarkington. (Fadiman) 11:57-8*Ja18'36. B 14922
Lorenzo in Taos. by Mable Dodge Luhan. (Coates) 8:59-61*Mr12 '32. B 14923
Lorenzo the magnificent. by David Loth. (Smith) 5:120 N2'29. B 14924
Lost. by A. E. Thomas and George Agnew Chamberlain. (Brackett) 3:33-4 Ap9'27. 14924A
Lost--a wife. (Shane) 1:17 Jy4'25. CC 14925
Lost boy. by T. C. Upham. (Benchley) 7:26 Ja16'32. 14925A
Lost horizon. (Mosher) 13:62*Mr6 '37. CC 14926
Lost horizon. by James Hilton. (Fadiman) 9:74 S30'33. B 14927
Lost in the Arctic. (Claxton) 4:59 Ag4'28. CC 14928
A lost lady. (Mosher) 10:103 O13 '34. CC 14929
Lost laughter. by Mateel Howe Farnham. (Coates) 9:56 Ap1'33. B 14930
Lost sheep. by Belford Forrest. (Benchley) 6:34-6 My17'30. T 14930A
The lost squadron. (Mosher) 8:77*

Mr19'32. CC 14931
Lot in Sodom. (Mosher) 9:69 S9 '33. CC 14932
The lottery bride. (Mosher) 6:119 D6'30. CC 14933
Louder, please. by Norman Krasna. (Benchley) 7:30 N21'31. T 14934
Loudspeaker. by John Howard Lawson. (Brackett) 3:33 Mr12 '27. T 14935
Louie the 14th. by Arthur Wimperis and Sigmund Romberg. (Anon.) 1:13 Mr14'25. T 14936
Louis Beretti. by Donald Henderson Clarke. (Gannett) 5:168 D7 '29. B 14937
Louisa May Alcott. by Katharine Anthony. (Fadiman) 13:61*F12 '38. B 14938
Love. (Claxton) 3:111 D10'27. CC 14939
Love. by William Lyon Phelps. (Parker) 4:99 O20'28. B 14940
Love affair. (Mosher) 15:66*Mr18 '39. CC 14941
Love and babies. by Herbert P. Mc Cormack. (Gibbs) 9:22 S2 '33. T 14942
The love call. by Edward Locke and Harry B. Smith. (Brackett) 3:25 N5'27. T 14943
The love duel. by Lili Hatvany and Zoë Akins. (Brackett) 5: 29-30 Ap27'29. T 14944
Love 'em and leave 'em. (Claxton) 2:96 D11'26. CC 14945
Love 'em and leave 'em. by George Abbott and John V. A. Weaver. (Gabriel) 2:33 F20'26. T 14946
Love for love. by William Congreve. (Anon.) 1:13 Ap11'25. T 14947
Love for two. by Mildred Gilman. (Coates) 8:66*Ap23'32. B 14948
Love from a stranger. (Mosher) 13:64*Ap24'37. CC 14949
Love from a stranger. by Frank Vosper. (Gibbs) 12:30*O10'36. T 14950
Love goes past. by Ursula Parrott. (Coates) 7:50-1 Ag22'31. B 14951
Love, here is my hat. by William Saroyan. (Fadiman) 14:63-4*Mr19'38. B 14952
Love, honor and betray. by André-Paul Antoine; Fanny Hatton, adapt. and Frederic Hatton, adapt. (Brackett) 6:29-30 Mr22 '30. T 14953
Love-in-a-mist. by Amélie Rives and Gilbert Emery. (Connelly) 2:26 Ap24'26. T 14954
Love in Chartres. by Nathan Asch. (Hoyt) 3:106-107 N26'27. B 14955
Love in the machine age. by Floyd Dell. (Smith) 6:102 Ap19 '30. B 14956
Love is enough. by Francis Brett Young. (Boyd) 3:120-1 Ap9'27. B 14957
Love is like that. by Kenyon Nicholson and S. N. Behrman. (Brackett) 3:33 Ap30'27. T 14958
The love letters of a living poet. by Benjamin De Casseres. (Coates) 7:109-10 D5'31. B 14959
Love, live and laugh. (Mosher) 5:113-15 N9'29. CC 14960
Love me forever. (Mosher) 11:45*Jy6'35. CC 14961
Love me tonight. (Mosher) 8:38 Ag20'32. CC 14962
The love nest. by Ring W. Lardner. (Dounce) 2:60-1 My8'26. B 14963
The love of Mario Ferraro. by Johan Fabricius. (Coates) 7:84 S19'31. B 14964
The love of the foolish angel. by Helen Beauclerk. (Smith) 5:103 S21'29. B 14965
Love of women. by Aimée Stuart and Philip Stuart. (Benchley) 13:26*D25'37. T 14966
Love on a bet. (Mosher) 12:63-4*Mr14'36. CC 14967
Love on the dole. by Ronald Gow and Walter Greenwood. (Benchley) 12:32*Mr7'36. T 14968
Love on the run. (Mosher) 12:65*N28'36. CC 14969
The love parade. (Mosher) 5:89-90 N30'29. CC 14970
Love sonnets of a cave man. by

Don Marquis. (Markey) 4:108 Ap21'28. B 14971
Love story. by Thelma Woodhill. (Smith) 5:56 Ag24'29. B 14972
Love without money. by Floyd Dell. (Coates) 7:79-80 O31'31. B 14973
Love-life in nature. by Wilhelm Bölsche. (Boyd) 2:110 D4'26. B 14974
The lovely lady. by D. H. Lawrence. (Coates) 8:62-3 F11'33. B 14975
Lovers. (Claxton) 3:103 Ap23'27. CC 14976
Love's greatest mistake. (Claxton) 3:65 F26'27. CC 14977
Loves of a dictator. (Mosher) 11:61*Je8'35. CC 14978
Loves of an actress. (Claxton) 4:59 Ag4'28. CC 14979
The loves of Lulu. by Frank Wedekind. (Anon.) 1:15 My23 '25. T 14980
Lovey Mary. (Shane) 2:41 Je26 '26. CC 14981
Luana. by Richard Walton Tully. (Benchley) 6:34 S27'30. T 14982
Lucienne. by Jules Romains. (Anon.) 1:28 Mr21'25. B 14983
Luck. by Lothrop Stoddard. (Smith) 5:117 O5'29. B 14984
Lucky. by Otto Harbach; Bert Kalmar; Harry Ruby and Jerome Kern. (Brackett) 3:34 Ap2'27. T 14985
A lucky break. by Zelda Sears. (Anon.) 1:15 Ag22'25. T 14986
The lucky devil. (Shane) 1:17 Jy 11'25. CC 14987
Lucky Sam Mc Carver. by Sidney Howard. (Mankiewicz) 1:19-20 O31'25. T 14988
Lucky Sambo. by Porter Grainger and Freddie Johnson. (Mankiewicz) 1:15 Je20'25. T 14989
Lucky star. (Mosher) 5:35 Jy27 '29. CC 14990
Lucrece. by Thornton Wilder. (Benchley) 8:22-4 D31'32.T 14991
Lucretia Borgia. (Mosher) 4:50 D29'28. CC 14992
Lucy Church Amiably. by Gertrude Stein. (Coates) 8:69-70* F20'32. B 14993
Lucy Gayheart. by Willa Cather. (Fadiman) 11:46-7*Ag3'35. B 14994
Luigi Pirandello. by Walter Starkie. (Boyd) 2:69 Ja15'27. B 14995
Luise Königin von Preussen. (Mosher) 8:68 O15'32. CC 14996
Lulu Belle. by Edward Sheldon and Charles MacArthur. (Gabriel) 2:33 F20'26. T 14997
Lummox. (Mosher) 6:56-7 Mr29 '30. CC 14998
Lust for life. by Irving Stone. (Fadiman) 10:81 S29'34.B 14999
Luxury liner. (Mosher) 8:53 F11 '33. CC 15000
Lyric drama. by Irene Lewisohn. (Brackett) 3:33-4 Ap16'27. T 15001
Lysistrata. by Aristophanes and Gilbert Seldes, adapt. (Benchley) 6:32-3 My10'30; 6:30 Je14 '30. T 15002

M

M. (Mosher) 9:69 Ap8'33. CC 15003
Macbeth. by William Shakespeare. (Brackett) 4:38-40 D1'28.T 15004
Machinal. by Sophie Treadwell. (Brackett) 4:34 S15'28.T 15005
Mackerel skies. by John Haggart. (Benchley) 9:32 F3'34.T 15006
Mackerel sky. by Helen Ashton. (Coates) 6:72 Ja17'31. B 15007
Mad about music. (Mosher) 14:56-7*Mr12'38. CC 15008
The mad genius. (Mosher) 7:73-4 O31'31. CC 15009
The mad hopes. by Romney Brent. (Lockridge) 8:30 D10'32.T 15010
Mad hour. (Claxton) 4:93 Ap21'28. CC 15011
The mad Miss Manton. (Mosher) 14:58*O29'38. CC 15012
The mad professor. by Hermann Sudermann. (Lowrie) 4:58 D29 '28. B 15013
The mad whirl. (Shane) 1:17 Jy4 '25. CC 15014

Madame Bovary. by Gaston Baty and Benn W. Levy, adapt. (Benchley) 13:30*N27'37.T 15015

Madame Capet. by Marcelle Maurette. (Gibbs) 14:30*N5'38. T 15016

Madame Curie. by Eve Curie. (Fadiman) 13:74-8*N27'37. B 15017

Madame de Pompadour. by Marcelle Tinayre. (Dounce) 2:52 Ap10'26. B 15018

Madame Pompadour. (Mosher) 3:50-1 Ag13'27. CC 15019

Madame Sans Gene. (Anon.) 1:31 My2'25. CC 15020

Madame Satan. (Mosher) 6:87 O11 '30. CC 15021

Madame X. (Mosher) 13:90*O30 '37. CC 15022

Madame X. by Alexandre Bisson and John Raphael. (White) 3:37 Jy23'27. T 15023

Mädchen in uniform. (Mosher) 8:64 S17'32. CC 15024

Made for each other. (Mosher) 15:66-7*F18'39. CC 15025

Made in France. by Jack Larric. (Benchley) 6:33 N22'30. T 15026

Made in U. S. A. by Hans Otto Storm. (Fadiman) 15:67-8*O28 '39. B 15027

Mademoiselle. by Jacques Deval and Grace George, adapt. (Benchley) 8:24-6 O29'32.T 15028

Mlle. Modiste. by Henry Blossom and Victor Herbert. (Benchley) 5:42 O26'29. T 15029

Madison Square Garden. (Mosher) 8:57 O22'32. CC 15030

Madonna of the sleeping cars. by Murice Dekobra. (Boyd) 3:101 My14'27. B 15031

Madonna without child. by Myron Brinig. (Lowrie) 4:92 F16'29. B 15032

Maggie, the magnificent. by George Kelly. (Benchley) 5:34-8 N2'29. T 15033

The magic island. by William Seabrook. (Lowrie) 4:69 Ja12 '29. B 15034

The magic mountain. by Thomas Mann. (Boyd) 3:81 Je25'27. B 15035

Magic night. (Mosher) 8:68 N12 '32. CC 15036

The magic of monarchy. by Kingsley Martin. (Fadiman) 13:63-4* Je5'37. B 15037

The magician. (Claxton) 2:43 O30 '26. CC 15038

The magnificent flirt. (Claxton) 4: 59 Je30'28. CC 15039

The magnificent idler. by Cameron Rogers. (Dounce) 2:64 My22'26. B 15040

Magnificent obsession. (Mosher) 11: 64*Ja11'36. CC 15041

Magnus Merriman. by Eric Linklater. (Fadiman) 10:100-102 Mr 17'34. B 15042

Magpie: the autobiography of a nymph errant. by Lois Vidal. (Fadiman) 10:65-6 Jy14'34. B 15043

Mahogany Hall. by Charles Robinson. (Benchley) 9:28-30 Ja27'34. T 15044

Maid in waiting. by John Galsworthy. (Coates) 7:87-8 N28'31; 7:80 D19'31. B 15045

Maid of Salem. (Mosher) 13:61-2* Mr6'37. CC 15046

The maiden voyage. by Felix Riesenberg and Archie Binns. (Coates) 7:87-8 Mr14'31.B 15047

The main event. (Claxton) 3:87 N5 '27. CC 15048

Main line West. by Paul Horgan. (Anon.) 12:72*Mr21'36.B 15049

Mainly for lovers. by Philip Johnson. (Benchley) 12:26*F29'36. T 15050

Maisie. (Mosher) 15:65*Je24'39. CC 15051

Maitresse de roi. by Adolphe Aderer and Armand Ephraim. (Brackett) 2:42-4 D11'26.T 15052

Major Barbara. by George Bernard Shaw. (Brackett) 4:40 D8 '28. T 15053

Make a wish. (Mosher) 13:60*O2 '37. CC 15054

The making of a king. (Mosher) 11:73*D21'35. CC 15055

The making of Americans. by Gertrude Stein. (Fadiman) 9: 84-7 F10'34. B 15056
Makropoulos secret. by Karel Capek. (Gabriel) 1:27 F6'26. T 15057
Malaisie. by Henri Fauconnier. (Coates) 7:89 N28'31. B 15058
The male animal. by James Thurber and Elliott Nugent. (Benchley) 15:30*Ja20'40. T 15059
Mama loves Papa. by John Mc Gowan and Mann Page. (Gabriel) 2:23 Mr6'26. T 15060
Mamba's daughters. by Dorothy Heyward and DuBose Heyward. (Benchley) 14:28*Ja14'39.T 15061
Mamba's daughters. by DuBose Heyward. (Lowrie) 4:87 F2'29. B 15062
Mammy. (Mosher) 6:99 Ap5'30. CC 15063
Man about town. (Mosher) 15:65* Je24'39. CC 15064
Man and maid. (Anon.) 1:31 Ap18 '25. CC 15065
Man and mask. by Feodor Chaliapin and Phyllis Mégroz, trans. (Coates) 8:46 D24'32. B 15066
Man and woman. by Havelock Ellis. (Gannett) 5:106-107 N30 '29. B 15067
A man called Cervantes. by Bruno Frank. (Fadiman) 11:62*Mr2'35. B 15068
A man can build a house. by Nathalie Colby. (Leonard) 4:107 N24'28. B 15069
A man could stand up--. by Ford Madox Ford. (Dounce) 2:98 N13 '26. B 15070
The man from Blankley's. (Mosher) 6:99-100 Ap5'30. CC 15071
The man from Toronto. by Douglas Murray. (Brackett) 2:25 Je 26'26. T 15072
A man from Wyoming. (Mosher) 6:54 Jy19'30. CC 15073
The man I killed. (Mosher) 7:51-2 Ja30'32. CC 15074
The man in possession. (Mosher) 7:54*Jy25'31. CC 15075
The man in possession. by H. M. Harwood. (Benchley) 6:30 N15 '30. T 15076
The man in the iron mask. (Mosher) 15:57-8*Jy15'39. CC 15077
The man Mencken. by Isaac Goldberg. (Dounce) 1:22-3 Ja16'26. B 15078
Man of Aran. (Mosher) 10:84 O27 '34. CC 15079
The man of destiny. by George Bernard Shaw. (Mankiewicz) 1:14 D5'25. T 15080
The man of the Renaissance. by Ralph Roeder. (Fadiman) 9:92-3 D2'33. B 15081
Man of two worlds. (Mosher) 9:59 Ja20'34. CC 15082
The man on stilts. by Edwin Barker and Albert Barker. (Benchley)7:30-4 S19'31.T 15083
The man on the box. (Shane) 1:22 O3'25. CC 15084
Man on the flying trapeze. (Mosher) 11:41*Ag10'35. CC 15085
Man or devil? by Jerome K. Jerome. (Anon.) 1:15 My30'25. T 15086
Man-proof. (Mosher) 13:55-6*Ja22 '38. CC 15087
A man scans his past. by Maurice Constantin-Weyer. (Smith) 5:64 Jy6'29. B 15088
Man the miracle maker. by Hendrick Willem van Loon. (Lowrie) 4:100-101 Ja5'29. B 15089
A man to remember. (Mosher) 14: 95*N12'38. CC 15090
The man who came to dinner. by George S. Kaufman and Moss Hart. (Gibbs) 15:30*O28'39. T 15091
The man who changed his name. by Edgar Wallace. (Benchley) 8:26-8*My14'32. T 15092
The man who could work miracles. (Maloney) 13:60*F20'37.CC 15093
The man who dared. (Mosher) 9: 74 S16'33. CC 15094
The man who died. by D. H. Lawrence. (Coates) 7:87 My16'31. B 15095
The man who found himself.

(Shane) 1:19 Ag29'25. CC 15096
The man who had everything. by Louis Bromfield. (Fadiman) 11:76-8*My18'35. B 15097
The man who killed Lincoln. by Philip Van Doren Stern. (Fadiman) 14:58*F4'39. B 15098
The man who knew Coolidge. by Sinclair Lewis. (Parker) 4: 106-107 Ap7'28. B 15099
The man who laughs. (Claxton) 4: 93 My12'28. CC 15100
The man who lost himself. by Osbert Sitwell. (Smith) 6:99 Mr 5'30. B 15101
The man who played God. (Mosher) 8:61-2*F20'32. CC 15102
The man who reclaimed his head. by Arthur Hammerstein and L. Lawrence Weber. (White) 8:26-8 S17'32. T 15103
The man with a load of mischief. by Ashley Dukes. (Mankiewicz) 1:19 N7'25. T 15104
A man with red hair. by Benn W. Levy. (Brackett) 4:34-6 N24'28. T 15105
Man, woman, and sin. (Claxton) 3:111-13 D10'27. CC 15106
Manhattan cocktail. by Edward Hope. (Lowrie) 5:105 Ap13'29. B 15107
Manhattan Mary. by B. G. De Sylva, et al. (Brackett) 3:32 O8'27. T 15108
Manhattan melodrama. (Mosher) 10:94 My12'34. CC 15109
Manhattan transfer. by John Dos Passos. (Dounce) 1:18 N28'25; 1:21-2 Ja2'26. B 15110
The Manhatters. by Aline Erlanger and George S. Oppenheimer. (White) 3:33-4 Ag6'27. T 15111
Mannequin. (Shane) 1:27 Ja16'26. CC 15112
Mannequin. by Fannie Hurst. (Dounce) 2:53-4 Ag21'26.B 15113
Man's estate. by Beatrice Blackmar and Bruce Gould. (Brackett) 5:29-30 Ap13'29. T 15114
Man's fate. by André Malraux and Haakon M. Chevalier, trans. (Fadiman) 10:69-70 Je23'34. B 15115
Man's hope. by André Malraux. (Fadiman) 14:67*N5'38.B 15116
A man's man. by Patrick Kearney. (Mankiewicz) 1:19 O24'25. T 15117
A man's past. (Claxton) 3:84 O8 '27. CC 15118
The man's town. by Willard Robertson. (Brackett) 6:30 Mr22 '30. T 15119
Mansion on the Hudson. by Cornelia Otis Skinner. (Gibbs) 11: 32-4*Ap13'35. T 15120
The mansions of philosophy. by Will Durant. (Smith) 5:103 Je15 '29. B 15121
Manslaughter. (Gibbs) 6:54-5 Ag2 '30. CC 15122
Mantis. by Ethelreda Lewis. (Lowrie) 4:74 Ja19'29. B 15123
Mantrap. by Sinclair Lewis. (Dounce) 2:87-8 Je5'26.B 15124
Many a slip. by Edith Fitzgerald and Robert Riskin. (Benchley) 5:28 F15'30. T 15125
Many mansions. by Eckert Goodman and Jules Eckert Goodman. (Gibbs) 13:28-30*N6'37.T 15126
Many thousands gone. by John Peale Bishop. (Coates) 7:77*My 23'31. B 15127
Many waters. by Monckton Hoffe. (Benchley) 5:36-8 O5'29.T 15128
Mape; the world of illusion. by André Maurois. (Dounce) 2:49-50 Jy3'26. B 15129
Marcel Proust: his life and work. by Léon Pierre Quint. (Boyd) 3:100-101 My14'27. B 15130
March hares. by Harry Wagstaff Gribble. (Brackett) 4:34 Ap21 '28. T 15131
The march of time. (Mosher) 10: 59*F9'35. CC 15132
Marching by. by Ernst Neubach, et al. (Benchley) 8:26*Mr12'32. T 15133
Marching! marching! by Clara Weatherwax. (Anon.) 11:54*Ja 4'36. B 15134
Marching song. by John Howard

Lawson. (Benchley) 13:30*Mr 6'37. T 15135

Marco millions. by Eugene O'Neill. (Boyd) 3:88-9 My28'27. B 15136 (Brackett) 3:25-6 Ja21'28. 15137

Mare nostrum. (Shane) 2:44 F27 '26. CC 15138

Margin for error. by Clare Boothe. (Gibbs) 15:25*N11'39. T 15139

Marginal land. by Horace Kramer. (Fadiman) 15:70*Ap1'39. B 15140

Maria. by Alfred Savoir. (Flanner) 9:71 O28'33. T 15141

Maria Capponi. by René Schickele. (Hoyt) 4:97 Mr3'28. B 15142

Marianne. (Mosher) 5:107-109 O 26'29. CC 15143

Marie Antoinette. (Mosher) 14:40-1*Ag20'38. CC 15144

Marie Antoinette. by Stefan Zweig. (Coates) 9:78 Ap8'33. B 15145

Mariners. by Clemence Dane. (Brackett) 3:33 Ap9'27. T 15146

Marked woman. (Mosher) 13:63-5*Ap17'37. CC 15147

Marlborough. by Donald Barr Chidsey. (Smith) 5:96 S28'29. B 15148

Marquis preferred. (Mosher) 4:67 Ja26'29. CC 15149

The marquise. by Noel Coward. (Brackett) 3:34 N26'27. T 15150

The marriage bed. by Ernest Pascal. (Brackett) 4:28-30 Ja19 '29. T 15151

Marriage for three. by Elmer Harris. (Benchley) 7:28-30 N21 '31. T 15152

Marriage in blue. by A. E. Fisher. (Coates) 7:50 Ag22'31. B 15153

Marriage license. (Claxton) 2:44 O30'26. CC 15154

The marriage playground. (Mosher) 5:75 D21'29. CC 15155

Married in Hollywood. (Gibbs) 5: 80 S28'29. CC 15156

Marry the man! by Jean Archibald. (Brackett) 5:29-30 My4'29. T 15157

Marseilles. by Sidney Howard and Marcel Pagnol. (Benchley) 6:37-8 N29'30. T 15158

The martial spirit. by Walter Millis. (Coates) 7:78*Je6'31. B 15159

Martin's Summer. by Vicki Baum. (Coates) 7:51 Ag22'31. B 15160

The martyr. by Liam O'Flaherty. (Fadiman) 9:67 Je10'33. B 15161

Mary and Martha. by J. Anker Larsen. (Dounce) 2:53-4 Ag28 '26. B 15162

Mary Baker Eddy. by Lyman P. Powell. (Coates) 6:135-6 D6'30. B 15163

Mary Burns, fugitive. (Mosher) 11:80*N23'35. CC 15164

Mary Gladstone: her diaries and letters. by Mary Gladstone and Lucy Masterman, ed. (Smith) 6:82 My31'30. B 15165

Mary Lincoln, wife and widow. by Carl Sandburg. (Coates) 8:81 N 19'32. B 15166

Mary of Scotland. (Maloney) 12:48-9*Ag8'36. CC 15167

Mary of Scotland. by Maxwell Anderson. (Benchley) 9:34 D9'33. T 15168

Mary, Queen of Scotland. by Stefan Zweig. (Fadiman) 11:48-9*Ag31 '35. B 15169

Mary, wife of Lincoln. by Katherine Helm. (Lowrie) 4:114 D1 '28. B 15170

The mask and the face. by Luigi Chiarelli and W. Somerset Maugham, trans. (Benchley) 9: 30 My20'33. T 15171

Masks and faces. by A. J. Minor. (Benchley) 9:26 Mr25'33. T 15172

The masque of kings. by Maxwell Anderson. (Benchley) 13:28*F20 '37. T 15173

The masque of Venice. by George Dunning Gribble. (Gabriel) 2:22 Mr13'26. T 15174

Masquerade in Vienna. (Mosher) 12:63*Ja23'37. CC 15175

Master Kung. by Carl Crow. (Fadiman) 14:74*My14'38. B 15176

The master of destiny. by Frederick Tilney. (Smith) 5:74 F1 '30. B 15177

Master of Manhattan. by Lothrop

Stoddard. (Coates) 7:88 Mr28 '31. B 15178
The master of the house. by Radclyffe Hall. (Coates) 8:70-1*My7'32. B 15179
Mata Hari. (Mosher) 7:75 Ja9'32. CC 15180
The mating season. by William A. Grew. (White) 3:34 Ag6'27. T 15181
Matriarch. by G. B. Stern. (Boyd) 2:68 Ja15'27. B 15182
The matriarch. by G. B. Stern. (Benchley) 6:27-8 Mr29'30. T 15183
Matrimony, pfd. by Louis Verneuil. (Benchley) 12:35*N21'36. T 15184
Matthew Arnold. by Lionel Trilling. (Fadiman) 14:61-3*Ja21 '39. B 15185
Matthias at the door. by Edwin Arlington Robinson. (Bogan) 7:62 F13'32. B 15186
The Maurizius case. by Jacob Wassermann. (Smith) 5:122 N23 '29. B 15187
The mauve decade. by Thomas Beer. (Dounce) 2:62-4 My1'26. B 15188
May fair. by Michael Arlen. (Dounce) 1:15 Je6'25. B 15189
May Flavin. by Myron Brinig. (Kronenberger) 14:57*Je25'38. B 15190
May wine. by Frank Mandel; Sigmund Romberg and Oscar Hammerstein, II. (Benchley) 11:36*D14'35. T 15191
Maya. by Simon Gantillon and Ernest Boyd, trans. (Brackett) 4:33 Mr3'28. T 15192
Mayerling. (Mosher) 13:69*S18 '37. CC 15193
Mayflowers. by Clifford Grey and Edward Kunneke. (Mankiewicz) 1:14-15 D5'25. T 15194
Maytime. (Mosher) 13:54-5*Mr 27'37. CC 15195
Mayor Harding of New York. by Stephen Endicott. (Coates) 7:51-2*Jy18'31. B 15196
The mayor of Hell. (Mosher) 9:46 Jy8'33. CC 15197
Me, gangster. (Mosher) 4:81 O27 '28. CC 15198
The medieval feast. by William Mead. (Coates) 7:50 Ag29'31. B 15199
The Mediterranean and other poems. by Allen Tate. (Bogan) 12:61*Ag22'36. B 15200
Meet General Grant. by W. E. Woodward. (Lowrie) 4:114 D1 '28. B 15201
Meet Nero Wolfe. (Mosher) 12:56-7*Jy25'36. CC 15202
Meet the Baron. (Mosher) 9:80 N4 '33. CC 15203
Mein Kampf. by Adolf Hitler. (Fadiman) 15:77-8*Mr11'39. B 15204
Mélo. by Henri Bernstein and Arthur Pollock. (Benchley) 7:28-30 Ap25'31. T 15205
Melody. by Edward Childs Carpenter; Irving Caesar and Sigmund Romberg. (Benchley) 9:28-30 F25'33. T 15206
The melody of love. (Mosher) 4:82 O27'28. CC 15207
Memoirs of a fox-hunting man. by Siegfried Sassoon. (Fadiman) 14:62-3*Ja14'39. B 15208
Memoirs of a terrorist. by Boris Savinkov. (Coates) 7:77*Je6'31. B 15209
Memoirs of an infantry officer. by Siegfried Sassoon. (Smith) 6:102 O18'30. B 15210
The memoirs of Lorenzo da Ponte. by Arthur Livingston, ed. (Gannett) 5:137-8 D14'29. B 15211
Memoirs of Marmontel. by Jean François Marmontel and Richard Aldington, ed. (Coates) 6:116 N8'30. B 15212
The memoirs of Marshal Foch. by Ferdinand Foch. (Coates) 7:88-9 Ap4'31. B 15213
Memoirs of the court of England in 1675. by Marie Catherine d' Aulnoy. (Boyd) 3:70-1 S3'27. B 15214
Memories and vagaries. by Axel Munthe. (Smith) 6:88 N29'30. B 15215

Memories of Manhattan. by Charles T. Harris. (Leonard) 4:65 Jy21'28. B 15216
Memory lane. (Shane) 1:35 F6'26. CC 15217
Men and brethren. by James Gould Cozzens. (Anon.) 11:54* Ja4'36. B 15218
Men dislike women. by Michael Arlen. (Coates) 7:106-108 Ap11 '31. B 15219
Men in battle. by Alvah Bessie. (Fadiman)15:92-3*O14'39.B 15220
Men in white. (Mosher) 10:87-8 Je16'34. CC 15221
Men in white. by Sidney Kingsley. (Gibbs) 9:34-5 O7'33.T 15222
(Benchley) 9:25-6 D23'33. 15223
Men must fight. by S. K. Lauren and Reginald Lawrence. (Benchley) 8:28 O22'32. T 15224
Men of good will. by Jules Romains. and Warre B. Wells, trans. (Fadiman) 9:70 Je3'33. B 15225
Men of music. by Wallace Brockway and Herbert Weinstock. (Fadiman) 15:69*N4'39. B 15226
Men of science. by J. G. Crowther. (Fadiman)12:72*Mr14'36.B 15227
Men with wings. (Mosher) 14:58* O29'38. CC 15228
Men without names. (Mosher) 11: 45*Jy6'35. CC 15229
Men without women. (Mosher) 5: 77 F8'30. CC 15230
Men without women. by Ernest Hemingway. (Parker) 3:92-4 O 29'27. B 15231
Menace. by Arthur M. Brilant. (Brackett) 3:33 Mr26'27.T 15232
Mercenary Mary. by William B. Friedlander; Con Conrad and Isabel Leighton. (Mankiewicz) 1:15 Jy25'25. T 15233
The merchant of Venice. by William Shakespeare. (Mankiewicz) 1:24 Ja23'26. T 15234
(Brackett) 3:25 Ja28'28. 15235
The merchant of Yonkers. by Thornton Wilder. (Benchley) 14:26*Ja7'39. T 15236
Merchants of glory. by Marcel Pagnol and Marcel Nivoix. (Mankiewicz) 1:19-20 D26'25. T 15237
Merrily we roll along. by George S. Kaufman and Moss Hart. (Gibbs) 10:32 O6'34. T 15238
Merry Andrew. by Lewis Beach. (Brackett) 4:28 F2'29. T 15239
Merry-go-round. by Morrie Ryskind and Howard Dietz. (Long) 3:36 Je11'27. T 15240
Merry-go-round. by Albert Maltz and George Sklar. (Benchley) 8:26*My7'32. T 15241
The merry Malones. by George M. Cohan. (Brackett) 3:32 O8 '27. T 15242
The merry widow. (Shane) 1:17 S5'25. CC 15243
The merry widow. (Mosher) 10: 87-8 O20'34. CC 15244
The merry wives of Windsor. by William Shakespeare. (Brackett) 4:32 Mr31'28. T 15245
The merry world. by Maurice Rubens and Clifford Grey. (Brackett) 2:32-3 Je19'26. T 15246
The messenger of the gods. by Phyllis Bottome. (Hoyt) 3:114-15 N12'27. B 15247
Meteor. by S. N. Behrman. (Benchley) 5:27-8 Ja4'30. T 15248
The method of freedom. by Walter Lippmann. (Fadiman) 10: 92-4 Je9'34. B 15249
The Methodist faun. by Anne Parrish. (Smith) 5:127-8 O19'29. B 15250
A Methodist saint. by Herbert Asbury. (Boyd) 3:104 Ap2'27. B 15251
Metropolis. (Claxton) 3:80-1 Mr12 '27. CC 15252
Mexicana. by Celestino Gorostiza, et al. (Gibbs) 15:36*Ap29'39. T 15253
Mexico. by Stuart Chase. (Coates) 7:51*Ag15'31. B 15254
Michael and Mary. by A. A. Milne. (Benchley) 5:25 D28'29.T 15255
Michael Strogoff. (Claxton) 2:95-6

D11'26. CC 15256
Michel Auclair. by Charles Vildrac. (Anon.) 1:13 Mr14'25. T 15257
Microbe hunters. by Paul de Kruif. (Dounce) 2:68 F20'26. B 15258
The Midas touch. by Margaret Kennedy. (Fadiman) 15:71-2* Ap8'39. B 15259
Mid-channel. by Ludwig Lewisohn. (Lowrie) 5:115 My18'29. B 15260
The middle watch. by Ian Hay and Stephen King-Hall. (Benchley) 5:40 O26'29. T 15261
Midnight. (Mosher) 15:70* Ap8'39. CC 15262
Midnight. by Claire Sifton and Paul Sifton. (Benchley) 6:27-8 Ja10'31. T 15263
Midnight alibi. (Mosher) 10:60 Jy 14'34. CC 15264
Midnight Club. (Mosher) 9:40 Ag5 '33. CC 15265
Midnight in the desert. by J. B. Priestley. (Fadiman) 13:59* Mr27'37. B 15266
The midnight sun. (Shane) 2:55 My1'26. CC 15267
The midnight taxi. (Mosher) 4:84 N3'28. CC 15268
Midstream. by Helen Keller. (Smith) 5:136 D14'29. B 15269
Midsummer night. by John Masefield. (Lowrie) 4:143-4 D8'28. B 15270
A midsummer night's dream. (Mosher) 11:67*O19'35.CC 15271
A midsummer night's dream. by William Shakespeare. (Wright) 3:41 Jy9'27. T 15272
(Brackett) 3:34 D3'27. 15273
Mid-west. by James Hagan. (Benchley) 11:24*Ja18'36.T 15274
The mighty. (Mosher) 5:71 Ja11 '30. CC 15275
The mighty Barnum. (Mosher) 10:69*Ja5'35. CC 15276
The Mikado. (Mosher) 15:72*Je3 '39. CC 15277
The Mikado. by William S. Gilbert and Arthur Sullivan. (Anon.) 1:11 Ap25'25. T 15278
(Brackett) 3:26 O1'27. 15279
The milk and honey route. by Nels Anderson. (Coates) 7:109 Ap11'31. B 15280
The Milky Way. (Mosher) 12:71* Ap4'36. CC 15281
The Milky Way. by Lynn Root and Harry Clork. (Benchley) 10:30 My19'34. T 15282
A million and one nights. by Terry Ramsaye. (Boyd) 2:56 Ja 1'27. B 15283
A million bid. (Claxton) 3:69 Je11 '27. CC 15284
The millionaire. (Mosher) 7:85-6 Ap18'31. CC 15285
Mima. by David Belasco, adapt. (Brackett) 4:26-30 D22'28. T 15286
Mimie Scheller. by Alfred L. Golden. (Gibbs) 12:32*O10'36. T 15287
Min and Bill. (Mosher) 6:75 N29 '30. CC 15288
Miracle at Verdun. by Hans Chlumberg. (Parker) 7:30-4 Mr28'31. T 15289
The miracle man. (Mosher) 8:53* Ap30'32. CC 15290
The miracle of England. by André Maurois. (Fadiman) 13:73*Ap24 '37. B 15291
The miracle of the wolves. (Hays) 1:27 Mr7'25. CC 15292
A mirror for witches. by Esther Forbes. (Markey) 4:104 My12 '28. B 15293
Mirrors. by Milton Herbert Gropper. (Brackett) 3:25-6 Ja28'28. T 15294
Mirrors of the year. by Grant Overton, ed. (Boyd) 3:102 Ap2 '27. B 15295
Mirthful haven. by Booth Tarkington. (Smith) 6:106-107 O25'30. B 15296
The misleading lady. (Mosher) 8: 56-7*Ap16'32. CC 15297
Miss America. by W. J. Turner. (Bogan) 7:80 Mr21'31.B 15298
Miss Fane's baby is stolen. (Mosher) 9:61 Ja27'34.CC 15299
Miss Gulliver travels. by George

Ford and Ethel Taylor. (White) 7:30 D5'31. T 15300
Miss Lonelyhearts. by Nathanael West. (Coates) 9:67 Ap15'33. B 15301
Miss Mole. by Emily Hilda Young. (Smith) 6:100 O18'30. B 15302
Miss Quis. by Ward Morehouse. (Benchley) 13:26*Ap17'37. T 15303
Miss Swan expects. by Samuel Spewack and Bella Spewack. (Benchley) 15:28*Mr4'39. T 15304
The missing link. (Claxton) 3:91 My14'27. CC 15305
The Mississippi gambler. (Mosher) 5:107 N2'29. CC 15306
Missouri legend. by E. B. Ginty. (Gibbs) 14:28*O1'38. T 15307
Mr. Bisbee's princess. by Julian Street. (Dounce) 1:17 Jy25'25. B 15308
Mr. Charles, King of England. by John Drinkwater. (Boyd) 2:115 D11'26. B 15309
Mr. Darby. by Martin Armstrong. (Coates) 7:54-5 Ja30'32. B 15310
Mr. Deeds goes to town. (Mosher) 12:48*Ap25'36. CC 15311
Mr. Emmanuel. by Louis Golding. (Kronenberger) 15:65*Jy22'39. B 15312
Mr. Fothergill's plot. by Anon. (Coates) 7:110-11 D5'31. B 15313
Mr. Fortune's maggot. by Sylvia Townsend Warner. (Boyd) 3:116 Ap23'27. B 15314
Mr. Gilhooley. by Frank B. Elser. (Benchley) 6:34-6 O11'30. T 15315
Mr. Gilhooley. by Liam O'Flaherty. (Boyd) 3:94-5 F19'27. B 15316
Mr. Godly beside himself. by Gerald Bullett. (Anon.) 1:26 Ap 11'25. B 15317
Mr. Hodge and Mr. Hazard. by Elinor Wylie. (Parker) 4:98-9 Mr31'28. B 15318
Mr. Isaacs. (Mosher) 7:45*Ag1 '31. CC 15319
Mr. Moneypenny. by Channing Pollock. (Brackett) 4:34 O27 '28. T 15320
Mr. Pim passes by. by A. A. Milne. (Brackett) 3:34 Ap30'27. T 15321
Mister Romeo. by Harry Wagstaff Gribble and Wallace A. Manheimer. (Brackett) 3:61 S17 '27. T 15322
Mr. Smith goes to Washington. (Mosher) 15:73-4*O21'39. CC 15323
Mr. Weston's good wine. by T. F. Powys. (Hoyt) 4:107-108 Ap7 '28. B 15324
Mrs. Craddock. by W. Somerset Maugham. (Hoyt) 3:79-80 F18 '28. B 15325
Mrs. Dane's defense. by Henry Arthur Jones. (Brackett) 3:25 F18'28. T 15326
Mrs. Eddy. by Edwin Franden Dakin. (Smith) 5:87-8 S7'29. B 15327
Mrs. Haney. by Foxhall Daingerfield. (Fadiman) 9:96-7 N18'33. B 15328
Mrs. Moonlight. by Benn W. Levy. (Benchley) 6:36 O11'30. T 15329
Mrs. O'Brien entertains. by Harry Madden. (Benchley) 15:30* F18'39. T 15330
Mrs. Socrates. by Fritz Mauthner. (Boyd) 2:61 D25'26. B 15331
Mrs. Taylor. by Marjorie Worthington. (Coates) 8:42-3 Ag20'32. B 15332
Mrs. Wiggs of the cabbage patch. (Mosher) 10:87-8 N3'34. CC 15333
Mitsou. by Sidonie Gabrielle Colette. (Smith) 6:69-70 Jy12'30. B 15334
Mitya's love. by Ivan Bunin. (Dounce) 2:90-1 N6'26. B 15335
Mixed doubles. by Frank Stayton. (Brackett) 3:29 My7'27. T 15336
Moana. (Shane) 1:36 F13'26. CC 15337
The mob. by Blasco Ibáñez. (Boyd 3:66 Ag13'27. B 15338
Moby Dick. (Shane) 1:39 Ja23'26. CC 15339
Moby Dick. (Mosher) 6:58 Ag23 '30. CC 15340
Mockery. (Claxton) 3:57 S3'27. CC 15341

Modern American poetry. by Louis Untermeyer, ed. (Smith) 6:62 Ag16'30. B 15342
A modern hero. by Louis Bromfield. (Coates) 8:60*Ap30'32. B 15343
Modern man: his belief and behavior. by Harvey Fergusson. (Fadiman) 11:60*Ja25'36.B15344
Modern man in the making. by Otto Neurath. (Fadiman) 15: 69-70*S16'39. B 15345
Modern times. (Mosher) 11:57-8* F15'36. CC 15346
A modern virgin. by Elmer Harris. (Benchley) 7:28*My30'31. T 15347
Molders of American thought. by William H. Cordell, ed. (Fadiman) 10:54-6*D29'34. B 15348
Moment in Peking. by Lin Yutang. (Fadiman) 15:87-9*N18'39.15349
Money from home. by Frank Craven. (Brackett) 3:33 Mr12 '27. T 15350
The money lender. by Roy Horniman. (White) 4:25 S8'28.T 15351
Money of her own. by Margaret Culkin Banning. (Leonard) 4: 104 S15'28. B 15352
Money writes. by Upton Sinclair. (Parker) 3:122-3 D10'27.B 15353
Monkey. by Sam Janney. (Benchley) 8:30*F20'32. T 15354
Monkey business. (Mosher) 7:73-4 O17'31. CC 15355
Monkey business. by Oscar Carter. (Gabriel) 1:24 Ja30'26. T 15356
The monkey talks. by René Fauchois and Gladys Unger. (Mankiewicz) 1:20 Ja16'26. T 15357
Monsieur de Pourceaugnac. by Jean Baptiste Poquelin Molière. (Flanner) 9:60 F18'33. T 15358
Monte Carlo. (Mosher) 6:67 S6 '30. CC 15359
A month in the country. by Ivan Turgenev. (Benchley) 6:27 Mr 29'30. T 15360
The moon in the Yellow River. by Denis Johnston. (Benchley) 8:26-8*Mr12'32. T 15361
The moon is a gong. by John Dos Passos. (Gabriel) 2:25 Mr27'26. T 15362
Moon over Mulberry Street. by Nicholas Cosentino. (Gibbs) 11:38*S14'35. T 15363
Moonblind. by Theodore Wilde. (Parker) 7:89-90 O10'31. B 15364
Moor born. by Dan Totheroh. (Benchley) 10:32 Ap14'34. T 15365
Morals. by Charles Recht and Sidney Howard. (Mankiewicz) 1:23 D12'25. T 15366
More joy in heaven. by Morley Callaghan. (Fadiman) 13:92-3* N20'37. B 15367
More or less about myself. by Margot Asquith. (Fadiman) 9: 84-7 F10'34. B 15368
More poems. by A. E. Housman. (Bogan) 12:64-5*O31'36. B 15369
More than a secretary. (Mosher) 12:88-9*D19'36. CC 15370
Morgan the magnificent. by John K. Winkler. (Smith) 6:76 S6'30. B 15371
The morning after. by Len D. Hollister and Leona Stephens. (Mankiewicz) 1:15 Ag8'25. T 15372
Morning glory. (Mosher) 9:45 Ag26 '33. CC 15373
Morning shows the day. by Helen Hull. (Fadiman) 10:96-7 N3'34. B 15374
Morning's at seven. by Paul Osborn. (Benchley) 15:36*D9'39. T 15375
Morocco. (Mosher) 6:101 N22'30. CC 15376
Morocco. (Mosher) 12:64*Ap18'36. CC 15377
Morrow's almanack for 1930. by Thayer Hobson, ed. (Smith) 5: 123-4 O26'29. B 15378
Mosaic. by G. B. Stern. (Smith) 6:104 O25'30. B 15379
Moscow laughs. (Maloney) 11:63* Mr30'35. CC 15380
Moscow skies. by Maurice Hindus. (Anon.) 12:72*S26'36. B 15381
Moses and monotheism. by Sigmund

Freud. (Anon.) 15:72*Je24'39. B 15382
A most immoral lady. by Townsend Martin. (Brackett) 4:38-40 D8'28. T 15383
Most of the game. by John van Druten. (Benchley) 11:30*O12 '35. T 15384
The most powerful man in the world. by Glyn Roberts. (Fadiman) 14:61-2*Je4'38. B 15385
Mother. by Bertolt Brecht and Hanns Eisler. (Benchley) 11:25*N30'35. T 15386
The mother. by Pearl S. Buck. (Fadiman) 9:84 Ja13'34. B 15387
The mother. by Karel Capek; Paul Selver and Miles Malleson. (Gibbs) 15:30*My6'39. T 15388
Mother Carey's chickens. (Maloney) 14:41-2*Ag6'38. CC 15389
Mother knows best. (Mosher) 4:80-1 S22'28. CC 15390
Mother of mine. (Mosher) 4:92 Ja5'29. CC 15391
Mothers cry. by Helen Grace Carlisle. (Smith) 5:82 Ja18'30. B 15392
Moulin rouge. (Mosher) 10:76 F17 '34. CC 15393
The mountain and the plain. by Herbert Gorman. (Fadiman) 12:48-9*Ag15'36. B 15394
Mountain justice. (Mosher) 13:64* My8'37. CC 15395
Mountain music. (Mosher) 13:49* Jy3'37. CC 15396
Mourning becomes Electra. by Eugene O'Neill. (Benchley) 7:28-30 N7'31. T 15397
The mouthpiece. (Mosher) 8:53* Ap30'32. CC 15398
Move on. by Charles Bamfield Hoyt. (Gabriel) 1:23 Ja30'26. T 15399
Move on, Sister. by Daniel N. Rubin. (Benchley) 9:28 N4'33. T 15400
Move over. by Ethel Pettit Roche. (Hoyt) 3:73 Ja21'28. B 15401
Movers and shakers. by Mabel Dodge Luhan. (Fadiman) 12:88-90*N21'36. B 15402
The movies march on. (Mosher) 15:58*Jy15'39. CC 15403
Mozart. by Ashley Dukes and Sacha Guitry. (Brackett) 2:39-40 O4'26. T 15404
Mozart. by Sacha Guitry. (Brackett) 2:29 Ja8'27. T 15405
The mud turtle. by Elliott Lester. (Mankiewicz) 1:16 Ag29'25. T 15406
The mulberry bush. by Edward Knoblock. (Brackett) 3:33-4 N12 '27. T 15407
Mulliner nights. by P. G. Wodehouse. (Coates) 9:62 F25'33. B 15408
Murder at the vanities. by Rufus King. (Gibbs) 9:26-7 S23'33. T 15409
Murder by the clock. (Mosher) 7:53-4*Jy25'31. CC 15410
Murder in Manhattan. by Arthur Procter. (Smith) 6:59 Ag2'30. B 15411
Murder in the cathedral. by T. S. Eliot. (Benchley) 12:32*Mr28 '36; 14:30*F26'38. T 15412
The murder man. (Mosher) 11:41* Jy27'35. CC 15413
Murder on a honeymoon. (Mosher) 11:61-2*F23'35. CC 15414
Murder on the blackboard. (Mosher) 10:64 Je30'34. CC 15415
Murder on the second floor. by Frank Vosper. (Benchley) 5:38-40 S21'29. T 15416
Murders in the Rue Morgue. (Mosher) 8:62*F20'32. CC 15417
Murray Anderson's almanac. by Noel Coward, et al. (Brackett) 5:39 Ag24'29. T 15418
Murray Hill. by Leslie Howard. (Brackett) 3:32 O8'27. T 15419
Muscling in. by Fred D. Pasley. (Coates) 7:102-103 D12'31. B 15420
Music at midnight. by Muriel Draper. (Lowrie) 4:88 F2'29. B 15421
Music for madame. (Mosher) 13:89*O30'37. CC 15422
The music from behind the moon. by James Branch Cabell.

(Dounce) 2:80 S18'26. B 15423
The music goes 'round. (Mosher) 12:50-1*F29'36. CC 15424
Music in the air. (Mosher) 10: 34*D22'34. CC 15425
Music in the air. by Oscar Hammerstein, II and Jerome Kern. (Benchley) 8:22 N19'32. T 15426
The music master. (Claxton) 2: 70-2 Ja22'27. CC 15427
Mutiny in the big house. (Mosher) 15:58-9*D16'39. CC 15428
Mutiny on the Bounty. (Mosher) 11:79-80*N16'35. CC 15429
My America. by Louis Adamic. (Fadiman) 14:61-2*My28'38. B 15430
My best girl. (Claxton) 3:70 N12 '27. CC 15431
My Bill. (Mosher) 14:45*Jy16'38. CC 15432
My brother, A. E. Housman. by Laurence Housman. (Bogan) 14:64-5*Ap23'38. B 15433
My country. by William J. Perlman. (Brackett) 2:38 Ag28'26. T 15434
My dear children. by Catherine Turney and Jerry Horwin. (Gibbs) 15:28 F10'40. T 15435
My dear Cornelia. by Stuart P. Sherman. (Anon.) 1:28 Mr21 '25. B 15436
My ears are bent. by Joseph Mitchell. (Fadiman) 13:62-3* Ja22'38. B 15437
My first husband. by Marie A. Essipov. (Coates) 8:70 Ap9'32. B 15438
My friendly contemporaries. by Hamlin Garland. (Coates) 8: 66 N26'32. B 15439
My girl. by Harlan Thompson and Harry Archer. (Mankiewicz) 1:15 Jy25'25. T 15440
My girl Friday. by William A. Grew. (Brackett) 5:28 F23'29. T 15441
My heart's in the highlands. by William Saroyan. (Gibbs) 15: 28-30*Ap22'39. T 15442
My heresy. by William Montgomery Brown. (Dounce) 2:70 S25 '26. B 15443
My jungle book. by Herbert S. Dickey. (Coates) 8:83*Mr19'32. B 15444
My life. by Isadora Duncan. (Parker) 3:69-71 Ja14'28. B 15445
My life. by Leon Trotsky. (Smith) 6:92 Ap26'30. B 15446
My life is in your hands. by Eddie Cantor. (Lowrie) 4:129 D15'28. B 15447
My lucky star. (Mosher) 14:63* S17'38. CC 15448
My magnolia. by Alex C. Rogers and Eddie Hunter. (Brackett) 2:36 Jy31'26. T 15449
My man. (Mosher) 4:50 D29'28. CC 15450
My man Godfrey. (Mosher) 12:67* S26'36. CC 15451
My Maryland. by Dorothy Donnelly and Sigmund Romberg. (Brackett) 3:32 S24'27. T 15452
My memoir. by Edith Bolling Wilson. (Fadiman) 15:69*Mr18'39. B 15453
My next bride. by Kay Boyle. (Fadiman) 10:110-11 N10'34. B 15454
My princess. by Dorothy Donnelly and Sigmund Romberg. (Brackett) 3:34 O15'27. T 15455
My shadow as I pass. by Sybil Bolitho. (Fadiman) 10:101-102 S22'34. B 15456
My sin. (Mosher) 7:79-80 S19'31. CC 15457
My son. (Anon.) 1:31 My2'25. CC 15458
My son, my son! by Howard Spring. (Fadiman) 14:64*My21 '38. B 15459
My Thirty Years' War. by Margaret Anderson. (Smith) 6:82 My31'30. B 15460
My tropical air castle. by Frank M. Chapman. (Gannett) 5:86-7 D21'29. B 15461
Myron T. Herrick. by T. Bentley Mott. (Smith) 5:66-7 D28'29. B 15462
The mysterious Dr. Fu Manchu.

(Mosher) 5:35 Jy27'29. CC 15463
The mysterious island. (Mosher) 5:57-9 D28'29. CC 15464
The mysterious madame. by C. E. Bechhofer Roberts. (Coates) 7:83 My9'31. B 15465
The mysterious universe. by James Jeans. (Coates) 6:134 D6'30. B 15466
Mystery moon. by Frederick Herendeen. (Benchley) 6:26 Jy5'30. T 15467
The mystery of Edwin Drood. (Maloney) 11:64*Mr30'35. CC 15468
The mystery of life. (A. Gibbs) 6:57 D20'30. CC 15469
The mystery of life. (Mosher) 7:48*Jy4'31. CC 15470
The mystery of the wax museum. (Mosher) 9:56 F25'33. CC 15471
The mystery ship. by Edgar M. Schoenberg and Milton Silver. (Brackett) 3:33-4 Mr26'27. T 15472
Mystery Square. by Hugh A. Anderson and George Bamman. (Brackett) 5:30 Ap20'29. T 15473
The mystic. (Shane) 1:17 S5'25. CC 15474
Myths about Lincoln. by Lloyd Lewis. (Smith) 5:81 Je1'29. B 15475

N

N by E. by Rockwell Kent. (Smith) 6:120 D13'30. B 15476
Nagana. (Mosher) 9:55 F25'33. CC 15477
Naked. by Luigi Pirandello. (Brackett) 2:33-4 N20'26. T 15478
Naked on roller skates. by Maxwell Bodenheim. (Coates) 6:60-1 Ja31'31. B 15479
The name and nature of poetry. by A. E. Housman. (Fadiman) 9:66-7 Je10'33. B 15480
Nameless men. (Claxton) 4:84 Mr31'28. CC 15481
Nancy Steele is missing. (Mosher) 13:77-8*Mr13'37. CC 15482
Nancy's private affair. by Myron C. Fagan. (Benchley) 5:28 Ja25'30. T 15483
Napi. by Julius Berstl and Brian Marlow, adapt. (Parker) 7:32-4 Mr21'31. T 15484
Napoleon, the man of destiny. by Emil Ludwig. (Boyd) 2:66 Ja15'27. B 15485
Napoleon. by B. Harrison Orkow. (Brackett) 4:32 Mr17'28. T 15486
The narrow corner. by W. Somerset Maugham. (Coates) 8:73 N12'32. B 15487
National Velvet. by Enid Bagnold. (Fadiman) 11:78-9*Ap27'35. B 15488
A native argosy. by Morley Callaghan. (Lowrie) 5:104-105 Ap13'29. B 15489
The native's return. by Louis Adamic. (Fadiman) 9:69-70 F3'34. B 15490
The natural mother. by Dominique Dunois. (Smith) 5:122 N23'29. B 15491
Naughty Riquette. by Harry B. Smith. (Brackett) 2:29 S25'26. T 15492
Naughty-naught '00. by John Van Antwerp. (Benchley) 12:26*Ja30'37. T 15493
Navy blue & gold. (Mosher) 13:45*D25'37. CC 15494
Navy blues. (Mosher) 5:73 Ja18'30. CC 15495
The Nazarine. by Sholem Asch. (Fadiman) 15:76*O21'39. B 15496
Ned Mc Cobb's daughter. by Sidney Howard. (Brackett) 2:39 D11'26. T 15497
Ned Wayburn's gambols. by Ned Wayburn. (Brackett) 4:28 Ja26'29. T 15498
Negro. by Nancy Cunard, ed. (Flanner) 10:55-6 Ap28'34. B 15499
Nell Gwyn. (Claxton) 2:32 Jy24'26. CC 15500
Nell Gwyn. (Mosher) 11:54*Je29'35. CC 15501
Nelson W. Aldrich. by Nathaniel Wright Stephenson. (Coates) 6:114-15 N22'30. B 15502
Nero, the singing emperor of Rome. by Arthur Weigall.

(Coates) 6:89-90 N29'30.B 15503
Never ask the end. by Isabel Paterson. (Coates) 8:87 Ja7 '33. B 15504
Never enough. by Leane Zugsmith. (Coates) 8:63 O29'32. B 15505
Never no more. by James Knox Millen. (Benchley) 7:26 Ja16 '32. T 15506
Never the twain shall meet. (Mosher) 7:64*Je13'31.CC 15507
New adventures of Get-Rich-Quick Wallingford. (Mosher) 7:75 O17'31. CC 15508
The new American credo. by George Jean Nathan. (Boyd) 3:115-16 Ap23'27. B 15509
A new American history. by W. E. Woodward. (Fadiman) 12: 115*D5'36. B 15510
A new anthology of modern poetry. by Selden Rodman, ed. (Bogan) 14:58-9*Jy23'38. B 15511
The new book of English verse. by Charles Williams, ed. (Bogan) 12:72-3*F22'36. B 15512
New directions in prose and poetry. by James Laughlin. (Fadiman) 13:62*Ja15'38B 15513
New England holiday. by Charles Allen Smart. (Coates) 7:51 Ag 22'31. B 15514
New faces. by Leonard Sillman, et al. (Benchley) 10:28 Mr24 '34. T 15515
New faces of 1936. by June Sillman, et al. (Gibbs) 12:39*My 30'36. T 15516
New frontiers of the mind. by J. B. Rhine. (Fadiman) 13:72-3*O9'37. B 15517
The new generation. by V. F. Calverton and Samuel D. Schmalhausen, ed. (Smith) 6: 108 My10'30. B 15518
The new Gulliver. (Flanner) 11: 38*O26'35. CC 15519
The new Gulliver. (Mosher) 11: 77-8*N9'35. CC 15520
The new Klondike. (Shane) 2:49 Mr27'26. CC 15521
New medical follies. by Morris Fishbein. (Boyd) 3:96 My7'27. B 15522
New moon. (Mosher) 6:68 Ja3'31. CC 15523
The new moon. by Oscar Hammerstein, II; Frank Mandel and Laurence Schwab. (Brackett) 4:32 S29'28. T 15524
New morals for old. (Mosher) 8: 34 Jy2'32. CC 15525
New pathways in science. by Arthur Eddington. (Fadiman) 11: 84-6*Mr16'35. B 15526
New wine. by Geoffrey Moss. (Hoyt) 3:125-6 D3'27. B 15527
New worlds to conquer. by Richard Halliburton. (Smith) 5:164-5 D7'29. B 15528
New writing. by John Lehmann, ed. (Fadiman) 14:90-1*D17'38. B 15529
New York. (Claxton) 2:75 F5'27. CC 15530
New-York. by Paul Morand. (Flanner) 6:57 F22'30. B 15531
(Coates) 6:100 N15'30. 15532
New York exchange. by Peter Glenny. (Brackett) 2:26 Ja15 '27. T 15533
New York nights. by Stephen Graham. (Hoyt) 3:113-14 N12'27. B 15534
A New York tempest. by Manuel Komroff. (Coates) 8:44 Ag27'32. B 15535
The New Yorkers. by Curtis Arnoux Peters. (Benchley) 6:29-30 D20'30. T 15536
Newly rich. (Mosher) 7:47-8*Jy4 '31. CC 15537
News from Tartary: a journey from Peking to Kashmir. by Peter Fleming. (Anon.) 12:65* O24'36. B 15538
The next hundred years. by C. C. Furnas. (Fadiman) 11:53-4* Ja 14'36. B 15539
Next time we love. (Mosher) 11: 61*F8'36. CC 15540
Nic-nax of 1926. by Paul W. Porter, et al. (Brackett) 2:43 Ag 14'26. T 15541
Nice women. by William A. Grew.

(Brackett) 5:46 Je29'29. T 15542
Nigger heaven. by Carl Van Vechten. (Dounce) 2:61-2 S4 '26. B 15543
Night after night. (Mosher) 8:78 N5'32. CC 15544
Night angel. (Mosher) 7:54-5*Je 20'31. CC 15545
A night at the opera. (Mosher) 11:92-3*D14'35. CC 15546
The night club. (Anon.) 1:31 My 16'25. CC 15547
The night club era. by Stanley Walker. (Fadiman) 9:81-2 N11 '33. B 15548
Night clubs. by Jimmy Durante and Jack Kofoed. (Coates) 7: 88 Mr7'31. B 15549
Night court. (Mosher) 8:59-60 Je 4'32. CC 15550
Night flight. (Mosher) 9:70 O14 '33. CC 15551
Night hostess. by Philip Dunning. (Brackett) 4:27-8 S22'28.T15552
A night in Kurdistan. by Jean-Richard Bloch. (Coates) 7:74 F28'31. B 15553
A night in Paris. by Harold Atteridge, et al. (Mankiewicz) 1:19 Ja16'26. T 15554
(Brackett) 15555
A night in Spain. by Harold Atteridge. (Brackett) 3:29-30 My 14'27. T 15556
Night in the hotel. by Eliot Crawshaw-Williams. (Coates) 7:62-3* Je27'31. B 15557
Night in the house. by Rodney Acklund. (Benchley) 11:32-4*N 16'35. T 15558
A night in Venice. by J. Keirn Brennan, et al. (Brackett) 5:28 Je1'29. T 15559
The night is filled. (Mosher) 14: 65*S24'38. CC 15560
The night is young. (Mosher) 10: 59*Ja19'35. CC 15561
Night must fall. (Mosher) 13:63-4*My8'37. CC 15562
Night must fall. by Emlyn Williams. (Gibbs) 12:32*O10'36. T 15563
A night of Barrie. by James M. Barrie. (Benchley) 8:30*Mr19 '32. T 15564
Night of January 16. by Ayn Rand. (Gibbs) 11:29*S28'35. T 15565
The night of June 13th. (Gibbs) 8:53 S24'32. CC 15566
The night of love. (Claxton) 2:68 Ja29'27. CC 15567
Night of the poor. by Frederic Prokosch. (Fadiman) 15:68* O7'39. B 15568
Night over Taos. by Maxwell Anderson. (Benchley) 8:30*Mr19 '32. T 15569
The night remembers. by Martha Madison. (Benchley) 10:36†D15 '34. T 15570
Night riders. by Robert Penn Warren. (Fadiman) 15:68-9*Mr18 '39. B 15571
The night visitor. by Arnold Bennett. (Coates) 7:91 N14'31. B 15572
The nightingale. by Guy Bolton and P. G. Wodehouse. (Brackett) 2:25 Ja15'27. T 15573
The night's candles. by René Roy. (Coates) 7:67*My30'31. B 15574
Nightstick. by John Wray; Elliott Nugent; J. C. Nugent and Elaine Sterne Carrington. (Brackett) 3:34-5 N26'27. T 15575
Nightwood. by Djuna Barnes. (Flanner) 13:57*F20'37.B15576
(Fadiman) 13:83-4*Mr13'37. 15577
The Nile: the life-story of a river. by Emil Ludwig. (Fadiman) 12: 62*F13'37. B 15578
Nina Rosa. by Otto Harbach; Sigmund Romberg and Irving Caesar. (Benchley) 6:38 S27'30. T 15579
Nine chains to the moon. by R. Buckminster Fuller. (Fadiman) 14:69*S10'38. B 15580
Nine days a queen. (Mosher) 12: 66-7*S26'36. CC 15581
Nine etched from life. by Emil Ludwig. (Fadiman) 10:109-10 My5'34. B 15582
Nine Pine Street. by John Colton

and Carleton Miles. (Benchley) 9:32-4 My6'33. T 15583
Nine till six. by Aimée Stuart and Philip Stuart. (Benchley) 6:36 O4'30. T 15584
Nine-fifteen revue. by Ruth Selwyn. (Benchley) 6:34 F22'30. T 15585
1900. by Paul Morand. (Flanner) 7:49*Jy18'31. B 15586
1900 A. D. by Paul Morand. (Coates) 7:91 O10'31. B 15587
1919. by John Dos Passos. (Coates) 8:59-60*Mr26'32. B 15588
1935. by Anon. (Gibbs) 12:31*My 23'36. T 15589
1931--. by Claire Sifton and Paul Sifton. (White) 7:28 D19'31. T 15590
The nineteenth hole. by Frank Craven. (Brackett) 3:29 O22'27. T 15591
Ninth Avenue. by Maxwell Bodenheim. (Boyd) 2:114 D11'26. B 15592
The 9th guest. by Owen Davis. (Benchley) 6:28 S6'30. T 15593
90 horse power. by Francis De Witt. (Gabriel) 2:26 Mr27'26 T 15594
Ninotchka. (Mosher) 15:85-6*N18 '39. CC 15595
Nirvana. by John Howard Lawson. (Gabriel) 2:22-3 Mr13'26. T 15596
No arms, no armour. by Robert Henriques. (Fadiman) 15:52*Ja6'40. B 15597
No castle in Spain. by William McFee. (Fadiman) 9:90-1 O7 '33. B 15598
No enemy. by Ford Madox Ford. (Smith) 5:127-8 N23'29. B 15599
No foolin'. by Rudolph Friml and Gene Buck. (Brackett) 2:32 Jy 3'26. T 15600
No goodness in the worm. by Gay Taylor. (Coates) 6:66 Ja 24'31. B 15601
No greater glory. (Mosher) 10:94 My12'34. CC 15602
No limit. (Mosher) 6:59 Ja24'31. CC 15603
No love. by David Garnett. (Smith) 5:104-105 Je8'29. B 15604
No marriage ties. (Mosher) 9:43 Ag12'33. CC 15605
No more ladies. by A. E. Thomas. (Benchley) 9:28-30 F3'34. T 15606
No more parades. by Ford Madox Ford. (Dounce) 1:21 N21'25. B 15607
No more women. by Samuel Shipman and Neil Twomey. (Brackett) 2:42-3 Ag14'26. T 15608
The no-nation girl. by Evans Wall. (Smith) 5:121 N2'29. B 15609
No other woman. (Mosher) 8:53 F4'33. CC 15610
No peace with Napoleon! by Armand Augustin Caulaincourt. (Fadiman) 12:74-5*N28'36. B 15611
No quarter given. by Paul Horgan. (Fadiman) 10:66*F2'35. B 15612
No questions asked. by Anne Morrison Chapin. (Benchley) 10:28-30 F17'34. T 15613
No star is lost. by James T. Farrell. (Fadiman) 14:72-3*S17'38. B 15614
No stone unturned. by Patrick Carleton. (Fadiman) 15:68-9*Ap 22'39. B 15615
No time for comedy. by S. N. Behrman. (Gibbs) 15:34*Ap29 '39. T 15616
No time like the present. by Storm Jameson. (Fadiman) 9: 72 Je24'33. B 15617
No tresspassing. by John Hunter Booth. (Brackett) 2:32 S18'26. T 15618
No villain need be. by Vardis Fisher. (Anon.) 12:76-7*Mr7'36. B 15619
Noah. by André Obey. (Benchley) 11:26†F23'35. T 15620
Noah's ark. (Mosher) 5:105 Mr23 '29. CC 15621
Noah's ark. by Amabel Williams-Ellis. (Dounce) 2:44 Mr6'26. B 15622
Nomad's land. by Mary Roberts Rinehart. (Dounce) 2:46-7 Jy24 '26. B 15623
Nona. by Gladys Unger. (White)

8:28 O15'32. T 15624
None but the brave. by Arthur Schnitzler. (Dounce) 2:90 O2 '26. B 15625
None shall look back. by Caroline Gordon. (Fadiman) 13:62-3*F20'37. B 15626
Nonsuch: the land of water. by William Beebe. (Coates) 8:59-60*Ap2'32. B 15627
The noose. by Willard Mack. (Brackett) 2:34-6 N6'26. T 15628
North of Suez. by William McFee. (Smith) 6:100 My3'30. B 15629
North to the Orient. by Anne Morrow Lindbergh. (Fadiman) 11:50-1*Ag17'35. B 15630
Northcliffe. by Hamilton Fyfe. (Smith) 6:104-106 O25'30. B 15631
Northwest passage. by Kenneth Roberts. (Fadiman) 13:54-5* Jy3'27. B 15632
Not for heaven. by Dorothy McCleary. (Fadiman) 11:63-4* My4'35. B 15633
Not I, but the wind. by Frieda Lawrence. (Fadiman) 10:118 O13'34. B 15634
Not peace but a sword. by Vincent Sheean. (Kronenberger) 15:58-9*Jy29'39. B 15635
Not so dumb. (Mosher) 5:83 F15 '30. CC 15636
Not to eat, not to love. by George Weller. (Coates) 9:66-7 Ap29 '33. B 15637
Not under forty. by Willa Cather. (Fadiman) 12:74*N28'36. B 15638
Not without laughter. by Langston Hughes. (Smith) 6:58 Ag2 '30. B 15639
A note in music. by Rosamond Lehmann. (Smith) 6:103-104 S13'30. B 15640
Notes on democracy. by H. L. Mencken. (Boyd) 2:90-2 N27 '26. B 15641
Nothing is sacred. by Josephine Herbst. (Leonard) 4:116 O13 '28. B 15642
Nothing sacred. (Mosher) 13:100-101*D4'37. CC 15643
The notorious lady. (Claxton) 3:101-103 Ap9'27. CC 15644
Notorious literary attacks. by Albert Mordell, ed. (Dounce) 2:61 My29'26. B 15645
The notorious Sophie Lang. (Mosher) 10:51 Jy28'34. CC 15646
November. by Gustav Flaubert. (Coates) 8:52*F27'32. B 15647
November night. by Anon. (Hoyt) 3:77-8 F4'28. B 15648
Now and forever. (Mosher) 10:88 O20'34. CC 15649
Now we are six. by A. A. Milne. (Parker) 3:112-13 N12'27. B 15650
Now you've done it. by Mary Coyle Chase. (Benchley) 13:28-30*Mr13'37. T 15651
Nowhere bound. by Leo Birinski. (Benchley) 10:30†F2'35. T 15652
Now-a-days. by Arthur F. Brash. (Brackett) 5:44 Ag17'29. T 15653
Nowhere else in the world. by Gordon Enders and Edward Anthony. (Anon.) 11:114*D7'35. B 15654
Nudism comes to America. by Frances Merrill and Mason Merrill. (Coates) 8:66-7*Ap16 '32. B 15655
Number 7. by Joseph Jefferson Farjeon. (Brackett) 2:33 O2'26. T 15656
Numbered men. (Mosher) 6:80 Je 14'30. CC 15657
Nurse Edith Cavell. (Mosher) 15:57-8 S23'39. CC 15658

O

O evening star. by Zoë Akins. (Benchley) 11:24*Ja18'36. T 15659
O rare Ben Jonson. by Byron Steel. (Boyd) 3:95-6 S24'27. B 15660
Oberlin's three stages. by Jacob

Wassermann. (Dounce) 2:53 Je 19'26. B 15661
Obscure destinies. by Willla Cather. (Coates) 8:46 Ag6'32. B 15662
Octavia. by Margot Asquith. (Markey) 4:87-8 Je9'28. B 15663
The octoroon. by Dion Boucicault. (Brackett) 5:28 Mr23'29. T 15664
Odalisque. by L. M. Hussey. (Boyd) 2:80 Ja29'27. B 15665
Odd man out. by Paul Hervey Fox and George Tilton. (Mankiewicz) 1:13 Je6'25. T 15666
Ode to liberty. by Sidney Howard. (Benchley) 10:30-4†Ja5'35. T 15667
The odyssey of a nice girl. by Ruth Suckow. (Dounce) 1:22 N7'25. B 15668
Of ants and men. by Caryl P. Haskins. (Fadiman) 15:74-5* Je3'39. B 15669
Of human bondage. (Mosher) 10: 64 Jy7'34. CC 15670
(Mosher) 11:56*Je1'35. 15671
Of human hearts. (Mosher) 13: 59*F12'38. CC 15672
Of Lena Geyer. by Marcia Davenport. (Fadiman) 12:84*S19 '36. B 15673
Of many things. by Otto Kahn. (Dounce) 2:45 Jy24'26. B 15674
Of mice and men. by John Steinbeck. (Fadiman) 13:67*F27'37. B 15675
(Benchley) 13:38*D4'37. T 15676
Of thee I sing. by George S. Kaufman; Morrie Ryskind; George Gershwin and Ira Gershwin. (White) 7:26-8 Ja2 '32. T 15677
(Benchley) 7:28 Ja9'32. 15678
Of time and the river. by Thomas Wolfe. (Fadiman) 11:68-70* Mr9'35. B 15679
Off key. by Arthur Caesar. (Brackett) 3:33-4 F19'27. T 15680
Off to Buffalo! by Max Liebman and Allen Boretz. (Benchley) 15:28*Mr4'39. T 15681
Off with their heads. by Peggy Bacon. (Fadiman) 10:87*N24 '34. B 15682
The office wife. (Mosher) 6:95 O4 '30. CC 15683
Oh, Ernest! by Francis DeWitt. (Brackett) 3:29-30 My21'27. T 15684
Oh glory! by Harford Powel, Jr. (Coates) 7:55*Jy4'31. B 15685
Oh Kay. (Claxton) 4:66 S1'28. CC 15686
Oh, Kay! by Guy Bolton; P. G. Wodehouse; George Gershwin and Ira Gershwin. (Brackett) 2:33 N20'26. T 15687
Oh Mama. by Wilton Lackaye and Harry Wagstaff Gribble. (Mankiewicz) 1:16 Ag29'25. T 15688
Oh, please. by Maurice Hennequin and Pierre Veber. (Brackett) 2:23 Ja1'27. T 15689
Oh, promise me! by Howard Lindsay and Bertrand Robinson. (Benchley) 6:35-6 D6'30. T 15690
Oil for the lamps of China. (Mosher) 11:62*Je15'35. CC 15691
Oklahoma town. by George Milburn. (Coates) 7:89-90 Mr14 '31. B 15692
Ol' man Satan. by Donald Heywood. (White) 8:28 O15'32. T 15693
Old Adam's likeness. by Lucy Poate Stebbins. (Leonard) 4:77 Jy14'28. B 15694
Old Bill, M. P. by Bruce Bairnsfather. (Brackett) 2:33 N20'26. T 15695
The old bunch. by Meyer Levin. (Fadiman) 13:83*Mr20'37. B 15696
The old dark house. (Mosher) 8: 77-8 N5'32. CC 15697
Old English. (Mosher) 6:49 Ag30 '30. CC 15698
The old-fashioned way. (Mosher) 10:56 Jy21'34. CC 15699
Old father of waters. by Alan

Le May. (Hoyt) 4:85 Mr10'28. B 15700
Old Ironsides. (Claxton) 2:82 D18 '26. CC 15701
(Claxton) 3:66-7 N26'27. 15702
Old Jules. by Mari Sandoz. (Fadiman) 11:83*N2'35. B 15703
Old loves and new. (Shane) 2:51 Ap24'26. CC 15704
The old maid. (Maloney) 15:52-3* Ag19'39. CC 15705
The old maid. by Zoë Akins. (Benchley) 10:28-30†Ja19'35. T 15706
Old man Murphy. by Patrick Kearney and Harry Wagstaff Gribble. (Benchley) 7:26 My30 '31. 15707
The old people. by J. D. Beresford. (Coates) 8:60-1*Ap30'32. B 15708
The old rascal. by William Hodge. (Benchley) 6:27-8 Ap5 '30. T 15709
Old San Francisco. (Claxton) 3:61 Jy2'27. CC 15710
Old ship. by Lennox Kerr. (Coates) 7:88-9 Mr14'31. B 15711
Old soldier Sahib. by Frank Richards. (Fadiman) 12:76*Ap 11'36. B 15712
Old wine. by Phyllis Bottome. (Anon.) 1:26 My9'25. B 15713
Old wine and new. by Warwick Deeping. (Coates) 8:71*My7 '32. B 15714
The old woman. by André de Lorde. (Gibbs) 11:32*Jy20'35. T 15715
The olive field. by Ralph Bates. (Anon.) 12:49*Ag15'36. B 15716
The olive tree. by Aldous Huxley. (Fadiman) 13:70*Mr6'37. B 15717
Oliver Twist. (Mosher) 9:62 Ap22'33. CC 15718
Olympia. by Ferenc Molnar. (Brackett) 4:33-4 O27'28. T 15719
The omnibus of adventure. by John Grove, ed. (Smith) 6:132 D6'30. B 15720
The omnibus of crime. by Dorothy L. Sayers. (Smith) 5:65-6 Ag31'29. B 15721
On a Paris roundabout. by Jan Gordon. (Hoyt) 3:81 F11'28. B 15722
On approval. by Frederick Lonsdale. (Brackett) 2:31 O30'26. T 15723
On borrowed time. (Mosher) 15: 69*Jy8'39. CC 15724
On borrowed time. by Paul Osborn. (Benchley) 13:28-30*F12 '38. T 15725
On borrowed time. by Lawrence Edward Watkin. (Fadiman) 13: 63*S4'37. B 15726
On doing the right thing. by Albert Jay Nock. (Lowrie) 4:130 D15'28. B 15727
On Forsyte 'change. by John Galsworthy. (Coates) 6:103-104 O18'30. B 15728
On stage. by B. M. Kaye. (Benchley) 11:28-30*N9'35. T 15729
On the Avenue. (Mosher) 12:60* F13'37. CC 15730
On the bottom. by Edward Ellsberg. (Smith) 5:80 Je1'29. B 15731
On the decks of Old Ironsides. by Eliot Snow and Allen H. Gosnell. (Coates) 8:61*Ap2'32. B 15732
On the rocks. by George Bernard Shaw. (Gibbs) 14:24*Je25'38. T 15733
On the spot. by Edgar Wallace. (Benchley) 6:33 N8'30. T 15734
On the Volga. by Panteleimon Romanof. (Fadiman) 10:66 Jy14 '34. B 15735
On this island. by W. H. Auden. (Bogan) 12:63-4*F13'37. B 15736
On to fortune. by Lawrence Langner and Armina Marshall. (Benchley) 11:28†F16'35. T 15737
On trial. (Mosher) 4:92-3 N24'28. CC 15738
On with the show. (Mosher) 5:97-

8 Je8'29. CC 15739

On your toes. (Mosher) 15:64*O 28'39. CC 15740

On your toes. by Richard Rodgers; Lorenz Hart and George Abbott. (Gibbs) 12:28*Ap18'36. T 15741

Once a clown always a clown. by De Wolf Hopper. (Boyd) 2:91 F5'27. B 15742

Once a lady. (Mosher) 7:81 N14 '31. CC 15743

Once a sinner. (Mosher) 6:55 Ja 24'31. CC 15744

Once in a lifetime. by Moss Hart and George S. Kaufman. (Benchley) 6:34 O4'30. T 15745

Once is enough. by Frederick Lonsdale. (Benchley) 14:30*F 26'38. T 15746

Once on a time. by A. A. Milne. (Dounce) 2:69-70 S25'26. B 15747

Once there was a man—Napoleon. by Joseph Delteil. (Smith) 5: 84-5 F8'30. B 15748

Once we had a child. by Hans Fallada and Eric Sutton, trans. (Anon.) 12:73-4*Mr14'36. B 15749

One day in October. by Sigurd Hoel. (Coates) 8:62-3 O29'32. B 15750

One day more. by Joseph Conrad. (Gabriel) 2:27-8 Ap3'26. T 15751

The one-eyed moon. by Marguerite Steen. (Fadiman) 11: 77-8*Ap13'35. B 15752

One glorious hour. by Ella Barnett, trans. and Gerhardt Falkenberg. (Brackett) 3:33-4 Ap 23'27. T 15753

One hour with you. (Mosher) 8: 56*Ap2'32. CC 15754

100 men and a girl. (Mosher) 13: 69*S18'37. CC 15755

One man's journey. (Mosher) 9: 69-70 S9'33. CC 15756

One minute to play. (Claxton) 2: 51-2 S18'26. CC 15757

One more river. (Mosher) 10:64 Ag18'34. CC 15758

One more Spring. (Mosher) 11: 56*Mr2'35. CC 15759

One more Spring. by Robert Nathan. (Coates) 8:59 F4'33. B 15760

One night of love. (McKelway) 10: 79-80 S15'34. CC 15761

One of the family. by Kenneth Webb. (Mankiewicz) 1:20 Ja2 '26. T 15762

One rainy afternoon. (Mosher) 12: 62*My16'36. CC 15763

One romantic night. (Mosher) 6: 87 Je7'30. CC 15764

One Sunday afternoon. (Mosher) 9:70 S9'33. CC 15765

One Sunday afternoon. by James Hagan. (Benchley) 9:28 Mr4'33. T 15766

One-third of a nation. (Mosher) 15:67*F18'39. CC 15767

One-third of a nation. by Arthur Arent. (Benchley) 13:23*Ja29 '38. T 15768

One, two, three! by Ferenc Molnar. (Benchley) 6:34 O11'30. T 15769

One, two, three. by Paul Selver. (Boyd) 2:81 Ja29'27. B 15770

One's company. by Peter Fleming. (Fadiman) 10:80-1 S29'34. B 15771

The only girl. by Henry Blossom and Victor Herbert. (Benchley) 10:28 Je2'34. T 15772

Only saps work. by Courtenay Terrett. (Smith) 6:59 Jy26'30. B 15773

Only the brave. (Mosher) 6:95 Mr 15'30. CC 15774

Only yesterday. by Frederick Lewis Allen. (Coates) 7:110 D 5'31; 8:93 D3'32. B 15775

Open house. by Samuel R. Golding. (Mankiewicz) 1:19-20 Ja2 '26. T 15776

The open secret. by Oliver Onions. (Smith) 6:112 N22'30. B 15777

Operator 13. (Mosher) 10:64 Je30 '34. CC 15778

The Oppenheim family. (Mosher) 15:72-3*Je3'39. CC 15779

The Oppermanns. by Lion Feuchtwanger. (Fadiman) 10:101-102 Mr24'34. B 15780

The optimists. by Clifford Grey; Greatex Newman and Austin Melford. (Brackett) 3:25 F18 '28. 15780A

Opus 7. by Sylvia Townsend Warner. (Bogan) 7:82-3 Mr21'31. B 15781

Oranges and lemons. by A. A. Milne. (Dounce) 1:17 Ag1'25. B 15782

The orchid. by Robert Nathan. (Coates) 7:61*Je20'31. B 15783

Ordeal: the story of my life. by Maria, queen consort of Ferdinand I, King of Rumania. (Fadiman) 11:76-8*Ap27'35. B 15784

Orlando. by Virginia Woolf. (Leonard) 4:123 N10'28. B 15785

The orphan angel. by Elinor Wylie. (Dounce) 2:88 N20'26. B 15786

Oscar Wilde. by Leslie Stokes and Sewell Stokes. (Gibbs) 14:34-6*O 22'38. T 15787

Oscar Wilde discovers America (1882). by Lloyd Lewis. (Fadiman) 12:74-5*My23'36.B 15788

Oscar Wilde, from purgatory. by Hester Travers Smith. (Dounce) 2:55-6 Mr27'26. B 15789

O' Shaughnessy's boy. (Mosher) 11:68*O12'35. CC 15790

Other man's saucer. by Keith Winter. (Smith) 6:130 D6'30. B 15791

Other men's wives. by Walter Hackett. (Benchley) 5:36-8 N23 '29. T 15792

Other women's husbands. (Shane) 2:55 My1'26. CC 15793

Our betters. (Mosher) 9:56 Mr4 '33. CC 15794

Our betters. by W. Somerset Maugham. (Brackett) 4:33 Mr3 '28. T 15795

Our business civilization. by James Truslow Adams. (Smith) 5:127 N23'29. B 15796

Our daily bread. (Mosher) 10:103 O13'34. CC 15797

Our dancing daughters. (Mosher) 4:93 O20'28. CC 15798

Our modern maidens. (Mosher) 5:91-2 S14'29. CC 15799

Our lawless police. by Ernest Jerome Hopkins. (Coates) 7:89 N7'31. B 15800

Our leading citizen. (Mosher) 15:52*S2'39. CC 15801

Our little girl. (Mosher) 11:62* Je15'35. CC 15802

Our master's voice: advertising. by James Rorty. (Fadiman) 10:102-103 My19'34. B 15803

Our Mr. Dormer. by R. H. Mottram. (Hoyt) 3:119-20 N19'27. B 15804

Our times. by Mark Sullivan. (Coates) 8:81-2 N19'32. B 15805

Our town. by Thornton Wilder. (Benchley) 13:28*F12'38. T 15806

Ourselves alone. (Maloney) 13:33*Ag7'37. CC 15807

Out of a blue sky. by Hans Chlumberg and Leslie Howard, trans. (Benchley) 6:34 F22'30. T 15808

Out of Africa. by Isak Dinesen. (Fadiman) 14:60*Mr5'38. B 15809

Out of the sea. by Don Marquis. (Brackett) 3:32-3 D17'27. T 15810

Out West with the Hardys. (Mosher) 14:87-8*D17'38. CC 15811

The outlaw years. by Robert M. Coates. (Smith) 6:62 Ag16'30. B 15812

Outlaws of the Orient. (Mosher) 13:60*O2'37. CC 15813

Outposts of science. by Bernard Jaffe. (Fadiman) 11:78*N30'35. B 15814

Outside looking in. by Maxwell Anderson. (Mankiewicz) 1:19 S 19'25. T 15815

The outsider. by Dorothy Brandon (Brackett) 4:34 Ap21'28. T 15816

Outward bound. (Mosher) 6:75 S2'

'30. CC 15817

Outward bound. by Sutton Vane. (Benchley) 14:26*D31'38. T 15818

Over here. by Mark Sullivan. (Fadiman) 9:96 N18'33. B 15819

Overshadowed. by Eugene Löhrke. (Smith) 5:56-7 Jy27'29. B 15820

Overture. by William Bolitho. (Benchley) 6:30-2 D20'30. T 15821

Owen D. Young. by Ida M. Tarbell. (Coates) 8:58-9 Je18'32. B 15822

The Oxford book of light verse. by W. H. Auden, ed. (Bogan) 14:50-1*D24'38. B 15823

The Oxford book of modern verse. by William Butler Yeats, ed. (Bogan) 12:115-17*N14'36. B 15824

The Ozarks. by Vance Randolph. (Coates) 7:92-3 O10'31. B 15825

P

Pacific liner. (Mosher) 14:59*Ja21'39. CC 15826

Padlocked. (Claxton) 2:35 Ag7'26. CC 15827

Padlocks of 1927. by Paul Gerard Smith, et al. (White) 3:34-6 Jy23'27. T 15828

The pagan. (Mosher) 5:107 My18'29. CC 15829

Pagan interval. by Frances Winwar. (Smith) 5:96 Je22'29. B 15830

Pagan lady. by William Du Bois. (Benchley) 6:27-8 N1'30. T 15831

Page Miss Glory. by Joseph Schrank and Philip Dunning. (Benchley) 10:36†D8'34. T 15832

Pagliacci. (Mosher) 7:76 Mr7'31. CC 15833

Paid. (Mosher) 6:57 Ja10'31. CC 15834

Paid. by Sam Forrest. (Mankiewicz) 1:14 D5'25. T 15835

The painted city. by Mary Badger Wilson. (Boyd) 3:93 Mr5'27. B 15836

The painted room. by Margaret Wilson. (Dounce) 2:68-9 S25'26. B 15837

The painted veil. (Mosher) 10:83*D8'34. CC 15838

The painted veil. by W. Somerset Maugham. (Anon.) 1:26 Ap4'25. B 15839

Painting the town. (Mosher) 3:51 Ag13'27. CC 15840

Pale horse, pale rider. by Katherine Anne Porter. (Fadiman) 15:69-70*Ap1'39. B 15841

Palm Beach. by Cornelius Vanderbilt, Jr. (Parker) 6:57-9 Ja31'31. B 15842

The Palm Beach girl. (Shane) 2:40 Je26'26. CC 15843

Palmerston. by Philip Guedalla. (Boyd) 2:82-4 F12'27. B 15844

Palmy days. (Mosher) 7:78 O3'31. CC 15845

Palooka. (Mosher) 10:88 Mr10'34. CC 15846

Panic! by Archibald Mac Leish. (Gibbs) 11:28*Mr30'35. T 15847

The panther. by Gerald Bullett. (Hoyt) 3:92-3 N5'27. B 15848

Paolo and Francesca. by Stephen Phillips. (Brackett) 5:30-2 Ap13'29. T 15849

Parade. by Paul Peters, et al. (Gibbs) 11:26*Je1'35. T 15850

Paradise. by Esther Forbes. (Anon.) 13:69-70*F27'37. B 15851

Paradise city. by Henry Channon. (Coates) 6:61-3 Ja31'31. B 15852

Paradise for three. (Mosher) 14:58-9*F19'38. CC 15853

Paradise for two. (Claxton) 2:68 Ja29'27. CC 15854

Paradise lost. by Clifford Odets. (Benchley) 11:24*D21'35. T 15855

Paramount on parade. (Mosher) 6:89 Ap26'30. CC 15856

Pardon my English. by Herbert

Fields; George Gershwin and Ira Gershwin. (Benchley) 8:26 Ja28'33. T 15857

Paris. (Shane) 2:63 Je5'26. CC 15858

Paris. (Mosher) 5:103-104 N16 '29. CC 15859

Paris. by Martin Brown. (Brackett) 4:27 O20'28. T 15860

Paris bound. (Gibbs) 5:79 S28'29. CC 15861

Paris bound. by Philip Barry. (Brackett) 3:26 Ja7'28. T 15862

The Paris gun. by Henry W. Miller. (Smith) 6:103 Mr8'30. B 15863

Paris in Spring. (Mosher) 11:48* Jy20'35. CC 15864

Paris interlude. (Mosher) 10:51 Ag4'34. CC 15865

Paris with the lid off. by Bruce Reynolds. (Hoyt) 3:81 Ja7'28. B 15866

Parlor, bedroom and bath. (Mosher) 7:101 Ap11'31. CC 15867

Parnell. by Elsie Schauffler. (Benchley) 11:30*N23'35. T 15868

A party. by Ivor Novello. (Gibbs) 9:22 S2'33. T 15869

The party dress. by Joseph Hergesheimer. (Smith) 6:120-2 Ap12'30. B 15870

The party's over. by Daniel Kusell. (Benchley) 9:30 Ap8'33. T 15871

The Pasquier chronicles. by Georges Duhamel. (Fadiman) 14:64-5*Mr19'38. B 15872

Passing. by Nella Larsen. (Lowrie) 5:104-105 My11'29. B 15873

The passing of the Essenes. by George Moore. (Coates) 7:70 F21'31. B 15874

The passing present. by Gretchen Damrosch. (White) 7:28-30 D 19'31. T 15875

The passing show. by Henry Russell. (Boyd) 2:91-3 F5'27. B 15876

Passion flower. (Mosher) 6:30 D 27'30. CC 15877

The passion of Joan of Arc. (Mosher) 5:47 Ap6'29. CC 15878

The passionate plumber. (Mosher) 8:77*Mr19'32. CC 15879

Passion's pilgrims. by Jules Romains. (Fadiman) 9:69 F3'34. B 15880

The past recaptured. by Marcel Proust and Frederick A. Blossom, trans. (Coates) 8:66 S10 '32. B 15881

Past years. by Oliver Lodge. (Coates) 8:67*Mr5'32. B 15882

Pastoral. by Victor Wolfson. (Gibbs) 15:25*N11'39. T 15883

The pastures of heaven. by John Steinbeck. (Coates) 8:62-3 O22 '32. B 15884

Paths of glory. by Humphrey Cobb. (Fadiman) 11:70-1*Je8'3 B 15885

Paths of glory. by Sidney Howard. (Gibbs) 11:34-6*O5'35. T 15886

Patience. by William S. Gilbert and Arthur Sullivan. (Long) 3: 34 Je11'27. T 15887

The patriot. (Claxton) 4:40 Ag25 '28. CC 15888

The patriot. (Seldes) 4:40-6 S15 '28. CC 15889

The patriot. by Pearl Buck. (Fadiman) 15:66*Mr4'39. B 15890

The patriot. by Ashley Dukes. (Brackett) 3:25-6 F4'28. T 15891

The patriot's progress. by Henry Williamson. (Smith) 6:70 Jy12'30. B 15892

The patsy. by Barry Conners. (Mankiewicz) 1:19 Ja2'26. T 15893

Paul Bunyan. by James Stevens. (Anon.) 1:26 My30'25. B 15894

Paul Robeson, Negro. by Eslanda Goode Robeson. (Smith) 6:58 Ag2'30. B 15895

Pay day. by Nathan Asch. (Smith) 6:101 F22'30. B 15896

Payment deferred. (Mosher) 8:68

N12'32. CC 15897
Payment deferred. by Jeffrey Dell. (Benchley) 7:34 O10'31. T 15898
Peace is where the tempests blow. by Valentine Kataev. (Fadiman) 13:75-6*Ap3'37. B 15899
Peace it's wonderful. by William Saroyan. (Fadiman) 15:68*Ap 22'39. B 15900
Pearl diver. by Victor Berge and Henry Wysham Lanier. (Smith) 5:77 Ja11'30. B 15901
The pearl of great price. by Robert McLaughlin. (Brackett) 2: 34 N13'26. T 15902
Pearls, arms and hashish. by Henri de Monfried. (Coates) 6:105 O18'30. B 15903
The pearls of the crown. (Mosher) 14:52*Ap23'38. CC 15904
A peculiar treasure. by Edna Ferber. (Fadiman) 14:58-9*F4 '39. B 15905
Peder victorious. by O. E. Rölvaag. (Lowrie) 4:76 Ja19'29. B 15906
Pedlar's progress. by Odell Shepard. (Fadiman) 13:88-90* My15'37. B 15907
The peep show. by Alice Dudeney. (Lowrie) 4:92 F16'29. B 15908
Peking picnic. by Ann Bridge. (Coates) 8:61-2 S24'32. B 15909
The pelican. by F. Tennyson Jesse and H. M. Harwood. (Mankiewicz) 1:19-20 O3'25. T 15910
Pending heaven. by William Gerhardi. (Smith) 6:99 Mr15'30. B 15911
Penelope's man. by John Erskine. (Lowrie) 4:114-15 D1'28. B 15912
Penny wise. by Jean Ferguson Black. (Gibbs) 13:32*My1'37. T 15913
Penrod and Sam. (Mosher) 7:78-9 O3'31. CC 15914
Penrod Jashber. by Booth Tarkington. (Smith) 5:122-3 O12'29. B 15915
People round the corner. by Thyra Samter Winslow. (Boyd) 3: 79 Je11'27. B 15916
The people, yes. by Carl Sandburg. (Bogan) 12:59-61*Ag22 '36. B 15917
Pepita. by Victoria Sackville-West. (Fadiman) 13:119*D4'37. B 15918
The perfect alibi. (Mosher) 7:82 Ap25'31. CC 15919
The perfect alibi. by A. A. Milne. (Brackett) 4:38 D15'28. T 15920
The perfect crime. (Claxton) 4:55 Ag11'28. CC 15921
The perfect gentleman. (Mosher) 11:49*D28'35. CC 15922
The perfect marriage. by Arthur Goodrich. (Benchley) 8:22-3 N 26'32. T 15923
The perfect sap. (Claxton) 2:61 Ja 15'27. CC 15924
Perfectly scandalous. by William Gerhardi. (Leonard) 4:95 N3'28. B 15925
The perfumed lady. by Harry Wagstaff Gribble. (Benchley) 10: 28 Mr24'34. T 15926
Perhaps I am. by Edward W. Bok. (Parker) 4:81-3 Mr10'28. B 15927
Perhaps women. by Sherwood Anderson. (Coates) 7:81 S26'31. B 15928
Period piece. by Jenny Ballou. (Fadiman) 15:68-70 F3'40. B 15929
Peripherie. by Frantisek Langer. (Brackett) 3:24 Ja14'28. T 15930
Perish in their pride. by Henry de Montherlant. (Anon.) 11:61* Ja25'36. B 15931
Personal appearance. by Lawrence Riley. (Benchley) 10:28 O27'34. T 15932
Personal history. by Vincent Sheean. (Fadiman) 10:64*F2'35. B 15933
Personalities of antiquity. by Arthur Weigall. (Lowrie) 4:73 Ja 26'29. B 15934

Peter Abelard. by Helen Waddell. (Fadiman) 9:74 S30'33. B 15935

Peter Ashley. by DuBose Heyward. (Coates) 8:61-2 O29'32. B 15936

Peter Ibbetson. (Mosher) 11:80*N 16'35. CC 15937

Peter Ibbetson. by John Raphael and Constance Collier. (Benchley) 7:28-30 Ap18'31. T 15938

Peter Pan. by James M. Barrie. (Brackett) 4:38 D15'28. T 15939

Peter the Czar. by Alfred Henschke. (Dounce) 1:44 Ja30 '26. B 15940

Peter the First. (Mosher) 13:43* Ja1'38. CC 15941

Peter the Great. by Georges Oudard. (Smith) 5:162 D7'29. B 15942

Petersburg nights. (McKelway) 10:68 S22'34. CC 15943

The petrified forest. by Robert E. Sherwood. (Benchley) 10: 28†Ja19'35. T 15944

Petticoat fever. (Mosher) 12:56* Mr28'36. CC 15945

Petticoat fever. by Mark Reed. (Benchley) 11:34*Mr16'35. T 15946

Petticoat influence. by Neil Grant. (Benchley) 6:25-6 D27'30. T 15947

Phantom crown. by Bertita Harding. (Fadiman) 13:64*F20'37. B 15948

The phantom lover. by Georg Kaiser. (Brackett) 4:36 S15'28. T 15949

The phantom of the opera. (Shane) 1:24 S12'25. CC 15950

The Philadelphia story. by Philip Barry. (Gibbs) 15:30-2*Ap8'39. T 15951

Philip goes forth. by George Kelly. (Benchley) 6:29-30 Ja24'31. T 15952

Philippa. by Anne Douglas Sedgwick. (Smith) 6:112-13 N8'30. B 15953

Philosopher's holiday. by Irwin Edman. (Fadiman) 14:67-8*N5 '38. B 15954

Phoenix. by Edward D. McDonald, ed. (Fadiman) 12:82-3*O17'36. B 15955

Picadilly. (Mosher) 5:69-70 Jy20 '29. CC 15956

Piccadilly Jim. (Mosher) 12:46* Ag29'36. CC 15957

Picasso. by Gertrude Stein. (Fadiman) 15:68-9*F18'39. B 15958

Pickwick. by Cosmo Hamilton and Frank C. Reilly. (Brackett) 3: 60 S17'27. T 15959

Picture book. by Murdock Pemberton. (Smith) 6:89 S27'30. B 15960

Picture snatcher. (Mosher) 9:48-9 My27'33. CC 15961

The pieces of a fan. by Vincent Sheean. (Fadiman) 13:77-8*N6 '37. B 15962

Pig iron. by Charles G. Norris. (Dounce) 2:63-4 Ap17'26. B 15963

The pig is fat. by Lawrance M. Maynard. (Hellman) 6:104-105 Ap5'30. B 15964

Pigeons and people. by George M. Cohan. (Benchley) 8:24 Ja 28'33. T 15965

Piggy. by William B. Friedlander and Daniel Kusell. (Brackett) 2:36 Ja29'27. T 15966

Pigsties with spires. by Georgina Garry. (Leonard) 4:62 Ag11'28. B 15967

The pilgrim of eternity: Byron—a conflict. by John Drinkwater. (Dounce) 1:23 D26'25. B 15968

Pilgrimmage. (Mosher) 9:46 Jy22 '33. CC 15969

Pinocchio. (Mosher) 15:74 F10'40. CC 15970

Pins and needles. by Arthur Arer et al. (Benchley) 13:34*D18'37; 15:38-40*D2'39. T 15971
(Gibbs) 15:36 Ap29'39. 15972

Pinwheel. by Francis Edwards Faragoh. (Brackett) 3:33 F26'2 T 15973

Pipe all hands. by H. M. Tomlinson. (Fadiman) 13:68-9*My1'3 B 15974

The pirates of Penzance. by William S. Gilbert and Arthur Sullivan. (Brackett) 2:35 D18 '26. T 15975
Pity is not enough. by Josephine Herbst. (Fadiman) 9:55-6 My 27'33. B 15976
The place called Dagon. by Herbert Gorman. (Hoyt) 3:123-4 D 3'27. B 15977
The plainsman. (Mosher) 12:61-3* Ja23'37. CC 15978
The plastic age. (Claxton) 2:32 Jy24'26. CC 15979
The platinum tower. by Jerome Bahr. (Fadiman) 15:61-2*F25 '39. B 15980
Plato's Britannia. by Douglas Woodruff. (Coates) 7:50-1 Ag 29'31. B 15981
Play parade. by Noel Coward. (Fadiman) 9:100-102 D16'33. B 15982
A play without a name. by Austin Strong. (Brackett) 4:40 D8'28. T 15983
Playboy of Paris. (Mosher) 6:101 N8'30. CC 15984
The playboy of the western world. by John Millington Synge. (Benchley) 5:28 Ja11'30. T 15985
Playing with love. by Arthur Schnitzler. (Brackett) 5:32 Mr9 '29. T 15986
The play's the thing. by Ferenc Molnar. (Brackett) 2:33-4 N13 '26. T 15987
Pleased to meet you. by Christopher Morley. (Boyd) 3:110-11 Ap30'27. B 15988
Pleasure bound. by Harold Atteridge, et al. (Brackett) 5:30 Mr2'29. T 15989
Pleasure man. by Mae West. (Brackett) 4:32 O13'28. T 15990
The plot thickens. (Mosher) 12: 89*D19'36. CC 15991
The plough and the stars. (Mosher) 12:60*F6'37. CC 15992
The plough and the stars. by Sean O'Casey. (Brackett) 3:34 D10'27. T 15993
Plum bun. by Jessie Fauset. (Lowrie) 5:85-6 Mr9'29. B 15994
The plumed serpent. by D. H. Lawrence. (Dounce) 2:55-6 Ap 3'26. B 15995
Plumes in the dust. by Sophie Treadwell. (Benchley) 12:38* N14'36. T 15996
The plutocrat. by Arthur Goodrich. (Benchley) 6:28-30 Mr1 '30. T 15997
The plutocrat. by Booth Tarkington. (Boyd) 2:77 Ja22'27. B 15998
Pocahontas. by Nathalia Crane. (Bogan) 7:80-2 Mr21'31. B 15999
Pocahontas: or the nonpareil of Virginia. by David Garnett. (Coates) 8:62 F11'33. B 16000
Poems. by Louis Mac Neice. (Bogan) 13:93-4*D18'37. B 16001
Poems in praise of practically nothing. by Samuel Hoffenstein. (Parker) 4:99-100 Mr31'28. B 16002
Poems, 1911-1936. by John Hall Wheelock. (Bogan) 12:66-7*O3 '36. B 16003
Poems, 1919-1934. by Walter de la Mare. (Bogan) 12:61-2*Je20 '36. B 16004
Poems, 1924-1933. by Archibald Mac Leish. (Bogan) 10:114 Ap7 '34. B 16005
Poems of Gerard Manley Hopkins. by Gerard Manley Hopkins. (Bogan) 7:84-5 Mr21'31. B 16006
The poet's tongue. by W. H. Auden. (Bogan) 14:58*Jy23'38. B 16007
Point counter point. by Aldous Huxley. (Leonard) 4:116 O13'28. B 16008
A point of honor. by Jo Eisinger and Stephen Van Gluck. (Benchley) 13:30-3*F20'37. T 16009
Point Valaine. by Noel Coward. (Benchley) 10:28†Ja26'35. T 16010
Poker faces. (Claxton) 2:60 S25

'26. CC 16011
The politicos. by Matthew Josephson. (Fadiman) 14:73-5*Ap9'38. B 16012
Politics. (Mosher) 7:49*Ag8'31. CC 16013
Polk: the diary of a President. by Allan Nevins, ed. (Smith) 5: 127 N23'29. B 16014
Polly. by Guy Bolton and George Middleton. (Brackett) 4:32 Ja 19'29. T 16015
Polly of the circus. (Mosher) 8: 52*Mr26'32. CC 16016
Polonaise: the life of Chopin. by Guy de Pourtalès. (Boyd) 3:94-6 My7'27. B 16017
Polykushka. (Claxton) 2:70 Ja22 '27. CC 16018
Pomeroy's past. by Clare Kummer. (Gabriel) 2:26 My1'26. T 16019
Pomp and circumstance. by E. de Gramont. (Smith) 5:77 Jy20 '29. B 16020
The pony express. (Shane) 1:21-2 S19'25. CC 16021
Poor devil. by Henry Justin Smith. (Smith) 5:63 Ag10'29. B 16022
The poor little rich girl. (Mosher) 12:45*Jy4'36. CC 16023
The poor nut. (Claxton) 3:34 Jy30 '27. CC 16024
The poor nut. by J. C. Nugent and Elliott Nugent. (Anon.) 1: 11 My9'25. T 16025
Poor splendid wings. by Frances Winwar. (Fadiman) 9:81 S23 '33. B 16026
Pope or Mussolini. by John Hearley. (Smith) 5:65-6 Jy13'29. B 16027
Poppa. by Bella Spewack and Samuel Spewack. (Brackett) 4: 26 Ja12'29. T 16028
Poppy. (Mosher) 12:61*Je27'36. CC 16029
The popular sin. (Claxton) 2:58-9 D25'26. CC 16030
Porgy. by Dorothy Heyward and DuBose Heyward. (Brackett) 3: 29 O22'27. T 16031
Porgy and Bess. by DuBose Heyward; Dorothy Heyward; George Gershwin and Ira Gershwin. (Benchley) 11:32*O19'35. T 16032
Port o' London. by George W. Oliver. (Gabriel) 2:25 F27'26. T 16033
Port of shadows. (Mosher) 15:66-7*N4'39. CC 16034
Portage, Wisconsin; and other essays. by Zona Gale. (Leonard) 4:111-12 N17'28. B 16035
Portia on trial. (Mosher) 13:102* D11'37. CC 16036
Portrait by Caroline. by Sylvia Thompson. (Coates) 6:64-6 Ja 10'31. B 16037
Portrait of a diplomatist. by Harold Nicholson. (Smith) 6:88 S27 '30. B 16038
Portrait of a man with red hair. by Hugh Walpole. (Dounce) 1: 22 O24'25. B 16039
Portrait of America. by Diego Rivera. (Fadiman) 10:109 My12 '34. B 16040
Portrait of Jennie. by Robert Nathan. (Fadiman) 15:62-3*Ja20 '40. B 16041
Portrait of Lady Mary Montagu. by Iris Barry. (Hoyt) 4:100-101 Mr31'28. B 16042
Portrait of New York. by Felix Riesenberg. (Fadiman) 15:80* My13'39. B 16043
Portraits and prayers. by Gertrude Stein. (Fadiman) 10:86*N17'34. B 16044
Portraits in miniature. by Lytton Strachey. (Coates) 7:58*Jy25'31. B 16045
Possessed. (Mosher) 7:107-108 D 5'31. CC 16046
Possession. by Louis Bromfield. (Dounce) 1:21-2 O31'25. B 16047
Possession. by Edgar Selwyn. (Brackett) 4:32 O13'28. T 16047A
Post mortems of mere mortals. by C. MacLaurin. (Hellman) 6: 104 My3'30. B 16048

Post Road. by Wilber Daniel Steele and Norma Mitchell. (Benchley) 10:34†D15'34. T 16049

The postman always rings twice. by James M. Cain. (Fadiman) 10:86 F24'34. B 16050
(Benchley) 12:32*Mr7'36. T 16051

Potash and Perlmutter, detectives. by Montague Glass and Jules Eckert Goodman. (Brackett) 2:33 S11'26. T 16052

Potemkin. (Claxton) 2:54 S11'26. CC 16053
(Claxton) 2:94 D11'26. 16054

Potterism. by Rose Macaulay. (Markey) 4:94 Ap28'28. B 16055

The potters. (Claxton) 2:72 Ja22 '27. CC 16056

Power. (Mosher) 10:103 O13'34. CC 16057

The power and secret of the Jesuits. by René Fülöp-Miller. (Smith) 6:107 My10'30. B 16058

Praying curve. by Martin Brown. (Brackett) 2:33 F5'27. T 16059

Precious. by James Forbes. (Brackett) 4:26 Ja26'29. T 16060

Preface to a life. by Zona Gale. (Dounce) 2:98-100 N13'26. B 16061

Pre-honeymoon. by Anne Nichols. (Gibbs) 12:32*My9'36. T 16062

Prejudices: fifth series. by H. L. Mencken. (Boyd) 2:92 N26'27. B 16063

Prelude to exile. by William McNally. (Benchley) 12:52-6*D12 '36. T 16064

Present arms. by Herbert Fields; Richard Rodgers and Lorenz Hart. (Brackett) 4:33-4 My5'28. T 16065

Present indicative. by Noel Coward. (Fadiman) 13:59-60*Mr27 '37. B 16066

Presenting Lily Mars. by Booth Tarkington. (Fadiman) 9:54-5 Ag19'33. B 16067

A president is born. by Fannie Hurst. (Parker) 3:76-7 Ja28 '28. B 16068

The President vanishes. (Mosher) 10:99*D15'34. CC 16069

The President's daughter. by Nan Britton. (Parker) 3:105-108 O 15'27. B 16070

The President's mystery. (Mosher) 12:58*O24'36. CC 16071

The pretender. by Lion Feuchtwanger. (Fadiman) 13:72*My22'37. B 16072

Pride and prejudice. by Helen Jerome. (Benchley) 11:30-2*N 16'35. T 16073

Priest or pagan. by John Rathbone Oliver. (Fadiman) 9:55 Ag 26'33. B 16074

Prima donna. by Pitts Sanborn. (Simon) 4:92-3 F16'29. B 16075

A primer for lovers. by William Hurlbut. (Benchley) 5:34-6 N30 '29. T 16076

The primrose path. by Robert Buckner and Walter Hart. (Benchley) 14:28*Ja14'39. T 16077

The prince and the pauper. (Mosher) 13:85-6*My15'37. CC 16078

The prince of tempters. (Claxton) 2:68 O23'26. CC 16079

The prince of Washington Square. by Harry F. Liscomb. (Dounce) 1:26 F28'25. B 16080

Princess Charming. by Jack Donahue, et al. (Benchley) 6:35-6 O25'30. T 16081

Princess Flavia. by Harry B. Smith and Sigmund Romberg. (Mankiewicz) 1:20 N14'25. T 16082

Princess Ida. by William S. Gilbert and Arthur Sullivan. (Anon.) 1:11-12 My16'25. T 16083

Princess September and the nightingale. by W. Somerset Maugham. (Fadiman) 15:73*N25'39. B 16084

Princess Turandot. by Harry Alsberg and Isaac Don Levine. (Brackett) 2:33-4 N27'26. T 16085

Prison days and nights. by Victor

F. Nelson. (Coates) 9:61-2 Mr4'33. B 16086
Prison without bars. (Mosher) 15:66-7*Mr25'39. CC 16087
The prisoner of Shark Island. (Mosher) 12:65-6*F22'36. CC 16088
The prisoner of Zenda. (Mosher) 13:66*S11'37. CC 16089
Prisoners. by Franz Molnar. (Anon.) 1:28 Mr28'25. B 16090
Private detective 62. (Mosher) 9:42 Jy15'33. CC 16091
Private Jones. (Mosher) 9:54 Ap1 '33. CC 16092
The private life of Don Juan. (Mosher) 10:99*D15'34. CC 16093
The private life of Frank Harris. by Samuel Roth. (Coates) 7:81 Ja9'32. B 16094
The private life of Helen of Troy. by John Erskine. (Dounce) 1:22 D26'25. B 16095
The private life of Henry VIII. (Mosher) 9:80-1 O21'33. CC 16096
The private life of Henry VIII. (Flanner) 9:72-3 O28'33. CC 16097
The private life of Lady Hamilton. by Albert Flament. (Smith) 5:67 D28'29. B 16098
Private lives. (Mosher) 7:49 D26 '31. CC 16099
Private lives. by Noel Coward. (Benchley) 6:28-30 F7'31; 7:26 My23'31. T 16100
The private lives of Elizabeth & Essex. (Mosher) 15:97-8*D9 '39. CC 16101
Private number. (Mosher) 12:55-6*Je20'36. CC 16102
Private worlds. (Maloney) 11:77-8*Ap6'35. CC 16103
Private worlds. by Phyllis Bottome. (Fadiman) 10:69-70 Mr 31'34. B 16104
The prizefighter and the lady. (Mosher) 9:84 N18'33. CC 16105
Procession of lovers. by Lloyd Morris. (Lowrie) 5:116-17 Mr 23'29. B 16106
Processional. by John Howard Lawson. (Gibbs) 13:28*O23'37. T 16107
The prodigal. (Mosher) 7:47-8*Jy 4'31. CC 16108
The prodigal parents. by Sinclair Lewis. (Fadiman) 13:61*Ja22 '38. B 16109
Professional soldier. (Mosher) 11:61*F8'36. CC 16110
The professor. by Rex Warner. (Fadiman) 15:62*F25'39. B 16111
Professor Bernardi. by Arthur Schnitzler. (Leonard) 4:63 Ag 25'28. B 16112
Professor, beware. (Mosher) 14:45*Jy16'38. CC 16113
The professor's house. by Willa Cather. (Dounce) 1:20-1 S19 '25. B 16114
A program for America. by Will Durant. (Coates) 7:88-9 N21'31. B 16115
Proletarian literature in the United States. by Granville Hicks, ed. (Fadiman) 11:74-5* O12'35. B 16116
Prologue to glory. by Ellsworth Prouty Conkle. (Benchley) 14:28*Mr26'38. T 16117
Promise. by Henri Bernstein. (Benchley) 12:28*Ja9'37. T 16118
Promise not to tell. by Nancy Hoyt. (Smith) 5:74-5 F1'30. B 16119
The promises men live by. by Harry Scherman. (Anon.) 14:61-2*Mr5'38. B 16120
Prosper Mérimée: a mask and a face. by G. H. Johnstone. (Boyd) 3:120 Ap9'27. B 16121
Prosperity. (Mosher) 8:84-5 D3'32. CC 16122
The proud and the meek. by Jules Romains. (Fadiman) 10:99-101 O20'34. B 16123
Proud flesh. (Anon.) 1:31 Ap25'25. CC 16124
Proud heart. (Shane) 1:22-3 N7'25. CC 16125

A proud woman. by Arthur Richman. (Brackett) 2:33 N27'26. T 16126
The provincial lady in America. by E. M. Delafield. (Fadiman) 10:94-5 Je16'34. B 16127
Psyche. by Pierre Louÿs. (Coates) 7:85 My9'31. B 16128
The public enemy. (Mosher) 11:6* F16'35. CC 16129
Public hero number 1. (Mosher) 11:61*Je15'35. CC 16130
Public papers and addresses of Franklin D. Roosevelt. by Samuel I. Rosenman, ed. (Fadiman) 14:61*Ap30'38. B 16131
Public speech. by Archibald MacLeish. (Bogan) 12:79-80*My23 '36. B 16132
Pull devil, pull baker. by Stella Benson and Nikolai Gerasimovich Savin. (Fadiman) 9:50-1 Jy1'33. B 16133
The pumpkin coach. by Louis Paul. (Fadiman) 11:88*Ap6'35. B 16134
Puppets. (Shane) 2:41 Je26'26. CC 16135
Puppets and passions. by Roso di San Secondo. (Brackett) 3:33-4 Mr5'27. T 16136
(No entry) 16137
Pure gold. by O. E. Rölvaag. (Smith) 5:88 F15'30. B 16138
The pure in heart. by John Howard Lawson. (Benchley) 10:28 Mr31'34. T 16139
The puritan. by Chester Erskin. (Benchley) 11:28-30*F1'36. T 16140
The puritan. by Liam O'Flaherty. (Coates) 8:68-9*Mr5'32. B 16141
A puritan in Babylon. by William Allen White. (Fadiman) 14:88-9*N19'38. B 16142
Purity. by René Wachthausen. (Benchley) 6:31-2 Ja3'31. T 16143
Purse strings. by Edith Stern. (Boyd) 3:97 S10'27. B 16144
Purslane. by Bernice Kelly Harris. (Fadiman) 15:78*My13 '39. B 16145
The pursuer. by Louis Golding. (Fadiman) 11:68*Ja11'36. B 16146
The pursuit of happiness. by Alan Child and Isabelle Louden. (Gibbs) 9:32 O21'33. T 16147
Puttin' on the ritz. (Mosher) 5:88 F22'30 CC 16148
Puzzles of 1925. by Elsie Janis. (Parker) 1:13 F21'25. T 16149
Pygmalion. (Mosher) 14:100-101* D3'38. CC 16150
Pygmalion. by George Bernard Shaw. (Brackett) 2:33 N27'26. T 16151
Pylon. by William Faulkner. (Fadiman) 11:73-4*Mr30'35. B 16152
Pyramid and temple. by Julius Meier-Graefe. (Coates) 6:107-108 O25'30. B 16153
Pyramids. by Samuel Ruskin Golding. (Brackett) 2:37-8 Jy31'26. T 16154

Q

Quality Street. (Claxton) 3:68-9 N 12'27. CC 16155
Quality Street. (Mosher) 13:70*Ap 10'37. CC 16156
Quatorze juillet. (Mosher) 9:81 O 21'33. CC 16157
Queen Christina. (Mosher) 9:69-70 Ja6'34. CC 16158
Queen Elizabeth. by Katharine Anthony. (Smith) 5:128-9 O19 '29. B 16159
Queen high. (Mosher) 6:56 Ag16 '30. CC 16160
Queen high. by Laurence Schwab and B. G. De Sylva. (Brackett) 2:31-2 S18'26. T 16161
The queen of cooks. by Mary Lawton. (Dounce) 1:17 Jy4'25. B 16162
Queen of the night clubs. (Mosher) 5:105-106 Mr23'29. CC 16163
The Queen's husband. by Robert E. Sherwood. (Brackett) 3:25 F 4'28. T 16164
Queer books. by Edmund Pearson.

(Leonard) 4:107 N24'28. B 16165
The quick and the dead. by Claire Spencer. (Coates) 8:39 Jy2'32. B 16166
Quick millions. (Mosher) 7:82 Ap25'31. CC 16167
Quicksand. by Warren F. Lawrence. (Brackett) 4:28 F25'28. T 16168
Quiet street. by Michael Ossorgin. (Smith) 6:98-100 O11 '30. B 16169
Quo vadis. (Hays) 1:27 Mr7'25. CC 16170

R

R. F. D. by Charles Allen Smart. (Fadiman) 14:59-60*Mr5'38. B 16171
Rachel's children. by Harriet Hassell. (Fadiman) 14:60*Ap30 '38. B 16172
The racket. (Claxton) 4:69 Jy14 '28. CC 16173
The racket. by Bartlett Cormack. (Brackett) 3:34-5 D3'27. T 16174
Rackety rax. (Mosher) 8:68 N12 '32. CC 16175
Rackety rax. by Joel Sayre. (Coates) 8:52-3*F27'32. B 16176
Radetzky march. by Joseph Roth. (Fadiman) 9:94-5 O21'33. B 16177
Raffles. (Gibbs) 6:54 Ag2'30. CC 16178
Raffles. (Mosher) 15:51*Ja6'40. CC 16179
The rage of Paris. (Mosher) 14: 52-3*Je25'38. CC 16180
Raggle-taggle. by Walter Starkie. (Fadiman) 9:82-3 O14'33. B 16181
Rain. (Claxton) 3:67 F11'28. CC 16182
Rain. (Mosher) 8:56-7 O22'32. CC 16183
Rain. by John Colton and Clemence Randoph. (Benchley) 11: 26-8†F23'35. T 16184
Rain from heaven. by S. N. Behrman. (Benchley) 10:30†Ja5'35. T 16185
The rain girl: the tragic story of Jeanne Eagels. by Edward Doherty. (Parker) 7:84-6 Ap4 '31. B 16186
Rain or shine. (Mosher) 6:55-6 Ag16'30. CC 16187
Rain or shine. by James Gleason and Maurice Marks. (Brackett) 3:25-6 F18'28. T 16188
Rain upon Godshill. by J. B. Priestley. (Fadiman) 15:60-1* S23'39. B 16189
Rainbow. by Laurence Stallings; Oscar Hammerstein, II and Vincent Youmans. (Brackett) 4:40 D1'28. T 16190
The rainbow man. (Mosher) 5:64 Ap27'29. CC 16191
Rainbow on the river. (Mosher) 12:49-51*D26'36. CC 16192
The rainmaker. (Claxton) 2:59 My 22'26. CC 16193
The rains came. (Mosher) 15:61-2*S16'39. CC 16194
The rains came. by Louis Bromfield. (Fadiman) 13:68*O23'37. B 16195
Ramona. (Claxton) 4:84 My19'28. CC 16196
The ramparts we watch. by George Fielding Eliot. (Fadiman) 14:98*N12'38. B 16197
Rang tang. by Kaj Gynt. (White) 3:36-7 Jy23'27. T 16198
Rango. (Mosher) 7:67 F28'31. CC 16199
Rapid transit. by Lajos N. Egri. (Brackett) 3:34 Ap16'27. T 16200
Rasputin. (Mosher) 15:74*O21'39. CC 16201
Rasputin. by Felix Youssoupoff. (Hoyt) 3:115-16 N12'27. B 16202
Rasputin and the empress. (Mosher) 8:79 Ja7'33. CC 16203
Rats, lice, and history. by Hans Zinsser. (Fadiman) 10:68-9* F9'35. B 16204
The rats of Norway. by Keith

Winter. (Coates) 8:59*Ap2'32. B 16205
Rattling the cup on Chicago crime. by Edward Dean Sullivan. (Smith) 5:103 Je15'29. B 16206
The raven. (Mosher) 11:52*Jy13 '35. CC 16207
Reaching for the moon. (Mosher) 6:57 Ja10'31. CC 16208
Reaching for the stars. by Nora Waln. (Fadiman) 15:68*Mr4 '39. B 16209
Read America first. by Robert Littell. (Dounce) 2:77-8 O23 '26. B 16210
Read 'em and weep. by Sigmund Spaeth. (Boyd) 2:116 D11'26. B 16211
Rearguard. by Compton Pakenham. (Smith) 6:101 O11'30. B 16212
Rebecca of Sunnybrook farm. (Mosher) 8:41 Ag6'32. CC 16213
The rebel generation. by Jo van Ammers-Küller. (Lowrie) 4:100 Ja5'29. B 16214
The rebellious puritan. by Lloyd Morris. (Boyd) 3:102 Mr26'27. B 16215
Rebound. (Gibbs) 7:54-5 S5'31. CC 16216
Rebound. by Donald Ogden Stewart. (Benchley) 5:27-8 F15'30. T 16217
Recapture. by Preston Sturges. (Benchley) 5:27 F8'30. T 16218
Recaptured. by Sidonie Gabrielle Colette and Viola Garvin, trans. (Coates) 7:61 Ja23'32. B 16219
Reckless. (Mosher) 11:70*Ap27'35. CC 16220
The reckless lady. (Shane) 1:40 Ja30'26. CC 16221
The reckless lady. by Philip Gibbs. (Anon.) 1:26 Ap18'25. B 16222
Recognition of Robert Frost. by Richard Thornton, ed. (Bogan) 13:94*D18'37. B 16223
The rector of Wyck. by May Sinclair. (Anon.) 1:26 Ap25'25. B 16224
Red blinds. by Lord Lathom. (Brackett) 2:33-4 O16'26. T 16225
The red cat. by Rudolph Lothar and Hans Adler. (Gibbs) 10:26 S29'34. T 16226
Red cavalry. by I. Babel. (Smith) 5:89 S7'29. B 16227
The red dance. (Claxton) 4:59 Jy 7'28. CC 16228
Red dust. (Mosher) 8:68 N12'32. CC 16229
Red harvest. by Walter Charles Roberts. (Benchley) 13:30-2* Ap10'37. T 16230
Red headed woman. (Mosher) 8:48 Jy9'32. CC 16231
The red hills. by Rhys Davies. (Coates) 8:59-60 F4'33. B 16232
Red, hot and blue. by Cole Porter; Howard Lindsay and Russel Crouse. (Benchley) 12:28-32*N7 '36. T 16233
The red lamp. by Mary Roberts Rinehart. (Dounce) 1:15 Ag15 '25. B 16234
The red mill. (Claxton) 3:82 F19 '27. CC 16235
The red pavilion. by John Gunther. (Boyd) 2:74-6 Ja22'27. B 16236
The red robe. by Harry B. Smith and Edward Delaney Dunn. (Brackett) 4:30-2 Ja5'29. T 16237
The red room. by Geoffrey Dennis. (Coates) 8:60*Mr26'32. B 16238
Red rust. by V. Kirchon and A. Ouspensky. (Benchley) 5:26 D28 '29. T 16239
Red sky at morning. by Margaret Kennedy. (Hoyt) 3:111-12 D17 '27. B 16240
Red star over China. by Edgar Snow. (Fadiman) 13:63-5*Ja8 '38. B 16241
Red virtue. by Ella Winter. (Coates) 9:66-7 Ap22'33. B 16242

Re-echo. by I. J. Golden. (Benchley) 9:22-4 Ja20'34. T 16243
Reflected glory. by George Kelly. (Gibbs) 12:28*O3'36. T 16244
A regular fellow. (Shane) 1:20 O 10'25. CC 16245
A regular guy. by Patrick Kearney. (Benchley) 7:26*Je20'31. T 16246
Relations. by Willard Mack. (White) 4:41 S1'28. T 16247
Rembrandt. (Mosher) 12:102*D5 '36. CC 16248
Remember? (Mosher) 15:53*D23 '39. CC 16249
Remember the day. by Philip Dunning and Philo Higley. (Gibbs) 11:30*S28'35. T 16250
Remember the night. (Mosher) 15:50*Ja20'40. CC 16251
Remembering laughter. by Wallace Stegner. (Fadiman) 13:63-4*O2'37. B 16252
Remote control. (Gibbs) 6:109-11 D13'30. CC 16253
Remote control. by Clyde North; Albert C. Fuller and Jack T. Nelson. (Benchley) 5:34-6 S21 '29. T 16254
Remous. (Flanner) 11:54*Mr16'35. CC 16255
Rendezvous. (Mosher) 11:75-6* N2'35. CC 16256
Rendezvous. by Barton MacLane. (Benchley) 8:28 O22'32. T 16257
Renegades. (Mosher) 6:84-5 N15 '30. CC 16258
The rescue. (Mosher) 4:70 Ja19 '29. CC 16259
Restless days. by Lilo Linke. (Fadiman) 11:76*Ap13'35. B 16260
Resurrection. (Claxton) 3:89-91 My21'27. CC 16261
Resurrection. (Mosher) 6:51 Ja31 '31. CC 16262
Retreat. by C. R. Benstead. (Smith) 6:102-103 Mr8'30. B 16263
Retreat from glory. by Bruce Lockhart. (Fadiman) 10:100 O6'34. B 16264
Return I dare not. by Margaret Kennedy. (Coates) 7:91-2 N14 '31. B 16265
The return of Dr. X. (Mosher) 15:93*D2'39. CC 16266
The return of Sherlock Holmes. (Mosher) 5:107 O26'29. CC 16267
The return of Sophie Lang. (Maloney) 12:39*Ag1'36. CC 16268
The return of the prodigal son. by André Gide. (Flanner) 9:40 Mr18'33. T 16269
The return of the Scarlet Pimpernel. (Mosher) 14:55*Ap16'38. CC 16270
Reunion in Vienna. (Mosher) 9:61-2 My6'33. CC 16271
Reunion in Vienna. by Robert E. Sherwood. (Benchley) 7:28-30 N28'31. T 16272
Revelry. by Maurine Watkins. (Brackett) 3:31-2 S24'27. T 16273
Revenge with music. by Howard Dietz and Arthur Schwartz. (Benchley) 10:34-6†D8'34. T 16274
Revolt. by Harry Wagstaff Gribble. (Brackett) 4:34 N10'28. T 16275
Revolt in the arts. by Oliver M. Sayler. (Coates) 6:100-101 N15 '30. B 16276
Revolt in the desert. by T. E. Lawrence. (Boyd) 3:102 Ap2'27. B 16277
The revolution of nihilism. by Hermann Rauschning. (Fadiman) 15:62*S9'39. B 16278
The rhapsody. by Louis K. Anspacher. (Benchley) 6:34 S27 '30. T 16279
Rhapsody. by Otto Schinnerer. (Boyd) 3:96 Mr12'27. B 16280
Rhapsody in black. by Lew Leslie. (Benchley) 7:28-30 My16 '31. T 16281
Rhodes. (Mosher) 12:51*F29'36. CC 16282
Rhododendron pie. by Margery Sharp. (Smith) 6:58-9 Ag2

'30. B 16283
Rich brat. by Forrest Wilson. (Smith) 5:104 N30'29. B 16284
Rich land, poor land. by Stuart Chase. (Anon.) 12:85-6*S19'36. B 16285
Rich man, poor girl. (Mosher) 14:52-3*Ag27'38. CC 16286
A rich man's daughter. by R. H. Mottram. (Smith) 6:100-102 O18'30. B 16287
Rich man's folly. (Mosher) 7:108 D5'31. CC 16288
Richard Harding Davis: his day. by Fairfax Downey. (Fadiman) 9:81 S23'33. B 16289
Richard of Bordeaux. by Gordon Daviot. (Benchley) 10:28 F24 '34. T 16290
Richelieu. (Mosher) 11:70*Ap27 '35. CC 16291
Richelieu: a study. by Hilaire Belloc. (Gannett) 5:105 N30'29. B 16292
The richest girl in the world. (McKelway) 10:56 S29'34. CC 16293
Riddle me this! by Daniel N. Rubin. (Benchley) 8:32-4*Mr5 '32. T 16294
Riddles of silence. by Arthur J. Thomson. (Coates) 8:62*My14 '32. B 16295
Riders of the purple sage. (Mosher) 7:79 O3'31. CC 16296
Riffraff. (Mosher) 11:52-3*Ja18 '36. CC 16297
The right age to marry. by H. F. Maltby. (Gabriel) 2:24 F27'26. T 16298
Right of happiness. by Roy Daavidson. (Parker) 7:38 Ap11'31. T 16299
Right this way. by Marianne Brown Waters, et al. (Benchley) 13:32*Ja15'38. T 16300
The right to live. (Mosher) 11: 62*F23'35. CC 16301
The right to love. (Mosher) 6:59 Ja10'31. CC 16302
The right to love. by Sheldon White. (Mankiewicz) 1:15 Je20 '25. T 16303
Right you are if you think you are. by Luigi Pirandello. (Brackett) 3:33 Mr5'27. T 16304
The ring is closed. by Knut Hamsun. (Fadiman) 13:90-1*My15 '37. B 16305
The ring of the Löwenskölds. by Selma Lagerlöf. (Coates) 6:64 Ja10'31. B 16306
Ringside. by Edward E. Paramore, Jr.; Hyatt Daab and George Abbott. (White) 4:25-6 S8'28. T 16307
Rio. (Mosher) 15:67*N4'39. CC 16308
Rio Rita. (Mosher) 5:113-14 O19 '29. CC 16309
Rio Rita. by Guy Bolton and Fred Thompson. (Brackett) 3:33 F19 '27. T 16310
Ripeness is all. by Eric Linklater. (Fadiman) 11:82*My11 '35. B 16311
Ripples. by William Anthony McGuire, et al. (Benchley) 6: 33 F22'30. T 16312
Riptide. (Mosher) 10:97-8 Ap7'34. CC 16313
The rise and fall. by Robertus Love. (Dounce) 2:49 Jy3'26. B 16314
Ritzy. (Claxton) 3:51-2 Je25'27. CC 16315
The rivals. by Richard Brinsley Sheridan. (Brackett) 6:29 Mr22 '30. T 16316
The river. (Mosher) 4:92 Ja5'29. CC 16317
The river. (A. Gibbs) 6:57 D20'30. CC 16318
The river. (Mosher) 13:53-4*F5 '38. CC 16319
The river pirate. (Mosher) 4:80 S22'28. CC 16320
The road back. (Mosher) 13:63* Je26'37. CC 16321
The road back. by Erich Maria Remarque. (Coates) 7:76*My23 '31. B 16322
Road end. by Woods Morrison. (Boyd) 3:80 Je25'27. B 16323
The road leads on. by Knut Hamsun and Eugene Gay-Tifft, trans.

(Fadiman) 10:93-4 Je16'34. B 16324

Road of ages. by Robert Nathan. (Fadiman) 10:64-5*F2'35. B 16325

The road to En-Dor. by Louis Joseph Vance. (Anon.) 1:26 Ap 11'25. B 16326

The road to glory. (Mosher) 12: 44*Ag15'36. CC 16327

The road to happiness. by Gregorio Martinez Sierra and Eduardo Marquina. (Brackett) 3: 29 My14'27. T 16328

The road to heaven. by Thomas Beer. (Markey) 4:87-8 Je2'28. B 16329

Road to life. (Mosher) 7:58-9 F6 '32. CC 16330

(Mosher) 8:57*Ap23'32. 16331

The road to oblivion. by Vladimir Zenzinov. (Coates) 7:52-3*Jy4 '31. B 16332

The road to Reno. (Mosher) 7:75-6 O17'31. CC 16333

The road to Rome. by Robert E. Sherwood. (Brackett) 2:33 F12 '27. T 16334

The road to Singapore. (Mosher) 7:79 O10'31. CC 16335

Road to war. by Walter Millis. (Fadiman) 11:64-5*My4'35. B 16336

The road to yesterday. (Shane) 1:29 D5'25. CC 16337

Roadhouse nights. (Mosher) 6:75 Mr1'30. CC 16338

Roadside. by Lynn Riggs. (Benchley) 6:37-8 O4'30. T 16339

Roar China! by S. Tretyakov; Leo Lania and Ruth Langner. (Benchley) 6:33-4 N8'30; 7:24* Jy25'31. T 16340

The roaring twenties. (Mosher) 15:59*N11'39. CC 16341

The robber barons. by Matthew Josephson. (Fadiman) 10:76-8 Mr3'34. B 16342

Roberta. (Maloney) 11:70-1*Mr16 '35. CC 16343

Roberta. by Otto Harbach and Jerome Kern. (Benchley) 9:30-2 N25'33. T 16344

Robespierre's rise and fall. by Louis Gosselin. (Hoyt) 3:73 Ja 21'28. B 16345

Robin Hood. by Reginald DeKoven and Harry B. Smith. (Benchley) 7:28 F6'32. T 16346

Rock me, Julie. by Kenneth Raisbeck. (Benchley) 6:28 F14'31. T 16347

Rockefeller: giant, dwarf, symbol. by William H. Allen. (Smith) 6:104-105 My24'30. B 16348

Rocket to the moon. by Clifford Odets. (Benchley) 14:36*D3'38. T 16349

Roll, Jordan, roll. by Julia Peterkin. (Fadiman) 9:49-50 D30'33. B 16350

Roll, sweet chariot. by Paul Green. (Benchley) 10:38 O13'34. T 16351

Rolled stockings. (Claxton) 3:34 Jy30'27. CC 16352

Rolling home. (Shane) 2:35 Je12 '26. CC 16353

A Roman holiday. by Don Ryan. (Smith) 5:89 F15'30. B 16354

Romance. (Mosher) 6:50 Ag30'30. CC 16355

The romantic comedians. by Ellen Glasgow. (Dounce) 2:88-9 O2'26. B 16356

The romantic exiles. by Edward Hallett Carr. (Fadiman) 9:55-6 Je17'33. B 16357

A Romany life. by Gipsy Petulengro. (Fadiman) 12:76-8*Ap11'36. B 16358

Rome express. (Mosher) 9:55-6 Mr4'33. CC 16359

Rome haul. by Walter D. Edmonds. (Lowrie) 5:85 Mr9'29. B 16360

Romeo and Juliet. (Mosher) 12: 36-8*Ag22'36. CC 16361

Romeo and Juliet. by William Shakespeare. (Benchley) 10:28† D29'34. T 16362

The roof. by John Galsworthy. (Benchley) 7:28-30 N14'31. T 16363

A room in Berlin. by Gunther

Birkenfeld. (Smith) 6:82 N1'30. B 16364
A room in red and white. by Roy Hargrave. (Benchley) 11:26-8* Ja25'36. T 16365
A room of one's own. by Virginia Woolf. (Smith) 5:124 N9 '29. B 16366
Room service. (Mosher) 14:65* S24'38. CC 16367
Room service. by John Murray and Allen Boretz. (Gibbs) 13: 28*My29'37. T 16368
Room 349. by Mark Linder. (Benchley) 6:28-30 My3'30. T 16369
Roosevelt: a study in fortune and power. by Emil Ludwig. (Fadiman) 14:58-9*Je11'38. B 16370
Roosevelt omnibus. by Don Wharton, ed. (Fadiman) 10:90-4 O 27'34. B 16371
Roosevelt: the story of a friendship. by Owen Wister. (Smith) 6:84 Je21'30. B 16372
The root and the flower. by L. H. Meyers. (Fadiman) 11:74-5*S7'35. B 16373
Roots. by Eduardo Zamacois. (Smith) 5:162 D7'29. B 16374
Rope. by David Wallace and T. S. Stribling. (Brackett) 4:34 Mr3 '28. T 16375
Rope enough. by Dorothy Parker. (Boyd) 2:84 Ja8'27. B 16376
Rope of gold. by Josephine Herbst. (Anon.) 15:70*Mr4'39. B 16377
Rope's end. by Patrick Hamilton. (Benchley) 5:36-8 S28'29. T 16378
Rosa. by Knut Hamsun. (Dounce) 2:56 Ap3'26. B 16379
Rosalie. (Mosher) 13:61-2*Ja8'38. CC 16380
Rosalie. by George Gershwin and Sigmund Romberg. (Brackett) 3:26 Ja21'28. T 16381
The Rosalie Evans letters from Mexico. by Rosalie Evans. (Dounce) 2:57-9 Ap24'26. B 16382
Rose Marie. (Mosher) 11:60*F8 '36. CC 16383
Rose of the rancho. (Mosher) 11: 63*Ja11'36. CC 16384
Rose of Washington Square. (Mosher) 15:77*My13'39. CC 16385
Rosmersholm. by Henrik Ibsen. (Anon.) 1:11-12 My16'25. T 16386
Rough house Rosie. (Claxton) 3: 79 My28'27. CC 16387
Rough justice. by C. E. Montague. (Dounce) 2:61 My8'26; 2:59-60 My15'26. B 16388
The rough riders. (Claxton) 3:85-7 Mr26'27. CC 16389
Rough romance. (Mosher) 6:80 Je 21'30. CC 16390
Round up. by Ring W. Lardner. (Parker) 5:105-106 Ap27'29. B 16391
Roundabout. by Nancy Hoyt. (Dounce) 2:85-6 Je5'26. B 16392
The royal family. by Edna Ferber and George S. Kaufman. (Brackett) 3:25 Ja7'28. T 16393
The royal family of Broadway. (Mosher) 6:67 Ja3'31. CC 16394
Royal progress. by Hector Bolitho. (Fadiman) 13:69*My8'37. B 16395
The royal virgin. by Harry Wagstaff Gribble. (Benchley) 6:27 Mr29'30. T 16396
The royal way. by André Malraux. (Fadiman) 11:64-5*F23 '35. B 16397
Rubber! a story of glory and greed. by Howard Wolf and Ralph Wolf. (Anon.) 12:83*S12 '36. B 16398
"Ruby Robert" alias Bob Fitzsimmons. by Robert Hobart Davis. (Dounce) 2:59 My29'26. B 16399
Ruddigore. by William S. Gilbert and Arthur Sullivan. (Long) 3: 34 Je11'27. T 16400
The rueful mating. by G. B. Stern. (Coates) 8:50 Jy9'32. B 16401
Rufus LeMaire's affairs. by Martin Broones and Ballard Mac-

donald. (Brackett) 3:34 Ap9'27. T 16402
Ruggles of Red Gap. (Maloney) 11:70*Mr16'35. CC 16403
The ruin. by Edward Sackville-West. (Boyd) 2:67-8 Ja15'27. B 16404
Rulers of the sea. (Mosher) 15:69*N11'39. CC 16405
The ruling voice. (Mosher) 7:81 N14'31. CC 16406
Rum, romance and rebellion. by Charles William Taussig. (Markey) 4:107-108 Ap21'28. B 16407
Rumbin galleries. by Booth Tarkington. (Fadiman) 13:93*O30 '37. B 16408
Rumour at nightfall. by Graham Greene. (Coates) 7:65 F6'32. B 16409
Run, little chillun! by Hall Johnson. (Benchley) 9:24 Ap15'33. T 16410
Run sheep run. by Raymond Knight. (Gibbs) 14:32-4*N12 '38. T 16411
The runaway. (Shane) 2:55 My1 '26. CC 16412
The runaways. by George A. Birmingham. (Leonard) 4:66 Ag18'28. B 16413
Running wild. (Claxton) 3:81 Je18 '27. CC 16414
Runt. by Hatcher Hughes. (Anon.) 1:11 Ap18'25. T 16415
Russet mantle. by Lynn Riggs. (Benchley) 11:26*Ja25'36. T 16416
Russian somersault. by Ivor Schwezoff. (Fadiman) 12:74-6* Mr7'36. B 16417

S

SOS tidal wave. (Mosher) 15:57* Jy1'39. CC 16418
S. S. San Pedro. by James Gould Cozzens. (Coates) 7:84-5 S12 '31. B 16419
The sacred flame. (Mosher) 5:91 N30'29. CC 16420
The sacred flame. by W. Somerset Maugham. (Brackett) 4:37-8 D1'28. T 16421
The sacred tree. by Arthur Waley, trans. (Dounce) 2:56-7 Je26'26. B 16422
Sadie McKee. (Mosher) 10:89-90 My26'34. CC 16423
The saga of Billy the Kid. by Walter Noble Burns. (Dounce) 2:45 Mr6'26. B 16424
The saga of Cimba. by Richard Maury. (Anon.) 15:79*Mr11'39. B 16425
The saga of Frank Dover. by Johannes Bucholtz. (Fadiman) 14:81*O22'38. B 16426
Sagittarius rising. by Cecil Lewis. (Anon.) 12:85*O17'36. B 16427
Sailor, beware! by Courtney Burr. (Gibbs) 9:35 O7'33. T 16428
Sailors of Cattaro. by Friedrich Wolf. (Benchley) 10:26†D22'34. T 16429
St. George of Weldon. by Robert Rylee. (Fadiman) 13:60-1* Mr 27'37. B 16430
St. Helena. by R. C. Sherriff and Jeanne Casalis. (Benchley) 12:27*O17'36. T 16431
Saint Joan. by George Bernard Shaw. (Benchley) 12:24*Mr21 '36. T 16432
Saint Joan of Arc. by Victoria Sackville-West. (Fadiman) 12:70-1*S26'36. B 16433
Saint Johnson. by William Riley Burnett. (Coates) 6:104 O18'30. B 16434
St. Mawr. by D. H. Lawrence. (Dounce) 1:17 Je27'25. B 16435
Saint Wench. by John Colton. (Benchley) 8:26 Ja14'33. T 16436
Salar the salmon. by Henry Williamson. (Fadiman) 12:72-3*Je 13'36. B 16437
Sally. (Mosher) 5:48 Ja4'30. CC 16438
Sally, Irene and Mary. (Shane) 1:34-5 D19'25. CC 16439
Sally of the sawdust. (F. J. S.) 1:

16 Je27'25. CC 16440
Sally of the sawdust. (Shane) 1: 16-17 Ag8'25. CC 16441
Sally: the story of a foster girl. by John Metcalfe. (Fadiman) 12:78-9*My9'36. B 16442
The saloon in the home. by Ridgely Hunt, ed. and George S. Chappell, ed. (Coates) 6: 55 D27'30. B 16443
Salt walter taffy. by Corey Ford. (Smith) 5:103-104 Je15'29. B 16444
Saluta. by Will Morrissey, et al. (Gibbs) 10:34-5 S8'34. T 16445
Salute to freedom. by Eric Lowe. (Fadiman) 14:72-3*F11'39. B 16446
Salvation. by Sidney Howard and Charles MacArthur. (Brackett) 3:24-5 F11'28. T 16447
The salvation hunters. (Hays) 1: 28 F21'25. CC 16448
The Salzburg tales. by Christina Stead. (Fadiman) 10:79-80 S29 '34. B 16449
Sam Abramovitch. by François Porché and Charlton Andrews. (Brackett) 2:33 Ja29'27. T 16450
The same person. by Anna Robeson Burr. (Coates) 7:80-1 My2 '31. B 16451
Samuel Butler: a mid-Victorian modern. by Clara Greuning Stillman. (Coates) 8:69-70 O8 '32. B 16452
Samuel Drummond. by Thomas Boyd. (Dounce) 1:17-18 S5'25. B 16453
San Francisco. (Mosher) 12:45* Jy4'36. CC 16454
San Quentin. (Maloney) 13:33*Ag 7'37. CC 16455
Sanatorium. by D. Stewart. (Smith) 6:63 Ag23'30. B 16456
Sanctuary. by William Faulkner. (Coates) 7:86 Mr7'31. B 16457
(Flanner) 9:27 Ja20'34. 16458
Sandalwood. by Owen Davis. (Brackett) 2:33 O2'26. T 16459
Sanders of the river. (Mosher) 11:45*Jy6'35. CC 16460
Sanfelice. by Vincent Sheean. (Fadiman) 12:59-60*Je20'36. B 16461
Sang et lumières. by Joseph Peyré. (Flanner) 11:51*F15'36. B 16462
The Santa Fe Trail. by R. L. Duffus. (Smith) 6:63 Ag23'30. B 16463
The sap from Syracuse. (Gibbs) 6:55 Ag2'30. CC 16464
Sarah and son. (Mosher) 6:61 Mr 22'30. CC 16465
Saratoga. (Mosher) 13:64*Jy24'37. CC 16466
Sardinian sideshow. by Amelie Posse-Brázdová. (Coates) 8:59-60 Ja14'33. B 16467
Sari. by Julius Wilhelm and Fritz Greenbaum. (Benchley) 5:28 F8 '30. T 16468
Satan met a lady. (Maloney) 12: 39*Ag1'36. CC 16469
Saturday night. by Jacinte Benavente. (Brackett) 2:34 N6'26. T 16470
A Saturday night. by Owen Davis. (Benchley) 9:28 Mr11'33. T 16471
The Saturday night kid. (Mosher) 5:110-11 N23'29. CC 16472
Saturday to Monday. by Newman Levy. (Smith) 6:104 My24'30. B 16473
Saturday's children. by Maxwell Anderson. (Brackett) 2:33 F5 '27. T 16474
Savage messiah. by H. S. Ede. (Parker) 7:82-6 Mr14'31. B 16475
Save me the waltz. by Katherine Dayton. (Benchley) 14:28*Mr 12'38. T 16476
Sawdust Caesar. by George Seldes. (Fadiman) 11:77*N30 '35. B 16477
The sawdust paradise. (Claxton) 4:66 S1'28. CC 16478
Say it again. (Shane) 2:35-6 Je12 '26. CC 16479
Say it with songs. (Mosher) 5:63 Ag17'29. CC 16480
Say when. by Calvin Brown.

(Long) 4:42 Jy14'28. T 16481
Say when. by John McGowan and Ray Henderson. (Benchley) 10: 30†N17'34. T 16482
Scarface. (Mosher) 8:51-2 My28 '32. CC 16483
The scarlet empress. (McKelway) 10:67-8 S22'34. CC 16484
The scarlet fox. by Willard Mack. (Brackett) 4:33 Ap7'28. T 16485
The scarlet letter. (Claxton) 2: 35 Ag21'26. CC 16486
Scarlet pages. by Samuel Shipman and John B. Hymer. (Benchley) 5:34 S21'29. T 16487
The scarlet pimpernel. (Mosher) 10:58-9*F9'35. CC 16488
Scarlet seas. (Mosher) 4:60 Ja12 '29. CC 16489
Scarlet Sister Mary. by Julia Peterkin. (Benchley) 6:35 D6 '30. T 16490
Scènes de la vie future. by Georges Duhamel. (Flanner) 6: 35-6 S6'30. B 16491
Schliemann. by Emil Ludwig. (Coates) 7:67*My30'31. B 16492
The school for directors. by Ignazio Silone. (Fadiman) 14:75-8*N26'38. B 16493
The school for husbands. by Jean Baptiste Poquelin Molière and Arthur Guiterman, adapt. (Gibbs) 9:28-9 O28'33. T 16494
The school for scandal. by Richard Brinsley Sheridan. (Mankiewicz) 1:15 D5'25. T 16495
School for virtue. by Arthur Ebenhack. (Benchley) 7:24 My2 '31. T 16496
School for wives. by André Gide. (Smith) 5:97 S28'29. B 16497
Schoolhouse on the lot. by Joseph A. Fields and Jerome Chodorov. (Benchley) 14:25-30*Ap 2'38. T 16498
Schools. by A. B. See. (Parker) 4: 104-106 My26'28. B 16499
Schumann. by Victor Basch. (Coates) 7:51 Ag29'31. B 16500
Schweiger. by Franz Werfel. (Gabriel) 2:27 Ap3'26. T 16501
Science for the citizen. by Lancelot Hogben. (Fadiman) 14:71-2*S24'38. B 16502
The science of life. by H. G. Wells; G. P. Wells and Julian S. Huxley. (Coates) 7:74 F28 '31. B 16503
The scientific detective and the expert witness. by C. Ainsworth Mitchell. (Coates) 7:50* Ag15'31. B 16504
Scoop. by Evelyn Waugh. (Fadiman. 14:56*Jy23'38. B 16505
Scotch mist. by Patrick Hastings. (Brackett) 2:33 O2'26. T 16506
A Scottie's Saturday night. by Harold Willard Gleason. (Lowrie) 4:76 F9'29. B 16507
The scoundrel. (Mosher) 11:66-7* My11'35. CC 16508
Sculpture inside and out. by Malvina Hoffman. (Anon.) 15:71-2*Ap22'39. B 16509
Sea fever. (Mosher) 5:107 N2'29. CC 16510
The sea god. (Mosher) 6:90 S13 '30. CC 16511
The sea gull. by Anton Chekhov. (Benchley) 5:41 S28'29; 14:24* Ap9'38. T 16512
Sea legs. by Arthur Swanstrom. (Gibbs) 13:28*My29'37. T 16513
The sea of grass. by Conrad Richter. (Fadiman) 12:62-3*F 13'37. B 16514
The sea tyrant. by Peter Freuchen. (Coates) 8:42 Ag20'32. B 16515
The sealers. by Peter Tutein. (Fadiman) 14:67*Mr26'38. B 16516
Seaports in the moon. by Vincent Starrett. (Markey) 4:108-109 Ap21'28. B 16517
Search for beauty. (Mosher) 10: 77 F17'34. CC 16518
Searching for the sun. by Dan Totheroh. (Benchley) 12:26*F29 '36. T 16519

A season in hell. by Jean-Marie Carré. (Coates) 7:76 O24'31. B 16520
Seasoned timber. by Dorothy Canfield. (Anon.) 15:70*Mr4'39. B 16521
The second comin'. by George Bryant. (White) 7:30-2 D19'31. T 16522
The second little show. by Dwight D. Wiman, et al. (Benchley) 6:34 S13'30. T 16523
The second man. by S. N. Behrman. (Brackett) 3:33 Ap23'27. T 16524
The second prince. by Thomas Bell. (Anon.) 11:70*Mr23'35. B 16525
Secret agent. (Mosher) 12:67*Je 13'36. CC 16526
The secret of Dr. Kildare. (Mosher) 15:58*D16'39. CC 16527
Secret sentence. by Vicki Baum. (Coates) 8:47 Jy16'32. B 16528
Secrets. (Mosher) 9:49 Mr25'33. CC 16529
Security. by Esme Wynne-Tyson. (Brackett) 5:30 Ap13'29. T 16530
See how they run. by Helen Grace Carlisle. (Smith) 5:77 Jy20'29. B 16531
See my lawyer. by Richard Maibaum and Harry Clork. (Gibbs) 15:30*O7'39. T 16532
See Naples and die. by Elmer Rice. (Benchley) 5:38-40 O5'29. T 16533
See you in jail. (Claxton) 3:101 Ap9'27. CC 16534
Seed. (Mosher) 7:70*My23'31. CC 16535
Seed of the brute. by Knowles Entrikin. (Brackett) 2:33 N13 '26. T 16536
Seeds of revolt. by Mauritz A. Hallgren. (Fadiman) 9:79 S9 '33. B 16537
Seeds of tomorrow. by Mikhail Sholokhov. (Fadiman) 11:83*N 2'35. B 16538
Seen but not heard. by Marie Baumer and Martin Berkeley. (Gibbs) 12:24*S26'36. T 16539
Segelfoss Town. by Knut Hamsun. (Anon.) 1:24 Mr14'25. B 16540
The Selbys. by Anne Green. (Smith) 6:100 My3'30. B 16541
Selected poems. by Oliver St. John Gogarty. (Bogan) 10:113 Ap7'34. B 16542
Selected poems. by Marianne Moore. (Bogan) 11:66-7*My4 '35. B 16543
Selected poems. by Edith Sitwell. (Bogan) 13:70*My8'37. B 16544
Selected short stories. by Sinclair Lewis. (Fadiman) 11:56-8*Jy13'35. B 16545
The Senate and the League of Nations. by Henry Cabot Lodge. (Dounce) 1:21-2 N7'25. B 16546
Señor daredevil. (Claxton) 2:36 Ag 21'26. CC 16547
Serena Blandish. by S. N. Behrman. (Brackett) 4:27-8 F2'29. T 16547A
The serenade. by Harry B. Smith and Victor Herbert. (Brackett) 6:28 Mr15'30. T 16548
The servant in the house. by Charles Rann Kennedy. (Gabriel) 2:26 My15'26. T 16549
Servants' entrance. (McKelway) 10:88 O6'34. CC 16550
Serve it forth. by M. F. K. Fisher. (Fadiman) 13:65*Je19'37. B 16551
Service de luxe. (Mosher) 14:58* O29'38. CC 16552
Service for two. by Martin Flavin. (Brackett) 2:33 S11'26. T 16553
Set a thief. by Edward E. Paramore, Jr. (Brackett) 3:34 Mr5 '27. T 16554
Set to music. by Noel Coward. (Benchley) 14:26*Ja28'39. T 16555
The set-up. by Joseph Moncure March. (Leonard) 4:110 N17'28. B 16556
Seven brothers. by Alexis Kivi.

(Lowrie) 5:96 Mr2'29. B 16557
Seven days. by Andreas Latzko. (Coates) 7:47*Ag1'31. B 16558
Seven days' darkness. by Gunnar Gunnarsson. (Smith) 6:96 N15 '30. B 16559
Seven days leave. (Mosher) 5:62-4 F1'30. CC 16560
Seven days whipping. by John Biggs, Jr. (Leonard) 4:59 Jy28 '28. B 16561
Seven faces. (Mosher) 5:111 N23 '29. CC 16562
Seven keys to Baldpate. (Shane) 1:23 N7'25. CC 16563
Seven keys to Baldpate. by George M. Cohan. (Gibbs) 11: 28*Je8'35. T 16564
Seven iron men. by Paul de Kruif. (Smith) 5:116-17 O5'29. B 16565
Seven pillars of wisdom. by T. E. Lawrence. (Fadiman) 11:65-8* S28'35. B 16566
Seven poor men of Sydney. by Christina Stead. (Fadiman) 11: 62*Mr2'35. B 16567
The seven vices. by Guglielmo Ferrero. (Smith) 5:64 Jy13'29. B 16568
The seven who fled. by Frederic Prokosch. (Fadiman) 13:49-51* Ag28'37. B 16569
The seventh gate. by Muriel Harris. (Smith) 6:100-102 Ap19'30. B 16570
Seventh heaven. (Claxton) 3:59 Je 4'27. CC 16571
Seventh heaven. (Mosher) 13:55* Mr27'37. CC 16572
Sex. by Jane Mast. (Gabriel) 2: 26 My8'26. T 16573
The sex fable. by Edouard Bourdet. (Benchley) 7:28 O31'31. T 16574
Shadow and substance. by Paul Vincent Carroll. (Benchley) 13:26*F5'38. T 16575
The shadow before. by William Rollins, Jr. (Fadiman) 10:102 Mr17'34. B 16576
The shadow flies. by Rose Macaulay. (Coates) 8:63 O22 '32. B 16577
Shadows of men. by Jim Tully. (Smith) 5:76 Ja11'30. B 16578
Shadows on the rock. by Willa Cather. (Coates) 7:49-50*Ag15 '31. B 16579
A shadowy third. by Elizabeth Sprigge. (Boyd) 3:89-90 Je18 '27. B 16580
Shady lady. by Estelle Morando, et al. (White) 9:24 Jy22'33. T 16581
Shake hands with the devil. by Reardon Conner. (Fadiman) 9: 70-1 F3'34. B 16582
Shakespeare. by Mark Van Doren. (Fadiman) 15:61*S30'39. B 16583
Shall we dance. (Mosher) 13:86-7* My15'37. CC 16584
Shanghai. (Mosher) 11:42*Jy27'35. CC 16585
Shanghai express. (Mosher) 8:48-9*F27'32. CC 16586
The Shanghai gesture. by John Colton. (Gabriel) 1:23 F13'26. T 16587
The Shannons of Broadway. by James Gleason. (Brackett) 3: 31 O8'27. T 16588
The shape of things to come. by H. G. Wells. (Fadiman) 9:78-9 S9'33. B 16589
Shatter the dream. by Norah C. James. (Coates) 6:73 Ja17'31. B 16590
Shattered. (Shane) 2:52 My8'26. CC 16591
The shattered lamp. by Leslie Reade. (Benchley) 10:30 Mr31 '34. T 16592
She couldn't say no. by B. M. Kaye. (Brackett) 2:31 S18'26. T 16593
She done him wrong. (Mosher) 9: 59 F18'33. CC 16594
She goes to war. (Mosher) 5:61 Je15'29. CC 16595
She had to know. by Paul Geraldy. (Parker) 1:13 F21'25. T 16596
She loves me not. (McKelway) 10: 80 S15'34. CC 16597
She loves me not. by Howard Lind-

say. (Benchley) 9:28-30 D2'33. T 16598
She married her boss. (Mosher) 11:69-70*O5'35. CC 16599
She shall have music. by Alyse Gregory. (Dounce) 2:80-1 S18 '26. B 16600
She stoops to conquer. by Oliver Goldsmith. (Brackett) 4:50 My 26'28. T 16601
She walks in beauty. by Dawn Powell. (Hoyt) 4:108 Ap7'28. B 16602
The she-wolf. (Mosher) 7:69-70* Je6'31. CC 16603
The shelf. by Dorrance Davis. (Brackett) 2:34 O9'26. T 16604
The sheltered life. by Ellen Glasgow. (Coates) 8:44 Ag27'32. B 16605
Sherlock Holmes. by William Gillette and Arthur Conan Doyle. (Benchley) 5:40 D7'29. T 16606
Sherman, fighting prophet. by Lloyd Lewis. (Coates) 8:95 D3 '32. B 16607
Sherman: soldier, realist, American. by B. H. Liddell Hart. (Gannett) 5:137 D14'29. B 16608
Sherwood Anderson's notebook. by Sherwood Anderson. (Dounce) 2:65 My22'26. B 16609
She's my baby. by Guy Bolton; Bert Kalmar and Harry Ruby. (Brackett) 3:24 Ja14'28. T 16610
Shining scabbard. by R. C. Hutchinson. (Fadiman) 12:54-5*D26 '36. B 16611
The shining hour. (Mosher) 14: 51*Ja28'39. CC 16612
The shining hour. by Keith Winter. (Benchley) 10:28-30 F24 '34. T 16613
A ship comes in. by Joseph Anthony. (Gibbs) 10:28 S29'34. T 16614
The ship from Shanghai. (Mosher) 6:98 My3'30. CC 16615
Shipwreck in Europe. by Josef Bard. (Hoyt) 4:95-6 Mr24'28. B 16616
The shoals of honour. by Elizabeth Sanxay Holding. (Dounce) 2:64 Ap17'26. B 16617
The shock punch. (Anon.) 1:31 My 23'25. CC 16618
The shoemaker's holiday. by Thomas Dekker. (Benchley) 13: 32*Ja8'38. T 16619
Shoot the works. (Mosher) 10:60 Jy14'34. CC 16620
Shoot the works. by Heywood Broun and Milton Raison. (White) 7:28-9 Ag1'31. T 16621
Shooting star. by Noel Pierce and Bernard C. Schoenfeld. (White) 9:24-6 Je24'33. T 16622
The shop around the corner. (Mosher) 15:49*Ja27'40. CC 16623
The shopworn angel. (Mosher) 4: 61 Ja12'29. CC 16624
The shopworn angel. (Mosher) 14: 49*Jy9'38. CC 16625
Shore leave. (Shane) 1:22 S19'25. CC 16626
Short as any dream. by Elizabeth Shepley Sergeant. (Smith) 5:128 O19'29. B 16627
A short history of Julia. by Isa Glenn. (Smith) 6:88 N29'30. B 16628
A short introduction to the history of human stupidity. by Walter B. Pitkin. (Coates) 8:66*Ap23 '32. B 16629
Short stories, scraps and shavings. by George Bernard Shaw. (Fadiman) 10:90-1 Je2'34. B 16630
The shortest night. by G. B. Stern. (Coates) 7:59*Jy25'31. B 16631
Should ladies behave. (Mosher) 9:49 D23'33. CC 16632
The show. (Claxton) 3:83 Mr19'27. CC 16633
Show boat. (Mosher) 5:63-4 Ap27 '29. CC 16634
Show boat. (Mosher) 12:67-9*My 23'36. CC 16635
Show boat. by Edna Ferber. (Dounce) 2:60-1 S4'26. B 16636

Show boat. by Oscar Hammerstein, II and Jerome Kern. (Brackett) 3:25-6 Ja7'28. T 16637
Show boat. by Jerome Kern and Oscar Hammerstein, II. (Benchley) 8:26 My28'32. T 16638
Show business. by Thyra Samter Winslow. (Dounce) 2:60 Mr20 '26. B 16639
Show girl. by William Anthony McGuire and George Gershwin. (Brackett) 5:46 Jy13'29. T 16640
The show is on. by Vincente Minnelli, et al. (Benchley) 12:26-8*Ja2'37. T 16641
Show of shows. (Mosher) 5:90-1 N30'29. CC 16642
The show-off. (Claxton) 2:36 Ag 28'26. CC 16643
The show-off. (Mosher) 10:89 Mr 24'34. CC 16644
Show people. (Mosher) 4:95 N17 '28. CC 16645
Show them no mercy! (Mosher) 11:93*D14'35. CC 16646
The Shrewsbury edition of the works of Samuel Butler. by Samuel Butler; Henry Festing Jones, ed. and A. T. Bartholomew, ed. (Boyd) 3:86-8 My 28'27. B 16647
Shuffle along of 1933. by Flournoy E. Miller. (Benchley) 8:30 Ja7'33. T 16648
Shule agra. by Kathleen Coyle. (Boyd) 3:108 Ap16'27. B 16649
The sidewalks of New York. by Eddie Dowling and Jimmy Hanley. (Brackett) 3:34 O15'27. T 16650
Siege. (F. J. S.) 1:16 Je27'25. CC 16651
Siegfried. (Hays) 1:30 F28'25. CC 16652
Siegfried. (F.J.S.) 1:15 Je13'25. CC 16653
Siegfried. (Shane) 1:17 S5'25. CC 16654
Siegfried. by Jean Giraudoux. (Benchley) 6:34 D13'30. T16655
The sign of the cross. (Mosher) 8:85 D10'32. CC 16656
The sign of the leopard. by Edgar Wallace. (Brackett) 4:30 D22'28. T 16657
Silas Crockett. by Mary Ellen Chase. (Fadiman) 11:85-6* N23'35. B 16658
Silence. (Claxton) 2:55 My29'26. CC 16659
The silent enemy. (Mosher) 6:96 My24'30. CC 16660
The silent house. by John G. Brandon and George Pickett. (Brackett) 3:25 F18'28. T 16661
The silent witness. by Jack DeLeon and Jack Celestin. (Parker) 7:32-4 Ap4'31. T 16662
Silken shackles. (Claxton) 2:56 My29'26. CC 16663
The silver box. by John Galsworthy. (Brackett) 3:25 Ja28 '28. T 16664
The silver cord. (Mosher) 9:64 My13'33. CC 16665
The silver cord. by Sidney Howard. (Brackett) 2:23 Ja1'27. T 16666
Silver dollar. (Mosher) 8:40 D31 '32. CC 16667
The silver spoon. by John Galsworthy. (Dounce) 2:49-50 Ag14 '26. B 16668
The silver stallion. by James Branch Cabell. (Dounce) 2:59-60 My8'26. B 16669
The silver tassie. by Sean O'Casey. (Benchley) 5:36-8 N9 '29. T 16670
The silver Virgin. by Ida A. R. Wylie. (Lowrie) 4:92 F16'29. B 16671
Simba. (Claxton) 3:65 F4'28. CC 16672
Simon Girty. by Thomas Boyd. (Lowrie) 4:73 Ja26'29. B 16673
Simonetta Perkins. by L. P. Hartley. (Dounce) 2:86-7 Je5'26. B 16674
Simple Simon. by Ed Wynn; Guy Bolton; Richard Rodgers and

Lorenz Hart. (Benchley) 6:27 Mr1'30. T 16675
The simpleton of the Unexpected Isles. by George Bernard Shaw. (Benchley) 11:26†Mr2'35. T 16676
The sin of Madelon Claudet. (Mosher) 7:79-81 N7'31. CC 16677
Since Ibsen. by George Jean Nathan. (Coates) 9:67-8 Ap15 '33. B 16678
Since yesterday. by Frederick Lewis Allen. (Fadiman) 15:77 F10'40. B 16679
Sing and like it. (Mosher) 10:92 Ap21'34. CC 16680
Sing and whistle. by Milton Herbert Gropper. (Benchley) 10:30 F17'34. T 16681
Sing, baby, sing. (Mosher) 12:67* S26'36. CC 16682
Sing for your supper. by Harold Hecht, et al. (Gibbs) 15:30*My 6'39. T 16683
Sing high, sing low. by David Boehm and Murdock Pemberton. (Benchley) 7:30 N21'31. T 16684
Sing me a love song. (Mosher) 12:50*Ja2'37. CC 16685
Sing out the news. by Charles Friedman and Harold Rome. (Gibbs) 14:28*O1'38. T 16686
Singermann. by Myron Brinig. (Smith) 5:88 S7'29. B 16687
Singin' the blues. by John McGowan. (Benchley) 7:34 O3'31. T 16688
The singing fool. (Mosher) 4:77-8 S29'28. CC 16689
The single standard. (Mosher) 5:38-9 Ag3'29. CC 16690
Sinner. by Thompson Buchanan. (Brackett) 3:33-4 F26'27. T 16691
Sinners' holiday. (Mosher) 6:92 O18'30. CC 16692
Sinners in Summertime. by Sigurd Hoel. (Smith) 6:58-9 Jy26 '30. B 16693
Sins of man. (Mosher) 12:61*Je 27'36. CC 16694
Sins of the fathers. (Mosher) 4:78 F2'29. CC 16695
Sir Billy Howe. by Bellamy Partridge. (Coates) 8:72*Ap9'32. B 16696
Sir Francis Bacon. by Byron Steel. (Smith) 5:74 F1'30. B 16697
Sir! she said. by Alec Waugh. (Smith) 6:102 O18'30. B 16698
Sirocco. by Ralph Bates. (Fadiman) 14:72*F11'39. B 16699
The sisters. (Mosher) 14:62-3* O15'38. C 16700
The sisters. by Myron Brinig. (Fadiman) 12:62-3*F6'37. B 16701
Six characters in search of an author. by Luigi Pirandello. (Benchley) 7:30-2 Ap25'31. T 16702
Six hours to live. (Mosher) 8:60 O29'32. CC 16703
Six Mrs. Greenes. by Lorna Rea. (Lowrie) 5:108-109 Ap27'29. B 16704
Six of a kind. (Mosher) 10:87 Mr 17'34. CC 16705
6000 enemies. (Mosher) 15:76*Je 17'39. CC 16706
Sixty glorious years. (Mosher) 14:73-4*N26'38. CC 16707
Skerrett. by Liam O'Flaherty. (Coates) 8:74 O15'32. B 16708
Sketch of a sinner. by Frank Swinnerton. (Smith) 5:129 O19 '29. B 16709
Skidding. by Aurania Rouverol. (Brackett) 4:52 Je2'28. T 16710
Skin and bones. by Thorne Smith. (Fadiman) 9:49 D30'33. B 16711
Skin-deep. by Naomi Royde-Smith. (Boyd) 2:79-80 Ja29'27. B 16712
Skin deep. by Lynn Starling. (Brackett) 3:29 O29'27. T 16713
Skinner steps out. (Mosher) 5:76 D14'29. CC 16714
Skippy. (Mosher) 7:99 Ap11'31. CC 16715

The sky but not the heart. by R. L. Duffus. (Anon.) 12:49-50* Ag15'36. B 16716

Sky devils. (Mosher) 8:55-6*Mr12 '32. CC 16717

The sky hawk. (Mosher) 5:73-5 D21'29. CC 16718

The sky rocket. (Shane) 1:40 Ja 30'26. CC 16719

Skylark. by Samson Raphaelson. (Gibbs) 15:30*O21'39. T 16720

Skyscraper. (Claxton) 4:91-2 Ap 14'28. CC 16721

Skyscraper souls. (Mosher) 8:37 Ag13'32. CC 16722

The sky's the limit! by Pierce Johns and Hendrik Booraem. (Benchley) 10:28-30†D29'34. T 16723

Skyward. by Richard E. Byrd. (Markey) 4:95 Ap28'28. B 16724

A slave of fashion. (Shane) 1:17 Ag1'25. CC 16725

Slave ship. (Mosher) 13:64*Je26 '37. CC 16726

Slaves all. by Edward Percy. (Brackett) 2:36 D18'26. T 16727

A sleeping clergyman. by James Bridie. (Benchley) 10:32-4 O 20'34. T 16728

The sleeping fury. by Louise Bogan. (Fadiman) 13:84-5*Mr 20'37. B 16729

Slide Kelly slide. (Claxton) 3:88-9 Ap2'27. CC 16730

A slight case of murder. (Mosher) 14:47*Mr5'38. CC 16731

A slight case of murder. by Howard Lindsay and Damon Runyon. (Gibbs) 11:32*S21'35. T 16732

Slightly scarlet. (Mosher) 6:97 Mr8'30. CC 16733

Slim. by William Wister Haines. (Fadiman) 10:54-7 Ag4'34. B 16734

The slower Judas. by G. B. Stern. (Lowrie) 4:87 F2'29. B 16735

The slums of Berlin. (Claxton) 2:68 Ja29'27. CC 16736

Small miracle. by Norman Krasna. (Gibbs) 10:34 O6'34. T 16737

The smart set. (Claxton) 4:63 Mr 10'28. CC 16738

A smattering of ignorance. by Oscar Levine. (Fadiman) 15: 54-6*Ja13'36. B 16739

Smile, brother, smile. (Claxton) 3:89 S10'27. CC 16740

Smiles. by William Anthony McGuire, et al. (Benchley) 6:33-4 N29'30. T 16741

The smiling lieutenant. (Mosher) 7:60*My30'31. CC 16742

Smirt: an urbane nightmare. by James Branch Cabell. (Fadiman) 10:100-101 Mr10'34. B 16743

The snake pit. by Sigrid Undset. (Lowrie) 4:72-3 Ja26'29. B 16744

Snakes of the world. by Raymond L. Ditmars. (Coates) 7:89 N21 '31. B 16745

The snare of the fowler. by Gerald Bullett. (Anon.) 12:64*O24 '36. B 16746

Snow White and the seven dwarfs. (Gibbs) 13:30*F5'38. CC 16747

Snow White and the seven dwarfs. (Mosher) 13:52*Ja15'38. CC 16748

The snows of Helicon. by H. M. Tomlinson. (Fadiman) 9:46 Ag 12'33. B 16749

So big. (Mosher) 8:63*My7'32. CC 16750

So many paths. by Irving Kaye Davis. (Benchley) 10:34-6†D15 '34. T 16751

So proudly we hail. by Joseph M. Viertel. (Gibbs) 12:28*O3'36. T 16752

So red the rose. (Mosher) 11:73-4*N30'35. CC 16753

So red the rose. by Stark Young. (Fadiman) 10:57 Jy28'34. B 16754

So this is Paris. (Claxton) 2:35-6 Ag21'26. CC 16755

So was Napoleon. by Jack O'Donnell and John Wray. (Benchley) 5:32-5 Ja18'30. T 16756

Sob sister. (Mosher) 7:79-81 O10

'31. CC 16757
Sober feast. by Barbara Blackburn. (Smith) 5:123 O12'29. B 16758
A social celebrity. (Shane) 2:51 Ap24'26. CC 16759
The social highwayman. (Shane) 2:37 Je19'26. CC 16760
The social lion. (Mosher) 6:79-80 Je21'30. CC 16761
The social register. by Anita Loos and John Emerson. (Benchley) 7:30 N21'31. T 16762
Soft cushions. (Claxton) 3:79 S17 '27. CC 16763
The soft spot. by A. S. M. Hutchinson. (Fadiman) 9:46 Ag12'33. B 16764
Soil. (Mosher) 6:94 O25'30. CC 16765
Sold out to the future. by Roy Helton. (Fadiman) 10:64*Ja12 '35. B 16766
The soldier and the lady. (Mosher) 13:65*Ap17'37. CC 16767
Soldiers and women. by Paul Hervey Fox and George Tilton. (Benchley) 5:40 S14'29. T 16768
Soldier's pay. by William Faulkner. (Dounce) 2:54 Ap3'26. B 16769
Solid South. by Lawton Campbell. (Benchley) 6:36 O25'30. T 16770
The somber flame. by Samuel Rogers. (Boyd) 3:96-7 My7'27. B 16771
Some do not . . . by Ford Madox Ford. (Dounce) 1:26 F28'25. B 16772
Some folks won't work. by Clinch Calkins. (Coates) 6:114 N8'30. B 16773
Some other beauty. by Ida A. R. Wylie. (Smith) 6:115 My17'30. B 16774
Some people. by Harold Nicholson. (Boyd) 3:90-1 S17'27. B 16775
Something about Eve. by James Branch Cabell. (Parker) 3:94-5 O29'27. B 16776
Something always happens. (Claxton) 4:92 My26'28. CC 16777
Something gay. by Adelaide Heilbron. (Gibbs) 11:34*My11'35. T 16778
Something more important. by H. F. Maltby. (Gibbs) 11:32*Jy 20'35. T 16779
Something of myself for my friends known and unknown. by Rudyard Kipling. (Fadiman) 13:70*Mr6'37. B 16780
Something to brag about. by Edgar Selwyn and William Le Baron. (Anon.) 1:15 Ag22'25. T 16781
Something to sing about. (Mosher) 13:65*S25'37. CC 16782
The Somme. (Mosher) 4:125 D8 '28. CC 16783
The son of Marietta. by Johan Fabricius. (Fadiman) 11:67-8* Ja11'36. B 16784
The son of the Grand Eunuch. by Charles Pettit. (Boyd) 3:54 Jy 30'27. B 16785
The son of the sheik. (Claxton) 2:34 Jy31'26. CC 16786
Son of woman. by John Middleton Murry. (Coates) 7:87-8 My 16'31. B 16787
Song o' my heart. (Mosher) 6:61 Mr22'30. CC 16788
The song of songs. (Mosher) 9:44 Jy29'33. CC 16789
Song of the flame. by Otto Harbach; Oscar Hammerstein, II and George Gershwin. (Mankiewicz) 1:20 Ja9'26. T 16790
Song of the wheatfields. by Ferenc Móra. (Coates) 6:114-15 N8'30. B 16791
The song of the world. by Jean Giono. (Fadiman) 13:53-4*Ag 21'37. B 16792
Song on your bugles. by Eric Knight. (Fadiman) 13:61-2*Ag 14'37. B 16793
The song writer. by Crane Wilbur. (White) 4:32 Ag25'28. T 16794
The sonnets of Petrarch. by

Francesco Petrarca and Joseph Auslander, trans. (Bogan) 7:63 F13'32. B 16795
Sons o' guns. by Fred Thompson and Jack Donahue. (Benchley) 5:39 D7'29. T 16796
Sons of the puritans. by Don Marquis. (Fadiman) 15:69-70* F18'39. B 16797
Sophie Lang goes West. (Mosher) 13:67*O9'37. CC 16798
Sorrell and son. (Claxton) 3:99-101 N19'27. CC 16799
The sorrows of Satan. (Claxton) 2:66 O23'26. CC 16800
So's your old man. (Claxton) 2: 77-8 N6'26. CC 16801
The soul enchanted. by Romain Rolland. (Boyd) 3:113 Ap30'27. B 16802
Soul-fire. (Anon.) 1:31 My9'25. CC 16803
Soul mates. (Shane) 1:31 Ja9'26. CC 16804
Souls at sea. (Mosher) 13:51*Ag 21'37. CC 16805
The sound and the fury. by William Faulkner. (Smith) 5:116-18 N16'29. B 16806
The sound wagon. by T. S. Stribling. (Fadiman) 11:52-3*Ja4 '36. B 16807
Sounding brass. by Ethel Mannin. (Dounce) 2:46 Jy24'26. B 16808
Soundings. by Arthur Hamilton Gibbs. (Anon.) 1:28 Mr28'25. B 16809
Sour grapes. by Vincent Lawrence. (Brackett) 2:31 S18'26. T 16810
Sous les toits de Paris. (Mosher) 6:29 D27'30. CC 16811
South. by Frederick Wright. (Fadiman) 11:72*S14'35. B 16812
South Sea Rose. (Mosher) 5:74-6 D14'29. CC 16813
Southern charm. by Isa Glenn. (Hoyt) 3:80 Ja7'28. B 16814
Southways. by Erskine Caldwell. (Kronenberger) 14:56*Je25'38. B 16815
The Spanish earth. (Mosher) 13: 51-2*Ag21'37. CC 16816
Spanish prelude. by Jenny Ballou. (Fadiman) 13:84*Mr20'37. B 16817
Sparken broke. by Charles Morgan. (Fadiman) 12:70-2*Ap18 '36. B 16818
Sparrows. (Claxton) 2:59 S25'26. CC 16819
Speak easily. (Mosher) 8:38 Ag27 '32. CC 16820
Special agent. (Mosher) 11:64*S28 '35. CC 16821
Special delivery. by James Branch Cabell. (Coates) 9:55 Mr25'33. B 16822
The speckled band. (Mosher) 7:81 N14'31. CC 16823
The specter. by Maxim Gorky. (Fadiman) 14:75-6*Ap9'38. B 16824
Speedy. (Claxton) 4:91 Ap14'28. CC 16825
Spell against death. by Harold Lewis Cook. (Bogan) 9:48 Jy15 '33. B 16826
Spellbound. by Frank Vosper. (Brackett) 3:34 N26'27. T 16827
Spendthrift. (Maloney) 12:39*Ag1 '36. CC 16828
The sphinx. (Mosher) 9:42 Jy15 '33. CC 16829
The spider. by Fulton Oursler and Lowell Brentano. (Brackett) 3:33-4 Ap2'27. T 16830
The spinner of the years. by Phyllis Bentley. (Lowrie) 5: 108 Mr16'29. B 16831
The spirit of America. by William Edwin Rudge. (Smith) 6:77-8 S6'30. B 16832
The spirit of Notre Dame. (Mosher) 7:69 O24'31. CC 16833
Spitfire. (Mosher) 10:87 Mr17'34. CC 16834
Spook house. by Joe Byron Totten. (Benchley) 6:26 Je14'30. T 16835
Spooks. by Robert J. Sherman. (Mankiewicz) 1:15 Je13'25. T 16836
$port$. by John R. Tunis. (Leo-

nard) 4:95-6 O27'28. B 16837
Sporting goods. (Claxton) 4:70 F25'28. CC 16838
Spread eagle. by George S. Brooks and Walter B. Lister. (Brackett) 3:33 Ap16'27. T 16839
Spring dance. by Eleanor Golden; Eloise Barrangon and Philip Barry. (Gibbs) 12:26*S5'36. T 16840
Spring fever. by Vincent Lawrence. (Mankiewicz) 1:13 Ag15 '25. T 16841
Spring freshet. by Owen Davis. (Benchley) 10:38 O13'34. T 16842
Spring in Autumn. by Gregorio Martinez Sierra; Blanche Yurka, adapt. and Nene Belmonte, adapt. (Benchley) 9:26-8 N4 '33. T 16843
Spring is here. by Owen Davis; Richard Rodgers and Lorenz Hart. (Brackett) 5:28 Mr23'29. T 16844
Spring madness. (Mosher) 14:101* D3'38. CC 16845
Spring meeting. by M. J. Farrell and John Perry. (Benchley) 14:28-30*D17'38. T 16846
Spring of youth. by Wyn Griffith. (Fadiman) 11:50*Ag17'35. B 16847
Spring song. by Virginia Farmer. (Brackett) 3:24 D31'27. T 16848
Spring song. by Bella Spewack and Samuel Spewack. (Gibbs) 10:40 O13'34. T 16849
Spring storm. by Alvin Johnson. (Fadiman) 12:68*Ap28'36. B 16850
The springboard. by Alice Duer Miller. (Brackett) 3:29 O22'27. T 16851
Springboard. by Robert Wolf. (Boyd) 3:104-105 Ap2'27. B 16852
Springtime for Henry. by Benn W. Levy. (White) 7:30 D19'31. T 16853
The squall. (Mosher) 5:108 My18 '29. CC 16854
The squall. by Jean Bart. (Brackett) 2:34 N20'26. T 16855
Square crooks. by James P. Judge. (Gabriel) 2:22 Mr13'26. T 16856
Squaring the circle. by Valentine Kataev. (Benchley) 11:30*O12 '35. T 16857
The squealer. by Mark Linder. (Brackett) 4:36 N24'28. T 16858
Stagecoach. (Mosher) 15:64*Mr4 '39. CC 16859
Stage door. (Mosher) 13:67*O9 '37. CC 16860
Stage door. by George S. Kaufman and Edna Ferber. (Benchley) 12:26*O31'36. T 16861
Stalin. by Isaac Don Levine. (Coates) 7:77-8*Je6'31. B 16862
Stalin. by Boris Souvarine. (Fadiman) 15:66-8*S16'39. B 16863
Stamboul quest. (Mosher) 10:56 Jy 21'34. CC 16864
The stammering century. by Gilbert Seldes. (Leonard) 4:103 S15'28. B 16865
Stand-in. (Mosher) 13:88*N20'37. CC 16866
Stand up and cheer. (Mosher) 10: 89 Ap28'34. CC 16867
Stanley and Livingston. (Maloney) 15:47-8 *Ag12'39. CC 16868
Star-begotten. by H. G. Wells. (Fadiman) 13:66-7*Je12'37. B 16869
The star-gazer. by Zsolt de Harsanyi. (Fadiman) 15:68 F3'40. B 16870
A star is born. (Mosher) 13:63* My1'37. CC 16871
The star maker. (Mosher) 15:51* S2'39. CC 16872
Star of midnight. (Mosher) 11:71-2*Ap20'35. CC 16873
Star spangled. by Robert Ardrey. (Benchley) 12:24*Mr21'36. T 16874
The star spangled manner. by Beverley Nichols. (Leonard) 4:95 O27'28. B 16875

The star-wagon. by Maxwell Anderson. (Gibbs) 13:28*O9'37. T 16876
The star witness. (Mosher) 7:42-43*Ag15'31. CC 16877
Stark love. (Claxton) 3:77-8 Mr5 '27. CC 16878
Starlight. by Gladys Unger. (Anon.) 1:13 Mr14'25. T 16879
The starling. by Doris Leslie. (Boyd) 3:89 My28'27. B 16880
Stars fell on Alabama. by Carl Carmer. (Fadiman) 10:67-9 Je 30'34. B 16881
The stars in their courses. by James Jeans. (Coates) 7:92-3 Ap18'31. B 16882
Stars in your eyes. by J. P. Mc Evoy. (Benchley) 15:28*F18'39. T 16883
The stars look down. by A. J. Cronin. (Fadiman) 11:65-6*S 14'35. B 16884
The start of the road. by John Erskine. (Fadiman) 14:81-2*O 22'38. B 16885
Starting point. by Cecil Day-Lewis. (Anon.) 14:62 F19'38. B 16886
State fair. (Mosher) 8:53 F4'33. CC 16887
State fair. by Phillip D. Stong. (Coates) 8:69-70*My7'32. B 16888
State Street Sadie. (Claxton) 4:91-2 S15'28. CC 16889
State's attorney. (Mosher) 8:51* My14'32. CC 16890
Staying with relations. by Rose Macaulay. (Smith) 6:80 N1'30. B 16891
Steamboat Bill, Jr. (Claxton) 4: 83 My19'28. CC 16892
Steamboat round the bend. (Mosher) 11:63*S28'35. CC 16893
Stella Dallas. (Shane) 1:26 N28'25. CC 16894
Stella Dallas. (Maloney) 13:49*Jy 31'37. CC 16895
Stepdaughters of the war. by Kenyon Nicholson. (Benchley) 6:34 O18'30. T 16896
Stephen Escott. by Ludwig Lewisohn. (Smith) 6:98 Mr22'30. B 16897
Stepping high. by Gene Markey. (Lowrie) 5:116 Mr23'29. B 16898
Stepping out. by Elmer Harris. (Brackett) 5:28-30 Je1'29. T 16899
Stepping sisters. by Howard Warren Comstock. (Benchley) 6:30-2 My3'30. T 16900
Steps going down. by John T. McIntyre. (Fadiman) 12:62-4* S5'36. B 16901
(Bogan) 14:56-8*Jy23'38. 16902
Stevedore. by Paul Peters and George Sklar. (Benchley) 10: 30 Ap28'34. T 16903
Still waters. by Augustus Thomas. (Gabriel) 2:22 Mr13'26. T 16904
Stolen heaven. (Mosher) 7:61-3 F 21'31. CC 16905
Stolen heaven. (Mosher) 14:56*My 21'38. CC 16906
Stolen life. (Mosher) 15:75*Je17 '39. CC 16907
Stone Daugherty. by John P. Fort. (Lowrie) 5:103-104 My11'29. B 16908
Stop-over. by Matt Taylor and Sam Taylor. (Benchley) 13:28-30*Ja22'38. T 16909
The store. by T. S. Stribling. (Coates) 8:39 Jy2'32. B 16910
Stories of three decades. by Thomas Mann and H. T. Lowe-Porter trans. (Fadiman) 12:64-5*Je6 '36. B 16911
The stork is dead. by Frederic Hatton and Fanny Hatton. (White) 8:28 O1'32. T 16912
Storm at daybreak. (Mosher) 9: 44 Jy29'33. CC 16913
Storm in a teacup. (Mosher) 14: 57*Mr19'38. CC 16914
Storm over Asia. (Mosher) 6:89-90 S13'30. CC 16915
Storm over Patsy. by Bruno Frank. (Benchley) 13:36*Mr20 '37. T 16916
Storm over the Constitution. by Irving Brant. (Anon.) 12:55*Jy

11'36. B 16917

The story of a cheat. (Mosher) 14:48*O1'38. CC 16918

The story of a lake. by Negley Farson. (Fadiman) 15:61*F25 '39. B 16919

The story of a wonder man. by Ring W. Lardner. (Boyd) 3: 105 Mr26'27. B 16920

The story of Irving Berlin. by Alexander Woollcott. (Anon.) 1:26 Ap4'25. B 16921

The story of Louis Pasteur. (Mosher) 12:65*F22'36. CC 16922

Story of philosophy. by Will Durant. (Dounce) 2:57 Je26'26. B 16923

The story of San Michele. by Axel Munthe. (Gannett) 5:138 D14'29. B 16924

The story of surgury. by Harvey Graham. (Fadiman) 15:62-4* S9'39. B 16925

The story of surnames. by William Dodgson Bowman. (Coates) 7:50 Ag29'31. B 16926

The story of Temple Drake. (Mosher) 9:63-4 My13'33. CC 16927

The story of the Borgias. by Lacy Collison-Morley. (Coates) 9:71 My20'33. B 16928

The story of Vernon and Irene Castle. (Mosher) 15:69-70*Ap 8'39. CC 16929

A story-teller's holiday. by George Moore. (Coates) 7:69-70 F21'31. B 16930

Stowaway. (Mosher) 12:49*D26'36. CC 16931

Straight is the way. (Mosher) 10: 88 S8'34. CC 16932

Straight, place, and show. (Mosher) 14:55-6*O8'38. CC 16933

Straight thru the door. by William Hodge. (Brackett) 4:33 O 13'28. T 16934

Stranded. (Mosher) 11:54-5*Je29 '35. CC 16935

Stranded in Paris. (Claxton) 2:83 D18'26. CC 16936

Strange bedfellows. by Don Herold. (Hellman) 6:94-5 Ap26'30. B 16937

The strange case of Captain Ramper. (Claxton) 4:80 Je9'28. CC 16938

The strange case of Miss Annie Spragg. by Louis Bromfield. (Parker) 4:87-8 S29'28. B 16939

Strange fugitive. by Morley Callaghan. (Leonard) 4:80-1 S8'28. B 16940

Strange houses. by Cora Jarrett. (Anon.) 12:66 Je27'36. B 16941

Strange interlude. (Mosher) 8:43 S3'32. CC 16942

Strange interlude. by Eugene O'Neill. (Brackett) 3:24 F11'28; 4:26 D29'28. T 16943

Strange woman. by Elmer Davis. (Boyd) 3:92-3 S17'27. B 16944

Strangers and lovers. by Edwin Granberry. (Markey) 4:98 Ap 14'28. B 16945

Strangers at home. by Charles Divine. (Gibbs) 10:34 S22'34. T 16946

The stranger's return. (Mosher) 9:40 Ag5'33. CC 16947

Stranger's return. by Phillip D. Stong. (Fadiman) 9:50-1 Jy8 '33. B 16948

The straw hat review. by Max Liebman, et al. (Gibbs) 15:30-2*O7'39. T 16949

The strawberry blonde. by Martin Brown. (Brackett) 3:34 F26 '27. T 16950

Street angel. (Claxton) 4:91-3 Ap 21'28. CC 16951

The street of chains. by Lillian Lauferty. (Smith) 5:126-7 N9 '29. B 16952

Street of chance. (Mosher) 5:77-9 F8'30. CC 16953

The street of forgotten men. (Shane) 1:17 Ag1'25. CC 16954

The street of sin. (Claxton) 4:79-80 Je9'28. CC 16955

The street of the fishing cat. by Jolán Földes. (Fadiman) 12:

53-5*Ja2'37. B 16956
Street scene. (Gibbs) 7:53-4 S5 '31. CC 16957
Street scene. by Elmer Rice. (Brackett) 4:26-8 Ja19'29. T 16958
(Benchley) 6:28 Ap19'30. 16959
The streets of New York. by Dion Boucicault. (Benchley) 7:28 O 17'31. T 16960
Streets of Paris. by Charles Sherman, et al. (Gibbs) 15:28* Jy1'39. T 16961
Stretchers. by Frederick A. Pottle. (Smith) 5:121 N2'29. B 16962
The stricken deer. by David Cecil. (Hellman) 6:102 My3'30. B 16963
Strictly dishonorable. by Preston Sturges. (Benchley) 5:34-6 S28 '29. T 16964
Strictly dynamite. (Mosher) 10: 60 Jy14'34. CC 16965
Stride of man. by Thames Williamson. (Lowrie) 4:59 D29'28. B 16966
Strike! by Mary Heaton Vorse. (Smith) 6:96 N15'30. B 16967
Strike me pink. (Mosher) 11:55* Ja25'36. CC 16968
Strike me pink. by Lew Brown and Ray Henderson. (Benchley) 9:24-6 Mr18'33. T 16969
Strike up the band. by Morrie Ryskind; Ira Gershwin and George Gershwin. (Benchley) 5:27-8 Ja25'30. T 16970
Strip girl. by Henry Rosendahl. (Benchley) 11:32*O26'35. T 16971
Stroke of luck. by Arnold Bennett. (Coates) 8:65 Je4'32. B 16972
The strong man. (Claxton) 2:50-1 S18'26. CC 16973
A strong man's house. by Lee Wilson Dodd. (Benchley) 5:36 S28'29. T 16974
Stronger than love. by Dario Niccodemi. (Mankiewicz) 1:19-20 Ja16'26. T 16975
The struggle. (Mosher) 7:74 D19 '31. CC 16976
Struggles and triumphs, or the life of P. T. Barnum. by George S. Bryan, ed. (Boyd) 3:87-8 Je18'27. B 16977
The student prince in old Heidelberg. (Claxton) 3:83 O1'27. CC 16978
A study in scarlet. (Mosher) 9: 60-1 Je10'33. CC 16979
Stürme der leidenschaft. (Mosher) 8:52*Mr26'32. CC 16980
Submarine. (Claxton) 4:90-1 S15 '28. CC 16981
Substitute for murder. by William Jourdan Rapp and Leonardo Bercovici. (Benchley) 11:30* N2'35. T 16982
The subway. by Elmer Rice. (Brackett) 4:23-4 F9'29. T 16983
Subway Sadie. (Claxton) 2:50 S18 '26. CC 16984
Success. by Lion Feuchtwanger. (Smith) 6:112 N8'30. B 16985
Success story. by John Howard Lawson. (White) 8:26 O8'32. T 16986
Such is life. by Peter Glenny and Marie Armstrong Hecht. (Long) 3:72-3 S10'27. T 16987
Such men are dangerous. (Mosher) 6:95 Mr15'30. CC 16988
Sucker's progress. by Herbert Asbury. (Fadiman) 14:97-8* N12'38. B 16989
Suez. (Mosher) 14:56*O22'38. CC 16990
Summer bachelors. (Claxton) 2:59 D25'26. CC 16991
Summer night. by Vicki Baum and Benjamin Glazer. (Gibbs) 15: 25*N11'39. T 16992
Summer storm. by Frank Swinnerton. (Dounce) 2:80 O16'26. B 16993
Summer time ends. by John Hargrave. (Fadiman) 11:77-80*O5 '35. B 16994
Summer will show. by Sylvia Townsend Warner. (Kronenberger) 12:48-9 *Jy4

'36. B 16995
Summers night. by Sylvia Thompson. (Coates) 7:55 Ja30'32. B 16996
The summing up. by W. Somerset Maugham. (Fadiman) 14: 66*Mr26'38. B 16997
The sun also rises. by Ernest Hemingway. (Dounce) 2:88-90 N20'26. B 16998
(Parker) 3:92-3 O29'27. 16999
Sun and moon. by Vincent H. Gowen. (Boyd) 3:90 Je18'27. B 17000
The sun cure. by Alfred Noyes. (Smith) 5:70 Ag17'29. B 17001
The sun in splendor. by Thomas Burke. (Dounce) 2:79-80 O23 '26. B 17002
Sun kissed. by Raymond Van Sickle. (Benchley) 13:34*Mr20 '37. T 17003
The sun never sets. (Mosher) 15: 74-5*Je10'39. CC 17004
Sunday nights at nine. by Catherine Bammen, et al. (Benchley) 10:34 My5'34; 10:38†D1 '34. T 17005
Sunny. by Jerome Kern; Otto Harbach and Oscar Hammerstein, II. (Mankiewicz) 1:20 O3'25. T 17006
Sunny days. by Clifford Grey and William Cary Duncan. (Brackett) 3:26 F18'28. T 17007
Sunny side up. (Mosher) 5:62 O12 '29. CC 17008
Sunrise. (Claxton) 3:81-3 O1'27. CC 17009
Sunset gun. by Dorothy Parker. (White) 4:88-9 Je9'28. B 17010
Sunshine. by Henry C. White. (Brackett) 2:39 Ag28'26. T 17011
Super-sleuth. (Mosher) 13:64*Jy 24'37. CC 17012
Susan and God. by Rachel Crothers. (Gibbs) 13:28*O16'37. T 17013
Susan Lenox. (Mosher) 7:68-9 O 24'31. CC 17014
Susan Spray. by Sheila Kaye-Smith. (Coates) 7:84 S12 '31. B 17015
Suspense. by Joseph Conrad. (Dounce) 1:18 S26'25. B 17016
Suspense. by Patrick MacGill. (A. Gibbs) 6:82-3 My10'30. T 17017
(Brackett) 6:24-6 Ag23'30. 17018
Sutter's gold. (Mosher) 12:72*Ap 4'36. CC 17019
Suwannee River. by Cecil H. Matschat. (Fadiman) 14:46*Ag6'38. B 17020
Suzy. (Maloney) 12:39*Ag1'36. CC 17021
Svengali. (Mosher) 7:77-8 My9'31. CC 17022
The swan. (Hays) 1:27 Mr14'25. CC 17023
Swan song. by John Galsworthy. (Leonard) 4:64 Jy21'28. B 17024
Swanee River. (Mosher) 15:51* Ja6'40. CC 17025
Swear by the night. by Nathalia Crane. (Bogan) 12:73*F22'36. B 17026
Sweden, land of the Vikings. (Mosher) 9:79 Ja13'34. CC 17027
Sweepstakes. (Mosher) 7:47*Jy4 '31. CC 17028
Sweet Adeline. (Mosher) 10:34*D 22'34. CC 17029
Sweet Adeline. by Oscar Hammerstein, II and Jerome Kern. (Benchley) 5:38-40 S14'29. T 17030
Sweet aloes. by Jay Mallory. (Benchley) 12:28*Mr14'36. T 17031
Sweet and low. by David Freedman. (Benchley) 6:36 D6'30. T 17032
Sweet land of liberty. by Philip Dunning. (Benchley) 5:38 O5'29. T 17033
Sweet man. by Gilmore Millen. (Smith) 6:70-1 Je28'30. B 17034
Sweet music. (Mosher) 11:55-6* Mr2'35. CC 17035
Sweet mystery of life. by Richard

Maibaum; Michael Wallach and George Haight. (Benchley) 11:34-6*O19'35. T 17036

Sweetheart time. by Harry B. Smith; Ballard Macdonald and Irving Caesar. (Gabriel) 1:23-4 Ja30'26. T 17037

Sweetie. (Mosher) 5:107 N2'29. CC 17038

The swing Mikado. by Harry Minturn, et al. (Benchley) 15:32-3*Mr11'39. T 17039
(Gibbs) 15:28 Ap1'39. 17040

Swing time. (Mosher) 12:59*S5'36. CC 17041

Swing your lady. (Mosher) 13:48* Ja29'38. CC 17042

Swing your lady! by Kenyon Nicholson and Charles Robinson. (Benchley) 12:26-8*O31'36. T 17043

Swingin' the dream. by Gilbert Seldes and Erik Charell. (Benchley) 15:34-6*D9'39. T 17044

Swiss family Manhattan. by Christopher Morley. (Coates) 7:60-1 Ja16'32. B 17045

Swiss Family Robinson. (Mosher) 15:75 F10'40. CC 17046

The sword in the stone. by T. H. White. (Fadiman) 14:45*Ja7'39. B 17047

Swords and roses. by Joseph Hergesheimer. (Middleton) 5:115 Ap20'29. B 17048

Sworn enemy. (Mosher) 12:79*S19'36. CC 17049

Sylvia Scarlett. (Mosher) 11:53* Ja18'36. CC 17050

Symphony. by Charles March. (Gibbs) 11:26*My4'35. T 17051

Symphony in two flats. by Ivor Novello. (Benchley) 6:34-6 S27'30; 7:24*Jy18'31. T 17052

Syncopating Sue. (Claxton) 2:78 N6'26. CC 17053

Synthetic sin. (Mosher) 4:61 Ja12'29. CC 17054

T

Taboo. by Wilbur Daniel Steele. (Dounce) 1:23 S12'25. B 17055

Tabu. (Mosher) 7:79-81 Mr28'31. CC 17056

Take a chance. by B. G. DeSylva and Laurence Schwab. (Lockridge) 8:36 D3'32. T 17057

Take my tip. by Nat N. Dorfman. (Benchley) 8:26*Ap23'32. T 17058

Take the air. by Anne Caldwell and Gene Buck. (Brackett) 3:35 D3'27. T 17059

Tale of Bali. by Vicki Baum. (Fadiman) 13:50*Ja1'38. B 17060

The tale of Chicago. by Edgar Lee Masters. (Fadiman) 9:47 Ag12'33. B 17061

A tale of two cities. (Mosher) 11:49-50*D28'35. CC 17062

Tale without end. by Lilo Linke. (Fadiman) 10:62-3 Ag11'34. B 17063

The tales of the 1001 nights. (Claxton) 2:67-8 Ja29'27. CC 17064

Talk about girls. by John Hunter Booth. (Wright) 3:67-8 Je25'27. T 17065

The taming of the shrew. (Mosher) 5:96 D7'29. CC 17066

The taming of the shrew. by William Shakespeare. (Brackett) 3:24-5 N5'27. T 17067
(Benchley) 11:30*O12'35. 17068

Tammany Hall. by M. R. Werner. (Markey) 4:99 My5'28. B 17069

Tapestry in gray. by Martin Flavin. (Benchley) 11:22-3*Ja4'36. T 17070

Taps. by Franz Adam Beyerlein. (Anon.) 1:12 Ap25'25. T 17071

Tar. by Sherwood Anderson. (Boyd) 2:108 D4'26. B 17072

Tarnished lady. (Mosher) 7:75-7 My9'31. CC 17073

Tartuffe, the hypocrite. (Claxton) 3:50-1 Ag6'27. CC 17074

Tarzan and his mate. (Mosher) 10:88-9 Ap28'34. CC 17075

Tarzan escapes. (Mosher) 12:65* N28'36. CC 17076

Tarzan finds a son. (Mosher) 15: 75-6*Je17'39. CC 17077
Tarzan, the ape man. (Mosher) 8:56*Ap2'32. CC 17078
Tattle tales. by Frank Fay and Nick Copeland. (White) 9:26 Je 10'33. T 17079
Tattoo: secrets of strange art as practised by the natives of the United States. by Albert Parry. (Fadiman) 9:50 D30'33. B 17080
The tavern. by George M. Cohan. (Benchley) 6:28 My31'30. T 17081
Taxi, taxi. (Claxton) 3:65 F26'27. CC 17082
Technics and civilization. by Lewis Mumford. (Fadiman) 10: 98-9 Ap28'34. B 17083
Teeftallow. by T. S. Stribling. (Dounce) 2:63 Ap17'26. B 17084
Tell it to Sweeney. (Claxton) 3: 87 O22'27. CC 17085
Tell it to the Marines. (Claxton) 2:48 Ja1'27. CC 17086
Tell me more. by Fred Thompson; William K. Wells; George Gershwin and Ira Gershwin. (Anon.) 1:11-12 My9'25. T 17087
Tell me, pretty maiden. by Dorothy Day Wendell. (Benchley) 13:26*D25'37. T 17088
Tell no tales. (Mosher) 15:75*Je 10'39. CC 17089
The tell-tale heart. (Mosher) 10: 62 Je23'34. CC 17090
Telling the world. (Claxton) 4:57-9 Jy21'28. CC 17091
Tempest. (Claxton) 4:91 My26'28. CC 17092
The temptress. (Claxton) 2:41 O16 '26. CC 17093
The ten commandments. by Warwick Deeping. (Coates) 7:83-4 S19'31. B 17094
Ten days that shook the world. (Mosher) 4:107-108 N10'28. CC 17095
Ten minute alibi. by Anthony Armstrong. (Gibbs) 9:26-8 O28 '33. T 17096
Ten nights in a barroom. (Mosher) 7:73-5 Mr7'31. CC 17097
Ten nights in a barroom. by William W. Pratt. (Brackett) 4:34 Ap7'28. T 17098
The ten principal Upanishads. by William Butler Yeats, trans. (Bogan) 13:73-4*S25'37. B 17099
1066 and all that. by W. C. Sellar and R. J. Yeatman. (Coates) 7:91 Ap4'31. B 17100
Ten thousand shall fall. by David King. (Smith) 6:99-100 F22'30. B 17101
Ten to one in Sweden. by Paddy Sylvanus. (Smith) 5:105 S21'29. B 17102
The tender enemy. (Mosher) 14: 69*Ap9'38. CC 17103
Tender is the night. by F. Scott Fitzgerald. (Fadiman) 10:112-15 Ap14'34. B 17104
Tenderloin. (Claxton) 4:77 Mr24 '28. CC 17105
Tenth Avenue. by John McGowen and Lloyd Griscom. (Long) 3:47-8 Ag27'27. T 17106
Tents in Mongolia. by Henning Haslund. (Fadiman) 10:80 S29 '34. B 17107
The terrible siren. by Emanie Sachs. (Lowrie) 4:142 D8'28. B 17108
Test pilot. (Mosher) 14:52*Ap23 '38. CC 17109
Testament. by R. C. Hutchinson. (Fadiman) 14:63*O29'38. B 17110
Testament of a critic. by George Jean Nathan. (Coates) 6:63 Ja 31'31. B 17111
Testimony against Gertrude Stein. Anon. (Fadiman) 11:86*Mr16'35. B 17112
The Texans. (Maloney) 14:41*Ag6 '38. CC 17113
Texts and pretexts. by Aldous Huxley. (Bogan) 9:66-7 F18'33. B 17114
Thank you, Jeeves! by P. G. Wodehouse. (Fadiman) 10:108 My5 '34. B 17115

Thanks for everything. (Mosher) 14:87*D17'38. CC 17116
Thanks for the memory. (Mosher) 14:97*D10'38. CC 17117
That certain age. (Mosher) 14: 58*N5'38. CC 17118
That devil Wilkes. by R. W. Postgate. (Gannett) 5:85-6 D21'29. B 17119
That French lady. by Samuel Shipman and Neil Twomey. (Brackett) 3:33 Mr26'27. T 17120
That girl from Paris. (Mosher) 12:64*Ja9'37. CC 17121
That last infirmity. by Charles Brackett. (Dounce) 2:68 S25'26. B 17122
That nice young couple. by Francis Hackett. (Anon.) 1:26 My23 '25. B 17123
That Royle girl. (Shane) 1:26 Ja 16'26. CC 17124
That they may live. (Mosher) 15: 86*N18'39. CC 17125
That's gratitude. by Frank Craven. (Benchley) 6:30-2 S20 '30. T 17126
That's the woman. by Bayard Veiller. (Benchley) 6:34-5 S13 '30. T 17127
Theater. by W. Somerset Maugham. (Fadiman) 13:69-70*Mr6'37. B 17128
The theatre of George Jean Nathan. by Isaac Goldberg. (Boyd) 2:114-15 D11'26. B 17129
Theatre Street. by Tamara Karsavina. (Coates) 7:76 F28'31. B 17130
The theatre: three thousand years of drama, acting and stagecraft. by Sheldon Cheney. (Smith) 5:127 N9'29. B 17131
Their eyes were watching God. by Zora N. Hurston. (Fadiman) 13:73*S18'37. B 17132
Their own desire. (Mosher) 5:64 F1'30. CC 17133
Theodora goes wild. (Mosher) 12: 81*N21'36. CC 17134
There goes my heart. (Mosher) 14:63*O15'38. CC 17135
There you are. by Carl Bartfield, et al. (Benchley) 8:27-8 My28 '32. T 17136
There's always a woman. (Mosher) 14:52*Ap23'38. CC 17137
There's always Juliet. by John van Druten. (Benchley) 8:26* F27'32. T 17138
There's that woman again. (Mosher) 14:61*Ja14'39. CC 17139
There's wisdom in women. by Joseph O. Kesselring. (Benchley) 11:30-2*N9'35. T 17140
Theresa. by Arthur Schnitzler. (Leonard) 4:99-100 O6'28. B 17141
These bars of flesh. by T. S. Stribling. (Anon.) 14:62-3*Ap16 '38. B 17142
These charming people. by Michael Arlen. (Mankiewicz) 1:19 O17'25. T 17143
These foreigners. by William Seabrook. (Fadiman) 14:62-3*Mr12 '38. B 17144
These modern women. by Lawrence Langner. (Brackett) 4: 26-7 F25'28. T 17145
These two. by Lionel Hale. (Benchley) 10:30 My19'34. T 17146
They came like swallows. by William Maxwell. (Fadiman) 13: 67-8*My1'37. B 17147
They don't mean any harm. by A. A. Milne. (Benchley) 8:30* Mr5'32. T 17148
They gave him a gun. (Mosher) 13:70-1*My22'37. CC 17149
They knew what they wanted. by Sidney Howard. (Gibbs) 15:39* O14'39. T 17150
They shall have music. (Mosher) 15:57*Jy29'39. CC 17151
They shall not die. by John Wexley. (Benchley) 10:30 Mr3'34. T 17152
They still fall in love. by Jesse Lynch Williams. (Lowrie) 5:11 Mr23'29. B 17153
They stooped to folly. by Ellen Glasgow. (Smith) 5:60 Ag3

'29. B 17154

They walk in the city. by J. B. Priestley. (Fadiman) 12:58-9*Ag22'36. B 17155

They were still dancing. by Evelyn Waugh. (Coates) 7:60 Ja16 '32. B 17156

They won't forget. (Mosher) 13: 56*Jy17'37. CC 17157

The Thibaults. by Roger Martin du Gard. (Fadiman) 15:68*Mr 25'39. B 17158

The thief. by Henri Bernstein. (Brackett) 3:34 Ap30'27. T 17159

The thin man. (Mosher) 10:64 Jy 7'34. CC 17160

(Mosher) 11:75*N2'35. 17161

(No entry) 17162

Things greater than he. by Luciano Zuccoli. (Dounce) 2:60-1 My29'26. B 17163

Things to come. (Mosher) 12:45-7*Ap25'36. CC 17164

The thinking reed. by Rebecca West. (Fadiman) 12:74*Mr7 '36. B 17165

The third degree. (Claxton) 3:80 F19'27. CC 17166

The third degree. by Emanuel H. Lavine. (Smith) 6:82-3 N1'30. B 17167

The third hour. by Geoffrey Household. (Fadiman) 13:65* Ja8'38. B 17168

The third little show. by Dwight D. Wiman, et al. (Benchley) 7:28-30*Je13'31; 7:24-6*Jy25 '31. T 17169

The thirsty earth. (Flanner) 9: 73 O28'33. CC 17170

The thirteen. (Mosher) 13:49*Jy 3'37. CC 17171

The 39 steps. (Mosher) 11:63-4* S14'35. CC 17172

This country of yours. by Morris Markey. (Coates) 8:62 S24 '32. B 17173

This delicate creature. by Con O'Leary. (Lowrie) 5:115-16 Mr 23'29. B 17174

This is America. (Mosher) 9:46 Jy22'33. CC 17175

This is my affair. (Mosher) 13: 58*My29'37. CC 17176

This is my story. by Eleanor Roosevelt. (Fadiman) 13:91-2* N20'37. B 17177

This is New York. by Robert E. Sherwood. (Benchley) 6:37 D13 '30. T 17178

This mad ideal. by Floyd Dell. (Anon.) 1:26 Ap18'25. B 17179

This man's art. by Walton Hall Smith. (Coates) 7:59-61*Je20 '31. B 17180

This one man. by Sidney Buchman. (Benchley) 6:26 N1'30. T 17181

This side idolatry. by C. E. Bechofer-Roberts. (Leonard) 4:88 S22'28. B 17182

This side of heaven. (Mosher) 10: 76-7 F17'34. CC 17183

This strange adventure. by Mary Roberts Rinehart. (Lowrie) 5:117 Mr23'29. B 17184

This thing called love. by Edwin Burke. (Brackett) 4:32 S29'28. T 17185

This was a man. by Noel Coward. (Brackett) 2:39 D4'26. T 17186

This was Ivor Trent. by Claude Houghton. (Fadiman) 10:65-6* F2'35. B 17187

This way out. by Philip Littell. (Leonard) 4:100-101 O20'28. B 17188

This way to the big show. by Dexter W. Fellows and Andrew A. Freeman. (Fadiman) 12:64-5*My30'36. B 17189

This woman business. by Benn W. Levy. (Brackett) 2:35-6 D18 '26. T 17190

This year of grace. by Noel Coward. (Brackett) 4:32-3 N17'28. T 17191

Thomas Paine: prophet and martyr of democracy. by Mary Agnes Best. (Boyd) 3:76-8 Je11 '27. B 17192

Thoreau. by Henry Seidel Canby. (Fadiman) 15:65-8*O7'39. B 17193

Thoroughbred. by Doty Hobart. (Benchley) 9:34-6 N18'33. T 17194

Thoroughbreds don't cry. (Mosher) 13:101*D4'37. CC 17195

Those barren leaves. by Aldous Huxley. (Dounce) 1:26 F21'25. B 17196

Those high grey walls. (Mosher) 15:64*O28'39. CC 17197

Those three French girls. (Mosher) 6:92 O18'30. CC 17198

Those we love. by George Abbott and Sidney Howard. (Benchley) 6:28 Mr1'30. T 17199

Thou desperate pilot. by Zoë Akins. (Brackett) 3:33 Mr19 '27. T 17200

A thousand Summers. by Merrill Rogers. (Benchley) 8:26 Je4 '32. T 17201

Three American plays. by Maxwell Anderson and Laurence Stallings. (Dounce) 2:80 O23 '26. B 17202

Three and one. by Denys Amiel; Lewis Galantiere, trans. and John Houseman, trans. (Benchley) 9:32 N11'33. T 17203

Three bad men. (Claxton) 2:78 N6 '26. CC 17204

Three cheers. by Anne Caldwell and R. H. Burnside. (Brackett) 4:33 O27'28. T 17205

Three comrades. (Maloney) 14:49*Je4'38. CC 17206

Three comrades. by Erich Maria Remarque. (Fadiman) 13:66-7*My1'37. B 17207

Three-cornered moon. (Mosher) 9:49 Ag19'33. CC 17208

Three-cornered moon. by Gertrude Tonkonogy. (Benchley) 9:24-6 Mr25'33. T 17209

Three faces East. (Shane) 2:54 F20'26. CC 17210

Three faces East. (Mosher) 6:90-1 S13'30. CC 17211

Three hours. (Claxton) 3:83 Mr12 '27. CC 17212

Three kingdoms. by Storm Jameson. (Dounce) 2:44-5 Mr6'26. B 17213

Three little girls. by Herman Feiner and Bruno Hardt-Warden. (Benchley) 6:28-30 Ap26 '30. T 17214

Three live ghosts. (Mosher) 5:66-8 O5'29. CC 17215

Three loves. by Max Brod. (Smith 5:63 Ag10'29. B 17216

Three men on a horse. by John Cecil Holm and George Abbott. (Benchley) 10:30†F9'35. T 17217

The three musketeers. (Mosher) 11:78*N9'35. CC 17218

The three musketeers. by William Anthony McGuire and Rudolph Friml. (Brackett) 4:29 Mr24 '28. T 17219

The 3-penny opera. by Bertolt Brecht and Kurt Weill. (Benchley) 9:24 Ap22'33. T 17220

Three plays. by George Bernard Shaw. (Fadiman) 10:85-6 F17 '34. B 17221

Three rogues. (Mosher) 7:99 Ap11 '31. CC 17222

Three sinners. (Claxton) 4:90 Ap 28'28. CC 17223

The three sisters. by Anton Chekhov. (Gibbs) 15:30-2*O21 '39. T 17224

The three Sitwells. by R. L. Mégroz. (Boyd) 3:95 S10'27. B 17225

Three smart girls grow up. (Mosher) 15:66*Mr25'39. CC 17226

Three times the hour. by Valentine Davies. (Benchley) 7:28-30 S5'31. T 17227

Three virgins of Haworth. by Emile Romieu and Georges Romieu. (Coates) 6:105*O18'3 B 17228

Three waltzes. by Clare Kumme and Rowland Leigh. (Benchley 13:28*Ja1'38. T 17229

The three wax-works. (Shane) 2:49 Mr27'26. CC 17230

Three week ends. (Mosher) 4:118 D15'28. CC 17231

Three wise fools. by Austin Strong. (Benchley) 12:33*Mr7

'36. T 17232

Three wives. by Beatrice Kean Seymour. (Boyd) 3:91-2 S17'27. B 17233

Three women. (Mosher) 12:66*F 22'36. CC 17234

Three worlds. by Carl Van Doren. (Fadiman) 12:82*S19'36. B 17235

Three's a crowd. (Claxton) 3:84 O8'27. CC 17236

Three's a crowd. by Howard Dietz and Arthur Schwartz. (Benchley) 6:34 O25'30. T 17237

Thrice a stranger. by Vera Brittain. (Fadiman) 14:69-70*S10 '38. B 17238

Through beds of stone. by M. L. Haskins. (Lowrie) 4:76-7 Ja19 '29. B 17239

Through English eyes. by J. A. Spender. (Lowrie) 4:60-1 D29 '28. B 17240

Through the wheat. by Thomas Boyd. (Markey) 4:83 Je23'28. B 17241

Through the years. by Brian Hooker and Vincent Youmans. (Benchley) 7:27-8 F6'32. T 17242

Thumbs up. by H. I. Phillips, et al. (Benchley) 10:34†Ja5'35. T 17243

Thunder. (Mosher) 5:59-60 Jy13 '29. CC 17244

Thunder afloat. (Mosher) 15:74* O21'39. CC 17245

Thunder in the air. by Robins Millar. (Benchley) 5:36 N23'29. T 17246

Thunder on the left. by Jean Ferguson Black. (Benchley) 9:30-2 N11'33. T 17247

Thunder on the left. by Christopher Morley. (Dounce) 1:18 N28'25. B 17248

Thunder over Mexico. (White) 9:64-5 S30'33. CC 17249

Thunder Rock. by Robert Ardrey. (Benchley) 15:28*N25'39. T 17250

Thunderbolt. (Mosher) 5:66 Je29 '29. CC 17251

The thundering herd. (Hays) 1:27 Mr7'25. CC 17252

Thunderstorm. by G. B. Stern. (Dounce) 1:17 Jy11'25. B 17253

Thy dark freight. by Vere Hutchinson. (Lowrie) 5:108-109 Mr 16'29. B 17254

Thy servant a dog. by Rudyard Kipling. (Smith) 6:120 D13'30. B 17255

Tide rising. by George Brewer, Jr. (Benchley) 12:26*F6'37. T 17256

Tides. by Ada Street and Julian Street. (Dounce) 2:90-2 N20'26. B 17257

Tiger shark. (Gibbs) 8:55 O1'32. CC 17258

Tiger! Tiger! by Honoré Willsie Morrow. (Smith) 5:88 F15'30. B 17259

Tight britches. by John Tainter Foote and Hubert Hayes. (Gibbs) 10:34 S22'34. T 17260

The tightwad. by Robert Keith. (Brackett) 3:33 Ap30'27. T 17261

Till the day I die. by Clifford Odets. (Fadiman) 11:62-3*Je1 '35. B 17262

Till we meet again. (Mosher) 12:63*My16'36. CC 17263

Tillie the toiler. (Claxton) 3:71 Je11'27. CC 17264

Timber House. by John Boruff. (Gibbs) 12:24*S26'36. T 17265

Time and the Conways. by J. B. Priestley. (Benchley) 13:30-2* Ja15'38. T 17266

The time of man. by Elizabeth Madox Roberts. (Dounce) 2:83-4 O9'26. B 17267

The time of your life. by William Saroyan. (Gibbs) 15:27*N4'39. T 17268

Times have changed. by Louis Bromfield. (Benchley) 11:26† Mr9'35. T 17269

Timetable for tramps. by Tibor Koeves. (Fadiman) 15:96-7*D2 '39. B 17270

The tin box parade. by Milton Mackaye. (Fadiman) 10:110-11*D8'34. B 17271
Tin gods. (Claxton) 2:60 S25'26. CC 17272
Tin Pan Alley. by Isaac Goldberg. (Smith) 6:112-13 N22'30. B 17273
Tin Pan Alley. by Hugh Stanislaus Stange. (Brackett) 4:34-6 N10'28. T 17274
Tin wedding. by Margaret Leech. (Boyd) 2:60 D25'26. B 17275
Tip-toes. by Guy Bolton; Fred Thompson; George Gershwin and Ira Gershwin. (Mankiewicz) 1:19-20 Ja9'26. T 17276
'Tis pity. by John Ford. (Gabriel) 2:25 F27'26. T 17277
Titans of literature. by Burton Rascoe. (Coates) 8:73-4 N12 '32. B 17278
To have and have not. by Ernest Hemingway. (Fadiman) 13:76-7*O16'37. B 17279
To Mary—with love. (Mosher) 12:59*S5'36. CC 17280
To Quito and back. by Ben Hecht. (Gibbs) 13:28-30*O16 '37. T 17281
To raise these halt. by Fred Rothermell. (Anon.) 12:74*O10 '36. B 17282
To see ourselves. by E. M. Delafield. (Gibbs) 11:34-6*My11'35. T 17283
To the market place. by Berry Fleming. (Fadiman) 14:64*O 29'38. B 17284
To the pure. by Morris L. Ernst and William Seagle. (Leonard) 4:95-6 N3'28. B 17285
The toast of New York. (Maloney) 13:49*Jy31'37. CC 17286
Tobacco Road. by Jack Kirkland. (Benchley) 9:30 D16'33. T17287
Today and tomorrow. by Henry Ford and Samuel Crowther. (Dounce) 2:45-6 Jy24'26. B 17288
Today we live. (Mosher) 9:62-3 Ap22'33. CC 17289
Together again. by Helen Grace Carlisle. (Smith) 6:87-8 N29 '30. B 17290
Together and apart. by Margaret Kennedy. (Fadiman) 13:75*Ap 3'37. B 17291
Tol'able David. (Mosher) 6:103-104 N22'30. CC 17292
Tolerance. by Hendrik William van Loon. (Dounce) 1:23 Ja16 '26. B 17293
Tolstoy, the inconstant genius. by Alexander Nazaroff. (Gannett) 5:87-8 D21'29. B 17294
Tom Sawyer. (Mosher) 6:29 D27 '30. CC 17295
Tommy. by Howard Lindsay and Bertrand Robinson. (Brackett) 2:26 Ja22'27. T 17296
Tomorrow and tomorrow. by Philip Barry. (Benchley) 6:26-9 Ja24'31; 7:24-6*Je27'31. T 17297
Tomorrow morning. by Anne Parrish. (Boyd) 2:54-5 Ja1'27. B 17298
Tomorrow's a holiday! by Romney Brent. (Benchley) 11:26* Ja11'36. T 17299
Tonight at 8:30. by Noel Coward. (Benchley) 12:46-8*D5'36. T 17300
Tonight at twelve. (Gibbs) 5:79-80 S28'29. CC 17301
Tonight at 12. by Owen Davis. (Brackett) 4:33 N24'28. T 17302
Tonight or never. by Lili Hatvany. (Benchley) 6:34 N29'30. T 17303
Tongues of fire. by Algernon Blackwood. (Anon.) 1:26 My16 '25. B 17304
Too hot to handle. (Mosher) 14: 65-6*S24'38. CC 17305
Too many boats. by Owen Davis. (Gibbs) 10:34 S22'34. T 17306
Too many girls. by George Marion, Jr.; Richard Rodgers, and Lorenz Hart. (Gibbs) 15:30* O28'39. T 17307
Too many heroes. by Dore Schary (Benchley) 13:32*N27'

'37. T 17308

Too true to be good. by George Bernard Shaw. (Benchley) 8: 26*Ap16'32. T 17309

Top hat. (Mosher) 11:62*S7'35. CC 17310

Top speed. by Guy Bolton. (Benchley) 5:28-30 Ja4'30. T 17311

Topaze. (Mosher) 9:58-9 F18'33. CC 17312

Topaze. by Marcel Pagnol and Benn W. Levy, trans. (Benchley) 6:35-6 F22'30. T 17313

Topper. (Mosher) 13:46*Ag28'37. CC 17314

Topper takes a trip. (Mosher) 14:43-4*Ja7'39. CC 17315

Topsy and Eva. (Mosher) 3:64 Ag 20'27. CC 17316

Torch song. by Kenyon Nicholson. (Benchley) 6:28 S6'30. T 17317

The torches flare. by Stark Young. (Markey) 4:108 My26 '28. B 17318

The Torguts. by W. L. River. (Fadiman) 15:90-2*O14'39. B 17319

Torrent. (Shane) 2:44 F27'26. CC 17320

Tortilla Flat. by Jack Kirkland. (Benchley) 13:28*Ja22'38. T 17321

A touch of brimstone. by Leonora Kaghan and Anita Philips. (Gibbs) 11:30*S28'35. T 17322

Tovarich. (Mosher) 13:43*Ja1'38. CC 17323

Tovarich. by Jacques Deval and Robert E. Sherwood, trans. (Benchley) 12:26-8*O24'36. T 17324

Towards a better life. by Kenneth Burke. (Coates) 8:68-9* F20'32. B 17325

The tower of lies. (Shane) 1:22 O3'25. CC 17326

Tower of London. (Mosher) 15: 98*D9'39. CC 17327

The toy wife. (Mosher) 14:53-4* Je18'38. CC 17328

Tracked in the snow country. (Shane) 1:17 Jy25'25. CC 17329

Tracking down the enemies of man. by Arthur Torrance. (Smith) 5:65 Jy6'29. B 17330

Trade winds. (Mosher) 14:60-1* Ja14'39. CC 17331

Trader Horn. (Mosher) 6:71 F14 '31. CC 17332

Trader Horn. by Ethelreda Lewis. (Boyd) 3:64-6 Jy16'27. B 17333

The tragedy of Edward VII. by W. E. Edwards. (Lowrie) 4:67 D22'28. B 17334

The tragedy of the Italia. by David Giudice. (Lowrie) 4:75 F9'29. B 17335

The tragedy of Tolstoy. by Alexandra Tolstoy. (Coates) 9:55 Mr25'33. B 17336

Tragic America. by Theodore Dreiser. (Coates) 7:53-4 Ja 30'32. B 17337

The tragic era. by Claude G. Bowers. (Smith) 5:103-104 S21 '29. B 17338

Tragic mansions. by Rita de Acosta Lydig. (Boyd) 3:86-7 Je4'27. B 17339

The tragic pursuit of perfection. by Antonia Vallentin. (Fadiman) 14:105-106*D3'38. B 17340

The trail of '98. (Claxton) 4:82-3 Mr31'28. CC 17341

The trail of the lonesome pine. (Mosher) 12:51*F29'36. CC 17342

Tramp, tramp, tramp. (Claxton) 2:55-6 My29'26. CC 27343

Transatlantic. (Mosher) 7:48-9* Ag8'31. CC 17344

Transfiguration. by Sergeev Tzensky. (Dounce) 2:91-2 N6 '26. B 17345

The transients. by Mark Van Doren. (Fadiman) 10:81*Ja5 '35. B 17346

Transition. by Will Durant. (Parker) 3:96-7 O8'27. B 17347

Translations and tomfooleries. by George Bernard Shaw. (Dounce) 2:89-90 N6

'26. B 17348
Translations from the Chinese. by Christopher Morley. (Hoyt) 3:94-5 N5'27. B 17349
Translations from the poetry of Ranier Maria Rilke. by Ranier Maria Rilke and M. D. Herter Norton, trans. (Bogan) 14:52*D 24'38. B 17350
Transport. by Isa Glenn. (Lowrie) 4:87 F2'29. B 17351
The trap. by Delfino Cinelli. (Smith) 6:54 Ag30'30. B 17352
Trapped. by Samuel Shipman and Max Marcin. (Brackett) 4:28 S22'28. T 17353
Travel diary of a philosopher. by Hermann Alexander Keyserling. (Boyd) 2:108-10 D4'26. B 17354
Travels in the Congo. by André Gide. (Smith) 5:80-1 Je1'29. B 17355
Travels in two democracies. by Edmund Wilson. (Fadiman) 12: 65 *My30'36. B 17356
Treadmill. by Lola Jean Simpson. (Lowrie) 5:107-108 Ap27'29. B 17357
Treasure girl. by Fred Thompson; Vincent Lawrence; George Gershwin and Ira Gershwin. (Brackett) 4:33 N17'28. T 17358
Treasure Island. (Mosher) 10:63-4 Ag18'34. CC 17359
The treasure of the Sierra Madre. by B. Traven. (Fadiman) 11: 66-7*Je15'35. B 17360
The treasurer's report. by Robert Benchley. (Smith) 6:113 N 8'30. B 17361
A treasury of art masterpieces. by Thomas Craven. (Fadiman) 15:58-9*S30'39. B 17362
Treatise on right and wrong. by H. L. Mencken. (Fadiman) 10: 106 Ap7'34. B 17363
The tree. by Richard Maibaum. (Benchley) 8:26-8*Ap23'32. T 17364
The tree of liberty. by Elizabeth Page. (Fadiman) 15:66-7*Mr4 '39. B 17365
Trelawny of the Wells. by Arthur Wing Pinero. (Brackett) 2:33-4 F12'27. T 17366
Trending into Maine. by Kenneth Roberts. (Kronenberger) 14:57-8*Je25'38. B 17367
The trespasser. (Mosher) 5:112 N9'29. CC 17368
The trial. by Franz Kafka. (Fadiman) 13:68-9*O23'37. B 17369
Trial of a judge. by Stephen Spender. (Bogan) 14:64-5*O1'38. B 17370
The trial of Mary Dugan. (Mosher) 5:47-8 Ap6'29. CC 17371
The trial of Mary Dugan. by Bayard Veiller. (Brackett) 3: 25 O1'27. T 17372
Trick for trick. by Vivian Crosby; Shirley Warde and Harry Wagstaff Gribble. (Benchley) 8:27* F27'32. T 17373
Tricks of women, and other Albanian tales. by Paul Fenimore Cooper, trans. (Leonard) 4:89 S29'28. B 17374
Trigger. by Lula Vollmer. (Brackett) 3:33 D17'27. T 17375
Triple crossed. by Frank Merlin. (Brackett) 3:30 My14'27. T 17376
Triple fugue. by Osbert Sitwell. (Anon.) 1:26 Ap25'25. B 17377
The triple thinkers. by Edmund Wilson. (Fadiman) 14:65-6*Mr 19'38. B 17378
Triplets. by Mark Linder. (White) 8:28 O1'32. T 17379
Triumph over pain. by René Fülop Miller. (Fadiman) 14:53-4*S3 '38. B 17380
Triumphal march. by T. S. Eliot. (Bogan) 7:64-5 F13'32. B 17381
The triumphant bachelor. by Owen Davis. (Brackett) 3:32 S24'27. T 17382
A Trojan ending. by Laura Riding. (Fadiman) 13:60-1*Ag14'37. B 17383
Trojan incident. by Philip H. Davis and Wallingford Riegger. (Gibbs) 14:28*Ap30'38. T 17384

Troopship. (Mosher) 14:53*Ap30 '38. CC 17385
Tropic death. by Eric Walrond. (Dounce) 2:100 N13'26. B 17386
Trouble for two. (Mosher) 12:63* Je6'36. CC 17387
The trouble I've seen. by Martha Gellhorn. (Anon.) 12:72-3*S26 '36. B 17388
The trouper. by J. C. Nugent and Elliott Nugent. (Gabriel) 2:27 Mr20'26. T 17389
Troupers of the Gold Coast. by Constance Rourke. (Lowrie) 4:75-6 F9'29. B 17390
Troyka. by Lula Vollmer. (Benchley) 6:33 Ap12'30. T 17391
True confession. (Mosher) 13:45* D25'37. CC 17392
The true heart. by Sylvia Townsend Warner. (Lowrie) 5:83-4 Mr9'29. B 17393
True heaven. (Mosher) 4:83-4 F 16'29. CC 17394
A true story. by Stephen Hudson. (Smith) 6:100 My3'30. B 17395
True to the Navy. (Brackett) 6: 73 My31'30. CC 17396
The truth about Blayds. by A. A. Milne. (Benchley) 8:28*Ap23 '32. T 17397
The truth game. by Ivor Novello. (Benchley) 6:28-30 Ja10'31. T 17398
Try the sky. by Francis Stuart. (Fadiman) 9:51-2 Jy22'33. B 17399
Tsushima. by A. Novikoff-Priboy. (Fadiman) 12:61-2*F6'37. B 17400
Tugboat Annie. (Mosher) 9:49 Ag 19'33. CC 17401
Tumbleweeds. (Shane) 1:23 Ja2 '26. CC 17402
Tumbling in the hay. by Oliver St. John Gogarty. (Fadiman) 15:78-9*Je17'39. B 17403
The tumult and the shouting. by George Slocombe. (Anon.) 12: 66*Je27'36. B 17404
Tunnel Hill. by Harlan Hatcher. (Coates) 7:96-7 Ap25'31. B 17405
The turn of the century: 1900-1904. by Mark Sullivan. (Dounce) 2:54 Mr27'26. B 17406
The turning wheels. by Stuart Cloete. (Fadiman) 13:77*N6'37. B 17407
A turning wind. by Muriel Rukeyser. (Bogan) 15:100-101*D16 '39. B 17408
Twelfth night. by William Shakespeare. (Brackett) 2:24 Ja1'27. T 17409
(Benchley) 6:36 O25'30. 17410
Twelve against the gods. by William Bolitho. (Smith) 5:119-20 N16'29. B 17411
Twelve miles out. by William Anthony McGuire. (Mankiewicz) 1:15 N28'25. T 17412
Twelve thousand. by Bruno Frank. (Brackett) 4:29 Mr24'28. T 17413
20th Century. (Mosher) 10:94 My 12'34. CC 17414
20th Century. by Ben Hecht and Charles MacArthur. (Benchley) 8:30 Ja7'33. T 17415
Twentieth Century crimes. by Frederick A. Mackenzie. (Boyd) 3:95-6 S10'27. B 17416
$25 an hour. by Gladys Unger and Leyla Georgie. (Benchley) 9:30-2 My20'33. T 17417
Twenty-five years with Earl Haig. by T. Secrett. (Smith) 5:73 Je 29'29. B 17418
24 hours. (Mosher) 7:79 O10'31. CC 17419
Twenty-four hours. by Louis Bromfield. (Smith) 6:97 S20'30. B 17420
20,000 leagues under the sea or David Copperfield. by Robert Benchley. (Lowrie) 4:143 D8 '28. B 17421
Twenty thousand years in Sing-Sing. by Lewis E. Lawes. (Coates) 8:61-2*My14'32. B 17422
Twenty years a-growing. by Maurice O'Sullivan. (Fadiman) 9: 47 Ag5'33. B 17423

Twilight of man. by Earnest Albert Hooton. (Fadiman) 15:59-61*S30'39. B 17424
Twilight sleep. by Edith Wharton. (Boyd) 3:87-8 Je4'27. B 17425
Twinkle twinkle. by Harlan Thompson and Harry Archer. (Brackett) 2:33 N27'26. T 17426
Two Arabian knights. (Claxton) 3:89 O29'27. CC 17427
The two bouquets. by Eleanor Farjeon and Herbert Farjeon. (Gibbs) 14:24*Je11'38. T 17428
Two days. (Mosher) 4:71 F9'29. CC 17429
Two for tonight. (Mosher) 11:64* S14'35. CC 17430
Two girls wanted. by Gladys Unger. (Brackett) 2:32 S18'26. T 17431
200 were chosen. by Ellsworth Prouty Conkle. (Benchley) 12:26-8*N28'36. T 17432
Two kinds of women. (Mosher) 7:56 Ja23'32. CC 17433
Two living and one dead. by Sigurd Christiansen. (Coates) 8:59*Ap2'32. B 17434
Two lovers. (Claxton) 4:83 Mr31 '28. CC 17435
Two on an island. by Elmer Rice. (Gibbs) 15:30 F3'40. T 17436
Two or three graces. by Aldous Huxley. (Dounce) 2:59-60 My 29'26. B 17437
The two orphans. by A. D'Ennery and Eugene Corman. (Gabriel) 2:28 Ap17'26. T 17438
Two seconds. (Mosher) 8:52 My 28'32. CC 17439
The two sisters. by H. E. Bates. (Boyd) 2:55-6 Ja1'27. B 17440
Two strange women. by Edwin B. Self. (Benchley) 8:28 Ja21'33. T 17441
Two thieves. by Manuel Komroff. (Coates) 7:74-6 F28'31. B 17442
2 X 2 = 5. by Gustav Wied. (Brackett) 3:35 D10'27. T 17443
Two who dared. (Mosher) 13:56* Jy17'37. CC 17444
Two worlds. by Lester Cohen. (Anon.) 12:51-2*Jy4'36. B 17445
Two years. by Liam O'Flaherty. (Smith) 6:100-101 O11'30. B 17446
Twopence coloured. by Patrick Hamilton. (Leonard) 4:73 S1 '28. B 17447
The tyranny of words. by Stuart Chase. (Fadiman) 13:61-2*Ja 22'38. B 17448

U

U-Boats westward. by Ernst Hashagen. (Coates) 7:76 O24'31. B 17449
The ugly duchess. by Lion Feuchtwanger. (Hoyt) 3:71-2 Ja14'28. B 17450
Ultima Thule. by Henry Handel Richardson. (Smith) 5:103-104 S14'29. B 17451
Ulysses. by James Joyce. (Fadiman) 9:69 Ja27'34. B 17452
Un carnet de bal. (Flanner) 13:59*O2'37. CC 17453
Un soir de rafle. (Mosher) 7:69 O24'31. CC 17454
Unashamed. (Mosher) 8:45 Jy23 '32. CC 17455
The uncertain trumpet. by A. S. M. Hutchinson. (Smith) 5:117-18 O5'29. B 17456
The unchastened woman. by Louis K. Anspacher. (Gabriel) 2:24 F27'26. T 17457
Uncle Sham. by Kanhaya Lal Gauba. (Smith) 5:61-2 Ag3'29. B 17458
Uncle Tom's cabin. (Claxton) 3:69-70 N12'27. CC 17459
Uncle Tom's cabin. by G. L. Aiken and A. E. Thomas. (White) 9:24-6 Je10'33. T 17460
Uncle Vanya. by Anton Chekhov. (Benchley) 6:27-8 Ap26'30; 6:29-30 Ja3'31. T 17461
Under a Texas moon. (Mosher) 6:111-12 Ap12'30. CC 17462
Under glass. by Eva Kay Flint and George Bradshaw. (Bench-

ley) 9:32 N11'33. T 17463
Under the gaslight. by Augustin Daly. (Brackett) 5:32 Ap13'29. T 17464
Under the North Pole. by Hubert Wilkins. (Coates) 7:84-5 My9 '31. B 17465
Under the pampas moon. (Mosher) 11:62*Je8'35. CC 17466
Under the rose. by Anatole France. (Dounce) 2:49 Jy17'26. B 17467
Underground. (Mosher) 5:74-5 Mr 9'29. CC 17468
Underworld. (Claxton) 3:56-7 S3 '27. CC 17469
The underworld of Paris. by Alfred Morain. (Coates) 6:78 F 14'31. B 17470
An undesirable lady. by Leon Gordon. (Gibbs) 9:35 O21'33. T 17471
Undine. by Olive Schreiner. (Lowrie) 4:129-30 D15'28. B 17472
Une saison en enfer. by Arthur Rimbaud and Delmore Swartz, trans. (Bogan) 15:52-4*Ja27'40. B 17473
Unexpected husband. by Barry Conners. (Benchley) 7:30 Je13 '31. T 17474
Unfinished cathedral. by T. S. Stribling. (Fadiman) 10:88-9 Je2'34. B 17475
Unforbidden fruit. by Warner Fabian. (Leonard) 4:63-4 Je30 '28. B 17476
The unguarded hour. (Mosher) 12:69-70*Ap11'36. CC 17477
The unholy three. (Anon.) 1:31 My 23'25. CC 17478
The unholy three. (Shane) 1:15 Ag 15'25. CC 17479
Union Depot. (Mosher) 7:55-6 Ja 23'32. CC 17480
Union Pacific. (Mosher) 15:76-7* My13'39. CC 17481
Union Square. by Albert Halper. (Coates) 9:66-7 Mr11'33. B 17482
The United States of Europe. by Edouard Herriot. (Coates) 6: 121-2 D13'30. B 17483
Unkind star. by Nancy Hoyt. (Boyd) 3:54-5 Jy30'27. B 17484
The unknown. (Claxton) 3:81-3 Je 18'27. CC 17485
The unknown quantity. by Hermann Broch. (Fadiman) 11:83* My11'35. B 17486
The unknown soldier. (Shane) 2:61-3 Je5'26. CC 17487
The unlit lamp. by Radclyffe Hall. (Smith) 5:56 Jy27'29. B 17488
Untamed. (Mosher) 5:96 D7'29. CC 17489
The untamed lady. (Shane) 2:51 Mr20'26. CC 17490
Unto the third. by J. N. Gilchrist. (Benchley) 9:28 Ap29'33. T 17491
The untried case: the Sacco-Vanzetti case and the Morelli gang. by Herbert B. Ehrmann. (Fadiman) 9:55 Ag26'33. B 17492
The unvanquished. by William Faulkner. (Fadiman) 14:60 F19 '38. B 17493
Unveiled. by Beatrice Kean Seymour. (Anon.) 1:26 My30'25. B 17494
Unweave a rainbow. by Edgar Johnson. (Coates) 6:66-7 Ja24 '31. B 17495
The up and up. by Eva Kay Flint and Martha Madison. (Benchley) 6:30 S20'30. T 17496
Up pops the devil. by Albert Hackett and Frances Goodrich. (Benchley) 6:34 S13'30. T 17497
Up the Congo. (Mosher) 5:72 Ja25 '30. CC 17498
Up the line. by Henry Fisk Carlton. (Brackett) 2:40 D4'26. T 17499
Up the river. (Mosher) 6:91-2 O18 '30. CC 17500
Up the river. (Mosher) 14:96*D10 '38. CC 17501
Up to now. by Alfred E. Smith. (Smith) 5:123-4 O12'29. B 17502

Upper world. (Mosher) 10:80 Je2 '34. CC 17503
Upstage. (Claxton) 2:78-80 N20 '26. CC 17504

V

The vagabond duchess. by Cyril Hughes Hartmann. (Boyd) 2: 115-16 D11'26. B 17505
The vagabond king. (Mosher) 6: 75-6 Mr1'30. CC 17506
Vagabonds. by Knut Hamsun. (Smith) 6:132 D6'30. B 17507
Valencia. (Claxton) 2:49 Ja1'27. CC 17508
The valiant. (Mosher) 5:107 My18 '29. CC 17509
Valiant is the word for Carrie. (Mosher) 12:77*O17'36. CC 17510
Valley Forge. by Maxwell Anderson. (Benchley) 10:24-6†D22 '34. T 17511
The valley of the kings. by Marmaduke Pickthall. (Dounce) 2: 68-9 O23'26. B 17512
The Vanderbilt revue. by Lew Fields, et al. (Benchley) 6:31 N15'30. T 17512A
Vanessa. (Mosher) 11:72*Ap20'35. CC 17513
The vanguard. by Arnold Bennett. (Hoyt) 3:112 D17'27. B 17514
Vanished fleets. by Alan J. Villiers. (Coates) 7:97 Ap25'31. B 17515
The vanishing American. (Shane) 1:22-3 O24'25. CC 17516
Vanity under the sun. by Dale Collins. (Leonard) 4:72 S1'28. B 17517
Variety. (Claxton) 2:34 Jy3'26. CC 17518
Variety. (Claxton) 2:35 Jy17'26. CC 17519
A variety of things. by Max Beerbohm. (Leonard) 4:100 O6'28. B 17520
Vasco. by Marc Chadourne. (Leonard) 4:80 S8'28. B 17521
The vegetable, or from President to postman. by F. Scott Fitzgerald. (Brackett) 5:30 Ap20 '29. T 17522
Vein of iron. by Ellen Glasgow. (Fadiman) 11:49-51*Ag31'35. B 17523
Veneer. by Hugh Stanislaus Stange. (Benchley) 5:36 N23'29. T 17524
The Venetian glass nephew. by Eugene Bonner and Ruth Hale. (Parker) 7:34 Mr7'31. T 17525
Venus invisible. by Nathalia Crane. (Leonard) 4:100 O20'28. B 17526
The verdict of Bridlegoose. by Llewelyn Powys. (Dounce) 2: 52-3 Je12'26. B 17527
Verdun. by Jules Romains. (Fadiman) 15:49-51*D30'39. B 17528
Vermont. by A. E. Thomas. (Brackett) 4:30 Ja19'29. T 17529
Very heaven. by Richard Aldington. (Fadiman) 13:84*Mr13'37. B 17530
Very warm for May. by Oscar Hammerstein, II and Jerome Kern. (Benchley) 15:28*N25'39. T 17531
A very wise virgin. by Sam Janney. (Long) 3:36-8 Je11'27. T 17532
The vessel of wrath. (Mosher) 14: 48-9*D31'38. CC 17533
Vestal fire. by Compton Mackenzie. (Hoyt) 3:125-6 D10'27. B 17534
The viaduct murder. by Ronald A. Knox. (Dounce) 2:62-3 Ap 17'26. B 17535
The vice squad. (Mosher) 7:63-4* Je13'31. CC 17536
A victim of circumstances. by George Gissing. (Boyd) 3:72-3 S3'27. B 17537
Victoria of England. by Edith Sitwell. (Anon.) 12:54*Ag8'36. B 17538
Victoria Regina. by Laurence Housman. (Benchley) 11:22*Ja 4'36. T 17539

W

(Benchley) 8:26-8 D17'32. T 17578
Walk like a mortal. by Dan Wickenden. (Fadiman) 15:78-9 F10'40. B 17579
Wall Street. by James N. Rosenberg. (Brackett) 3:33 Ap30'27. T 17580
The walls of Jericho. by Rudolph Fisher. (Leonard) 4:63 Ag11'28. B 17581
The waltz dream. (Claxton) 2:34 Jy31'26. CC 17582
The waltz of the dogs. by Leonid Andreyev. (Brackett) 4:33 My 5'28. T 17583
Waltz time. (White) 9:78 O7'33. CC 17584
The wanderer. (Shane) 1:19 Ag29 '25. CC 17585
The wanderer of Liverpool. by John Masefield. (Coates) 6:99 N15'30. B 17586
The waning sex. (Claxton) 2:59-60 S25'26. CC 17587
Wanted men. (Mosher) 12:45*Jy18 '36. CC 17588
Wanton Mally. by Booth Tarkington. (Coates) 8:73 N12'32. B 17589
War. by Ludwig Renn. (Smith) 5:57-8 Jy27'29. B 17590
War among ladies. by Eleanor Scott. (Leonard) 4:76-7 Jy14 '28. B 17591
War bugs. by Charles MacArthur. (Smith) 5:64-5 Jy6'29. B 17592
The war goes on. by Sholem Asch. (Anon.) 12:65-6*O31'36. B 17593
War letters of fallen Englishmen. by Laurence Housman, ed. (Coates) 6:115-16 N8'30. B 17594
War nurse. (Mosher) 6:77-8 N1 '30. CC 17595
The war song. by Samuel Spewack; Bella Spewack and George Jessel. (Brackett) 4:34 O6'28. T 17596
War with the newts. by Karel Capek. (Fadiman) 13:73-4*O9 '37. B 17597
(No entry) 17598
Ward eight. by Joseph F. Dineen. (Anon.) 12:83-4*O17'36. B 17599
The warrior's husband. by Julian Thompson. (Benchley) 8:30-1* Mr19'32. T 17600
Warming up. (Claxton) 4:57 Jy21 '28. CC 17601
Washington jitters. by John Boruff and Walter Hart. (Gibbs) 14:30*My14'38. T 17602
The Washington masquerade. (Mosher) 8:36 Jy30'32. CC 17603
Washington merry-go-round. (Mosher) 8:59 O29'32. CC 17604
Watch for the dawn. by Stuart Cloete. (Fadiman) 15:54*S2'39. B 17605
The water gipsies. by A. P. Herbert. (Smith) 6:110 N22'30. B 17606
The water hole. (Claxton) 4:91 S15'28. CC 17607
The water wheel. by Julian L. Shapiro. (Coates) 9:68 Mr18'33. B 17608
Waterloo. by Manuel Komroff. (Kronenberger) 12:49-51*Jy4 '36. B 17609
Waterloo Bridge. by Robert E. Sherwood. (Benchley) 5:30-2 Ja18'30. T 17610
The waters under the earth. by Martha Ostenso. (Smith) 6:80 N1'30. B 17611
The wave. (Mosher) 13:64-5*Ap 24'37. CC 17612
The wave. by Evelyn Scott. (Smith) 5:77 Jy20'29. B 17613
The waves. by Virginia Woolf. (Coates) 7:87-8 N7'31; 7:80 D19 '31. B 17614
The way of a transgressor. by Negley Farson. (Fadiman) 11:64-5*F15'36; 13:62-3*Ja15'38. B 17615
The way of all flesh. (Claxton) 3:61 Jy2'27. CC 17616

The way of Ecben. by James Branch Cabell. (Smith) 5:120 N2'29. B 17617
The way of sacrifice. by Fritz von Unruh. (Markey) 4:83-4 Je23'28. B 17618
The way things are. by E. M. Delafield. (Hoyt) 3:80-1 F18 '28. B 17619
The way to strength and beauty. (Claxton) 3:51 Ag6'27. CC 17620
The wayward man. by St. John Ervine. (Hoyt) 3:112-13 D17 '27. B 17621
We. by Eugene Zamiatin. (Dounce) 1:28 Mr7'25. B 17622
We all do. by Knud Wiberg and Marcel Strauss. (Brackett) 3: 34 Mr12'27. T 17623
We Americans. (Claxton) 4:95 Ap 7'28. CC 17624
We are from Kronstadt. (Mosher) 12:69-70*My9'36. CC 17625
We are incredible. by Margery Latimer. (Markey) 4:108-109 My26'28. B 17626
We are not alone. (Mosher) 15: 92-3*D2'39. CC 17627
We are not alone. by James Hilton. (Fadiman) 13:84*Mr13 '37. B 17628
We in captivity. by Kathleen Pawle. (Fadiman) 12:71-2*Mr 21'36. B 17629
We live again. (Mosher) 10:106 N10'34. CC 17630
We moderns. (Shane) 1:35 O19'25. CC 17631
We shall live again. by Maurice Hindus. (Fadiman) 15:78-80*My 13'39. B 17632
We take to bed. by Marshall McClintock. (Coates) 7:76-7 F28 '31. B 17633
We, the people. by Elmer Rice. (Benchley) 8:32 F4'33. T 17634
We who are about to die. (Mosher) 12:65*Ja9'37. CC 17635
A weak woman. by Jacques Deval and Ernest Boyd. (Gabriel) 1: 27 F6'26. T 17636
Weary River. (Mosher) 4:79 F2 '29. CC 17637
The weather in the streets. by Rosamond Lehmann. (Fadiman) 12:74*My23'36. B 17638
The weather tree. by Mary Chapman and John Stanton Chapman. (Coates) 7:60 Ja23'32. B 17639
The web and the rock. by Thomas Wolfe. (Fadiman) 15:69-70*Je 24'39. B 17640
Wedding bill$. (Claxton) 3:61 Jy2 '27. CC 17641
The wedding march. (Mosher) 4: 92-3 O20'28. CC 17642
The wedding night. (Maloney) 11: 61-2*Mr23'35. CC 17643
The wedding of Palo. (Mosher) 13:77*Mr13'37. CC 17644
The wedge. by Hermann B. Deutsch. (Fadiman) 11:51*Ag17 '35. B 17645
Wedlock. by Jacob Wassermann and Ludwig Lewisohn, trans. (Boyd) 2:96 D18'26. B 17646
Wednesday's child. by Leopold Atlas. (Benchley) 9:28 Ja27'34. T 17647
Week-end. by Charles Brackett. (Dounce) 1:22-3 S12'25. B 17648
Week-end. by Hugh O'Connell. (Benchley) 5:34 N2'29. T 17649
Week-end. by Phillip D. Stong. (Fadiman) 10:80-1*Ja5'35. B 17650
Weep for the virgins. by Nellise Child. (Benchley) 11:48 D7'35. T 17651
Weep no more. by Ward Greene. (Coates) 7:64-5 F6'32. B 17652
The weigher of souls. by André Maurois. (Coates) 7:92 Ap18 '31. B 17653
Welcome danger. (Mosher) 5:107 O26'29. CC 17654
Welcome home. (Anon.) 1:31 My 30'25. CC 17655
The well of loneliness. by Radclyffe Hall. (Lowrie) 4:58-9 D29'28. B 17656

(Flanner) 6:84 O4'30. 17657
Wells Fargo. (Mosher) 13:62*Ja 8'38. CC 17658
We're in the Navy now. (Claxton) 2:85-6 N13'26. CC 17659
We're not dressing. (Mosher) 10: 96-7 My5'34. CC 17660
West of Zanzibar. (Mosher) 4:60 Ja12'29. CC 17661
West Point of the air. (Mosher) 11:63-4*Ap13'35. CC 17662
West-running brook. by Robert Frost. (Lowrie) 4:131 D15'28. B 17663
The wet Flanders Plain. by Henry Williamson. (Gannett) 5:168 D7'29. B 17664
Wet paint. (Claxton) 2:59 My22'26. CC 17665
The wet parade. (Mosher) 8:52-3*Ap30'32. CC 17666
The wet parade. by Upton Sinclair. (Coates) 7:79-80 S26'31. B 17667
Wharf angel. (Mosher) 10:89 Ap 28'34. CC 17668
What a life! (Mosher) 15:89*O14 '39. CC 17669
What a life. by Clifford Goldsmith. (Gibbs) 14:30*Ap23'38. T 17670
What every woman knows. (Mosher) 10:87 N3'34. CC 17671
What every woman knows. by James Barrie. (Connelly) 2: 26 Ap24'26. T 17672
What is your emotional age? by J. George Frederick. (Leonard) 4:108 N24'28. B 17673
What me befell. by Jean Jules Jusserand. (Fadiman) 9:50-2 D30'33. B 17674
What never dies. by Alexander Engel and Ernest Boyd, trans. (Brackett) 2:29-30 Ja8'27.T 17675
What people said. by W. L. White. (Fadiman) 14:60-1*Ap 16'38. B 17673
What price glory. (Anon.) 1:26 Mr28'25. CC 17677
What price glory. (Claxton) 2:72 D4'26. CC 17678
What price glory. by Maxwell Anderson and Laurence Stallings. (Mankiewicz) 1:15 Jy11'25. T 17679
What price Hollywood. (Mosher) 8:45 Jy23'32. CC 17680
What shall the children read? by Laura E. Richards. (Fadiman) 15:74*N25'39. B 17681
What the doctor ordered. by Caesar Dunn. (Long) 3:48 Ag27 '27. T 17682
What we live by. by Ernest Dimnet. (Coates) 8:50-1 Jy9'32. B 17683
What women do? Anon. (Mankiewicz) 1:15 Ag1'25. T 17684
What would be the character of a new war? Anon. (Fadiman) 9:81-3 S16'33. B 17685
Whatever goes up. by Milton Lazarus. (Benchley) 11:46*D7 '35. T 17686
Whatever we do. by Allen Updegraff. (Hoyt) 3:54 D31'27. B 17687
Wheat and soldiers. by Ashihei Hino. (Fadiman) 15:82-3*My27 '39. B 17688
When a man loves. (Claxton) 2:51 F12'27. CC 17689
When James Gordon Bennett was Caliph of Bagdad. by Albert Stevens Crockett. (Dounce) 2: 65 My22'26. B 17690
When ladies meet. (Mosher) 9:45 Jy1'33. CC 17691
When ladies meet. by Rachel Crothers. (White) 8:28 O15'32. T 17692
When ships were ships. by William Morris Barnes. (Coates) 6:99-100 N15'30. B 17693
When the Daltons rode. by Emmet Dalton and Jack Jungmeyer. (Coates) 6:81 F14'31. B 17694
When they love. by Maurice Baring. (Leonard) 4:88 S29'28. B 17695
When tomorrow comes. (Maloney) 15:53*Ag19'39. CC 17696
When turtles sing. by Don Marquis. (Leonard) 4:90-1 S29'28. B 17697
When we are married. by J. B. Priestley. (Benchley) 15:28*Ja 6'40. T 17698

When you're in love. (Maloney) 13:60-1*F27'37. CC 17699
Where do we go from here? by William Bowers. (Benchley) 14:28*N26'38. T 17700
Where Paris dines. by Julian Street. (Smith) 5:96-7 Je22'29. B 17701
Where sinners meet. (Mosher) 10:79-80 Je2'34. CC 17702
While parents sleep. by Anthony Kimmins. (Benchley) 10:26 Je 16'34. T 17703
While the bridegroom tarried. by Edna Bryner. (Lowrie) 4:74-6 Ja19'29. B 17704
While the city sleeps. (Mosher) 4:81 O27'28. CC 17705
Whipsaw. (Mosher) 11:46-7*F1 '36. CC 17706
Whirlpool. by William Jourdan Rapp and Walter Marquiss. (Benchley) 5:36-8 D14'29. T 17707
The whirlwind of youth. (Claxton) 3:70-1 Je11'27. CC 17708
Whisky. by Aeneas MacDonald. (Fadiman) 9:60-2 Ja20'34. B 17709
Whispering friends. by George M. Cohan. (Brackett) 4:33-4 Mr3 '28. T 17710
The whispering gallery. Anon. (Boyd) 2:112 D4'26. B 17711
The whispering gallery. by Percy Robinson and Terence de Marney. (Brackett) 5:28 F23'29. T 17712
The whistler's room. by Paul Alverdes. (Smith) 6:100 F22'30. B 17713
Whistling in the dark. (Mosher) 8:53 F4'33. CC 17714
Whistling in the dark. by Laurence Gross and Edward Childs Carpenter. (Benchley) 7:24-6 Ja30'32. T 17715
The white angel. (Mosher) 12:45* Jy4'36. CC 17716
White banners. (Mosher) 14:53* Je25'38. CC 17717
White cargo. (Mosher) 6:76 Mr1 '30. CC 17718
The white desert. (Shane) 1:17 Jy18'25. CC 17719
The white eagle. by Edwin Milton Royle and Rudolph Friml. (Brackett) 3:25 Ja14'28. T 17720
White gold. (Claxton) 3:93 Ap16'27. CC 17721
The white hell of Pitz Palu. (Mosher) 6:96 O4'30. CC 17722
White Horse Inn. by Hans Mueller, et al. (Gibbs) 12:31-2*O10'36. T 17723
White lilacs. by Harry B. Smith. (Brackett) 4:28 S22'28. T 17724
White mule. by William Carlos Williams. (Fadiman) 13:65-6* Je19'37. B 17725
The white parade. (Mosher) 10:78*N17'34. CC 17726
White shadows of the seven seas. (Claxton) 4:54-5 Ag11'28. CC 17727
The white sister. (Mosher) 9:49 Mr25'33. CC 17728
The white steed. by Paul Vincent Carroll. (Benchley) 14:30-2* Ja21'39. T 17729
White wings. by Philip Barry. (Brackett) 2:31 O30'26. T 17730
White zombie. (Mosher) 8:41 Ag6 '32. CC 17731
Whiteoaks. by Mazo de la Roche. (Benchley) 14:26*Ap2'38. T 17732
Who cares? by Edward Clarke Lilley, et al. (Benchley) 6:26-8 Jy19'30. T 17733
Whom the gods destroy. (Mosher) 10:56 Jy21'34. CC 17734
Whoopee. (Mosher) 6:87-8 O11'30. CC 17735
Whoopee. by William Anthony McGuire. (Brackett) 4:37-8 D 15'28. T 17736
Whoops dearie! by Peter Arno. (Boyd) 3:100-101 My21'27. B 17737
Who's who. by Leonard Sillman. (Benchley) 14:28*Mr12'38. T 17738

Whose constitution? by Henry A. Wallace. (Anon.) 12:52*Jy4 '36. B 17739
Why girls go back home. (Claxton) 2:58-9 My22'26. CC 17740
Why keep them alive? by Paul de Kruif. (Anon.) 12:77-8*Mr 7'36. B 17741
Why should penguins fly? and other stories. by Dwight Fiske. (Anon.) 12:67-8*O31'36. B 17742
A wicked woman. (Mosher) 10:57-8*Ja12'35. CC 17743
Wickford Point. by John P. Marquand. (Fadiman) 15:67-8*Mr 18'39. B 17744
Wide open town. by Myron Brinig. (Coates) 7:89 Mr14'31. B 17745
Wife, doctor, and nurse. (Mosher) 13:73*O16'37. CC 17746
Wife insurance. by Frederick Jackson. (Benchley) 10:28-9 Ap21'34. T 17747
Wife of General Ling. (Mosher) 14:59*F19'38. CC 17748
Wife vs. secretary. (Mosher) 12:63-4*Mr7'36. CC 17749
The wife who wasn't wanted. (Shane) 1:25 S12'25. CC 17750
Wild. by Carol Denny Hill. (Boyd) 3:97 S10'27. B 17751
Wild birds. by Dan Totheroh. (Anon.) 1:11-12 Ap25'25. T 17752
Wild cargo. (Mosher) 10:96-7 Ap 7'34. CC 17753
Wild company. (Mosher) 6:54 Jy 26'30. CC 17754
The wild duck. by Henrik Ibsen. (Gabriel) 1:22 F13'26. T 17755
The wild goose chase. by Rex Warner. (Fadiman) 13:52-3*Ja 29'38. B 17756
Wild innocence. (Mosher) 14:87* N19'38. CC 17757
Wild metal. by Charles Gilson. (Coates) 8:62 My28'32. B 17758
The wild palms. by William Faulkner. (Fadiman) 14:60-1* Ja21'39. B 17759
The wild party. by Joseph Moncure March. (Markey) 4:96 Ap 28'28. B 17760
The wild rose. by Otto Harbach; Oscar Hammerstein, II and Rudolph Friml. (Brackett) 2:32 O30'26. T 17761
Wild talents. by Charles Fort. (Coates) 8:65-6 Je11'32. B 17762
Wild waves. by William Ford Manley. (Benchley) 8:30-2*Mr 5'32. T 17763
The wilderness woman. (Shane) 2:52-3 My15'26. CC 17764
Wilhelm Hohenzollern, the last of the Kaisers. by Emil Ludwig. (Boyd) 3:94-5 Mr12'27. B 17765
William Pitt, the younger. by P. W. Wilson. (Smith) 6:100 Mr15 '30. B 17766
Win that girl. (Mosher) 4:85-7 O 6'28. CC 17767
The wind and the rain. by Merton Hodge. (Benchley) 9:30 F10'34. T 17768
The wind from the mountains. by Trygve Gulbranssen. (Fadiman) 13:72-4*My22'37. B 17769
Wind over Wisconsin. by August Derleth. (Fadiman) 14:60*Ap30 '38. B 17770
Wind, sand and stars. by Antoine de Saint-Exupéry. (Anon.) 15:72*Je24'39. B 17771
Wind without rain. by Herbert Krause. (Fadiman) 14:73*F11 '39. B 17772
Windjammer. by Kenneth Attiwill. (Coates) 6:67 Ja10'31. B 17773
Windlestraws. by Phyllis Bottome. (Smith) 5:124-6 N9'29. B 17774
Winds of chance. (Shane) 1:17 Ag 22'25. CC 17775
The Windsor tapestry. by Compton Mackenzie. (Fadiman) 14:97-8*N12'38. B 17776
Wine of choice. by S. N. Behrman. (Benchley) 14:30*Mr5'38. T 17777
Wine, women and war. Anon.

(Boyd) 2:94-5 D18'26. B 17778
Wines. by Julian Street. (Fadiman) 9:62 Ja20'34. B 17779
Winged pharaoh. by Joan Grant. (Fadiman) 14:67*Mr26'38. B 17780
The wingless victory. by Maxwell Anderson. (Benchley) 12:26*Ja 2'37. T 17781
Wings. (Mosher) 3:63 Ag20'27. CC 17782
The wings of the eagle. by Gilbert Seldes. (Smith) 5:129-30 O19'29. B 17783
Wings of the Navy. (Mosher) 14: 53*F4'39. CC 17784
Wings of wax. by Janet Hoyt. (Lowrie) 5:107 Ap27'29. B 17785
Wings over Europe. by Robert Nichols and Maurice Browne. (Brackett) 4:25-6 D22'28. T 17786
Wining and dining with rhyme and reason. by D. T. Carlisle and Elizabeth Dunn. (Fadiman) 9:62-3 Ja20'34. B 17787
Winner take all. (Mosher) 8:49 Je25'32. CC 17788
Winner take nothing. by Ernest Hemingway. (Fadiman) 9:74-5 O28'33. B 17789
Winnie-the-Pooh. by A. A. Milne. (Dounce) 2:78 O30'26. B 17790
Winter wheat. by Almey St. John Adcock. (Dounce) 2:46 Jy24'26. B 17791
Winterset. (Mosher) 12:64-5*N28 '36. CC 17792
Winterset. by Maxwell Anderson. (Gibbs) 11:36-8*O5'35. T 17793
(Benchley) 12:41-2*My2'36. 17794
The wisdom tooth. by Marc Connelly. (Gabriel) 2:24 F27'26. T 17795
The wiser sex. (Mosher) 8:76* Mr19'32. CC 17796
The wiser they are. by Sheridan Gibney. (Benchley) 7:28 Ap18 '31. T 17797
The witch. by John Mansfield. (Brackett) 2:34 N27'26. T 17798
The witch in the wood. by T. H. White. (Fadiman) 15:68-9*N4 '39. B 17799
Witchcraft through the ages. (Mosher) 5:75 Je1'29. CC 17800
Witches still live. by Theda Kenyon. (Gannett) 5:166 D7'29. B 17801
With malice toward some. by Margaret Halsey. (Fadiman) 14:47-8*Ag20'38. B 17802
With Napoleon in Russia. by Napoleon Bonaparte and Jean Hanoteau, ed. (Fadiman) 11: 77-8*N30'35. B 17803
With pencil, brush and chisel. by Emil Fuchs. (Anon.) 1:26 Ap11 '25. B 17804
With Williamson beneath the sea. (Mosher) 8:85 D3'32. CC 17805
The withered root. by Rhys Davies. (Markey) 4:100 My5'28. B 17806
Within the gates. by Sean O'Casey. (Benchley) 10:30-2 Mr10'34; 10: 29 N3'34. T 17807
Within the law. by Bayard Veiller. (Brackett) 4:32 Mr17'28. T 17808
Within the web. by Joan Sutherland. (Coates) 8:61-2 My28'32. B 17809
Without warning. by Ralph Spencer Zink. (Gibbs) 13:28*My8'37. T 17810
The wizard. (Claxton) 3:111-13 D3 '27. CC 17811
The wizard of Oz. (Maloney) 15: 52*Ag19'39. CC 17812
Wolf Solent. by John Cowper Powys. (Smith) 5:103 Je8'29. B 17813
Wolf's clothing. (Claxton) 3:91 Ap 2'27. CC 17814
Wolves. by Romain Rolland. (Benchley) 7:26 Ja16'32. T 17815
The woman accused. (Mosher) 9: 63 Mr18'33. CC 17816
The woman between. (Mosher) 7: 74 O31'31. CC 17817

Woman chases man. (Mosher) 13: 64*Je19'37. CC 17818
A woman denied. by Gennaro Mario Curci. (Parker) 7:33-4 Mr7'31. T 17819
The woman disputed. (Mosher) 4:95-7 N17'28. CC 17820
A woman disputed. by Denison Clift. (Brackett) 2:33-4 O9'26. T 17821
A woman of affairs. (Mosher) 4: 65-7 Ja26'29. CC 17822
The woman of Andros. by Thornton Wilder. (Smith) 6:81 Mr1 '30. B 17823
The woman of bronze. by Paul Kester. (Wright) 3:66 Je25'27. T 17824
A woman of the world. (Shane) 1:34 D19'25. CC 17825
The woman on the balcony. by Rose Caylor. (Boyd) 3:111-12 Ap30'27. B 17826
A woman rebels. (Mosher) 12:70* N7'36. CC 17827
Woman to woman. (Mosher) 5:111 N23'29. CC 17828
Woman trap. (Mosher) 5:75-6 S7 '29. CC 17829
The woman who invented love. by Guido Da Verona. (Leonard) 4:60-1 Jy7'28. B 17830
The woman who rode away. by D. H. Lawrence. (Markey) 4: 86-7 Je9'28. B 17831
The woman who stole everything. by Arnold Bennett. (Boyd) 3:97 My7'27. B 17832
A woman with white eyes. by Mary Borden. (Smith) 6:110-12 N22'30. B 17833
A woman's a fool—to be clever. by Dorothy Bennett and Link Hannah. (Gibbs) 14:32*O29'38. T 17834
The women. (Mosher) 15:61*S16 '39. CC 17835
The women. by Clare Boothe. (Benchley) 12:26*Ja2'37. T 17836
Women and monks. by Joseph Kallinikov. (Smith) 6:96 N15 '30. B 17837
Women go on forever. by Daniel N. Rubin. (Brackett) 3:59-60 S17'27. T 17838
Women have been kind. by Lou Tellegen. (Parker) 7:64-7 F21 '31. B 17839
The women have their way. by Serafin Quintero and Joaquin Alvarez Quintero. (Benchley) 5:27-8 F8'30. T 17840
Women must work. by Richard Aldington. (Fadiman) 10:111 N 10'34. B 17841
Wonder bar. (Mosher) 10:89 Mr 10'34. CC 17842
The wonder bar. by Irving Caesar, adapt. and Aben Kandel, adapt. (Parker) 7:34-5 Mr28 '31. T 17843
Wonder boy. by Edward Chodorov and Arthur Barton. (Benchley) 7:28-30 O31'31. T 17844
Wonder of women. (Mosher) 5:34-5 Jy27'29. CC 17845
A wonderful night. by Fanny Todd Mitchell. (Benchley) 5:34-6 N9 '29. T 17846
The wooden kimono. by John H. Floyd. (Brackett) 2:30 Ja8'27. T 17847
The woods colt. by Thames Williamson. (Fadiman) 9:89-90 O7 '33. B 17848
Woof, woof. by Estelle Hunt; Sam Summers and Cyrus Wood. (Benchley) 5:28 Ja4'30. T 17849
Work. by Adriano Tilgher and Dorothy Canfield trans. (Coates) 7:87 Mr28'31. B 17850
Work of art. by Sinclair Lewis. (Fadiman) 9:69-71 Ja27'34. B 17851
The work of Stephen Crane. by Stephen Crane and Wilson Follett, ed. (Dounce) 1:22 Ja2'26. B 17852
The work, wealth and happiness of mankind. by H. G. Wells. (Coates) 7:53-5 D26'31. B 17853
The world and the flesh. (Mosher)

8:50-1*My14'32. CC 17854
World champions. by Paul Morand. (Coates) 7:67*My30'31. B 17855
The world changes. (Mosher) 9: 79-80 N4'33. CC 17856
The world does move. by Booth Tarkington. (Lowrie) 4:129 D 15'28. B 17857
World from below. by Jules Romains. (Fadiman) 11:76-7*O5 '35. B 17858
A world I never made. by James T. Farrell. (Fadiman) 12:64* O31'36. B 17859
The world is round. by Gertrude Stein. (Fadiman) 15:72-3*N25 '39. B 17860
The world moves on. (Mosher) 10:64 Jy7'34. CC 17861
The world of William Clissold. by H. G. Wells. (Dounce) 2:89 O2'26. B 17862
World panorama: 1918-1933. by Gilbert Seldes. (Fadiman) 9: 66 Je10'33. B 17863
The world waits. by George F. Hummel. (Benchley) 9:28 N4 '33. T 17864
The world we make. by Sidney Kingsley. (Benchley) 15:38*D2 '39. T 17865
The world's delight. by Fulton Oursler. (Smith) 5:66 Ag31'29. B 17866
The works of François Rabelais. by François Rabelais; Albert Jay Nock, ed. and Catherine Rose Wilson, ed. (Coates) 7: 93 O10'31. B 17867
The worm ouroboros. by E. R. Eddison. (Dounce) 2:49-50 Jy 10'26. B 17868
The would-be gentleman. by F. Anstey. (Brackett) 4:32-3 O13 '28. T 17869
A wreath of cloud. by Arthur Waley, trans. (Boyd) 3:102-103 Mr26'27. B 17870
The wreck of the Hesperus. (Claxton) 3:113 D3'27. CC 17871
The wrecker. by Arnold Ridley and Bernard Merivale. (Brackett) 4:33 Mr10'28. T 17872
Wuthering Heights. (Mosher) 15: 79-80*Ap15'39. CC 17873
Wuthering Heights. by Randolph Carter. (Gibbs) 15:30*My6'39. T 17874

Y

Yama. by Alexandre Kuprin. (Smith) 5:76-7 Ja11'30. B 17875
Yang and yin. by Alice Tisdale Hobart. (Anon.) 12:80*N7'36. B 17876
A Yank at Oxford. (Mosher) 14: 48 Mr5'38. CC 17877
The Yankee clipper. (Claxton) 3: 87 My7'27. CC 17878
The year of grace. by Noel Coward. (Brackett) 4:32-3 N17'28. T 17879
The yearling. by Marjorie Kinnan Rawlings. (Fadiman) 14:60-1* Ap2'38. B 17880
The years. by Virginia Woolf. (Fadiman) 13:76-7*Ap10'37. B 17881
Years are so long. by Josephine Lawrence. (Fadiman) 10:70-1 Jy7'34. B 17882
Years of grace. by Margaret A. Barnes. (Smith) 6:58 Ag2'30. B 17883
The years of the locust. by Gilbert Seldes. (Coates) 8:62 F11 '33. B 17884
Yellow. by Maraget Vernon. (Brackett) 2:34 O2'26. T 17885
Yellow gentians and blue. by Zona Gale. (Parker) 3:91-2 N5 '27. B 17886
Yellow Jack. (Mosher) 14:59 My 28'38. CC 17887
Yellow Jack. by Sidney Howard. (Benchley) 10:32-4 Mr17'34. T 17888
The yellow jacket. by George C. Hazelton and J. H. Benrimo. (Brackett) 4:33-4 N24'28. T 17889
The yellow lily. (Claxton) 4:92

My26'28. CC 17890
The yellow ticket. (Mosher) 7:81 N7'31. CC 17891
Yes, my darling daughter. by Mark Reed. (Benchley) 13:28-30*F20'37. T 17892
Yesterday's burdens. by Robert M. Coates. (Fadiman) 9:118 D9'33. B 17893
Yokel boy. by Lew Brown; Charles Tobias and Samuel H. Stept. (Gibbs) 15:28*Jy15'39. T 17894
You and heredity. by Amram Scheinfeld. (Fadiman) 15:56* S2'39. B 17895
You and me. (Maloney) 14:50-1* Je11'38. CC 17896
You belong to me. (McKelway) 10:68 S22'34. CC 17897
You can escape. by Edward H. Smith. (Smith) 5:97 S28'29. B 17898
You can't cheat an honest man. (Mosher) 15:58*F25'39. CC 17899
You can't get away with it. (Mosher) 12:97*D12'36. CC 17900
You can't get away with murder. (Mosher) 15:68*Ap1'39. CC 17901
You can't print that! by George Seldes. (Lowrie) 4:92 F16'29. B 17902
You can't sleep here. by Edward Newhouse. (Fadiman) 10:88* N24'34. B 17903
You can't take it with you. (Mosher) 14:59*S10'38. CC 17904
You can't take it with you. by Moss Hart and George S. Kaufman. (Benchley) 12:26*D26'36. T 17905
You never know. by Cole Porter and Rowland Leigh. (Gibbs) 14: 28-9*O1'38. T 17906
You never know women. (Claxton) 2:35-6 Ag7'26. CC 17907
You only live once. (Mosher) 12: 52-3*Ja30'37. CC 17908
You said it. by Jack Yellen and Sid Silvers. (Benchley) 6:28 Ja 31'31. T 17909
You'd be surprised. (Claxton) 2:75 O2'26. CC 17910
Young Alexander. by Hardwick Nevin. (Brackett) 5:28 Mr23'29. T 17911
Young and healthy. by Donald Henderson Clarke. (Parker) 7:88-9 O10'31. B 17912
Young Apollo. by Anthony Gibbs. (Smith) 5:124 O26'29. B 17913
The young at heart. (Mosher) 14: 94*N12'38. CC 17914
The young Cosima. by Henry Handel Richardson. (Fadiman) 15:68-9*Mr25'39. B 17915
Young couple wanted. by Arthur Wilmurt. (Gibbs) 15:30 F3'40. T 17916
Young Dr. Kildare. (Mosher) 14: 57-8*N5'38. CC 17917
Young eagles. (Mosher) 6:57 Mr29 '30. CC 17918
Young Henry of Navarre. by Heinrich Mann and Eric Sutton, trans. (Anon.) 13:65*O2'37. B 17919
Young in the Nineties. by Una Hunt. (Boyd) 3:100 Mr19'27. B 17920
Young Joseph. by Thomas Mann. (Fadiman) 11:63*My4'35. B 17921
Young love. by Samson Raphaelson. (Brackett) 4:33-4 N10'28. T 17922
Young Madame Conti. by Hubert Griffith and Benn W. Levy. (Benchley) 13:30*Ap10'37. T 17923
Young man of Manhattan. by Katharine Brush. (Smith) 5:77 Ja11'30. B 17924
Young man with a horn. by Dorothy Baker. (Fadiman) 14:60*Je 4'38; 14:49*D24'38. B 17925
The young may moon. by Martha Ostenso. (Smith) 5:59 Ag24'29. B 17926
The young Melbourne. by David Cecil. (Fadiman) 15:54*S2'39. B 17927
Young men in love. by Michael

Arlen. (Boyd) 3:97 My7'27. B 17928
Young Mr. Lincoln. (Mosher) 15: 74*Je10'39. CC 17929
Young Mrs. Greeley. by Booth Tarkington. (Smith) 5:105 Je8 '29. B 17930
Young nowheres. (Mosher) 5:60-2 O12'29. CC 17931
Young Orland. by Herbert Asquith. (Hoyt) 3:119 N19'27. B 17932
Young sinners. (Mosher) 7:82 My 16'31. CC 17933
Young sinners. by Elmer Harris. (Benchley) 5:36 D14'29. T 17934
Young woman of 1914. by Arnold Zweig and Eric Sutton, trans. (Coates) 8:78 D17'32. B 17935
Young Woodley. by John van Druten. (Mankiewicz) 1:19 N14 '25. T 17936
The youngest camel. by Kay Boyle. (Fadiman) 15:73*N25 '39. B 17937
The youngest one. by Katherine Haviland Taylor. (Leonard) 4: 58 Jy28'28. B 17938
Your days are numbered. by Florence Campbell. (Coates) 7:83-4 S12'31. B 17939
Your life lies before you. by Harry Hansen. (Fadiman) 11: 82-3*N2'35. B 17940
Your Uncle Dudley. (Mosher) 11: 74*D21'35. CC 17941
Your Uncle Dudley. by Howard Lindsay and Bertrand Robinson. (Benchley) 5:36 N30'29. T 17942
You're telling me. (Mosher) 10: 95 Ap14'34. CC 17943
Yours for the asking. (Mosher) 12:46*Ag29'36. CC 17944
Yours truly. by Clyde North and Anne Caldwell. (Brackett) 2:33-4 F5'27. T 17945
Youth astray. (Claxton) 4:81 Je9 '28. CC 17946
The youth of Maxim. (Mosher) 11:58-9*My4'35. CC 17947

Z

Zaza. (Mosher) 14:43*Ja7'39. CC 17948
Zeppelin. by McElbert Moore; Earle Crooker and Lowell Brentano. (Brackett) 4:26-8 Ja26'29. T 17949
Zest. by Frank Norris. (Fadiman) 9:55 My27'33. B 17950
Ziegfeld follies. by Irving Berlin and Harold Atteridge. (Long) 3: 48-9 Ag27'27. T 17951
Ziegfeld follies, 1931. by Florenz Ziegfeld. (Benchley) 7:26-8*Jy 4'31. T 17952
Ziegfeld follies of 1936-1937. by Ira Gershwin and David Freedman. (Benchley) 11:28-30*F8 '36. T 17953
Zombie. by Kenneth Webb. (Benchley) 8:32*F20'32. T 17954
Zoo in Budapest. (Mosher) 9:61 My6'33. CC 17955
Zwei herzen im 3-4 takt. (Mosher) 6:93 O25'30. CC 17956
(Mosher) 7:48 Jy18'31. 17957

Initials, Pseudonyms and Abbreviations of Names

A.	Katharine S. Angell White
A. A.	Anthony Armstrong
AE	George Russell
A. G.	Anthony Gibbs
A. GIBBS	Anthony Gibbs
A. G. L.	A. G. Lockhart
AGNI	Alva Johnston
A. H. F.	Arthur H. Folwell
A. K. L.	A. K. Laing
ALCESTE	Ernest Boyd
ALESSIA	Irma Brandeis
ALISON WNDRLAND	Arthur Kober
A. M. L.	Arthur Moss
A. M. M.	Adrienne M. Murphy
A. N. B.	A. N. Bass
ANDERSON, MR.	Paul Hollister
ANGELA CYPHER	Marjorie Allen Seiffert
ANGELINA	Katharine S. Angell White
ANGELL, KATHARINE S.	Katharine S. Angell White
ANONYMOUS	E. B. White
ARNO, PETER	Curtis Arnoux Peters
ASPER	Morris Markey
AUDAX MINOR	G. F. T. Ryall
A. W. S.	Agnes W. Smith
BARON IRELAND	Nate Salisbury
BEAUGIBBS	Wolcott Gibbs
BAEDEKER JONES	E. B. White
B. C.	Brownell Carr
BENCHLEY	Robert Benchley
B. G. L.	Edith Owen
B. H.	Baird Hall

BIRDSEYE and BIRDSEYE 2nd	Gilbert Seldes
B. L.	Baird Leonard
BLISS, TIP	T. H. Bliss
B. N.	Beverly Nichols
BOGAN	Louis Bogan
BOYD	Ernest Boyd
BRACKETT	Charles Brackett
B. R. R.	Ben Ray Redman
BUNNY	Eleanor W. Koehler
C. B.	Charles Brackett
C. C.	Carroll Carroll
C. COUPON	M. B. O'Shea
C. D.	Caroline Duer
C. F. L.	C. F. Looms
C. G.	Charles Graves
C. G. S.	Charles G. Shaw
CHARLOT, GENOVA	Grace Hazard Conkling
CHARON, JR.	Stanley Walker
C. H. F.	Charles Henri Ford
CHILDE HAROLD	James Thurber
C. J.	Clara Janson
CLAXTON	Oliver Claxton
C. L. Q.	C. Lee Quong
C. M.	Charles MacArthur
COATES	Robert M. Coates
COL. BOLTON FIELD-FIELD	James Thurber
CONNELLY	Marc Connelly
CONNOISSEUR	Willa K. Smith
CONSTANT READER	Dorothy Parker
COUPON, C.	M. B. O'Shea
CYPHER, ANGELA	Marjorie Allen Seiffert
D. B. W. L.	D. B. Wyndham Lewis
D. C.	Donald Cameron
D. D.	Dorothy Dow
D. H.	Dorothy Homans
D. K.	Doris Kirkpatrick

D. K. R.	Dorothy Kidder Riggs
DOUNCE	Harry Esty Dounce
D. T.	Dorothy Thompson
D. W.	Dearing Ward, or Douglas Watts
E. & O. E.	Samuel James
E. B. M. D.	Ernest Boyd
E. B. S.	Elizabeth B. Sayre
E. B. W.	E. B. White
E. C.	Elizabeth Coatsworth
E. D.	Elmer Davis
EDEN, PATIENCE	Martha Banning Thomas
E. J.	Elizabeth Jordan
ELSPETH	Elspeth O'Halloran
E. M. C.	E. M. Cody
EUSTACE TILLEY	E. B. White
E. W.	Elinor Wylie
EXTRA	Thomas Longan
FADIMAN	Clifton Fadiman
F. A. F.	F. A. Fender
FALSTAFF, JAKE	Herman Fetzer
FAWKES, GUY	Robert Benchley
F. D.	Fairfax Downey
F. H.	Fillmore Hyde
FIELD-FIELD, COL. BOLTON	James Thurber
FINNY, S.	E. B. White
FLANNER	Janet Flanner
FROST, JACK	Carl Brandt
F. S.	Florence Stone
F. T.	Ferdinand Touhy
GABRIEL	Gilbert W. Gabriel
GANNETT	Louis S. Gannett
G. C. R.	Gertrude Curtis Ryan
GENÊT	Janet Flanner
GENOVA CHARLOT	Grace Hazard Conkling
G. F. R.	G. F. Riegel

G. H.	George Hellman
G. H. C.	Grace Hazard Conkling
GIBBS	Wolcott Gibbs
GIBBS, A.	Anthony Gibbs
GOLLY WOGG	Gilbert W. Gabriel
GREELEY, HORACE, JR.	Philip G. Wylie
GRIFFITH, MADDY VEGTEL	Maddy Vegtel
GROVER, JAMES	Gorham, James
G. S.	G. Schwabe
GUIDO	Guy Du Bois
G. W. G.	Gilbert W. Gabriel
HABAKKUK JONES	Elmer Davis
HAROLD, CHILDE	James Thurber
HAWTHORNE	Ruth Hawthorne
HAY	Newman Levy
HAYS	Will Hays, Jr.
H. C.	Howard Cushman
H. D.	Harry Esty Dounce
HELLMAN	George Hellman
H. E. Y.	H. E. Yates
HIPPOLYTA	Janet Flanner
H. J. D.	Homer Joseph Dodge
H. J. L.	H. J. Littlefield
H. J. M.	Herman J. Mankiewicz
HORACE GREELEY, JR.	Philip G. Wylie
HORVENDILE	Gilmer V. Black
HOYT	Nancy Hoyt
H. R.	Herbert Reed
I. B.	Irma Brandeis or Iris Barry
IRELAND, BARON	Nate Salisbury
I. V. V.	J. W. Harrington
JACK FROST	Carl Brandt
JAKE FALSTAFF	Herman Fetzer
JAM	Aimee Whitalser
JARED L. MANLEY	James Thurber

J. C.	John Cowmos
J. C. M.	John Chapin Mosher
J. C. N.	J. C. Norton
J. C. O.	James C. Oestreicher
JEAKE, SAMUEL, JR.	Conrad Aiken
J. F. F.	Joseph Fulling Fishman
J. G. T.	James Thurber
J. M.	Jo U. Milward
J. M. M.	Joseph Moncure March
JOHN SWIFT	Gilbert Seldes
JONES, BAEDEKER	E. B. White
JONES, HABAKKUK	Elmer Davis
J. S. N.	John Strong Newberry
J. T.	James Thurber
J. X. J.	John J. Holzinger
K. C.	Kathleen Cannell
K. P. B.	Kenneth Phillips Britton
KRONENBERGER	Louis Kronenberger
K. S. & H. S.	Katherine Sproehnle
K. S. A.	Katharine S. Angell White
K. WHITE	Katharine S. Angell White
L. B.	Louise Bogan or Lisle Bell
LEONARD	Baird Leonard
LEONARD Q. ROSS	Leo Rosten
L. H.	Lois Long and Nancy Hardin
LIPSTICK	Lois Long
L. N. J.	Leslie Nelson Jennings
LOCKRIDGE	Richard Lockridge
LONG	Lois Long
LORD STITES	Donald Stites Fairchild
LOWRIE	Rebecca L. Lowrie
L. S. G.	Louis S. Gannett
L. S. P.	Leslie S. Pearl
M.	Joseph Moncure March
Mc GREGOR	G. M. Hurley

Mc KELWAY	St. Clair Mc Kelway
MAJOLICA WATTLES	Clinch Calkins
MALONEY	Russell Maloney
THE MAN WHO CAME BACK	C. Hovey
MANHATTAN	Berry Fleming
MANKIEWICZ	Herman J. Mankiewicz
MANLEY, JARED L.	James Thurber
MARCH	Joseph Moncure March
MARGARETTA	Margaretta Manning
MARGO	Frances M. Frost
MARKEY	Morris Markey
MARNE	Margaret Fishback
M. C.	Marc Connelly
M. C. D.	Mary Carolyn Davies
M. G.	Marie Gilchrist
MIDDLETON	Scudder Middleton
MR. ANDERSON	Paul Hollister
M. K. L.	Margaret K. Leech
M. M. W.	Myra M. Waterman
MOSHER	John Chapin Mosher
M. W.	Margaret Widdemer
N. C.	Nigel Cauchy
NET STAR	Franklin P. Adams
NETTLES	Clara Janson
N. H.	Nancy Hoyt
N. L.	Newman Levy
N. N. D.	Nat N. Dorfman
N. S.	G. Beck
O. C.	Oliver Claxton
PARKER	Dorothy Parker
PATIENCE EDEN	Martha Banning Thomas
P. C.	Parke Cummings
P. E.	Martha Banning Thomas
THE PERENNIAL BACHELOR	Ordway Teed
PETER ARNO	Curtis Arnoux Peters

P. G.	Paul Gould
P. G. A.	Persis Greely Anderson
P. G. G.	Paul G. Gumbinner
P. G. W.	Philip G. Wylie
PLUSUPER	Francis Steegmuller
POLY	L. C. Meyers
QUID	Marquis James
R. A.	Heywood Broun
R. A. S.	Robert A. Simon
R. B.	Robert Benchley
R. B. P.	Ruth B. Parr
R. C. W.	R. C. Washburn
R. H.	Ruth Hawthorne
R. L.	Richard Lockridge
R. L. J.	Ruth Lambert Jones
R. L. L.	Rebecca L. Lowrie
R. M.	Russell Maloney
R. M. C.	Robert M. Coates
ROSS, LEONARD Q.	Leo Rosten
ROTO	T. H. Bosworth
SAM	Frank Sullivan
SAMUEL JEAKE, JR.	Conrad Aiken
S. C. M.	St. Clair McKelway
SEARCH-LIGHT	Waldo Frank
S. FINNY	E. B. White
SGANARELLE	Gilbert Seldes
SHANE	Theodore Shane
S. H. H.	Stewart Hyde Hawkins
SIG	Sigmund Spaeth
SIMON	Robert A. Simon
SIMPLE SUSAN, SPINSTER	Florence Helm
S. M.	Scudder Middleton
SMITH	Agnes W. Smith
S. S. J.	S. S. Jones
STARHILL	Gilbert Seldes

STITES, LORD	Donald Stites Fairchild
STOWAWAY	Sam Marx
SUPER	Henry Carlton
S. W.	Sterling Wilson
SWIFT, JOHN	Gilbert Seldes
TELEMAQUE	Harold Wengler
T. H. B.	T. H. Bliss
T. H. L.	Tracy Hammond Lewis
TILLEY, EUSTACE	E. B. White
TIMOTHY VANE	Alexander Woollcott
TIP BLISS	T. H. Bliss
TOP HAT	Lois Long
TOUCHSTONE	Harry Esty Dounce
T. S.	Theodore Shane
TYMPANI	Robert A. Simon
VAN GOGH	Murdock Pemberton
VANE, TIMOTHY	Alexander Woollcott
V. P.	Viola Paradise
V. T.	V. L. Parsons
WATTLES, MAJOLICA	Clinch Calkins
W. G.	Wolcott Gibbs
WHITE	E. B. White
WHITE, K.	Katharine S. Angell White
WNDRLAND, ALISON	Arthur Kober
WOOLLCOTT	Alexander Woollcott
WORRIED	Robert Benchley
WRIGHT	Saul Wright

A.
see White, Katharine S. Angell
A. A.
see Armstrong, Anthony
A. B. B.
9140
AE
see Russell, George
A. G.
see Gibbs, Anthony
A. G. L.
see Lockhart, A. G.
A. H. F.
see Folwell, Arthur H.
A. J. O.
7980
A. K. L.
see Laing, A. K.
A. L. L.
4661, 4666, 4699, 10653
A. M.
see Moss, Arthur
A. M. M.
see Murphy, Adrienne M.
A. N. B.
see Bass, A. N.
A. O. N.
884
A. R. T.
7579
A. T.
14251r
A. W. S.
see Smith, Agnes W.
Abbott, Berenice
12716
Abbott, C. C.
12899, 14779
Abbott, George
12500, 12546, 12893, 13433, 13641, 14051, 14571, 14643, 14836, 14946, 15741, 16307, 17199, 17217
Abell, George
2097
Abrahams, S. M.
1251
Abrams, Leon
14051
Achard, Marcel
13187, 14739
Acheson, Edward
9576, 11615
Ackerley, J. R.
14135
Acklund, Rodney
15558
Adair, A. H.
13136
Adamic, Louis
12917, 13262, 13896, 15430, 15490
Adams, Felicia
97
Adams, Franklin P.
95, 257, 602, 673, 699, 1022, 1461, 1473, 1924, 1925, 2029, 2106, 2286, 2705, 2792, 3179, 3240, 4099, 4218, 4804, 4810, 4811, 4812, 4813, 4924, 5045, 5308, 5351, 5774, 5943, 6054, 6449, 6682, 6683, 7824, 7967, 8562, 9041, 9547, 9627, 9646, 9647, 9974, 10709, 10720, 11188, 11238, 11274, 11662, 11736, 11762, 12872, 13129
Adams, Henry
14780
Adams, James Truslow
11919, 14895, 15796
Adams, Samuel Hopkins
1292, 6469, 8004
Adcock, Almey St. John
17791
Addington, Sarah
9044, 10541
Adee, William T.
9014

Aderer, Adolphe
15052
Adler, Hans
16226
Aesop III
2736
AGNI
see Johnston, Alva
Ahearn, Danny
14242
Aiken, Conrad
1065, 2803, 5101, 5375, 5886, 6134, 8498, 8581-8598, 12036, 12452, 12539, 12842, 12903, 13909, 14483
Aiken, G. L.
17460
Aikman, Duncan
12615
Akeley, Mary L. Jobe
12654
Akins, Zoë
12951, 13530, 13690, 13943, 14944, 15659, 15706, 17200
Albert, Herman W.
10449
Albright, Hardie
11984
Aldington, Richard
11976, 12831, 13059, 15212, 17530, 17841
Aldis, Dorothy
541, 10340
Aleichem, Sholem
14307
Alexander, Irene
13942
Alexander, Jack
162, 433, 869, 1419, 2027, 2036, 2078, 2131, 2209, 2213, 2244, 4032, 4067, 4186, 4212, 4541, 5033, 5403, 6170, 6504, 8099, 8853, 9127, 9230, 10937, 11104, 11307, 11707
Alger, Joseph
516, 2109, 4625, 7762, 9096
Alison Wndrland
see Kober, Arthur
Allen, Fred
2325
Allen, Frederick Lewis
4016, 5807, 8204, 10592, 11455, 11475, 12025, 15775, 16679
Allen, George
3956, 4352, 7531, 10893
Allen, Hervey
11916, 12090
Allen, Robert S.
4794, 11150
Allen, Sara Van Alstyne
3041
Allen, William H.
16348
Allingham, Philip
12726
Allvine, Glendon
14618
Alsberg, Harry
16085
Altalena
see Zhabotinskii, Vladimir
Alton, Maxine
12131
Alverdes, Paul
17713
Amiel, Denys
17203
Amis, A.
7350
Ammers-Küller, Jo Van
14233, 14459
Anderson, Hugh A.
15473
Anderson, Margaret
15460
Anderson, Maxwell
12487, 12574, 13326, 13819, 13978, 14129, 14561, 14615, 15168, 15173, 15569, 15815, 16474, 16876, 17202, 17511, 17679, 17781, 17793, 17794
Anderson, Mr.
see Hollister, Paul
Anderson, Nels
15280
Anderson, Persis Greely
174, 395, 415, 918, 1227, 1397, 1775, 2099, 2189, 2469, 2537, 2593, 2732, 2778, 2883, 2953, 3012, 3924, 3953, 4264, 5032, 5239, 5481, 5559, 5578, 6310, 6481, 7053, 7234, 7494, 7523, 8187, 8235, 8698, 8789, 8793, 9004, 9012, 9556, 10157, 10277, 10544, 10599, 10730,

10772, 10846, 10920, 11246, 11517, 11631
Anderson, Sherwood
2121, 5488, 6328, 7396, 7695, 8485, 10079, 13012, 13058, 14075, 14609, 15928, 16609, 17072
Andersson, J. G.
12056
Andrews, Amos
8040
Andrews, C. E.
14365
Andrews, Charlton
1693, 8897, 13765, 16450
Andrews, F. Emerson
7587, 7853, 10947
Andreyev, Leonid
14550, 17583
Angela Cypher
see Seiffert, Marjorie Allen
Angelina
see White, Katharine S. Angell
Angell, Hildegarde
4, 7492
Angell, Katharine S.
see White, Katharine S. Angell
Angly, Edward
1674, 8635
Angoff, Charles
4510
Angus, Bernie
12063
Anonymous
see White, E. B.
Ansky, S.
13260, 13261
Anspacher, Louis K.
16279, 17457
Anstey, F.
17869
Anthony, C. L.
12194
Anthony, Edward
15654
Anthony, Joseph
583, 16614
Anthony, Katharine
14938, 16159
Anthony, Norman B.
12237
Antoine, André-Paul
14953
Anton, Henry
529, 1787, 2787, 5355, 5356, 5841, 6262, 6332, 8638, 9364, 10992, 11885
Antongini, Tom
12996
Appel, Benjamin
12502
Applegate, Frank G.
14352
Aragon, Louis
12316, 14760
Araminta
11403
Archer, Harry
15440, 17426
Archibald, Jean
15157
Ardrey, Robert
12670, 14243, 16874, 17250
Arent, Arthur
15768, 15971, 15972
Argus
3230
Aristophanes
15002
Arlen, Harold
14803
Arlen, Michael
13572, 13950, 14838, 15189, 15219, 17143, 17928
Armour, Richard
386, 525, 2729, 3080, 5298, 5683, 7471, 7506, 7885, 8188, 8332, 8864, 9299, 9398, 9797, 9812, 10515, 10943
Armstrong, Anthony
206, 790, 1208, 1332, 2387, 2719, 3901, 4588, 5087, 6491, 7207, 8326, 8369, 9750, 10153, 10253, 17096
Armstrong, Charlotte
2785, 7195, 8927, 14000
Armstrong, Elizabeth
7205
Armstrong, Margaret
13447, 13542
Armstrong, Martin
12174, 15310
Arno, Peter
5879, 11437, 14107, 15536, 17737
Arnold, Marion E.

1686
Arnold, Thurman W.
13582
Asbury, Herbert
16, 442, 829, 1103, 1393, 1881, 2383, 2442, 2637, 2962, 2978, 3039, 3152, 4153, 5433, 7744, 8781, 9132, 9644, 10119, 10418, 10520, 11061, 11122, 11528-11533, 11606, 12519, 12658, 13665, 13707, 15251, 16989
Asch, Nathan
2102, 6511, 7051, 11020, 14955, 15896
Asch, Sholem
15496, 17593
Ashton, Helen
13173, 13256, 15007
Ashton, Herbert, Jr.
12561
Asper
see Markey, Morris
Asquith, Herbert
17932
Asquith, Margot
14737, 15368, 15663
Atherton, Gertrude
11924
Atkinson, J. Brooks
13294
Atkinson, Oriana
2275, 6355, 8899, 9882
Atlas, Leopold
12593, 17647
Atteridge, Harold
12146, 13400, 13726, 13935, 13962, 15554, 15555, 15556, 15989, 17951
Attiwill, Kenneth
17773
Atwater, Florence Carroll
863, 5629B, 7891
Atwater, Richard
9275, 9611
Auden, W. H.
4974, 9778, 11128, 12163, 14510, 15736, 15823, 16007
Aughinbaugh, William E.
14286
Aulnoy, Marie Catherine d'
15214
Auslander, Joseph
2693, 4572, 16795
Austin, Kay
4984
Axelson, Mary Macdougal
14802
Azoy, A. C. M., Jr.
4527, 8905

B

B. B.
584
B. C.
see Carr, Brownell
B. G. L.
see Owen, Edith
B. H.
see Hall, Baird
B. L.
see Leonard, Baird
B. N.
see Nichols, Beverly
B. R. R.
see Redman, Ben Ray
Babel, I.
16227
Bachman, Eleanor
10001, 11353
Backer, George
14185
Bacon, Frank
14828
Bacon, Josephine Daskam
7895-7897, 7900, 7906, 7909
Bacon, Leonard
12074, 13972
Bacon, Peggy
249, 282, 409, 906, 1342, 1530, 1544, 1560, 1904, 2161, 2470, 2485, 2763, 2868, 2955, 3057, 3199, 3232, 4214, 4402, 4934, 5085, 6289, 6392, 8297, 8950, 10083, 11135, 11877, 15682
Baedeker Jones
see White, E. B.
Baerlein, Henry
13228
Bagby, George
13516
Bagger, Eugene
13646
Bagnold, Enid

13204, 15488
Bahr, Jerome
15980
Bailey, H. C.
14616
Bailey, Le Roy
12966
Bairnsfather, Bruce
15695
Baker, Dorothy
17925
Baker, Rug Dept.
see Wengler, Harold
Balderston, John L.
12326, 13220
Baldwin, Faith
13152
Balieff, Nikita
7144
Ballard, Fred
14646
Ballou, Jenny
11619, 15929, 16817
Bamman, George
15473
Bamman, Catherine
17005
Banks, Polan
13738
Banning, Margaret Culkin
15352
Baragwanath, John
11981
Barber, Frederick
14197
Barbican, James
12863
Barbusse, Henri
14283
Bard, Josef
16616
Baring, Maurice
12686, 13669, 14331, 17695
Barker, Albert
15083
Barker, Edwin
15083
Barnard, Edward W.
10249
Barnard, Harry
13270
Barnard, Seymour
7790, 7791
Barnes, Djuna
5434, 8988, 11703, 15576, 15577
Barnes, Margaret A.
11947, 13143, 14458, 17883
Barnes, William Morris
17693
Barnett, Ella
15753
Baron Ireland
see Salisbury, Nate
Barrangon, Eloise
16840
Barras, Charles M.
12403
Barrie, James M.
11920, 11967, 13453, 14753, 14873, 15564, 15939, 17672
Barrington, E.
see Beck, Lily Adams
Barry, Griffin
6445, 11267
Barry, Iris
3135, 14704, 16042
Barry, Jerome
665, 725, 750, 1637, 1754, 1969, 2992, 4255, 4468, 5224, 5748, 8381, 8445, 9368, 9558, 10271, 10872, 11792, 11808
Barry, Philip
12072, 12537, 12805, 14103, 14169, 14216, 14327, 14480, 14518, 15862, 15951, 16840, 17297, 17730
Barry, Robert
3
Barry, Tom F.
7759, 11696
Barry, William E.
14004
Barrymore, John
12864
Bart, Jean
16855
Bartfield, Carl
17136
Bartholomae, Philip
14612
Bartholomew, A. T.
16647
Bartlett, Arthur
825, 1008, 3161, 5414, 5756, 5768, 9215, 10065, 11789
Bartlett, Ruth Fitch
104, 135, 1501, 3218, 5503, 5978, 7586, 10427

Barton, Arthur
17844
Barton, Ralph
1385, 5063, 5064, 5065, 5066, 5407, 6250, 7640, 8341, 10215, 13816
Basch, Victor
16500
Bass, A. N.
10452
Basshe, Em Jo
12697, 13287
Basso, Hamilton
14347
Batchelor, Jean
32, 52, 64, 317, 377, 428, 467, 742, 980, 1132, 1509, 1799, 1843, 1869, 2251, 2478, 2529, 2968, 3075, 3273, 4231, 4463, 4467, 4919, 5027, 5028, 5039, 6233, 8141, 8189, 8207, 8277, 8989, 9155, 9480, 9638, 9734, 10142, 10780, 10877, 10904, 11088, 11232, 11767
Bates, Ernest Sutherland
12354
Bates, H. E.
13041, 17440
Bates, Ralph
14749, 15716, 16699
Battle, John Tucker
2526, 3917
Battle, Kemp P.
11282
Baty, Gaston
15015
Baudelaire, Charles
13564
Baum, Vicki
13156, 13886, 15160, 16528, 16992, 17060
Baumer, Marie
16539
Bayer, Charles M.
8049
Beach, Lewis
15239
Beahan, Charles
14441, 14876
Beals, Carleton
12014, 12935
Beard, Charles A.
12004, 12021
Beard, William
12021
Beaton, George
14431
Beauclerk, Helen
14965
Beaugibbs
see Gibbs, Wolcott
Bechofer-Roberts, C. E.
17182
Beck, G.
1930
Beck, Lily Adams
13805
Beck, Miriam
788
Bedel, Maurice
14461
Beebe, Lucius
10444
Beebe, William
12114, 13983, 14536, 15627
Beer, Thomas
4144, 7558, 13995, 15188, 16329
Beerbohm, Max
17520
Begouën, Max
12394
Behrman, S. N.
37, 1480, 2258, 4758, 4960, 6536, 10996, 12041, 12383, 12530, 13350, 14958, 15248, 15616, 16185, 16524, 16547A, 17777
Bein, Albert
14767, 14875
Beith, Ian Hay
14002
Belasco, David
13446, 15286
Bell, Clive
12782
Bell, Lisle
117, 8087
Bell, Thomas
11971, 16525
Bellamann, Henry
12929
Bellamy, Virginia Woods
121, 315, 648, 2296, 2496, 4122, 7077, 7745, 8146, 9684, 11586

Belloc, Hilaire
16292
Belmonte, Juan
12184
Belmonte, Nene
16843
Bemelmans, Ludwig
1039, 2305, 5165, 8813, 11590
Benavente, Jacinte
16470
Benchley, Robert
41, 131, 136, 150, 345, 425, 542, 643, 681, 762, 812, 927, 956, 978, 1053, 1058, 1164, 1228, 1403, 1641, 1659, 1712, 1732, 1885, 1919, 2153, 2372, 2406, 2452, 2455, 2477, 2500, 2512, 2564, 2689, 2720, 2882, 2900, 2934, 2937, 3116, 3120, 3132, 3198, 3208, 3251, 3928, 4098, 4241, 4316, 4346, 4383, 4389, 4390, 4493, 4517, 4641, 4727, 4894, 5094, 5125, 5187, 5203, 5335, 5352, 5402, 5508, 5540, 5606, 5686, 5965, 6108, 6140, 6168, 7030, 7071, 7073, 7132, 7295, 7304, 7321, 7360, 7361, 7372, 7374, 7385, 7465, 7487, 7512, 7577, 7584, 7600, 7608, 7610, 7686, 7703, 7868, 7926, 7928, 7955, 8249, 8262, 8380, 8401, 8536, 8556, 8617-8623, 8628, 8657, 8702, 8742, 8809, 8872, 8910, 8971, 9058, 9104, 9220, 9360, 9422, 9425, 9478, 9523, 9616, 9702, 9871, 9993, 10013, 10029, 10047, 10214, 10325, 10470-10475, 10530, 10546, 10583, 10809, 10882, 11095, 11137, 11155, 11210, 11354, 11400, 11431, 11505, 11512, 11578, 11580, 11612, 11753, 11766, 11896r, 11907r, 11912r, 11917r, 11944r, 11950r, 11965r, 11968r, 11969r, 11973r, 11980r, 11981r, 11982r, 11984r, 11988r, 12000r, 12013r, 12019r, 12031r, 12037r, 12039r, 12041r, 12043r, 12048r, 12050r, 12054r, 12072r, 12083r, 12094r, 12096r, 12103r, 12106r, 12127r, 12128r, 12136r, 12147r, 12150r, 12160r, 12199r, 12207r, 12209r, 12213r, 12227r, 12235r, 12243r, 12248r, 12259r, 12270r, 12302r, 12315r, 12326r, 12328r, 12335r, 12342r, 12343r, 12344r, 12364r, 12369r, 12373r, 12380r, 12381r, 12383r, 12387r, 12390r, 12391r, 12392r, 12396r, 12397r, 12409r, 12421r, 12422r, 12429r, 12440r, 12450r, 12487r, 12496r, 12500r, 12503r, 12505r, 12513r, 12520r, 12530r, 12535r, 12537r, 12544r, 12553r, 12558r, 12560r, 12566r, 12582r, 12593r, 12598r, 12604r, 12612r, 12619r, 12622r, 12628r, 12630r, 12631r, 12632r, 12659r, 12663r, 12670r, 12680r, 12692r, 12703r, 12704r, 12715r, 12717r, 12739r, 12741r, 12746r, 12756r, 12760r, 12783r, 12799r, 12836r, 12839r, 12841r, 12847r, 12851r, 12882r, 12885r, 12888r, 12896r, 12905r, 12912r, 12915r, 12922r, 12931r, 12934r, 12937r, 12939r, 12946r, 12970r, 12985r, 12993r, 13011r, 13016r, 13019r, 13028r, 13046r, 13051r, 13052r, 13053r, 13068r, 13079r, 13091r, 13104r, 13109r, 13123r, 13135r, 13143r, 13150r, 13151r, 13156r, 13161r, 13170r, 13181r, 13184r, 13210r, 13239r, 13244r, 13279r, 13281r, 13286, 13297r, 13302r, 13304r, 13309r, 13314r, 13326r, 13350r, 13370r, 13379r, 13380r, 13390r, 13395r, 13400r, 13401r, 13402r, 13413r, 13428r, 13435r, 13438r, 13442r, 13449r, 13457r, 13463r, 13466r,

13471r, 13475r, 13477r,
13493r, 13494r, 13500r,
13510r, 13528r, 13532r,
13533r, 13547r, 13568r,
13591r, 13592r, 13603r,
13608r, 13610r, 13615r,
13651r, 13657r, 13660r,
13667r, 13688r, 13691r,
13703r, 13715r, 13717r,
13736r, 13747r, 13758r,
13761r, 13769r, 13770r,
13774r, 13785r, 13807r,
13825r, 13830r, 13835r,
13850r, 13853r, 13858r,
13864r, 13868r, 13886r,
13911r, 13921r, 13942r,
13943r, 13946r, 13949r,
13959r, 13960r, 13965r,
13969r, 13980r, 13982r,
13988r, 14004r, 14030r,
14032r, 14033r, 14039r,
14041r, 14062r, 10464r,
14070r, 14084r, 14097r,
14099r, 14103r, 14107r,
14121r, 14129r, 14132r,
14133r, 14136r, 14143r,
14155r, 14185r, 14193r,
14212r, 14216r, 14222r,
14227r, 14230r, 14238r,
14239r, 14241r, 14243r,
14246r, 14255r, 14263r,
14276r, 14279r, 14282r,
14288r, 14289r, 14293r,
14301r, 14308r, 14316r,
14324r, 14328r, 14357r,
14372r, 14373r, 14374r,
14376r, 14384r, 14394r,
14404r, 14406r, 14424r,
14429r, 14444r, 14458r,
14460r, 14470r, 14473r,
14474r, 14486r, 14492r,
14494r, 14498r, 14518r,
14522r, 14531r, 14533r,
14535r, 14540r 14546r,
14549r, 14561r, 14575r,
14587r, 14606r, 14637r,
14643r, 14646r, 14657r,
14659r, 14671r, 14672r,
14686r, 14687r, 14705r,
14711r, 14726r, 14727r,
14728r, 14748r, 14750r,
14752r, 14757r, 14765r,
14767r, 14785r, 14787r,
14802r, 14833r, 14863r, 14875r,
14876r, 14893r, 14900r,
14914r, 14925Ar, 14930Ar,
14934r, 14966r, 14968r,
14982r, 14991r, 15002r,
15006r, 15015r, 15026r,
15028r, 15029r, 15033r,
15044r, 15050r, 15059r,
15061r, 15076r, 15083r,
15092r, 15125r, 15128r,
15133r, 15135r, 15152r,
15158r, 15168r, 15171r,
15172r, 15173r, 15183r,
15184r, 15191r, 15205r,
15206r, 15223r, 15224r,
15236r, 15241r, 15248r,
15255r, 15261r, 15263r,
15274r, 15282r, 15303r,
15304r, 15315r, 15329r,
15330r, 15347r, 15354r,
15360r, 15361r, 15365r,
15375r, 15384r, 15386r,
15397r, 15400r, 15412r,
15416r, 15426r, 15467r,
15483r, 15493r, 15506r,
15515r, 15536r, 15558r,
15564r, 15569r, 15570r,
15579r, 15583r, 15584r,
15585r, 15593r, 15606r,
15613r, 15620r, 15651r,
15652r, 15659r, 15667r,
15676r, 15678r, 15681r,
15690r, 15706r, 15707r,
15709r, 15725r, 15729r,
15734r, 15737r, 15745r,
15746r, 15766r, 15768r,
15769r, 15772r, 15792r,
15806r, 15808r, 15818r,
15821r, 15831r, 15832r,
15855r, 15857r, 15868r,
15871r, 15898r, 15923r,
15926r, 15932r, 15939r,
15944r, 15946r, 15947r,
15952r, 15965r, 15971r,
15985r, 15996r, 15997r,
16009r, 16010r, 16032r,
16049r, 16051r, 16064r,
16073r, 16076r, 16077r,
16081r, 16100r, 16117r,
16118r, 16139r, 16140r,
16143r, 16184r, 16185r,
16217r, 16218r, 16230r,
16233r, 16239r, 16243r,

17889
Benson, E. F.
12158
Benson, Sally
287, 321, 388, 591, 794, 800, 852, 1284, 1711, 1810, 1981, 2301, 2741, 2806, 3142, 3148, 3211, 3978, 4010, 4220, 4250, 4379, 4410, 4514, 4602, 4800, 5302, 5706, 5835, 5864, 5981, 6063, 6212, 6419, 6556, 7026, 7151, 7797, 8200, 8245, 8264, 8386, 8483, 8550, 8671, 8878, 9141, 9165, 9613, 9768, 9961, 10100, 10201, 10212, 10216, 10234, 10415, 10676, 11156, 11242, 11287, 11538, 11621, 11691, 11706
Benson, Stella
7364, 7769, 13448, 16133
Benstead, C. R.
16263
Bentley, Phyllis
13663, 16831
Benton, Tom
12143
Beppo
7559
Bercovici, Leonardo
16982
Beresford, J. D.
11990, 15708
Berg, Camillo
489
Berge, Victor
15901
Berger, Meyer
163, 657, 719, 748, 1073, 3242, 5421, 8195, 8468, 8773, 9572, 10074, 10341, 10362, 11018
Bergman, Harold
1594, 9730
Berkeley, Martin
16539
Berlin, Irving
12157, 12809, 12810, 13428, 17951
Berman, Berel Vladimir
2188
Berman, Philip
2602
Bernard, Jean-Jacques
14846
Bernd, A. B.
26, 278, 536, 808, 1833, 1929, 1931, 3083, 4424, 5113, 9399, 9787
Berndorff, H. R.
13374
Bernstein, Aline
14508
Bernstein, Henri
14738, 14741, 14742, 15205, 16118, 17159
Bernstein, Walter
4605
Berstl, Julius
15484
Besier, Rudolf
12256-59
Bessie, Alvah C.
13259, 15220
Best, Mary Agnes
17192
Beuick, Marshall D.
1681, 5386, 10163
Beveridge, Albert J.
11901
Beyerlein, Franz Adam
17071
Bianchi, Martha Dickinson
13339
Bibesco, Marthe
12684, 13957
Bibesco, Prince
14639
Bickford, Charles A.
11543
Bierstadt, Edward Hale
12964
Biggs, John, Jr.
16561
Biggs, Rachel
9513, 10097
Binns, Archie
14831, 15047
Birabeau, André
12977
Birdseye and Birdseye 2nd
see Seldes, Gilbert
Birinski, Leo
15652
Birk, Genevieve Blane
662

Birkenfeld, Gunther
16364
Birmingham, George A.
16413
Birmingham, Michael
13449
Bisch, Louis E.
14572
Bishop, Elizabeth
1493
Bishop, Helen
577
Bishop, John Peale
7292, 11610, 15127
Bishop, Morris
266, 304, 608, 766, 802, 965, 1202, 1256, 1396, 1432, 1763, 1792, 2004, 2056, 2417, 2489, 2638, 2639, 2675, 3014, 3147, 3203, 3207, 4171, 4208, 4238, 4289, 4290, 4460, 4765, 4818, 4975, 5104, 5179, 5321, 5496, 5531, 5536, 5711, 5712, 5713, 5714, 5715, 5716, 5717, 5718, 5719, 5720, 5721, 5722, 5723, 5724, 5725, 5726, 5727, 5728, 5729, 5730, 5731, 5732, 5733, 5734, 5735, 5736, 5854, 5933, 6181, 6232, 6294, 6316, 6432, 6655, 7347, 7430, 7670, 7852, 8023, 8115, 8126, 8148, 8167, 8439, 8576, 8651, 8676, 8957, 9032, 9040, 9196, 9276, 9660, 9843, 9849, 10174, 10286, 10432, 10455, 10590, 10697, 11105, 11393, 11488, 11568, 11577, 11755, 11856
Bisson, Alexandre
15023
Black, Dorothy
14298
Black, Gilmer V.
8469
Black, Loring M.
1715, 8464
Black, Jean Ferguson
15913, 17247
Blackburn, Barbara
16758
Blackburn, Philip C.
14899
Blackmar, Beatrice
15114
Blackwell, Donald
13151
Blackwood, Algernon
17304
Blaine, Harriet Offen
5689
Blaisdell, Elinore
925
Blake, Barry
992, 993
Blake, George
13766
Blake, Hugh
7298, 7571, 8901
Blaker, Richard
12592, 14110
Blassingame, Lurton
3158, 10559, 10958, 11045, 11077
Bliss, T. H.
1050, 1163, 2625, 4160, 7203, 7309, 8174, 9254, 9740, 10463, 11513, 11732
Bliss, Tip
see Bliss, T. H.
Blitzstein, Marc
12922
Blixen, Karen
see Dinesen, Isak
Bloch, Bertram
4568, 13019, 13808, 14470, 14494
Bloch, Jean-Richard
11890, 15553
Blood, Leighton H.
307
Blossom, Frederick A.
15881
Blossom, Henry
15029, 15772
Blow, Katharine
9633
Blum, Edwin
14263
Blumberg, Flossie Jane
7021
Blumenfield, R. D.
14341
Boas, Louise Schutz
13325, 13934
Bodenheim, Maxwell
1402, 1692, 3114, 5860, 7876, 9073, 9188, 10183, 13250,

13762, 15479, 15592
Boehm, David
5188, 5189, 5190, 5191, 16684
Boettiger, John
14435
Bogan, Louise
531, 1285, 1625, 1766, 1983, 2342, 2574, 2887, 3102, 3991, 4437, 4542, 4747, 5278, 5288, 5515, 5603, 6144, 7127, 7734, 8077, 8792, 9067, 9139, 9233, 9546, 9548, 9743, 9903, 10236, 10758, 10769, 10789, 10814, 11215, 11883, 11954r, 12006r, 12042r, 12087r, 12088r, 12163r, 12169r, 12234r, 12311r, 12470r, 12516r, 12587r, 12623r, 12634r, 12812r, 12813r, 12815r, 12816r, 12818r, 12819r, 12820r, 12821r, 12842r, 12878r, 12887r, 12899r, 13094r, 13249r, 13443r, 13497r, 13553r, 13564r, 13713r, 13800r, 14118r, 14259r, 14317r, 14398r, 14483r, 14690r, 14698r, 14720r, 14776r, 14779r, 15186r, 15200r, 15298r, 15369r, 15433r, 15511r, 15512r, 15736r, 15781r, 15823r, 15824r, 15917r, 15999r, 16001r, 16003r, 16004r, 16005r, 16006r, 16007r, 16132r, 16223r, 16542r, 16543r, 16544r, 16729, 16795r, 16826r, 16902r, 17026r, 17099r, 17114r, 17350r, 17370r, 17381r, 17408r, 17473r
Bohm, Elizabeth
617
Bojer, Johan
13337
Bok, Edward W.
13183, 15927
Bolitho, Hector
14578, 16395
Bolitho, Sybil
15456
Bolitho, William
15821, 17411
Bölsche, Wilhelm
14974
Bolton, Guy
12096, 13785, 15573, 15687, 16015, 16310, 16610, 16675, 17276, 17311
Bonaparte, Napoleon
17803
Bonnell, Mariana
8243
Bonner, Eugene
17525
Bonner, Paul Hyde
4801, 5438, 6069
Booraem, Hendrik
16723
Booth, John Hunter
15618, 17065
Boothe, Clare
11896, 14607, 15139, 17836
Borden, Mary
17833
Borden, Oliver
6033
Boretz, Allen
13715, 15681, 16368
Borg, Gil
4209
Boruff, John
17265, 17602
Bosworth, Francis
13493
Bosworth, Thomas S.
211, 1356, 4656, 7066, 9662, 10245, 11044
Bottome, Phyllis
15247, 15713, 16104, 17774
Boucicault, Dion
11939, 15664, 16960
Bourdet, Edouard
12645, 14627, 16574
Bowen, Elizabeth
13064, 14225
Bowen, Frank C.
12698
Bower, Marian
13877
Bowers, Claude G.
14455, 17338
Bowers, William
17700
Bowie, John
14543
Bowman, William Dodgson

16926
Boyce, Burke
133, 707, 708, 987, 1045, 1100, 1146, 1147, 1378, 1409, 1439, 1478, 1504, 1519, 1571, 2138, 2345, 2357, 2449, 2699, 2760, 2961, 2998, 3010, 3043, 3191, 4252, 4281, 4576, 4712, 5034, 6095, 6444, 7004, 7070, 7216, 7239, 7301, 7357, 7384, 7421, 8217, 8384, 8411, 8456, 8466, 8632, 9106, 9289, 9315, 9359, 9824, 9877, 10055, 10138, 10179, 10209, 11244, 11363, 11452, 11655, 11723
Boyd, Ernest
180, 696, 1349, 4367, 4484, 6165, 6431, 11991r, 12047r, 12059r, 12074r, 12092r, 12132r, 12155r, 12167r, 12183r, 12186r, 12190r, 12204r, 12242r, 12252r, 12273r, 12304r, 12313r, 12325r, 12329r, 12334r, 12394r, 12452r, 12493r, 12511r, 12514r, 12554r, 12555r, 12702r, 12742r, 12771r, 12817r, 12822r, 12829r, 12856r, 12860r, 12926r, 12940r, 12953r, 12968r, 13002r, 13006r, 13056r, 13072r, 13077r, 13147r, 13185r, 13257r, 13286r, 13296r, 13330r, 13429r, 13519r, 13645r, 13654r, 13751r, 13778r, 13780r, 13790r, 13810r, 13863r, 13895r, 13947r, 13972r, 14009r, 14044r, 14149r, 14177r, 14190r, 14229r, 14272r, 14287r, 14339r, 14385r, 14465r, 14475r, 14490r, 14596r, 14699r, 14723r, 14846r, 14877r, 14919r, 14957r, 14974r, 14995r, 15031r, 15035r, 15130r, 15136r, 15182r, 15192r, 15214r, 15251r, 15283r, 15295r, 15309r, 15314r, 15316r, 15331r, 15338r, 15485r, 15509r, 15522r, 15592r, 15641r, 15660r, 15665r, 15742r, 15770r, 15836r, 15844r, 15876r, 15916r, 15988r, 15998r, 16017r, 16063r, 16121r, 16144r, 16211r, 16215r, 16236r, 16277r, 16280r, 16323r, 16376r, 16404r, 16580r, 16647r, 16649r, 16712r, 16771r, 16775r, 16785r, 16802r, 16852r, 16880r, 16920r, 16944r, 16977r, 17000r, 17072r, 17129r, 17192r, 17225r, 17233r, 17275r, 17298r, 17333r, 17339r, 17354r, 17416r, 17425r, 17440r, 17484r, 17505r, 17537r, 17566r, 17636, 17646r, 17675, 17711r, 17737r, 17751r, 17765r, 17778r, 17826r, 17832r, 17870r, 17920r, 17928r
Boyd, Hutcheson
14655
Boyd, James
12395, 13235, 14909
Boyd, Thomas
16453, 16673, 17241
Boyer, Richard O.
270, 647, 1002, 1017, 1604, 1834, 3040, 3946, 5067, 5325, 5595, 6064, 6094, 6302, 6326, 6411, 7232, 7241, 7617, 9663, 10528, 11756
Boyle, Kay
483, 698, 774, 871, 1455, 2456, 2990, 4430, 4913, 5369, 5391, 5810, 7865, 8482, 9415, 11301, 11347, 11553, 11659, 13060, 13190, 13742, 13800, 15454, 17937
Brackett, Charles
11898r, 11921r, 11930r, 11939r, 11947r, 11952r, 11972r, 11983r, 12009, 12029r, 12032r, 12052r, 12069r, 12077r, 12211r, 12215r, 12236r, 12240r, 12251r, 12292r, 12297r, 12301r, 12310r, 12312r, 12322r, 12348r, 12351r, 12363r, 12367r, 12379r, 12386r, 12402r, 12403r, 12424r, 12427r, 12448r, 12474r,

12482r, 12488r, 12517r,
12522r, 12546r, 12561r,
12564r, 12600r, 12601r,
12602r, 12605r, 12625r,
12637r, 12638r, 12645r,
12656r, 12676r, 12695r,
12697r, 12725r, 12728r,
12733r, 12750r, 12772r,
12801r, 12805r, 12810r,
12840r, 12846r, 12849r,
12865r, 12866r, 12868r,
12871r, 12881r, 12883r,
12893r, 12909r, 12913r,
12921r, 12928r, 12945r,
12951r, 12976r, 12978r,
12990r, 12999r, 13003r,
13090r, 13103r, 13122r,
13149r, 13154r, 13178r,
13199r, 13206r, 13220r,
13264r, 13273r, 13277r,
13287r, 13288r, 13320r,
13331r, 13346r, 13355r,
13366r, 13410r, 13434r,
13437r, 13445r, 13446r,
13470r, 13474r, 13481r,
13516r, 13530r, 13557r,
13574r, 13579r, 13580r,
13587r, 13600r, 13641r,
13662r, 13664r, 13671r,
13689r, 13690r, 13714r,
13746r, 13759r, 13765r,
13771r, 13772r, 13795r,
13815r, 13819r, 13837r,
13848r, 13855r, 13857r,
13860r, 13876r, 13889r,
13891r, 13892r, 13897r,
13904r, 13929r, 13962r,
13964r, 13973r, 13978r,
13981r, 13984r, 13994r,
14003r, 14014r, 14035r,
14048r, 14055r, 14057r,
14061r, 14073r, 14083r,
14091r, 14113r, 14122r,
14127r, 14134r, 14153r,
14163r, 14169r, 14171r,
14180r, 14183r, 14187r,
14189r, 14202r, 14208r,
14211r, 14232r, 14235r,
14237r, 14245r, 14252r,
14299r, 14303r, 14326r,
14354r, 14361r, 14362r,
14380r, 14382r, 14420r,
14425r, 14430r, 14432r,
14441r, 14448r, 14450r,
14454r, 14462r, 14480r,
14493r, 14514r, 14521r,
14523r, 14527r, 14530r,
14539r, 14543r, 14550r,
14552r, 14553r, 14555r,
14557r, 14572r, 14581r,
14592r, 14628r, 14638r,
14639r, 14648r, 14651r,
14652r, 14653r, 14655r,
14656r, 14667r, 14688r,
14753r, 14775r, 14823r,
14834r, 14839r, 14846r,
14850r, 14856r, 14882r,
14883r, 14918r, 14935r,
14943r, 14944r, 14953r,
14958r, 14985r, 15001r,
15004r, 15005r, 15052r,
15053r, 15072r, 15105r,
15108r, 15114r, 15119r,
15131r, 15146r, 15150r,
15151r, 15157r, 15192r,
15232r, 15235r, 15239r,
15242r, 15245r, 15246r,
15273r, 15279r, 15286r,
15294r, 15320r, 15321r,
15322r, 15326r, 15336r,
15350r, 15383r, 15404r,
15405r, 15407r, 15418r,
15419r, 15434r, 15441r,
15449r, 15452r, 15455r,
15472r, 15473r, 15478r,
15486r, 15492r, 15497r,
15498r, 15524r, 15533r,
15541r, 15542r, 15552r,
15555r, 15556r, 15559r,
15573r, 15575r, 15591r,
15600r, 15608r, 15618r,
15628r, 15653r, 15656r
15664r, 15680r. 15684r,
15687r, 15689r, 15695r,
15719r, 15723r, 15753r,
15780Ar, 15795r, 15810r,
15816r, 15849r, 15860r,
15862r, 15891r, 15902r,
15920r, 15930r, 15939r,
15949r, 15959r, 15966r,
15973r, 15975r, 15983r,
15986r, 15987r, 15989r,
15990r, 15993r, 16015r,
16028r, 16031r, 16052r,
16059r, 16060r, 16065r,
16085r, 16126r, 16136r,

16137r, 16151r, 16154r, 16161r, 16164r, 16168r, 16174r, 16188r, 16190r, 16200r, 16225r, 16237r, 16273r, 16275r, 16304r, 16310r, 16316r, 16328r, 16334r, 16375r, 16381r, 16393r, 16402r, 16421r, 16447r, 16450r, 16459r, 16470r, 16474r, 16485r, 16506r, 16524r, 16530r, 16536r, 16547Ar, 16548r, 16553r, 16554r, 16588r, 16593r, 16601r, 16604r, 16610r, 16637r, 16640r, 16650r, 16657r, 16661r, 16664r, 16666r, 16691r, 16710r, 16713r, 16727r, 16810r, 16827r, 16830r, 16839r, 16844r, 16848r, 16851r, 16855r, 16858r, 16899r, 16934r, 16943r, 16950r, 16958r, 16983r, 17007r, 17011r, 17018r, 17059r, 17067r, 17098r, 17120r, 17122, 17145r, 17159r, 17185r, 17186r, 17190r, 17191r, 17200r, 17205r, 17219r, 17261r, 17274r, 17296r, 17302r, 17353r, 17358r, 17366r, 17372r, 17375r, 17376r, 17382r, 17396r, 17409r, 17413r, 17426r, 17431r, 17443r, 17464r, 17499r, 17522r, 17529r, 17556r, 17571r, 17580r, 17583r, 17596r, 17623r, 17648, 17675r, 17710r, 17712r, 17720r, 17730r, 17736r, 17761r, 17786r, 17798r, 17808r, 17821r, 17838r, 17847r, 17869r, 17872r, 17879r, 17885r, 17889r, 17911r, 17922r, 17945r, 17949r

Braddell, Maurice
14429

Bradford, Gamaliel
14504

Bradford, Roark
14486

Bradshaw, George
17463

Braley, Berton
5462, 8177

Bramah, Ernest
14547

Brammer, Julius
12722

Brand, Millen
14119

Brandeis, Irma
184, 656, 1726, 2134, 3020, 4581, 5011, 7812, 8529, 8530, 9301, 9597, 10892, 11068, 11265

Brandon, Dorothy
15816

Brandon, John G.
16661

Brandt, Carl
1346, 11149

Brant, Irving
16917

Brash, Arthur F.
15653

Brecht, Bertolt
15386, 17220

Brecht, Harold
13217

Breen, Bernice
3138, 6300, 7085, 8342, 11198

Brennan, Frederick Hazlett
12270

Brennan, J. Keirn
15559

Brent, Romney
15010, 17299

Brentano, Lowell
13438, 13921, 16830, 17949

Breuer, Bessie
1572, 1577, 2655, 4406, 4587

Brewer, George, Jr.
13019, 17256

Briant, Roy
11921

Bridge, Ann
13784, 15909

Bridgers, Ann Preston
12893

Bridie, James
16728

Brieux, Eugene
11910

Briffault, Robert

13384, 13385
Bright, John
14158
Brilant, Arthur M.
15232
Brill, Leighton K.
12235
Bringolf, Hans
14271
Brinig, Myron
15032, 15190, 16687, 16701, 17745
Brittain, Vera
14191, 17238
Britton, Kenneth Phillips
1474, 2617, 2618, 4798, 5084, 5749, 7018, 8082, 8083, 8978 14238
Britton, Nan
16070
Brobeck, Florence
1088
Broch, Hermann
17486
Brock, Louis
2698
Brock, Lynn
14596
Brockway, Wallace
15226
Brod, Max
17216
Brokaw, Clare Boothe
see Boothe, Clare
Bromfield, Louis
12198, 13079, 13282, 13462, 13863, 14235, 15097, 15343, 16047, 16195, 16939, 17269, 17420
Bronz
2958, 5417
Brooks, Alden
12153
Brooks, Cyrus
13163
Brooks, George S.
16839
Brooks, Matt
13760
Brooks, Van Wyck
13561, 14504, 14808
Broomell, Myron H.
3092
Broones, Martin
16402
Brougham, Philip
5642
Broun, Edmund R.
1108
Broun, Heywood
1109, 1110, 2270, 2271, 2272, 2273, 2274, 2527, 7989, 8178, 8321, 8818, 11021, 11582, 11819, 12092, 14422, 16621
Brousson, Jean-Jacques
12044, 12045
Brown, Anthony
14239
Brown, Beth
12101
Brown, Bob
14770
Brown, Calvin
16481
Brown, Carlton
269, 571, 1624, 2656, 2945, 3963, 4613, 5195, 8873, 9054, 9560
Brown, Constantine
12010
Brown, Harry
333, 7433, 8160, 9413
Brown, Henry Collins
6430, 14342
Brown, Katharine Holland
13473
Brown, Lew
12622, 13574, 13761, 14212, 16969, 17894
Brown, Martin
13003, 15860, 16059, 16950
Brown, Mary
5613
Brown, R. T.
2129
Brown, Ruth
2888, 2889, 3264, 5214, 5447, 8181, 9655, 9785, 10604, 11384, 11385
Brown, William Montgomery
15443
Browne, Maurice
17786
Browne, Robert Gore
14320
Browne, Waldo R.

12252
Brownell, Harriett
3174, 7474, 9402, 9692, 10484, 10561
Brownell, John Charles
12503
Brubaker, Howard
1040
Bruen, E. J.
7782
Brúland, Ragnhilde
13691
Bruncken, Herbert Gerhard
8513
Brush, Katharine
21, 3076, 6154, 9249, 10219, 10538, 11371, 11780, 17924
Bryan, George S.
16977
Bryan, Joseph, III
7964
Bryant, George
14372, 16522
Bryner, Edna
12059, 17704
Buchanan, Charles L.
7713
Buchanan, Thompson
12150, 16691
Buchman, Sidney
17181
Buchner, Georg
12998, 12999
Bucholtz, Johannes
16426
Buck, Gene
15600, 17059
Buck, Pearl S.
11975, 13414, 13504, 14224, 15387, 15890
Buckner, Robert
8916, 16077
Bugnet, Charles
13578
Bullett, Gerald
14150, 15317, 15848, 16746
Bullock, Turner
14663
Bunin, Ivan
15335
Bunny
see Koehler, Eleanor W.
Burgoyne, J. M.
7872
Burke, Edwin
17185
Burke, Kenneth
12908, 17325
Burke, Thomas
11795, 12469, 17002
Burnet, Dana
13641
Burnett, Whit
13577
Burnett, William Riley
13008, 13777, 13870, 14402, 14859, 16434
Burns, Paul A.
2981
Burns, Walter Noble
16424
Burnside, R. H.
17205
Burr, Anna Robeson
16451
Burr, Courtney
16428
Burt, Struthers
13077
Busch, Niven, Jr.
210, 272, 759, 977, 1117, 1777, 2358, 2531, 2921, 2965, 3243, 4158, 4353, 5333, 5839, 5970, 6156, 6645, 7296, 7826, 8041, 8092, 8103, 8123, 8366-8368, 8510, 8909, 9479, 9581, 9625, 9640, 9686, 9904-9921, 9968, 9971, 11058, 11558, 11559, 11797
Busch, Noel F.
243, 973
Busey, Garreta
5275, 10008, 10794
Bushnell, Adelyn
14282
Bussiere, Tadema
13509
Butler, Ellis Parker
1733, 1967, 5102, 5601, 9795
Butler, Hilton
3154
Butler, Samuel
16647
Butts, Mary
12165
Buzzell, Eddie

14653
Byers, Margaretta
8185, 10410
Bynner, Witter
878, 1546, 2158, 2723, 3923, 5440, 6404, 7729, 8761, 9959, 10250, 10717, 10838, 11147
Byrd, Richard E.
13140, 14857, 16724
Byrd, William
11995
Byrne, Donn
12957, 13097, 13993

C

C. B. E.
6022, 9461
C. B. T.
5887, 5888, 5906, 6439
C. B. W.
5907
C. C.
see Carroll, Carroll
C. Coupon
see O'Shea, M. B.
C. D.
see Duer, Caroline or Day, Clarence
C. F. L.
see Looms, C. F.
C. G.
see Graves, Charles
C. G. S.
see Shaw, Charles G.
C. H. F.
see Ford, Charles Henri
C. J.
see also Janson, Clara
C. J.
3233-35
C. L. Q.
see Quong, C. Lee
C. M.
see MacArthur, Charles
C. P.
7108
Cabell, James Branch
15423, 16669, 16743, 16776, 16822, 17617
Caesar, Arthur
4502, 15680
Caesar, Irving
13761, 15206, 15579, 17037, 17843
Cain, James M.
576, 9386, 16050, 16051
Caldwell, Anne
12777, 17059, 17205, 17945
Caldwell, Erskine
6147, 7411, 9664, 14512, 16815
Caldwell, Taylor
13264, 13272
Calkins, Clinch
20, 1529, 2049, 4607, 4987, 5062, 5209, 6014, 6442, 7819, 7899, 8151, 8278-8281, 8565, 8784, 8790, 9142, 9603, 9604, 9809, 10195, 10764, 10791, 10793, 11023, 16773
Callaghan, Morley
27, 214, 1038, 1447, 2024, 2397, 2511, 2631, 2759, 6026, 7871, 8908, 8948, 9522, 9582, 9682, 10478, 10690, 11309, 11563, 11855, 11861, 14427, 15367, 15489, 16940
Calmer, Edgar
12352
Calverton, V. F.
15518
Cambridge, Elizabeth
14201
Cameron, Donald
7081
Campbell, Allen
854, 1275, 1870, 4103, 4480, 4828, 5409, 5419, 5455, 6004, 7228, 8390, 8495, 8731, 9227, 9234, 9951, 10512, 11839
Campbell, David B.
4853
Campbell, Dorothy de Brissac
14387
Campbell, Florence
17939
Campbell, J. L.
13429
Campbell, Kane
13344
Campbell, Kenneth
4145, 9738, 9878
Campbell, Lawton
14316, 16770
Canby, Henry Seidel

1235, 1236, 17193
Canby, Marion
2032, 10059
Cane, Melville
127, 412, 5754, 7050, 7954
Canfield, Dorothy
13075, 16521, 17850
Cannell, Kathleen
7084, 9594
Cantor, Eddie
15447
Cantwell, Robert
14696, 14730
Cape, Vandy
11283
Capek, Karel
14622, 15057, 15388, 17597
Caplan, Arthur
14821
Carleton, Patrick
15615
Carlisle, D. T.
17787
Carlisle, Helen Grace
15392, 16531, 17290
Carlton, Henry
1868
Carlton, Henry Fisk
1868, 17499
Carman, Dorothy Walworth
8001
Carmer, Carl
1426, 2781, 2817, 3173, 7110, 11300, 11702, 14247, 14852, 16881
Carneal, Georgette
13910
Carpenter, Edward Childs
12215, 15206, 17715
Carples, Esther
454
Carr, Brownell
546, 7495, 8359, 9061, 10060, 10414, 10416, 10746
Carr, Edward Hallett
16357
Carré, Jean-Marie
16520
Carrington, Elaine Sterne
15576
Carroll, Albert
44, 1742, 5430, 8066, 10020, 11351
Carroll, Carroll
768, 879, 1075, 1645, 1800, 1825, 1836, 2017, 2233, 2745, 3159, 3260, 4060, 4125, 4657, 5181, 5850, 6204, 7069, 7133, 7517, 7685, 7772, 8000, 8382, 8993, 9821, 10122, 10706, 10707, 11200
Carroll, Earl
13273, 13275, 13277, 13278, 13279, 13516
Carroll, Gladys Hasty
2901, 12156, 13490A
Carroll, Lewis
14899
Carroll, Paul Vincent
14575, 16575, 17729
Carson, Velma
8298, 10223
Carstarphen, Frank E.
12315
Carten, Audrey
14728
Carten, Waveney
14728
Carter, Desmond
13243
Carter, Jay Franklin
2528
Carter, Oscar
15356
Carter, Randolph
12127, 17874
Carter, Sherman
5588
Carver, Gertrude
810, 1632, 3169, 6210, 7436, 7570, 9157, 10379, 10548
Cary, Joyce
11936
Casanova, Eve
4654
Casella, Alberto
13068
Caspary, Vera
959, 9639, 10382
Castelhun, Dorothea
5643, 7532
Cather, Willa
13056, 14994, 15638, 15662, 16114, 16579
Catlin, Stanton L.
6288

Catto, Max
13960
Cauchy, Nigel
3905, 5126
Caulaincourt, Armand Augustin
15611
Cavett, Frank
13615
Caylor, Rose
17826
Cecil, David
16963, 17927
Celestin, Jack
16662
Céline, Louis-Ferdinand
12231, 13066, 14511
Cendrars, Blaise
14271
Chadourne, Marc
17521
Chaliapin, Feodor
15066
Chamberlain, George Agnew
14924A
Chamberlain, John
8250-8252, 13459
Chamberlain, Neville
14338
Channon, Henry
15852
Chapin, Anne Morrison
15613
Chapin, Katherine Garrison
9537
Chapman, Arthur
10910, 11544
Chapman, Frank M.
15461
Chapman, John Stanton
17639
Chapman, Maristan
14005, 14182
Chapman, Mary
17639
Chappell, George S.
3066, 13175, 16443
Chardonne, Jacques
13387
Charell, Erik
17044
Charles, Theodore
14448
Charlot, Genova
see Conkling, Grace Hazard
Charon, Jr.
see Walker, Stanley
Chase, Eleanor
9460
Chase, Mary Coyle
15651
Chase, Mary Ellen
16658
Chase, Stuart
13303, 15254, 16285, 17448
Chater, Arthur G.
12586
Cheever, John
1102, 1128, 4282, 4990, 5207, 8385
Chekhov, Anton
92730A, 10360, 16512, 17224, 17461
Cheney, Sheldon
17131
Chesterton, Gilbert Keith
12185
Chevalier, Haakon M.
12316, 13043, 15115
Chiarelli, Luigi
15171
Chidsey, Donald Barr
7985, 15148
Child, Alan
12708, 16147
Child, Nellise
17651
Childe Harold
see Thurber, James
Childe, Stark
10595
Chilton, Eleanor Carroll
12588, 13585
Chirico, Giorgio de
14059
Chlumberg, Hans
15289, 15808
Chodorov, Edward
14574, 17844
Chodorov, Jerome
16498
Chotzinoff, Samuel
1690, 8559, 9129, 13364, 14185
Christiansen, Sigurd
17434
Chubb, Thomas Caldecot

14810
Churchward, James
12744
Cianelli, Eduardo
13592
Cinelli, Delfino
17352
Civitas
4486
Clark, Alexander, Jr.
9867
Clark, Gill
12644
Clark, James B.
9062
Clark, Maurice
12598
Clarke, Beverly L.
1226, 4347, 7187, 7513, 8448, 9931, 10339
Clarke, Donald Henderson
14344, 14937, 17912
Clarke, Harold
12703
Clarke, Marcia
10860
Claxton, Oliver
230, 231, 323, 799, 1267, 1375, 2093, 2094, 2256, 2262, 2300, 2674, 4614, 4710, 4768, 4943, 5528, 5596, 5607, 5844, 5946, 6271, 7393, 7540, 7712, 7969, 8375, 10436, 10628, 11146, 11498, 11897r, 11911r, 11915r, 11923r, 11932r, 11951r, 11953r, 11962r, 11992r, 11997r, 12064r, 12080r, 12176r, 12195r, 12205r, 12220r, 12249r, 12269r, 12271r, 12279r, 12281r, 12319r, 12340r, 12353r, 12360r, 12366r, 12370r, 12432r, 12435r, 12439r, 12446r, 12609r, 12610r, 12626r, 12642r, 12655r, 12669r, 12678r, 12700r, 12713r, 12729r, 12732r, 12736r, 12768r, 12779r, 12824r, 12838r, 12889r, 12919r, 12947r, 12961r, 12973r, 13032r, 13102r, 13117r, 13119r, 13137r, 13189r, 13200r, 13202r, 13213r, 13221r, 13230r, 13231r, 13238r, 13246r, 13271r, 13295r, 13308r, 13332r, 13349r, 13353r, 13396r, 13431r, 13441r, 13468r, 13480r, 13483r, 13498r, 13506r, 13512r, 13517r, 13556r, 13599r, 13609r, 13611r, 13612r, 13640r, 13643r, 13644r, 13672r, 13711r, 13718r, 13721r, 13727r, 13728r, 13740r, 13745r, 13779r, 13788r, 13806r, 13862r, 13874r, 13990r, 13999r, 14008r, 14046r, 14065r, 14101r, 14154r, 14164r, 14186r, 14206r, 14214r, 14249r, 14306r, 14334r, 14399r, 14408r, 14413r, 14421r, 14446r, 14516r, 14562r, 14563r, 14585r, 14600r, 14620r, 14644r, 14658r, 14702r, 14712r, 14724r, 14725r, 14754r, 14755r, 14762r, 14768r, 14829r, 14837r, 14848r, 14867r, 14894r, 14903r, 14904r, 14911r, 14928r, 14939r, 14945r, 14976r, 14977r, 14979r, 15011r, 15038r, 15039r, 15048r, 15100r, 15106r, 15118r, 15154r, 15252r, 15256r, 15284r, 15305r, 15341r, 15427r, 15431r, 15481r, 15500r, 15530r, 15567r, 15644r, 15686r, 15701r, 15702r, 15710r, 15757r, 15827r, 15854r, 15888r, 15921r, 15924r, 15979r, 16011r, 16018r, 16024r, 16030r, 16053r, 16054r, 16056r, 16079r, 16155r, 16173r, 16182r, 16193r, 16196r, 16228r, 16235r, 16261r, 16315r, 16352r, 16387r, 16389r, 16414r, 16478r, 16486r, 16534r, 16547r, 16571r, 16633r, 16643r, 16659r, 16663r, 16672r, 16721r, 16730r, 16736r, 16738r,

16740r, 16755r, 16763r, 16777r, 16786r, 16799r, 16800r, 16801r, 16819r, 16825r, 16838r, 16878r, 16889r, 16892r, 16936r, 16938r, 16951r, 16955r, 16973r, 16978r, 16981r, 16984r, 16991r, 17009r, 17053r, 17064r, 17074r, 17082r, 17085r, 17086r, 17091r, 17092r, 17093r, 17105r, 17166r, 17204r, 17212r, 17223r, 17236r, 17264r, 17272r, 17341r, 17343r, 17427r, 17435r, 17459r, 17469r, 17485r, 17504r, 17508r, 17518r, 17519r, 17568r, 17582r, 17587r, 17601r, 17607r, 17616r, 17620r, 17624r, 17641r, 17659r, 17665r, 17678r, 17689r. 17708r, 17721r, 17727r, 17740r, 17811r, 17814r, 17871r, 17878r, 17890r, 17907r, 17910r, 17946r

Cleaves, Bess
3184

Clemenceau, Georges
13893, 13894

Clemenceau-Jacquemaire, Madeleine
14814

Clemens, Le Roy
11993

Clendening, Logan
3192, 5018, 12305, 13989

Cleveland, John
9283

Clift, Denison
17821

Clifton, Violet
12473

Cline, Leonard
13814

Cloete, Stuart
17407, 17605

Clork, Harry
15282, 16532

Cluett, Jack
227, 232, 625, 1459, 1514, 1746, 2126, 2327, 2598, 3017, 3034, 4524, 4904, 5047, 5167, 5641, 5920, 7831, 8050, 8051, 9166, 9512, 9726, 10369, 10476, 10556, 10659, 11583

Cluett, John P.
3167, 3168

Coates, Robert M.
8, 29, 33, 496, 753, 899, 995, 1138, 1716, 1831, 1978, 1979, 1980, 1991, 2040, 2197, 2321, 2331, 2468, 2552, 2972, 3131, 3194, 3277, 3995, 4293, 4636, 4655, 5138, 5368, 5569, 5655, 5695, 6137, 6564, 6649, 7257, 7439, 7590-7592, 7757, 7839, 8114, 8164, 8798, 8879, 9072, 9191, 9197, 9439, 9769, 10180, 10246, 10668, 10785, 11056, 11106, 11293, 11331, 11332, 11622, 11826, 11909r, 11924r, 11928r, 11940r, 12002r, 12008r, 12018r, 12021r, 12023r, 12035r, 12038r, 12049r, 12056r, 12057r, 12076r, 12098r, 12109r, 12152r, 12156r, 12158r, 12180r, 12203r, 12232r, 12300r, 12308r 12330r, 12358r, 12388r, 12411r, 12438r, 12507r, 12534r, 12536r, 12563r, 12568r, 12571r, 12577r, 12583r, 12586r, 12591r, 12595r, 12617r, 12646r, 12662r, 12675r, 12686r, 12698r, 12706r, 12744r, 12785r, 12831r, 12852r, 12854r, 12891r, 12901r, 12908r, 12974r, 13057r, 13058r, 13062r, 13074r, 13092r, 13125r, 13144r, 13152r, 13163r, 13175r, 13190r, 13192r, 13224r, 13228r, 13241r, 13250r, 13258r, 13262r, 13294r, 13301, 13311r, 13317r, 13339r, 13348r, 13363r, 13382r, 13387r, 13398r, 13419r, 13425r, 13432r, 13439r, 13440r, 13452r, 13453r, 13456r, 13458r, 13459r, 13484r, 13492r, 13543r, 13562r, 13569r, 13593r, 13616r, 13624r,

13669r, 13673r, 13685r, 13709r, 13735r, 13748r, 13777r, 13782r, 13818r, 13881r, 13894r, 13901r, 13909r, 13910r, 13928r, 13939r, 14007r, 14013r, 14034r, 14038r, 14052r, 14112r, 14135r, 14151r, 14159r, 14197r, 14200r, 14207r, 14210r, 14264r, 14269r, 14271r, 14290r, 14300r, 14331r, 14335r, 14346r, 14360r, 14368r, 14386r, 14387r, 14396r, 14435r, 14440r, 14452r, 14453r, 14456r, 14467r, 14469r, 14499r, 14502r, 14509r, 14519r, 14537r, 14545r, 14650r, 14701r, 14730r, 14736r, 14747r, 14770r, 14772r, 14793r, 14800r, 14808r, 14822r, 14841r, 14842r, 14854r, 14889r, 14905r, 14917r, 14923r, 14930r, 14948r, 14951r, 14959r, 14964r, 14973r, 14975r, 14993r, 15007r, 15045r, 15047r, 15058r, 15066r, 15095r, 15127r, 15145r, 15153r, 15159r, 15160r, 15163r, 15166r, 15178r, 15179r, 15196r, 15199r, 15209r, 15212r, 15213r, 15219r, 15254r, 15280r, 15301r, 15310r, 15313r, 15332r, 15343r, 15408r, 15420r, 15438r, 15439r, 15444r, 15465r, 15466r, 15479r, 15487r, 15502r, 15503r, 15504r, 15505r, 15514r, 15532r, 15535r, 15549r, 15553r, 15557r, 15572r, 15574r, 15587r, 15588r, 15601r, 15627r, 15637r, 15647r, 15655r, 15662r, 15685r, 15692r, 15708r, 15711r, 15714r, 15728r, 15732r, 15750r, 15760r, 15775r, 15783r, 15800r, 15805r, 15812r, 15822r, 15825r, 15852r, 15874r, 15881r, 15882r, 15884r, 15903r, 15909r, 15928r, 15936r, 15981r, 16000r, 16037r, 16086r, 16094r, 16115r, 16128r, 16141r, 16153r, 16166r, 16176r, 16205r, 16219r, 16232r, 16238r, 16242r, 16265r, 16276r, 16295r, 16306r, 16322r, 16332r, 16401r, 16409r, 16419r, 16434r, 16443r, 16451r, 16452r, 16457r, 16467r, 16492r, 16500r, 16503r, 16504r, 16515r, 16520r, 16528r, 16558r, 16577r, 16579r, 16590r, 16605r, 16607r, 16629r, 16631r, 16678r, 16696r, 16708r, 16745r, 16773r, 16787r, 16791r, 16822r, 16862r, 16882r, 16888r, 16910r, 16926r, 16928r, 16930r, 16972r, 16996r, 17015r, 17045r, 17094r, 17100r, 17111r, 17130r, 17156r, 17173r, 17180r, 17228r, 17278r, 17325r, 17336r, 17337r, 17405r, 17422r, 17434r, 17442r, 17449r, 17465r, 17470r, 17482r, 17483r, 17495r, 17515r, 17570r, 17586r, 17589r, 17594r, 17608r, 17614r, 17633r, 17639r, 17652r, 17653r, 17667r, 17683r, 17693r, 17694r, 17745r, 17758r, 17762r, 17773r, 17809r, 17850r, 17853r, 17855r, 17867r, 17884r, 17935r, 17939r

Coatsworth, Elizabeth
108, 786, 1390, 1634, 1656, 1747, 1926, 2168, 2346, 2445, 2802, 2911, 4181, 4362, 4458, 4962, 5463, 5478, 6015, 7518, 7861, 7945, 8427, 8940, 9013, 9020, 9074-9083, 9770, 10089, 10101, 10235, 10649, 10767, 10806, 10824, 10832, 11214, 11618

Cobb, Humphrey
15885

Cobb, Julia

14778, 15751, 17016
Conroy, E. T.
466, 2717, 8064, 11591
Conroy, Jack
2229, 13144A
Constant Reader
see Parker, Dorothy
Constantin-Weyer, Maurice
15088
Cook, Harold Lewis
1646, 2623, 5009, 7434, 7632, 8499, 9511, 9801, 10935, 11102, 11355, 16826
Cooke, Charles
9168, 12374, 14205
Cooke, Le Baron
2690, 10741, 11325
Coombs, Kelly
3001, 3921, 6303
Coon, Horace
12891
Cooper, Louise Field
628, 814, 2225, 2557, 4109, 4149, 5292, 5441, 8372
Cooper, Paul Fenimore
17374
Cooper, Willard
9579, 9728
Copeau, Jacques
12564
Copeland, Nick
17079
Corbin, Alice
2471, 4378, 7581, 8955
Corbin, Harold Standish
1507, 7253
Cordell, William H.
15348
Corle, Edwin
4095, 4163, 5499, 6051
Corley, Donald
14229
Cormack, Bartlett
16174
Cormon, Eugene
17438
Corse, Elizabeth
11063
Cort, David
3906, 4063, 7508, 9586, 10495, 10946, 11171
Cortis, Ernest
11972
Cortis, Louise
11972
Cosentino, Nicholas
15363
Coughlan, Robert
6507
Coupon, C.
see O'Shea, M. B.
Cover, Louise S.
5921
Coward, Noel
12397, 12888, 13091, 13300, 13434, 14031, 14032, 15150, 15418, 15982, 16010, 16066, 16100, 16555, 17186, 17191, 17300, 17573, 17879
Cowen, William Joyce
13442
Cowing, George Cecil
539, 578, 593, 1160, 1486, 1687, 1839, 2291, 2367, 2786, 2791, 4071, 4169, 4276, 4338, 4809, 4980, 5105, 5204, 5317, 6086, 6357, 8238, 8975, 9665, 9884, 9934, 10036, 10884, 10886, 11098, 11815
Cowl, Jane
14448
Cowles, Albert
14652
Cowley, Malcolm
13415
Cowmos, John
2361, 5376, 5750, 5889, 5890
Cox, Wallace
1643, 2192
Coyle, Kathleen
13558, 16649
Cozzens, James Gould
12672, 14701, 15218, 16419
Craig, Mollie
10095
Crane, Carl
8861
Crane, Frances
156, 518, 865, 886, 924, 1066, 1304, 1562, 1628, 2145, 2654, 2810, 3909, 4135, 4288, 4320, 4321, 4403, 4414, 4714, 4953, 4961, 4963, 5344, 5378, 5883, 5885, 5958, 5959, 6031, 6034, 6059, 6280, 6291, 6427, 6582, 7190, 7451, 7453, 7483, 7490

7650, 7730, 8033, 8078, 8096, 8291, 8546, 8712, 8844, 8861, 9182, 9209, 9363, 9756, 9992, 10319, 10329, 10497, 10622, 10696, 10986, 11337, 11422, 11758
Crane, Hart
12812
Crane, Nathalia
15999, 17026, 17526
Crane, Stephen
17852
Craven, Frank
15350, 15591, 17126
Craven, John V.
14747
Craven, Thomas
17362
Crawford, Alice
12328
Crawford, Elizabeth
2725, 4551, 4959, 11837
Crawshaw-Williams, Eliot
15557
Crawshay, Eliot
13265
Crockett, Albert Stevens
17690
Cronin, A. J.
12774, 16884
Cronyn, George
10879, 13590
Crooker, Earle
13438, 13921, 17949
Crooker, Herbert
10098
Crosby, Vivian
17373
Cross, Victoria
13321
Crothers, Rachel
12151, 14680, 17013, 17692
Croué, Jean
12564
Crouse, Russel
986, 2982, 5248, 6189, 7942, 10456-10461, 10521-10527, 11330, 11367, 12096, 13705, 14165, 14193, 14819, 16233
Crow, Carl
12749, 15176
Crowell, Chester T.
579, 1301, 5171, 6135, 9698, 14851
Crowell, Evelyn Miller
6413
Crowther, J. G.
15227
Crowther, Samuel
17288
Croy, Homer
246, 8730
Crozier, F. P.
12506
Crump, John
14136
Cullinan, Ralph
12649
cummings, e. e.
13317, 14134
Cummings, Parke
520, 832, 1135, 1414, 1470, 1555, 1714, 1736, 1783, 2375, 2418, 2588, 2783, 3067, 3180, 3185, 3900, 4083, 4318, 4461, 4489, 4753, 4869-4880, 5008, 5048, 5304, 5313, 5367, 5589, 5782, 5831, 6185, 6297, 6657, 7082, 7113, 7548, 7662, 8572, 8673, 8812, 8823, 8856, 8898, 8937, 9307, 9348, 9397, 9401, 9464, 9631, 9779, 9938, 10610, 10614, 10728, 10754, 10763, 10807, 10865, 11041, 11042, 11425, 11438, 11507, 11634, 11786, 11840
Cunard, Nancy
15499
Cuppy, Will
620, 891, 1279, 1570, 2092, 2797, 2996, 4068, 4429, 6136, 6343, 6464, 7012, 8350, 9269, 9889, 10081, 10280, 10615
Curci, Gennaro Mario
13592, 17819
Curie, Eve
15017
Curley, Jack
447
Currier, Isabel
10503
Curry, Robert
9228
Curtis, Frank
5827
Curtiss, Philip

1295, 7903
Cushing, Tom
13103, 14628
Cushman, Howard
1850, 2440, 3262, 4507, 6023, 8858, 9047, 10733, 10915, 11033
Cypher, Angela
see Seiffert, Marjorie Allen
Czernin, Ferdinand
11375

D

D. B. W. L.
see Lewis, D. B. Wyndham
D. C.
see Cameron, Donald
D. D.
see Dow, Dorothy
D. D. P.
11806
D. H.
see Homans, Dorothy
D. K.
see Kirkpatrick, Doris
D. K. R.
see Riggs, Dorothy Kidder
D. M.
848, 6441, 10836
D. T.
see Thompson, Dorothy
D. W.
see Ward, Dearing
Daab, Hyatt
16307
Daavidson, Roy
16299
Dahlberg, Edward
12489
Daingerfield, Foxhall
15328
Dakin, Edwin Franden
15327
Dale, Felix
5289
Dalton, Emmet
17694
Daly, Augustin
17464
Daly, Grace L.
892
Damrosch, Gretchen
15875
Dane, Clemence
12212, 12836, 13897, 14686, 15146
D'arcy, Jack
4018
Daugherty, Sonia
290
Davenport, Marcia
1677, 9783, 15673
DaVerona, Guido
17830
Davidson, Gustav
1247
Davidson, Louise
221
Davies, Mary Carolyn
1157, 2484, 5276, 8294, 11668
Davies, Rhys
16232, 17806
Davies, Valentine
12442, 14556, 17227
Daviot, Gordon
16290
Davis, Brion
13907
Davis, Burton
11292
Davis, Donald
13380, 13853
Davis, Dorrance
12106, 14659, 16604
Davis, Eddie
13760
Davis, Elmer
396, 680, 1087, 1556, 1891, 4535, 4592, 4692, 4875, 4881, 5910, 5923, 7023, 7161, 7563, 7604, 7657, 7803, 7817, 7984, 8524, 8647, 8711, 8921, 9088, 9219, 9585, 9642, 9745, 10564, 11592, 11822, 13670, 13776, 16944
Davis, Harold
14184
Davis, Irving Kaye
8740, 11980, 12915, 13123, 16751
Davis, Nathalie C.
4808
Davis, Owen

13199, 13380, 13853, 13915, 14473, 14546, 15593, 16459, 16471, 16842, 16844, 17302, 17306, 17382, 17558
Davis, Philip H.
17384
Davis, Robert Hobart
12617, 16399
Dawson, Mitchell
856
Day, Clarence
67, 250, 277, 298, 512, 2821, 2822, 2823, 2824, 2825, 2826, 2827, 2828, 2829, 2830, 2831, 2833, 2834, 2835, 2836, 2839, 2840, 2841, 2842, 2843, 2844, 2845, 2846, 2847, 2848, 2849, 2850, 2851, 2852, 2853, 2854, 2855, 2856, 2857, 2858, 2859, 2860, 2861, 2862, 2863, 2864, 2865, 2866, 2867, 3150, 3937, 4129, 4130, 4131, 4146, 4164, 4405, 4474, 4475, 4476, 4604, 4616, 4920, 6211, 6313, 6314, 6482, 6699, 7062, 7285, 7358, 7464, 7620, 8407, 8819, 8946, 9331-9337, 9353, 9410, 9565, 9870, 10050, 10254, 10804, 10861, 10873, 11474
Day, Dorothy
8484
Day, Gerald M.
1341
Day, Lillian
1912, 2451, 5415, 5838, 9387, 11297
Day, Price
18, 484, 3163, 7043, 9373, 9813, 9816, 9830, 10826
Day-Lewis, Cecil
16886
Dayton, Katharine
4782, 11569, 13528, 16476
Dazy, Jack
12402
de Acosta, Mercedes
14432
Dean, Basil
12881
Deane, Hamilton
13220
Dearden, Harold
14380
de Casalis, Jeanne
16431
De Casseres, Benjamin
14959
De Costa, Leon
14621
Deeping, Warwick
15714, 17094
de Forest, Marian
14886
de Gramont, E.
16020
de Harsanyi, Zsolt
16870
Dekker, Thomas
16619
Dekobra, Maurice
15031
DeKoven, Reginald
16346
De Kruif, Paul
13503, 15258, 16565, 17741
Delafield, E. M.
12751, 13531, 14475, 16127, 17283, 17619
de la Mare, Walter
12311, 13553, 16004
De Lano, Allen
13600
de la Roche, Mazo
17732
DeLeon, Jack
16662
de Lichtervelde, Louis
14758
Dell, Floyd
12799, 14856, 14956, 14973, 17179
Dell, Jeffrey
15898
Delmar, Viña
12226, 12227
de Lorde, André
15715
Delteil, Joseph
13190, 14477, 15748
Demaison, André
12275
de Marney, Terence
17712
de Montherlant, Henry
12581, 15931
de Morinni, Clara

8076
Denig, Lynde
6282
D'Ennery, A.
17438
Dennis, Geoffrey
12897, 13351, 16238
Denny, Harold Norman
4635
de Pourtalès, Guy
16017
Derleth, August
17770
De Sylva, B. G.
13244, 13574, 13587, 13860, 14163, 15108, 16161, 17057
Deutsch, Babette
139, 1548, 2927, 3141, 3916, 4294, 4969, 5800, 6356, 7316, 7320, 7412, 7799, 8205, 8213, 8807, 8902, 9374, 10004, 10160, 10482, 10663, 11002, 11478, 11491, 14339
Deutsch, Hermann B.
17645
Deval, Jacques
14091, 15028, 17324, 17636
De Vine, John F.
10042
De Witt, Francis
15594, 15684
Dibble, R. F.
14488
Dibble, Theodore
4107
Dickens, Elizabeth
6209, 8403
Dickenson, May Freud
12107
Dickey, Herbert S.
15444
Dietz, Howard
12171, 12243, 12343, 13570, 14882, 15240, 16274, 17237
Dillon, George
13564
Dilworthy, Roger
14772
Dimmitt, Harrison S.
153
Dimnet, Ernest
17683
Dineen, Joseph F.
17599
Dinesen, Isak
15809
di San Secondo, Roso
16136
Ditmars, Raymond L.
16745
Divine, Charles
16946
Dock, George, Jr.
11047
Dr. Winkle
10024
Dodd, Lee Wilson
1765, 2363, 2551, 3074, 3252, 3253, 4302, 4704, 5267, 6330, 7510, 8547, 8575, 8709, 8966, 10699, 10766, 10810, 11187, 16974
Dodge, Homer Joseph
15, 1906
Doherty, Brian
13477
Doherty, Edward
16186
Dolson, Hildegarde
981, 1149, 4199, 4472, 4797, 5605, 7196, 8286, 8668, 9187, 10578
Donahue, Jack
16081, 16796
Donnell, Cushing
12750
Donnelly, Dorothy
14074, 15452, 15455
Dorfman, Nat N.
2368, 4858, 17058
Dos Passos, John
11925, 11952, 12368, 13619, 14329, 15110, 15362, 15588
Dostoievsky, Fyodor
12931
Dostoyevsky, Anna Grigorevna
13128
Doten, Dana
12138
Dottin, Paul
14799
Douglas, Charles Noel
13622
Douglas, Jane
6584-6586, 7164
Douglas, Joan

2211
Douglas, Norman
13866, 14340, 14917
Dounce, Harry Esty
11893r, 11903r, 11985r, 11990r, 12024r, 12028r, 12045r, 12061r, 12099r, 12114r, 12122r, 12123r, 12165r, 12174r, 12268r, 12278r, 12291r, 12377r, 12419r, 12467r, 12484r, 12508r, 12510r, 12648r, 12677r, 12724r, 12731r, 12751r, 12752r, 12798r, 12864r, 12872r, 12880r, 12886r, 12895r, 12942r, 12956r, 13001r, 13012r, 13017r, 13070r, 13085r, 13127r, 13164r, 13166r, 13183r, 13222r, 13242r, 13282r, 13305r, 13328r, 13337r, 13408r, 13424r, 13450r, 13478r, 13548r, 13655r, 13670r, 13681r, 13695r, 13750r, 13752r, 13805r, 13836r, 13905r, 13993r, 14016r, 14028r, 14082r, 14102r, 14209r, 14220r, 14388r, 14433r, 14442r, 14455r, 14477r, 14536r, 14616r, 14622r, 14682r, 14796r, 14845r, 14881r, 14901r, 14963r, 15018r, 15040r, 15070r, 15078r, 15110r, 15113r, 15124r, 15129r, 15162r, 15188r, 15189r, 15258r, 15308r, 15335r, 15423r, 15443r, 15543r, 15607r, 15622r, 15623r, 15625r, 15645r, 15661r, 15668r, 15674r, 15747r, 15782r, 15786r, 15789r, 15837r, 15940r, 15963r, 15968r, 15995r, 16039r, 16047r, 16061r, 16080r, 16095r, 16114r, 16162r, 16210r, 16234r, 16314r, 16356r, 16379r, 16382r, 16388r, 16392r, 16399r, 16422r, 16424r, 16435r, 16453r, 16546r, 16600r, 16609r, 16617r, 16636r, 16639r, 16668r, 16669r, 16674r, 16769r, 16772r, 16808r, 16923r, 16993r, 16998r, 17002r, 17016r, 17055r, 17084r, 17122r, 17163r, 17196r, 17202r, 17213r, 17248r, 17253r, 17257r, 17267r, 17288r, 17293r, 17345r, 17348r, 17386r, 17406r, 17437r, 17467r, 17512r, 17527r, 17535r, 17557r, 17622r, 17648r, 17690r, 17790r, 17791r, 17852r, 17862r, 17868r
Dow, Dorothy
418, 735, 1882, 3226, 4764, 4958, 5967, 5980, 6157, 7545, 8500, 9607, 9749, 10560, 10936, 11100
Dowd, Harrison
1357, 3160, 5522, 9661, 11373
Dowling, Eddie
14187, 16650
Downey, Fairfax
1457, 4663, 4695, 4725, 4952, 6366, 7293, 7649, 7929, 8209, 8602, 8636, 9589, 10015, 12591, 16289
Doyle, Arthur Conan
16606
Doyle, Mary
4838
Doyle, William R.
12656, 14649
Drake, William A.
13379, 13886
Draper, Muriel
15421
Dreher, Carl
2726
Dreiser Committee
14013
Dreiser, Theodore
12028, 12702, 13033, 13229, 13699, 17337
Drinkwater, John
12386, 12387, 14360, 15309, 15968
Driscoll, Louis
4833
Du Bois, Guy
4227
Du Bois, William

13980, 14279, 15831
Dudeney, Alice
15908
Dudley, Bide
12482, 12605
Duer, Caroline
630, 5465, 7103
Duff, James L.
502
Duffey, Vincent
13942
Duffus, R. L.
16463, 16716
Dugan, William Francis
17556
du Gard, Roger Martin
17158
du Maurier, Daphne
13251, 13763, 14439
Duhamel, Georges
15872, 16491
Dukes, Ashley
14498, 15104, 15404, 15891
Dulles, Foster Rhea
2985
Dunbar, L. D.
471
Duncan, Isadora
15445
Duncan, William Cary
13911, 17007
Dunlop, Geoffrey
12998
Dunn, Caesar
17682
Dunn, Edward Delaney
16237
Dunn, Elizabeth
17787
Dunning, Decla
286, 4988
Dunning, Philip
12546, 13765, 14571, 14836, 15552, 15832, 16250, 17033
Dunois, Dominique
15491
Dunsany, Edward John
10660, 12724, 14299
Dunsany, Lord
see Dunsany, Edward John
Dupree, Frank
13981
Durant, Harry
11921
Durant, Will
12662, 14811, 15121, 16115, 16923, 17347
Durante, Jimmy
15549
Duranty, Walter
14291
Duryee, Mary Ballard
302, 2651, 3094, 7233, 10388, 11074
Dyson, Will
12142

E

E. B. M. D.
see Boyd, Ernest
E. B. S.
see Sayre, Elizabeth B.
E. B. W.
see White, E. B.
E. C.
see Coatsworth, Elizabeth
E. C. S.
9777
E. D.
see Davis, Elmer
E. E.
3247, 4253, 6001, 7282, 9130, 11205
E. F. H.
10358
E. F. K.
490, 5143, 8689, 9761, 10819
E. G. N.
8296
E. J.
see Jordan, Elizabeth
E. L.
5092
E. M. C.
see Cody, E. M.
E. O.
6016
E. & O. E.
see James, Samuel
E. W.
see Wylie, Elinor
Eames, Hamilton
10096
Eastman, Max
4088, 11000, 12087, 13361,

14854
Eastman, Rebecca Hooper
324, 7883
Eaton, Walter Prichard
1972
Ebenhack, Arthur
16496
Eberhart, Richard
10736
Eckstein, Gustav
12756, 14889
Eddington, Arthur
15526
Eddison, E. R.
17868
Ede, H. S.
16475
Eden, Patience
see Thomas, Martha Banning
Edgar, Day
14337
Edgelow, Thomas
2421
Editors
311, 5199, 7986
Edman, Irwin
15954
Edmonds, Walter D.
13237, 13363, 16360
Edsall, Florence S.
559, 2248, 8377
Edson, Charles Leroy
13905
Edwards, Bob
7268
Edwards, W. E.
17334
Egan, Cyril B.
6305, 9962
Egan, Michael
13186
Egri, Lajos N.
16200
Ehrenburg, Ilya
13420
Ehrmann, Herbert B.
17492
Eichel, Leslie P.
13215
Eiker, Mathilde
14665
Eilert, Andrée L.
11735
Einstein, Albert
12901
Eisenberg, Emanuel
789, 1407, 1549, 1596, 1666, 2003, 2605, 4345, 4763, 8293
Eisenberg, Frances
4549
Eisinger, Jo
16009
Eisler, Hanns
15386
Eldridge, Paul
12803
Eliot, George Fielding
16197
Eliot, H. W., Jr.
2504, 5360
Eliot, T. S.
12042, 12164, 12813, 13443, 15412, 17381
Eliscu, Edward
13657
Elizabeth
see Russell, Mary Annette
Ellis, Havelock
15067
Ellsberg, Edward
14072, 15731
Elser, Frank B.
2239, 13466, 15315
Elspeth
see O'Halloran, Elspeth
Embry, Jacqueline
806, 1144, 2735, 4436, 5389, 5789, 5954, 7629, 10795
Emerson, John
13746, 16762
Emery, Dorothy Mills
2941, 7606, 10575
Emery, Gilbert
13449, 14954
Emery, John C.
1057, 2405, 2447, 7150, 8106-8109, 10226, 10669
Enders, Gordon
15654
Endicott, Stephen
15196
Endore, S. Guy
12660
Engel, Alexander
12990, 17675
Engle, Paul

12516
English, Maurice
3146
Entrikin, Knowles
16536
Ephraim, Armand
15052
Ephron, Henry
2124
Epicure
1866
Eppley, Louise
1347
Epstein, Julius J.
12054
Epstein, Philip
12054
Erlanger, Aline
15111
Ernst, Morris L.
17285
Erskin, Chester
13846, 14276, 16140
Erskine, John
11918, 12764, 13695, 15912, 16095, 16885
Ertz, Susan
13697
Ervine, St. John
13532, 14484, 17621
Eshenfelder, George
9451
The eskimo
7936
Esler, Lemist
13964
Esmond, H. V.
14234
Essipov, Marie A.
15438
Esty, Lucien
12167
Eulenberg, Herbert
14162
Euripides
11954
Eustace Tilley
see White, E. B.
Evans, Rosalie
16382
Evarts, Esther
519, 1091, 5098
Evreinoff, Nicholas
12738
Ewing, Annemarie
2489, 11577
Ewing, Max
13891
Extra
see Longan, Thomas

F

F. A. F.
see Fender, F. A.
F. B. M.
733, 10364
F. D.
see Downey, Fairfax
F. G. S.
4876
F. J. S.
12293r, 13086r, 13240r, 16440r, 16651r, 16653r
F. H.
see Hyde, Fillmore
F. S.
see Stone, Florence
F. T.
see Tuohy, Ferdinand
Fabian, Warner
10602, 17476
Fabricius, Jan
14376
Fabricius, Johan
14964, 16784
Fadiman, Clifton
710, 2000, 4285, 4399, 4650, 5227, 5545, 7623, 11903Ar, 11905r, 11916r, 11925r, 11931r, 11934r, 11941r, 11942r, 11948r, 11975r, 11976r, 11986r, 11989r, 11995r, 11996r, 12003r, 12004r, 12010r, 12011r, 12012r, 12020r, 12025r, 12036r, 12051r, 12053r, 12067r, 12073r, 12082r, 12090r, 12098r, 12105r, 12110r, 12111r, 12112r, 12113r, 12130r, 12138r, 12142r, 12143r, 12154r, 12166r,

12170r, 12184r, 12185r,
12188r, 12191r, 12197r,
12223r, 12274r, 12284r,
12289r, 12290r, 12298r,
12299r, 12303r, 12305r,
12311r, 12316r, 12324r,
12332r, 12341r, 12349r,
12352r, 12368r, 12374r,
12399r, 12406r, 12407r,
12412r, 12413r, 12414r,
12458r, 12468r, 12471r,
12473r, 12492r, 12494r,
12497r, 12502r, 12504r,
12509r, 12512r, 12519r,
12526r, 12562r, 12597r,
12616r, 12636r, 12640r,
12644r, 12651r, 12653r,
12671r, 12672r, 12682r, 12683r,
12685r, 12726r, 12743r,
12749r, 12753r, 12757r,
12761r, 12770r, 12774r,
12778r, 12788r, 12792r,
12811r, 12830r, 12833r,
12835r, 12845r, 12853r,
12873r, 12884r, 12897r,
12902r, 12906r, 12911r,
12917r, 12935r, 12944r,
12952r, 12962r, 12967r,
12996r, 13000r, 13008r,
13013r, 13021r, 13026r,
13037r, 13038r, 13039r,
13042r, 13043r, 13055r,
13061r, 13064r, 13066r,
13067r, 13073r, 13076r,
13080r, 13129r, 13144Ar,
13160r, 13168r, 13171r,
13188r, 13203r, 13204r,
13237r, 13248r, 13251r,
13253r, 13254r, 13259r,
13264r, 13267r, 13270r,
13272r, 13289r, 13303r,
13306r, 13310r, 13312r,
13316r, 13319r, 13345r,
13347r, 13352r, 13359r,
13360r, 13368r, 13373r,
13384r, 13385r, 13393r,
13397r, 13414r, 13415r,
13416r, 13444r, 13447r,
13462r, 13476r, 13479r,
13488r, 13490r, 13490Ar,
13496r, 13502r, 13503r,
13504r, 13508r, 13515r,
13524r, 13535r, 13537r,
13538r, 13541r, 13545r,
13549r, 13552r, 13561r,
13566r, 13567r, 13572r,
13577r, 13582r, 13583r,
13588r, 13590r, 13617r,
13621r, 13623r, 13626r,
13631r, 13649r, 13663r,
13674r, 13686r, 13687r,
13710r, 13719r, 13742r,
13763r, 13784r, 13870r,
13880r, 13896r, 13899r,
13907r, 13930r, 13932r,
13936r, 13952r, 13954r,
13956r, 13975r, 13983r,
13989r, 13996r, 14001r,
14017r, 14019r, 14021r,
14022r, 14036r, 14056r,
14058r, 14072r, 14105r,
14109r, 14110r, 14116r,
14131r, 14175r, 14178r,
14184r, 14194r, 14195r,
14198r, 14201r, 14215r,
14221r, 14224r, 14233r,
14240r, 14247r, 14254r,
14266r, 14267, 14268r,
14284r, 14286r, 14291r,
14294r, 14308r, 14309r,
14318r, 14321r, 14325r,
14329r, 14338r, 14347r,
14350r, 14351r, 14359r,
14366r, 14367r, 14369r,
14370r, 14391r, 14417r,
14422r, 14431r, 14439r,
14451r, 14468r, 14487r,
14496r, 14503r, 14504r,
14506r, 14508r, 14511r,
14512r, 14578r, 14609r,
14610r, 14611r, 14683r,
14692r, 14694r, 14696r,
14700r, 14713r, 14722r,
14734r, 14749r, 14769r,
14782r, 14794r, 14801r,
14811r, 14831r, 14853r,
14870r, 14895r, 14899r,
14912r, 14913r, 14915r,
14922r, 14927r, 14938r,
14952r, 14994r, 14999r,
15017r, 15027r, 15037r,
15042r, 15043r, 15056r,
15068r, 15081r, 15097r,
15098r, 15115r, 15116r,
15140r, 15161r, 15169r,
15176r, 15185r, 15204r,

17803r, 17841r, 17848r, 17851r, 17858r, 17859r, 17860r, 17863r, 17880r, 17881r, 17882r, 17893r, 17895r, 17903r, 17915r, 17921r, 17925r, 17927r, 17937r, 17940r, 17950r
Fagan, James B.
12052
Fagan, Myron C.
14354, 14883, 15483
Fairbank, Janet Ayer
12534
Fairchild, Donald Stites
9946, 14385
Falkenberg, Gerhardt
15753
Fallada, Hans
14870, 15749
Falstaff, Jake
see Fetzer, Herman
Fangen, Ronald
13248
Faragoh, Francis Edwards
15973
Farbstein, W. E.
380, 612, 645, 765, 1195, 1579, 1890, 2242, 2491, 2573, 2695, 4558, 4559, 4560, 4565, 4906, 5495, 6252, 6363, 8220, 8629, 8630, 8779, 9654, 10037, 10099, 10438-10441, 10945, 11010, 11011
Farigoule, Louis
see Romains, Jules
Farjeon, Eleanor
17428
Farjeon, Herbert
17428
Farjeon, Joseph Jefferson
13346, 15656
Farley, James
12303
Farmer, Virginia
16848
Farnham, Mateel Howe
14930
Farrell, James T.
13786, 15614, 17859
Farrell, M. J.
16846
Farson, Negley
13002, 16919, 17615
Fauchois, René
14726, 15357
Fauconnier, Henri
15058
Faulkner, William
11905, 12152, 13168, 14822, 16152, 16457, 16458, 16769, 16806, 17493, 17759
Fauset, Jessie
15994
Fawkes, Guy
see Benchley, Robert
Fay, Bernard
13653
Fay, Frank
13651, 17079
Fay, Judith
1018
Fayard, Jean
13092
Fearing, Kenneth
384, 1151, 2289, 2572, 4509, 5223, 5322, 7258, 7944, 8079, 8501, 8822, 8868, 11805
Federn, Karl
12253
Feiner, Herman
17214
Feld, Rose C.
1631, 2683, 2772, 4077, 4258, 5476, 7851, 8479, 8548
Feldkamp, Fred J.
784
Fellowes, Daisy
12687, 14761
Fellows, Dexter W.
17189
Fender, F. A.
35, 8985, 9281
Ferber, Edna
8021, 10624, 11564, 12762, 12833, 13135, 15905, 16393, 16636, 16861
Ferguson, Charles W.
861
Fergusson, Harvey
14209, 15344
Ferrero, Guglielmo
16568
Ferris, Walter
14523
Fessier, Michael
13687

Fetzer, Herman
89, 111, 728, 2152, 5133, 7189, 7594, 9308, 10078, 10390, 10755, 11177, 11470, 11769
Feuchtwanger, Lion
14468, 14499, 15780, 16072, 16985, 17450
Ficke, Arthur Davison
1497, 2796, 8475
Field, Rachel
600, 2414, 2877, 7628, 8190, 9789, 11986
Field-Field, Col. Bolton
see Thurber, James
Fields, Dorothy
12424
Fields, Herbert
12034, 12728, 12871, 13054, 13244, 13500, 13787, 14073, 14153, 15857, 16065
Fields, Joseph A.
16498
Fields, Lew
17512A
Finan, James
11614
Fineman, Irving
13160
Finklehoffe, Fred F.
12560
Finn, Jonathan
12704
Finney, Charles G.
12770
Finny, S.
see White, E. B.
Fishback, Margaret
71, 102, 130, 202, 261, 284, 296, 383, 405, 445, 465, 503, 521, 524, 562, 565, 596, 626, 715, 757, 777, 850, 853, 938, 1016, 1034, 1059, 1239, 1244, 1312, 1315, 1363, 1379, 1381, 1433, 1438, 1460, 1464, 1511, 1525, 1565, 1647, 1649, 1657, 1661, 1844, 1879, 1987, 2020, 2051, 2053, 2128, 2156, 2212, 2395, 2542, 2544, 2687, 2692, 2752, 2798, 2909, 2946, 2960, 2997, 3030, 3035, 3155, 3181, 3195, 3971, 4038, 4082, 4104, 4225, 4284, 4317, 4420, 4446, 4522, 4540, 4577, 4825, 4970, 4971, 5123, 5201, 5217, 5320, 5340, 5341, 5363, 5654, 5751, 5752, 5758, 5763, 5770, 5772, 5773, 5775, 5776, 5778, 5779, 5783, 5784, 5785, 5787, 5792, 5795, 5930, 5942, 6096, 6097, 6192, 6193, 6194, 6195, 6336, 6393, 6424, 6480, 7028, 7029, 7061, 7134, 7200, 7229, 7231, 7235, 7269, 7407, 7447, 7449, 7463, 7470, 7481, 7493, 7651, 7701, 7710, 7768, 7786, 7796, 7800, 7806, 7809, 7838, 7840, 8026, 8080, 8379, 8397, 8544, 8606, 8714, 8715, 8754, 8775, 8788, 8800, 8811, 8843, 8934, 8935, 8953, 8961, 8963, 8973, 8996, 9015, 9025, 9207, 9247, 9251, 9264-9266, 9290, 9293, 9390, 9419, 9454, 9532, 9533, 9544, 9545, 9596, 9620, 9622, 9623, 9643, 9742, 9874, 9949, 9960, 9984, 9987, 9995, 10032, 10052, 10091, 10139, 10162, 10176, 10196, 10228, 10231, 10251, 10295, 10326, 10387, 10391, 10407, 10579, 10611, 10672, 10700, 10701, 10705, 10713, 10727, 10742, 10750, 10760, 10768, 10781, 10837, 10921, 10922, 10940, 10960-10978, 11004, 11038, 11169, 11189, 11190, 11255, 11272, 11360, 11440, 11520, 11630, 11763, 11823, 11863, 11881
Fishbein, Morris
15522
Fisher, A. E.
3954, 15153
Fisher, Dorothy Canfield
see Canfield, Dorothy
Fisher, M. F. K.
16551
Fisher, Rudolph
17581
Fisher, Vardis
12743, 15619
Fishman, Joseph Fulling
534, 1377, 1454, 2165, 2166, 2206, 2453, 3281, 3283, 3284, 3285, 3286, 3897, 3898, 4115, 4325, 4449, 5197, 5345, 5815,

13818, 13881
Foch, Ferdinand
15213
Fodor, Ladilaus
12760
Foerster, Norman
14251
Földes, Jolán
16956
Foley, Martha
13577
Follett, John D.
1116
Follett, Wilson
17852
Folwell, Arthur H.
36, 126, 507, 535, 1153, 1485, 2018, 2238, 2536, 2984, 3925, 4157, 4176, 4994, 5112, 5342, 6374, 6378, 7291, 7351, 7352, 8052, 9939, 9940, 10400, 10638, 10788, 10890, 10902, 11454
Foote, John Tainter
17260
Forbes, Anne
8046, 10820, 11415
Forbes, Esther
15293, 15851
Forbes, James
16060
Forbes, John
746, 747, 1024, 1458, 1737, 1738, 2479, 3197, 3976, 5836, 6600, 9259, 9535, 9767, 9881, 10005, 10116, 11220-11222, 11510
Ford, Charles Henri
5006, 5090, 13713
Ford, Corey
40, 134, 212, 331, 492, 720, 840, 849, 888, 889, 890, 908, 1131, 1265, 1490, 1741, 1852, 1947, 2101, 2199, 3918, 3975, 4089, 4454, 4455, 4456, 4611, 4615, 4639, 4694, 4701, 4746, 4850, 4905, 4936, 5073, 5154, 5533, 5680, 5861, 5871, 6083, 6327, 6646, 7288, 7354, 7355, 7390, 7511, 7943, 8452, 8659, 9148, 9286, 9414, 9488, 9510, 9518, 9760, 9936, 10189, 10406, 10657, 11346, 11426, 11492-11495, 11504, 11745, 14165, 16444
Ford, Ford Madox
1042, 14721, 15070, 15599, 15607, 16772
Ford, George
15300
Ford, Harry Chapman
13302, 13403
Ford, Henry
17288
Ford, John
12940, 17277
Ford, Margaret
1006, 2317, 4491, 5688, 6027, 7551, 8210, 8900, 9484, 10543, 10551
Ford, Worthington Chauncey
14780
Forester, C. S.
12640, 13729, 13975
Forks
11318
Forrest, Belford
14930A
Forrest, Sam
15835
Forster, E. M.
13378
Fort, Charles
17762
Fort, Garrett
14441
Fort, John P.
16908
Foster, Michael
12012
Fowler, Gene
13476, 13923, 13928
Fox, Douglas C.
394
Fox, Paul Hervey
13610, 15666, 16768
France, Anatole
14309, 17467
Frances, Countess of Warwick
see Warwick, Frances Evelyn
Francis, J. O.
12277
Frank, Bruno
15068, 16916, 17413
Frank, Florence Kiper
1417, 7047, 7612, 10301, 11656

Frank, Gerold
2676, 6603, 9043, 10053
Frank, Leonhard
12785, 14549
Frank, Waldo
93, 147, 709, 1386, 1608, 2378, 2587, 3269, 4951, 4997, 5012, 5286, 5361, 5657, 5868, 6075, 6177, 6465, 6643, 7102, 7271, 7854, 8218, 8319, 8480, 8852, 8866, 9287, 9311, 11067, 11211, 12003, 12526, 13055, 17557
Frankau, Gilbert
12981
Franken, Rose
12083
Frankforter, Alice
172, 209, 247, 381, 472, 528, 679, 783, 957, 989, 1043, 1162, 1220, 1445, 1512, 1578, 1588, 1593, 1620, 1805, 1880, 1943, 2008, 2304, 2306, 2381, 2475, 2509, 2545, 2811, 2974, 2994, 3042, 3105, 3151, 3968, 3972, 3974, 4029, 4059, 4155, 4161, 4595, 4944, 5005, 5161, 5332, 5343, 5394, 5486, 5505, 5927, 6088, 6256, 6276, 6473, 6605, 7014, 7118, 7614, 7615, 7925, 8042, 8111, 8335, 8519, 8527, 8708, 9034, 9156, 9260, 9279, 9376, 9406, 9573, 9773 9948, 9967, 10159, 10306, 10412, 10888, 11140, 11165, 11289, 11677, 11761, 11843, 11850, 11853
Frankfurter, Marion D.
14781
Frederick, J. George
17673
Fredric, Helene
2069
Freedman, David
14803, 17032, 17953
Freeman, Andrew A.
5849, 12571, 17189
Freeman, H. W.
13214, 14495
Freeman, Joseph
12026
Freuchen, Peter
12113, 13373, 16515
Freud, Sigmund
15382
Freudy
2694, 9221
Friebus, Florida
11966
Friedkin, Emily Z.
7990
Friedlander, William B.
15223, 15966
Friedman, Charles
16686
Friml, Rudolph
13522, 15600, 17219, 17720, 17761
Frost, Frances M.
48, 61, 68, 101, 319, 429, 431, 603, 604, 844, 911, 914, 1001, 1047, 1204, 1270, 1557, 1722, 1730, 1821, 1857, 1858, 1913, 2085, 2107, 2139, 2147, 2633, 2634, 2805, 2910, 2993, 3053, 3093, 3157, 3182, 3217, 4005, 4569, 4726, 4759, 4928, 5035, 5134, 5473, 5562, 5571, 5985, 6017, 6138, 6304, 6308, 6477, 7035, 7072, 7444, 7496, 7554, 7687, 7780, 7889, 8155, 8158, 8333, 8376, 8424, 8425, 8476, 8515, 8567, 8603, 8661, 8703, 8718, 8817, 8829, 8833, 8835, 8841, 8942, 9000, 9009, 9116, 9131, 9383, 9389, 9408, 9427, 9476, 9563, 9588, 9803, 9826, 10056, 10092, 10093, 10227, 10655, 10714, 10839, 11231, 11356, 11624, 11663, 11695, 11715, 11733, 11739, 11740, 14363
Frost, Jack
see Brandt, Carl
Frost, Robert
12814, 12821, 17663
Frost, Walter
12635
Fuchs, Daniel
391, 1862, 4501, 5977, 6153, 7046, 8248
Fuchs, Emil
17804
Fuller, Barbara Anne
9626

Fuller, Albert C.
16254
Fuller, Hector
11904
Fuller, R. Buckminster
15580
Fuller, Sylvia
1651, 2652, 3236, 6249, 8065, 8744, 8941, 9421, 11490, 11508
Fülöp-Miller, René
16058, 17380
Funk, Wilfred J.
2349, 6606, 7708, 7808
Furnas, C. C.
15539
Furnas, Marthedith
7580
Furth, Albert
4126
Fyfe, Hamilton
15631

G

G. C. R.
see Ryan, Gertrude Curtis
G. F. R.
see Riegel, G. F.
G. H.
see Hellman, George
G. H. C.
see Conkling, Grace Hazard
G. L. H.
1468
G. S.
see Schwabe, G.
G. W. G.
see Gabriel, Gilbert W.
Gabriel, Gilbert W.
185, 876, 6080, 7408, 10501, 10880, 12172r, 12228r, 12277r, 12280r, 12283r, 12423r, 12521r, 12584r, 12738r, 12927r, 12972r, 13114r, 13196r, 13226r, 13292r, 13298r, 13333r, 13509r, 13716r, 13772r, 13787r, 13808r, 13813r, 13915r, 13917r, 13936r, 13979r, 14002r, 14060r, 14323r, 14397r, 14443r, 14464r, 14485r, 14538r, 14612r, 14862r, 14946r, 14997r, 15057r, 15060r, 15174r, 15356r, 15362r, 15399r, 15594r, 15596r, 15751r, 16019r, 16033r, 16298r, 16501r, 16549r, 16573r, 16587r, 16856r, 16904r, 17037r, 17277r, 17389r, 17438r, 17457r, 17554r, 17636r, 17755r, 17795r
Galantiere, Lewis
6583, 12048, 17203
Gale, Zona
12477, 16035, 16061, 17886
Gallagher, Francis
14404
Gallico, Paul
5479, 8656, 13460
Galsworthy, John
12630, 12648, 13366, 13562, 15045, 15728, 16363, 16664, 16668, 17024
Gandera, Felix
14048
Gannett, Lewis
258, 4552, 8981, 12189r, 12459r, 12660r, 13028r, 13159r, 13653r, 14479r, 14589r, 14937r, 15067r, 15211r, 15461r, 16292r, 16608r, 16924r, 17119r, 17294r, 17562r, 17664r, 17801r
Gantillon, Simon
15192
Garçon, Maurice
13099
Gardiner, Alexander
12633
Gardner, Mona
11773, 11889
Garland, George White
11264
Garland, Hamlin
15439
Garnett, David
13810, 13901, 14782, 15604, 16000
Garnett, Edward
14778
Garrett, Oliver H. P.
248, 285, 348, 1231, 1360, 3171, 7441, 7866, 10338, 11690

12532r, 12567r, 12590r, 12652r, 12694r, 12708r, 12767r, 12834r, 12848r, 12966r, 12977r, 12982r, 12998r, 13110r, 13148r, 13155r, 13186r, 13209r, 13223r, 13229r, 13232r, 13265r, 13274r, 13371r, 13426r, 13451r, 13525r, 13551r, 13565r, 13666r, 13675r, 13733r, 13749r, 13760r, 13775r, 13839r, 13846r, 13871r, 13938r, 13945r, 13967r, 14000r, 14047r, 14051r, 14077r, 14081r, 14096r, 14165r, 14192r, 14205r, 14280r, 14296r, 14310r, 14515r, 14526r, 14554r, 14556r, 14571r, 14574r, 14607r, 14615r, 14618r, 14640r, 14661r, 14663r, 14766r, 14795r, 14803r, 14819r, 14821r, 14828r, 14855r, 14942r, 14950r, 15016r, 15091r, 15120r, 15122r, 15126r, 15139r, 15156r, 15222r, 15238r, 15253r, 15287r, 15307r, 15363r, 15388r, 15409r, 15435r, 15442r, 15516r, 15563r, 15565r, 15566r, 15589r, 15616r, 15715r, 15733r, 15741r, 15787r, 15847r, 15850r, 15861r, 15869r, 15883r, 15886r, 15913r, 15951r, 15972r, 16062r, 16107r, 16147r, 16178r, 16216r, 16226r, 16244r, 16250r, 16253r, 16368r, 16411r, 16428r, 16445r, 16464r, 16494r, 16513r, 16532r, 16539r, 16564r, 16614r, 16683r, 16686r, 16720r, 16732r, 16737r, 16747r, 16752r, 16778r, 16779r, 16840r, 16849r, 16876r, 16946r, 16949r, 16957r, 16961r, 16992r, 17013r, 17040r, 17051r, 17096r, 17150r, 17224r, 17258r, 17260r, 17265r, 17268r, 17281r, 17283r, 17301r, 17306r, 17307r, 17322r, 17384r, 17428r, 17436r, 17471r, 17540r, 17558r, 17575r, 17602r, 17670r, 17723r, 17810r, 17834r, 17874r, 17894r, 17906r, 17916r

Gibney, Sheridan
17797

Gide, André
14308, 16269, 16497, 17355

Gilbert, Edwin
13839

Gilbert, Morris
896, 2896

Gilbert, William S.
13357, 13843, 13979, 14397, 15278, 15279, 15887, 15975, 16083, 16400

Gilchrist, Eleanor
1476, 2394, 8772, 11456

Gilchrist, J. N.
17491

Gilchrist, Marie
419, 1910, 3109, 10011

Gilcrest, Julia
10712

Gilder, Rodman
1339

Gill, Brendan
157, 1238, 1306, 1664, 1710, 1818, 2037, 2332, 2538, 2682, 2761, 2820, 2948, 5328, 5658, 7691, 7963, 9302, 9356, 11790

Gillen, James
9618

Gillette, William
16606

Gilligan, Edmund
12492

Gillis, William R.
13833

Gilman, Mildred
2560, 3037, 3931, 5366, 6067, 7582, 8259, 9436, 11399, 14948

Gilmore, Louis
11423

Gilson, Charles
17758

Gingrich, Arnold
12671

Ginty, E. B.

15307
Giono, Jean
14021, 16792
Giraudoux, Jean
12041, 12313, 14528, 16655
Girdler, Catherine
10823
Gisnet, Morris
14736
Gissing, George
17537
Giudice, Davide
17335
Gladstone, Mary
15165
Glaenzer, Richard Butler
8258, 10570
Glasgow, Ellen
12254, 16356, 16605, 17154, 17523
Glaspell, Susan
11969, 12002, 12557, 12841, 13684, 14361
Glass, Montague
7310, 16052
Glazer, Benjamin
16992
Gleason, Harold Willard
169, 392, 1526, 2190, 2200, 2708, 3056, 4981, 5845, 6056, 6471, 7723, 8159, 8299, 8328, 9039, 9323, 9447, 10421, 11632, 16507
Gleason, James
13433, 14409, 16188, 16588
Glenn, Isa
14877, 16628, 16814, 17351
Glenny, Peter
15533, 16987
Glutz, Ambrose
5676
Glyn, Elinor
14414
Goddard, Pliny Earle
374, 8284
Godden, Rumer
12414
Godwin, A. H.
13780
Goetel, Ferdynand
13673
Goethe, Johann Wolfgang von
13481
Goetz, E. Ray
14667
Gogarty, Oliver St. John
10665, 12154, 16542, 17403
Gogol, Nikolai
14373
Gold, Michael
13494, 14471
Goldberg, Arthur Gerald
4299
Goldberg, Hyman
5926, 6152, 9340, 10151
Goldberg, Isaac
15078, 17129, 17273
Goldberg, Rube
438, 8913
Golden, Alfred L.
15287
Golden, Eleanor
16840
Golden, Ernie
12147
Golden, I.J.
16243
Golden, John
11944, 13156
Golding, Louis
13545, 15312, 16146
Golding, Samuel Ruskin
15776, 16154
Goldman, Harold
12896
Goldring, Douglas
13427
Goldschmidt, Lena
12663
Goldsmith, Clifford
17670
Goldsmith, Margaret
12753
Goldsmith, Oliver
16601
Goldstrom, John
11402
Goll, Claire
14469
Gollomb, Joseph
2967, 7317, 8412
Golly-Wogg
see Gabriel, Gilbert W.
Goodhue, Willis Maxwell
12342, 14553
Goodman, Arthur

14301
Goodman, Eckert
15126
Goodman, Jules Eckert
15126, 16052
Goodrich, Arthur
12637, 15923, 15997
Goodrich, Frances
12520, 17497
Goodwin, Shaun
452
Goold, Helen
5819, 8053
Gordon, Ann
11752
Gordon, Caroline
13710, 15626
Gordon, Jan
15722
Gordon, Leon
17471
Gordon, Taylor
12479
Gordy, Donald
2250
Gordy, Edward L.
38, 5640, 8570, 10539, 11435
Gore-Browne, R. F.
12970
Gorer, Geoffrey
11934, 12233
Gorham, James
1140
Gorky, Maxim
12608, 13072, 16824
Gorman, Herbert
545, 14349, 15394, 15977
Gorostiza, Celestino
15253
Gosnell, H. Allen
15732
Gosse, Philip
14151
Gosselin, Louis
16345
Gotham
552
Gottwald, Fritz
12846
Gould, Bruce
473, 15114
Gould, Paul
79, 80, 81, 1387, 1703, 4034, 7702, 11817
Gow, Ronald
14968
Gowen, Emmett
13013
Gowen, Vincent H.
17000
Grace, Dick
14264
Grafton, Samuel
5180
Graham, Al
1384, 1705, 8067, 10542
Graham, Ed. B.
24
Graham, Eleanor
11574
Graham, Gordon
293
Graham, Harvey
16925
Graham, Stephen
1446, 4942, 9169, 10916, 15534
Grainger, Porter
14989
Granberry, Edwin
12047, 16945
Grannis, Anita
5120
Grant, Joan
17780
Grant, Neil
15947
Granville-Barker, Harley
12043
Grattan, Lawrence
13876
Graves, Charles
5892, 5893, 5894, 5895, 5896, 5897, 9492, 9493, 11759
Graves, Robert
12595, 12788, 12906, 13865, 14735
Gray, A. Barr
1777
Gray, Don
8437
Greeley, Dana Watterson
14362
Greeley, Horace, Jr.
see Wylie, Philip G.
Green, Anne

16541
Green, Howard J.
9051
Green, Julian
12196, 12754, 12795
Green, Paul
14227, 14328, 14492, 16351
Greenbaum, Fritz
16468
Greene, Graham
12538, 16409
Greene, Ward
17652
Greenfield, Will H.
4741
Greensfelder, Elmer
12558
Greenwood, C. T.
8604
Greenwood, Walter
14969
Gregg, F. B.
5765
Gregory, Alyse
16600
Gregory, Frank
14893
Gregory, Horace
7951
Grew, William A.
13276, 14462, 15181, 15441, 15542
Grey, Clifford
14534, 14601, 15194, 15246, 15780A, 17007
Gribble, Francis
12239
Gribble, George Dunning
15174
Gribble, Harry Wagstaff
12146, 15131, 15322, 15688, 15707, 15926, 16275, 16396, 17373
Grice, Jess Nancy
5534, 8100, 8806
Griffith, Hubert
17923
Griffith, Maddy Vegtel
see Vegtel, Maddy
Griffith, Wyn
16847
Griscom, Lloyd
17106
Gropper, Milton Herbert
12363, 12582, 14374, 15294, 16681
Groseclose, Elgin
12110
Gross, Kathleen Cotter
9804
Gross, Laurence
17715
Gross, Milt
14034
Gross, Stephen
14192
Grove, John
15720
Grover, J. P.
144, 5472, 8650, 10148
Grover, James
see Gorham, James
Gruening, Ernest
7318
Grunauer, Milton
8726, 11526
Grunwald, Alfred
12772, 12990
Guedalla, Philip
13478, 14254, 15844
Guido
see Du Bois, Guy
Guilloux, Louis
12399, 14634
Guiterman, Arthur
53, 448, 468, 504, 637, 672, 676, 690, 739, 842, 902, 1067, 1122, 1134, 1274, 1391, 1405, 1420, 1648, 1650, 1669, 1694, 1945, 2220, 2302, 2370, 2467, 2492, 2601, 2642, 2919, 3274, 3922, 4064, 4140, 4172, 4448, 4466, 4469, 4596, 4752, 4890, 4931, 4932, 4933, 5038, 5040, 5216, 5293, 5615, 5644, 5646, 5647, 5648, 5650, 6042, 6196, 6312, 7002, 7116, 7143, 7477, 7552, 7668, 7669, 7675, 7677, 7680, 7725, 7776, 7833, 7870, 7877, 7907, 7912-7914, 8017, 8289, 8308, 8318, 8400, 8451, 8563, 8687, 8688, 8691, 8735, 8748, 8837, 8925, 8954, 8964, 9026, 9063, 9243, 9379, 9462, 9707, 9711, 9727, 9853, 9998, 10154, 10282, 10378,

10426, 10756, 10774, 11130, 11132, 11197, 11447, 11557, 11716, 11743, 11748, 16494
Guitry, Sacha
14744, 14834, 15404, 15405
Gulbranssen, Trygve
12349, 17769
Gumbinner, Paul G.
592, 2167, 2789, 2925, 4555, 5487, 7699, 8054, 8509, 9143, 10186, 10555, 10630, 10930, 10990, 11446
Gunn, Elizabeth
1502, 6667, 10749
Gunnarsson, Gunnar
16559
Gunther, John
7244, 13838, 14369, 14370, 16236
Gusev, Sergiei Ivanovich
14697
Guthrie, Thomas Anstey
see Anstey, F.
Gwynne
5111
Gynt, Kaj
16198

H

H. A. M.
7937
H. C.
see Cushman, Howard
H. C. N.
1041
H. D.
14398
H. D.
see also Dounce, Harry Esty
H. E. S.
7588
H. E. Y.
see Yates, H. E.
H. H. G.
4655
H. J. D.
see Dodge, Homer Joseph
H. J. L.
see Littlefield, H. J.
H. J. M.
see Mankiewicz, Herman J.
H. L. B.
5259
H. L. M.
see Mencken, H. L.
H. R.
see Reed, Herbert
Haardt, Sara
4892, 5210
Habakkuk, Jones
see Davis, Elmer
Hackett, Albert
12520, 17497
Hackett, Francis
1015, 13649, 14089, 17123
Hackett, Walter
15792
Hagan, James
13977, 15274, 15766
Haggart, John
15006
Hahn, Emily
84, 1296, 1322, 1416, 2074, 2276, 2768, 3125, 3962, 3981, 4003, 4363, 4371, 4372, 4451, 5016, 5093, 5226, 5229, 5254, 5258, 5452, 5535, 5990, 6011, 6229, 6263, 6539, 6651, 7060, 7090, 7098, 7192, 7217, 7302, 7690, 7886, 8069, 8212, 8441, 8653, 8696, 9087, 9159, 9170, 9190, 9224, 9452, 9486, 9880, 10129, 11049, 11143, 11270, 11626, 11931
Haight, George
13868, 17036
Haines, William Wister
16734
Haisley, Wayne G.
10684
Hale, Agnes Burke
3044
Hale, Hope
7130, 9490
Hale, Lionel
17146
Hale, Nancy
1554, 2991, 3106, 4156, 6421, 6509, 8271, 10454
Hale, R.
1422, 10686
Hale, Ruth
17525
Hale, William Harlan
12706, 13996

Hall, Baird
2434, 2435, 2436
Hall, James Norman
4237, 6368, 8933, 14261
Hall, Leonard
1809, 5984, 7387
Hall, Radclyffe
15179, 17488, 17656, 17657
Hallgren, Mauritz A.
16537
Halliburton, Richard
13569, 15528
Halper, Albert
12761, 13626, 17482
Halsey, Margaret
11296, 17802
Hamilton, Anne
991, 7873
Hamilton, Cosmo
12673, 12860, 12970, 15959
Hamilton, Patrick
16378, 17447
Hamlin, Talbot Faulkner
7045
Hammerstein, Arthur
15103
Hammerstein, Oscar, II
13090, 13297, 13660, 13705, 13837, 13848, 15191, 15426, 15524, 16190, 16637, 16638, 16790, 17006, 17030, 17531, 17761
Hammett, Dashiell
13802
Hammond, Percy
2174, 8465, 9253
Hamp, Pierre
14610
Hamsun, Knut
16305, 16324, 16379, 16540, 17507
Handley, Alan
9369
Hanley, Jimmy
16650
Hannah, Link
17834
Hanoteau, Jean
17803
Hansen, Harry
17940
Harbach, Otto
12680, 13090, 13522, 13608, 13837, 13848, 14612, 14985, 15579, 16344, 16790, 17006, 17761
Harbour, F. F.
128
Hardin, Nancy
8514, 8797, 11502
Hardin, Taylor Scott
1221
Harding, Bertita
85, 15948
Harding, T. Swann
13430
Hardt-Warden, Bruno
17214
Hardy, Florence Emily
13283, 14729
Hargrave, John
16994
Hargrave, Roy
14238, 16365
Harkins, John
836
Harkness, Marjorie Gane
11588
Harlow, Alvin F.
3221, 4151, 11725, 11771
Harold, Childe
see Thurber, James
Harpie
4748
Harriman, Margaret Case
624, 1005, 1618, 1993, 2313, 2377, 3104, 4020, 4310, 4396, 4500, 6486, 6638, 7336, 7440, 8739, 9134, 10088, 10290, 10834, 11097, 11229, 11294, 11737
Harrington, J. W.
517
Harrington, Jonathan
4078
Harrington, Joseph
6205
Harris, Bernice Kelly
16145
Harris, Charles T.
15216
Harris, Elmer
13929, 14639, 15152, 15347, 16899, 17934
Harris, Frank
12330

Harris, Lewis
8055
Harris, Mildred
10381, 12896
Harris, Muriel
16570
Hart, Frances Noyes
12315, 14124
Hart, Henry
13932
Hart, Lorenz
12207, 12500, 12728, 12871, 13054, 13716, 13787, 14041, 14280, 14293, 15741, 16065, 16675, 16844, 17307
Hart, Moss
12031, 12034, 12157, 13426, 13428, 14522, 15091, 15238, 15745, 17905
Hart, Walter
16077, 17602
Hartley, L. P.
16674
Hartmann, Cyril Hughes
17505
Harvey, Alice
10351
Harvey, Frank
14705
Harwood, H. M.
12970, 14606, 14661, 15076, 15910
Hasek, Jaroslav
13861
Hasenclever, Walter
14096
Hashagen, Ernst
17449
Haskell, Loney
1789, 11251
Haskins, Caryl P.
15669
Haskins, M. L.
17239
Haslund, Henning
17107
Hassell, Harriet
16172
Hastings, Patrick
16506
Hatch, Leonard
1127, 2814, 3156, 5346, 6103, 6235, 11335
Hatcher, Harlan
17405
Hatton, Fanny
12990, 14902, 14953, 16912
Hatton, Frederic
12990, 14902, 14953, 16912
Hatvany, Lili
14944, 17303
Hauser, Heinrich
12400, 13432
Hawkins, Maxwell
12934
Hawkins, Stuart Hyde
4642, 6395, 7539, 10145, 10876, 11665, 11738
Hawthorne, Hazel
4047, 9751
Hawthorne, Ruth
12814r
Hay
see Levy, Newman
Hay, Ian
12213, 15261
Hay, Sara Henderson
487, 745, 2042, 2080, 2195, 4007, 5075, 5708, 7644, 7785, 7793, 7814, 8305, 8347, 8553, 8747, 9675, 9786, 9851, 10702, 10759, 10762, 10796-10803, 10805, 11352
Haydon, Robert
12186
Hayes, Alfred
5088
Hayes, Hubert
17260
Haynes, Annie
12953
Hays, Will, Jr.
14666r, 14710r, 15292r, 16170r, 16448r, 16652r, 17023r, 17252r,
Hazelton, George C.
17889
Hazzard, John E.
14237
Head, Cloyd
12108
Hearley, John

16027
Heath, Horton
482, 1019, 1367, 2335, 2914, 4416, 5707, 6537, 6589, 7542, 7764, 8877, 11417, 11779
Hecht, Ben
271, 718, 1219, 2885, 4037, 5814, 6173, 7781, 8327, 8395, 9239, 11605, 11616, 12471, 12554, 13677, 13923, 14467, 14533, 14640, 17281, 17415
Hecht, Harold
16683
Hecht, Marie Armstrong
16987
Hedge, Charlcie
10646
Hedgehog
5962
Hedin, Sven
14456
Heggie, Barbara
2533, 4649, 7209
Heijermans, Herman
13112, 13857
Heilbron, Adelaide
16778
Heimann, Philip
13525
Heiser, Victor
12011
Held, John, Jr.
4774, 5359
Hellman, Geoffrey T.
561, 683, 874, 999, 1097, 1662, 1832, 2023, 2295, 2307, 2463, 2473, 2568, 3111, 3945, 4203, 4247, 4272, 4333, 4700, 4717, 5059, 5115, 5448, 5709, 6148, 6519, 6614, 7067, 7250, 7616, 8117, 8693, 8705, 9066, 9252, 9352, 9590, 9591, 9956, 10831, 10995, 11016, 11451, 11535, 11635, 11658, 11679
Hellman, George S.
3153, 12181r, 12754r, 12796r, 12850r, 12991r, 13343r, 13374r, 13559r, 13638r, 14242r, 14427r, 14471r, 14623r, 14851r, 15964r, 16048r, 16937r, 16963r
Hellman, Lillian
12746, 14863
Helm, Florence
224, 6243, 10048
Helm, Katherine
4739, 15170
Helser, Laura McGuffey
8428
Heltai, Jeno
12974
Helton, Roy
16766
Hemingway, Ernest
4306, 5649, 7178, 13057, 13455, 13456, 13496, 13952, 14335, 15231, 16998, 16999, 17279, 17789
Henderson, Ray
16482, 16969
Henderson, Robert
7414
Henderson, W. J.
6654, 7939, 11607
Hennequin, Maurice
15689
Henriot, Émile
12122
Henriques, Robert
15597
Henschke, Alfred
15940
Herbert, A. P.
14175. 17606
Herbert, Conrad
252
Herbert, Victor
12209, 15029, 15772, 16548
Herbst, Josephine
15642, 15976, 16377
Herendeen, Anne
1280
Herendeen, Frederick
11982, 15467
Hergesheimer, Joseph
14841, 15870, 17048
Herman, Alexander C.
13215
Herman, Justin
300
Herold, Don
4784, 7303, 9186, 11561, 16937
Herrick, Robert
13348
Herriot, Edouard

6099, 6190, 6472, 7536, 7704, 7979, 9094, 9100, 9614, 9784, 10165, 10170, 10288, 10514, 11523, 11546, 11682
Hollister, Len D.
15372
Hollister, Paul
1636
Holm, John Cecil
17217
Holmes, John
464, 530, 954, 1427, 1431, 1771, 1828, 1895, 1900, 2207, 2336, 2738, 2753, 6220, 6460, 6478, 6479, 7044, 7555, 7763, 7904, 8093, 8247, 8253, 8462, 8660, 8770, 10291, 10313, 10545, 10568, 11072, 11744
Holmes, John Haynes
14310
Holroyd-Reece, John
17551
Homans, Dorothy
2558, 4133, 5500, 11345
Holzinger, John J.
17, 245, 435, 614, 1044, 1155, 1889, 2348, 2388, 2426, 2427, 2428, 2429, 2430, 2431, 2432, 2433, 2660, 2969, 3072, 4070, 5379, 5697, 7223, 8360, 9450, 9593, 9831, 9963, 10150, 10411, 10465, 10868, 11350, 11887
Hone, Philip
13130
Honeycutt, Ann
11005, 11012
Hood, Ann
9444
Hooker, Brian
13437, 17242
Hooton, Earnest Albert
12097, 17424
Hoover, Irwin Hood
13623
Hope, Edward
11133, 15107
Hopkins, Arthur
12585
Hopkins, Ernest Jerome
15800
Hopkins, Gerard Manley
12899, 14779, 16006
Hopper, De Wolf
15742
Hopwood, Avery
12262, 13714
Horace Greeley, Jr.
see Wylie, Philip G.
Horan, Charles
13113
Horgan, Paul
573, 1248, 2578, 7112, 8144, 8639, 9027, 10666, 10954, 11585, 13479, 15049, 15612
Horine, J. Max
1154
Hornblow, Arthur, Jr.
12645, 14606
Horner, Harry
13371
Hornet
7820
Horniman, Roy
15351
Horton, Edward
9657
Horton, Kate
12236
Horton, Philip
14019
Horvendile
see Black, Gilmer V.
Horwin, Jerry
15435
Houghton, Claude
17187
Hoult, Norah
12796, 14176
Household, Geoffrey
17168
Houseman, John
12048, 17203
Housman, A. E.
15369, 15480
Housman, Laurence
4608, 15433, 17539, 17540, 17594
Hovey, C.
5474
Howard, Garland
12715
Howard, John Tasker
7805
Howard, L. O.
14368

12604
Hurlbut, William
12521, 14122, 16076
Hurley, G. M.
1591, 1963, 3996, 5669, 6349
Hurst, Fannie
12099, 14420, 15113, 16068
Hurston, Zora N.
17132
Hussey, L. M.
15665
Hutchens, John K.
1811, 8549, 10997
Hutchings, Edward, Jr.
5914, 6255
Hutchinson, A. S. M.
12358, 16764, 17456
Hutchinson, R. C.
16611, 17110
Hutchinson, Vere
17254
Hutchison, Howard B.
4179
Hutty, Leigh
14232
Huxley, Aldous
11941, 12507, 12529, 13159, 13352, 13422, 14465, 15717, 16008, 17114, 17196, 17437
Huxley, Julian S.
16503
Hyde, Agnes Rogers
4619
Hyde, Fillmore
22, 485, 654, 864, 1404, 1552, 1691, 1696, 1894, 2288, 2577, 2718, 2954, 3058, 4006, 4166, 4287, 4295, 4780, 5260, 5594, 5971, 5991, 5997, 6517, 6609, 6610, 6647, 7000, 7001, 7124, 7199, 7326, 7718, 7940, 8199, 8318, 8577, 8580, 8684, 9112, 9163, 9732, 9859, 9885, 10028, 10057, 10220, 10330, 10502, 10506, 10593, 10694, 10729, 11050, 11144, 11421, 11782
Hyde, Robert
1878, 2127, 5350, 10356, 12955
Hymer, John B.
11993, 13470, 14004, 16487
Hynd, Alan
10034

I

I. B.
see Brandeis, Irma or Barry, Iris
I. V. V.
see Harrington, J. W.
Ibáñez, Blasco
15538
Ibsen, Henrik
13184, 13355, 13772, 13773, 13774, 13775, 14060, 14061, 14062, 14485, 14656, 14657, 14862, 16386, 17545, 17755
Inge, Benson
12450
Ingersoll, Ralph McAllister
8633
Inglis, William
5266, 11522
Ireland, Baron
see Salisbury, Nate
Irving, Lawrence
14252
Irwin, Wallace
14786
Ish-Kishor, Sulamith
499
Isherwood, Christopher
4766, 12163, 14510, 14713

J

J. B. C.
7890, 9107, 11046
J. C.
see Cowmos, John
J. C. D.
10342
J. C. M.
see Mosher, John Chapin
J. C. N.
see Norton, J. C.
J. C. O.
see Oestreicher, James C.
J. F.
1210, 5186
J. F. F.
see Fishman, Joseph Fulling
J. G. T.
see Thurber, James
J. H.
1970, 7327

J. M.
see Milward, Jo U.
J. M. C.
4198
J. M. M.
see March, Joseph Moncure
J. R. P.
6524
J. S. N.
see Newberry, John Strong
J. S. P.
7006
J. T.
see Thurber, James
J. X. J.
see Holzinger, John J.
Jabotinsky, Vladimir
see Zhabotinskii, Vladimir
Jack Frost
see Brandt, Carl
Jackson, Frederick
12392, 17747
Jackson, Gardner
14781
Jaffe, Bernard
12954, 15814
Jaffray, Norman R.
1060
Jake Falstaff
see Fetzer, Herman
Jalonack, H. M.
3029
Jam
see Whitalser, Aimee
James, Marquis
42, 1914, 2041, 2645, 3952, 5543, 5544, 5681, 7565, 8646, 10276, 10582, 12057
James, Norah C.
16590
James, Samuel
2944, 4571
James, Will
14906
Jameson, Harry
5959
Jameson, Storm
13461, 15617, 17213
Janis, Elsie
16149
Janney, Sam
14918, 15354, 17532
Janson, Clara
778, 946, 3233, 3234, 3235, 8827, 10377
Jared L. Manley
see Thurber, James
Jarrett, Cora
16941
Jeake, Samuel, Jr.
see Aiken, Conrad
Jean
960
Jean-Jacques
11136
Jeans, James
15466, 16882
Jeans, Ronald
12603, 14748
Jellife, Belinda
13601
Jenkins, Elizabeth
14017
Jenkins, Oliver
2589, 5051, 5568, 7497, 7526, 8153, 8528, 10673
Jennings, Dean S.
10076
Jennings, Leslie Nelson
393, 976, 1194, 1212, 1213, 1214, 1215, 1216, 1217, 1218, 1410, 1494, 1606, 1719, 1938, 2090, 2191, 2462, 2503, 3007, 3121, 4278, 4377, 4417, 4496, 4497, 4498, 5053, 5859, 6554, 7467, 7599, 7639, 7747, 7898, 8179, 8776, 8824, 8884, 8986, 9326, 9549, 10489, 10931, 11233, 11458
Jerard, Elise
2926, 5570, 5975, 6320, 7119, 8915, 11547
Jerome, Helen
16073
Jerome, Jerome K.
15086
Jesse, F. Tennyson
15910
Jessel, George
4799, 17596
Joad, Cyril Michinson
12204
Job, Thomas
12248
Joffe, Eugene
233, 4132, 7409

Johannsen, Ernst
13638
John Swift
see Seldes, Gilbert
Johns, Pierce
16723
Johnson, Alvin
16850
Johnson, Chic
14081
Johnson, Edgar
17495
Johnson, Freddie
14989
Johnson, Hall
16410
Johnson, Hugh S.
12447
Johnson, James Weldon
12190, 12410
Johnson, Laurence E.
14425
Johnson, Marcy
10063
Johnson, Martin
14847
Johnson, Nunnally
158, 1290, 2278, 3254, 4081, 4719, 4832, 6130, 6399, 6487, 7063, 7359, 9863
Johnson, Owen
12742
Johnson, Philip
15050
Johnson, Spud
138, 276, 341, 1011, 1175, 2765, 4326, 4640, 4877, 4883, 5291, 6290, 6679, 6697, 7255, 7524, 7775, 7933, 8101, 8803, 9689, 10368, 11013, 11344
Johnsrud, Harold
9384
Johnston, Alva
260, 340, 554, 740, 741, 818, 833, 834, 921, 969, 970, 1129, 1302, 1328, 1329, 1351, 1607, 1744, 1801, 1835, 1975, 1976, 2055, 2458, 2913, 2973, 3904, 3982, 3997, 4042, 4331, 4354, 4370, 4626, 5297, 5364, 5372, 5384, 5437, 5509, 5575, 5593, 5656, 5837, 5940, 6058, 6260, 6261, 6265, 6299, 7091, 7168, 7382, 7461, 7486, 8003, 8015, 8939, 9001, 9180, 9195, 9206, 9256, 9341, 9358, 9567, 9571, 9674, 9869, 9876, 10232, 10304, 10348, 10552, 10883, 11048, 11315, 11341, 11579, 11693
Johnston, Denis
15361
Johnston, Esther
1644
Johnston, Reed
60, 244, 469, 2799, 3204, 4485, 4690, 6454, 7462, 7765, 11057
Johnstone, G. H.
16121
Johnstone, Nancy
14215
Jones, Baedeker
see White, E. B.
Jones, Habakkuk
see Davis, Elmer
Jones, Henry Arthur
15326
Jones, Henry Festing
16647
Jones, Paul
6006
Jones, Ruth Lambert
189, 332, 397, 566, 607, 1499, 1720, 1813, 1971, 2044, 2240, 2309, 2599, 2608, 2611, 2711, 2767, 2809, 2884, 3101, 3124, 4268, 5074, 5374, 5408, 5466, 6375, 6474, 6678, 7279, 7525, 7858, 8232, 8287, 8300, 8727, 8766, 8990, 9144, 9338, 10307, 10612, 10636, 10771, 10815, 10898, 10941, 10956, 11305, 11882
Jones, S. S.
6360
Jones, Stacy V.
4439, 6637
Jones, Stanley
1186, 1373, 1855, 2196, 2727, 4336, 4855, 5049, 5590, 5929, 6109, 6110, 6111, 6112, 6113, 6114, 6115, 6116, 6117, 6118, 6119, 6120, 6121, 6122, 6123, 6124, 6125, 7068, 7251, 7643, 7742, 7987, 8889, 8995, 9712-

9724, 9953, 10041, 10224, 10494
Jonson, Ben
17571
Jordan, Elizabeth
328, 6490, 8163, 10031, 10270
Josephson, Matthew
2928, 3926, 4204, 5270, 5271, 8911, 14452, 16012, 16342
Joyce, James
12815, 13515, 17452
Judge, James P.
16856
Jungmeyer, Jack
17694
Jusserand, Jean Jules
17674

K

K. C.
see Cannell, Kathleen
K. P. B.
see Britton, Kenneth Phillips
K. S. & H. S.
see Sproehnle, Katherine
K. S. A.
see White, Katharine S. Angell
K. S. W.
6348
Kafka, Franz
12674, 17369
Kaghan, Leonora
17322
Kahler, Wood
2677, 13285
Kahn, E. J., Jr.
538, 2748, 4040, 4303, 4566, 5310, 5358, 6331, 7139, 7894, 9319, 10046, 11851
Kahn, Otto
15674
Kaiser, Georg
15949
Kaiser, Stuart B.
1323
Kallesser, Michael
14037
Kallinikov, Joseph
17837
Kalman, Emmerich
12909
Kalmar, Bert
14172, 14985, 16610
Kamban, Gudmundur
14284
Kandel, Aben
17843
Kantor, MacKinlay
12130, 13153, 14913
Karsavina, Tamara
17130
Kataev, Valentine
13334, 15899, 16857
Katz, H. W.
13538
Katzenellenbogen, Zebulon Q.
7206
Katzin, Olga
5424
Kaufman, Beatrice
2678, 8330, 9706, 10365, 13155
Kaufman, Charles
3220
Kaufman, George S.
217, 5798, 12031, 12069, 12243, 12596, 12717, 12809, 12810, 13016, 13135, 13426, 13528, 13855, 14293, 14535, 14727, 14766, 15091, 15238, 15677, 15678, 15745, 16393, 16861, 17905
Kaufman, Lionel M.
9930
Kaus, Gina
12685
Kaverin, Benjamin
14700
Kay, Helen
7
Kaye, B. M.
14289, 15729, 16593
Kaye-Smith, Sheila
13750, 17015, 17547
Kearney, Patrick
12029, 13329, 15117, 15707, 16246
Kearton, Cherry
14411
Keating, Laurence J.
13925
Keefe, Willard
12695
Keith, Agnes Newton
14694

Keith, Robert
17261
Keller, Helen
15269
Kelley, Ethel
7741
Kelley, Robert F.
7733
Kellock, Harold
14217
Kelly, George
11891, 12310, 12925, 12976, 15033, 15952, 16244
Kemp, Harry
10600, 10757
Kennedy, Aubrey
12312
Kennedy, Charles Rann
16549
Kennedy, Margaret
12880, 12881, 13370, 13589, 15259, 16240, 16265, 17291
Kent, Rockwell
15476
Kenyon, Bernice
10
Kenyon, Theda
17801
Kerby, Philip
12350
Kern, Jerome
12680, 12777, 14985, 15426, 16344, 16637, 16638, 17006, 17030, 17531
Kerr, Laura Nowak
703
Kerr, Geoffrey
2932, 7165
Kerr, Lennox
15711
Kerr, Sophie
12364
Kesselring, Joseph O.
17140
Kester, Paul
14651, 17824
Kettering, Ralph Thomas
12801
Keyserling, Hermann Alexander
12005, 17354
Kiefer, Edmund J.
7784
Kiki
see Prin, Alice
Kimmins, Anthony
17703
King, Alexander
5353
King, David
17101
King, Rufus
14288, 14394, 15409
King-Hall, Magdalen
13127, 14287
King-Hall, Stephen
15261
Kingsland, Dorothea
11410
Kingsley, Sidney
13046, 15222, 15223, 17865
Kinkead, Eugene F.
10792, 11394
Kinkead, Robin
1802, 4603, 9136
Kinne, Burdette
942, 3130, 4488, 7148, 7163, 10639, 10866
Kipling, Rudyard
13070, 14842, 16780, 17255
Kirby, Madison
9395
Kirby, Rollin
1283, 1928, 2393, 2480, 4105, 4948, 7137, 7362, 7405, 8337, 8893, 9128, 11750
Kirchon, V.
16239
Kirkland, Jack
17287, 17321
Kirkpatrick, Doris
4606, 9729
Kirkpatrick, John
11917, 12466
Kivi, Alexis
16557
Klinger, George A.
1314
Knapp, Clarence
168, 549, 1564, 1755, 4202, 4239, 4348, 4820, 4844, 4849, 4909, 4911, 4912, 4914, 5061, 5442, 5443, 5444, 5445, 7167, 7237, 7314, 7455, 7466, 7732, 7737, 7994, 8266, 9103, 9295, 9507, 9902, 9924, 9965, 10104, 10133, 10289, 10380, 10383,

10466, 10858, 11395, 11518, 11599, 11868, 11870
Knickerbocker, H. R.
12458
Knight, Bruce Winton
14244
Knight, Eric
16793
Knight, Raymond
16411
Knoblock, Edward
12086, 13390, 13850, 15407
Knopf
12484
Knox, Cleone
see King-Hall, Magdalen
Knox, Ronald A.
17535
Knox, William Boardman
2920, 5504
Kober, Arthur
45, 46, 486, 551, 574, 627, 691, 796, 932, 1010, 1090, 1094, 1096, 1099, 1130, 1198, 1241, 1318, 1448, 1452, 1621, 1695, 1748, 1759, 1996, 2103, 2204, 2214, 2382, 2399, 2636, 2879, 2897, 2986, 2988, 3278, 3896, 3943, 4004, 4056, 4114, 4139, 4269, 4343, 4423, 4916, 5095, 5152, 5213, 5221, 5253, 5307, 5312, 5327, 5420, 5561, 5577, 5579, 5635, 5993, 6025, 6107, 6325, 6453, 6617, 6618, 6671, 7031, 7086, 7117, 7125, 7253, 7294, 7297, 7822, 7867, 7930, 7931, 8056-8058, 8095, 8161, 8202, 8338, 8363, 8487, 8613, 8616, 8699, 8700, 8834, 8977, 9030, 9199, 9211, 9449, 9519, 9529, 9554, 9555, 9557, 9652, 9709, 9862, 9935, 10018, 10019, 10103, 10203, 10210, 10238, 10240, 10314, 10695, 10998, 11031, 11277, 14030
Koehler, Eleanor W.
4898
Koeves, Tibor
17270
Kofoed, Jack
15549
Komroff, Manuel
12898, 15535, 17442, 17609
Kramer, Horace
15140
Krasna, Norman
14934, 16737
Krause, Herbert
17772
Krauss, William A.
19, 34, 1590, 1600, 2075, 5934, 7915, 8405, 9525
Kreymborg, Alfred
31, 967, 1092, 1918, 2081, 5549, 7345, 7731, 9350, 10146, 11008, 12007, 12008
Krock, Arthur
1115, 2284, 4332, 6010, 11086
Kronenberger, Louis
12538r, 13316, 13422r, 13845r, 14087r, 14267r, 14273r, 14510r, 15190r, 15312r, 15635r, 16815r, 16995r, 17367r, 17609r
Krutch, Joseph Wood
13305, 13543
Kummer, Clare
14097, 16019, 17229
Kuncz, Aladar
12412
Kunneke, Edward
15194
Kuprin, Alexandre
17875
Kusell, Daniel
12945, 15871, 15966

L

L. B.
see Bogan, Louise or Bell, Lisle
L. B. G.
4877, 4884, 10778
L. H.
see Long, Lois and Hardin, Nancy
L. L. B.
7328
L. M.
6278, 10311
L. N. J.
see Jennings, Leslie Nelson
L. S. G.
see Gannett, Louis S.
L. S. P.
see Pearl, Leslie S.

17673r, 17695r, 17697r, 17830r, 17938r
Leonard, Dorothy
2401, 5089, 11268
Leonard, Jonathan
12221
Leonard Q. Ross
see Rosten, Leo
Leroy, Nat
12542
Leslie, Doris
13686, 16880
Leslie, Lew
12422, 12423, 14384, 14785, 16281
Leslie, Shane
13751
Lester, Elliott
15406
Levey, Harold
13963
Levien, Sonya
2815
Levin, Meyer
15696
Levine, Isaac Don
16085, 16862
Levine, Oscar
16739
Levy, Benn W.
12136, 13109, 15015, 15105, 15329, 16853, 17190, 17313, 17923
Levy, Leon
6468
Levy, Melvin
13830
Levy, Newman
91, 176, 187, 220, 283, 476, 527, 702, 837, 838, 1036, 1353, 1545, 2135, 2185, 2569, 2912, 3051, 3144, 3993, 4221, 4222, 4226, 4357, 5306, 5538, 5986, 6045, 6596, 7111, 7941, 7974-7978, 8387, 9049, 9110, 9339, 9517, 9800, 9842, 10266, 10918, 11235, 14554, 16473
Lewi, Grant
50
Lewis, Cecil
16427
Lewis, Cecil Day
see Day-Lewis, Cecil
Lewis, D. B. Wyndham
704, 2007, 5255, 9118, 9294, 13650, 14589
Lewis, Ethelreda
15123, 17333
Lewis, Grace Hegger
8119, 11225
Lewis, Lloyd
12735, 14444, 15475, 15788, 16607
Lewis, Raymond
11514
Lewis, Seaman
12210
Lewis, Sinclair
301, 11201, 12076, 12133, 13182, 13330, 14417, 14444, 15099, 15124, 16109, 16545, 17851
Lewis, Therese
2808, 10315
Lewis, Tracy Hammond
594, 10113
Lewisohn, Irene
15001
Lewisohn, Ludwig
11996, 12665, 13419, 14412, 15260, 16897, 17646
Liddell Hart, Basil Henry
12830, 16608
Lieberman, Elias
2543, 9680, 9814, 10833
Liebling, A. J.
155, 289, 755, 990, 1007, 1086, 1254, 1500, 3193, 4292, 4361, 4419, 5398, 5401, 5566, 5624, 5625, 5631, 5744, 6158, 6272, 6526, 7240, 7479, 7535, 7753, 7856, 7938, 8201, 8746, 8987, 9891, 10505, 11026, 11029, 11573, 11754, 11791, 11866
Liebman, Max
15681, 16949
Lief, Max
2658, 5277, 14121
Lief, Nathaniel
14121
Lieferant, Henry
14132
Lieferant, Sylvia
14132
Lilley, Edward Clarke

17733
Lincoln, Victoria
327, 6591, 7156, 11322
Lindbergh, Anne Morrow
14853, 15630
Linder, Mark
16369, 16858, 17379
Lindsay, Howard
12096, 14193, 14819, 15690, 16233, 16598, 16732, 17296, 17942
Lindsay, Norman
13394
Lindsay, Philip
14105
Lindsey, Walter O.
13196
Linington, Ann
575, 10331
Linke, Lilo
16260, 17063
Linklater, Eric
14325, 14519, 15042, 16311
Lippmann, Arthur L.
10743
Lippmann, Walter
12017, 15249
Lipstick
see Long, Lois
Liscomb, Harry F.
16080
Lister, Walter B.
16839
Littell, Philip
17188
Littell, Robert
3213, 5162, 16210
Little, Clarence C.
12201
Little, Katharine Day
10242
Little Rodgers
2995
Littlefield, H. J.
402, 11724
Littlefield, Jack
831, 8560
Livingston, Arthur
15211
Livingstone, Tristram
8923
Llewellyn, Richard
14240
Lobrano, Gustave
7509
Locke, Edward
12793, 14943
Locke, William J.
12046, 14500
Lockhart, A. G.
6652, 8608
Lockhart, Bruce
16264
Lockhart, Gene
12584
Lockridge, Frances
8919
Lockridge, Richard
70, 107, 470, 714, 732, 928, 1141, 1307, 1352, 1629, 1933, 2096, 2108, 2210, 2315, 2497, 2555, 2563, 2940, 3031, 3136, 4123, 4340, 4393, 4490, 4941, 4957, 5076, 5160, 5279, 5323, 5446, 5573, 6251, 6309, 6483, 6505, 6513, 6514, 6515, 6566-6577, 6619, 6629-6634, 6696, 7145, 7397, 7521, 7522, 7530, 7716, 7850, 7874, 7916-7918, 7923, 8561, 8733, 8912, 9091, 9366, 9367, 9605, 9739, 9973, 9980, 10010, 10082, 10296, 10499, 10596, 10895, 11180, 11342, 11457, 11477, 11697, 12194r, 13243r, 13520r, 13725r, 13754r, 13923r, 15010r, 17057r
Lockwood, Sally
7491
Lodge, Henry Cabot
16546
Lodge, Oliver
15882
Loeder, Richard
17572
Löhrke, Eugene
12125, 13074, 15820
Long, Dillard
13864
Long, Haniel
10723
Long, Huey P.
13393

Long, J. C.
12573
Long, Lois
55, 275, 734, 1242, 4728, 5205, 6036, 8125, 8132, 8470, 8797, 10299, 11502, 11829, 11891r, 11987r, 12210r, 12437r, 12585r, 13138r, 13595r, 13757r, 13890r, 14093r, 15240r, 15887r, 16400r, 16481r, 16987r, 17106r, 17532r, 17682r, 17950r
Longan, Thomas
1701, 1704, 7022
Longstreth, Edward
9651
Longwell, Daniel
5377
Longworth, Alice Roosevelt
13094
Lonsdale, Frederick
12628, 14127, 14552, 14716, 15723, 15746
Loomis, Frederic
12884
Looms, C. F.
7171
Loos, Anita
12594, 13746, 16762
Lopez y Fuentes, Gregorio
13319
Lorca, Federico García
12396, 14690
Lord, Douglas
17552
Lord, Russell
1934, 2706, 6065, 6443, 9216, 13311
Lord Stites
see Fairchild, Donald Stites
Lorentz, Pare
4814, 8022
Loth, David
14924
Lothar, Rudolph
12077, 12846, 16226
Lottman, George D.
9808, 10981
Louden, Isabelle
16147
Louÿs, Pierre
14759, 16128
Love, Robertus
16314
Lowe, Eric
16446
Lowell, Joan
12918
Lowe-Porter, H. T.
16911
Lowrie, Rebecca
11908r, 12089r, 12149r, 12221r, 12425r, 12572r, 12588r, 12624, 12667r, 12691r, 12918r, 13009r, 13015r, 13020r, 13024r, 13048r, 13096r, 13128r, 13136r, 13217r, 13283r, 13324r, 13417r, 13472r, 13473r, 13531r, 13698r, 13816r, 13922r, 14054r, 14089r, 14117r, 14160r, 14283r, 14344r, 14495r, 14500r, 14624r, 14781r, 14807r, 14838r, 15013r, 15032r, 15034r, 15062r, 15089r, 15107r, 15123r, 15170r, 15201r, 15260r, 15270r, 15421r, 15447r, 15489r, 15727r, 15873r, 15906r, 15908r, 15912r, 15934r, 15994r, 16106r, 16214r, 16360r, 16507r, 16557r, 16671r, 16673r, 16704r, 16735r, 16744r, 16831r, 16898r, 16908r, 16966r, 17108r, 17153r, 17174r, 17184r, 17239r, 17240r, 17254r, 17334r, 17335r, 17351r, 17357r, 17390r, 17393r, 17421r, 17472r, 17547r, 17574r, 17656r, 17663r, 17704r, 17785r, 17857r, 17902r
Luce, Clare Boothe
see Boothe, Clare
Ludwig, Emil
12792, 13124, 13820, 14532, 14844, 15485, 15578, 15582, 16370, 16492, 17765
Luhan, Mabel Dodge
12222, 13306, 14923, 15402
Lundbergh, Holger
5139
Lunn, Arnold

12854
Luria, Lajos
12840
Lurie, Charles N.
4554
Lydig, Mrs. Philip
see Lydig, Rita de Acosta
Lydig, Rita de Acosta
17339
Lyles, Aubrey
14555
Lynch, Bohun
14149
Lynch, Denis
12485
Lynch, Frances
14037
Lynch, Katherine
4337
Lyndon, Barré
12000

M

M.
see March, Joseph Moncure
M. B.
7505
M. C.
see Connelly, Marc
M. C. D.
see Davies, Mary Carolyn
M. F.
51, 1104, 6423, 6426
M. G.
see Gilchrist, Marie
M. J.
10398
M. K. L.
see Leech, Margaret K.
M. M.
905, 2266, 2590, 3893, 6402, 6623, 7204, 7828, 8137, 8313, 8314, 9121, 9776, 11154, 11162
M. M. W.
see Waterman, Myra M.
M. McL. L.
11560
M. R. A.
6340
M. R. C.
4262
M. S.
6030
M. W.
see Widdemer, Margaret
McAfee, Helen
9983
McAlbert, Cora
8413
MacArthur, Charles
1615, 1708, 13677, 14533, 14640, 14997, 16447, 17415, 17592
Macaulay, Rose
16055, 16577, 16891
McCall, Mary C., Jr.
432, 1177, 2105, 8225, 8290, 9466
McCarten, John
2014, 2686, 4174, 6538, 6598, 6599, 6601, 6602, 6639, 7681, 8156, 9060
McCarthy, Neil
3133
McCleary, Dorothy
15633
McClellan, Jack
14652
McClellan, Ruth
109, 10721
McClinchey, Florence E.
14479
McClintock, Marshall
17633
McClure, Robert E.
13425, 14660
McColl, John
7996, 11334
McConnell, Oviatt
5405
McCord, David
675, 736, 767, 1142, 1435, 1449, 1717, 1750, 1751, 1752, 1753, 2132, 2936, 3038, 3899, 4251, 4720, 5079, 5080, 5081, 6664, 8072, 8336, 8494, 8891, 9064, 9146, 9845, 9854, 9855, 9860, 9861, 9966, 10247, 10264, 10273, 10481, 10894, 10939, 11798, 11858
McCord, Raphael
1471, 6132
McCormack, Herbert P.
14942

McCormick, Elsie
178, 1487, 3200, 6362
McCoy, Homer
9365
McCoy, Samuel
7109, 10849
McCullough, Marvin
2224
MacDonald, Aeneas
17709
Macdonald, Ballard
16402, 17037
Macdonald, Dwight
6394, 7242
McDonald, Edward D.
15955
McDonald, Laetitia
14648
MacDonald, Murray
14687
Macdonough, Glen
12209
Macdougall, Allan Ross
13878
McEvoy, J. P.
11987, 13815, 16883
McFadden, Elizabeth
13209
McFadden, Frances
9736
McFee, William
14007, 15598, 15629
McGeehan, W. O.
6641, 9089
MacGill, Patrick
17017, 17018
McGill, V. J.
12181
McGinley, Phyllis
57, 65, 100, 160, 390, 404, 423, 660, 663, 664, 867, 1064, 1170, 1173, 1205, 1222, 1338, 1429, 1495, 1658, 1660, 1709, 1873, 1923, 2070, 2217, 2218, 2237, 2360, 2494, 2495, 2586, 2620, 2704, 2983, 3019, 3267, 3276, 4271, 4543, 4582, 4841, 4903, 5023, 5370, 5411, 5467, 5468, 5469, 5519, 5587, 5614, 5651, 5955, 6231, 6246, 6329, 6344, 6422, 6452, 6669, 6680, 7129, 7184, 7429, 7501, 7557, 7595, 7621, 7625, 7673, 7678, 7679, 7715, 7778, 7779, 7956, 8192, 8315, 8414, 8502, 8640, 8760, 8887, 9242, 9262, 9435, 9539, 9735, 9788, 9791, 9806, 9822, 9945, 9990, 10038, 10084, 10430, 10692, 10731, 10738, 10841, 10950, 11195, 11237, 11357, 11359, 11467, 11527, 11774, 11775
McGovern, Margaret
3984
McGowan, John
12373, 13280, 13410, 13574, 13785, 14041, 14064, 14163, 15060, 16482, 16688, 17106
Macgowan, Kenneth
88, 1250, 2162, 11069, 13596
McGrath, Frank
12659
McGregor
see Hurley, G. M.
MacGregor, Charles W.
10181, 11673
McGuinness, James Kevin
375, 610, 751, 926, 1266, 4438, 5010, 5527, 6659, 8346, 8663, 8903, 8968, 10027, 10255, 10302
McGuire, William Anthony
14303, 16312, 16640, 16741, 17219, 17412, 17736
MacGunigle, Robert
17578
McHugh, Jimmy
12424
McHugh, Vincent
5172, 10773, 11062, 12616
McIntyre, John T.
13490, 16901, 16902
Mack, Willard
12849, 13446, 13662, 13704, 13994, 14189, 14839, 15628, 16247, 16485
Mackall, Virginia Woods
5705
Mackaness, George
14818
McKay, Agnes
10448
McKay, Claude
12244, 12837

14418r, 14489r, 14517r, 14568r, 14626r, 14715r, 14860r, 14896r, 15093r, 15167r, 15380r, 15389r, 15468r, 15705r, 15807r, 16103r, 16268r, 16343r, 16403r, 16455r, 16469r, 16828r, 16868r, 16895r, 17021r, 17113r, 17206r, 17286r, 17564r, 17643r, 17696r, 17699r, 17812r, 17896r

Malraux, André
13043, 14746, 14764, 15115, 15116, 16397

Maltby, H. F.
13053, 16298, 16779, 17556

Maltz, Albert
5022, 12416, 15241

The man who came back
see Hovey, C.

Mandel, Frank
13090, 13297, 15191, 15524

Mandley, Percy G.
13314

Mangham, Herbert J.
10467

Manhattan
see Fleming, Berry

Manheimer, Wallace A.
15322

Manhood, H. A.
13720

Mankiewicz, Herman J.
815, 4761, 7349, 11683, 11910r, 12058r, 12093r, 12108r, 12126r, 12146r, 12217r, 12466r, 12574r, 12596r, 12603r, 12620r, 12721r, 12777r, 12809r, 12920r, 12925r, 13054r, 13093r, 13112r, 13215r, 13260r, 13275r, 13276r, 13300r, 13344r, 13354r, 13357r, 13628r, 13726r, 13756r, 13803r, 13855r, 13884r, 13888r, 13950r, 13963r, 13987r, 14031r, 14074r, 14172r, 14234r, 14327r, 14409r, 14447r, 14534r, 14601r, 14621r, 14680r, 14716r, 14878r, 14988r, 14989r, 15080r, 15104r, 15117r, 15194r, 15233r, 15234r, 15237r, 15357r, 15366r, 15372r, 15406r, 15440r, 15554r, 15666r, 15688r, 15762r, 15776r, 15815r, 15835r, 15893r, 15910r, 16082r, 16303r, 16495r, 16790r, 16836r, 16841r, 16975r, 17006r, 17143r, 17276r, 17412r, 17573r, 17679r, 17684r, 17936r

Manley, Jared L.
see Thurber, James

Manley, William Ford
17763

Mann, Heinrich
14087, 17919

Mann, Thomas
12845, 14496, 15035, 16911, 17921

Manners-Sutton, D.
12406

Mannes, Marya
633, 756, 4426, 5791, 9846, 12612

Mannin, Ethel
12930, 16808

Manning, Frederic
14098

Manning, Margaretta
410, 505, 1368, 1413, 2045, 2385, 2688, 5780, 6244, 6245, 6658, 6672, 8886, 9160, 9222, 9458, 10881, 11163, 11625

Mansfield, John
17798

Mansfield, Katherine
1331, 5982, 8306, 14505

Mantle, Burns
12334

March
see March, Joseph Moncure

March, Charles
17051

March, Joseph Moncure
148, 772, 1380, 4058, 5159, 5702, 6039, 7356, 8838, 9982, 16556, 17760

March, William
12835

Marcin, Max
12363, 17353

Marconnier, Byrne
385
Marcus, D. Frank
12240
Margaretta
see Manning, Margaretta
Margo
see Frost, Frances M.
Maria, queen consort of Ferdinand I, king of Rumania
15784
Marie, Queen of Rumania
see Maria, queen consort of Ferdinand I, king of Rumania
Mariéjol, Jean H.
13027
Mariia, grand duchess of Russia
13311
Marion, George, Jr.
17307
Marjorie
4817
Markey, Gene
16898
Markey, Morris
118, 170, 424, 609, 622, 682, 706, 749, 811, 824, 827, 870, 875, 885, 898, 961, 963, 997, 1009, 1052, 1069, 1125, 1185, 1188, 1277, 1300, 1319, 1350, 1366, 1369, 1370, 1371, 1450, 1547, 1679, 1768, 1883, 1887, 1888, 1892, 1893, 1932, 1954, 1955, 1956, 1957, 1958, 1959, 1960, 1961, 1965, 2022, 2028, 2163, 2179, 2254, 2261, 2303, 2310, 2334, 2347, 2352, 2386, 2422, 2424, 2554, 2565, 2691, 2702, 2758, 2876, 2878, 2930, 2949, 2971, 2979, 3027, 3069, 3082, 3088, 3112, 3891, 3902, 4054, 4061, 4120, 4180, 4242, 4334, 4482, 4511, 4575, 4579, 4586, 4806, 4985, 4992, 4999, 5000, 5001, 5002, 5003, 5004, 5135, 5184, 5218, 5228, 5241, 5252, 5261, 5290, 5303, 5330, 5555, 5710, 5747, 5952, 6037, 6089, 6169, 6206, 6230, 6236, 6361, 6376, 6428, 6437, 6496, 6512, 7052, 7100, 7101, 7106, 7120, 7202, 7254, 7270, 7274, 7330-7335, 7363, 7389, 7400, 7404, 7417, 7498, 7572, 7609, 7634, 7663, 7689, 7811, 7864, 7961, 7992, 8145, 8241, 8255, 8257, 8472, 8541, 8551, 8569, 8612, 8624, 8626, 8654, 8657, 8707, 8738, 8745, 8763, 8795, 8826, 8938, 8952, 8962, 9048, 9052, 9053, 9059, 9109, 9117, 9162, 9193, 9194, 9237, 9317, 9322, 9329, 9354, 9355, 9420, 9453, 9467, 9469, 9524, 9526, 9530, 9531, 9553, 9636, 9641, 9666, 9763, 9883, 10006, 10021, 10061, 10105, 10190, 10191, 10218, 10241, 10261, 10336, 10372, 10389, 10408, 10424, 10533, 10572, 10623, 10651, 10658, 10878, 10889, 10891, 10897, 10899, 10900, 10909, 10913, 10917, 10949, 10951, 10955, 10983, 10987, 10993, 11019, 11064, 11175, 11185, 11206, 11262, 11317, 11321, 11366, 11382, 11545, 11620, 11751, 11788, 11842, 11849, 11867, 11970r, 12017r, 12044r, 12226r, 12242, 12266r, 12464r, 12594r, 12624r, 12684r, 12795r, 12957r, 13378r, 13707r, 14027r, 14043r, 14217r, 14340r, 14365r, 14378r, 14547r, 14735r, 14778r, 14798r, 14971r, 15293r, 15663r, 16055r, 16329r, 16407r, 16517r, 16724r, 16945r, 17069r, 17173r, 17241r, 17318r, 17550r, 17618r, 17626r, 17760r, 17806r, 17831r
Marks, Florence
1126
Marks, Marjorie
5989, 6622
Marks, Maurice
16188
Marks, Percy
13048, 14919
Marlow, Brian
12227, 13858, 15484
Marlowe, Christopher
13161
Marmontel, Jean François

12600, 12920
Meehan, John
12427
Mégroz, Phyllis
15066
Mégroz, R. L.
17225
Meier-Graefe, Juilus
13207, 16153, 17550, 17551
Melford, Austin
15780A
Mencken, H. L.
75, 76, 77, 78, 555, 1048, 1201, 2255, 2657, 3987, 4196, 4991, 5057, 5168, 5249, 5498, 6070, 6337, 6347, 7958, 8815, 8860, 8894, 8980, 9204, 9349, 11230, 12020, 14001, 15641, 16063, 17363
Merivale, Bernard
17872
Meriwether, Susan
13557
Merlin, Frank
13858, 14161, 17376
Merling, Howard
14572
Merrick, Leonard
14861
Merrill, Frances
12038, 15655
Merrill, Mason
12038, 15655
Merz, Charles
5585, 13241, 13906
Metcalfe, Felicia
12834
Metcalfe, John
16442
Metzl, Lothar
13675
Meyers, L. C.
4660
Meyers, L. H.
16373
Michaud, Régis
13335
Middleton, George
12372, 12437, 16015
Middleton, Lamar
688, 8130
Middleton, Scudder
389, 2263, 3960, 4462, 4270, 4570, 9941, 11534, 13141r, 13838r, 14364r, 14847r, 17048r
Milburn, George
400, 1786, 2779, 9442, 12682, 15692
Miles, Carleton
15583
Miles, Hamish
13312, 13439
Millar, Robins
17246
Millay, Cora B.
6446
Millay, Edna St. Vincent
12576, 12887, 13564, 14259
Millen, Gilmore
17034
Millen, James Knox
15506
Miller, Alice Duer
1152, 13953, 16851
Miller, Flourney E.
14555, 16648
Miller, Henry W.
12902, 15863
Miller, Max
1520, 3128, 3959, 5121, 6284, 12299, 14038, 14269
Millin, Sarah Gertrude
12144, 12844, 13491
Millis, Walter
15159, 16336
Mills, Dorothy
1432, 8439, 9843
Milne, A. A.
12120, 13631, 13799, 14171, 14223, 14430, 15255, 15321, 15650, 15747, 15782, 15920, 17148, 17397, 17790
Milward, Jo U.
8133
Minelli, Vincente
16641
Minnigerode, Meade
11893, 12895, 14890
Minor, A. J.
15172
Minturn, Harry
17039, 17040
Mirbeau, Octave
12696
Misch, Robert Jay

6127, 6128, 6197, 6198, 6199, 6200, 6201, 6218, 6219, 6668, 7019, 7020, 8048, 8649, 9701, 10121, 11878
Misrock, Henry R.
12532
Mr. Anderson
see Hollister, Paul
Mitchell, C. Ainsworth
16504
Mitchell, Dodson L.
14348
Mitchell, Fanny Todd
12474, 17846
Mitchell, John
6408
Mitchell, Joseph
218, 686, 1326, 1467, 2356, 4113, 4481, 4520, 4583, 4590, 4769, 4776, 5362, 5830, 6234, 6391, 6506, 6530, 6607, 7639, 10243, 10507, 11096, 15437
Mitchell, Margaret
13845
Mitchell, Norma
12600, 12920, 16049
Mitchell, Susanna Valentine
10363
Mitchell, Thomas
12799, 13808, 14856
Mitchell, Zelpha
7982
Mitchison, Naomi
12798
Mochrie, Margaret
11540
Modell, Merriam
5822
Moeller, Philip
12638
Moffat, Donald
262, 509, 792, 841, 901, 1336, 1462, 1884, 2146, 2340, 2474, 2583, 2950, 3920, 3955, 4055, 4955, 5056, 5170, 5404, 5510, 5556, 6074, 6321, 6382, 6562, 6563, 6625-6627, 7075, 7155, 7256, 7343, 7773, 7848, 7919, 8136, 8219, 8309, 8324, 8325, 8331, 8450, 9229, 10309, 10835, 11256-11261, 11304, 11660
Moffatt, S. M.
1622
Mohr, Max
14326
Molière, Jean Baptiste Poquelin
15358, 16494
Molnar, Ferenc
13803, 13854, 14833, 15719, 15769, 15987
Molnar, Franz
13085, 16090
Monfried, Henri de
15903
Monk, Philip
10080
Monks, John, Jr.
12560
Monro, Hector H.
12853
Montague, C. E.
16388
Montgomery, James
12777
Montross, Lois
3913
Moon, Lorna
13015
Moore, George
14082, 15874, 16930
Moore, Leslie
7605
Moore, McElbert
17949
Moore, Marianne
16543
Moore, Rosalie
11485
Moore, Samuel Taylor
1757, 14120
Móra, Ferenc
16791
Morain, Alfred
17470
Morand, Paul
14351, 15531, 15587, 17855
Morando, Estelle
16581
Mordell, Albert
15645
Morehouse, Ward
253, 13744, 15303
Morgan, Agnes
13888-13891
Morgan, Charles

13551, 16818
Morley, Christopher
669, 2600, 2643, 8216, 10991, 11720, 12132, 14274, 14611, 15988, 17045, 17248, 17349
Morley, F. V.
13398
Mornay, Alastair
13126
Morris, Lloyd
16106, 16215
Morrissey, Will
16445
Morrison, Anne
14493
Morrison, Chester L.
1670, 7094
Morrison, Woods
16323
Morrow, Betty
2508, 11369, 11370
Morrow, Honoré Willsie
17259
Morse, Katharine D.
406, 510, 974, 1441, 5994, 7714, 9592, 9981, 9997
Morse, N. Brewster
13984
Morton, Charles W., Jr.
182, 7166, 11503, 11834
Morton, David
917, 4612, 4927, 7278, 8152, 8764
Morton, Michael
13471
Mosher, John Chapin
372, 446, 540, 564, 582, 717, 791, 877, 903, 941, 1033, 1133, 1159, 1345, 1598, 1762, 2033, 2034, 2065, 2173, 2205, 2318, 2559, 2662, 2819, 2952, 3003, 3023, 3046, 3270, 3892, 3949, 4039, 4052, 4102, 4291, 4442, 4464, 4512, 4513, 4526, 4599, 4965, 5037, 5116, 5157, 5238, 5326, 5425, 5454, 5458, 5493, 5497, 5678, 5995, 6183, 6184, 6247, 6387, 6388, 6418, 6590, 7003, 7104, 7138, 7177, 7198, 7249, 7445, 7655, 7658, 7660, 7717, 7727, 7750, 7836, 7845, 7892, 7927, 7935, 8024, 8043, 8081, 8263, 8599, 9022, 9151, 9161, 9226, 9231, 9261, 9271, 9324, 9380, 9412, 9440, 9472, 9487, 9610, 9656, 9695, 9703, 9894, 10102, 10117, 10166, 10211, 10262, 10370, 10413, 10516, 10517, 10571, 10619, 10845, 10857, 10980, 10982, 11015, 11279, 11328, 11562, 11681, 11731, 11770, 11892r, 11906r, 11914r, 11922r, 11926r, 11927r, 11929r, 11935r, 11943r, 11945r, 11946r, 11949r, 11955r, 11956r, 11959r, 11960r, 11961r, 11963r, 11964r, 11965r, 11978r, 11994r, 11998r, 12022r, 12027r, 12032r, 12040r, 12055r, 12060r, 12068r, 12070r, 12071r, 12078r, 12079r, 12081r, 12084r, 12085r, 12091r, 12095r, 12102r, 12117r, 12118r, 12119r, 12121r, 12124r, 12129r, 12134r, 12135r, 12159r, 12161r, 12168r, 12173r, 12175r, 12177r, 12193r, 12200r, 12202r, 12206r, 12208r, 12214r, 12216r, 12218r, 12219r, 12225r, 12229r, 12230r, 12238r, 12241r, 12245r, 12246r, 12247r, 12250r, 12260r, 12263r, 12264r, 12265r, 12267r, 12272r, 12276r, 12282r, 12287r, 12288r, 12307r, 12318r, 12321r, 12327r, 12333r, 12338r, 12339r, 12347r, 12357r, 12359r, 12361r, 12362r, 12365r, 12375r, 12376r, 12378r, 12382r, 12398r, 12405r, 12408r, 12420r, 12426r, 12428r, 12430r, 12433r, 12434r, 12444r, 12445r, 12449r, 12454r, 12457r, 12460r, 12461r, 12463r, 12475r, 12476r, 12478r, 12480r, 12481r, 12491r, 12495r, 12498r, 12499r, 12501r, 12515r, 12524r, 12525r, 12527r, 12531r, 12540r, 12541r, 12545r, 12547r, 12548r,

12550r, 12551r, 12552r,
12559r, 12565r, 12575r,
12578r, 12579r, 12580r,
12589r, 12606r, 12613r,
12618r, 12621r, 12627r,
12629r, 12639r, 12641r,
12643r, 12661r, 12664r,
12666r, 12668r, 12679r,
12681r, 12688r, 12689r,
12693r, 12701r, 12705r,
12707r, 12709r, 12710r,
12711r, 12714r, 12718r,
12723r, 12727r, 12740r,
12745r, 12747r, 12748r,
12755r, 12758r, 12759r,
12763r, 12769r, 12773r,
12775r, 12776r, 12780r,
12781r, 12789r, 12791r,
12794r, 12800r, 12804r,
12806r, 12807r, 12808r,
12823r, 12825r, 12827r,
12828r, 12832r, 12859r,
12862r, 12867r, 12869r,
12870r, 12874r, 12875r,
12876r, 12877r, 12879r,
12892r, 12900r, 12904r,
12910r, 12916r, 12923r,
12924r, 12932r, 12933r,
12936r, 12938r, 12941r,
12948r, 12958r, 12960r,
12965r, 12969r, 12975r,
12980r, 12983r, 12984r,
12987r, 12988r, 12992r,
12994r, 12995r, 12997r,
13010r, 13014r, 13018r,
13022r, 13023r, 13027r,
13029r, 13031r, 13034r,
13035r, 13036r, 13044r,
13045r, 13049r, 13050r,
13065r, 13069r, 13081r,
13082r, 13083r, 13084r,
13087r, 13089r, 13095r,
13098r, 13100r, 13105r,
13106r, 13107r, 13108r,
13111r, 13116r, 13118r,
13120r, 13121r, 13132r,
13133r, 13134r, 13139r,
13142r, 13145r, 13157r,
13158r, 13162r, 13169r,
13172r, 13174r, 13176r,
13179r, 13180r, 13201r,
13205r, 13208r, 13211r,
13212r, 13216r, 13218r,

13219r, 13225r, 13226r,
13234r, 13236r, 13245r,
13247r, 13255r, 13266r,
13269r, 13284r, 13290r,
13291r, 13293r, 13299r,
13307r, 13315r, 13318r,
13323r, 13340r, 13341r,
13342r, 13365r, 13369r,
13372r, 13375r, 13376r,
13377r, 13388r, 13389r,
13391r, 13392r, 13399r,
13404r, 13406r, 13409r,
13412r, 13418r, 13423r,
13454r, 13464r, 13465r,
13469r, 13485r, 13487r,
13489r, 13495r, 13499r,
13501r, 13505r, 13507r,
13513r, 13514r, 13518r,
13521r, 13523r, 13526r,
13527r, 13529r, 13534r,
13539r, 13540r, 13544r,
13546r, 13554r, 13560r,
13563r, 13571r, 13573r,
13575r, 13576r, 13584r,
13586r, 13604r, 13606r,
13607r, 13613r, 13614r,
13618r, 13620r, 13625r,
13627r, 13629r, 13630r,
13632r, 13634r, 13635r,
13636r, 13637r, 13639r,
13642r, 13652r, 13656r,
13661r, 13676r, 13678r,
13679r, 13680r, 13683r,
13692r, 13693r, 13694r,
13702r, 13706r, 13708r,
13712r, 13722r, 13723r,
13724r, 13730r, 13731r,
13732r, 13741r, 13743r,
13755r, 13764r, 13768r,
13781r, 13783r, 13789r,
13791r, 13792r, 13793r,
13794r, 13796r, 13797r,
13798r, 13801r, 13804r,
13809r, 13812r, 13817r,
13822r, 13823r, 13824r,
13827r, 13829r, 13831r,
13834r, 13841r, 13842r,
13844r, 13851r, 13852r,
13856r, 13869r, 13872r,
13873r, 13879r, 13882r,
13885r, 13887r, 13898r,
13912r, 13913r, 13914r,
13918r, 13919r, 13920r,

13924r, 13926r, 13931r, 13933r,
13937r, 13940r, 13944r, 13948r,
13951r, 13958r, 13961r, 13968r,
13970r, 13971r, 13974r, 13976r,
13985r, 13986r, 14010r, 14011r,
14012r, 14020r, 14023r, 14024r,
14025r, 14026r, 14029r, 14049r,
14050r, 14063r, 14066r, 14068r,
14069r, 14071r, 14076r, 14078r,
14079r, 14080r, 14085r,
14095r, 14100r, 14104r,
14106r, 14108r, 14115r,
14125r, 14126r, 14128r,
14137r, 14138r, 14139r,
14140r, 14141r, 14144r,
14152r, 14156r, 14157r,
14166r, 14167r, 14168r,
14170r, 14173r, 14174r,
14179r, 14181r, 14188r,
14199r, 14204r, 14213r,
14219r, 14226r, 14231r,
14236r, 14250r, 14253r,
14256r, 14260r, 14262r,
14265r, 14270r, 14275r,
14277r, 14278r, 14281r,
14285r, 14292r, 14295r,
14297r, 14302r, 14304r,
14305r, 14311r, 14312r,
14313r, 14315r, 14319r,
14332r, 14333r, 14336r,
14343r, 14353r, 14358r,
14371r, 14375r, 14379r,
14381r, 14383r, 14392r,
14393r, 14400r, 14401r,
14403r, 14405r, 14410r,
14419r, 14423r, 14426r,
14428r, 14434r, 14436r,
14438r, 14445r, 14449r,
14457r, 14463r, 14466r,
14472r, 14476r, 14478r,
14501r, 14513r, 14520r,
14525r, 14541r, 14542r,
14548r, 14551r, 14558r,
14559r, 14560r, 14564r,
14565r, 14566r, 14567r,
14573r, 14576r, 14579r,
14582r, 14584r, 14588r,
14590r, 14593r, 14595r,
14597r, 14598r, 14605r,
14614r, 14617r, 14619r,
14629r, 14641r, 14645r,
14647r, 14654r, 14664r,
14668r, 14670r, 14673r,

14674r, 14678r, 14679r,
14685r, 14693r, 14695r,
14703r, 14707r, 14708r,
14709r, 14714r, 14717r,
14718r, 14732r, 14733r,
14743r, 14756r, 14763r,
14771r, 14773r, 14774r,
14777r, 14784r, 14788r,
14790r, 14791r, 14804r,
14805r, 14809r, 14812r,
14815r, 14816r, 14817r,
14824r, 14827r, 14832r,
14835r, 14840r, 14843r,
14858r, 14864r, 14865r,
14868r, 14869r, 14871r,
14872r, 14874r, 14880r,
14884r, 14885r, 14887r,
14888r, 14891r, 14897r,
14898r, 14907r, 14908r,
14920r, 14926r, 14929r,
14931r, 14932r, 14933r,
14941r, 14949r, 14960r,
14961r, 14962r, 14967r,
14969r, 14970r, 14978r,
14990r, 14992r, 14996r,
14998r, 15000r, 15003r,
15008r, 15009r, 15012r,
15019r, 15021r, 15022r,
15024r, 15025r, 15030r,
15036r, 15041r, 15046r,
15051r, 15054r, 15055r,
15063r, 15064r, 15071r,
15073r, 15074r, 15075r,
15077r, 15079r, 15082r,
15085r, 15087r, 15090r,
15094r, 15102r, 15109r,
15132r, 15143r, 15144r,
15147r, 15149r, 15155r,
15164r, 15175r, 15180r,
15193r, 15195r, 15197r,
15198r, 15202r, 15203r,
15207r, 15221r, 15228r,
15229r, 15230r, 15244r,
15262r, 15264r, 15265r,
15268r, 15271r, 15275r,
15276r, 15277r, 15281r,
15285r, 15288r, 15290r,
15297r, 15299r, 15306r,
15311r, 15319r, 15323r,
15333r, 15340r, 15346r,
15355r, 15359r, 15370r,
15373r, 15376r, 15377r,
15390r, 15391r, 15393r,

15395r, 15396r, 15398r,
15403r, 15410r, 15413r,
15414r, 15415r, 15417r,
15422r, 15424r, 15425r,
15428r, 15429r, 15432r,
15448r, 15450r, 15451r,
15457r, 15463r, 15464r,
15470r, 15471r, 15477r,
15482r, 15494r, 15495r,
15501r, 15507r, 15508r,
15520r, 15523r, 15525r,
15537r, 15540r, 15544r,
15545r, 15546r, 15550r,
15551r, 15560r, 15561r,
15562r, 15581r, 15595r,
15602r, 15603r, 15605r,
15610r, 15621r, 15636r,
15643r, 15646r, 15649r,
15657r, 15658r, 15670r,
15671r, 15672r, 15683r,
15691r, 15697r, 15698r,
15699r, 15718r, 15724r,
15730r, 15738r, 15739r,
15740r, 15743r, 15744r,
15745r, 15755r, 15756r,
15758r, 15759r, 15763r,
15764r, 15765r, 15767r,
15774r, 15778r, 15779r,
15790r, 15794r, 15797r,
15798r, 15799r, 15801r,
15802r, 15811r, 15813r,
15817r, 15826r, 15829r,
15833r, 15834r, 15838r,
15840r, 15845r, 15846r,
15853r, 15856r, 15859r,
15864r, 15865r, 15867r,
15877r, 15878r, 15879r,
15897r, 15904r, 15914r,
15919r, 15922r, 15937r,
15941r, 15945r, 15956r,
15958r, 15961r, 15969r,
15970r, 15978r, 15984r,
15991r, 15992r, 16013r,
16016r, 16023r, 16029r,
16034r, 16036r, 16046r,
16057r, 16069r, 16071r,
16078r, 16087r, 16088r,
16089r, 16091r, 16092r,
16093r, 16096r, 16099r,
16101r, 16102r, 16105r,
16108r, 16110r, 16113r,
16122r, 16129r, 16130r,
16148r, 16150r, 16156r,
16157r, 16158r, 16160r,
16163r, 16167r, 16175r,
16179r, 16180r, 16183r,
16187r, 16191r, 16192r,
16194r, 16199r, 16201r,
16203r, 16207r, 16208r,
16213r, 16220r, 16229r,
16231r, 16248r, 16249r,
16251r, 16256r, 16258r,
16259r, 16262r, 16266r,
16267r, 16270r, 16271r,
16282r, 16286r, 16288r,
16291r, 16296r, 16297r,
16301r, 16302r, 16308r,
16309r, 16313r, 16317r,
16319r, 16320r, 16321r,
16327r, 16330r, 16331r,
16333r, 16335r, 16338r,
16341r, 16355r, 16359r,
16361r, 16367r, 16380r,
16383r, 16384r, 16385r,
16390r, 16394r, 16405r,
16406r, 16418r, 16420r,
16423r, 16438r, 16454r,
16460r, 16465r, 16466r,
16472r, 16480r, 16483r,
16488r, 16489r, 16508r,
16510r, 16511r, 16518r,
16526r, 16527r, 16529r,
16535r, 16552r, 16560r,
16562r, 16572r, 16584r,
16585r, 16586r, 16594r,
16595r, 16599r, 16603r,
16612r, 16615r, 16620r,
16623r, 16624r, 16625r,
16632r, 16634r, 16635r,
16642r, 16644r, 16645r,
16646r, 16656r, 16660r,
16665r, 16667r, 16677r,
16680r, 16682r, 16685r,
16689r, 16690r, 16692r,
16694r, 16695r, 16700r,
16703r, 16705r, 16706r,
16707r, 16714r, 16715r,
16717r, 16718r, 16722r,
16726r, 16731r, 16733r,
16742r, 16748r, 16750r,
16753r, 16757r, 16761r,
16765r, 16767r, 16782r,
16783r, 16788r, 16789r,
16798r, 16805r, 16811r,
16813r, 16816r, 16820r,
16821r, 16823r, 16829r,

16833r, 16834r, 16845r, 16854r, 16859r, 16860r, 16864r, 16866r, 16867r, 16871r, 16872r, 16873r, 16877r, 16887r, 16890r, 16893r, 16905r, 16906r, 16907r, 16913r, 16914r, 16915r, 16918r, 16922r, 16927r, 16929r, 16931r, 16932r, 16933r, 16935r, 16942r, 16947r, 16953r, 16965r, 16968r, 16976r, 16979r, 16980r, 16988r, 16990r, 17004r, 17008r, 17012r, 17014r, 17019r, 17022r, 17025r, 17027r, 17028r, 17029r, 17035r, 17038r, 17041r, 17042r, 17046r, 17049r, 17050r, 17054r, 17056r, 17062r, 17066r, 17073r, 17075r, 17076r, 17077r, 17078r, 17089r, 17090r, 17095r, 17097r, 17103r, 17109r, 17116r, 17117r, 17118r, 17121r, 17125r, 17133r, 17134r, 17135r, 17137r, 17139r, 17149r, 17151r, 17157r, 17160r, 17161r, 17164r, 17171r, 17172r, 17175r, 17176r, 17183r, 17195r, 17197r, 17198r, 17208r, 17211r, 17215r, 17218r, 17222r, 17226r, 17231r, 17234r, 17244r, 17245r, 17251r, 17263r, 17280r, 17289r, 17292r, 17295r, 17305r, 17310r, 17312r, 17314r, 17315r, 17316r, 17323r, 17327r, 17328r, 17331r, 17332r, 17342r, 17344r, 17359r, 17368r, 17371r, 17385r, 17387r, 17392r, 17394r, 17401r, 17414r, 17419r, 17429r, 17430r, 17433r, 17439r, 17444r 17454r, 17455r, 17462r, 17466r, 17468r, 17477r, 17480r, 17481r, 17489r, 17498r, 17500r, 17501r, 17503r, 17506r, 17509r, 17510r, 17513r, 17533r, 17536r, 17541r, 17542r, 17543r, 17544r, 17548r, 17559r, 17560r, 17563r, 17567r, 17577r, 17588r, 17595r, 17603r, 17604r, 17612r, 17625r, 17627r, 17630r, 17635r, 17637r, 17642r, 17644r, 17654r, 17658r, 17660r, 17661r, 17662r, 17666r, 17668r, 17669r, 17671r, 17680r, 17691r, 17702r, 17705r, 17706r, 17714r, 17716r, 17717r, 17718r, 17722r, 17726r, 17728r, 17731r, 17734r, 17735r, 17743r, 17746r, 17748r, 17749r, 17753r, 17754r, 17757r, 17767r, 17782r, 17784r, 17788r, 17792r, 17796r, 17800r, 17805r, 17816r, 17817r, 17818r, 17820r, 17822r, 17827r, 17828r, 17829r, 17835r, 17842r, 17845r, 17854r, 17856r, 17861r, 17874r, 17877r, 17887r, 17891r, 17899r, 17900r, 17901r, 17904r, 17908r, 17914r, 17917r, 17918r, 17929r, 17931r, 17933r, 17941r, 17943r, 17944r, 17947r, 17948r, 17955r, 17956r, 17957r

Moss, Arthur
3237

Moss, Geoffrey
15527

Mott, T. Bentley
15462

Mottram, R. H.
12675, 15804, 16287

Mount, Laura
8267

Much, Thomas
8084

Mueller, Hans
17723

Muir, Edwin
14509

Muir, Willa
14509

Mukerji, Dhan Gopal
13144, 17562

Mulheron, Mary
5582
Mullins, Helene
399, 569, 598, 919, 1951, 2059, 4159, 5015, 5091, 5146, 5274, 6224, 7036, 7547, 7688, 8171, 8542, 8666, 9033, 9210, 9645, 9847, 10202, 10213, 10907, 11227
Mumford, Lewis
2788, 3250, 7311, 8869, 12007, 12008, 12568, 12962, 14117, 17083
Munro, C. K.
12172, 12283
Munro, Hector H.
12853
Munthe, Axel
15215, 16924
Murphy, Adrienne M.
820
Murphy, Owen
13963
Murphy, Ralph
13992
Murray, D. L.
13147
Murray, Douglas
15072
Murray, John
16368
Murry, John Middleton
12191, 16787
Musser, Benjamin
2653
Mussolini, Benito
12650
Myers, Henry
13848

N

N. C.
see Cauchy, Nigel
N. H.
see Hoyt, Nancy
N. L.
see Levy, Newman
N. N. D.
see Dorfman, Nat N.
N. S.
see Beck, G.
Nabokov, Vladimir
14734
Nash, Ogden
2, 12, 219, 322, 444, 560, 595, 606, 619, 629, 684, 685, 1278, 1299, 1313, 1320, 1527, 1611, 1702, 1952, 2319, 2390, 2487, 2556, 2733, 2943, 2977, 3103, 3140, 3209, 3219, 3965, 4101, 4137, 4219, 4296, 4329, 4637, 4756, 4781, 4901, 4917, 5025, 5129, 5147, 5169, 5176, 5200, 5211, 5319, 5365, 5410, 5560, 5696, 5793, 5880, 5922, 5931, 5987, 6012, 6410, 7010, 7146, 7230, 7248, 7472, 7484, 7672, 8002, 8154, 8175, 8244, 8398, 8463, 8481, 8665, 8724, 8846-8851, 9780, 9823, 9985, 10230, 10260, 10419, 10510, 10511, 10569, 10626, 10677, 10740, 10927, 11087, 11091, 11239, 11320, 11368, 11414, 11536, 11542, 11575, 11685-11688, 11701, 11727, 11813, 11884
Nason, Leonard
12731
Nathan, George Jean
12141, 12197, 14699, 15509, 16678, 17111
Nathan, Robert
112, 1372, 2287, 2575, 2609, 2737, 4165, 4443, 8110, 10565, 12393, 15760, 15783, 16041, 16325
Nazaroff, Alexander
17294
Neale, Russell
14160
Nebel, Frederick
13502
Neisser, Edith
10934
Nelson, Jack T.
16254
Nelson, Victor F.
16086
Nemirovsky, Irene
13030
Net Star
see Adams, Franklin P.
Nettles
see Janson, Clara

Neubach, Ernst
15133
Neumann, Alfred
12082, 13719, 14580
Neumann, Robert
13559
Neurath, Otto
15345
Nevin, Hardwick
17911
Nevins, Allan
16014
The New Yorker
10283
Newberry, John Strong
265, 382, 414, 668, 984, 1734, 2415, 5513, 6166, 8285, 8446, 9212, 10086, 11032
Newhouse, Edward
4009, 7169, 7265, 11833, 17903
Newman, Frances
13047, 14009
Newman, Greatrex
15780A
Newman, R. H.
5215
Niccodemi, Dario
16975
Nicholl, Louise Townsend
11329
Nichols, Anne
11898, 11899, 11900, 16062
Nichols, Beverly
456, 5898, 5899, 5900, 5901, 5902, 5903, 12116, 12926, 16875
Nichols, Robert
17786
Nicholson, Frank
13482
Nicholson, Harold
16038, 16775
Nicholson, J. V.
12855
Nicholson, Kenyon
12251, 12292, 12982, 14958, 16896, 17043, 17317
Niles, Blair
13658
Nitti, Francesco
13367
Niven, Frederick
13328
Nivoix, Marcel
15237
Noble, Hollister
237, 3050, 7932
Nock, Albert Jay
13648, 14506, 15727, 17867
Nordhoff, Charles
14261
Norman, Charles
1071, 1095, 1496, 2149, 2612, 2668, 5240, 5387, 5599, 8512, 8716, 8765, 9309, 10531, 10607, 10629
Norris, Charles G.
15963
Norris, Frank
17950
Norris, Kathleen
12286, 14881
North, Clyde
14348, 16254, 17945
Norton, J. C.
1196, 8140
Norton, M. D. Herter
17350
Notch, Frank K.
14583
Novák, Sonia Ruthèle
9235, 9562, 11704
Novello, Ivor
13667, 15869, 17052, 17398
Novikoff-Priboy, A.
17400
Noyes, Alfred
17001
Nugent, Elliott
12517, 12602, 14557, 15059, 15575, 16025, 17389
Nugent, Homer
4019
Nugent, J. C.
12517, 12602, 13223, 14557, 15575, 16025, 17389
Nuhn, Ferner
7315, 9232
Nurnberg, Maxwell
12703
Nye, Edgar Wilson
12377

O

2420
One drinker
7569
O'Neil, George
12013
O'Neill, Charles
1193, 4051, 9710
O'Neill, Eugene
11950, 12351, 13093, 13263, 13628, 13917, 15136, 15137, 15397, 16943
O'Neill, Rose
7993
Onions, Oliver
15777
Oppenheim, James
12309
Oppenheimer, George S.
14111, 15111
Orenburgsky, Sergey Gussiev
see Gusev, Sergiei Ivanovich
Orkow, B. Harrison
15486
Orr, Clifford
712, 1333, 1626, 1973, 2057, 2076, 2203, 2773, 3145, 4112, 4195, 4495, 5684, 5908, 5999, 6628, 8237, 8371, 9310
Orr, Edith
4162
Osborn, Paul
14211, 15375, 15725, 17553
O'Shea, M. B.
4013
Ossorgin, Michael
16169
Ostenso, Martha
13006, 17611, 17926
Ostrow, Dmitri
12160
O'Sullivan, Maurice
17423
Otway, Thomas
12856
Oudard, Georges
15942
Oursler, Fulton
11983, 12312, 16830, 17866
Ouspensky, A.
16239
Overton, Grant
15295
Overton, Jacqueline
14910
Overton, Ruth
2501
Owen, Edith
804, 4796, 7568, 7653, 8222, 9772, 9933, 11269
Owen, Harrison
14003
Owen, Louise
8182
Owen, Russell
2364, 6264

P

P. C.
see Cummings, Parke
P. E.
see Thomas, Martha Banning
P. G.
see Gould, Paul
P. G. A.
see Anderson, Persis Greely
P. G. G.
see Gumbinner, Paul G.
P. G. W.
see Wylie, Philip G.
P. M. R.
1867
Packard, Frederick
288, 511, 1037, 1986, 2580, 3205, 3958, 4412, 4821, 5182, 5193, 5609, 5610, 6553, 8208, 8821, 9362, 9433, 9482, 9887, 9888, 10446, 10650, 10698
Page, Elizabeth
17365
Page, Mann
14222, 15060
Page, Will A.
12304
Pagnol, Marcel
15158, 15237, 17313
Paine, Albert Bigelow
9258
Pakenham, Compton
16212
Pálffy, Eleanor
3265
Palmer, Gretta
6038, 6401, 7406
Palmer, Paul
11698

15420
Paterson, Isabel
15504
Patience Eden
see Thomas, Martha Banning
Patrick, John
14070
Patrick, Ted
8920
Patter, Walter
6079
Patterson, Sterling
4525, 6207, 11794
Paul, Elliot
12858, 14794
Paul, Louis
16134
Paule, Kathleen
17629
Payne, George Henry
8972
Payne, Sevier
7795
Pearl, Leslie S.
2613, 8426
Pearson, Drew
12010
Pearson, Edmund
855, 1794, 1803, 2260, 4148, 4323, 5572, 5574, 6133, 6552, 7107, 8768, 9650, 9704, 10620, 16165
Peattie, Donald Culross
11989, 12468, 13954
Peck, George A.
2122, 4907
Peck, Raymond W.
12676
Peckham, Richard
113, 417, 1166, 1697, 4319, 4721, 7038, 7346, 9927, 9977, 10003
Peeler, Clare
7353
Peet, Creighton
436, 4387, 5564, 7080, 7099, 7276, 8681, 9986, 10577, 11027, 11764
Pelerin, James
5969
Pember, Clifford
12649
Pemberton, Brock
4265, 8645
Pemberton, Murdock
910, 1150, 1982, 2112, 3938, 4470, 5348, 5823, 5824, 6139, 6398, 8447, 15960, 16684
Pennington, Jo
10603
Perceval-Monger, W.
9394, 9864
Percy, Edward
16727
Perelman, Laura
11973
Perelman, S. J.
11, 616, 724, 743, 931, 1000, 1252, 1294, 1434, 1440, 2355, 3085, 3248, 4384, 5044, 5156, 5380, 6377, 6433, 7578, 7684, 7901, 8019, 8449, 8865, 9658, 9775, 9970, 10284, 10357, 10395-10397, 10529, 10852, 11323, 11471, 11551, 11650, 11787, 11796, 11811, 11835, 11973, 17578
The perennial bachelor
see Teed, Ordway
Perkins, Grace
12062
Perkins, Kenneth
12928, 12985
Perlman, William J.
14230, 15434
Perry, John
16846
Perse, St. John
12042
Pertwee, Roland
14053, 14380
Peter Pansy
1553
Peterkin, Julia
12536, 16350, 16490
Peters, Curtis Arnoux
see Arno, Peter
Peters, Paul
15850, 16903
Peterson, Houston
14027
Petrarca, Francesco
16795
Petrarch
see Petrarca, Francesco
Petrie, Elizabeth Link

Pottle, Frederick A.
12486, 16962
Pound, Ezra
12634, 12822, 13497
Pouquet, Jeanne Simone
14723
Powel, Harford, Jr.
15685
Powell, Dawn
500, 913, 939, 1616, 1988, 10193, 12369, 14474, 16602
Powell, Hickman
2208, 2567, 4118, 8018, 14719
Powell, Lyman P.
15163
Powell, William B.
11594
Powers, Roswell J.
9746, 10625
Powers, Tom
10123
Powys, John Cowper
17813
Powys, Llewelyn
12104, 14086, 17527
Powys, T. F.
15324
Pratt, Philip
497, 2155, 2807, 7953, 8147, 10016
Pratt, Theodore
479, 692, 912, 1293, 1790, 1853, 1854, 1946, 1968, 2481, 2482, 2483, 2502, 2581, 2873, 2931, 2959, 3275, 4173, 4457, 4757, 4783, 4897, 5124, 5329, 5371, 5418, 5685, 5938, 5944, 6396, 6510, 6685, 6686, 6687, 6688, 6689, 6690, 7160, 7247, 7342, 7395, 7454, 7965, 8030, 8059, 8104, 8180, 8274, 8334, 8453, 8568, 8719, 9122, 9126, 9138, 9152, 9284, 9520, 10252, 10333, 10335, 10908, 10929, 11030, 11173, 11280, 11284, 11348, 11372, 11550, 11816, 11820, 11832, 12355, 12356
Pratt, William W.
2221, 17098
Prenez Garde
1962
Prentice, Frances Woodward
1424, 4407, 7735, 9595, 11397, 11436, 11462
Prichard, Katharine Susannah
12890
Priestley, J. B.
12065, 12232, 12993, 13203, 13304, 13359, 13452, 13849, 13850, 14637, 14769, 15266, 16189, 17155, 17266, 17698
Prin, Alice
14570
Pringle, Henry F.
203, 236, 1062, 1063, 1156, 1418, 1567, 2046, 2832, 3889, 5183, 5235, 5460, 5851, 5873, 6588, 7450, 7458, 8610, 8611, 8706, 8918, 9463, 9667, 10854, 11460, 11521, 11803, 11958, 14801
Printzlau, Olga
14443
Private 19022
see Manning, Frederic
Procter, Arthur
15411
The professor
3063, 5737
Prokosch, Frederic
9781, 12166, 12169, 15568, 16569
Proust, Marcel
15881
Pulitzer, Ralph
5645, 10808
Pulsifer, Harold Trowbridge
7280
Putnam, J. Wesley
12483
Putnam, P. T. L.
8976
Puysange
5106, 9097
Pyne, Archibald
1550
Pynne, William
1640

Q

Quid
see James, Marquis
Quint, Léon Pierre
15130
Quintero, Joaquin Alvarez

14255, 17840
Quintero, Serafin
14255, 17840
Quong, C. Lee
7752, 10901

R

R. A.
see Broun, Heywood
R. A. S.
see Simon, Robert A.
R. B.
see Benchley, Robert
R. B. H.
4499
R. B. P.
see Parr, Ruth B.
R. C. W.
see Washburn, R. C.
R. H.
see Hawthorne, Ruth
R. L.
10942
R. L.
see also Lockridge, Richard
R. L. J.
see Jones, Ruth Lambert
R. L. L.
see Lowrie, Rebecca L.
R. M.
see Maloney, Russell
R. M. C.
see Coates, Robert M.
R. R.
5974, 9697
R. S. W.
6068
R. T. L.
5618
R. V. H.
6151
Rabelais, Francois
17867
Radin, Paul
12140
Raftery, Gerald
597, 1861, 4550
Raisbeck, Kenneth
16347
Raison, Milton
16621
Ramsaye, Terry
1229, 15283
Rand, Ayn
15565
Randole, Leo
12692
Randolph, Clemence
16184
Randolph, Vance
15825
Raphael, John
15023, 15938
Ralphaelson, Samson
11907, 14447, 16720, 17922
Rapp, William Jourdan
14014, 16982, 17707
Rascoe, Burton
8373, 12290, 17278
Rath, Frederick
13533
Rathbone, Basil
14523
Rattigan, Terence
13525, 13666
Raucat, Thomas
14190
Rauschning, Hermann
16278
Rawlings, Marjorie Kinnan
8229, 17880
Raymond, Ernest
13001
Raynolds, Robert
12563
Razaf, Andy
14202
Rea, Lorna
16704
Reade, Leslie
16592
Recht, Charles
15366
Rector, George
13790
Redman, Ben Ray
1137
Reed, Douglas
14367
Reed, Herbert
3894, 4072, 4200, 5964, 9179, 10588
Reed, Joseph Verner

12967
Reed, Mark
15946, 17892
Reese, S. Albert
2201
Reich, Edward
2324
Reid, James
2323
Reid, Laurence
9566
Reid, Phyllis
3224
Reilly, Frank C.
15959
Reiman, Corinna
6043
Reith, George
12139
Remarque, Erich Maria
11979, 16322, 17207
Renn, Ludwig
17590
Reynolds, Bruce
15866
Rhine, J. B.
15517
Rhys, Jean
11940
Ricardel, Molly
14279
Rice, Elinor
12332
Rice, Elmer
1399, 3919, 4150, 5283, 7319, 8682, 8801, 11310, 12019, 12344, 12805, 12905, 14321, 14526, 14752, 16533, 16958, 16959, 16983, 17436, 17634
Richards, Ben
3170
Richards, Frank
15712
Richards, Laura E.
17681
Richards, Ruth
7306, 9819, 10403, 11413
Richardson, Anna Steese
12364
Richardson, Henry Handel
12182, 13347, 17451, 17915
Richman, Arthur
13884, 14057, 16126
Richter, Conrad
16514
Rickman, Carl
12566
Riddell, John
14346
Rideout, Ransom
13821
Riding, Laura
12816, 17383
Ridley, Arnold
13771, 17872
Riegel, G. F.
4124, 5671, 11888
Riegger, Wallingford
17384
Riesenberg, Felix
13296, 15047, 16043
Riesenfeld, Helen
556, 1178, 5019
Riewerts, J. P.
12448
Rigg, H. K.
6162
Riggs, Dorothy Kidder
7843, 8060
Riggs, Lynn
5132, 12367, 13949, 16339, 16416
Riley, Lawrence
15932
Rilke, Rainer Maria
13249, 17350
Rimbaud, Arthur
17473
Rinehart, Mary Roberts
12262, 15623, 16234, 17184
Ripperger, Henrietta Sperry
7122
Rising, Lawrence
13436
Riskin, Robert
12427, 15125
River, W. L.
17319
Rivera, Diego
16040
Rives, Amélie
14954
Robbins, Charles
196, 11151
Robbins, James
9343

4427
Rose, Billy
12381
Rose, Carl
5924, 11828
Rosenberg, James N.
17580
Rosendahl, Henry
16971
Rosenfeld, Paul
12007, 12008
Rosenheck, Kenneth
8409
Rosenman, Samuel I.
16131
Ross, Florence W.
8061, 8062, 10618
Ross, Leonard Q.
see Rosten, Leo
Ross, Malcolm
4845, 5122, 9344
Ross, Nancy Wilson
8759, 11809
Ross, Virgilia Peterson
263, 1630
Rostand, Edmond
12972, 14686
Rosten, Leo
1197, 1472, 4750, 5220, 5336, 6440, 6540-6551, 7528, 7627, 8236, 8854, 9024, 9551, 10349, 10420, 11125
Roth, Henry
1093
Roth, Joseph
16177
Roth, Samuel
16094
Rothermell, Fred
17282
Roto
see Bosworth, T. H.
Roule, Louis
13537
Rourke, Constance
12179, 17390
Rouverol, Aurania
13965, 16710
Roy, René
15574
Royde-Smith, Naomi
16712
Royle, Edwin Milton
17720
Rubens, Maurice
15246
Rubin, Daniel N.
12783, 13114, 15400, 16294, 17838
Ruby, Harry
14172, 14985, 16610
Rudge, William Edwin
16832
Rug Dept. Baker
see Wengler, Harold
Rukeyser, Muriel
17408
Rumsey, Adeline
9637
Runyon, Damon
16732
Ruskin, Harry
12235
Russell, Charles Edward
12720
Russell, Frances
2661
Russell, Franklin
13908
Russell, George
2550
Russell, Henry
15876
Russell, Mary Annette
13417, 14388
Russell, Phillips
12325, 13336, 14490
Russell, Sydney King
1348, 1358, 1806, 6021, 8191, 8505, 8924, 10269, 10350, 11708
Rutt, Edwin
8655
Ryall, G. F. T.
721, 8348
Ryan, Don
10498, 16354
Ryan, Gertrude Curtis
1901, 2597, 3266, 3994, 7243, 9217, 9240
Ryan, Phyllis
2669, 2886, 3025, 4487
Rykert, C. Gurd
9954
Rylee, Robert
13073, 16430

Ryskind, Morrie
4633, 12069, 13705, 14766, 15240, 15677, 15678, 16970

S

S. A. T.
10716
S. C. M.
see McKelway, St. Clair
S. F.
2486, 2664
S. Finny
see White, E. B.
S. H. H.
see Hawkins, Stewart Hyde
S. M.
see Middleton, Scudder
S. S.
11469
S. S. J.
see Jones, S. S.
S. W.
see Wilson, Sterling
Saalburg, Allen
8275
Sabatini, Rafael
12657
Sacco, Nicola
14781
Sachs, Emanie
17108
Sackville-West, Edward
16404
Sackville-West, Victoria
8896, 13313, 13440, 15918, 16433
Saerchinger, César
7128
Sager, Gordon
813
St. Clair, Stewart
14638
Saint-Exupéry, Antoine de
17771
St. John, Theodore
13151
Saki
see Munro, Hector H.
Salisbury, Nate
1206, 1364, 1779, 3986, 4091, 7375-7379, 7388, 7402, 8554, 9113, 9799, 10274
Salten, Felix
14218
Sam
see Sullivan, Frank
Samstag, Nicholas
649, 653, 882, 1014, 1785, 5753, 6416, 10345, 11001
Samuel Jeake, Jr.
see Aiken, Conrad
Sanborn, Pitts
11253, 16075
Sandburg, Carl
11903, 11903A, 13859, 15166, 15917
Sandeen, Ernest E.
8142
Sandemose, Aksel
13682
Sanderson, Ivan T.
12073, 12653
Sandler, David
11092
Sandoz, Mari
12636, 15703
Santayana, George
14722
Sapieha, Princess Paul
2136
Sappington, K. C.
975
Sardou, Victorien
13138
Saroyan, William
4775, 14359, 14952, 15442, 15900, 17268
Sassoon, Siegfried
15208, 15210
Saunders, Paul M.
1829, 7040
Savage, Courtenay
12601
Savage, Joe W.
11181
Savarin Gibbs
see Gibbs, Wolcott
Savin, Nikolai Gerasimovich
16133
Savine, Nicholas de Toulouse Lautrec de
see Savin, Nikolai Gerasimovich
Savinkov, Boris
15209
Savoir, Alfred

Scott, Evelyn
12518, 17613
Scott, Noël
9733
Scott, Winfield Townley
1505
Scully, Michael
188, 1758, 1989, 2326, 6175, 6693, 8162, 8246, 9177, 9407
Seabrook, William
12170, 14537, 15034, 17144
Seagle, William
17285
Search-light
see Frank, Waldo
Searle, Margaret
7338
Sears, Zelda
14986
Seaver, Edwin
12850
Secrett, T.
17418
Sedgwick, Anne Douglas
15953
Sedgwick, Henry Dwight
13009, 14088
See, A. B.
16499
Seeds, Charmé
455, 586, 1939, 2148
Seeley, Evelyn
11374
Seff, Manuel
12429
Segall, Harry
12301
Seiffert, Marjorie Allen
96, 99, 440, 599, 1653, 1718, 1875, 2235, 2649, 2665, 2891, 4069, 4244, 4254, 5208, 5427, 5532, 5915, 5951, 6277, 7598, 7624, 7676, 7726, 7788, 7792, 7804, 7815, 8239, 8295, 8329, 8362, 8399, 8965, 9509, 9827, 10040, 10094, 10171, 10384, 10450, 10719, 10748, 10779, 10864, 11054, 11115, 11291, 11396, 11608, 11638, 11678, 11699
Seitz, Don
13222
Seldes, George
16477, 17902
Seldes, Gilbert
47, 197, 326, 498, 780, 1516, 1566, 1576, 1654, 1941, 2230, 2540, 2894, 2947, 3022, 3084, 3271, 4029, 4314, 4433, 4519, 4947, 5041, 5082, 5273, 5511, 5518, 5608, 5928, 6150, 6186, 6274, 6371, 6406, 6407, 7121, 7284, 8157, 8230, 8231, 9021, 9577, 9782, 10221, 10905, 11468, 11506, 11581, 15002, 15889r, 16865, 17044, 17783, 17863, 17884
Self, Edwin B.
17441
Sellar, W. C.
17100
Sellmer, Robert
5050, 8710
Selsey, E. W.
9890
Selver, Paul
15388, 15770
Selwyn, Arch
12721
Selwyn, Edgar
16047A, 16781
Selwyn, Ruth
15585
Sencourt, Robert Esmonde
14792
Senior, Elliot
10141
Sergeant, Elizabeth Shepley
13519, 16627
Seymour, Beatrice Kean
17233, 17494
Sganarelle
see Seldes, Gilbert
Shairp, Mordaunt
13945, 13946
Shakespeare, William
12094, 12162, 13987, 13988, 14084, 14531, 14581, 14587, 15004, 15234, 15235, 15245r, 15272, 15273, 16362, 17067, 17068, 17409, 17410
Shand, P. Morton
12472
Shane, Theodore
3183, 9244, 10513, 12030r, 12178r, 12261r, 12294r,

12306r, 12320r, 12323r, 12345r, 12371r, 12401r, 12415r, 12455r, 12569r, 12570r, 12690r, 12766r, 12786r, 12797r, 12802r, 12857r, 12950r, 12971r, 12986r, 12989r, 13004r, 13115r, 13268r, 13327r, 13467r, 13511r, 13550r, 13597r, 13602r, 13668r, 13811r, 13832r, 13847r, 13883r, 13902r, 13941r, 13991r, 14006r, 14067r, 14142r, 14146r, 14356r, 14544r, 14569r, 14586r, 14599r, 14604r, 14613r, 14625r, 14676r, 14677r, 14826r, 14830r, 14866r, 14879r, 14921r, 14925r, 14981r, 14987r, 15014r, 15084r, 15096r, 15112r, 15138r, 15217r, 15243r, 15267r, 15337r, 15339r, 15474r, 15521r, 15704r, 15793r, 15843r, 15858r, 15950r, 16021r, 16125r, 16135r, 16221r, 16245r, 16337r, 16353r, 16412r, 16439r, 16441r, 16479r, 16563r, 16591r, 16626r, 16654r, 16719r, 16725r, 16759r, 16760r, 16804r, 16894r, 16954r, 17124r, 17210r, 17230r, 17320r, 17326r, 17329r, 17402r, 17479r, 17487r, 17490r, 17516r, 17569r, 17585r, 17631r, 17719r, 17750r, 17764r, 17775r, 17825r

Shapiro, Julian L.
17608

Sharp, Margery
14015, 16283

Shattuck, Charles
9342

Shaw, A. H.
2125

Shaw, Charles G.
1684, 1685, 1698, 2714, 2771, 2774, 2899, 3238, 3239, 3272, 4620, 4621, 4622, 4623, 4624, 4630, 4779, 4785, 4786, 4787, 4788, 4789, 4790, 4791, 4792, 4793, 5382, 5432, 6085, 6141, 7218, 7834, 8032, 8094, 8339, 8340, 9029, 9923, 9926, 9928, 10534-10536, 10640-10643, 11071, 11094, 11319, 11420, 11519, 11598, 11821, 11846, 14044

Shaw, George Bernard
11928, 12058, 12103, 12126, 12611, 12631, 13178, 13733, 13767, 14047, 14241, 14378, 15053, 15080, 15733, 16151, 16432, 16630, 16676, 17221, 17309, 17348

Shaw, Irwin
966, 4014, 4822, 5576, 5829, 6100, 6225, 7452, 9028, 9250, 11428, 12590, 13736

Shaw, Leslie G.
1655, 5429, 9536, 11168

Shay, Edith
4100, 9441

Shay, Frank
14112

Sheahan, Henry Beston
12467

Sheean, Vincent
6642, 9448, 13038, 15635, 15933, 15962, 16461

Shelby, Ann
13825

Sheldon, Edward
13143, 14458, 14997

Shellhase, Jane Gilbert
3149, 4224, 7562

Shepard, Odell
15907

Shepherd, George
7654, 8804

Sherard, Robert Harborough
12331

Sheridan, Richard Brinsley
16316, 16495

Sherman, Charles
13274, 16961

Sherman, Clarke
4545

Sherman, Harold
14099

Sherman, Richard
6665

Sherman, Robert J.
16836

Sherman, Stuart P.
12942, 15436
Sherriff, R. C.
14195, 14514, 14515, 16431
Sherry, Edna
14374
Sherry, Gordon
12409
Sherwood, Robert E.
4505, 4754, 8261, 11894, 14296, 15944, 16164, 16272, 16334, 17178, 17324, 17610
Shipman, Samuel
12302, 12928, 13470, 15608, 16487, 17120, 17353
Shipp, Mary
1673
Sholokhov, Mikhail
12051, 16538
Shrdlu, Etaoin
1966, 7743, 11336
Shuman, Ik
2710, 6529, 7348
Sibley, R. B.
5996
Siegmeister, Alice Rayfiel
1282
Sierra, Gregorio Martinez
12921, 14592, 16328, 16843
Sierra, Marie Martinez
12921
Sifton, Claire
15263, 15590
Sifton, Paul
12322, 15263, 15590
Sig
see Spaeth, Sigmund
Silberer, Geza
12638
Sillman, June
15516
Sillman, Leonard
15515, 17738
Silone, Ignazio
12512, 13588, 16493
Sil-vara
see Silberer, Geza
Silver, Milton
15472
Silvers, Sid
17909
Simon, Louis
12605
Simon, Max
14602
Simon, Robert A.
401, 2488, 3927, 4528, 7468, 8683, 9624, 12555, 12708, 13843r, 16075r
Simple Susan, Spinster
see Helm, Florence
Simpson, Harold
12603
Simpson, Helen
10999, 12963
Simpson, Kenneth
11981
Simpson, Lola Jean
11254, 17357
Simpson, Reginald
14893
Sims, Tom
1070
Sinclair, Bettina
5097, 8755, 8917, 11145
Sinclair, Gordon
13593
Sinclair, May
13450, 14148, 16224
Sinclair, Upton
4652, 12023, 15353, 17667
Singer, I. J.
12562
Siste Viator
1111
Sitwell, Edith
16544, 17538
Sitwell, Osbert
11970, 12291, 15101, 17377
Sitwell, Sacheverell
11970
Skinner, Cornelia Otis
225, 817, 1158, 2245, 2411, 4044, 4205, 4930, 5198, 5917, 7097, 7844, 9167, 9534, 11224, 11810, 13309, 15120
Sklar, George
14795, 15241, 16903
Skolsky, Sidney
1764, 2443, 2684, 7033, 7538, 11075
Slade, Caroline

1483, 4598, 4795
Slesinger, Tess
5912, 6578
Slocombe, George
17404
Small, Florence S.
4538, 7079
Smart, Charles Allen
15514, 16171
Smedley, Agnes
13026
Smedley, Doree
3050
Smith, Agnes W.
11890r, 11895r, 11902r,
11919r, 11977r, 11979r,
12001r, 12005r, 12007r,
12009r, 12016r, 12046r,
12065r, 12086r, 12104r,
12125r, 12148r, 12153r,
12164r, 12182r, 12192r,
12198r, 12201r, 12224r,
12239r, 12244r, 12253r,
12275r, 12285r, 12295r,
12385r, 12400r, 12410r,
12417r, 12472r, 12477r,
12479r, 12489r, 12506r,
12518r, 12529r, 12533r,
12599r, 12607r, 12608r,
12614r, 12633r, 12654r,
12658r, 12674r, 12687r,
12699r, 12712r, 12719r,
12720r, 12730r, 12734r,
12735r, 12762r, 12764r,
12787r, 12861r, 12890r,
12894r, 12898r, 12930r,
12943r, 12954r, 12959r,
12981r, 13007r, 13030r,
13059r, 13075r, 13088r,
13099r, 13124r, 13126r,
13131r, 13173r, 13195r,
13214r, 13301r, 13313r,
13321r, 13325r, 13334r,
13335r, 13336r, 13338r,
13351r, 13356r, 13364r,
13367r, 13383r, 13394r,
13405r, 13407r, 13420r,
13430r, 13436r, 13448r,
13455r, 13491r, 13536r,
13542r, 13558r, 13578r,
13589r, 13596r, 13605r,
13619r, 13647r, 13648r,
13658r, 13684r, 13697r,
13699r, 13701r, 13734r, 13738r,
13753r, 13833r, 13849r,
13861r, 13865r, 13866r,
13878r, 13893r, 13925r,
13927r, 13934r, 13953r,
13957r, 13966r, 13995r,
13997r, 14018r, 14075r,
14088r, 14092r, 14098r,
14120r, 14123r, 14124r,
14150r, 14158r, 14162r,
14182r, 14203r, 14218r,
14248r, 14257r, 14258r,
14314r, 14320r, 14322r,
14330r, 14337r, 14341r,
14349r, 14352r, 14377r,
14395r, 14402r, 14407r,
14459r, 14482r, 14497r,
14507r, 14524r, 14532r,
14570r, 14580r, 14583r,
14591r, 14594r, 14608r,
14642r, 14662r, 14681r,
14691r, 14704r, 14719r,
14729r, 14731r, 14758r,
14780r, 14789r, 14792r,
14797r, 14799r, 14806r,
14810r, 14813r, 14814r,
14820r, 14844r, 14857r,
14859r, 14861r, 14892r,
14906r, 14909r, 14910r,
14916r, 14924r, 14956r,
14965r, 14972r, 14984r,
15088r, 15101r, 15121r,
15148r, 15165r, 15177r,
15187r, 15210r, 15215r,
15250r, 15269r, 15296r,
15302r, 15327r, 15334r,
15342r, 15371r, 15378r,
15379r, 15392r, 15411r,
15446r, 15460r, 15462r,
15475r, 15476r, 15491r,
15518r, 15528r, 15599r,
15604r, 15609r, 15629r,
15631r, 15639r, 15640r,
15720r, 15721r, 15731r,
15748r, 15773r, 15777r,
15791r, 15796r, 15812r,
15820r, 15830r, 15863r,
15870r, 15892r, 15895r,
15896r, 15901r, 15911r,
15915r, 15942r, 15953r,
15960r, 16014r, 16020r,
16022r, 16027r, 16038r,
16058r, 16098r, 16119r,

16138r, 16159r, 16169r, 16206r, 16212r, 16263r, 16227r, 16283r, 16287r, 16348r, 16354r, 16364r, 16366r, 16372r, 16374r, 16433r, 16444r, 16456r, 16463r, 16473r, 16497r, 16531r, 16541r, 16559r, 16565r, 16568r, 16570r, 16578r, 16627r, 16628r, 16687r, 16693r, 16697r, 16698r, 16709r, 16758r, 16774r, 16806r, 16891r, 16897r, 16952r, 16962r, 16832r, 16967r, 16985r, 17001r, 17034r, 17101r, 17102r, 17131r, 17154r, 17167r, 17216r, 17255r, 17259r, 17273r, 17290r, 17330r, 17338r, 17352r, 17355r, 17361r, 17395r, 17411r, 17418r, 17420r, 17446r, 17451r, 17456r, 17458r, 17488r, 17502r, 17507r, 17546r, 17555r, 17561r, 17565r, 17590r, 17592r, 17606r, 17611r, 17613r, 17617r, 17701r, 17713r, 17724r, 17766r, 17774r, 17783r, 17813r, 17823r, 17833r, 17837r, 17866r, 17875r, 17883r, 17898r, 17913r, 17924r, 17926r, 17930r

Smith, Alfred E.
17502

Smith, Bernard
4142

Smith, Beverly
6104

Smith, Dodie
12619, 13051

Smith, Edward H.
17898

Smith, H. S.
13239

Smith, Harry B.
12772, 12909, 13981, 15492, 16082, 16237, 16346, 16548, 17037, 17724

Smith, Helena Huntington
342, 590, 722, 968, 1807, 1872, 2337, 2628, 3936, 3944, 4324, 4394, 4729, 5416, 6270, 7305, 7488, 8221, 8677, 8845, 9470, 9628, 10518, 11070, 11083

Smith, Henry Justin
12735, 16022

Smith, Hester Travers
15789

Smith, Joe Bates
13110

Smith, Kent
1668, 10120

Smith, Mortimer
325

Smith, Paul Gerard
13689, 14041, 14113, 15828

Smith, Pauline
12273

Smith, Thorne
8121, 16711

Smith, Walton Hall
17180

Smith, Willa Kay
11537, 11539

Smith, Winchell
14828

Smoff
7841, 10090

Smolka, H. P.
13621

Smun, Sigi
1498

Snow, Edgar
16241

Snow, Eliot
15732

Sommerfield, John
13062

Sophocles
13320

Soussanin, Nicholas
14230

Souvarine, Boris
16863

Spaeth, Katie
1021

Spaeth, Sigmund
82, 1207, 1354, 1680, 1899, 2010, 2784, 3091, 6129, 6644, 7115, 8488, 9330, 9438, 10014, 10675, 10689, 10829, 11295,

11480, 11481, 11804, 16211
Spafford, Justin
12167
Sparkes, Boyden
14120
Sparling, Earl
2804
Spence, Ralph
13281, 13875
Spencer, Claire
13701, 16166
Spencer, Theodore
2021
Spender, J. A.
17240
Spender, Stephen
17370
Spengler, Oswald
14221
Spewack, Bella
12496, 12497, 12790, 14750, 15304, 16028, 16849, 17596
Spewack, Samuel
12496, 12497, 12790, 14750, 15304, 16028, 16849, 17596
Speyer, Leonora
845, 6380, 7692
Speyer, William
12914
Spie, Hugo
4995
Spiess, Jan
10035
Sprigge, Elizabeth
16580
Spring, Howard
15459
Springer, Fleta Campbell
585, 7478, 10308, 11909
Springs, Elliott White
14751
Sproehnle, Katherine
338, 350, 1061, 1430, 2942, 3065, 4154, 5523, 7261, 8124, 8150, 8172, 8173, 9868, 11082, 11768, 11784
Squire Cuthbert
7172
Squire, John Collings
14300
Stallings, Laurence
12574, 13457, 13535, 16190, 17202, 17558, 17679
Stange, Hugh Stanislaus
11944, 13435, 13580, 14039, 14914, 17274, 17524
Stanley, Martha
14765
Stanton, Olive
124, 4597
Starhill
see Seldes, Gilbert
Stark, Ora
10737
Starkie, Walter
14995, 16181
Starling, Lynn
16713
Starrett, Vincent
10744, 16517
Stayton, Frank
15336
Stead, Christina
12284, 16449, 16567
Stebbins, Lucy Poate
15694
Steegmuller, Francis
115, 1682, 2328, 3137, 3143, 3214, 5071, 7823, 7934, 8991, 9093, 9677, 11407, 11429, 13552
Steel, Byron
678, 9527, 10239, 15660, 16697
Steele, Porter
13437
Steele, Wilbur Daniel
9514, 14239, 16049, 17055
Steelman, Fred G.
200, 3036, 5339, 7308, 7329
Steen, Marguerite
13007, 15752
Stegner, Wallace
16252
Steig, Henry Anton
223, 4177, 4940, 6081, 8240
Stein, Gertrude
12187, 12188, 13397, 14993, 15056, 15958, 16044, 17860
Steinbeck, John
13899, 14915, 15675, 15676, 15884
Steiner, Robert
13371
Stengel, Hans
893, 8016

Stephens, James
4972, 5130, 6415, 8307, 8906, 9045, 9583, 12817
Stephens, Leona
15372
Stephenson, Nathaniel Wright
15502
Stept, Samuel H.
17894
Stern, Edith
16144
Stern, G. B.
2226, 2518, 2525, 4240, 4910, 6283, 6557, 7619, 11390, 12493, 13071, 15182, 15183, 15379, 16401, 16631, 16735, 17253
Stern, Harold
12147
Stern, Philip Van Doren
12519, 15098
Stevens, James
12508, 15894
Stewart, Charles Conger
13717
Stewart, D.
16456
Stewart, Donald Ogden
122, 1264, 2413, 2970, 3907, 4503, 4627, 4631, 4653, 4705, 4706, 4707, 5118, 5604, 6226, 7064, 7188, 7641, 8614, 9752, 9758, 10442, 11093, 11772, 13510, 16217
Stiff, Dean
see Anderson, Nels
Stillman, Clara Greuning
16452
Stillman, Henry
14688
Stites, Lord
see Fairchild, Donald Stites
Stix, Thomas L.
4667
Stockbridge, Frank Parker
295
Stoddard, Lothrop
14984, 15178
Stokes, Leslie
15787
Stokes, Sewell
15787
Stone, Florence
4556, 5099, 5639, 8859,
Stone, Grace Zaring
12811, 14054
Stone, Irving
14999
Stong, Phillip D.
5916, 12651, 16888, 16948, 17549, 17650
Storm, Hans Otto
15027
Storm, Lesley
12380, 14675
Storm, Marian
3950, 7157, 13698
Stowaway
see Marx, Sam
Stowell, Gordon
12599
Stoyle, Lewis E.
6660
Strachey, John
8983
Strachey, Lytton
13324, 16045
Strakosh, Avery
7213
Strauss, Marcel
17623
Street, Ada
17257
Street, Charles
3187, 4187, 4388, 9825
Street, Julian
15308, 17257, 17701, 17779
Street, Wolcott D.
11218
Stribling, T. S.
12224, 16375, 16807, 16910, 17084, 17142, 17475
Strindberg, August
13226, 13298, 13474, 13475
Strobel, Marion
10661
Strode, Hudson
14317
Strong, Anna Louise
14268
Strong, Austin
15983, 17232
Strong, L. A. G.

13192, 13709, 14706
Strouse, Don Muir
4024, 4025, 4026, 4027
Strunsky, Robert
2001
Stuart, Aimée
12390, 14966, 15584
Stuart, Francis
17399
Stuart, Philip
12390, 14966, 15584
Sturges, Lucy Hale
416
Sturges, Preston
12739, 13973, 16218, 16964
Sturges-Jones, Marion
491, 2776, 5597, 7175, 7789, 7997, 7998, 8364, 8685, 9164, 9285, 10152, 10817, 11037, 11434, 11441, 11499, 11645
Suckow, Ruth
962, 1667, 4646, 10200, 11601, 12894, 13583, 14623, 15668
Sudermann, Hermann
15013
Sugrue, Thomas
1262, 7646, 11121
Sullivan, Alan
14433
Sullivan, Arthur
13843, 13979, 14397, 15278, 15279, 15887, 15975, 16083, 16400
Sullivan, Edward Dean
12734, 16206
Sullivan, Frank
1, 54, 110, 152, 281, 488, 494, 515, 587, 588, 658, 771, 883, 909, 1106, 1165, 1255, 1518, 1531, 1532, 1533, 1534, 1535, 1536, 1537, 1538, 1539, 1540, 1541, 1542, 1580, 1699, 1788, 1804, 1871, 1897, 1937, 2054, 2063, 2066, 2232, 2280, 2311, 2351, 2392, 2396, 2514, 2640, 2679, 2716, 2903, 3077, 3139, 4127, 4138, 4143, 4152, 4188, 4194, 4349, 4425, 4483, 4506, 4553, 4618, 4638, 4644, 4645, 4658, 4760, 4767, 4829, 4839, 4895, 4899, 4956, 4982, 5140, 5145, 5151, 5155, 5470, 5547, 5586, 5591, 5602, 5687, 5828, 5863, 5949, 6000, 6044, 6082, 6409, 6463, 6493, 6527, 6532, 6595, 6648, 7154, 7266, 7307, 7392, 7394, 7435, 7442, 7473, 7482, 7500, 7661, 7740, 7835, 7875, 7881, 7920, 7971, 7991, 8047, 8234, 8273, 8432, 8460, 8461, 8533, 8535, 8644, 8874, 9057, 9173-9175, 9192, 9314, 9327, 9391, 9392, 9483, 9528, 9542, 9552, 9619, 9688, 9693, 9699, 9748, 9964, 10071, 10137, 10263, 10367, 10401, 10404, 10627, 10662, 10678, 10816, 10984, 11203, 11306, 11377, 11401, 11405, 11424, 11427, 11463, 11566, 11584, 11636, 11654, 11666, 11684, 11812, 11827, 11836, 11875
Sullivan, J. W. N.
12289
Sullivan, Mark
15805, 15819, 17406
Summers, Montague
12856
Summers, Sam
17849
Sundgaard, Arnold
13402
Super
see Carlton, Henry
Sutherland, Halliday
12111
Sutherland, Joan
17808
Sutton, Eric
13310, 15749, 17919, 17935
Swan, Mark
14245
Swanstrom, Arthur
16513
Swartz, Delmore
17473
Sweeney, J. L.
5457
Swerling, Jo
726, 11847
Swift, John
see Seldes, Gilbert
Swift, Michael
14208
Swift, Peter

5484
Swinnerton, Frank
12556, 14022, 16709, 16993
Sylvanus, Paddy
17102
Symons, Arthur
12861
Synge, John Millington
15985
Szczepkowska, Marja M.
13170

T

T. H. B.
see Bliss, T. H.
T. H. L.
see Lewis, Tracy Hammond
T. H. W.
650
T. S.
see Shane, Theodore
Tabor, Richard
14409
Taegen, Walter
7801
Taggard, Genevieve
1223, 6457, 6695, 8430, 9668, 10297, 10828, 12623, 14797
Tait, Agnes
4978, 8310, 9403
Talmey, Allene
6143
Tanenbaum, S. A.
2715
Tanner, Juanita
14377
Tarbell, Ida M.
6142, 15822
Tardieu, André
14745
Tarkington, Booth
12784, 14246, 14922, 15296, 15915, 15998, 16067, 16408, 17589, 17857, 17930
Tate, Allen
15200
Tatt, Agnes
6488
Tattner, Ernest R.
12112
Taussig, Charles William
16407
Taylor, Deems
4048
Taylor, Dwight
13725
Taylor, Ethel
15300
Taylor, Gay
15601
Taylor, Joe
6350, 6351, 6352, 6353, 6354
Taylor, Katherine Haviland
17938
Taylor, Matt
16909
Taylor, Rachel Annand
14395
Taylor, Sam
16909
Teasdale, Sara
12818
Tect, Archibald
5870
Teed, Ordway
1023
Teichner, Miriam
87, 1311, 2142
Telemaque
see Wengler, Harold
Tellegen, Lou
17839
Terrett, Courtenay
15773
Terwilliger, Ann
7921
Tetlow, Henry
8193, 11466
Thayer, Mary Van Rensselaer
7126
Thayer, Tiffany
12015
Thielen, Benedict
3052, 4286, 7719, 10885, 11449
Thirkell, Angela
12504
Thomas, A. E.
12372, 13333, 14924A, 15606, 17460, 17529
Thomas, Augustus
16904
Thomas, Bertram
12109
Thomas, Dorothy

3045, 3966, 8344, 11153, 14178
Thomas, Helen Noble
12155
Thomas, Jerry
12462
Thomas, John
13242
Thomas, Martha Banning
106, 132, 142, 205, 297, 801, 816, 900, 1167, 1171, 1181, 1225, 1365, 1488, 1528, 1707, 1819, 1824, 2013, 2150, 2176, 2243, 2437, 2438, 2561, 2566, 2595, 2614, 2647, 3047, 3078, 3118, 3908, 3933, 4012, 4217, 4356, 4411, 4546, 4634, 4922, 4946, 4996, 5017, 5042, 5055, 5069, 5072, 5083, 5287, 5413, 5699, 5755, 5799, 5882, 6365, 6459, 6663, 6681, 7015-7017, 7034, 7037, 7131, 7383, 7420, 7424, 7520, 7573, 7671, 7721, 7724, 7761, 7774, 7813, 7849, 8139, 8226, 8303, 8345, 8436, 8444, 8555, 8564, 8992, 8998, 9071, 9202, 9203, 9459, 9506, 9508, 9540, 9766, 9796, 9872, 9873, 9996, 10158, 10205, 10207, 10275, 10347, 10537, 10557, 10688, 10745, 10761, 10765, 10782, 10843, 10912, 10948, 11006, 11101, 11127, 11134, 11157, 11158, 11160, 11161, 11183, 11324, 11416, 11603, 11646, 11730, 11785
Thomas, Mrs. Edward
see Thomas, Helen Noble
Thomason, John W., Jr.
1589, 6499, 7550, 7553, 9465, 9485, 11364, 13548, 14453
Thompson, Charles Willis
9587
Thompson, Donald
255, 904, 1374, 2202, 2775, 4342, 4392, 6500, 8455, 11718
Thompson, Dorothy
1027, 7438
Thompson, Edward
13458
Thompson, Fred
13689, 14113, 16310, 16796, 17087, 17276, 17358
Thompson, Harlan
15440, 17426
Thompson, Julian
17600
Thompson, R. E. S.
11841
Thompson, Sylvia
12266, 12719, 14220, 16037, 16996
Thomson, Arthur J.
16295
Thorne, Anthony
13076
Thorne, David
12348, 13206
Thornton, Richard
16223
Thorp, Margaret Farrand
6091
Thurber, James
63, 83, 94, 105, 120, 141, 173, 186, 264, 303, 339, 427, 441, 634, 646, 651, 652, 687, 700, 754, 775, 881, 922, 988, 996, 1030, 1031, 1055, 1072, 1143, 1199, 1200, 1203, 1230, 1258, 1288, 1289, 1298, 1309, 1389, 1451, 1475, 1506, 1515, 1592, 1627, 1729, 1778, 1827, 1838, 1886, 1909, 1915, 1927, 1944, 1950, 2035, 2073, 2137, 2160, 2268, 2333, 2362, 2398, 2476, 2624, 2641, 2673, 2681, 2696, 2700, 2739, 2755, 2800, 2801, 2938, 2957, 3009, 3024, 3028, 3071, 3090, 3166, 3268, 3280, 3282, 3903, 3948, 3957, 4028, 4033, 4035, 4111, 4167, 4175, 4215, 4233, 4315, 4381, 4395, 4440, 4447, 4544, 4567, 4632, 4647, 4648, 4664, 4691, 4693, 4696, 4698, 4702, 4770, 4835, 4857, 4926, 5036, 5100, 5127, 5153, 5166, 5219, 5233, 5237, 5285, 5357, 5396, 5397, 5422, 5530, 5546, 5633, 5653, 5816, 5820, 5821, 5833, 5842, 5843, 5862, 5876, 5878, 5932, 6007, 6049, 6164, 6174, 6182, 6268, 6338, 6341, 6364, 6367, 6384, 6412, 6475, 6533, 6534, 6559-6561, 6579, 6587, 6635, 6684, 7011, 7013, 7024, 7057,

7083, 7152, 7173, 7193, 7341, 7373, 7380, 7418, 7419, 7431, 7459, 7476, 7515, 7544, 7556, 7593, 7720, 7739, 7855, 7860, 7863, 7884, 8008-8014, 8035, 8036, 8256, 8265, 8467, 8518, 8525, 8573, 8652, 8669, 8670, 8697, 8729, 8752, 8771, 8810, 8895, 8956, 8960, 9092, 9125, 9172, 9282, 9288, 9291, 9411, 9456, 9477, 9671, 9681, 9700, 9753, 9764, 9774, 9866, 9952, 9958, 10000, 10049, 10072, 10144, 10172, 10173, 10206, 10361, 10491, 10492, 10549, 10566, 10584, 10608, 10634, 10654, 10848, 10869-10870, 11073, 11116, 11228, 11266, 11276, 11299, 11327, 11473, 11479, 11482, 11496, 11500, 11548, 11549, 11572, 11600, 11602, 11623, 11714, 11719, 11824, 11864, 14407, 15059,

Thurman, Wallace
12425, 14014
Thurston, E. Temple
12451
Tickell, Jerrard
13567
Tietjens, Eunice
4263, 9471, 12108
Tilden, Ethel Arnold
5788, 8723
Tilgher, Adriano
17850
Tilley, Eustace
see White, E. B.
Tilney, Frederick
15177
Tilton, George
13610, 15666, 16768
Timoney, Alice
12488
Timothy Vane
see Woollcott, Alexander
Tinayre, Marcelle
15018
Tinckom-Fernandez, W. G.
6101
Tip Bliss
see Bliss, T. H.
Titzell, Josiah
635, 11124
Tobias, Charles
17894
Toch, Maximilian
9405
Toller, Ernst
12441
Tolstoi, Alexei
13021
Tolstoy, Alexandra
17336
Tolstoy, Sophie
13131
Tomlinson, H. M.
11977, 13037, 13700, 15974, 16749
Tonkonogy, Gertrude
17209
Toogood, Granville
14258
Toohey, John Peter
10644, 14493
Top Hat
see Long, Lois
Torrance, Arthur
17330
Tosbell, E. A.
11240
Totheroh, Dan
13150, 15365, 16519, 17752
Totten, Joe Byron
16835
Touchstone
see Dounce, Harry Esty
Toumey, William H.
2881, 11392
Tousseul, Jean
14451
Towne, Charles Hanson
670, 7736, 7810, 9612
Townley, Jean Graham
940
Tracy, Virginia
1678, 2989
Train, Arthur
14314
Trautwein, Susanne
14662
Traven, B.
13067, 17360
Treadwell, Sophie
15005, 15996

Trench
8686
Trench, P. S. Le Poer
6612, 8149
Tretyakov, S.
16340
Trevelyan, H. B.
13005
Trilling, Lionel
15185
Tripp, Dwight Kasson
9388
Trollope, Frances
13185
Trotsky, Leon
15446
Troy, Hugh
795
Truax, Rhoda
14200
Tschuppik, Karl
13343, 13647
Tuckerman, Gustavus
13253
Tully, Jim
12295, 12296, 12402, 12438, 12771, 14442, 16578
Tully, Richard Walton
14982
Tunis, John R.
199, 826, 2009, 2144, 2576, 4537, 6008, 6269, 7754, 8825, 11138, 11640, 11653, 12016, 16837
Tuohy, Ferdinand
2644, 7399, 8215, 9372, 10386
Turgenev, Ivan
15360
Turner, John Hastings
14145, 17576
Turner, Josie
1046, 2515, 2516, 2517, 2519, 2520, 2521, 2522, 2523, 2524, 2777, 2782, 10305
Turner, Nancy Byrd
39, 10631
Turner, W. J.
15298
Turney, Catherine
15435
Turney, Robert
13025
Tutein, Peter
16516
Twomey, Neil
15608, 17120
Tympani
see Simon, Robert A.
Tzensky, Sergeev
17345

U

Undset, Sigrid
12586, 14294, 16744
Unger, Gladys
14529, 15357, 15624, 16879, 17417, 17431
Untermeyer, Louis
437, 2939, 3015, 3225, 3934, 5250, 6052, 7059, 7630, 11164, 12470, 13197, 15342
Updegraff, Allen
17687
Upham, T. C.
14925A

V

V. P.
see Paradise, Viola
V. T.
see Parsons, V. L.
Vajda, Ernest
12951
Vallentin, Antonina
17340
van Ammers-Küller, Jo
16214
Van Antwerp, John
15493
Vance, Ethel
13368
Vance, Louis Joseph
16326
Van D.
10187
Vanderbilt, Cornelius, Jr.
15842
Vanderbilt, Sanderson
1667, 8073, 11141
van der Meersch, Maxence
14390, 14391
Van Dine, S. S.
see Wright, Willard Huntington

Van Doren, Carl
12324, 14440, 17235
Van Doren, Mark
994, 1362, 1508, 1561, 1773, 2635, 2770, 3110, 4085, 4092, 4261, 4422, 4478, 4518, 5567, 5598, 5611, 5832, 6666, 9005, 9037, 9409, 9672, 9972, 10332, 10519, 10562, 11633, 11637, 11746, 11859, 12089, 12189, 16583, 17346
van Druten, John
11938, 13148, 13154, 13565, 15384, 17138, 17936
Vane, Sutton
15818
Vane, Timothy
see Woollcott, Alexander
Van Etten, Winifred
14266
Van Gluck, Stephen
16009
Van Gogh
see Pemberton, Murdock
van Gogh, Vincent
14783, 17552
van Loon, Hendrick Willem
8680, 13748, 15089, 17293
van Messel, Rela
14783
van Paassen, Pierre
13042
Van Sickle, Raymond
12337, 17003
van Steenbergh, A.
5007, 5014, 6187, 8571, 9708, 9895, 11793
Van Vechten, Carl
13408, 15543
Vanzetti, Bartolomeo
14781
Vardi, David
14757
Vaughan, Hilda
12268, 14092, 14389
Veber, Pierre
15689
Vedder, Miriam
66, 279, 450, 1713, 1769, 1997, 2169, 2329, 2615, 2697, 2875, 2905, 4076, 4087, 4573, 4937, 4945, 5131, 5428, 6379, 7596, 7862, 7948, 7973, 8625, 9306, 9393, 9850, 10128, 11192, 11358
Vegtel, Maddy
25, 443, 537, 581, 1974, 2265, 2374, 2403, 3162, 3212, 4803, 5652, 5679, 5690, 5960, 6073, 6179, 6295, 6535, 7147, 7212, 7988, 8127, 8128, 9153, 9725, 10132, 10532, 10558, 10822, 11472, 11717
Veiller, Bayard
17127, 17372, 17808
Verdi, Francis M.
14372
Verneuil, Louis
15184
Vernon, Maraget
17885
Victor, Victor
13557
Vidal, Lois
15043
Viereck, George Sylvester
5968
Viertel, Joseph M.
16752
Vildrac, Charles
15257
Villard, Oswald Garrison
13508
Villiers, Alan J.
17515
Villon, François
12855
Vinchon, Jean
13099
Viner, Richard
7039
Vogdes, Walter
13922
Vollmer, Lula
13252, 14133, 17375, 17391
von Hofmannsthal, Hugo
14454
von Orbok, Attila
14143
von Schrader, Atreus
4382
von Unruh, Fritz
17618
Vorse, Ellen
2015
Vorse, Heaton
9443

Vorse, Mary Heaton
1123, 2584, 2762, 4444, 5175, 5338, 5918, 6438, 7585, 7748, 8947, 9473, 9521, 10022, 11076, 11080, 11139, 13598, 16967
Vosper, Frank
14950, 15416, 16827

W

W. B. C.
2685
W. G.
see Gibbs, Wolcott
W. G. H.
123, 2743, 8871, 11509
W. S.
1259, 1317
W. S. K.
7391, 7546
Wachthausen, René
16143
Waddell, Helen
15935
Waldorf, Wilella
7123
Waley, Arthur
16422, 17870
Walker, Charles R.
12511
Walker, Mildred
13171
Walker, Stanley
1998, 2341, 4170, 4182, 4662, 5945, 6390, 7027, 8543, 9893, 11079, 11576, 12778, 15548
Wall, Evans
15609
Wall, Fred
13992
Wallace, David
16375
Wallace, Edgar
6597, 12937, 15092, 15734, 16657
Wallace, Henry A.
17739
Wallace, Morgan
12868
Wallach, Michael
17036
Waln, Nora
14228, 16209
Walpole, Hugh
4350, 13616, 13997, 14016, 16039
Walrond, Eric
17386
Walsh, Richard J.
337
Walter, Eugene
14450
Walton, Georgina Jones
14823
Walton, Izaak
12852
Wandell, Samuel H.
11893
Ward, Christopher
6581, 7583, 8320, 10445, 10925
Ward, Dearing
421, 701, 785, 1056, 1842, 2703, 4515, 4921, 5026, 6087, 6317, 6319, 7142, 7696, 7758, 7829, 8102, 8351, 8876, 9272, 9580, 10344, 11007
Ward, Olive
632, 2198, 2410, 5244, 7283, 7648, 8383, 8478, 8490, 8757, 9382, 10423, 10547, 10770
Warde, Shirley
17373
Ware, Foster
2164, 2338. 3134, 4079, 4210, 4265, 6105
Ware, Leonard, Jr.
2141, 6691, 10911
Warfield, Frances
146, 320, 413, 513, 731, 1101, 1224, 1325, 1949, 2061, 2140, 2183, 2222, 2228, 2247, 2450, 2532, 2585, 2818, 2898, 3177, 4050, 4128, 4376, 4771, 4824, 5301, 5316, 5552, 5857, 6061, 6188, 6489, 6494, 6495, 7186, 7446, 7922, 8025, 8183, 8357, 8370, 8558, 8648, 9123, 9584, 9679, 9765, 9875, 9943, 9950, 10054, 10134, 10140, 10267, 10374, 10433, 10437, 11053, 11241, 11271, 11381, 11593, 11705
Warfield, Ruth White
12108
Warner, Rex

16111, 17756
Warner, Richard F.
5178, 7832, 8254
Warner, Sylvia Townsend
1308, 1797, 2100, 2194, 2535, 2751, 3061, 4066, 4629, 4893, 5245, 5483, 5950, 6062, 7174, 10033, 10776, 11066, 11109, 11110, 11379, 11942, 14901, 15314, 15781, 16995, 17393
Warren, Robert Penn
15571
Warrin, Frank L.
5551
Warwick, Frances Evelyn
14820
Warwick, James
12431
Washburn, R. C.
183, 267, 1330, 2084
Washburn, Robert Collyer
14800
Wassermann, Jacob
12577, 13163, 13195, 13424, 15187, 15661, 17646
Waterman, Myra M.
379, 5492, 8523, 9978, 10244
Waters, Hadley
13770, 14876
Waters, Marianne Brown
12453, 16300
Watkin, Lawrence Edward
15726
Watkins, Mary F.
1898, 2423, 6462
Watkins, Maurine
12733, 16273
Watson, A. M. K.
12385
Watson, E. L. Grant
12886
Watson, Forbes
1425, 10077
Watters, George Manker
12585
Wattles, Majolica
see Calkins, Clinch
Waugh, Alec
14203, 16698
Waugh, Evelyn
12411, 16505, 17156, 17546
Waxman, Percy
7275, 7882, 12584
Way, Isabelle Stewart
8720, 8721
Wayburn, Ned
15498
Wead, Frank
12694
Weatherwax, Clara
15134
Weaver, John V. A.
14095, 14946
Weaver, Raymond
12419
Weaver, Susan
2610
Webb, Kenneth
14183, 14237, 15762, 17954
Webb, Sherrill
14183
Webber, James Plaisted
13437
Weber, L. Lawrence
15103
Wedekind, Frank
14980
Weeks, Marie
9541
Weenolsen, Robert
14183
Weer, William
4856, 9569
Weidman, Jerome
1481, 1482, 2071, 2724, 4827, 5282, 5373, 5806, 7140, 8473, 11035, 11052
Weigall, Arthur
15503, 15934
Weill, Kurt
14615, 17220
Weimar, William
273, 11649
Weinstock, Herbert
15226
Weitzenkorn, Louis
13547
Welch, Douglass
689, 2460, 3201, 4000, 5020, 5021, 10656, 10926
Welch, Eddie
13281
Welch, Marie de L.
5941
Well known broker
7504

Weller, George
385A, 1675, 5222, 5225, 8134, 8736, 11391, 11642, 11652, 15637
Welles, Winifred
9, 851, 1321, 1921, 6485, 6624, 9404, 11664
Wells, Anna Mary
1688, 1841, 10667
Wells, Carolyn
2780, 8457, 9010
Wells, Carveth
14330
Wells, Catherine
12465
Wells, Emma
12604
Wells, G. P.
16503
Wells, H. G.
349, 12192, 12583, 12752, 12944, 13416, 14591, 16503, 16589, 16869, 17853, 17862
Wells, John
13911
Wells, Leigh Burton
11988
Wells, Oliver
12088
Wells, Warre B.
13092, 15225
Wells, William K.
13754, 13756, 13757, 13758, 17087
Wels, Beatrice
8830
Wembridge, Eleanor Rowland
14793
Wendel, Beth
167, 329, 8627, 11781
Wendell, Dorothy Day
17088
Wengler, Harold
4902, 5192, 8701
Wenning, T. H.
1603, 1613, 1808, 3018, 3210, 3985, 4842, 5314, 5855, 7722, 8203, 8609, 8674, 8944, 9280, 9468, 9649, 10312, 10373, 10896
Wenrich, Percy
12676
Wensley, Frederick Porter
13624
Werfel, Franz
13379, 13617, 13813, 14042, 14521, 16501
Werner, M. R.
4628, 4973, 5673, 7312, 7957, 8967, 10952, 12572, 17069
Wertenbaker, Charles
12464
Wescott, Glenway
13484, 13867, 13895
West, Edward Sackville
see Sackville-West, Edward
West, Mae
12882, 13122, 15990
West, Nathanael
13039, 15301
West, Rebecca
5675, 14018, 17165
West, Ruth
9815
Westbay, Annette
14055
Weston, Mildred
177, 299, 449, 860, 1246, 1484, 1551, 1725, 1795, 1922, 2089, 2444, 2592, 2603, 2630, 2757, 2880, 2893, 3002, 3008 3032, 3910, 4364, 4732, 5234, 5257, 5299, 6018, 6090, 6307, 6335, 6429, 6674, 7089, 7095, 7489, 7631, 7633, 7802, 8224, 8233, 8443, 8634, 8787, 8888, 8907, 9598, 9687, 9802, 9829, 9944, 9957, 9991, 9999, 10225, 10715, 10722, 10739, 10827, 10855, 11055, 11193, 11194, 11311, 11647, 11728, 11729, 11742, 11880
Weterstetten, Rudolph
12385
Wetjen, Albert R.
13492
Wexley, John
14711, 17152
Weybright, Victor
1599
Wharf, Michael
13588
Wharton, Don
11142, 16371
Wharton, Edith
12223, 12699, 14102, 14248,

1521, 1796, 2175, 2253, 2562, 2594, 4380, 4929, 5507, 5565, 6238, 7503, 8292, 9264, 9771, 10169
Willison, G. F.
1463
Willner, A. M.
13938
Wilmurt, Arthur
13969, 17916
Wilsey, M.
9245, 10073
Wilson, Alma
12851
Wilson, Bettina
727
Wilson, Catherine Rose
13648, 17867
Wilson, Doris J.
3119, 4778
Wilson, Edith Bolling
15453
Wilson, Edmund
474, 1145, 2376, 2490, 5909, 6055, 7286, 7783, 8440, 9316, 9325, 10589, 11639, 12018, 12203, 17356, 17378
Wilson, Forrest
12429, 16284
Wilson, Harry Leon
14246
Wilson, Margaret
15837
Wilson, Marjorie Damsey
11247-11250, 11252
Wilson, Mary Badger
15836
Wilson, P. W.
17766
Wilson, Romer
13063, 14798
Wilson, Sterling
344, 866, 8063, 10167, 10185, 11065
Wiman, Dwight D.
16523, 17169
Wimperis, Arthur
14936
Winkler, Cecelia
1727
Winkler, John K.
839, 3229, 4360, 4431, 4843, 6436, 7566, 7567, 8388, 9189, 9270, 9357, 9747, 10062, 14043, 14482, 15371
Winslow, Herbert Hall
14035
Winslow, Kent
6178
Winslow, Thyra Samter
137, 1168, 2182, 2548, 2907, 4834, 5537, 6502, 6640, 7025, 7087, 7179-7183, 7749, 8031, 8268, 8474, 9149, 9200, 9273, 9445, 11511, 11830, 11869, 15916, 16639
Winsmore, Robert S.
1964, 4993
Winter, Ella
16242
Winter, Keith
14318, 15791, 16205, 16613
Winterich, John T.
4735
Winwar, Frances
15830, 16026
Wister, Owen
16372
Witney, Frederick
11930
Wittels, Fritz
12943
Wndrland, Alison
see Kober, Arthur
Wodehouse, P. G.
12096, 12632, 13536, 14058, 14091, 14210, 15408, 15573, 15687, 17115, 17276
Wohlforth, Robert
2005, 2011, 2354, 5268, 5746, 7398, 8276, 9648, 10322, 11281
Wolf, Friedrich
16429
Wolf, Howard
16398
Wolf, Ralph
16398
Wolf, Robert
16852
Wolfe, Thomas
2408, 6555, 7887, 13674, 14916, 15679, 17640
Wolfson, Victor
13413, 15883
Wont Tell
1706

Y

Z